500 SLOW RECIPES

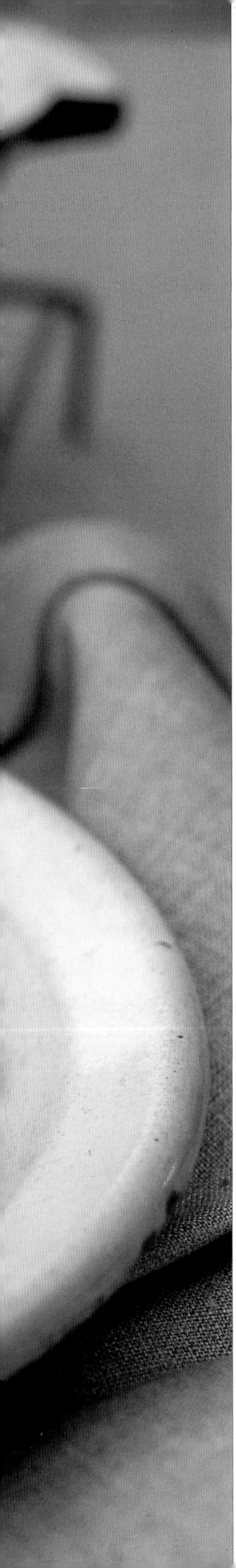

500 SLOW RECIPES

A COLLECTION OF SLOW-COOKED RECIPES, INCLUDING CASSEROLES, SOUPS, POT ROASTS AND PUDDINGS, WITH 500 PHOTOGRAPHS

CATHERINE ATKINSON & JENNI FLEETWOOD

greene&golden

This edition is published by greene&golden,
an imprint of Anness Publishing Ltd, Blaby Road, Wigston,
Leicestershire LE18 4SE; info@anness.com

www.annesspublishing.com

Publisher: Joanna Lorenz
Senior Editor: Felicity Forster
Recipes: Catherine Atkinson, Jane Bamforth, Alex Barker, Valerie Barrett, Judy Bastyra, Jacqueline Clark, Carole Clements, Joanna Farrow, Christine France, Brian Glover, Nicola Graimes, Juliet Harbutt, Christine Ingram, Becky Johnson, Lucy Knox, Christine McFadden, Marlene Spieler, Kate Whiteman, Rosemary Wilkinson, Elizabeth Wolf-Cohen and Jeni Wright
Photography: Karl Adamson, Edward Allwright, Steve Baxter, Nicki Dowey, James Duncan, Ian Garlick, Michelle Garrett, Amanda Heywood, Janine Hosegood, David Jordan, Dave King, Don Last, William Lingwood, Patrick McLeavey, Thomas Odulate, Craig Robertson, Bridget Sargeson and Sam Stowell
Copy Editor: Jay Thundercliffe
Production Controller: Mai-Ling Collyer

A CIP catalogue record for this book is available from the British Library.

NOTES

Bracketed terms are intended for American readers.
For all recipes, quantities are given in both metric and imperial measures and, where appropriate, in standard cups and spoons.
Follow one set of measures, but not a mixture, because they are not interchangeable.
Standard spoon and cup measures are level.
1 tsp = 5ml, 1 tbsp = 15ml, 1 cup = 250ml/8fl oz.
Australian standard tablespoons are 20ml.
Australian readers should use 3 tsp in place of 1 tbsp for measuring small quantities.
American pints are 16fl oz/2 cups. American readers should use 20fl oz/2.5 cups in place of 1 pint when measuring liquids.
Electric oven temperatures in this book are for conventional ovens. When using a fan oven, the temperature will probably need to be reduced by about 10–20°C/20–40°F. Since ovens vary, you should check with your manufacturer's instruction book for guidance.
The nutritional analysis given for each recipe is calculated per portion (i.e. serving or item), unless otherwise stated. If the recipe gives a range, such as Serves 4–6, then the nutritional analysis will be for the smaller portion size, i.e. 6 servings.
The analysis does not include optional ingredients, such as salt added to taste.
Medium (US large) eggs are used unless otherwise stated.

Front cover shows Anchovy and Roasted Pepper Salad – for recipe, see page 41.

PUBLISHER'S NOTE

Contents

Introduction

Slow cooking techniques have been used for hundreds of years and the renewed demand for natural food that is packed with flavour and goodness and free from artificial chemicals and additives means that many people are turning back to this wonderful method of cooking.

Slow-cooked recipes are perfectly suited to the modern world, where people often find that they do not have time to create complex or labour-intensive meals. The beauty of many of the recipes here is that they are prepared with an absolute minimum of fuss. For many dishes the ingredients can be put in a casserole in the oven, a large pan on the stove or in a specially designed slow cooker and then left to gently simmer away to make a fantastically tasty meal.

Slow cooking is perfect for everyone, from students, who may be using a minimalist kitchen, to busy families who are short of time and who may be forced to eat at different sittings. They are also ideal for dinner parties, freeing up the host to spend more time with their guests while a delicious meal is cooking away in the kitchen. As a bonus, after everybody has eaten, there will be less washing up than usual because many slow-cooked recipes only require a single pot.

As well as the nutritional and time-saving benefits of slow cooking, there is also an economical attraction because gently braising or simmering a piece of meat means that the cheaper, tougher cuts can be used, which become beautifully tender and tasty when cooked slowly. These cuts, such as brisket of beef, pork belly or lamb shanks, are often overlooked but they are in fact tastier than the leaner and more expensive cuts.

It is hard to go wrong with slow cooking and the finished meals will rarely spoil if not eaten the moment they are ready. Many can be cooked and then kept warm in the oven, slow cooker or pan, or quickly reheated on the stove or in a microwave. In fact, many dishes such as curries and casseroles will actually improve if they are made the day before, so that all the flavours can fully develop and blend together. Some dishes, such as those including rice or pasta, need some last-minute attention, but when the majority of the meal has been prepared in advance the effort is minimal.

Many recipes in this collection call for a slow cooker, an appliance that is becoming an essential addition to many kitchens. It is a superb way to experience the pleasures of leisurely cooking as it creates such a low, gentle heat that ingredients can be added to it many hours before the food is required. Its reputation for creating soups, succulent stews and pot roasts is well known, but there are many other recipes that highlight its extraordinary versatility.

The 500 deliciously tempting recipes included here are clearly explained in steps and feature a shot of the finished dish. They are divided into sections so that you can find the recipes you want, when you need them – Soups and Broths; Appetizers and Salads; Fish and Shellfish; Poultry; Meat and Game; Vegetarian and Side Dishes; Dessert and Cakes; and Preserves and Drinks.

There is a wide variety of classic dishes throughout the book, as well as delectable new creations for you to experience. The huge appeal of slow cooking means that there are dishes from a rich heritage of worldwide cuisines so you can be certain to find one that is perfect for any occasion. Start your meal with a sustaining soup, such as Scotch Broth or Seafood Chowder, or try an appetizing treat such as Country Game Terrine. The choice of main courses offers something for everybody, from Cod with Caramelized Onions and Coq au Vin to the classic Pot-roasted Brisket or a vegetarian Mixed Bean and Aubergine Tagine. Many traditional and enticing desserts are well-suited to slow cooking, such as Frosted Carrot and Parsnip Cake or Steamed Chocolate Puddings, and preserves and chutneys are also featured, including Mango Chutney, Whiskey Marmalade and the classic Lemon Curd.

So why not relax, make life easier for yourself and experience the simple and delicious pleasures of slow cooking with this fantastic collection of recipes aimed at the leisurely cook.

French Onion Soup with Cheese Croûtes

Probably the most famous of all onion soups, this is a hearty and warming dish, perfect for the slow cooker.

Serves 4

40g/1½oz/3 tbsp butter
10ml/2 tsp olive oil
1.2kg/2½lb onions, sliced
5ml/1 tsp caster (superfine) sugar
15ml/1 tbsp plain (all-purpose) flour
15ml/1 tbsp sherry vinegar
30ml/2 tbsp brandy
120ml/4fl oz/½ cup dry white wine
1 litre/1¾ pints/4 cups boiling beef, chicken or duck stock
5ml/1 tsp chopped fresh thyme
salt and ground black pepper

For the croûtes

4 slices day-old French stick or baguette, about 2.5cm/1in thick
1 garlic clove, halved
5ml/1 tsp French mustard
50g/2oz/½ cup grated Gruyère cheese

1 Put the butter and olive oil in the ceramic cooking pot and heat on high for about 15 minutes until melted. Add the onions and stir to coat in the butter and oil. Cover with the lid, then place a folded dish towel over the top to retain the heat and cook for 2 hours, stirring halfway through the cooking time.

2 Add the sugar and stir well. Cover again with the lid and dish towel and cook on high for 4 hours, stirring occasionally so the onions colour evenly. They should turn a dark golden colour.

3 Sprinkle the flour over the onions and stir. Next, stir in the vinegar followed by the brandy, then slowly blend in the wine. Stir in the stock and thyme and season with salt and pepper. Cook on high for 2 hours, or until the onions are very tender.

4 For the croûtes, place the bread slices under a low grill (broiler) and cook until lightly browned. Rub with the cut surface of the garlic and spread with mustard. Sprinkle the cheese over the top.

5 Turn the grill to high and cook the croûtes for 2–3 minutes, until the cheese is bubbling and brown. Ladle the soup into warmed bowls and float a croûte on top. Serve immediately.

Carrot and Coriander Soup

Root vegetables, such as carrots, are great for slow-cooker soups. Their earthy flavour becomes rich and sweet when cooked gently over a low heat.

Serves 4

450g/1lb carrots, preferably young and tender
15ml/1 tbsp sunflower oil
40g/1½oz/3 tbsp butter
1 onion, chopped
1 stick celery, plus 2–3 leafy tops
2 small potatoes, peeled
900ml/1½ pints/3¾ cups boiling vegetable stock
10ml/2 tsp ground coriander
15ml/1 tbsp chopped fresh coriander (cilantro)
150ml/¼ pint/⅔ cup milk
salt and ground black pepper

1 Trim and peel the carrots and cut into chunks. Heat the oil and 25g/1oz/2 tbsp of the butter in a pan and fry the onion over a gentle heat for 3–4 minutes until slightly softened. Do not let it brown.

2 Slice the celery and chop the potatoes, and add them to the onion in the pan. Cook for 2 minutes, then add the carrots and cook for a further minute. Transfer the fried vegetables to the ceramic cooking pot.

3 Pour the boiling stock over the vegetables, then season with salt and ground black pepper. Cover the pot with the lid and cook on low for 4–5 hours until the vegetables are tender.

4 Reserve 6–8 tiny celery leaves from the leafy tops for the garnish, then chop the remaining celery tops. Melt the remaining butter in a large pan and add the ground coriander. Fry for 1–2 minutes, stirring constantly, until the aromas are released.

5 Reduce the heat under the pan and add the chopped celery tops and fresh coriander. Fry for about 30 seconds, then remove the pan from the heat.

6 Ladle the soup into a food processor or blender and process until smooth, then pour into the pan with the celery tops and coriander. Stir in the milk and heat gently until piping hot. Adjust the seasoning and serve garnished with the reserved celery leaves.

French Onion Soup Energy 418kcal/1747kJ; Protein 11.5g; Carbohydrate 51.8g, of which sugars 19.4g; Fat 15.9g, of which saturates 8.2g; Cholesterol 33mg; Calcium 209mg; Fibre 5.3g; Sodium 1195mg.
Carrot and Coriander Soup Energy 168kcal/697kJ; Protein 3g; Carbohydrate 11.9g, of which sugars 9.2g; Fat 12.4g, of which saturates 6g; Cholesterol 24mg; Calcium 94mg; Fibre 3.1g; Sodium 758mg.

Tomato and Fresh Basil Soup

Peppery, aromatic basil is the perfect partner for sweet, ripe tomatoes – and it is easy to grow at home in a pot on a sunny kitchen windowsill. This slow-cooker soup is perfect in the late summer when fresh tomatoes are at their best and most flavoursome.

Serves 4

15ml/1 tbsp olive oil
25g/1oz/2 tbsp butter
1 onion, finely chopped
900g/2lb ripe tomatoes, roughly chopped
1 garlic clove, roughly chopped
about 600ml/1 pint/2½ cups vegetable stock
120ml/4fl oz/½ cup dry white wine
30ml/2 tbsp sun-dried tomato paste
30ml/2 tbsp shredded fresh basil
150ml/¼ pint/⅔ cup double (heavy) cream
salt and ground black pepper
whole basil leaves, to garnish

1 Heat the oil and butter in a large pan until foaming. Add the chopped onion and cook gently for about 5–7 minutes, stirring, until the onion is softened but not brown, then add the chopped tomatoes and garlic.

2 Add the vegetable stock, white wine and sun-dried tomato paste to the pan and stir to combine. Heat the mixture until just below boiling point, then carefully pour the mixture into the ceramic cooking pot.

3 Switch the slow cooker to the high or auto setting, cover with the lid and cook for 1 hour. Leave the slow cooker on automatic or switch to low and cook for a further 4–6 hours, until tender.

4 Leave the soup to cool for a few minutes, then ladle into a food processor or blender and process until smooth. Press the puréed soup through a sieve (strainer) into a clean pan.

5 Add the shredded basil and the cream to the soup and heat through, stirring. Do not allow the soup to reach boiling point. Check the consistency and add a little more stock if necessary. Season, then pour into warmed bowls and garnish with basil. Serve immediately.

Chilled Tomato and Sweet Pepper Soup

This delicious soup is made in the slow cooker before being chilled. Grilling the peppers gives a mild smoky flavour, but you can leave out this step, if you like.

Serves 4

2 red (bell) peppers
30ml/2 tbsp olive oil
1 onion, finely chopped
2 garlic cloves, crushed
675g/1½lb ripe tomatoes
120ml/4fl oz/½ cup red wine
450ml/¾ pint/scant 2 cups vegetable or chicken stock
2.5ml/½ tsp caster (superfine) sugar
salt and ground black pepper
chopped fresh chives, to garnish

For the croûtons

2 slices white bread, crusts removed
45ml/3 tbsp olive oil

1 Cut each pepper into quarters and remove the core and seeds. Place each quarter, skin side up, on a grill (broiler) rack. Grill (broil) until the skins are blistered and charred, then transfer to a bowl and cover with a plate.

2 Heat the oil in a frying pan. Add the onion and garlic and cook gently for about 10 minutes until soft, stirring occasionally. Meanwhile, remove the skin from the peppers and roughly chop the flesh. Cut the tomatoes into chunks.

3 Transfer the onions to the ceramic cooking pot and add the peppers, tomatoes, wine, stock and sugar. Cover and cook on high for 3–4 hours, or until the vegetables are very tender. Leave the soup to stand for about 10 minutes to cool slightly.

4 Ladle the soup into a food processor or blender and process until smooth. Press through a sieve (strainer) into a bowl. Leave to cool before chilling in the refrigerator for at least 3 hours.

5 Make the croûtons. Cut the bread into cubes. Heat the oil in a frying pan and fry the bread until golden. Drain on kitchen paper.

6 Season the soup to taste with salt and pepper, then ladle into chilled bowls. Top with croûtons and chopped chives and serve.

Tomato and Basil Soup Energy 335kcal/1387kJ; Protein 3.1g; Carbohydrate 11.7g, of which sugars 10.8g; Fat 28.9g, of which saturates 16.4g; Cholesterol 65mg; Calcium 50mg; Fibre 3g; Sodium 168mg.
Chilled Tomato Soup Energy 262kcal/1090kJ; Protein 3.5g; Carbohydrate 17.6g, of which sugars 11.5g; Fat 18g, of which saturates 2.6g; Cholesterol 0mg; Calcium 47mg; Fibre 3.4g; Sodium 499mg.

Spicy Pumpkin Soup

This stunning golden-orange soup has a smooth velvety texture and a delicate taste, which is subtly spiced with cumin and garlic. Gentle simmering in the slow cooker really gives the flavours time to develop to make a wonderful autumnal dish.

Serves 4

900g/2lb pumpkin, peeled and seeds removed
30ml/2 tbsp olive oil
2 leeks, trimmed and sliced
1 garlic clove, crushed
5ml/1 tsp ground ginger
5ml/1 tsp ground cumin
750ml/1¼ pints/3 cups near-boiling chicken stock
salt and ground black pepper
60ml/4 tbsp natural (plain) yogurt, to serve
coriander (cilantro) leaves, to garnish

1 Using a sharp knife, cut the pumpkin into large chunks. Place the chunks in the ceramic cooking pot.

2 Heat the oil in a large pan and add the leeks and garlic. Cook gently until softened but not coloured.

3 Add the ginger and cumin to the pan and cook, stirring, for a further minute. Transfer the mixture into the ceramic cooking pot, pour over the stock and season with salt and black pepper.

4 Cover the slow cooker with the lid, switch to the low setting and leave to cook for 6–8 hours, or until the pumpkin pieces are very tender.

5 Ladle the soup, in batches if necessary, into a food processor or blender and process until smooth. Return the soup to the rinsed out cooking pot, cover and cook on high for 1 hour, or until piping hot. Serve in warmed individual bowls, with a swirl of natural yogurt and a few coriander leaves.

Cook's Tip
To save time, reheat the soup on the stove rather than in the slow cooker.

Wild Mushroom Soup

This robust, creamy soup is ideal for the slow cooker. The rich flavour and colour of the soup are enhanced by adding dried wild mushrooms and a dash of Madeira.

Serves 4

15g/½oz/¼ cup dried wild mushrooms, such as morels, ceps or porcini
600ml/1 pint/2½ cups hot chicken or vegetable stock
25g/1oz/2 tbsp butter
1 onion, finely chopped
1 garlic clove, crushed
450g/1lb button (white) or other cultivated mushrooms, trimmed and sliced
15ml/1 tbsp plain (all-purpose) flour
fresh nutmeg
1.5ml/¼ tsp dried thyme
60ml/4 tbsp Madeira or dry sherry
60ml/4 tbsp crème fraîche or sour cream
salt and ground black pepper
chopped fresh chives, to garnish

1 Put the dried mushrooms in a sieve (strainer) and rinse under cold running water to remove any grit, then place in the ceramic cooking pot. Pour over half of the hot chicken or vegetable stock and cover with the lid. Switch the slow cooker to the auto or high setting.

2 Melt the butter in a large pan. Add the onion and cook for 5–7 minutes until softened. Add the garlic and fresh mushrooms to the pan and cook for 5 minutes. Sprinkle over the flour, grate in some nutmeg and add the thyme. Cook for 3 minutes more, stirring all the time, until blended.

3 Stir in the Madeira or sherry and the remaining stock, and season with salt and pepper. Bring to the boil, then transfer to the ceramic cooking pot. Cook for 1 hour, then switch to low or leave on auto and cook for 3–4 hours.

4 Ladle the soup into a food processor or blender and process until smooth. Strain it back into the pan, pressing it with the back of a spoon to force the purée through the sieve.

5 Reheat the soup until piping hot. Stir in half the crème fraîche or sour cream. Ladle into bowls, swirl a little of the remaining crème fraîche or sour cream on top and sprinkle with chives.

Spicy Pumpkin Soup Energy 89kcal/372kJ; Protein 2.3g; Carbohydrate 6.2g, of which sugars 4.7g; Fat 6.3g, of which saturates 1.1g; Cholesterol 0mg; Calcium 75mg; Fibre 3.1g; Sodium 127mg.
Wild Mushroom Soup Energy 143kcal/592kJ; Protein 3.7g; Carbohydrate 8.2g, of which sugars 3.2g; Fat 9g, of which saturates 5.3g; Cholesterol 22mg; Calcium 41mg; Fibre 2g; Sodium 174mg.

White Cabbage, Beetroot and Tomato Borscht

There are many versions of this classic soup, which originated in eastern Europe. Beetroot and sour cream are the traditional ingredients in every borscht, but other ingredients tend to be many and varied. This slow-cooker version has a sweet and sour taste and can be served piping hot or refreshingly chilled on a summer's day.

Serves 6

1 onion, chopped
1 carrot, chopped
6 raw or vacuum-packed (cooked, not pickled) beetroot (beets), 4 diced and 2 coarsely grated
400g/14oz can chopped tomatoes
6 new potatoes, cut into bitesize pieces
1 small white cabbage, thinly sliced
600ml/1 pint/2½ cups hot vegetable stock
45ml/3 tbsp sugar
30–45ml/2–3 tbsp white wine vinegar or cider vinegar
45ml/3 tbsp chopped fresh dill
salt and ground black pepper
sour cream and dill, to garnish
buttered rye bread, to serve

1 Put the onion, carrot, diced beetroot, tomatoes, new potatoes and cabbage into the ceramic cooking pot and pour over the hot vegetable stock. Cover the cooking pot with the lid and cook on the high setting for about 4 hours, or until the vegetables are just tender.

2 Add the grated beetroot, sugar and vinegar to the pot and stir until well combined. Cook for a further hour until the beetroot is cooked.

3 Taste the soup, checking for a good sweet and sour balance, and add a little more sugar and/or vinegar if necessary, tasting after each addition to check the balance. Season to taste with plenty of salt and ground black pepper.

4 Just before serving, stir the chopped dill into the soup and ladle into warmed soup bowls. Garnish each serving with a generous spoonful of sour cream and plenty more fresh dill, then serve with thick slices of buttered rye bread.

Spinach and Root Vegetable Soup

This is a deliciously rustic soup, traditionally prepared when the first vegetables of spring appear and the winter vegetables are still widely available. The slow cooker really helps to bring out the rich flavours of the root vegetables. You will need to use a large slow cooker to accommodate the spinach.

Serves 4

1 small turnip, cut into chunks
2 carrots, diced
1 small parsnip, cut into large dice
1 potato, diced
1 onion, chopped
1 garlic clove, finely chopped
¼ celeriac bulb, diced
750ml/1¼ pints/3 cups hot vegetable or chicken stock
175g/6oz fresh spinach, roughly chopped
1 small bunch fresh dill, chopped
salt and ground black pepper

For the garnish
2 hard-boiled eggs, sliced lengthways
1 lemon, sliced
30ml/2 tbsp chopped fresh parsley and dill

1 Put the turnip, carrots, parsnip, potato, onion, garlic, celeriac and vegetable or chicken stock into the ceramic cooking pot. Cook on the high or auto setting for about 1 hour, then either leave the cooker on auto or switch it to the low setting and cook for a further 5–6 hours, until all the vegetables are very soft and tender.

2 Stir the chopped spinach into the cooking pot and cook on the high setting for about 45 minutes, or until the spinach is tender but still green and leafy. Season with salt and plenty of ground black pepper.

3 Stir in the dill, then ladle the soup into warmed bowls and serve garnished with egg, lemon and a sprinkling of fresh parsley and dill.

Cook's Tip
For best results, use a really good-quality vegetable or chicken stock, preferably home-made, if possible.

White Cabbage Borscht Energy 125kcal/531kJ; Protein 3.5g; Carbohydrate 27.8g, of which sugars 7g; Fat 0.7g, of which saturates 0.1g; Cholesterol 0mg; Calcium 58mg; Fibre 3.2g; Sodium 357mg.
Spinach and Vegetable Soup Energy 67kcal/280kJ; Protein 3g; Carbohydrate 11.5g, of which sugars 7g; Fat 1.3g, of which saturates 0.1g; Cholesterol 0mg; Calcium 121mg; Fibre 3.9g; Sodium 499mg.

Spicy Red Lentil Soup with Onion

This wholesome soup is light and refreshing, and the slow cooking on top of the stove helps to bring out the subtly spiced flavour. It is delicious served as an appetizer or as a light lunch with chunks of fresh bread.

Serves 4

30–45ml/2–3 tbsp olive or vegetable oil
1 large onion, finely chopped
2 garlic cloves, finely chopped
1 fresh red chilli, seeded and chopped
5–10ml/1–2 tsp cumin seeds
5–10ml/1–2 tsp coriander seeds
1 carrot, finely chopped
scant 5ml/1 tsp ground fenugreek
5ml/1 tsp sugar
15ml/1 tbsp tomato purée (paste)
250g/9oz/generous 1 cup split red lentils
1.75 litres/3 pints/7½ cups chicken stock
salt and ground black pepper

To serve

1 small red onion, finely chopped
1 large bunch of fresh flat leaf parsley, finely chopped
4–6 lemon wedges

1 Heat the oil in a heavy pan and stir in the onion, garlic, chilli, cumin and coriander seeds. When the onion begins to colour slightly, toss in the carrot and cook for 2–3 minutes.

2 Add the ground fenugreek, sugar and tomato purée and stir in the lentils, until all the ingredients are well combined.

3 Pour in the stock, stir well and bring to the boil. Lower the heat, partially cover the pan with a lid and simmer for 35–45 minutes, until the lentils have broken up.

4 If the soup is too thick for your preference, thin it down to the desired consistency with a little water. Season with plenty of salt and ground black pepper.

5 Serve the soup as it is or, if you prefer a smooth texture, leave it to cool slightly, then pour it into a food processor or blender and process to the desired consistency. Reheat if necessary.

6 Ladle the soup into bowls and sprinkle with the chopped onion and parsley. Serve with lemon wedges to squeeze over.

Lentil and Pasta Soup

This rustic vegetarian soup makes a warming winter meal and goes especially well with Granary or crusty Italian bread.

Serves 4–6

175g/6oz/¾ cup brown lentils
3 garlic cloves, unpeeled
1 litre/1¾ pints/4 cups water
45ml/3 tbsp olive oil
25g/1oz/2 tbsp butter
1 onion, finely chopped
2 celery sticks, finely chopped
30ml/2 tbsp sun-dried tomato purée (paste)
1.75 litres/3 pints/7½ cups vegetable stock
a few fresh marjoram leaves
a few fresh basil leaves
leaves from 1 fresh thyme sprig
50g/2oz/½ cup dried small pasta shapes, such as macaroni or tubetti
salt and ground black pepper
fresh herb leaves, to garnish

1 Put the lentils in a large pan. Smash one of the garlic cloves using the blade of a large knife (there's no need to peel it first), then add it to the lentils.

2 Pour the water into the pan and bring to the boil. Simmer for about 20–25 minutes, or until the lentils are tender. Transfer the lentils into a sieve (strainer), remove the garlic and set it aside. Rinse the lentils under the cold tap and leave to drain.

3 Heat 30ml/2 tbsp of the oil with half the butter in the pan. Add the onion and celery and cook gently for 5 minutes until the onions have softened slightly.

4 Crush the remaining garlic, then peel and mash the reserved garlic. Add to the pan with the remaining oil, the sun-dried tomato purée and the lentils. Stir, then add in the stock, herbs and salt and pepper. Bring to the boil, stirring. Simmer for about 30–35 minutes, stirring occasionally.

5 Add the pasta and bring the soup back to the boil. Reduce the heat and simmer until the pasta is tender, for about 15 minutes. Add the remaining butter and stir until melted.

6 Taste the soup for seasoning, adjusting if necessary, then serve hot in warmed bowls, sprinkled with herb leaves.

Spicy Red Lentil Soup Energy 203kcal/856kJ; Protein 11.1g; Carbohydrate 31.8g, of which sugars 7.3g; Fat 4.4g, of which saturates 0.6g; Cholesterol 0mg; Calcium 45mg; Fibre 3.5g; Sodium 26mg.
Lentil and Pasta Soup Energy 206kcal/865kJ; Protein 8.1g; Carbohydrate 23.5g, of which sugars 1.7g; Fat 9.5g, of which saturates 3g; Cholesterol 9mg; Calcium 24mg; Fibre 1.9g; Sodium 42mg.

Potage of Lentils

In this soup, red lentils and vegetables are simmered in the slow cooker until very soft, then puréed to give a rich and velvety consistency. On a hot day, serve chilled with extra lemon juice.

Serves 4

45ml/3 tbsp olive oil
1 onion, chopped
2 celery sticks, chopped
1 carrot, sliced
2 garlic cloves, chopped
1 potato, diced
250g/9oz/generous 1 cup red lentils
750ml/1 ¼ pints/3 cups hot vegetable stock
2 bay leaves
1 small lemon
2.5ml/½ tsp ground cumin
cayenne pepper or Tabasco sauce, to taste
salt and ground black pepper
lemon slices and chopped fresh flat leaf parsley, to serve

1 Heat the oil in a frying pan. Add the onion and cook, stirring frequently, for 5 minutes, or until beginning to soften. Stir in the celery, carrot, garlic and potato. Cook for a further 3–4 minutes.

2 Transfer the fried vegetables to the ceramic cooking pot and switch to high. Add the lentils, hot vegetable stock, bay leaves and a pared strip of lemon rind and stir to combine. Cover the slow cooker with the lid and cook on the auto or high setting for about 1 hour.

3 Leave the cooker on auto or switch to low and cook for a further 4–5 hours, or until the vegetables and lentils are soft and very tender.

4 Remove and discard the bay leaves and the lemon rind. Process the soup in a food processor or blender until smooth. Transfer the soup back to the cleaned cooking pot, stir in the cumin and cayenne pepper or Tabasco, and season.

5 Cook the soup on high for a further 45 minutes, or until piping hot. Squeeze in lemon juice to taste and check the seasoning. Ladle into warmed bowls and top each portion with lemon slices and a sprinkling of chopped fresh parsley.

Minestrone with Pesto

Pesto is stirred into this slow-cooker version of minestrone to add extra flavour and colour. This soup makes an excellent supper dish when served with bread. To save time, you can use ready-made bottled pesto.

Serves 4

30ml/2 tbsp olive oil
1 onion, finely chopped
2 celery sticks, finely chopped
1 large carrot, finely chopped
1 potato, weighing about 115g/4oz, cut into 1cm/½in cubes
1 litre/1¾ pints/4 cups hot vegetable stock
75g/3oz green beans, cut into 5cm/2in pieces
1 courgette (zucchini), thinly sliced
2 Italian plum tomatoes, peeled and chopped
200g/7oz can cannellini beans, drained and rinsed
¼ Savoy cabbage, shredded
40g/1½oz dried 'quick-cook' spaghetti or vermicelli, broken into short lengths
salt and ground black pepper

For the pesto

about 20 fresh basil leaves
1 garlic clove
10ml/2 tsp pine nuts
15ml/1 tbsp freshly grated Parmesan cheese
15ml/1 tbsp freshly grated Pecorino cheese
30ml/2 tbsp olive oil

1 Heat the olive oil in a pan, then add the onion, celery and carrot and cook, stirring, for 7 minutes, until they begin to soften.

2 Transfer the fried vegetables to the ceramic cooking pot. Add the potato cubes and vegetable stock, cover the cooking pot with the lid and cook on high for 1¼ hours.

3 Add the green beans, courgette, tomatoes and cannellini beans to the pot. Cover and cook for 1 hour, then stir in the cabbage and pasta and cook for a further 20 minutes.

4 Meanwhile, place all the pesto ingredients in a food processor. Blend to a smooth sauce, adding 15–45ml/1–3 tbsp water through the feeder tube to loosen the mixture if necessary.

5 Stir 30ml/2 tbsp of the pesto sauce into the soup. Check the seasoning, adding more if necessary. Serve hot, in warmed bowls, with the remaining pesto spooned on top of each serving.

Potage of Lentils Energy 300kcal/1265kJ; Protein 15.8g; Carbohydrate 40.1g, of which sugars 3.6g; Fat 9.6g, of which saturates 1.3g; Cholesterol 0mg; Calcium 47mg; Fibre 3.9g; Sodium 456mg.
Minestrone Energy 263kcal/1098kJ; Protein 8.5g; Carbohydrate 25.1g, of which sugars 7g; Fat 14.9g, of which saturates 2.8g; Cholesterol 5mg; Calcium 103mg; Fibre 5.4g; Sodium 1034mg.

Italian Farmhouse Soup

Root vegetables form the base of this chunky, minestrone-style main meal soup. Cooked in one pot, it is simple to make as well as versatile – you can vary the vegetables according to what you have to hand.

Serves 4

30ml/2 tbsp olive oil
1 onion, roughly chopped
3 carrots, cut into large chunks
175–200g/6–7oz turnips, cut into large chunks
about 175g/6oz swede (rutabaga), cut into large chunks
400g/14oz can chopped Italian tomatoes
15ml/1 tbsp tomato purée (paste)
5ml/1 tsp dried mixed herbs
5ml/1 tsp dried oregano
50g/2oz dried (bell) peppers, washed and thinly sliced (optional)
1.5 litres/2½ pints/6¼ cups vegetable stock or water
50g/2oz/½ cup dried small macaroni or conchiglie
400g/14oz can red kidney beans, rinsed and drained
30ml/2 tbsp chopped fresh flat leaf parsley
salt and ground black pepper
freshly grated Parmesan cheese, to serve

1 Heat the olive oil in a large pan, add the onion and cook over a low heat for about 5 minutes until softened. Add the carrot, turnip and swede chunks, canned chopped tomatoes, tomato purée, dried mixed herbs, dried oregano and dried peppers, if using. Stir in salt and pepper to taste.

2 Pour in the vegetable stock or water and bring to the boil. Stir well, cover the pan, then lower the heat and simmer for 30–40 minutes, stirring occasionally.

3 Add the pasta to the pan and bring quickly to the boil, stirring. Lower the heat and simmer, uncovered, for about 5–7 minutes until the pasta is only just tender, or according to the instructions on the packet. Stir frequently.

4 Stir in the kidney beans. Heat through for 2–3 minutes, then remove the pan from the heat and stir in the parsley. Taste the soup for seasoning. Serve hot in warmed soup bowls, with grated Parmesan cheese handed separately.

Bean and Pistou Soup

This hearty vegetarian soup is typical of provençal-style cooking. It is cooked slowly in a bean pot in the oven and richly flavoured with a home-made garlic and fresh basil pistou sauce.

Serves 4–6

150g/5oz/scant 1 cup dried haricot (navy) beans, soaked overnight in cold water
150g/5oz/scant 1 cup dried flageolet or cannellini beans, soaked overnight in cold water
1 onion, chopped
1.2 litres/2 pints/5 cups hot vegetable stock
2 carrots, roughly chopped
225g/8oz Savoy cabbage, shredded
1 large potato, about 225g/8oz, roughly chopped
225g/8oz green beans, chopped
salt and ground black pepper
basil leaves, to garnish

For the pistou

4 garlic cloves
8 large sprigs basil leaves
90ml/6 tbsp olive oil
60ml/4 tbsp freshly grated Parmesan cheese

1 Soak a bean pot in cold water for 20 minutes then drain. Drain the soaked haricot and flageolet or cannellini beans and place in the bean pot. Add the onion and pour over sufficient cold water to come 5cm/2in above the beans. Cover and place the pot in an unheated oven. Set the oven to 200°C/400°F/Gas 6 and cook for about 1½ hours, or until the beans are tender.

2 Drain the beans and onion. Place half the beans and onion in a food processor and process to a paste. Return the drained beans and the bean paste to the pot. Add the vegetable stock.

3 Add the chopped carrots, shredded cabbage, chopped potato and green beans to the bean pot. Season with salt and pepper, cover and return the pot to the oven. Reduce the oven temperature to 180°C/350°F/Gas 4 and cook for 1 hour, or until all the vegetables are cooked right through.

4 Meanwhile, place the garlic and basil in a mortar and pound with a pestle, then gradually beat in the oil. Stir in the grated Parmesan. Stir half the pistou into the soup and then ladle into warmed soup bowls. Top each serving with a spoonful of the remaining pistou and serve garnished with basil.

Farmhouse Soup Energy 248kcal/1047kJ; Protein 10.2g; Carbohydrate 38.6g, of which sugars 14.9g; Fat 7g, of which saturates 1.1g; Cholesterol 0mg; Calcium 139mg; Fibre 10.6g; Sodium 422mg.
Bean and Pistou Soup Energy 305kcal/1281kJ; Protein 17.2g; Carbohydrate 34.6g, of which sugars 7.5g; Fat 11.8g, of which saturates 3.3g; Cholesterol 10mg; Calcium 215mg; Fibre 10.8g; Sodium 133mg.

Black-eyed Bean and Tomato Broth

This delicious soup, made with black-eyed beans and turmeric-tinted tomato broth, is flavoured with tangy lemon and speckled with chopped fresh coriander. It is ideal for serving at parties as it can be made in advance – simply multiply the quantities to the amount required.

Serves 4

175g/6oz/1 cup black-eyed beans (peas), soaked overnight
15ml/1 tbsp olive oil
2 onions, chopped
4 garlic cloves, chopped
1 medium-hot or 2–3 mild fresh chillies, chopped
5ml/1 tsp ground cumin
5ml/1 tsp ground turmeric
250g/9oz fresh or canned tomatoes, diced
600ml/1 pint/2½ cups chicken, beef or vegetable stock
25g/1oz fresh coriander (cilantro) leaves, roughly chopped
juice of ½ lemon
salt and ground black pepper
pitta bread, to serve

1 Put the black-eyed beans in a pan and add enough cold water to cover. Bring to the boil, then cook on a high heat for about 5–10 minutes, skimming off any foam that rises to the top. Remove from the heat, cover the pan with a tight-fitting lid and leave to stand for 2 hours.

2 Drain the beans, return to the pan, cover with fresh cold water, then simmer for 35–40 minutes, or until the beans are tender. Drain and set aside.

3 Heat the olive oil in a pan, add the chopped onions, garlic and fresh chilli and cook for 5 minutes, or until the onion has started to soften and turn translucent.

4 Stir the cumin and turmeric into the pan and cook, stirring, for a minute until the spices release their fragrances. Add the fresh or canned tomatoes, the meat or vegetable stock, half the chopped coriander and the drained beans, and simmer gently for 20–30 minutes.

5 Stir in the lemon juice, season with salt and pepper and add the remaining coriander. Serve immediately with pitta bread.

Old Country Mushroom, Bean and Barley Soup

This hearty and rustic soup is easy to make as all the ingredients are simply placed in one pot and then cooked together. It is perfect on a freezing cold day, when you can gather in the kitchen while it slowly cooks on the stove. Serve in warmed bowls, with plenty of rye or pumpernickel bread to mop up the delicious broth.

Serves 6–8

30–45ml/2–3 tbsp small haricot (navy) beans, soaked overnight
45–60ml/3–4 tbsp green split peas
45–60ml/3–4 tbsp yellow split peas
90–105ml/6–7 tbsp pearl barley
1 onion, chopped
2 carrots, sliced
3 celery sticks, diced or sliced
½ baking potato, peeled and cut into chunks
10g/¼oz or 45ml/3 tbsp mixed flavourful dried mushrooms
5 garlic cloves, sliced
2 litres/3½ pints/8 cups water
2 vegetable stock (bouillon) cubes
salt and ground black pepper
30–45ml/2–3 tbsp chopped fresh parsley, to garnish
rye or pumpernickel bread, to serve

1 Place the haricot beans, green and yellow split peas, pearl barley, chopped onion, carrots, celery, potato, mixed mushrooms and garlic into a large, heavy pan. Pour in the water.

2 Bring the mixture to the boil, then reduce the heat, cover with a tight-fitting lid and simmer gently for about 1½ hours, or until the beans are tender.

3 Crumble the stock cubes into the soup. Taste for seasoning, adjusting if necessary – remember the stock cubes will be quite salty. Ladle into warmed bowls, garnish with parsley and serve with rye or pumpernickel bread.

Cook's Tip
Ensure that you do not add the stock cubes until near the end of the cooking time as the salt will prevent the beans from becoming tender.

Bean Broth Energy 222kcal/934kJ; Protein 14.3g; Carbohydrate 31.8g, of which sugars 10.9g; Fat 5.1g, of which saturates 0.6g; Cholesterol 0mg; Calcium 273mg; Fibre 13.9g; Sodium 50mg.
Old Country Soup Energy 130kcal/553kJ; Protein 6.7g; Carbohydrate 26.1g, of which sugars 2.2g; Fat 0.6g, of which saturates 0.1g; Cholesterol 0mg; Calcium 24mg; Fibre 1.8g; Sodium 20mg.

Spicy Slow-cooked Soup

The great advantage of cooking soup in the slow cooker is that all the flavours have plenty of time to develop and mingle. This technique is particularly well suited to richer soups that have complex spicing, such as this vegetable soup that contains a variety of spices.

Serves 6

1 large onion, very finely chopped
1 litre/1¾ pints/4 cups near-boiling vegetable stock
5ml/1 tsp ground cinnamon
5ml/1 tsp ground turmeric
15ml/1 tbsp grated fresh root ginger
pinch cayenne pepper
2 carrots, finely diced
2 celery sticks, finely diced
400g/14oz can chopped tomatoes
450g/1lb potatoes, finely diced
400g/14oz can chickpeas, drained
5 threads saffron
30ml/2 tbsp chopped fresh coriander (cilantro)
15ml/1 tbsp lemon juice
salt and ground black pepper
fried wedges of lemon, to serve (optional)

1 Place the chopped onion in the ceramic pot of the slow cooker and add 600ml/1 pint/2½ cups of the near-boiling vegetable stock.

2 Switch the slow cooker to the high or auto setting, cover with the lid and cook for about 1 hour, until the onion is soft and translucent.

3 Mix together the cinnamon, turmeric, ginger, cayenne pepper and 30ml/2 tbsp of stock to form a paste, then add to the pot with the carrots, celery and remaining stock. Stir well and season. Cover and cook for 1 hour.

4 Add the chopped tomatoes, potatoes, chickpeas and saffron to the pot. Cook for about 4–5 hours until all the vegetables are very tender.

5 Stir the coriander and lemon juice into the pot, then check the seasoning and adjust as necessary. Ladle the soup into warmed bowls and serve piping hot, with fried wedges of lemon, if you like, for squeezing over.

Cannellini Bean Soup

This delicious soup is full of Mediterranean flavours. It is great served with bread and olives, and perhaps raw onion quarters (or even raw garlic for those with more robust palates).

Serves 4

275g/10oz/1½ cups dried cannellini beans, soaked overnight in cold water
1 large onion, thinly sliced
1 celery stick, sliced
2 or 3 carrots, sliced
400g/14oz can tomatoes
15ml/1 tbsp tomato purée (paste)
150ml/¼ pint/⅔ cup extra virgin olive oil
5ml/1 tsp dried oregano
30ml/2 tbsp finely chopped fresh flat leaf parsley
salt and ground black pepper

1 Drain the beans, rinse them under cold water and drain them again. Transfer them to a large pan, pour in enough water to cover and bring to the boil over a medium heat. Cook over a high heat for about 5–7 minutes, skimming off any foam, then drain.

2 Return the beans to the pan, pour in fresh water to cover them by about 3cm/1¼in, then add the sliced onion, celery and carrots, and the tomatoes, and stir to combine.

3 Stir in the tomato purée, extra virgin olive oil and dried oregano. Season to taste with a little ground black pepper, but don't add salt at this stage as it would toughen the skins of the beans and stop them becoming completely tender.

4 Bring to the boil, lower the heat and cook for about 1 hour, or until the beans are just tender. Season with salt, stir in the parsley and serve in warmed bowls.

Cook's Tip

For a more substantial meal you could serve this soup as the Greeks traditionally do, with fried squid, marinated anchovies or keftedes. It is also delicious served with chunks of freshly baked crusty bread, feta cheese and olives.

Spicy Slow-cooked Soup Energy 166kcal/705kJ; Protein 7.5g; Carbohydrate 30.3g, of which sugars 7.4g; Fat 2.5g, of which saturates 0.3g; Cholesterol 0mg; Calcium 62mg; Fibre 5.3g; Sodium 335mg.
Cannellini Bean Soup Energy 490kcal/2,051kJ; Protein 17.9g; Carbohydrate 47.8g, of which sugars 11.3g; Fat 26.6g, of which saturates 4.1g; Cholesterol 0mg; Calcium 89mg; Fibre 8.4g; Sodium 45mg.

Seafood Chowder

Like most chowders, this is a substantial dish, and benefits from being made in a slow cooker. It is great served with crusty bread for a tasty lunch or supper.

Serves 4

25g/1oz/2 tbsp butter
1 small leek, sliced
1 small garlic clove, crushed
1 celery stalk, chopped
2 rindless smoked streaky (fatty) bacon rashers (strips), finely chopped
200g/7oz/generous 1 cup drained, canned corn kernels
450ml/¾ pint/scant 2 cups milk
5ml/1 tsp plain (all-purpose) flour
450ml/¾ pint/scant 2 cups boiling chicken or vegetable stock
115g/4oz/generous ½ cup easy-cook (converted) rice
4 large scallops, preferably with corals
115g/4oz white fish fillet, such as monkfish
15ml/1 tbsp chopped fresh parsley, plus extra to garnish
pinch of cayenne pepper
45ml/3 tbsp single (light) cream (optional)
salt and ground black pepper

1 Melt the butter in a frying pan, add the leek, garlic, celery and bacon and cook for 10 minutes, until soft. Transfer the mixture to the ceramic cooking pot and switch the cooker on to high.

2 Place half the corn kernels in a food processor or blender. Add about 75ml/2½fl oz/⅓ cup of the milk and process until the mixture is well blended and fairly thick and creamy.

3 Sprinkle the flour over the leek mixture and stir in. Gradually add the remaining milk, stirring after each addition. Stir in the stock, followed by the corn mixture. Cover the slow cooker with the lid and cook for 2 hours.

4 Add the rice to the pot and cook for 30 minutes. Meanwhile, pull the corals away from the scallops and slice the white flesh into 5mm/¼in slices. Cut the fish fillet into bitesize chunks. Add the scallops and fish to the pot. Cover and cook for 15 minutes.

5 Stir the corals, parsley and cayenne pepper into the chowder and cook for 5–10 minutes. Stir in the cream, if using, and ladle into bowls. Sprinkle with chopped parsley and serve.

Bouillabaisse

Perhaps the most famous of all Mediterranean fish soups, this recipe, originating from Marseilles in the south of France, is a rich and colourful mixture of fish and shellfish, flavoured with tomatoes, saffron and orange.

Serves 4–6

1.3–1.6kg/3–3½lb mixed fish and shellfish, such as red mullet, John Dory, monkfish, large prawns (shrimp) and clams
1.2 litres/2 pints/5 cups water
225g/8oz tomatoes
pinch of saffron threads
90ml/6 tbsp olive oil
1 onion, sliced
1 leek, sliced
1 celery stick, sliced
2 garlic cloves, crushed
1 bouquet garni
1 strip pared orange rind
2.5ml/½ tsp fennel seeds
15ml/1 tbsp tomato purée (paste)
10ml/2 tsp Pernod
salt and ground black pepper
4–6 thick slices French bread
45ml/3 tbsp chopped fresh parsley

1 Remove the heads, tails and fins from the fish and put in a large pan with the water. Bring to the boil, and simmer for 15 minutes. Strain and reserve the liquid. Cut the fish into large chunks. Leave the shellfish in their shells.

2 Scald the tomatoes, then drain and refresh in cold water. Peel and chop them. Soak the saffron in 15–30ml/1–2 tbsp hot water. Heat the oil in the cleaned pan, add the onion, leek and celery and cook until softened.

3 Add the garlic, bouquet garni, orange rind, fennel seeds and tomatoes. Stir in the saffron and liquid and the fish stock. Season with salt and pepper, bring to the boil and simmer for 35 minutes.

4 Add the shellfish and boil for 6 minutes. Discard any clams that remain closed. Add the fish and cook for 6–8 minutes until it flakes easily. Using a slotted spoon, transfer the fish to a warmed serving platter. Keep the liquid boiling and add the tomato purée and Pernod, then check the seasoning.

5 Place a slice of bread in each soup bowl, pour the broth over and serve the fish separately, sprinkled with the parsley.

Bouillabaisse Energy 338kcal/1418kJ; Protein 42.2g; Carbohydrate 12.8g, of which sugars 3.8g; Fat 13.2g, of which saturates 1.9g; Cholesterol 100mg; Calcium 55mg; Fibre 1.6g; Sodium 239mg.
Seafood Chowder Energy 355kcal/1497kJ; Protein 18.5g; Carbohydrate 45.9g, of which sugars 10.8g; Fat 12.1g, of which saturates 5.8g; Cholesterol 49mg; Calcium 179mg; Fibre 1.5g; Sodium 655mg.

Coconut and Seafood Soup with Garlic Chives

The long list of ingredients in this recipe could mislead you into thinking that this soup is complicated. In fact, it is extremely easy to put together, and is cooked slowly on top of the stove.

Serves 4

600ml/1 pint/2½ cups fish stock
5 thin slices fresh root ginger
2 lemon grass stalks, chopped
3 kaffir lime leaves, shredded
25g/1oz garlic chives, chopped
15g/½oz fresh coriander (cilantro)
15ml/1 tbsp vegetable oil
4 shallots, chopped
400ml/14fl oz can coconut milk
30–45ml/2–3 tbsp Thai fish sauce
45–60ml/3–4 tbsp Thai green curry paste
450g/1lb uncooked large prawns (jumbo shrimp), peeled and deveined
450g/1lb prepared squid, cut into rings
a little lime juice (optional)
salt and ground black pepper
60ml/4 tbsp fried shallot slices, to serve

1 Pour the stock into a pan and add the slices of fresh ginger, the chopped lemon grass and half the lime leaves.

2 Add half the chopped chives to the pan with the stalks from the coriander. Bring to the boil, then reduce the heat. Cover the pan and simmer for 20 minutes. Strain the stock and reserve.

3 Rinse the pan, then add the oil and shallots. Cook over a medium heat for 5–10 minutes, stirring occasionally, until the shallots are just beginning to brown.

4 Stir in the stock, coconut milk, the remaining lime leaves and half the fish sauce. Heat gently until the soup is just simmering and cook over a low heat for 10–15 minutes.

5 Stir in the curry paste and the peeled prawns and cook for 3 minutes. Add the squid and cook for a further 2 minutes. Add the lime juice, if using, and season with salt and pepper.

6 Stir in the remaining fish sauce, chives and the coriander leaves. Serve in warmed bowls sprinkled with fried shallots.

Hot and Sour Prawn Soup

This salty, sour, spicy hot soup is a real classic. Cooking the stock in a slow cooker maximizes the flavour before the final ingredients are added.

Serves 4

450g/1lb raw king prawns (jumbo shrimp), thawed if frozen
900ml/1½ pints/3¾ cups near-boiling chicken stock or water
3 lemon grass stalks
6 kaffir lime leaves, torn in half
225g/8oz straw mushrooms, drained
45ml/3 tbsp Thai fish sauce
60ml/4 tbsp fresh lime juice
30ml/2 tbsp chopped spring onions (scallions)
15ml/1 tbsp fresh coriander (cilantro) leaves
4 fresh red chillies, seeded and thickly sliced
salt and ground black pepper

1 Peel the prawns, reserving the shells. Using a sharp knife, make a shallow cut along the back of each prawn and use the point of the knife to remove the thin black vein. Place the prawns in a bowl, cover and chill until ready to use.

2 Rinse the reserved prawn shells under cold running water, then put them in the ceramic cooking pot and add the chicken stock or water. Cover with the lid and switch to the high setting.

3 Using a pestle, bruise the bulbous end of the lemon grass stalks. Lift the lid of the ceramic pot and quickly add the lemon grass stalks and half the torn kaffir lime leaves to the stock. Stir well, then re-cover with the lid and cook for about 2 hours until the stock is fragrant and aromatic.

4 Strain the stock into a large bowl and rinse out the ceramic cooking pot. Pour the stock back into the cleaned pot. Add the drained mushrooms and cook on high for 30 minutes.

5 Add the prawns to the soup and cook for a further 10 minutes until the prawns turn pink and are cooked.

6 Stir the fish sauce, lime juice, spring onions, coriander, chillies and remaining lime leaves into the soup. Taste and adjust the seasoning if necessary. The soup should be sour, salty, spicy and hot.

Coconut Soup Energy 282kcal/1185kJ; Protein 37.9g; Carbohydrate 7.7g, of which sugars 6g; Fat 11.3g, of which saturates 1.9g; Cholesterol 473mg; Calcium 156mg; Fibre 0.7g; Sodium 451mg.
Hot and Sour Soup Energy 127kcal/536kJ; Protein 27g; Carbohydrate 1.4g, of which sugars 1.2g; Fat 1.4g, of which saturates 0.3g; Cholesterol 315mg; Calcium 133mg; Fibre 0.7g; Sodium 2715mg.

Tofu Soup with Mushrooms, Tomato, Ginger and Coriander

This is a deliciously rich clear soup, which is enhanced by a slowly cooked and well-flavoured aromatic stock.

Serves 4

115g/4oz/scant 2 cups dried shiitake mushrooms, soaked in water for 20 minutes
15ml/1 tbsp vegetable oil
2 shallots, halved and sliced
2 Thai chillies, seeded and sliced
4cm/1½in fresh root ginger, peeled and grated or finely chopped
15ml/1 tbsp nuoc mam
350g/12oz tofu, rinsed, drained and cut into bitesize cubes
4 tomatoes, skinned, seeded and cut into thin strips
salt and ground black pepper
1 bunch coriander (cilantro), stalks removed, finely chopped, to garnish

For the stock

1 meaty chicken carcass or 500g/1¼lb pork ribs
25g/1oz dried squid or shrimp, soaked in water for 15 minutes
2 onions, peeled and quartered
2 garlic cloves, crushed
7.5cm/3in fresh root ginger, chopped
15ml/1 tbsp nuoc mam
6 black peppercorns
2 star anise
4 cloves
1 cinnamon stick
sea salt

1 Make the stock. Put the chicken carcass or ribs in a deep pan. Drain and rinse the squid or shrimp and add to the pan with the remaining ingredients, except the salt. Pour in 2 litres/3½ pints/8 cups water. Bring to the boil, and boil for a few minutes, skim off any foam, then simmer, covered, for 1½–2 hours. Remove the lid and simmer for a further 30 minutes to reduce. Skim off any fat, season, strain and measure out 1.5 litres/2½ pints/6¼ cups.

2 Squeeze dry the soaked shiitake mushrooms, remove the stems and slice the caps into thin strips. Heat the oil in a large pan and stir in the shallots, chillies and ginger. As the fragrance begins to rise, stir in the nuoc mam, followed by the stock.

3 Add the tofu, mushrooms and tomatoes and bring to the boil. Reduce the heat and simmer for 5–10 minutes. Season to taste and sprinkle the finely chopped fresh coriander over the top. Serve piping hot in warmed bowls.

Winter Melon Soup with Tiger Lilies, Coriander and Mint

This soup uses two common South-east Asian ingredients – winter melon to absorb the flavours and tiger lilies for a floral scent. If you can't find winter melon, you could use another winter squash.

Serves 4

350g/12oz winter melon
25g/1oz light golden tiger lilies, soaked in hot water for 20 minutes
salt and ground black pepper
1 small bunch each coriander (cilantro) and mint, stalks removed, leaves chopped, to garnish

For the stock

25g/1oz dried shrimp, soaked in water for 15 minutes
500g/1¼lb pork ribs
1 onion, peeled and quartered
175g/6oz carrots, roughly chopped
15ml/1 tbsp nuoc mam
15ml/1 tbsp soy sauce
4 black peppercorns

1 Make the stock. Drain and rinse the dried shrimp. Put the ribs in a large pan and cover with 2 litres/3½ pints/8 cups water. Bring to the boil, skim off any fat, and add the shrimp and the remaining stock ingredients. Cover and simmer for 1½ hours, then skim off any foam or fat. Simmer, uncovered, for a further 30 minutes, then strain. You should have about 1.5 litres/2½ pints/6¼ cups.

2 Halve the winter melon lengthways and remove the seeds and inner membrane. Finely slice the flesh into half-moons. Squeeze the soaked tiger lilies dry and tie them in a knot.

3 Bring the stock to the boil in a deep pan. Reduce the heat and add the winter melon and tiger lilies. Simmer for 20 minutes, or until the winter melon is tender. Season and serve immediately with the herbs sprinkled over the top.

Cook's Tip
Tiger lilies are sometimes referred to as golden needles. When choosing them, make sure they are light gold in colour.

Tofu Soup Energy 220kcal/919kJ; Protein 12g; Carbohydrate 26g, of which sugars 4g; Fat 8g, of which saturates 1g; Cholesterol 0mg; Calcium 47.8mg; Fibre 1.1g; Sodium 500mg.
Winter Melon Soup Energy 46kcal/198kJ; Protein 2g; Carbohydrate 9g, of which sugars 4g; Fat 0g, of which saturates 0g; Cholesterol 0mg; Calcium 90mg; Fibre 1.4g; Sodium 400mg.

Avgolemono

This light chicken soup from Greece is a fine example of a few ingredients being combined in a slow cooker to make a fabulous dish.

Serves 4

900ml/1½ pints/3¾ cups near-boiling chicken stock
50g/2oz/⅓ cup easy-cook (converted) white rice
3 egg yolks
30–60ml/2–4 tbsp lemon juice
30ml/2 tbsp finely chopped fresh parsley
salt and ground black pepper
lemon slices and parsley sprigs, to garnish

1 Pour the hot chicken stock into the ceramic cooking pot of the slow cooker. Cover with a lid and cook on the high setting for 30 minutes, or until it reaches boiling point.

2 Stir the easy-cook rice into the stock, cover the slow cooker and cook for 45 minutes, or until the rice is tender. Season to taste with salt, if needed, and plenty of ground black pepper. Switch off the slow cooker, remove the lid and leave to stand for 5 minutes.

3 Meanwhile, whisk the egg yolks in a bowl, then add about 30ml/2 tbsp of the lemon juice, whisking constantly until the mixture is smooth and bubbly. Add a ladleful of the hot soup to the egg mixture, whisking continuously.

4 Slowly add the egg mixture to the soup in the ceramic cooking pot, whisking all the time. The soup will thicken slightly and turn a pretty yellow.

5 Taste and add more lemon juice and seasoning if necessary. Stir in the parsley and serve immediately, garnished with lemon slices and parsley sprigs.

Cook's Tip
When adding the egg mixture, be careful not to let the soup curdle. Allow the soup to cool slightly before whisking in the egg mixture in a slow, steady stream. Do not reheat the soup.

Chicken Soup with Knaidlach

If you have a large slow cooker you can double the quantities given here and use a small whole chicken.

Serves 4

2 chicken portions, about 275g/10oz each
1 onion
1.2 litres/2 pints/5 cups boiling chicken stock
2 carrots, thickly sliced
2 celery sticks, thickly sliced
1 small parsnip, cut into chunks
small pinch of ground turmeric
30ml/2 tbsp chopped fresh parsley, plus extra to garnish
15ml/1 tbsp chopped fresh dill
salt and ground black pepper

For the knaidlach
175g/6oz/¾ cup medium matzo meal
2 eggs, lightly beaten
45ml/3 tbsp vegetable oil
30ml/2 tbsp chopped fresh parsley
½ onion, finely grated
pinch of chicken stock (bouillon) cube (optional)
about 90ml/6 tbsp water
salt and ground black pepper

1 Place the chicken in the ceramic cooking pot. Peel the onion, keeping it whole. Cut a cross in the stem end and add to the pot with the stock, carrots, celery, parsnip, turmeric, salt and pepper. Cover and cook on high for 1 hour. Skim off the scum that rises.

2 Cook for a further 3 hours, or until the chicken is tender. Remove the chicken, discard the skin and bones and chop the flesh. Skim the fat off the soup, then return the chicken. Add the herbs and continue cooking while you make the knaidlach.

3 Mix all the knaidlach ingredients in a large bowl. It should be the consistency of a thick paste. Cover and chill for 30 minutes, until the mixture is firm. Bring a pan of water to the boil. Take a spoonful of the batter and roll into a ball, then add to the boiling water. Continue with the remaining batter, then cover the pan and simmer for 15–20 minutes.

4 Remove the knaidlach from the pan with a slotted spoon and divide between individual serving bowls. Leave them to firm up for a few minutes. Ladle the hot soup over the knaidlach and serve sprinkled with extra chopped parsley.

Avgolemono Energy 98kcal/410kJ; Protein 3.3g; Carbohydrate 11.1g, of which sugars 0.3g; Fat 4.8g, of which saturates 1.3g; Cholesterol 151mg; Calcium 26mg; Fibre 0.1g; Sodium 211mg.
Chicken Soup Energy 586kcal/2451kJ; Protein 38.2g; Carbohydrate 42.6g, of which sugars 6.3g; Fat 30.3g, of which saturates 7.7g; Cholesterol 272mg; Calcium 131mg; Fibre 3.7g; Sodium 802mg.

Chicken Soup with Prunes and Barley

The unusual combination of leeks and prunes in this one-pot soup is delicious.

Serves 6

115g/4oz/⅔ cup pearl barley
1 chicken, weighing about 2kg/4¼lb
900g/2lb leeks
1 fresh bay leaf
a few fresh parsley stalks and thyme sprigs
1 large carrot, thickly sliced
2.4 litres/4 pints/10 cups chicken or beef stock
400g/14oz ready-to-eat prunes
salt and ground black pepper
chopped fresh parsley, to garnish

1 Rinse the pearl barley then cook it in a pan of boiling water for 10 minutes. Drain, rinse well, then drain again and set aside.

2 Cut the breast portions off the chicken and set aside, then place the remaining chicken carcass in the pan. Cut half the leeks into 5cm/2in lengths and add to the pan. Tie the herbs into a bouquet garni and add to the pan with the carrot and stock.

3 Bring the stock to the boil, then reduce the heat and cover the pan. Simmer gently for 1 hour. Skim off any scum when the water first starts to boil and occasionally during simmering.

4 Add the chicken breast portions and cook for 30 minutes. Strain the stock. Reserve the breast portions and the meat from the carcass. Discard all the skin, bones, cooked vegetables and herbs. Skim the fat from the stock, then return it to the pan.

5 Add the pearl barley to the stock. Bring to the boil over a medium heat, then simmer gently for 15–20 minutes, until the barley is just cooked and tender. Season with salt and pepper.

6 Add the prunes to the pan, then thinly slice the remaining leeks and add to the pan. Bring to the boil, then cover and simmer gently for 10 minutes, or until the leeks are just cooked.

7 Slice the chicken breast portions and then add them to the soup with the remaining meat from the carcass, sliced or cut into pieces. Reheat the soup, if necessary, then ladle into warm soup bowls and sprinkle with chopped parsley to serve.

Chinese Chicken and Chilli Soup

Ginger and lemon grass add an aromatic note to this refreshing soup, which is traditionally cooked in a Chinese sand pot.

Serves 4

150g/5oz boneless chicken breast portion, cut into thin strips
2.5cm/1in piece fresh root ginger, finely chopped
5cm/2in piece lemon grass stalk, finely chopped
1 red chilli, seeded and thinly sliced
8 baby corn cobs, halved lengthways
1 large carrot, cut into thin sticks
1 litre/1¾ pints/4 cups hot chicken stock
4 spring onions (scallions), thinly sliced
12 small shiitake mushrooms, sliced
115g/4oz/1 cup vermicelli rice noodles
30ml/2 tbsp soy sauce
salt and ground black pepper

1 Place the chicken, ginger, lemon grass and sliced chilli in a Chinese sand pot or heavy non-stick pot with a lid. Add the baby corn and the carrot. Pour over the hot stock and cover the pot.

2 Place the pot in an unheated oven. Set the temperature to 200°C/400°F/Gas 6 and cook the soup for 35–45 minutes, or until the stock is simmering and the chicken and vegetables are tender.

3 Add the spring onions and mushrooms, cover and return the pot to the oven for 10–15 minutes. Meanwhile, place the noodles in a large bowl and cover with boiling water – soak for the required time, following the packet instructions.

4 Drain the noodles and divide among four warmed soup bowls. Stir the soy sauce into the soup and season with salt and pepper. Ladle the soup into the bowls and serve immediately.

Cook's Tip
Rice noodles are available in a variety of thicknesses and can be bought in straight lengths or in coils or loops. They are a creamy white colour and brittle in texture. Vermicelli rice noodles are very fine and only need to be soaked for a few minutes.

Chicken Soup with Prunes Energy 273kcal/1158kJ; Protein 21.7g; Carbohydrate 44.4g, of which sugars 27.2g; Fat 2.1g, of which saturates 0.4g; Cholesterol 47mg; Calcium 70mg; Fibre 7.5g; Sodium 55mg.
Chinese Chicken Soup Energy 168kcal/707kJ; Protein 13.7g; Carbohydrate 26.1g, of which sugars 3.1g; Fat 1g, of which saturates 0.2g; Cholesterol 26mg; Calcium 25mg; Fibre 1.7g; Sodium 853mg.

Asian-style Duck Consommé

The flavours of this soup are greatly enhanced by being made in a slow cooker.

Serves 4

1 small carrot
1 small leek, halved lengthways
4 shiitake mushrooms, thinly sliced
soy sauce
2 spring onions (scallions), thinly sliced
finely shredded watercress or Chinese leaves (Chinese cabbage)
ground black pepper

For the consommé

1 duck carcass (raw or cooked), plus 2 legs or giblets, trimmed of fat
1 large onion, unpeeled, with root end trimmed
2 carrots, cut into 2.5cm/1in pieces
1 parsnip, cut into 2.5cm/1in pieces
1 leek, cut into 2.5cm/1in pieces
2 garlic cloves, crushed
15ml/1 tbsp black peppercorns
2.5cm/1in piece fresh root ginger, peeled and sliced
4 thyme sprigs or 5ml/1 tsp dried thyme
1 bunch fresh coriander (cilantro)

1 Make the consommé. Put the duck carcass, legs or giblets, onion, carrots, parsnip, leek and garlic in the ceramic cooking pot. Add the peppercorns, ginger, thyme and coriander stalks (reserve the leaves) and enough cold water to cover the bones.

2 Cook, covered, on high or auto for 2 hours. Skim off any surface scum, then reduce the temperature to low or leave on auto. Cover and cook for 4 hours, removing the lid for the last hour.

3 Strain the consommé into a bowl, discarding the bones and vegetables. Leave to cool, then chill for several hours. Skim off any fat and blot with kitchen paper to remove all the fat.

4 Cut the carrot and leek into 5cm/2in pieces. Cut each piece lengthways into thin slices, then slice into thin julienne strips. Place in the clean ceramic cooking pot with the shiitake mushrooms.

5 Pour over the consommé and add a few dashes of soy sauce and some pepper. Cover and cook on high for 45 minutes, or until hot, skimming off any foam that rises to the surface.

6 Stir in the spring onions and watercress or Chinese leaves. Ladle into warmed bowls and sprinkle with the coriander leaves.

Aromatic Broth with Roast Duck

This slow-cooked broth makes a substantial autumn or winter meal. The home-made stock intensifies the delicious flavours of the soup.

Serves 4

15ml/1 tbsp vegetable oil
2 shallots, thinly sliced
4cm/1½in piece fresh root ginger, peeled and sliced
15ml/1 tbsp soy sauce
5ml/1 tsp five-spice powder
10ml/2 tsp sugar
175g/6oz pak choi (bok choy)
450g/1lb fresh egg noodles
350g/12oz roast duck, thinly sliced
sea salt

For the stock

1 chicken or duck carcass
2 carrots, peeled and quartered
2 onions, peeled and quartered
4cm/1½in fresh root ginger, peeled and cut into chunks
2 lemon grass stalks, chopped
30ml/2 tbsp nuoc mam
15ml/1 tbsp soy sauce
6 black peppercorns

For the garnish

4 spring onions (scallions), sliced
1–2 red Serrano chillies, seeded and finely sliced
1 bunch each coriander (cilantro) and basil, stalks removed, leaves chopped

1 Make the stock. Put the chicken or duck carcass into a deep pan. Add all the other stock ingredients and pour in 2.5 litres/4½ pints/10¼ cups water. Bring to the boil, and boil for a few minutes, skim off any foam, then simmer gently with the lid on for 2–3 hours. Continue to simmer uncovered for 30 minutes to reduce the stock. Skim off any fat, season with salt, then strain the stock. Measure out 2 litres/3½ pints/8 cups.

2 Heat the oil in a deep pan and stir in the shallots and ginger. Add the soy sauce, five-spice powder, sugar and stock and bring to the boil. Season with salt and simmer gently for 10–15 minutes.

3 Meanwhile, cut the pak choi diagonally into wide strips and blanch in boiling water to soften. Drain and refresh under cold running water. Bring a large pan of water to the boil, then add the fresh noodles. Cook for 5 minutes, then drain well.

4 Divide the noodles among four soup bowls, lay some of the pak choi and sliced duck over them, and then ladle over the broth. Garnish with spring onions, chillies and herbs, and serve.

Aromatic Broth with Roast Duck Energy 673kcal/2836kJ; Protein 37g; Carbohydrate 86g, of which sugars 22g; Fat 6g, of which saturates 1g; Cholesterol 81mg; Calcium 4mg; Fibre 0.7g; Sodium 700mg.
Duck Consommé Energy 96kcal/406kJ; Protein 7.1g; Carbohydrate 12.1g, of which sugars 7.9g; Fat 2.5g, of which saturates 0.6g; Cholesterol 28mg; Calcium 51mg; Fibre 4g; Sodium 47mg.

Beef and Barley Soup

This traditional farmhouse soup makes a wonderfully restorative dish on a cold winter day. It is slowly cooked to allow the flavours to develop, and it tastes even better if it is made in advance and then reheated before serving.

Serves 6–8

450–675g/1–1½lb rib steak, or other stewing beef on the bone
2 large onions
50g/2oz/¼ cup pearl barley
50g/2oz/½ cup green split peas
3 large carrots, chopped
2 white turnips, chopped
3 celery stalks, chopped
1 large or 2 medium leeks, thinly sliced
sea salt and ground black pepper
chopped fresh parsley, to garnish

1 Using a sharp knife, bone the meat, and put the bones and half an onion, roughly sliced, into a large pan. Cover the bones with cold water, season with salt and pepper and bring to the boil. Boil for a few minutes and skim off any foam that rises to the surface. Reduce the heat to low and then leave to simmer very gently for 1–2 hours.

2 Meanwhile, trim any fat or gristle from the meat and cut into small pieces. Chop the remaining onions finely. When the stock is ready, leave to cool slightly then strain into a bowl, discarding the bones and onion pieces. You will need about 2 litres/3½ pints/9 cups. If less, then make up that quantity by adding extra hot water. Return the strained stock to the rinsed pan with the chopped meat, onions, pearl barley and the green split peas.

3 Season the soup with salt and ground black pepper. Bring to the boil, and skim off any foam that rises to the surface if necessary. Reduce the heat, then cover the pan and simmer for about 30 minutes.

4 Add the rest of the vegetables to the pan and simmer for about 1 hour, or until the meat and all the vegetables are tender. Check the seasoning, adjusting if necessary Serve in large warmed bowls, generously sprinkled with parsley.

Oxtail Soup

Long, slow cooking gives this soup a rich flavour and meat that is beautifully tender.

Serves 4–6

1 oxtail, cut into joints, total weight about 1.3kg/3lb
25g/1oz/2 tbsp butter
2 medium onions, chopped
2 medium carrots, chopped
2 celery sticks, sliced
1 bacon rasher (strip), chopped
2 litres/3½ pints/8 cups beef stock
1 bouquet garni
2 bay leaves
30ml/2 tbsp flour
squeeze of fresh lemon juice
60ml/4 tbsp port, sherry or Madeira
salt and ground black pepper

1 Wash and dry the pieces of oxtail, trimming off any fat. Melt the butter in a large pan, add the oxtail in batches and brown them quickly on all sides. Lift the meat out on to a plate.

2 Add the onions, carrots, celery and bacon to the same pan. Cook over a medium heat for 5–10 minutes, stirring occasionally, until the vegetables are softened and golden brown.

3 Return the oxtail to the pan and add the stock, bouquet garni, bay leaves and seasoning. Bring just to the boil and skim off any foam. Cover and simmer gently for about 3 hours or until the meat is so tender that it is falling away from the bones.

4 Strain the mixture, discarding the vegetables, bouquet garni and bay leaves, and leave to cool slightly. When the oxtail has cooled enough to handle, pick all the meat off the bones and cut it into small pieces. Skim off any fat that has risen to the surface of the stock, then transfer to a large pan. Add the pieces of meat and reheat.

5 With a whisk, blend the flour with a little cold water to make a smooth paste. Stir in a little of the hot stock then stir the mixture into the pan. Bring the soup to the boil, stirring, until the soup thickens slightly. Reduce the heat and simmer gently for about 5–10 minutes.

6 Season with salt, pepper and lemon juice to taste. Stir in the port, sherry or Madeira and serve in warmed soup bowls.

Beef and Barley Soup Energy 194kcal/816kJ; Protein 20.3g; Carbohydrate 21.6g, of which sugars 12g; Fat 3.5g, of which saturates 1.2g; Cholesterol 50mg; Calcium 84mg; Fibre 5g; Sodium 88mg.
Oxtail Soup Energy 459kcal/1914kJ; Protein 45.4g; Carbohydrate 6.5g, of which sugars 2.6g; Fat 26.8g, of which saturates 11.8g; Cholesterol 176mg; Calcium 36mg; Fibre 0.7g; Sodium 403mg.

Beef Noodle Soup

The rare beef will cook gently under the steaming stock poured over it.

Serves 6

250g/9oz beef sirloin, thinly sliced
500g/1¼lb dried noodles, soaked for 20 minutes
1 onion, halved and finely sliced
6–8 spring onions (scallions), cut into long pieces
2–3 red Thai chillies, seeded and finely sliced
115g/4oz/½ cup beansprouts
1 large bunch each fresh coriander (cilantro) and mint, stalks removed, leaves chopped
2 limes, cut in wedges, and hoisin sauce or nuoc cham, to serve

For the stock

1.5kg/3lb 5oz oxtail, trimmed of fat and cut into thick pieces
1kg/2¼lb beef shank or brisket
2 large onions, quartered
2 carrots, cut into chunks
7.5cm/3in fresh root ginger, chopped
6 cloves
2 cinnamon sticks
6 star anise
5ml/1 tsp black peppercorns
30ml/2 tbsp soy sauce
45–60ml/3–4 tbsp nuoc mam
salt

1 Make the stock. Put the oxtail into a large pan and cover with water. Bring to the boil and blanch the meat for 10 minutes. Drain the meat, rinse off any scum and clean out the pan. Put the oxtail back into the pan with the other stock ingredients, apart from the nuoc mam and salt. Cover with 3 litres/5¼ pints/12 cups water. Bring to the boil, then simmer, covered, for 2–3 hours.

2 Remove the lid and simmer for another hour, until the stock has reduced to about 2 litres/3½ pints/8 cups. Skim off any fat and then strain the stock into another pan. Cut the beef sirloin across the grain into very thin pieces. Bring the stock to the boil once more, stir in the nuoc mam, season to taste, then reduce the heat and simmer until ready to use.

3 Meanwhile, bring a pan filled with water to the boil, drain the noodles and add to the water. Cook for 5 minutes or until tender. Drain the noodles and divide them among six soup bowls. Top with the beef sirloin, onion, spring onions, chillies and beansprouts. Ladle the stock over the top, sprinkle with the fresh herbs and serve with the lime wedges to squeeze over. Pass around the hoisin sauce or nuoc cham for diners to help themselves.

Salt Beef, Lamb and Chickpea Soup

This soup of savoury meats and vegetables is baked in a low oven for several hours.

Serves 8

45ml/3 tbsp olive oil
1 onion, chopped
10 garlic cloves, chopped
1 parsnip, sliced
3 carrots, sliced
5–10ml/1–2 tsp ground cumin
2.5ml/½ tsp ground turmeric
15ml/1 tbsp chopped fresh root ginger
250g/9oz/1 cup chickpeas, soaked overnight and drained
2 litres/3½ pints/8 cups beef stock
1 potato, peeled and diced
½ marrow (large zucchini), sliced or cut into chunks
400g/14oz fresh or canned tomatoes, diced
45–60ml/3–4 tbsp brown or green lentils
2 bay leaves
250g/9oz salted meat such as salt beef (or double the quantity of lamb)
250g/9oz piece of lamb
½ large bunch fresh coriander (cilantro), chopped
200g/7oz/1 cup long grain rice
8 lemon wedges and a spicy sauce such as zchug or fresh chillies, finely chopped, to serve

1 Preheat the oven to 120°C/250°F/Gas ½. Heat the oil in a large flameproof casserole, add the onion, garlic, parsnip, carrots, cumin, turmeric and ginger and cook for 2–3 minutes. Add the chickpeas, stock, potato, marrow, tomatoes, lentils, bay leaves, meats and coriander. Cook in the oven for 3 hours.

2 Put the rice on a double thickness of muslin (cheesecloth) and tie together at the corners, allowing enough room for the rice to expand while it is cooking.

3 Two hours before the end of cooking, remove the casserole from the oven. Place the rice parcel in the casserole, anchoring the edge of the muslin parcel under the lid so that the parcel is held above the soup and allowed to steam. Return the casserole to the oven and continue cooking for a further 2 hours.

4 Carefully remove the lid and the rice. Skim any fat off the top of the soup and ladle the soup into bowls with a scoop of the rice and one or two pieces of meat. Serve with lemon wedges and a spoonful of hot sauce or chopped fresh chillies.

Beef Noodle Soup Energy 391kcal/1635kJ; Protein 16g; Carbohydrate 74g, of which sugars 3g; Fat 2g, of which saturates 1g; Cholesterol 21mg; Calcium 62mg; Fibre 0.8g; Sodium 600mg.
Salt Beef Soup Energy 379kcal/1590kJ; Protein 25.9g; Carbohydrate 41.9g, of which sugars 4.9g; Fat 12.5g, of which saturates 3.3g; Cholesterol 47mg; Calcium 87mg; Fibre 5.1g; Sodium 369mg.

Lamb and Vegetable Broth

This is a modern adaptation of a traditional recipe for mutton broth. The home-made stock results in a tasty broth and beautifully tender pieces of lamb. It is a perfect soup for a cold winter's day and is delicious served with chunky wholemeal bread for a more substantial meal.

Serves 6

675g/1½lb neck (US shoulder or breast) of lamb on the bone
1 large onion, chopped
2 bay leaves
3 carrots, chopped
½ white turnip, diced
½ small white cabbage, shredded
2 large leeks, thinly sliced
15ml/1 tbsp tomato purée (paste)
30ml/2 tbsp chopped fresh parsley
salt and ground black pepper
wholemeal (whole-wheat) bread, to serve (optional)

1 Trim any excess fat from the neck of lamb. Put into a large pan with the onion and bay leaves. Add about 1.5 litres/ 2½ pints/6¼ cups water and bring to the boil.

2 Boil for a few minutes and skim off any scum that rises to the surface. Reduce the heat, cover the pan and simmer gently for about 1½–2 hours.

3 Remove the lamb from the stock and place on a chopping board and leave to cool. When it is cool enough to handle, remove the meat from the bones and cut into small pieces. Discard the bones and return the meat to the stock.

4 Add the carrots, white turnip, cabbage, leeks and tomato purée to the pan and stir well. Add the chopped parsley, and season well with salt and ground black pepper.

5 Bring the stock gently back to the boil, then reduce the heat and simmer, uncovered, for a further 30 minutes, until all the vegetables are tender.

6 Ladle the broth evenly among six warmed, deep soup bowls and serve with chunks of wholemeal bread, if you like.

Spiced Lamb Soup

Aromatic ginger, turmeric and cinnamon are slowly cooked with chickpeas and lamb to make this hearty, warming soup.

Serves 6

75g/3oz/½ cup chickpeas, soaked overnight
15g/½oz/1 tbsp butter
225g/8oz lamb, cut into cubes
1 onion, chopped
450g/1lb tomatoes, peeled and chopped
a few celery leaves, chopped
30ml/2 tbsp chopped fresh parsley
15ml/1 tbsp chopped fresh coriander (cilantro)
2.5ml/½ tsp ground ginger
2.5ml/½ tsp ground turmeric
5ml/1 tsp ground cinnamon
1.75 litres/3 pints/7½ cups water
75g/3oz/scant ½ cup green lentils
75g/3oz vermicelli or soup pasta
2 egg yolks
juice of ½–1 lemon
salt and ground black pepper
fresh coriander (cilantro), to garnish
lemon wedges, to serve

1 Drain the chickpeas, rinse under cold water and set aside. Melt the butter in a large flameproof casserole or pan and fry the lamb and onion for 2–3 minutes, stirring occasionally, until the lamb is just browned.

2 Add the chopped tomatoes, celery leaves, herbs and spices and season well with ground black pepper. Cook for about 1 minute, then stir in the water and add the green lentils and the soaked, drained and rinsed chickpeas.

3 Slowly bring to the boil and skim the surface to remove the froth. Boil for 10 minutes, then reduce the heat and simmer very gently for 2 hours, or until the chickpeas are very tender.

4 Season with salt and pepper, then add the vermicelli or soup pasta to the pan and cook for 5–6 minutes until it is just tender. If the soup is very thick at this stage, add a little more water.

5 Beat the egg yolks with the lemon juice and stir into the simmering soup. Immediately remove the soup from the heat and stir until thickened. Pour into warmed serving bowls and garnish with plenty of fresh coriander. Serve with lemon wedges for squeezing over the soup.

Spiced Lamb Soup Energy 248kcal/1042kJ; Protein 16.3g; Carbohydrate 25.8g, of which sugars 4.1g; Fat 9.5g, of which saturates 4g; Cholesterol 101mg; Calcium 64mg; Fibre 3.6g; Sodium 70mg.
Lamb Broth Energy 162kcal/675kJ; Protein 13.1g; Carbohydrate 8.5g, of which sugars 7g; Fat 8.6g, of which saturates 3.8g; Cholesterol 44mg; Calcium 42mg; Fibre 3g; Sodium 55mg.

Lamb Meatball and Vegetable Soup

A variety of vegetables makes a tasty base for meatballs in this substantial soup, which will make a hearty meal served with crusty bread.

Serves 4

1 litre/1¾ pints/4 cups lamb stock
1 onion, finely chopped
2 carrots, finely sliced
½ celeriac, finely diced
75g/3oz/¾ cup frozen peas
50g/2oz green beans, cut into 2.5cm/1in pieces
3 tomatoes, seeded and chopped
1 red (bell) pepper, seeded and diced
1 potato, coarsely diced
2 lemons, sliced
salt and ground black pepper
crusty bread, to serve

For the meatballs

225g/8oz/1 cup very lean minced (ground) lamb
40g/1½oz/¼ cup short grain rice
30ml/2 tbsp chopped fresh parsley
plain (all-purpose) flour, for coating

1 Pour the stock into a large pan and place over medium heat. Stir in the onion, carrot, celeriac and peas.

2 Add the beans, tomatoes, red pepper and potato with the slices of lemon. Stir in a little salt and freshly ground black pepper and bring the mixture to the boil. Reduce the heat, cover the pan and simmer for 15–20 minutes.

3 Meanwhile, prepare the meatballs. Mix the meat, rice and parsley together in a bowl and season well. The best way of mixing meat for meatballs is by hand, squeezing and kneading the mixture so that the meat mixes with the rice.

4 Take out a rounded teaspoon of the meat mixture and roll it into a small ball, roughly the size of a walnut. Toss it in the flour. Repeat with the remaining mixture.

5 Add the meatballs to the soup and simmer gently for 25–30 minutes, stirring occasionally, to prevent the meatballs from sticking. The rice should be plumped up and cooked in the meat. Adjust the seasoning and serve in warmed bowls, accompanied by crusty bread.

Irish Country Soup

Traditionally, buttered chunks of brown bread or Irish soda bread would be served with this hearty one-pot meal, which is based on the classic Irish stew.

Serves 4

15ml/1 tbsp vegetable oil
675g/1½lb boneless lamb chump chops, trimmed and cut into small cubes
2 small onions, quartered
2 leeks, thickly sliced
1 litre/1¾ pints/4 cups water
2 large potatoes, cut into chunks
2 carrots, thickly sliced
sprig of fresh thyme, plus extra to garnish
15g/½oz/1 tbsp butter
30ml/2 tbsp chopped fresh parsley
salt and ground black pepper
brown or Irish soda bread, to serve

1 Heat the oil in a large pan, add the lamb in batches and fry, turning occasionally, until well browned all over. Use a slotted spoon to remove the lamb from the pan and set aside.

2 Add the onions to the pan and cook for 4–5 minutes, until the onions are browned. Return the meat to the pan and add the leeks. Pour in the water, then bring to the boil. Reduce the heat, then cover and simmer for about 1 hour.

3 Add the potatoes, carrots and fresh thyme, and cook for 40 minutes, until the lamb is tender. Remove from the heat and leave to stand for 5 minutes, then skim off the fat.

4 Pour off the stock into a clean pan and whisk the butter into it. Stir in the parsley and season well, then pour the liquid back over the soup ingredients.

5 Ladle the soup into warmed bowls and garnish with sprigs of fresh thyme. Serve immediately with brown or soda bread.

Variation
The vegetables can be varied according to the season. Swede (rutabaga), turnip, celeriac and even cabbage could be added in place of some of those listed.

Lamb Soup: Energy 226kcal/948kJ; Protein 15.7g; Carbohydrate 25.1g, of which sugars 11.4g; Fat 7.7g, of which saturates 3.2g; Cholesterol 43mg; Calcium 75mg; Fibre 5.2g; Sodium 102mg.
Irish Country Soup Energy 453kcal/1893kJ; Protein 36.5g; Carbohydrate 20.5g, of which sugars 6.2g; Fat 25.6g, of which saturates 11.3g; Cholesterol 136mg; Calcium 53mg; Fibre 3.7g; Sodium 185mg.

Scotch Broth

Sustaining and warming, Scotch broth is custom-made for the chilly Scottish weather, and makes a tasty winter soup anywhere. Traditionally, a large pot of it is slowly cooked and this is dipped into throughout the next few days, the flavour improving all the time.

Serves 6–8

1kg/2¼lb lean neck (US shoulder or breast) of lamb, cut into large, even chunks
1.75 litres/3 pints/7½ cups cold water
1 large onion, chopped
50g/2oz/¼ cup pearl barley
1 bouquet garni
1 large carrot, chopped
1 turnip, chopped
3 leeks, chopped
1 small white cabbage, finely shredded
salt and ground black pepper
chopped fresh parsley, to garnish
wholemeal (whole-wheat) bread, to serve

1 Trim any fat from the chunks of lamb and place into a large, deep pan and cover with the measured water. Gently bring to the boil over medium heat. Continue to boil for a few minutes and skim off any scum that rises to the surface with a spoon. Add the chopped onion, pearl barley and bouquet garni to the pan, and stir in thoroughly.

2 Bring the soup back to the boil, then reduce the heat, partly cover the pan and simmer gently for a further 1 hour. Make sure that it does not boil too furiously. If the liquid begins to dry out then add in a little more water.

3 Add the carrot, turnip, leeks and white cabbage to the pan and season with salt and plenty of ground black pepper. Bring the mixture back to the boil, partly cover the pan again and simmer gently for about 35–45 minutes, until all the vegetables are tender.

4 Remove any excess fat from the surface of the soup by blotting it with a sheet of kitchen paper. Ladle the hot soup into warmed soup bowls, and garnish with chopped parsley. Serve with chunks of fresh wholemeal bread, if you like.

Sour Lamb Soup

This classic sour soup is made with lamb, although pork and poultry are popular alternatives. The paprika butter makes an unusual garnish.

Serves 4–5

30ml/2 tbsp oil
450g/1lb lean lamb, trimmed and cubed
1 onion, diced
30ml/2 tbsp plain (all-purpose) flour
15ml/1 tbsp paprika
1 litre/1¾ pints/4 cups hot lamb stock
3 sprigs of fresh parsley
4 spring onions (scallions)
4 sprigs of fresh dill
25g/1oz/scant ¼ cup long grain rice
2 eggs, beaten
30–45ml/2–3 tbsp vinegar or lemon juice
salt and ground black pepper

For the garnish
25g/1oz/2 tbsp butter, melted
5ml/1 tsp paprika
a little fresh parsley or lovage and dill

1 In a large pan heat the oil and fry the meat until brown. Add the onion and cook until it has softened. Sprinkle in the flour and paprika. Stir well, add the stock and cook for 10 minutes.

2 Tie the parsley, spring onions and dill together with string. Add to the large pan with the rice and season generously with salt and pepper. Bring to the boil, then simmer for about 35–45 minutes, or until the lamb is tender.

3 Remove the pan from the heat and stir in the eggs. Add the vinegar or lemon juice. Discard the tied herbs and season to taste.

4 For the garnish, melt the butter in a pan and blend in the paprika. Ladle the soup into warmed serving bowls. Garnish with the herbs and a little red paprika butter.

Cook's Tip
Add extra vinegar or lemon juice if you want the soup to have a more piquant flavour.

Scotch Broth Energy 387kcal/1619kJ; Protein 36.2g; Carbohydrate 17.7g, of which sugars 9.1g; Fat 19.5g, of which saturates 8.8g; Cholesterol 127mg; Calcium 86mg; Fibre 4.3g; Sodium 157mg.
Sour Lamb Soup Energy 314kcal/1309kJ; Protein 21.6g; Carbohydrate 10.1g, of which sugars 1.2g; Fat 21.1g, of which saturates 8.4g; Cholesterol 155mg; Calcium 49mg; Fibre 0.8g; Sodium 139mg.

Bacon Broth

A hearty meal in a soup bowl. The slow-cooked bacon hock contributes flavour and some meat to this dish, but it may be salty so remember to taste and add extra salt only if needed.

Serves 6–8

1 bacon hock, about 900g/2lb
75g/3oz/⅓ cup pearl barley
75g/3oz/⅓ cup lentils
2 leeks, sliced, or onions, diced
4 carrots, diced
200g/7oz swede (rutabaga), diced
3 potatoes, diced
small bunch of herbs (thyme, parsley, bay leaf)
1 small cabbage, trimmed, quartered or sliced
salt and ground black pepper
chopped fresh parsley, to garnish
brown bread, to serve

1 Soak the bacon in cold water overnight. Next morning, drain it and put it into a large pan with enough fresh cold water to cover it. Bring to the boil, skim off any scum that rises to the surface, and then add the barley and lentils. Bring back to the boil and simmer for about 15 minutes.

2 Add the leeks, carrots, swede and potatoes to the pan with some black pepper and the herbs. Bring back to the boil, reduce the heat and simmer gently for 1½–2 hours, or until the meat is tender.

3 Lift the bacon hock from the pan with a slotted spoon. Remove the skin, then take the meat off the bones and break it into bitesize pieces. Return to the pan with the cabbage. Discard the herbs and cook for a little longer until the cabbage is cooked to your liking.

4 Taste and adjust the seasoning if necessary. Ladle the hot soup into warmed soup bowls, garnish with parsley and serve with freshly baked brown bread.

Cook's Tip
Traditionally, the cabbage is simply trimmed and quartered, although it may be sliced if you prefer.

Gammon and Bean Broth

This tasty and substantial broth is made in a slow cooker to give the flavours time to develop fully.

Serves 6

450g/1lb gammon, in one piece, soaked overnight in cold water
2 bay leaves
2 onions, sliced
10ml/2 tsp paprika
675g/1½lb baking potatoes, cut into 2.5cm/1in chunks
225g/8oz spring greens (collards)
425g/15oz can haricot (navy) or cannellini beans, drained
ground black pepper

1 Drain the gammon and put it in the ceramic cooking pot with the bay leaves and onions. Pour over just enough fresh cold water to cover the meat. Switch to high, cover and cook for 1 hour.

2 Skim off any scum, then re-cover and cook for 3 hours. Check occasionally and skim the broth once or twice if necessary.

3 Using a slotted spoon and a large fork, carefully lift the gammon out of the slow cooker and on to a board. Add the paprika and potatoes to the broth and cook for 1 hour.

4 Meanwhile, discard the skin and fat from the gammon and cut the meat into chunks. Add it to the slow cooker and cook for a further 2 hours, or until the meat and potatoes are tender.

5 Remove the cores from the greens, then roll up the leaves and cut into thin shreds. Add to the slow cooker with the beans and cook for 30 minutes.

6 Remove the bay leaves from the broth, season with black pepper to taste and serve piping hot.

Cook's Tips
- *Bacon knuckles can be used instead of the gammon. The bones will give the stock a delicious flavour.*
- *Freeze leftover broth to use as stock for another soup.*

Bacon Broth Energy 306kcal/1284kJ; Protein 17.7g; Carbohydrate 33.5g, of which sugars 8.3g; Fat 12.1g, of which saturates 4.3g; Cholesterol 35mg; Calcium 74mg; Fibre 4.6g; Sodium 1.05g.
Gammon Broth Energy 273kcal/1147kJ; Protein 21.4g; Carbohydrate 33.7g, of which sugars 5.3g; Fat 6.7g, of which saturates 2g; Cholesterol 17mg; Calcium 113mg; Fibre 6.7g; Sodium 974mg.

Brown Lentil and Bacon Soup

This is a wonderfully hearty soup combining the earthy rustic taste of brown lentils with salty bacon. A lighter version can be made by omitting the frankfurters, if you prefer.

Serves 6

225g/8oz/1 cup brown lentils
15ml/1 tbsp sunflower oil
1 onion, finely chopped
1 leek, finely chopped
1 carrot, finely diced
2 celery sticks, chopped
115g/4oz piece of lean bacon
2 bay leaves
1.5 litres/2½ pints/6¼ cups water
30ml/2 tbsp chopped fresh parsley, plus extra to garnish
225g/8oz frankfurter, sliced
salt and ground black pepper

1 Rinse the brown lentils thoroughly under cold running water and drain. Set aside until required.

2 Heat the sunflower oil in a large, deep pan and gently fry the onion for about 5 minutes, until it turns soft and translucent. Add the leek, carrot, celery, bacon and bay leaves, and cook for 2 minutes, stirring to combine.

3 Add the lentils to the pan. Pour in the measured water, then slowly bring to the boil. Skim off any scum that rises to the surface, then reduce the heat and simmer, partly covered, for about 45–50 minutes, or until the lentils are soft.

4 Remove the piece of bacon from the soup and, when cool enough to handle, cut the meat into cubes. Trim off any fat.

5 Return the meat to the soup with the parsley and frankfurter, and season with salt and pepper. Simmer for 2–3 minutes, remove the bay leaves, and serve garnished with the parsley.

Cook's Tip
Unlike many other pulses, brown lentils do not need to be soaked before cooking. This makes them an ideal kitchen standby to use in an impromptu one-pot soup like this.

Split Pea and Bacon Soup

Victorian London was regularly covered with a thick winter fog, known as a 'pea-souper', because it had the colour and consistency of pea soup. The original version of this dish would probably have included pig's trotters and a marrow bone, which would have released their succulent flavours into the slowly cooked soup.

Serves 4–6

350g/12oz/1½ cups dried split yellow or green peas
25g/1oz/2 tbsp butter
6 rashers (strips) rindless lean streaky (fatty) bacon, finely chopped
1 medium onion, finely chopped
1 medium carrot, thinly sliced
1 celery stick, thinly sliced
1.75 litres/3 pints/7½ cups ham or chicken stock
60ml/4 tbsp double (heavy) cream
salt and ground black pepper
bread croûtons and fried bacon, to garnish

1 Place the split yellow or green peas into a large, heatproof bowl. Bring a pan of water to the boil, or boil it in a kettle, and pour the hot water over the peas in the bowl to cover. Set the bowl aside.

2 Meanwhile, melt the butter in a large, deep pan. Add the chopped bacon pieces, the onion, carrot and celery and cook over medium heat for about 10–15 minutes, stirring frequently, until the meat and vegetables are becoming soft and beginning to turn golden brown.

3 Drain the peas in the bowl and add them to the pan. Pour in the stock and stir well. Bring the soup to the boil, cover with a tight-fitting lid and reduce the heat. Simmer the soup gently for about 1 hour or until the peas are very soft.

4 Transfer the soup to a food processor or blender and process until smooth, then return the soup to the pan. Season to taste with salt and ground black pepper and stir in the cream. Heat until just bubbling and ladle into warmed soup bowls. Serve garnished with croûtons and pieces of crisp bacon.

Lentil Soup Energy 303kcal/1262kJ; Protein 12.7g; Carbohydrate 17.4g, of which sugars 3.4g; Fat 20.8g, of which saturates 5.1g; Cholesterol 29mg; Calcium 33mg; Fibre 3.4g; Sodium 359mg.
Split Pea Soup Energy 378kcal/1584kJ; Protein 20.2g; Carbohydrate 34.9g, of which sugars 3.1g; Fat 18.5g, of which saturates 8.7g; Cholesterol 47mg; Calcium 45mg; Fibre 3.4g; Sodium 527mg.

Spicy Carrot Dip

When carrots are cooked over a gentle heat in a slow cooker their flavour intensifies and becomes deliciously sweet, making them the perfect partner for hot, spicy flavourings.

Serves 4

1 onion, finely chopped
3 carrots, grated, plus extra to garnish (optional)
grated rind and juice of 1 orange
15ml/1 tbsp hot curry paste
150ml/¼ pint/⅔ cup natural (plain) yogurt
handful of fresh basil leaves
15ml/1 tbsp fresh lemon juice
dash Tabasco sauce (optional)
salt and ground black pepper

1 Put the onion, carrots, orange rind and juice, and curry paste in the ceramic cooking pot and stir well to combine. Cover with the lid and cook on high for 2 hours, or until the carrots are soft and tender.

2 Uncover the pot and leave to cool for about 10 minutes, then transfer the mixture to a food processor or blender and process until smooth.

3 Transfer the carrot purée to a mixing bowl and leave, uncovered, for about 1 hour to cool completely.

4 Add the yogurt to the cooled carrot purée. Tear the basil leaves roughly into small pieces, then stir them into the mixture until thoroughly combined.

5 Stir in the lemon juice and Tabasco, if using, then season to taste with salt and pepper. Serve at room temperature, within a few hours of making.

Cook's Tip
Serve this versatile dip as an appetizer or on its own with wheat crackers or fiery tortilla chips, or with a variety of raw vegetables for a healthy snack.

Cheese-stuffed Pears

These pears, made in the slow cooker, make a sublime dish with their scrumptious creamy topping. If you don't have a very large slow cooker, choose short squat pears rather than long, tapering ones, so that they will fit in a single layer.

Serves 4

50g/2oz/¼ cup ricotta cheese
50g/2oz/¼ cup dolcelatte cheese
15ml/1 tbsp honey
½ celery stick, finely sliced
8 green olives, pitted and roughly chopped
4 dates, pitted and cut into thin strips
pinch of paprika
2 medium barely ripe pears
150ml/¼ pint/⅔ cup fresh apple juice
mixed salad leaves, to serve (optional)

1 Place the ricotta cheese in a bowl and crumble in the dolcelatte. Add the honey, celery, olives, dates and paprika and mix together well until creamy and thoroughly blended.

2 Halve the pears lengthways. Use a melon baller or teaspoon to remove the cores and make a hollow for the filling.

3 Divide the ricotta filling equally between the pears, packing it into the hollow, then arrange the fruit in a single layer in the ceramic cooking pot.

4 Pour the apple juice around the pears, then cover with the lid. Cook on high for 1½–2 hours, or until the fruit is tender. (The cooking time will depend on the ripeness of the pears.)

5 Remove the pears from the slow cooker and brown them under a hot grill (broiler) for a few minutes. Serve with mixed salad leaves, if you like.

Cook's Tip
These pears go particularly well with slightly bitter and peppery leaves, such as chicory and rocket (arugula). Try them tossed in a walnut oil dressing.

Spiced Carrot Dip Energy 58kcal/241kJ; Protein 2.5g; Carbohydrate 9.5g, of which sugars 8.4g; Fat 1.3g, of which saturates 0.4g; Cholesterol 0mg; Calcium 80mg; Fibre 1.3g; Sodium 34mg.
Cheese-stuffed Pears Energy 236kcal/992kJ; Protein 6.9g; Carbohydrate 35.6g, of which sugars 35.6g; Fat 8.2g, of which saturates 5.0g; Cholesterol 24mg; Calcium 141mg; Fibre 4.1g; Sodium 261mg.

Mini Baked Potatoes with Blue Cheese

Baked potatoes are one of the ultimate slow-cooked foods. These mini versions are perfect as finger food for a party, especially as you can prepare them in advance.

Makes 20

20 small new or salad potatoes
60ml/4 tbsp vegetable oil
coarse salt
120ml/4fl oz/½ cup sour cream
25g/1oz blue cheese, such as Roquefort or Stilton, crumbled
30ml/2 tbsp chopped fresh chives, for sprinkling

1 Preheat the oven to 180°C/350°F/Gas 4. Wash and dry the potatoes. Pour the oil into a bowl. Add the potatoes and toss to coat thoroughly.

2 Dip the potatoes in the coarse salt to coat lightly. Spread out the potatoes in one layer on a baking sheet. Bake for about 45–50 minutes until tender.

3 Put the sour cream into a small bowl and add the blue cheese. Blend together until well combined.

4 Cut a cross in the top of each cooked potato with a sharp knife. Press the sides of each potato gently with your fingers to make them open up.

5 While the potatoes are still hot, top each one with a generous dollop of the blue cheese mixture. It will melt down into the potato nicely. Sprinkle with chives on a serving dish and serve hot or at room temperature.

Cook's Tip
This dish works just as well as a light snack. If you don't want to be bothered with lots of fiddly small potatoes, simply bake one large floury potato per person. Use whatever blue cheese is available to make the creamy topping.

Wild Mushroom and Sun-dried Tomato Soufflés

These impressive little soufflés are baked in individual earthenware pots. They are packed with rich, Italian flavours and are remarkably easy to prepare and cook.

Serves 4

25g/1oz/½ cup dried cep mushrooms
40g/1½oz/3 tbsp butter, plus extra for greasing
20ml/4 tsp grated Parmesan cheese
40g/1½oz/⅓ cup plain (all-purpose) flour
250ml/8fl oz/1 cup milk
50g/2oz/½ cup grated mature (sharp) Cheddar cheese
4 eggs, separated
2 sun-dried tomatoes in oil, drained and chopped
15ml/1 tbsp chopped fresh chives
salt and ground black pepper

1 Place the ceps in a bowl, pour over enough warm water to cover and leave to soak for 15 minutes. Grease four individual earthenware soufflé dishes with a little butter. Sprinkle the grated Parmesan into the soufflé dishes and rotate each dish to coat the sides with cheese. Preheat the oven to 190°C/375°F/Gas 5.

2 Melt the butter in a large pan, remove from the heat and stir in the flour. Cook over low heat for 1 minute, stirring constantly. Remove the pan from the heat and gradually stir in the milk. Return to the heat and bring to the boil, stirring constantly, until the sauce has thickened.

3 Remove the sauce from the heat, then stir in the grated Cheddar cheese and plenty of seasoning. Beat in the egg yolks, one at a time, then stir in the chopped sun-dried tomatoes and the chives. Drain the soaked mushrooms, then coarsely chop them and add them to the cheese sauce.

4 Whisk the egg whites until they stand in soft peaks. Mix one spoonful into the sauce then carefully fold in the rest. Divide the mixture among the soufflé dishes and bake for 25 minutes, or until the soufflés are golden brown on top, well risen and just firm to the touch. Serve immediately – before they sink.

Mini Baked Potatoes Energy 63kcal/262kJ; Protein 1.1g; Carbohydrate 6.3g, of which sugars 0.7g; Fat 3.9g, of which saturates 1.3g; Cholesterol 5mg; Calcium 14mg; Fibre 0.4g; Sodium 22mg.
Mushroom Soufflés Energy 290kcal/1207kJ; Protein 14.7g; Carbohydrate 11.6g, of which sugars 3.9g; Fat 20.8g, of which saturates 11.2g; Cholesterol 232mg; Calcium 274mg; Fibre 0.6g; Sodium 305mg.

Mushroom and Bean Pâté

Making pâté in the slow cooker results in this light and tasty version. It is delicious served on triangles of wholemeal toast for a vegetarian appetizer, or with crusty French bread as a light lunch served with salad.

Serves 8

450g/1lb/6 cups mushrooms, sliced
1 onion, finely chopped
2 garlic cloves, crushed
1 red (bell) pepper, seeded and diced
30ml/2 tbsp vegetable stock
30ml/2 tbsp dry white wine
400g/14oz can red kidney beans, rinsed and drained
1 egg, beaten
50g/2oz/1 cup fresh wholemeal (whole-wheat) breadcrumbs
10ml/2 tsp chopped fresh thyme
10ml/2 tsp chopped fresh rosemary
salt and ground black pepper
salad leaves, fresh herbs and tomato wedges, to garnish

1 Put the mushrooms, onion, garlic, red pepper, stock and wine in the ceramic cooking pot. Cover and cook on high for 2 hours, then set aside for about 10 minutes to cool.

2 Transfer the mixture to a food processor or blender and add the kidney beans. Process to make a smooth purée, stopping the machine once or twice to scrape down the sides.

3 Lightly grease and line a 900g/2lb loaf tin (pan). Put an inverted saucer or metal pastry ring in the bottom of the ceramic cooking pot. Pour in about 2.5cm/1in of hot water, and set to high.

4 Transfer the vegetable mixture to a bowl. Add the egg, breadcrumbs and herbs, and season. Mix thoroughly, then spoon into the loaf tin and cover with cling film (plastic wrap) or foil.

5 Put the tin in the slow cooker and pour in enough boiling water to come just over halfway up the sides of the tin. Cover with the lid and cook on high for 4 hours, or until lightly set.

6 Remove the tin and place on a wire rack until cool. Chill for several hours, or overnight. Turn the pâté out of the tin, remove the lining paper and serve garnished with salad leaves, herbs and tomato wedges.

Red Lentil and Goat's Cheese Pâté

The smoky, earthy flavour of red lentils is a perfect partner for tangy goat's cheese in this pâté that is made in the slow cooker.

Serves 8

225g/8oz/1 cup red lentils
1 shallot, very finely chopped
1 bay leaf
475ml/16fl oz/2 cups near-boiling vegetable stock
115g/4oz/½ cup soft goat's cheese
5ml/1 tsp ground cumin
3 eggs, lightly beaten
salt and ground black pepper
Melba toast and rocket (arugula) leaves, to serve

1 Rinse the lentils, drain, then place in the ceramic cooking pot and add the shallot, bay leaf and hot vegetable stock. Switch the slow cooker to high, cover and cook for 2 hours, or until the liquid has been absorbed and the lentils are soft and pulpy. Stir once or twice towards the end of cooking time.

2 Turn off the slow cooker. Transfer the lentil mixture to a bowl, remove the bay leaf and leave to cool uncovered. Meanwhile, wash and dry the ceramic cooking pot.

3 Lightly grease a 900ml/1½ pint/3¾ cup loaf tin (pan) with oil and line the base with baking parchment. Put an upturned saucer or metal pastry ring in the bottom of the ceramic cooking pot and pour in about 2.5cm/1in of hot water. Set the cooker to high.

4 Put the goat's cheese in a bowl with the cumin and beat together until creamy. Gradually mix in the eggs until blended. Stir in the lentil mixture and season well with salt and pepper.

5 Place the mixture in the tin. Cover with clear film (plastic wrap) or foil. Put the tin in the slow cooker and pour in boiling water to come just over halfway up the sides. Cover with the lid and cook for 3–3½ hours, until the pâté is lightly set.

6 Remove the tin from the slow cooker and place on a wire rack to cool completely. Chill for several hours, or overnight.

7 To serve, turn the pâté out of the tin, peel off the parchment and cut into slices. Serve with Melba toast and rocket leaves.

Mushroom and Bean Pâté Energy 85kcal/358kJ; Protein 5.5g; Carbohydrate 12.3g, of which sugars 3.8g; Fat 1.6g, of which saturates 0.4g; Cholesterol 28mg; Calcium 47mg; Fibre 3.7g; Sodium 187mg.
Red Lentil Pâté Energy 136kcal/573kJ; Protein 9.8g; Carbohydrate 16g, of which sugars 0.9g; Fat 4.1g, of which saturates 2.6g; Cholesterol 13mg; Calcium 34mg; Fibre 1.4g; Sodium 97mg.

Layered Vegetable Terrine

A combination of vegetables and herbs layered and slowly baked in a spinach-lined loaf tin. Delicious served hot or warm with a simple salad garnish.

Serves 6

3 red (bell) peppers, halved
450g/1lb main crop waxy potatoes
115g/4oz spinach leaves, trimmed
25g/1oz/2 tbsp butter
pinch grated nutmeg
115g/4oz/1 cup vegetarian Cheddar cheese, grated
1 courgette (zucchini), sliced lengthways and blanched
salt and ground black pepper
salad leaves and tomatoes, to serve

1 Preheat the oven to 180°C/350°F/Gas 4. Place the peppers in a roasting pan and roast, cores in place, for 30–45 minutes until charred. Remove from the oven. Place in a plastic bag to cool. Peel the skins and remove the cores. Halve the potatoes and boil in lightly salted water for 10–15 minutes.

2 Blanch the spinach for a few seconds in boiling water. Drain and pat dry on kitchen paper. Line the base and sides of a 900g/2lb loaf tin (pan) with the spinach, making sure the leaves overlap slightly.

3 Slice the potatoes thinly and lay one-third of the potatoes over the base, dot with a little of the butter and season with salt, pepper and nutmeg. Sprinkle a little cheese over.

4 Arrange three of the peeled pepper halves on top. Sprinkle a little cheese over and then a layer of courgettes. Lay another one-third of the potatoes on top with the remaining peppers and some more cheese, seasoning as you go. Lay the final layer of potato on top and scatter over any remaining cheese. Fold the spinach leaves over. Cover with foil.

5 Place the loaf tin in a roasting pan and pour boiling water around the outside, making sure the water comes to halfway up the sides of the tin. Bake for about 45 minutes to 1 hour. Remove from the oven and turn the loaf out on to a serving plate. Serve sliced with salad leaves and tomatoes.

Onion and Potato Cake

Serve this ever-popular dish with a salad accompaniment. It is also particularly good alongside sausages, lamb chops or roast chicken – in fact, any roast meat. The slow cooking time will vary a little depending on the potatoes and how thinly they are sliced: use a food processor or mandolin (if you have one) to make paper-thin slices. The mound of potatoes will cook down to make a thick buttery cake.

Serves 6

900g/2lb new potatoes, peeled and thinly sliced
2 medium onions, very finely chopped
salt and ground black pepper
115g/4oz/½ cup butter

1 Preheat the oven to 190°C/375°F/Gas 5. Lightly butter a 20cm/8in round cake tin (pan) and line the base with a circle of baking parchment.

2 Arrange some of the potato slices evenly in the bottom of the tin and then sprinkle some of the onions over them. Season with salt and pepper. Reserve 25g/1oz/2 tbsp of the butter and dot the mixture with tiny pieces of the remaining butter.

3 Repeat these layers, using up all the ingredients and finishing with a layer of potatoes. Melt the reserved butter and brush it over the top.

4 Cover the potatoes with foil, put in the hot oven and cook for 1–1½ hours, until tender and golden. Remove from the oven and leave to stand, still covered, for 10–15 minutes.

5 Carefully turn out the onion cake on to a warmed plate and serve with a salad or as an accompaniment to a main meal.

Cook's Tip
If using old potatoes, cook and serve in an earthenware or ovenproof glass dish. Then remove the cover for the final 10–15 minutes to lightly brown the top.

Vegetable Terrine Energy 205kcal/854kJ; Protein 8.3g; Carbohydrate 19.2g, of which sugars 7.7g; Fat 10.6g, of which saturates 6.6g; Cholesterol 27mg; Calcium 196mg; Fibre 3g; Sodium 203mg.
Onion and Potato Cake Energy 272kcal/1133kJ; Protein 3.5g; Carbohydrate 29.5g, of which sugars 5.8g; Fat 16.3g, of which saturates 10.1g; Cholesterol 41mg; Calcium 29mg; Fibre 2.4g; Sodium 135mg.

Baked Chickpea Purée with Lemon and Pine Nuts

This dish is a welcome change from the standard, cold hummus. Chickpeas, like many beans and peas, require slow cooking but their mildly nutty taste is well worth the effort.

Serves 4

225g/8oz/1¼ cups dried chickpeas, soaked in cold water for 6 hours or overnight
about 50ml/2fl oz/¼ cup olive oil
juice of 2 lemons
3–4 garlic cloves, crushed
10ml/2 tsp cumin seeds, crushed
30–45ml/2–3 tbsp light sesame paste (tahini)
45–60ml/3–4 tbsp thick and creamy natural (plain) yogurt
30–45ml/2–3 tbsp pine nuts
40g/1½oz/3 tbsp butter
5–10ml/1–2 tsp oiled or roasted Turkish red pepper or paprika
salt and ground black pepper

1 Drain the chickpeas, transfer them to a pan and fill the pan with plenty of cold water. Bring to the boil and boil for about 2–3 minutes, then lower the heat and partially cover the pan. Simmer the chickpeas for 1 hour, until they are soft and tender.

2 Drain the chickpeas, then rinse them well under cold running water. Remove any loose skins by rubbing the chickpeas in a clean dish towel. Preheat the oven to 200°C/400°F/Gas 6.

3 Using a large mortar and pestle, pound the chickpeas with the oil, lemon juice, garlic and cumin. Beat in the sesame paste, then beat in the yogurt until the purée is light and smooth. Season to taste. Transfer the purée to an ovenproof dish – preferably an earthenware one – and smooth the top with the back of a spoon.

4 Dry-roast the pine nuts in a small, heavy pan over a medium heat until golden brown. Lower the heat, add the butter and let it melt, then stir in the red pepper or paprika.

5 Pour the mixture over the purée and bake in the oven for about 25 minutes, until it has risen slightly and the butter has been absorbed. Serve straight from the oven.

Leek and Bacon Tart

This dish makes an ideal savoury first course served as small tartlets. It can also be served in larger portions with a mixed leaf salad as a light main course for lunch or supper.

Makes 6–8 small tartlets or 1 large tart serving 8–10

275g/10oz/2½ cups plain (all-purpose) flour
pinch of salt
175g/6oz/¾ cup butter
2 egg yolks
about 45ml/3 tbsp very cold water
lettuce leaves and tomatoes, to garnish

For the filling

225g/8oz streaky (fatty) bacon, diced
4 leeks, sliced
6 eggs
115g/4oz/½ cup cream cheese
15ml/1 tbsp mild mustard
pinch of cayenne pepper
salt and ground black pepper

1 Sift the flour and salt into a bowl, and rub in the butter until it resembles fine breadcrumbs. Add the egg yolks and just enough water to combine the dough. Wrap the dough in clear film (plastic wrap) and place in the refrigerator for 30 minutes.

2 Meanwhile, preheat the oven to 200°C/400°F/Gas 6. Roll out the pastry thinly and use to line 6–8 tartlet tins (muffin pans) or a 28cm/11in tart dish. Remove any air pockets and prick the base with a fork. Line the pastry loosely with baking parchment, weigh down with baking beans and bake the pastry shell blind for 15–20 minutes, or until golden.

3 To make the filling, cook the bacon in a hot pan until crisp. Add the leeks and continue to cook for 3–4 minutes until just softening. Remove from the heat. In a bowl, beat the eggs, cream cheese, mustard, cayenne pepper and seasoning together, then add the leeks and bacon.

4 Remove the paper and baking beans from the tartlet tins or tart dish, pour in the filling and bake for 35–40 minutes.

5 To serve, plate the tartlets on to individual serving plates or cut the tart into narrow wedges and serve warm, with a small salad garnish.

Baked Chickpea Purée Energy 433kcal/1803kJ; Protein 15g; Carbohydrate 29.5g, of which sugars 3g; Fat 29.2g, of which saturates 7.7g; Cholesterol 21mg; Calcium 160mg; Fibre 6.8g; Sodium 91mg.
Leek and Bacon Tart Energy 487kcal/2026kJ; Protein 15.4g; Carbohydrate 28.2g, of which sugars 1.6g; Fat 35.7g, of which saturates 19.1g; Cholesterol 265mg; Calcium 107mg; Fibre 2.1g; Sodium 681mg.

Pike and Salmon Mousse

This delicious mousse is slowly baked in a loaf tin in the oven. When sliced, this light-textured dish reveals a pretty layer of pink salmon. For a special occasion serve with red salmon caviar.

Serves 8

225g/8oz salmon fillets, skinned
600ml/1 pint/2½ cups fish stock
finely grated rind and juice of ½ lemon
900g/2lb pike fillets, skinned
4 egg whites
475ml/16fl oz/2 cups double (heavy) cream
30ml/2 tbsp chopped fresh dill
salt and ground black pepper
red salmon caviar or dill sprig, to garnish

1 Preheat the oven to 180°C/350°F/Gas 4. Oil a 900g/2lb loaf tin (pan), line with baking parchment and brush with more oil.

2 Cut the salmon into 5cm/2in strips. Place the stock and lemon juice in a pan and bring to the boil, then turn off the heat. Add the salmon strips, cover and leave for 2 minutes. Remove with a slotted spoon.

3 Cut the pike into cubes and process in a food processor or blender until smooth. Lightly whisk the egg whites with a fork. With the motor running, slowly pour in the egg whites, then the cream. Finally, add the lemon rind, dill and seasoning.

4 Spoon half of the pike mixture into the prepared loaf tin, levelling it with the back of the spoon.

5 Arrange the poached salmon strips on top, then carefully spoon in the remaining pike mixture and level the surface.

6 Cover the loaf tin with foil and put in a roasting pan. Add enough boiling water to come halfway up the sides of the loaf tin. Bake for about 45–50 minutes, or until firm.

7 Leave on a wire rack to cool, then chill for at least 3 hours. Turn out on to a serving plate and remove the lining paper. Serve the mousse cut in slices and garnished with red salmon caviar or a sprig of dill.

Three-fish Terrine

This striped terrine uses haddock, salmon and turbot and is slowly baked in the oven. Serve with a small salad, brown bread or Melba toast and butter.

Serves 8–10

450g/1lb spinach
350–450g/12oz–1lb haddock, cod or other white fish, skinned and chopped
3 eggs
115g/4oz/2 cups fresh breadcrumbs
300ml/½ pint/1¼ cups fromage blanc or low-fat cream cheese
a little freshly grated nutmeg
350–450g/12oz–1lb salmon fillet
350–450g/12oz–1lb fresh turbot fillet, or other flat fish
oil, for greasing
salt and ground black pepper
lemon wedges and rocket, to serve

1 Preheat the oven to 160°C/325°F/Gas 3. Remove the stalks from the spinach and cook the leaves briskly in a pan without any added water, shaking the pan occasionally, until the spinach is just tender. Drain and squeeze out the water.

2 Put the spinach into a food processor or blender with the haddock or other white fish, eggs, breadcrumbs, fromage blanc or cream cheese, salt, pepper and nutmeg to taste. Process until smooth. Skin and bone the salmon fillet and cut into long thin strips. Repeat with the turbot.

3 Oil a 900g/2lb loaf tin (pan) and line the base with baking parchment or foil. Make layers from the spinach mixture and the strips of salmon and turbot, starting and finishing with spinach.

4 Press down carefully and cover with oiled baking parchment. Prick a few holes in it, then put the terrine into a roasting pan and pour boiling water around it to come two-thirds of the way up the sides.

5 Bake in the preheated oven for 1–1½ hours, or until risen, firm and set. Leave to cool, then chill well before serving.

6 To serve, ease a sharp knife down the sides to loosen the terrine and turn out on to a flat serving dish. Slice the terrine and serve with lemon wedges and fresh rocket.

Pike Mousse Energy 477kcal/1977kJ; Protein 27.8g; Carbohydrate 1g, of which sugars 1g; Fat 40.3g, of which saturates 21.4g; Cholesterol 171mg; Calcium 89mg; Fibre 0g; Sodium 105mg.
Three-fish Terrine Energy 290kcal/1216kJ; Protein 32.5g; Carbohydrate 13.7g, of which sugars 2.8g; Fat 12.1g, of which saturates 3.9g; Cholesterol 112mg; Calcium 203mg; Fibre 1.5g; Sodium 306mg.

Cardamom Chicken Mousselines

These mousselines are made in the slow cooker and make an elegant appetizer. They should be served warm, not hot, so when they are cooked, turn off the slow cooker and leave to cool for half an hour before eating.

Serves 6

350g/12oz skinless chicken breast fillets
1 shallot, finely chopped
115g/4oz/1 cup full-fat soft cheese
1 egg, lightly beaten
2 egg whites
crushed seeds of 2 cardamom pods
60ml/4 tbsp white wine
150ml/¼ pint/⅔ cup double (heavy) cream
oregano sprigs, to serve

For the tomato vinaigrette
350g/12oz ripe tomatoes
10ml/2 tsp balsamic vinegar
30ml/2 tbsp olive oil
sea salt and ground black pepper

1 Chop the chicken and put it in a food processor with the shallot. Process until fairly smooth. Add the cheese, beaten egg, egg whites, cardamom seeds and wine and season with salt and pepper. Process again until the ingredients are thoroughly blended.

2 Gradually add the cream, using the pulsing action, until the mixture has a smooth and creamy texture. Transfer to a bowl, cover with clear film (plastic wrap) and chill for 30 minutes.

3 Meanwhile, prepare six 150ml/¼ pint/⅔ cup ramekins or dariole moulds that will all fit in the slow cooker. Lightly grease the base of each one, then line. Pour about 2cm/¾in hot water into the ceramic cooking pot and switch the cooker to high.

4 Divide the mixture among the dishes. Cover with foil and put in the ceramic cooking pot. Add more hot water to come halfway up the dishes. Cover and cook for 2½–3 hours until firm.

5 Meanwhile, peel, quarter, seed and dice the tomatoes. Place in a bowl, sprinkle with the vinegar and season with salt. Stir well.

6 To serve, unmould the mousselines on to warmed plates. Place tomato vinaigrette around each, then drizzle over a little olive oil and add black pepper. Garnish with sprigs of oregano.

Chicken and Pistachio Pâté

This delicious pâté is made in the slow cooker, and is ideal as an elegant appetizer for a special dinner.

Serves 8

oil, for greasing
800g/1¾lb boneless chicken meat
40g/1½oz/¾ cup fresh white breadcrumbs
120ml/4fl oz/½ cup double (heavy) cream
1 egg white
4 spring onions (scallions), finely chopped
1 garlic clove, finely chopped
75g/3oz cooked ham, cubed
75g/3oz/½ cup shelled pistachio nuts
30ml/2 tbsp green peppercorns in brine, drained
45ml/3 tbsp chopped fresh tarragon
pinch of grated nutmeg
salt and ground black pepper
French bread and salad, to serve

1 Line the base of a 1.2 litre/2 pint/5 cup round or oval ovenproof dish (such as a soufflé dish) with baking parchment, then brush the base and sides with oil. Put an upturned saucer or metal pastry ring in the base of the ceramic cooking pot and pour in 2.5cm/1in of hot water. Switch the slow cooker to high.

2 Cut the chicken meat into cubes, then put in a food processor and blend until fairly smooth. Remove any white stringy pieces from the minced (ground) meat. Place the breadcrumbs in a large mixing bowl, pour over the cream and leave to soak.

3 Meanwhile, lightly whisk the egg white with a fork, then add it to the breadcrumbs. Add the minced chicken, spring onions, garlic, ham, pistachio nuts, green peppercorns, tarragon, nutmeg, salt and pepper. Mix thoroughly.

4 Spoon the mixture into the prepared dish and cover with foil. Place the dish in the ceramic cooking pot and pour a little more boiling water around the dish to come just over halfway up the sides. Cover and cook for 4 hours, until the juices run clear when pierced with a skewer. Remove from the oven and leave to cool in the dish. Chill in the refrigerator, preferably overnight.

5 To serve, turn out the pâté on to a serving dish and cut into slices. Serve with crusty French bread and salad.

Mousselines Energy 191kcal/795kJ; Protein 18.1g; Carbohydrate 2g, of which sugars 2g; Fat 11.6g, of which saturates 5g; Cholesterol 96mg; Calcium 30mg; Fibre 0.7g; Sodium 130mg.
Chicken Pâté Energy 321kcal/1344kJ; Protein 36.6g; Carbohydrate 3.7g, of which sugars 1.2g; Fat 17.9g, of which saturates 7.7g; Cholesterol 125mg; Calcium 37mg; Fibre 0.7g; Sodium 379mg.

Chicken and Pork Terrine

This smooth terrine is baked in a loaf tin in the oven. It is an ideal appetizer with a delicate flavour and has a contrasting strip of coarser-textured meat running through the centre.

Serves 6–8

225g/8oz rindless streaky (fatty) bacon
375g/13oz skinless chicken breast fillet
15ml/1 tbsp lemon juice
225g/8oz lean minced (ground) pork
½ small onion, finely chopped
2 eggs, beaten
30ml/2 tbsp chopped fresh parsley
5ml/1 tsp salt
5ml/1 tsp green peppercorns, crushed
oil, for greasing
green salad, radishes and lemon wedges, to serve

1 Preheat the oven to 160°C/325°F/Gas 3. Put the bacon on a board and stretch it using the back of a heavy knife so that it can be arranged in overlapping slices over the base and sides of a 900g/2lb loaf tin (pan).

2 Cut 115g/4oz of the chicken into strips about 10cm/4in long. Sprinkle with lemon juice. Put the rest of the chicken in a food processor or blender with the minced pork and the onion. Process until fairly smooth.

3 Add the eggs, parsley, salt and peppercorns to the meat mixture, and process again briefly. Spoon half the mixture into the loaf tin and then level the surface.

4 Arrange the chicken strips on top, then spoon in the remaining meat mixture and smooth the top. Give the tin a couple of sharp taps to knock out any pockets of air.

5 Cover with a piece of oiled foil and put in a roasting pan. Pour in enough hot water to come halfway up the sides of the loaf tin. Bake for about 45–50 minutes, until firm.

6 Allow the terrine to cool in the tin before turning out and chilling. Serve sliced, with a green salad, radishes and wedges of lemon to squeeze over.

Turkey, Juniper and Green Peppercorn Terrine

This slow-cooked terrine is perfect for entertaining as it can be made several days in advance.

Serves 10–12

225g/8oz chicken livers, trimmed
450g/1lb minced (ground) turkey
450g/1lb minced (ground) pork
225g/8oz pancetta, diced
50g/2oz/½ cup shelled pistachio nuts, roughly chopped
5ml/1 tsp salt
2.5ml/½ tsp ground mace
2 garlic cloves, crushed
5ml/1 tsp green peppercorns in brine, drained
5ml/1 tsp juniper berries
120ml/4fl oz/½ cup dry white wine
30ml/2 tbsp gin
finely grated rind of 1 orange
8 large vacuum-packed vine leaves in brine
oil, for greasing
pickle or chutney, to serve

1 Chop the chicken livers finely. Put them in a bowl and add the turkey, pork, pancetta, pistachio nuts, salt, mace and garlic. Mix well. Lightly crush the peppercorns and juniper berries, and add them to the mixture. Stir in the wine, gin and orange rind. Cover and chill overnight.

2 Preheat the oven to 160°C/325°F/Gas 3. Rinse the vine leaves under cold running water. Drain them thoroughly. Lightly oil a 1.2 litre/2 pint/5 cup ovenproof terrine dish or loaf tin (pan). Line the terrine or tin with the leaves, letting the ends hang over the sides. Pack the meat mixture into the terrine or tin and fold the leaves over to enclose. Brush lightly with oil.

3 Cover the terrine. Place it in a roasting pan and pour in boiling water to come halfway up the sides of the terrine. Bake for 1¾ hours, checking the level of the water occasionally.

4 Leave the terrine to cool, then pour off the surface juices. Cover with clear film (plastic wrap), then foil, and place a weight on top. Chill overnight in the refrigerator.

5 Carefully turn out the terrine on to a serving plate and cut into slices. Serve at room temperature, with pickle or chutney.

Chicken Terrine Energy 191kcal/798kJ; Protein 22g; Carbohydrate 0.6g, of which sugars 0.4g; Fat 11.3g, of which saturates 3.8g; Cholesterol 115mg; Calcium 15mg; Fibre 0.1g; Sodium 417mg.
Turkey Terrine Energy 240kcal/1003kJ; Protein 25.3g; Carbohydrate 1.7g, of which sugars 1.5g; Fat 13.4g, of which saturates 4.1g; Cholesterol 153mg; Calcium 29mg; Fibre 0.8g; Sodium 316mg.

Country Game Terrine

The terrine dish must have a lid to seal in the flavours during the long cooking time.

Serves 8

225g/8oz unsmoked streaky (fatty) bacon rashers (strips), rind removed
225g/8oz chicken liver, minced (ground)
450g/1lb minced (ground) pork
1 small onion, finely chopped
2 garlic cloves, crushed
10ml/2 tsp dried mixed herbs
225g/8oz game (such as hare, rabbit, pheasant or pigeon)
60ml/4 tbsp port or sherry
1 bay leaf
50g/2oz/4 tbsp plain (all-purpose) flour
300ml/½ pint/1¼ cups aspic jelly, made up as packet instructions
salt and ground black pepper
fresh parsley and thyme sprigs, to garnish

1 Stretch each bacon rasher with the back of a heavy knife. Use to line a 1 litre/1¾ pint/4 cup ovenproof terrine dish.

2 In a bowl, mix together the minced liver and pork with the onion, garlic and dried herbs. Season with salt and pepper. Cut the game into thin strips and put it into another bowl with the port or sherry. Season with salt and pepper.

3 Put one-third of the minced mixture into the terrine. Cover with half the game and repeat the layers, ending with a minced layer. Level and lay the bay leaf on top.

4 Preheat the oven to 160°C/325°F/Gas 3. Put the flour into a bowl and mix to a dough with 30ml/2 tbsp cold water. Cover the terrine with a lid and seal it with the flour paste.

5 Place the terrine in a roasting pan and pour in enough hot water to come halfway up the sides of the dish. Cook in the oven for 2 hours.

6 Remove the lid and place a weight on top of the terrine. Leave to cool completely. Remove any fat, then cover with warmed aspic jelly. Cool once more, then chill in the refrigerator. To serve, carefully turn out on to a serving plate, cut into slices and garnish with parsley and thyme.

Duck and Calvados Terrine

This classic dish from Normandy, in France, uses the regional apple brandy, Calvados.

Serves 4

oil, for greasing
500g/1¼lb boneless duck meat, coarsely chopped
225g/8oz belly pork, minced (ground)
2 shallots, chopped
grated rind and juice of 1 orange
30ml/2 tbsp Calvados
10 rindless streaky (fatty) bacon rashers (strips)
2 eggs, beaten
30ml/2 tbsp chopped fresh parsley
salt and ground black pepper
mixed salad and hot toast, to serve

1 Grease and line a 900g/2lb loaf tin (pan) or ovenproof terrine dish with baking parchment. Place the duck meat in a bowl with the minced pork, shallots, orange rind and juice, Calvados and seasoning. Mix well, cover and chill for 1–2 hours.

2 Preheat the oven to 180°C/350°F/Gas 4. Stretch the bacon rashers with the back of a heavy knife and use them to line the loaf tin or dish, leaving any excess hanging over the edge.

3 Stir the eggs and parsley into the meat mixture, then spoon it into the prepared tin or dish. Smooth the surface, fold the bacon over, then cover with foil.

4 Stand the terrine in a roasting pan and pour in enough boiling water to come over halfway up the sides of the terrine.

5 Bake for 1¼ hours, then remove the terrine from the oven, lift off the foil and leave to cool. Cover with clean foil and a weight, and chill for 3–4 hours until firm.

6 Turn out the terrine on to a serving plate and cut it into slices. Serve with a mixed salad and hot toast.

Cook's Tip
Marinating the meat for a few hours will develop the flavours.

Game Terrine Energy 266kcal/1112kJ; Protein 27.1g; Carbohydrate 6.4g, of which sugars 1.4g; Fat 14g, of which saturates 5g; Cholesterol 182mg; Calcium 25mg; Fibre 0.3g; Sodium 432mg.
Duck Terrine Energy 585kcal/2431kJ; Protein 45.8g; Carbohydrate 1.5g, of which sugars 1.1g; Fat 44.3g, of which saturates 14.4g; Cholesterol 310mg; Calcium 66mg; Fibre 0.8g; Sodium 927mg.

Country-style Terrine with Leeks

This rustic terrine really benefits from being made in a slow cooker. Quatre épices is a French spice mix.

Serves 8

350g/12oz trimmed leeks
25g/1oz/2 tbsp butter
2 garlic cloves, finely chopped
900g/2lb lean pork leg or shoulder
115g/4oz rinded smoked streaky (fatty) bacon
5ml/1 tsp chopped fresh thyme
3 sage leaves, finely chopped
1.5ml/¼ tsp quatre épices (French spice mix)
1.5ml/¼ tsp ground cumin
2.5ml/½ tsp salt
2.5ml/½ tsp ground black pepper
3 bay leaves

1 Cut the leeks lengthways, wash and slice thinly. Melt the butter in a large pan, add the leeks, cover and cook for 10 minutes. Add the garlic and cook for 10 minutes. Set aside to cool.

2 Trim off any excess fat and gristle from the pork, then cut the meat into 2.5cm/1in cubes. Put the meat into a food processor and process to a coarse paste. Transfer the meat to a large bowl and remove any white stringy pieces.

3 Reserve two of the bacon rashers (strips) for the garnish, then finely chop the rest. Add to the pork mixture with the leeks, herbs, spices, salt and pepper, and mix thoroughly.

4 Grease a 1.2 litre/2 pint/5 cup heatproof dish or loaf tin (pan) with oil and line with baking parchment. Put an upturned saucer or metal pastry ring in the base of the ceramic cooking pot and pour in 2.5cm/1in of hot water. Turn the slow cooker to high.

5 Spoon the meat mixture into the prepared dish or tin. Tap firmly to settle the mixture, and smooth the top. Arrange the bay leaves and reserved bacon on top, then cover with foil.

6 Place in the slow cooker and pour in boiling water halfway up the sides. Cover and cook for 4–5 hours until the juices run clear when pierced with a skewer. Leave to cool in the dish or tin.

7 Place a weight on top and chill for several hours or overnight. Turn out on to a serving plate and cut into slices.

Herby Liver Pâté Pie

A delicious slow-baked dish, ideal as an appetizer or served as a light lunch.

Serves 10

675g/1½lb minced (ground) pork
350g/12oz pork liver
350g/12oz cooked ham, diced
1 small onion, finely chopped
30ml/2 tbsp chopped fresh parsley
5ml/1 tsp German mustard
30ml/2 tbsp Kirsch
5ml/1 tsp salt
beaten egg, for sealing and glazing
25g/1oz sachet aspic jelly
250ml/8fl oz/1 cup boiling water
ground black pepper
mustard, bread and dill pickles, to serve

For the pastry

450g/1lb/4 cups plain (all-purpose) flour
pinch of salt
275g/10oz/1¼ cups butter
2 eggs
1 egg yolk
30ml/2 tbsp water

1 Preheat the oven to 200°C/400°F/Gas 6. To make the pastry, sift the flour and salt into a bowl and rub in the butter. Beat the eggs, egg yolk and water, add to the dry ingredients and mix well. Knead the dough until smooth. Roll out two-thirds on a lightly floured surface and use to line a 10 × 25cm/4 × 10in hinged loaf tin (pan). Trim off any excess dough.

2 Process half the pork and the liver in a food processor until fairly smooth. Transfer to a bowl and add the remaining pork, ham, onion, parsley, mustard, Kirsch and seasoning. Spoon the filling into the tin, smoothing it down and levelling the surface.

3 Roll out the remaining pastry on the lightly floured surface and use it to top the pie, sealing the edges with some of the beaten egg. Decorate with the pastry trimmings and glaze with the remaining beaten egg. Make three or four holes in the top. Bake for 40 minutes, then reduce the oven to 180°C/350°F/Gas 4 and cook for a further hour. Leave to cool in the tin.

4 Make up the aspic jelly, using the boiling water. Stir to dissolve, then allow to cool. Make a small hole near the edge of the pie with a skewer, then pour in the aspic through a baking parchment funnel. Chill for at least 2 hours before serving the pie in slices with mustard, bread and dill pickles.

Country-style Terrine Energy 211kcal/884kJ; Protein 27.5g; Carbohydrate 1.3g, of which sugars 1g; Fat 10.7g, of which saturates 4.4g; Cholesterol 87mg; Calcium 20mg; Fibre 1.0g; Sodium 395mg.
Liver Pâté Pie Energy 577kcal/2411kJ; Protein 33g; Carbohydrate 36.1g, of which sugars 1.6g; Fat 33.7g, of which saturates 18.1g; Cholesterol 273mg; Calcium 96mg; Fibre 1.7g; Sodium 678mg.

Bon-bon Chicken with Sesame Sauce

This popular Chinese salad dish is full of Asian flavours. The chicken meat is tenderized by being beaten with a stick, called a bon – hence its name. Here, a rolling pin is used for the same effect after the chicken has been slowly poached in a pan on top of the stove.

Serves 6–8

1 chicken, about 1kg/2¼lb
1.2 litres/2 pints/5 cups water
15ml/1 tbsp sesame oil
½ cucumber, thinly sliced to garnish

For the sauce

30ml/2 tbsp light soy sauce
5ml/1 tsp sugar
15ml/1 tbsp finely chopped spring onions (scallions)
5ml/1 tsp red chilli oil
2.5ml/½ tsp ground Sichuan peppercorns
5ml/1 tsp white sesame seeds
10ml/2 tbsp sesame paste (tahini) or 30ml/2 tbsp peanut butter creamed with a little sesame oil

1 Clean the chicken well. In a wok or large pan, bring the water to a rolling boil, add the chicken, reduce the heat and gently cook, covered, for 40–45 minutes. Remove the chicken from the pan and immerse in cold water to cool.

2 After at least 1 hour, remove the chicken from the water and drain. Dry well with kitchen paper and brush on a coating of sesame oil. Carve the meat off the legs, wings and breast, and pull the meat off the rest of the bones.

3 On a flat work surface, cover the chicken meat with a piece of clear film (plastic wrap) and pound with a rolling pin. Tear the pounded meat into shreds with your fingers, or use two forks to shred it. Set aside.

4 To make the sauce, mix together all the ingredients in a large bowl until well combined, reserving a little of the chopped spring onion for the garnish.

5 Place the shredded chicken in a serving dish and arrange the cucumber around the edge. Pour the sauce over the chicken, garnish with the reserved spring onion and serve.

Chicken and Fruit Salad

An ideal party dish as the slow-roasted chickens can be cooked in advance and the salad finished off on the day. Serve with lots of warm garlic bread.

Serves 8

4 fresh tarragon or rosemary sprigs
2 x 1.6kg/3½lb chickens
65g/2½oz/5 tbsp softened butter
150ml/¼ pint/⅔ cup hot chicken stock
150ml/¼ pint/⅔ cup white wine
115g/4oz/1 cup walnut pieces
1 small Cantaloupe melon
450g/1lb seedless grapes or pitted cherries
salt and ground black pepper
mixed lettuce, to serve

For the dressing

30ml/2 tbsp tarragon vinegar
120ml/4fl oz/½ cup light olive oil
30ml/2 tbsp chopped mixed fresh herbs, such as parsley, mint and tarragon

1 Preheat the oven to 200°C/400°F/Gas 6. Put the sprigs of tarragon or rosemary inside the chickens and season. Tie the chickens in a neat shape with kitchen string, if necessary. Spread them with 50g/2oz/4 tbsp of the butter, place in a roasting pan and add the stock. Cover loosely with foil and roast for about 1½ hours, basting twice, until browned and the juices run clear. Remove the chickens from the roasting pan and leave to cool.

2 Add the wine to the juices in the roasting pan. Heat the pan on the stove, or transfer the juices to another pan, until the liquid has reduced and become syrupy. Strain and cool.

3 Heat the remaining butter in a frying pan and fry the walnuts until lightly browned. Drain on kitchen paper and cool. Scoop the melon into balls. Joint the chickens into eight portions.

4 To make the dressing, whisk the vinegar and oil together with a little salt and pepper. Remove all the fat from the cooled chicken juices and add to the dressing with the herbs.

5 Arrange the mixed lettuce on a serving plate. Put the chicken pieces on top and sprinkle over the grapes or cherries and the melon. Spoon over the dressing, sprinkle with walnuts and serve.

Bon-bon Chicken Energy 104kcal/437kJ; Protein 13g; Carbohydrate 1.4g, of which sugars 1.1g; Fat 5.2g, of which saturates 1g; Cholesterol 35mg; Calcium 6mg; Fibre 0.2g; Sodium 310mg.
Chicken Salad Energy 673kcal/2790kJ; Protein 33.3g; Carbohydrate 12.9g, of which sugars 12.8g; Fat 53.2g, of which saturates 14.1g; Cholesterol 177mg; Calcium 46mg; Fibre 1.2g; Sodium 197mg.

Anchovy and Roasted Pepper Salad

Slowly roasted sweet peppers, salty anchovies and plenty of garlic make an intensely flavoured salad that is delicious with meat, poultry or cheese. It also makes a tasty snack with olive bread and is excellent as part of a buffet or a picnic on a summer's day. Peeling the skin from the roasted peppers may seem arduous but the effort is well worthwhile.

Serves 4

2 red, 2 orange and 2 yellow (bell) peppers, halved and seeded
50g/2oz can anchovies in olive oil
2 garlic cloves
45ml/3 tbsp balsamic vinegar

1 Preheat the oven to 200°C/400°F/Gas 6. Place the peppers, cut side down, in a roasting pan. Roast for 30–40 minutes, until the skins are charred.

2 Transfer the peppers to a bowl, cover with clear film (plastic wrap) and leave for 15 minutes, until they have cooled down enough to handle.

3 Peel the peppers, then cut the flesh into chunky strips. Drain the anchovies and halve the fillets lengthways.

4 Slice the garlic as thinly as possible and place it in a large bowl. Add the olive oil, vinegar and a little ground black pepper. Stir gently until well combined.

5 Add the peppers and anchovies to the bowl and use a spoon and fork to fold the ingredients together. Cover and chill until ready to serve.

Cook's Tip
If you find that canned anchovies are a little too salty for your liking, you can reduce their saltiness by soaking them in milk for about 20 minutes. Rinse off the oil they are stored in before soaking, and then afterwards drain again and rinse them in plenty of cold running water.

Italian Salad

A combination of antipasto ingredients and slow-cooked potato wedges makes this a very substantial and popular dish.

Serves 6

1 aubergine (eggplant), sliced
75ml/5 tbsp olive oil
2 garlic cloves, cut into slivers
4 sun-dried tomatoes in oil, halved
2 red (bell) peppers, halved, seeded and cut into large chunks
2 large baking potatoes, cut into wedges
10ml/2 tsp mixed dried Italian herbs
30–45ml/2–3 tbsp balsamic vinegar
salt and ground black pepper

1 Preheat the oven to 200°C/400°F/Gas 6. Place the aubergines in a medium roasting pan with the olive oil, garlic slivers and sun-dried tomatoes. Lay the pepper chunks over the aubergines.

2 Lay the potato wedges on top of the other ingredients in the roasting pan. Sprinkle the herbs over and season with salt and black pepper.

3 Tightly cover the roasting pan with kitchen foil and bake in the preheated oven for about 45 minutes.

4 Remove the pan from the oven and gently turn the vegetables over. Then return to the oven and cook uncovered for 30 minutes more.

5 Take the vegetables out of the pan with a slotted spoon. Add the vinegar and seasoning to the pan, whisk and pour over the vegetables. Garnish with salt and black pepper.

Variation
There are many other vegetables that can be used in this dish. Roast some red onion wedges or chunks of courgette (zucchini) for the same amount of time. Small cherry tomatoes can be added to the pan for the last 20 minutes.

Anchovy Salad Energy 108kcal/453kJ; Protein 6g; Carbohydrate 16.4g, of which sugars 15.5g; Fat 2.4g, of which saturates 0.5g; Cholesterol 8mg; Calcium 83mg; Fibre 4.6g; Sodium 506mg.
Italian Salad Energy 154kcal/644kJ; Protein 2.2g; Carbohydrate 15.6g, of which sugars 3.1g; Fat 9.7g, of which saturates 1.5g; Cholesterol 0mg; Calcium 12mg; Fibre 2.2g; Sodium 17mg.

Creamy Anchovy and Potato Bake

This dish of potatoes, onions and anchovies with cream is made in the slow cooker and is ideal as a hearty winter lunch or simple supper, served with a refreshing salad.

Serves 4

1kg/2¼lb maincrop potatoes
2 onions
25g/1oz/2 tbsp butter
2 x 50g/2oz cans anchovy fillets
150ml/¼ pint/⅔ cup single (light) cream
150ml/¼ pint/⅔ cup double (heavy) cream
15ml/1 tbsp chopped fresh parsley
ground black pepper
fresh crusty bread, to serve

1 Peel the potatoes and cut them into slices slightly thicker than 1cm/½in. Cut the slices into strips slightly more than 1cm/½in wide. Peel the onions and cut into very thin rings.

2 Use half of the butter to grease the base and sides of the ceramic cooking pot, and layer half the potatoes and onions in the base of the dish.

3 Drain the anchovies, reserving about 15ml/1 tbsp of the oil. Cut the anchovies into thin strips and lay these over the potatoes and onions in the ceramic cooking pot, then layer the remaining potatoes and onions on top.

4 Combine the single cream and anchovy oil in a small jug (pitcher) and season with a little ground black pepper. Pour the mixture evenly over the potatoes and dot the surface with butter.

5 Cover and cook on high for 3½ hours, or until the potatoes and onions are tender. Brown under a hot grill (broiler), if you like, then drizzle over the double cream and sprinkle with parsley and pepper. Serve with fresh crusty bread.

Cook's Tip
This recipe can also be served as an appetizer for six, or as a side dish to accompany a main meal.

Baked Sardines with Caper and Tomato Stuffing

Sardines are often a popular choice for cooking on a summer barbecue, but you can enjoy these delicious oven-baked sardines all year round.

Serves 4

16 fresh sardines, cleaned
8–12 cherry tomatoes, on the vine, sliced
45ml/3 tbsp capers, chopped
½ small red onion, very finely chopped
60ml/4 tbsp olive oil
grated rind and juice of 1 lemon
45ml/3 tbsp chopped fresh parsley
15ml/1 tbsp chopped fresh basil
basil sprigs and lemon wedges, to garnish
crusty bread, to serve

1 Remove the backbone from the sardines by placing the fish slit side down on a chopping board. Using your fingers, push firmly along the length of the backbone to loosen it from the flesh. Turn the sardine over and pull out the bone; cut the ends with a sharp knife to release it. Repeat this process with the remaining sardines.

2 Place the tomato slices inside each sardine; they may stick out slightly, depending on the size of the fish. Lay the sardines in a single layer in a large earthenware dish.

3 Preheat the oven to 200°C/400°F/Gas 6. Mix the capers and red onion together and place on top of the tomatoes.

4 Mix together the olive oil, lemon rind and juice, parsley and basil and drizzle over the sardines. Bake the sardines for about 10 minutes, or until the fish flesh flakes easily. Garnish with basil and lemon wedges and serve with plenty of crusty bread to mop up the sauce.

Cook's Tip
Removing the bones before cooking, as in step 1 of this recipe, makes the sardines easier to eat.

Creamy Bake Energy 378kcal/1580kJ; Protein 11.3g; Carbohydrate 37.9g, of which sugars 6.4g; Fat 21.2g, of which saturates 11.4g; Cholesterol 54mg; Calcium 1460mg; Fibre 11.5g; Sodium 133mg.
Baked Sardines Energy 214kcal/887kJ; Protein 13.3g; Carbohydrate 3.4g, of which sugars 3g; Fat 16.4g, of which saturates 3.1g; Cholesterol 0mg; Calcium 89mg; Fibre 1.3g; Sodium 78mg.

Cannelloni Sorrentina-style

A slow-cooker dish of lasagne rolled around a tomato, ricotta and anchovy filling.

Serves 4–6

15ml/1 tbsp olive oil, plus extra for greasing
1 small onion, finely chopped
900g/2lb ripe Italian tomatoes, peeled and finely chopped
2 garlic cloves, crushed
5ml/1 tsp dried mixed herbs
150ml/¼ pint/⅔ cup hot vegetable stock
150ml/¼ pint/⅔ cup white wine
30ml/2 tbsp sun-dried tomato paste
2.5ml/½ tsp sugar
16 dried lasagne sheets
225g/8oz/1 cup ricotta cheese
130g/4½oz packet mozzarella cheese, drained and diced
30ml/2 tbsp shredded fresh basil, plus extra basil leaves to garnish
8 bottled anchovy fillets in olive oil, drained and halved lengthways
50g/2oz/⅔ cup freshly grated Parmesan cheese
salt and ground black pepper

1 Heat the oil in a pan and cook the onion for 5 minutes. Transfer to the ceramic cooking pot and switch on to high. Add the tomatoes, garlic and herbs, and season. Cover and cook for 1 hour.

2 Put half of the tomato mixture in a bowl and set aside to cool. Stir the stock, wine, tomato paste and sugar into the mixture in the slow cooker. Cover and cook for 1 hour. Turn off the cooker.

3 Meanwhile, cook the lasagne sheets according to the packet instructions. Lay them on a clean dish towel until needed.

4 Add the two cheeses and basil to the tomato mixture in the bowl. Spread a little of the mixture over each sheet. Place an anchovy fillet across each sheet and roll up.

5 Purée the tomato sauce from the slow cooker in a food processor or blender. Wash and dry the ceramic cooking pot, then lightly grease the base and halfway up the sides.

6 Spoon a third of the sauce into the ceramic cooking pot. Place the cannelloni on top and spoon over the remaining sauce. Sprinkle with the Parmesan. Cover and cook on high or auto for 1 hour. Switch to low or leave on auto and cook for a further hour. Serve garnished with basil.

Tuna Lasagne

This delicious dish is perfect for a family supper and is incredibly simple to make in a slow cooker.

Serves 6

65g/2½oz/5 tbsp butter, plus extra for greasing
1 small onion, finely chopped
1 garlic clove, finely chopped
115g/4oz mushrooms, thinly sliced
40g/1½oz/⅓ cup plain (all-purpose) flour
50ml/2fl oz/¼ cup dry white wine
150ml/¼ pint/⅔ cup double (heavy) cream
600ml/1 pint/2½ cups milk
45ml/3 tbsp chopped fresh parsley
2 x 200g/7oz cans tuna in oil
2 canned pimientos, cut into strips
115g/4oz/1 cup mozzarella cheese, grated
8–12 sheets pre-cooked lasagne
25g/1oz/3 tbsp freshly grated Parmesan cheese
salt and ground black pepper
Italian-style bread, such as ciabatta, and green salad, to serve

1 Lightly grease the base and halfway up the sides of the ceramic cooking pot. Melt 25g/1oz/2 tbsp of the butter in a large pan, add the onion and fry for 5 minutes until almost soft. Add the garlic and mushrooms and cook for 3 minutes, stirring occasionally. Transfer the vegetables to a bowl and set aside.

2 Melt the remaining butter in the pan and stir in the flour. Blend in the wine, then the cream and milk. Gently heat, stirring constantly, until it thickens. Stir in the parsley and season with salt and pepper. Reserve 300ml/½pint/1¼ cups of the sauce, then stir the mushroom mixture into the remaining sauce.

3 Drain the tuna and place into a bowl. Flake with a fork, then mix in the pimiento strips, mozzarella and a little salt and pepper.

4 Spoon a layer of the mushroom sauce over the base of the ceramic cooking pot and cover with 2–3 lasagne sheets followed by half of the tuna mixture. Spoon over half of the remaining sauce and add a layer of lasagne. Repeat, ending with lasagne. Pour over the reserved plain sauce. Sprinkle with the Parmesan.

5 Cover and cook on low for 2 hours, or until the lasagne is tender. If you like, brown the top of the lasagne under a medium grill (broiler) and serve with bread and a green salad.

Cannelloni Energy 546kcal/2293kJ; Protein 25.5g; Carbohydrate 54.3g, of which sugars 9.7g; Fat 24.1g, of which saturates 13.4g; Cholesterol 58mg; Calcium 301mg; Fibre 3.5g; Sodium 282mg.
Tuna Lasagne Energy 554kcal/2315kJ; Protein 32.2g; Carbohydrate 28.9g, of which sugars 7.4g; Fat 34.7g, of which saturates 18.5g; Cholesterol 110mg; Calcium 371mg; Fibre 0.6g; Sodium 616mg.

Poached Fish in Spicy Tomato Sauce

This slow-cooker dish can be served as a light lunch with flatbreads, such as pitta or matzos, but you can also serve it with plain boiled rice or noodles, if you are having it as part of a more substantial meal.

Serves 4

15ml/1 tbsp vegetable or olive oil
1 onion, finely chopped
150ml/¼ pint/⅔ cup passata (bottled strained tomatoes)
75ml/2½fl oz/⅓ cup boiling fish or vegetable stock
2 garlic cloves, crushed
1 small red chilli, seeded and finely chopped
pinch of ground ginger
pinch of curry powder
pinch of ground cumin
pinch of ground turmeric
seeds from 1 cardamom pod
juice of 1 lemon, plus extra if needed
900g/2lb mixed firm white fish fillets
30ml/2 tbsp chopped fresh coriander (cilantro)
30ml/2 tbsp chopped fresh parsley
salt and ground black pepper

1 Heat the oil in a frying pan, add the chopped onion and cook gently, stirring frequently, for 10 minutes until it is beginning to soften but not turn brown.

2 Transfer the onions to the ceramic cooking pot in the slow cooker. Stir in the passata, fish or vegetable stock, garlic, chilli, ginger, curry powder, cumin, turmeric, cardamom seeds and lemon juice, and season with salt and ground black pepper. Cover the slow cooker with the lid and cook on high or auto for 1½ hours, until the mixture is just simmering.

3 Add the fish fillets to the pot, cover and continue cooking on auto or switch to the low setting for 45 minutes to 1 hour, or until the fish fillets are just tender. Test by inserting a skewer or knife into the thickest part: the flesh should flake easily.

4 Lift the fish fillets out of the ceramic cooking pot on to warmed serving plates. Stir the coriander and parsley into the sauce. Taste and adjust the seasoning, if necessary, adding more lemon juice if the sauce requires it. Spoon the sauce over the fish and serve immediately.

Baked Cod with Horseradish Sauce

Cooking fish by baking it slowly in the oven in a sauce helps to keep it deliciously moist. In this recipe, a second, tangy horseradish sauce is served alongside for added flavour.

Serves 4

4 thick cod fillets or steaks
15ml/1 tbsp lemon juice
25g/1oz/2 tbsp butter
25g/1oz/¼ cup plain (all-purpose) flour, sifted
150ml/¼ pint/⅔ cup milk
150ml/¼ pint/⅔ cup fish stock
salt and ground black pepper
parsley sprigs, to garnish
potato wedges and chopped spring onions (scallions), fried, to serve

For the horseradish sauce
30ml/2 tbsp tomato purée (paste)
30ml/2 tbsp grated fresh horseradish
150ml/¼ pint/⅔ cup sour cream

1 Preheat the oven to 180°C/350°F/Gas 4. Place the fish in a buttered ovenproof dish in a single layer. Sprinkle all over with the lemon juice.

2 Melt the butter in a small, heavy pan. Stir in the flour and cook for 3–4 minutes until lightly golden. Stir constantly to stop the flour sticking to the pan. Remove from the heat.

3 Gradually whisk in the milk, and then the stock, into the flour mixture. Season with salt and pepper. Bring to the boil, stirring, and simmer for 3 minutes, still stirring.

4 Pour the sauce over the fish, ensuring it is evenly distributed, and bake for 20–25 minutes, depending on the thickness. Check by inserting a skewer in the thickest part: the flesh should be opaque and flake easily.

5 For the horseradish sauce, blend the tomato purée and horseradish with the sour cream in a small pan. Slowly bring to the boil, stirring, and then simmer for 1 minute.

6 Pour the horseradish sauce into a bowl and serve alongside the fish. Serve the fish hot, garnished with parsley sprigs and accompanied by potato wedges and fried spring onions.

Poached Fish Energy 224kcal/942kJ; Protein 42g; Carbohydrate 4.1g, of which sugars 3.1g; Fat 4.4g, of which saturates 0.6g; Cholesterol 104mg; Calcium 34mg; Fibre 0.8g; Sodium 151mg.
Baked Cod Energy 380kcal/1584kJ; Protein 40.7g; Carbohydrate 10.2g, of which sugars 5.4g; Fat 19.7g, of which saturates 11.7g; Cholesterol 145mg; Calcium 137mg; Fibre 0.5g; Sodium 222mg.

Onion and Fish Casserole

Choose a firm, meaty fish for this oven-baked casserole. Cod, grey mullet, red snapper or pompano would all work well in this hearty dish. Serve with fresh crusty bread to mop up the wonderful juices.

Serves 4

45ml/3 tbsp olive oil
4 onions, finely chopped
5ml/1 tsp sea salt
45ml/3 tbsp water
3 garlic cloves, crushed
1 bay leaf
6 allspice berries
2.5ml/½ tsp paprika
4 ripe plum tomatoes, seeded and diced
120ml/4fl oz/½ cup dry white wine, plus 45ml/3 tbsp
4 skinless fish steaks, about 175g/6oz each
lemon juice, for sprinkling
8 lemon slices
salt and ground black pepper
15ml/1 tbsp chopped fresh parsley, to garnish
crusty bread, to serve

1 Preheat the oven to 180°C/350°F/Gas 4. Put the oil, onion, sea salt and water in a heavy pan. Stir well and cook gently, covered, over a very low heat on the stove for 45 minutes but do not allow the onion to brown.

2 Stir in the garlic and cook for 1 minute before adding the bay leaf, allspice, paprika, tomatoes and the dry white wine, and season with salt and ground black pepper. Cook for about 10–15 minutes, stirring occasionally to prevent sticking. Remove and discard the allspice and bay leaf.

3 Spoon a layer of the onion mixture into the base of a shallow ovenproof dish and top with the fish steaks. Sprinkle with a little lemon juice and season with salt and black pepper.

4 Sprinkle over the remaining dry white wine and place two lemon slices overlapping on top of each of the fish steaks. Spoon the remaining onion sauce over the fish.

5 Bake the casserole in the oven for 15–20 minutes, or until the sauce thickens and the fish flakes easily when tested with a knife or skewer. Serve the fish topped with plenty of onion mixture. Garnish with parsley and serve with crusty bread.

Cod with Caramelized Onions

The slow cooker is ideal for this dish, resulting in onions that become caramelized and turn a deep golden colour with a fabulously rich, sweet flavour. Tangy caper and coriander butter adds a fresh, sharp contrast.

Serves 4

40g/1½oz/3 tbsp butter
10ml/2 tsp olive oil
1.2kg/2½lb yellow onions, peeled and finely sliced
5ml/1 tsp caster (superfine) sugar
30ml/2 tbsp balsamic vinegar
30ml/2 tbsp vegetable stock, white wine or water
4 x 150g/5oz thick cod fillets

For the butter
115g/4oz/½ cup butter, softened
30ml/2 tbsp capers, drained and chopped
30ml/2 tbsp chopped fresh coriander (cilantro)
salt and ground black pepper

1 Put the butter and oil in the ceramic cooking pot and heat on high for about 15 minutes, until melted. Add the onions and stir to coat well in the butter and oil. Cover the pot with the lid, then place a folded dish towel over the top to retain all the heat. Cook for 2 hours, stirring halfway through cooking time.

2 Sprinkle the sugar over the onions and mix well. Replace the lid and folded dish towel and cook on high for 4 hours, stirring two or three times. They should turn a dark golden colour.

3 Add the vinegar to the onions and stir in the stock, wine or water. Cover again and cook for 1 hour; the onions should now be fairly tender. Season with salt and pepper and stir well. Arrange the cod fillets on top of the onions and cook for a final 45 minutes to 1 hour, or until the fish flakes easily.

4 Meanwhile, make the butter. Place the soft butter in a bowl and beat in the capers, coriander, salt and pepper. Roll up the butter in foil or clear film (plastic wrap) to form a log shape, twisting the ends. Chill in the refrigerator or freezer until firm.

5 To serve, spoon the onions and fish on to warmed serving plates. Slice off discs of the butter and top each piece of fish with one or two slices. Serve immediately.

Fish Casserole Energy 307kcal/1283kJ; Protein 34.8g; Carbohydrate 14.5g, of which sugars 10.3g; Fat 10.5g, of which saturates 1.5g; Cholesterol 81mg; Calcium 64mg; Fibre 2.8g; Sodium 120mg.
Cod with Onions Energy 534kcal/2213kJ; Protein 31.3g; Carbohydrate 25g, of which sugars 18.1g; Fat 35g, of which saturates 20.6g; Cholesterol 152mg; Calcium 96mg; Fibre 4.2g; Sodium 334mg.

Haddock with Spicy Puy Lentils

Dark brown Puy lentils have a delicate taste and texture and hold their shape during cooking, which makes them particularly good for slow cooker dishes. Red chilli pepper and ground cumin add a hint of heat and spice without overpowering the flavour of the fish.

Serves 4

175g/6oz/¾ cup Puy lentils
600ml/1 pint/2½ cups near-boiling vegetable stock
30ml/2 tbsp olive oil
1 onion, finely chopped
2 celery sticks, finely chopped
1 red chilli, halved, seeded and finely chopped
2.5ml/ tsp ground cumin
4 thick pieces of haddock fillet or steak, each weighing about 150g/5oz
10ml/2 tsp lemon juice
25g/1oz/2 tbsp butter, softened
5ml/1 tsp finely grated lemon rind
salt and ground black pepper
lemon wedges, to garnish

1 Put the Puy lentils in a sieve (strainer) and rinse well under cold running water. Drain the lentils well, then transfer them to the ceramic cooking pot. Pour over the near-boiling vegetable stock, cover the slow cooker with the lid and switch on to the high setting.

2 Heat the oil in a frying pan, add the chopped onion and cook gently for about 8 minutes until soft. Stir in the celery, chilli and cumin, and cook for a further 2 minutes, or until soft but not coloured. Add the mixture to the lentils in the ceramic cooking pot, stir, re-cover and cook for about 2½ hours.

3 Meanwhile, rinse the haddock fillets under cold running water and pat dry on kitchen paper. Sprinkle them with the lemon juice. In a clean bowl, beat together the softened butter and lemon rind, and season with salt and a generous amount of ground black pepper.

4 Put the haddock on top of the lentils, then dot the lemon butter over the top. Cover and cook for 45 minutes to 1 hour, or until the fish flakes easily when tested with a knife, the lentils are tender and most of the stock has been absorbed. Serve immediately, garnished with the lemon wedges.

Red Mullet on a Bed of Fennel

These pretty pink fish are usually cooked whole, but you can remove the heads if there is not enough room in your slow cooker to fit them all in a single layer.

Serves 4

10ml/2 tsp fennel seeds
5ml/1 tsp chopped fresh thyme
30ml/2 tbsp chopped fresh parsley
1 clove garlic, crushed
10ml/2 tsp olive oil
4 red mullet or snapper, weighing about 225g/8oz each
lemon wedges, to serve

For the fennel
8 ripe tomatoes
2 fennel bulbs
30ml/2 tbsp olive oil
120ml/4fl oz/½cup boiling fish or vegetable stock
10ml/2 tsp balsamic vinegar
salt and ground black pepper

1 Crush the fennel seeds using a mortar and pestle, then work in the chopped thyme and parsley, garlic and olive oil.

2 Clean and scale the fish and trim off the fins. Cut slashes on each side of the fish. Push the herb paste into the cuts and spread any excess inside the body cavities. Place the fish on a plate, cover with clear film (plastic wrap) and leave to marinate.

3 Meanwhile, prepare the bed of fennel. Put the tomatoes in a heatproof bowl, cover with boiling water and leave for 1 minute. Drain and cool in cold water. Peel the skin off, quarter the tomatoes, discard the seeds and dice the flesh.

4 Trim the feathery fronds from the fennel (these can be kept for garnishing), then cut the bulbs into 1cm/½in slices from the top to the root end. Heat the oil in a frying pan and cook the slices over a medium heat for 10 minutes until starting to colour.

5 Transfer the fennel to the ceramic cooking pot. Add the diced tomatoes, hot stock, balsamic vinegar, salt and pepper, cover with the lid and cook on high for 2 hours.

6 Give the fennel sauce a stir, then place the fish on top in a single layer. Cover and cook for 1 hour, or until the fish is cooked through. Serve immediately, with lemon wedges.

Haddock with Lentils Energy 366kcal/1538kJ; Protein 38.9g; Carbohydrate 25.2g, of which sugars 3.2g; Fat 12.8g, of which saturates 4.3g; Cholesterol 82mg; Calcium 64mg; Fibre 4.7g; Sodium 353mg.
Red Mullet Energy 194kcal/816kJ; Protein 26.5g; Carbohydrate 4.2g, of which sugars 4.1g; Fat 8.1g, of which saturates 1.2g; Cholesterol 63mg; Calcium 95mg; Fibre 3.0g; Sodium 239mg.

Fish Balls with Cinnamon

This delicious dish featuring fish balls is a Jewish delicacy. The fish balls are slowly simmered in a pan on the stove and then combined with other vegetables. Chrain is a relish made with horseradish and beetroot, available from supermarkets and Jewish food stores.

Serves 8

1kg/2¼lb of 2–3 varieties of fish fillets, such as carp, whitefish, yellow pike, haddock and cod
2 eggs
120ml/4fl oz/½ cup cold water
30–45ml/2–3 tbsp medium matzo meal
15–45ml/1–3 tbsp sugar
fish stock, for simmering
2–3 onions, chopped
3 carrots, sliced
1–2 pinches of ground cinnamon
salt and ground black pepper
chrain or horseradish and beetroot (beets), to serve

1 Place the fish fillets on a plate, sprinkle with salt and chill for about 1 hour, or until the flesh has firmed. Rinse the fish well, then put in a food processor or blender and process until roughly minced (ground).

2 Put the fish into a bowl, add the eggs, mix well, then gradually add the water. Stir in the matzo meal, then the sugar and season with salt and pepper. Beat until light and aerated. Cover and chill for 1 hour.

3 Take 15–30ml/1–2 tbsp of the mixture and, with wet hands, roll into a ball. Continue with the remaining mixture.

4 Bring a large pan of fish stock to the boil, reduce to a simmer, then add the fishballs. Return to the boil, then simmer for 1 hour.

5 Add the onions, carrots, cinnamon and a little extra sugar, if you like, to the pan and simmer, uncovered, for 45–60 minutes. Add more water, if necessary, to keep the balls covered.

6 Leave the fish to cool slightly, then remove from the liquid with a slotted spoon. Serve warm or cold with the cooked vegetables and chrain or horseradish and beetroot.

Monkfish with Pesto

A slowly baked clay-pot dish of vegetables and monkfish stuffed with pesto.

Serves 4

900g/2lb monkfish tail, skinned
50g/2oz rocket (arugula)
30ml/2 tbsp pine nuts
1 garlic clove, chopped
25g/1oz/⅓ cup freshly grated Parmesan cheese
90ml/6 tbsp olive oil
45ml/3 tbsp lemon juice
2 red (bell) peppers, halved
2 yellow (bell) peppers, halved
1 red onion, cut into wedges
2 courgettes (zucchini), cut into 2.5cm/1in slices
4 fresh rosemary sprigs
salt and ground black pepper

1 Cut along one side of the central bone of the fish and remove the fillet. Repeat on the other side. Set aside. Soak a fish clay pot in cold water for 20 minutes, then set aside.

2 Make the pesto. Place the rocket, pine nuts, garlic, Parmesan, 45ml/3 tbsp of the oil and 15ml/1 tbsp of the lemon juice in a food processor or blender and process to form a smooth paste.

3 Lay a fish fillet out flat, cut side up and spread with pesto. Top with the other fillet, cut side down. Tie the fish with string to seal. Season with salt and pepper and set aside. Cut each pepper half into three lengthways. Remove the core and seeds.

4 Put the pepper pieces in the pot, add the onion and courgette. In a bowl, mix together 15ml/1 tbsp of the oil and the remaining lemon juice and sprinkle over the vegetables. Mix well and season.

5 Tuck the rosemary sprigs in among the vegetables. Cover the pot and place in an unheated oven. Set the temperature to 220°C/425°F/Gas 7 and cook the vegetables for 20 minutes.

6 Place the fish in the centre of the vegetables and brush with oil. Sprinkle the remaining oil over the vegetables. Cover and bake for 20–25 minutes until the fish is tender and opaque.

7 To serve, cut the fish into thick slices, removing the string if you like. Serve with the cooked vegetables from the pot.

Fish Balls Energy 146kcal/612kJ; Protein 25.2g; Carbohydrate 5.7g, of which sugars 2.1g; Fat 2.5g, of which saturates 0.5g; Cholesterol 105mg; Calcium 28mg; Fibre 0.6g; Sodium 94mg.
Monkfish with Pesto Energy 477kcal/1991kJ; Protein 47g; Carbohydrate 14.7g, of which sugars 13.7g; Fat 25.8g, of which saturates 4.5g; Cholesterol 42mg; Calcium 160mg; Fibre 4.3g; Sodium 139mg.

Skate with Tomato and Olive Sauce

The skate wings in this slow-cooker dish are given a Mediterranean twist with tomatoes, olives, orange and a dash of Pernod. If time allows, soak the skate in salted water for a few hours or overnight before cooking, to firm up the flesh.

Serves 4

15ml/1 tbsp olive oil
1 small onion, finely chopped
2 fresh thyme sprigs
grated rind of ½ orange
15ml/1 tbsp Pernod
400g/14oz can chopped tomatoes
50g/2oz/1 cup stuffed green olives
1.5ml/¼ tsp caster (superfine) sugar
4 small skate wings
plain (all-purpose) flour, for coating
salt and ground black pepper
15ml/1 tbsp basil leaves, to garnish
lime wedges, to serve

1 Heat the oil in a pan, add the onion and fry for 10 minutes. Stir in the thyme and orange rind and cook for 1 minute. Add the Pernod, tomatoes, olives, sugar and a little salt and pepper, and heat until just below boiling point. Transfer the mixture to the ceramic pot and switch the slow cooker on to the high setting. Cover with the lid and cook for 1½ hours.

2 Meanwhile, rinse the skate wings under cold water and pat dry on kitchen paper. Sprinkle the flour on a large, flat dish and season with salt and pepper. Coat each skate wing in the flour, shaking off any excess, then place on top of the tomato sauce.

3 Replace the cover on the ceramic cooking pot and reduce the temperature to low. Cook for 1½–2 hours, or until the skate is cooked and flakes easily.

4 Place the fish on to warmed serving plates and spoon over the sauce. Sprinkle over the basil leaves and serve with a wedge of lime for squeezing over.

Cook's Tip

Pernod gives this dish a distinctive taste of aniseed, but for those who don't like the flavour, use 15ml/1 tbsp vermouth instead.

Lemon Sole and Parma Ham Roulades

In this elegant slow-cooker dish, Parma ham and delicately textured lemon sole are rolled around a subtle herb and lemon stuffing. Serve this dish for a dinner party with new potatoes tossed in butter, and lightly steamed asparagus.

Serves 4

10ml/2 tsp unsalted (sweet) butter, at room temperature
120ml/4fl oz/½ cup dry white wine
4 large lemon sole fillets, about 150g/5oz each
8 thin slices of Parma ham, about 130g/4½oz in total
50g/2oz/½ cup chopped toasted walnuts
75g/3oz/1½ cups fresh white breadcrumbs
30ml/2 tbsp chopped fresh parsley
2 eggs, lightly beaten
5ml/1 tsp finely grated lemon rind
ground black pepper
new potatoes and steamed green vegetables, to serve

1 Smear the inside of the ceramic cooking pot with the butter. Pour in the wine and switch the slow cooker to high. Skin the fish fillets and check that all the bones have been removed, then pat dry with kitchen paper.

2 Remove most of the fat from the Parma ham. Lay two overlapping slices on a board and place a sole fillet on top, skinned side up.

3 Mix the walnuts, breadcrumbs, parsley, eggs, lemon rind and pepper together and spread a quarter of the mixture over the fish fillet, then press down gently. Starting at the thicker end of the fillet, carefully roll up the fish and ham to enclose the filling.

4 Repeat with the remaining Parma ham, fish and filling, then secure each roulade with a cocktail stick (toothpick). Place the roulades, seam side down, in the ceramic cooking pot. Cover with the lid, then turn the temperature down to low. Cook for 1½–2 hours, or until the fish flakes easily.

5 Remove the cocktail sticks from the roulades and serve immediately, accompanied by the freshly cooked vegetables.

Skate Energy 144kcal/606kJ; Protein 15.5g; Carbohydrate 8.1g, of which sugars 3.7g; Fat 4.8g, of which saturates 0.7g; Cholesterol 35mg; Calcium 37mg; Fibre 1.4g; Sodium 366mg.
Lemon Sole Roulades Energy 363kcal/1521kJ; Protein 38g; Carbohydrate 9.6g, of which sugars 1.5g; Fat 17.3g, of which saturates 3.6g; Cholesterol 201mg; Calcium 134mg; Fibre 0.8g; Sodium 714mg.

Swordfish in Barbecue Sauce

Using a slow cooker is an ideal way to prepare any firm fish steaks. The warmly spiced smoky sauce in this dish goes particularly well with meaty fish, such as swordfish, shark and tuna. Choose smaller, thicker fish steaks rather than large, thinner ones, so that they will fit in the slow cooker.

Serves 4

15ml/1 tbsp sunflower oil
1 small onion, very finely chopped
1 garlic clove, crushed
2.5ml/½ tsp chilli powder
15ml/1 tbsp Worcestershire sauce
15ml/1 tbsp soft light brown sugar
15ml/1 tbsp balsamic vinegar
15ml/1 tbsp American mustard
150ml/¼ pint/⅔ cup fresh tomato juice
4 swordfish steaks, about 115g/4oz each
salt and ground black pepper
fresh flat leaf parsley, to garnish
boiled or steamed rice, to serve

1 Heat the oil in a frying pan, add the onion and cook gently for 10 minutes, until soft. Stir in the garlic and chilli powder and cook for a few seconds, then add the Worcestershire sauce, sugar, vinegar, mustard and tomato juice. Heat gently, stirring, until nearly boiling.

2 Pour half the sauce into the ceramic cooking pot. Rinse the swordfish steaks, pat dry on kitchen paper and arrange in a single layer on top of the sauce. Top with the remaining sauce.

3 Cover the slow cooker with the lid and switch on to high. Cook for 2–3 hours, or until the fish is tender and cooked.

4 Carefully transfer the fish to warmed serving plates and spoon the barbecue sauce over the top. Garnish with sprigs of flat leaf parsley and serve immediately with boiled or steamed rice.

Cook's Tip
For a really smoky barbecue flavour, use a crushed dried chipotle chilli instead of the chilli powder.

Tuna with Tomatoes and Potatoes

The rich flavourings in this traditional fisherman's stew are given plenty of time to develop in the slow cooker. They are also the perfect partner to the robust taste of chunky tuna. Serve with plenty of fresh crusty bread for mopping up the juices.

Serves 4

30ml/2 tbsp olive oil
1 onion, finely chopped
1 clove garlic, finely chopped
75ml/2½fl oz/⅓ cup white wine
150ml/¼ pint/⅔ cup boiling fish or vegetable stock
200g/7oz can chopped tomatoes
5ml/1½ tsp paprika
2.5ml/½ tsp dried crushed chillies
450g/1lb waxy new potatoes, cut into 1cm/½in chunks
1 red and 1 yellow (bell) pepper, seeded and chopped
1 small sprig of fresh rosemary
1 bay leaf
450g/1lb fresh tuna, cut into 2.5cm/1in chunks
salt and ground black pepper
crusty bread, to serve

1 Heat the oil in a large frying pan, add the onion and fry gently, stirring frequently, for 8–10 minutes until it has turned soft and translucent.

2 Stir in the garlic, followed by the white wine, hot fish or vegetable stock, tomatoes, paprika and chillies. Bring to just below boiling point, then carefully pour the mixture into the ceramic cooking pot.

3 Add the chunks of new potato, the red and yellow peppers, sprig of fresh rosemary and the bay leaf to the slow cooker pot and stir to combine.

4 Cover the slow cooker with the lid and cook on high for 2–2½ hours, or until the potatoes are just tender, then season the sauce to taste with salt and a little ground black pepper.

5 Stir the chunks of tuna into the sauce. Cover and cook for 15–20 minutes, or until the fish is firm and opaque.

6 Remove the rosemary and bay leaf, then ladle the stew into warmed dishes, grind over a little more black pepper and serve with crusty bread.

Tuna Energy 297kcal/1256kJ; Protein 30.1g; Carbohydrate 27.5g, of which sugars 9.6g; Fat 6.g, of which saturates 1.2g; Cholesterol 57mg; Calcium 39mg; Fibre 3.2g; Sodium 397mg.
Swordfish Energy 158kcal/670kJ; Protein 27.3g; Carbohydrate 4.9g, of which sugars 4.5g; Fat 3.5g, of which saturates 0.6g; Cholesterol 59mg; Calcium 21mg; Fibre 0.2g; Sodium 414mg.

Spinach and Nut Stuffed Herrings

It is hard to cook large whole fish in a slow cooker, but herrings are ideal. Their oily flesh is perfectly suited to slow cooking as it keeps the fish wonderfully moist.

Serves 4

40g/1½oz/3 tbsp unsalted (sweet) butter
5ml/1 tsp sunflower oil
25g/1oz/¼ cup pine nuts
1 small onion, finely chopped
175g/6oz frozen spinach, thawed
50g/2oz/1 cup white breadcrumbs
25g/1oz/⅓ cup grated Parmesan cheese
pinch of freshly grated nutmeg
75ml/5 tbsp fish or vegetable stock or white wine
4 herrings, heads removed, and boned
salt and ground black pepper
lemon wedges, to serve

1 Heat 25g/1oz/2 tbsp of the butter and the oil in a frying pan. Add the pine nuts and gently fry for 3–4 minutes until golden. Lift them from the pan with a slotted spoon and place in a bowl. Add the onion to the pan and cook for 10 minutes until soft.

2 Meanwhile, place the thawed spinach in a fine sieve (strainer) and press out as much liquid as possible. Put the onion and spinach in the bowl with the pine nuts and add the breadcrumbs, cheese, nutmeg, salt and pepper. Mix until thoroughly combined.

3 Smear the remaining 15g/½oz/1 tbsp of butter over the base of the ceramic cooking pot and pour in the stock or wine. Cover with the lid and switch the slow cooker on to high.

4 Using a sharp knife, make three shallow cuts down each side of the fish, then spoon the stuffing into the cavities, packing it in quite firmly. Bring the edges of the fish together and secure with wooden cocktail sticks (toothpicks).

5 Arrange the fish on the base of the ceramic cooking pot in a single layer. Cover the pot with the lid and cook for 1½–2½ hours, or until the fish is tender and the flesh flakes easily in the thickest part when tested with a knife.

6 Carefully lift the stuffed fish out of the slow cooker on to warmed serving plates, and serve with lemon wedges.

Fillets of Brill in Red Wine Sauce

Forget the old maxim that red wine and fish do not go well together. The sauce adds colour and richness to this excellent dish. It is ideal for a dinner party, and simple to make as you only need one pot.

Serves 4

4 fillets of brill, about 175–200g/6–7oz each, skinned
150g/5oz/10 tbsp chilled butter, diced, plus extra for greasing
115g/4oz shallots, thinly sliced
200ml/7fl oz/scant 1 cup robust red wine
200ml/7fl oz/scant 1 cup fish or vegetable stock
salt and ground black and white pepper
fresh flat leaf parsley leaves or chervil, to garnish

1 Preheat the oven to 180°C/350°F/Gas 4. Season the fish fillets on both sides with salt and ground black pepper. Generously butter a shallow flameproof dish, which is large enough to take all the brill fillets in a single layer.

2 Spread the sliced shallots in an even layer in the dish and lay the fish fillets on top. Pour in the red wine and fish stock, cover the dish with a lid or foil and then bring the liquid to just below boiling point.

3 Transfer the dish to the oven and bake for about 6–8 minutes, or until the brill is just cooked and the flesh flakes easily in the thickest part when tested with a knife.

4 Using a metal spatula, lift the fish and the shallots out of the pan on to a serving dish, cover with foil and keep hot.

5 Transfer the dish to the stove and bring the cooking liquid to the boil over a high heat. Let it bubble until it has reduced by half. Lower the heat and whisk in the chilled butter, one piece at a time, to make a smooth, shiny sauce. Season with salt and ground white pepper, set the sauce aside and keep hot.

6 Divide the shallots among four warmed plates and lay the brill fillets on top. Pour the sauce over and around the fish and garnish with the fresh flat leaf parsley or chervil.

Stuffed Herrings Energy 351kcal/1462kJ; Protein 24g; Carbohydrate 7.6g, of which sugars 1.9g; Fat 23.9g, of which saturates 6.9g; Cholesterol 78mg; Calcium 619mg; Fibre 1.5g; Sodium 624mg.
Fillets of Brill Energy 515kcal/2142kJ; Protein 35.6g; Carbohydrate 2.6g, of which sugars 1.9g; Fat 36.7g, of which saturates 19.5g; Cholesterol 156mg; Calcium 98mg; Fibre 0.4g; Sodium 452mg.

Salmon Risotto with Cucumber

A classic risotto is time-consuming to make because the stock needs to be added gradually and requires constant stirring. Here, the wine and stock are added in one go into the slow cooker, making it far easier, yet still giving a delicious, creamy texture.

Serves 4

25g/1oz/2 tbsp butter
small bunch of spring onions (scallions), finely sliced
½ cucumber, peeled, seeded and chopped
225g/8oz/generous 1 cup easy-cook (converted) Italian rice
750ml/1¼ pints/3 cups boiling vegetable or fish stock
120ml/4fl oz/½ cup white wine
450g/1lb salmon fillet, skinned and diced
45ml/3 tbsp chopped fresh tarragon
salt and ground black pepper

1 Put the butter in the ceramic cooking pot and switch the slow cooker to high. Leave to melt for 15 minutes, then stir in the spring onions and cucumber. Cover and cook for 30 minutes.

2 Add the rice to the pot and stir, then pour in the stock and wine. Cover with the lid and cook for 45 minutes, stirring once halfway through cooking.

3 Stir the diced salmon into the risotto and season with salt and pepper. Cook for a further 15 minutes, or until the rice is tender and the salmon just cooked. Switch off the slow cooker and leave the risotto to stand for 5 minutes.

4 Remove the lid, add the chopped tarragon and mix lightly. Spoon the risotto into individual warmed serving bowls or plates and serve immediately.

Variation
Frozen peas can be used instead of cucumber, if you like. These should be defrosted and stirred into the risotto at the same time as the salmon.

Coconut Salmon

Salmon is quite a robust fish, and responds well to being cooked with this fragrant blend of spices, garlic and chilli in the slow cooker. Coconut milk adds a mellow touch and a creamy taste.

Serves 4

15ml/1 tbsp oil
1 onion, finely chopped
2 fresh green chillies, seeded and chopped
2 garlic cloves, crushed
2.5cm/1in piece fresh root ginger, grated
175ml/6fl oz/¾ cup coconut milk
10ml/2 tsp ground cumin
5ml/1 tsp ground coriander
4 salmon steaks, each 175g/6oz
10ml/2 tsp chilli powder
2.5ml/½ tsp ground turmeric
15ml/1 tbsp white wine vinegar
1.5ml/¼ tsp salt
fresh coriander (cilantro) sprigs, to garnish
rice tossed with spring onions (scallions), to serve

1 Heat the oil in a pan, add the onion, chillies, garlic and ginger and fry for 5–6 minutes, until fairly soft. Place in a food processor with 120ml/4fl oz/½ cup of the coconut milk and blend until smooth.

2 Transfer the paste to the ceramic cooking pot. Add 5ml/1 tsp of the cumin, the ground coriander and the rest of the coconut milk. Cover with the lid and cook on high for 1½ hours.

3 About 20 minutes before the end of cooking time, arrange the salmon steaks in a single layer in a shallow glass dish. Combine the remaining 5ml/1 tsp cumin, the chilli powder, turmeric, vinegar and salt in a bowl to make a paste. Rub the mixture over the salmon steaks and leave to marinate at room temperature while the sauce finishes cooking.

4 Add the salmon steaks to the sauce, arranging them in a single layer, and spoon some of the coconut sauce over the top to keep the fish moist while it cooks. Cover with the lid, reduce the temperature to low and cook for 45 minutes to 1 hour, or until the salmon is opaque and tender.

5 Transfer the fish to a serving dish, spoon over the sauce and garnish with fresh coriander. Serve with the spring onion rice.

Coconut Salmon Energy 363kcal/1512kJ; Protein 35.9g; Carbohydrate 5.1g, of which sugars 4.2g; Fat 22.2g, of which saturates 3.8g; Cholesterol 88mg; Calcium 59mg; Fibre 0.5g; Sodium 275mg.
Salmon Risotto Energy 506kcal/2122kJ; Protein 28.4g; Carbohydrate 51.3g, of which sgars 2.8g; Fat 20g, of which saturates 5.9g; Cholesterol 70mg; Calcium 91mg; Fibre 1.4g; Sodium 266mg.

Thai Fish Curry

Thin, soupy, strongly flavoured curries are typical of Thailand. Fragrant lemon grass, zesty galangal and salty Thai fish sauce come together to give this slow-cooker dish a deliciously distinct flavour.

Serves 4

450g/1lb salmon fillet
475ml/16fl oz/2 cups near-boiling vegetable stock
4 shallots, very finely chopped
1 garlic clove, crushed
2.5cm/1in piece fresh galangal or ginger, finely chopped
1 lemon grass stalk, finely chopped
2.5ml/½ tsp dried chilli flakes
15ml/1 tbsp Thai fish sauce
5ml/1 tsp palm sugar (jaggery) or light muscovado (brown) sugar

1 Wrap the salmon fillet in clear film (plastic wrap) and place in the freezer for 30–40 minutes to firm up slightly.

2 Unwrap the fish, and carefully remove and discard the skin. Using a sharp knife, cut the fish into 2.5cm/1in cubes and remove any stray bones with your fingers or a pair of tweezers.

3 Place the cubed fish in a bowl, cover with clear film (plastic wrap) and leave to stand at room temperature.

4 Meanwhile, pour the hot vegetable stock into the ceramic cooking pot and switch the slow cooker to high.

5 Add the shallots, garlic, galangal or ginger, lemon grass, chilli flakes, fish sauce and sugar to the pot and stir to combine. Cover with the lid and cook for 2 hours.

6 Add the salmon to the stock and cook for 15 minutes. Turn off the slow cooker and leave to stand for a further 10–15 minutes, or until the fish is cooked through. Serve immediately.

Cook's Tip
Make sure the fish has returned to room temperature before adding to the stock, so that the temperature of the liquid doesn't fall below simmering point.

Green Fish Curry

This slow-cooker version of a Thai green curry uses desiccated coconut and cream to give a rich taste.

Serves 4

1 onion, chopped
1 fresh green chilli, seeded and chopped, plus slices to garnish
1 garlic clove, crushed
50g/2oz/½ cup cashew nuts
2.5ml/½ tsp fennel seeds
30ml/2 tbsp desiccated (dry unsweetened shredded) coconut
150ml/¼ pint/⅔ cup water
30ml/2 tbsp vegetable oil
1.5ml/¼ tsp cumin seeds
1.5ml/¼ tsp ground coriander
1.5ml/¼ tsp ground cumin
150ml/¼ pint/⅔ cup double (heavy) cream
4 white fish fillets, such as cod or haddock, skinned
1.5ml/¼ tsp ground turmeric
30ml/2 tbsp lime juice
salt
45ml/3 tbsp chopped fresh coriander (cilantro), plus extra to garnish
boiled rice, to serve

1 Place the onion, chilli, garlic, cashew nuts, fennel seeds and desiccated coconut in a food processor with 45ml/3 tbsp of the water and blend to a smooth paste. Alternatively, work the dry ingredients to a paste with a mortar and pestle, then add water.

2 Heat the oil in a pan and fry the cumin seeds for 1 minute, until they give off their aroma. Add the coconut paste and fry for 5 minutes, then stir in the ground coriander, cumin and remaining water. Bring to the boil and cook for 1 minute.

3 Transfer the mixture to the ceramic cooking pot. Stir in the cream, cover and set to high. Cook for 1½ hours.

4 Towards the end of cooking time, prepare and marinate the fish. Cut the fillets into 5cm/2in chunks and put them in a glass bowl. Combine the turmeric, lime juice and a pinch of salt in a separate bowl and pour it over the fish, rubbing it in well. Cover with clear film (plastic wrap) and marinate for 15 minutes.

5 Stir the fish into the sauce, re-cover and cook for 30 minutes to 1 hour, or until the fish flakes easily. Stir in the coriander. Spoon the curry into warmed bowls. Garnish with chopped coriander and sliced green chilli, and serve with rice.

Fish Curry Energy 216kcal/902kJ; Protein 23.2g; Carbohydrate 2.7g, of which sugars 2.2g; Fat 12.6g, of which saturates 2.1g; Cholesterol 56mg; Calcium 30mg; Fibre 0.2g; Sodium 522mg.
Green Fish Curry Energy 511kcal/2118kJ; Protein 36.1g; Carbohydrate 6.4g, of which sugars 3.9g; Fat 37.9g, of which saturates 18.8g; Cholesterol 132mg; Calcium 50mg; Fibre 2g; Sodium 153mg.

Spicy Fish Tagine

This aromatic one-pot dish proves how good fish can be. Serve with couscous, which can be steamed over the cooking pot.

Serves 8

1.3kg/3lb firm fish fillets, skinned and cut into 5cm/2in chunks
60ml/4 tbsp olive oil
1 large aubergine (eggplant), cut into 1cm/½in cubes
2 courgettes (zucchini), cut into 1cm/½in cubes
4 onions, chopped
400g/14oz can chopped tomatoes
400ml/14fl oz/1⅔ cups passata (bottled strained tomatoes)
200ml/7fl oz/scant 1 cup fish stock
1 preserved lemon, chopped
90g/3½oz/scant 1 cup olives
60ml/4 tbsp chopped fresh coriander (cilantro), plus extra coriander leaves to garnish
salt and ground black pepper

For the harissa

3 large fresh red chillies, seeded and chopped
3 garlic cloves, peeled
15ml/1 tbsp ground coriander
30ml/2 tbsp ground cumin
5ml/1 tsp ground cinnamon
grated rind of 1 lemon
30ml/2 tbsp sunflower oil

1 Make the harissa. Whizz everything in a food processor to a smooth paste. Put the fish in a wide bowl and add 30ml/2 tbsp of the harissa. Toss to coat, cover and chill for at least 1 hour.

2 Heat half the oil in a heavy pan. Add the aubergine cubes and fry for 10 minutes, or until they are golden brown. Add the courgettes and fry for 2 minutes. Remove the vegetables from the pan using a slotted spoon and set aside.

3 Add the remaining oil to the pan, add the onions and cook gently for about 10 minutes until golden brown. Stir in the remaining harissa and cook for 5 minutes, stirring occasionally.

4 Add the vegetables to the pan, then stir in the tomatoes, the passata and stock. Bring to the boil, then simmer for 20 minutes.

5 Stir the fish chunks and preserved lemon into the pan. Add the olives. Cover and simmer over a low heat for 15–20 minutes. Season to taste with salt and pepper. Stir in the coriander. Serve with couscous, if you like, and garnish with coriander leaves.

Baked Sea Bream with Tomatoes

John Dory, halibut or sea bass can all be baked this way. If you prefer to use filleted fish, choose a chunky fillet, such as cod, and roast it skin side up. Roasting the tomatoes brings out their sweetness, which contrasts beautifully with the flavour of the fish.

Serves 4–6

8 ripe tomatoes
10ml/2 tsp sugar
200ml/7fl oz/scant 1 cup olive oil
450g/1lb new potatoes
1 lemon, sliced
1 bay leaf
1 fresh thyme sprig
8 fresh basil leaves
1 sea bream, about 900g–1kg/2–2¼lb, cleaned and scaled
150ml/¼ pint/⅔ cup dry white wine
30ml/2 tbsp fresh white breadcrumbs
2 garlic cloves, crushed
15ml/1 tbsp finely chopped fresh parsley
salt and ground black pepper
fresh flat parsley or basil leaves, chopped, to garnish

1 Preheat the oven to 240°C/475°F/Gas 9. Cut the tomatoes in half lengthways and arrange them in a single layer in a baking dish, cut side up. Sprinkle with sugar, salt and pepper and drizzle over a little of the olive oil.

2 Roast in the oven for about 30–40 minutes, until lightly browned all over and tender. Remove the tomatoes from the dish and set aside.

3 Meanwhile, cut the potatoes into 1cm/½in slices. Place them in a large pan of salted water and par-boil for 5 minutes. Drain and set aside.

4 Grease the baking dish with a little more of the oil. Arrange the potatoes in a single layer with the lemon slices over and sprinkle on the herbs. Season and drizzle with half the remaining oil. Lay the fish on top and season. Pour over the wine and the rest of the oil. Arrange the tomatoes around the fish.

5 Mix together the breadcrumbs, garlic and parsley; sprinkle over the fish. Bake for 30 minutes until the fish is cooked and flakes easily. Garnish with chopped parsley or basil and serve.

Spicy Fish Tagine Energy 263kcal/1099kJ; Protein 32.3g; Carbohydrate 8.3g, of which sugars 7g; Fat 11.3g, of which saturates 1.7g; Cholesterol 75mg; Calcium 57mg; Fibre 3.2g; Sodium 360mg.
Baked Sea Bream Energy 440kcal/1840kJ; Protein 26g; Carbohydrate 21.5g, of which sugars 6.6g; Fat 26.7g, of which saturates 3.4g; Cholesterol 51mg; Calcium 76mg; Fibre 2g; Sodium 205mg.

Salmon Baked with Potatoes and Thyme

This is clay-pot cooking at its most sophisticated. Potatoes and onions are slowly braised in a delicious thyme-flavoured stock and topped with tender, pepper-crusted salmon fillets.

Serves 4

675g/1½lb waxy potatoes, thinly sliced
1 onion, thinly sliced
10ml/2 tsp fresh thyme leaves
450ml/¾ pint/scant 2 cups vegetable or fish stock
40g/1½oz/3 tbsp butter, finely diced
4 skinless salmon fillets, about 150g/5oz each
30ml/2 tbsp olive oil
15ml/1 tbsp black peppercorns, roughly crushed
salt and ground black pepper
fresh thyme, to garnish
mangetouts (snow peas) or sugar snap peas, to serve

1 Soak a clay pot, large enough to fit the fish in a single layer, in cold water for 20 minutes, then drain.

2 Layer the potato and onion slices in the clay pot, seasoning each layer with salt and ground black pepper and sprinkling with thyme. Pour over the stock, dot with butter, cover and place in an unheated oven.

3 Set the oven to 190°C/375°F/Gas 5. Bake the potatoes for 40 minutes then remove the lid and bake for a further 20 minutes, or until they are almost cooked.

4 Meanwhile, brush the salmon fillets with olive oil and coat with crushed black peppercorns, pressing them in, if necessary, with the back of a spoon.

5 Place the salmon on top of the potatoes, cover and return to the oven for 15 minutes, or until the salmon is opaque and flakes easily, removing the lid for the last 5 minutes.

6 Spoon the potatoes and onions on to four serving plates and top each with a salmon fillet. Serve garnished with thyme sprigs, and with mangetouts or sugar snap peas to accompany.

Baked Salmon with a Herb and Lemon Mayonnaise

Whole fish are ideal for slowly baking in the oven. Leave the head on or take it off, as you prefer. This dish can be made with either salmon or sea trout, and is a family favourite served either hot or cold.

Serves 6

1.35kg/3lb fresh whole salmon or sea trout, cleaned
1 small lemon, thinly sliced
handful of parsley sprigs
salt and ground black pepper
butter or oil, for greasing

For the herb and lemon mayonnaise

300ml/½ pint/1¼ cups mayonnaise
30ml/2 tbsp natural (plain) yogurt or single (light) cream
finely grated rind of ½ lemon
30ml/2 tbsp chopped fresh chives
15ml/1 tbsp chopped fresh parsley
squeeze of lemon juice (optional)

1 Preheat the oven to 180°C/350°F/Gas 4. Rinse the cleaned salmon or sea trout, both inside and out, under cold running water, and then pat it dry with kitchen paper.

2 Season the fish cavity with salt and pepper and then spread half the lemon slices and the parsley sprigs inside the fish.

3 Grease a large sheet of foil and lay the fish on it. Put the remaining lemon slices and parsley on top. Fold the foil over to make a loose parcel. Transfer to the hot oven for 40 minutes.

4 Meanwhile, make the herb and lemon mayonnaise. Place the mayonnaise in a bowl and blend in the yogurt or cream, lemon rind and herbs, adding lemon juice to taste.

5 Lift the fish from the oven and tear open the foil. Peel away the skin, cutting around the head and tail with a sharp knife and discarding the parsley and lemon from the top of the fish. Carefully turn the fish over and repeat with the other side.

6 Lift the fish carefully on to a warmed serving plate and serve with the herb and lemon mayonnaise.

Salmon with Potatoes Energy 517kcal/2160kJ; Protein 33.4g; Carbohydrate 28.4g, of which sugars 3.1g; Fat 30.8g, of which saturates 9g; Cholesterol 96mg; Calcium 47mg; Fibre 1.9g; Sodium 147mg.
Baked Salmon Energy 551kcal/2289kJ; Protein 35.9g; Carbohydrate 1.5g, of which sugars 1.2g; Fat 44.7g, of which saturates 7.3g; Cholesterol 182mg; Calcium 84mg; Fibre 0.4g; Sodium 362mg.

Baked Sea Bass with Lemon Grass and Red Onions

Moist, tender sea bass is flavoured with a combination of Thai ingredients in this mouthwatering clay-pot dish.

Serves 2–3

1 sea bass, about 675g/1½lb, cleaned and scaled
30ml/2 tbsp olive oil
2 lemon grass stalks, finely sliced
1 red onion, finely shredded
1 chilli, seeded and finely chopped
5cm/2in piece fresh root ginger, finely shredded
45ml/3 tbsp chopped fresh coriander (cilantro)
rind and juice of 2 limes
30ml/2 tbsp light soy sauce
salt and ground black pepper

1 Soak a fish clay pot in cold water for 20 minutes, then drain. Make four to five diagonal slashes on both sides of the fish. Repeat the slashes on one side in the opposite direction to give an attractive cross-hatched effect. Rub the sea bass inside and out with salt, pepper and 15ml/1 tbsp of the olive oil.

2 Mix together the Thai ingredients – the lemon grass, red onion, chilli, ginger, coriander and lime rind.

3 Place a little of the lemon grass and red onion mixture in the base of the clay pot, then lay the fish on top. Sprinkle the remaining mixture over the fish, then sprinkle over the lime juice, soy sauce and the remaining olive oil. Cover and place in an unheated oven.

4 Set the oven to 220°C/425°F/Gas 7 and cook the fish for 30–40 minutes, or until the flesh flakes easily when tested with a knife. Serve immediately.

Variation
This recipe will taste delicious using a variety of fish, such as red or grey mullet, red snapper, pompano, salmon or tilapia. Depending on the weight of the fish you may need to use two smaller fish rather than one whole one.

Baked Monkfish with Potatoes and Garlic

This dish is easy to prepare as most of the ingredients are slowly baked in the oven in the same dish.

Serves 4

50g/2oz/¼ cup butter
2 onions, thickly sliced
1kg/2¼lb waxy potatoes, cut into small chunks
4 garlic cloves
a few fresh thyme sprigs
2–3 fresh bay leaves
450ml/¾ pint/scant 2 cups vegetable or fish stock, plus 45ml/3 tbsp
900g/2lb monkfish tail in one piece, membrane removed
30–45ml/2–3 tbsp white wine
50g/2oz/1 cup fresh white breadcrumbs
15g/½oz fresh flat leaf parsley, finely chopped
15ml/1 tbsp olive oil
salt and ground black pepper

1 Preheat the oven to 190°C/375°F/Gas 5. Melt half the butter in a shallow flameproof dish and cook the onions for 5 minutes until soft. Stir in the potatoes. Slice two of the garlic cloves and add them to the dish with the thyme and bay leaves, and season.

2 Pour the main batch of stock over the potatoes and bake, uncovered, stirring once or twice, for about 50 minutes, or until the potatoes are just tender.

3 Nestle the monkfish tail into the potatoes and season well with salt and pepper. Bake the monkfish and potatoes for 10–15 minutes. Mix the 45ml/3 tbsp stock with the wine and use to baste the monkfish two or three times during cooking.

4 Finely chop the remaining garlic. Melt the remaining butter and toss it with the breadcrumbs, garlic, most of the parsley and seasoning. Spread the mixture over the monkfish.

5 Drizzle olive oil over the crumb-covered fish, then return the dish to the oven and bake for 10–15 minutes, or until the breadcrumbs are crisp and brown and the liquid has been absorbed. Sprinkle the remaining parsley on to the potatoes and fish and serve immediately.

Baked Sea Bass Energy 298kcal/1248kJ; Protein 43.7g; Carbohydrate 1.6g, of which sugars 1.1g; Fat 13g, of which saturates 1.9g; Cholesterol 180mg; Calcium 298mg; Fibre 0.3g; Sodium 156mg.
Baked Monkfish Energy 529kcal/2230kJ; Protein 45.8g; Carbohydrate 54g, of which sugars 6.5g; Fat 15g, of which saturates 7.4g; Cholesterol 63mg; Calcium 67mg; Fibre 3.5g; Sodium 245mg.

Foil-baked Salmon

Slowly baking a whole salmon in a foil package ensures that the flesh remains wonderfully moist. It can be served hot, with new potatoes and cucumber salad, or is equally delicious eaten cold with a salad for a summer lunch.

Serves 6

1 whole salmon, total weight about 1kg/2¼lb, cleaned and trimmed
1 small bunch fresh dill, roughly chopped
4 garlic cloves, finely chopped
115g/4oz/½ cup unsalted (sweet) butter, softened
50ml/2fl oz/¼ cup dry white wine
juice of ½ lemon
10–12 black peppercorns
4–5 fresh bay leaves
salt and ground black pepper
slices of lemon, to garnish
boiled new potatoes and cucumber salad, to serve

1 Preheat the oven to 200°C/400°F/Gas 6. Place the salmon in the centre of a large piece of heavy foil.

2 Put the dill, garlic and softened butter into a small mixing bowl and mix well until a smooth paste forms. Gradually pour in the dry white wine and the lemon juice, and mix until thoroughly combined.

3 Using your hands, rub the mixture inside the cavity of the fish, and all over the outside. Put the peppercorns and bay leaves inside the cavity, then season the skin with salt and ground black pepper.

4 Bring the edges of the foil up and seal to make a loose but secure parcel around the fish.

5 Put the fish in the preheated oven and cook for about 30–40 minutes, or until the fish is tender and the flesh flakes easily in the thickest part when tested with a knife.

6 Remove the fish from the oven and divide into six even portions. Transfer the fish pieces to warmed serving plates. Pour over any juices caught in the foil, and serve immediately with boiled new potatoes and a cucumber salad.

Haddock and Beer Casserole

The earthy flavour of wild mushrooms perfectly complements the delicate taste of the haddock steaks and creamy sauce in this oven-baked dish. Cooking it in beer ensures that the flesh is moist, and it also makes an unusual addition to the sauce.

Serves 4

150g/5oz/2 cups wild mushrooms
50g/2oz/¼ cup butter
2 large onions, roughly chopped
2 celery sticks, sliced
2 carrots, sliced
4 haddock steaks, about 185g/6½oz each
300ml/½ pint/1¼ cups light lager
4 bay leaves
25g/1oz/¼ cup plain (all-purpose) flour
200ml/7fl oz/scant 1 cup double (heavy) cream
salt and ground black pepper
dill sprigs, to garnish

1 Preheat the oven to 190°C/375°F/Gas 5. Brush the wild mushrooms to remove any grit and only wash the caps briefly if necessary. Dry with kitchen paper and chop them.

2 Melt 25g/1oz/2 tbsp butter in a flameproof casserole, then add the onions, mushrooms, celery and carrots. Fry for about 8 minutes, or until golden brown.

3 Place the haddock steaks on top of the vegetables, then pour over the lager. Add the bay leaves and season with salt and pepper. Put the casserole in the preheated oven and cook for 20–25 minutes, or until the fish flakes easily when tested.

4 Remove the fish and vegetables from the casserole with a slotted spoon and transfer to a serving dish. Cover and keep warm while you make the sauce.

5 Melt the remaining butter in a medium pan, then stir in the flour and cook, stirring, for 2 minutes. Pour in the liquid from the casserole, mix well and simmer for 2–3 minutes. Add the cream to the sauce and heat briefly, without boiling.

6 Serve the haddock steaks and vegetables on warmed plates, with the sauce poured over and garnished with sprigs of dill.

Foil-baked Salmon Energy 242kcal/1005kJ; Protein 20.3g; Carbohydrate 0.1g, of which sugars 0.1g; Fat 17.9g, of which saturates 6.2g; Cholesterol 68mg; Calcium 23mg; Fibre 0g; Sodium 96mg.
Haddock Casserole Energy 503kcal/2097kJ; Protein 36.6g; Carbohydrate 15.5g, of which sugars 1.2g; Fat 33.2g, of which saturates 19.6g; Cholesterol 191mg; Calcium 92mg; Fibre 1g; Sodium 207mg.

Sour Fish and Vegetable Bake

This layered eel and vegetable bake is slowly baked in the oven, resulting in marvellously tender fish that is full in flavour.

Serves 4

675g/1½lb eel, skinned and boned
900ml/1½ pints/3¾ cups fish or vegetable stock
1.2 litres/2 pints/5 cups water
450g/1lb/4 cups shredded white cabbage
50g/2oz/¼ cup butter
1 large onion, chopped
2 pickled cucumbers, sliced
12 green olives
15ml/1 tbsp capers, drained
75g/3oz/1½ cups fresh white breadcrumbs
salt and ground black pepper
parsley, to garnish

1 Cut the eel into large pieces. Bring the fish or vegetable stock to a gentle simmer in a large, heavy pan, then add the eel and cook for about 4 minutes.

2 Remove the fish pieces from the pan with a slotted spoon. Reserve 150ml/¼ pint/⅔ cup of the stock and set aside, leaving the remaining stock in the pan.

3 Pour the measured water into the pan of stock. Bring to the boil, then add the shredded cabbage. Simmer for 2 minutes, then strain well.

4 Melt half of the butter in the pan. Cook the onion for about 5 minutes, stirring occasionally, until beginning to turn soft. Stir in the strained cabbage and reserved stock, then bring to the boil. Cover the pan with a tight-fitting lid and cook over low heat for about 1 hour, until tender. Season with salt and plenty of ground black pepper.

5 Preheat the oven to 200°C/400°F/Gas 6. Spoon half the cabbage into a baking dish. Top with the eel and the cucumbers. Spoon over the remaining cabbage and any remaining stock.

6 Sprinkle the olives, capers and the breadcrumbs over the top. Melt the remaining butter and drizzle over the top. Bake for 25–30 minutes, or until the breadcrumbs are lightly browned. Garnish with parsley sprigs.

Stuffed Red Snapper

A number of delectable flavours are combined in this unusual recipe – the red snapper filled with carp, sharpened by the salty cheese and dill pickle. Slow baking in the oven means that all these flavours are intensified, resulting in a dish that is perfect for a special occasion, particularly if you include the edible flowers as a garnish.

Serves 4

4 small red snapper, about 450g/1lb each, filleted and heads and fins removed
juice of 1 lemon
25g/1oz/2 tbsp butter, melted
sprigs of tarragon or sweet cicely plus pansies or other edible flowers, to garnish
lemon wedges, to serve

For the stuffing

350g/12oz fish fillets, such as carp, pike or sole, skinned
1 egg white
2.5ml/½ tsp chopped fresh tarragon
1 dill pickle, sliced
40g/1½oz/¾ cup fresh breadcrumbs
40g/1½oz/¼ cup feta cheese or brinza, roughly crumbled
salt and ground white pepper

1 Preheat the oven to 180°C/350°F/Gas 4. Wipe out the red snapper and pat dry, removing any membrane with a little salt. Liberally rub the lemon juice inside the fish.

2 Make the stuffing. Put the other fish fillets in a food processor and process with the egg white, tarragon, dill pickle, fresh breadcrumbs, cheese and a little salt and ground white pepper, until a smooth paste is formed.

3 Using a spoon, fill the red snapper with an equal amount of the fish fillet mixture and lay them in a single layer in a lightly oiled ovenproof dish.

4 Secure the fish with wooden cocktail sticks (toothpicks) and bake for 40–50 minutes. Spoon over the melted butter halfway through cooking.

5 Transfer the fish carefully to a serving plate. Serve with lemon wedges and garnish with fresh sprigs of tarragon or sweet cicely and edible flowers.

Fish Bake Energy 508kcal/2117kJ; Protein 33.1g; Carbohydrate 25.2g, of which sugars 9.9g; Fat 31.2g, of which saturates 11.8g; Cholesterol 282mg; Calcium 146mg; Fibre 4.2g; Sodium 623mg.
Red Snapper Energy 500kcal/2108kJ; Protein 82g; Carbohydrate 8g, of which sugars 0.5g; Fat 16g, of which saturates 6.2g; Cholesterol 176mg; Calcium 194mg; Fibre 0.2g; Sodium 621mg.

Fish with Fregola

Slowly simmered on top of the stove, this dish is a cross between a soup and a stew. Serve it with crusty bread to mop up the juices.

Serves 4–6

75ml/5 tbsp olive oil
4 garlic cloves, finely chopped
½ small fresh red chilli, seeded and finely chopped
1 large handful fresh flat leaf parsley, roughly chopped
1 red snapper, about 450g/1lb, cleaned, with head and tail removed
1 grey mullet or pompano, about 500g/1¼lb, cleaned, with head and tail removed
350–450g/12oz–1lb thick cod, monkfish or haddock fillet
400g/14oz can chopped plum tomatoes
175g/6oz/1½ cups dried fregola
250ml/8fl oz/1 cup water
salt and ground black pepper

1 Heat 30ml/2 tbsp of the oil in a large flameproof casserole. Add the chopped garlic and chilli, with half the parsley. Fry over medium heat, stirring occasionally, for about 5 minutes.

2 Cut all of the fish into large chunks – including the skin and the bones in the case of the snapper and mullet – and add the pieces to the casserole. Sprinkle with a further 30ml/2 tbsp of the oil and fry for a few minutes more.

3 Add the tomatoes, then fill the empty can with water and add to the pan. Bring to the boil. Season to taste with salt and pepper, lower the heat and cook for 10 minutes.

4 Add the fregola and simmer for 5 minutes, then add the water and the remaining oil. Simmer for 15 minutes until the fregola is just tender.

5 If the sauce gets too thick, add more water. Taste for seasoning, then serve immediately, sprinkled with the remaining parsley.

Cook's Tips
Fregola is a tiny pasta shape from Sardinia. If you can't get it, use a tiny soup pasta, such as corallini or semi de melone.

Stuffed Squid in Tomato Sauce

Squid are stuffed with ham and raisins in this delicious, slowly simmered dish.

Serves 4

2 squid, about 275g/10oz each
60ml/4 tbsp olive oil
1 small onion, finely chopped
2 garlic cloves, finely chopped
50g/2oz Serrano ham or gammon steak, diced small
75g/3oz/scant ½ cup long grain rice
30ml/2 tbsp raisins, chopped
30ml/2 tbsp chopped fresh parsley
½ small (US medium) egg, beaten
plain (all-purpose) flour, for dusting
250ml/8fl oz/1 cup white wine
1 bay leaf
30ml/2 tbsp chopped fresh parsley
salt, paprika and black pepper

For the tomato sauce
30ml/2 tbsp olive oil
1 onion, finely chopped
2 garlic cloves, finely chopped
200g/7oz can tomatoes
salt and cayenne pepper

1 Make the tomato sauce. Heat the oil in a flameproof casserole large enough to hold the squid. Cook the onion and garlic over low heat. Add the tomatoes and cook for 10–15 minutes. Season with salt and cayenne pepper.

2 Meanwhile, prepare the squid. Use the tentacles to pull out the body. Cut off the tentacles and reserve, discarding the eyes and everything below. Flex the bodies to pop out the spinal structure. Chop the fin flaps and rinse the bodies well.

3 Heat half the oil in a pan and gently fry the onion and garlic. Add the ham and squid tentacles and stir-fry. Off the heat, stir in the rice, raisins and parsley. Season and add the egg to bind.

4 Spoon the mixture into the squid bodies, then stitch them shut using a small poultry skewer. Blot the bodies with kitchen paper, then flour them very lightly. Heat the remaining oil in a frying pan and fry the squid, turning until coloured on all sides.

5 Arrange the squid in the tomato sauce. Add the wine and bay leaf. Cover the casserole tightly and simmer for 30 minutes, turning the squid over halfway through cooking if the sauce does not cover them completely. Serve sliced into rings, surrounded by the sauce and garnished with parsley.

Fish with Fregola Energy 300Kcal/1256kJ; Protein 29.6g; Carbohydrate 17.3g, of which sugars 2.3g; Fat 12.9g, of which saturates 1.7g; Cholesterol 44mg; Calcium 79mg; Fibre 1.1g; Sodium 126mg.
Stuffed Squid Energy 433kcal/1809kJ; Protein 26.8g; Carbohydrate 26.4g, of which sugars 9.1g; Fat 20.4g, of which saturates 3.3g; Cholesterol 340mg; Calcium 61mg; Fibre 1.5g; Sodium 325mg.

Octopus and Red Wine Stew

Fresh octopus is slowly simmered in a rich wine sauce in this traditional Greek one-pot dish.

Serves 4
900g/2lb prepared octopus
450g/1lb onions, sliced
2 bay leaves
450g/1lb ripe tomatoes
60ml/4 tbsp olive oil
4 garlic cloves, crushed
5ml/1 tsp sugar
15ml/1 tbsp chopped fresh oregano or rosemary
30ml/2 tbsp chopped fresh parsley
150ml/¼ pint/⅔ cup red wine
30ml/2 tbsp red wine vinegar
chopped fresh herbs, to garnish
warm bread and pine nuts, to serve

1 Put the octopus in a large pan of gently simmering water with one-quarter of the onions and the bay leaves. Cover the pan and cook gently for 1 hour.

2 While the octopus is cooking, plunge the tomatoes into boiling water for 30 seconds, then refresh in cold water. Peel away the skins and chop roughly.

3 Drain the octopus and, using a small sharp knife, cut it into bitesize pieces. Discard the head.

4 Heat the oil in the pan and fry the octopus, the remaining onions and the garlic for 3 minutes. Add the tomatoes, sugar, herbs, wine and vinegar and cook, stirring, for 5 minutes.

5 Cover the pan and cook over the lowest possible heat for 1½ hours until the sauce is thickened and the octopus is tender.

6 To serve, garnish with fresh herbs and serve with plenty of warm bread, and pine nuts to sprinkle on top.

Cook's Tip
The octopus, along with cuttlefish and squid, is a member of the mollusc family – their main shared characteristic is that they have no shell. Octopus can be very tough, so it needs long, slow cooking to tenderize it.

Fish Goulash

This mixed-fish dish is a cross between a stew and a soup, and benefits from making with a slowly simmered stock. It is traditionally served with half a hot cherry pepper in the centre of the serving bowl, with the goulash ladled over it and topped with sour cream.

Serves 6
2kg/4½lb mixed fish
4 large onions, sliced
2 garlic cloves, crushed
½ small celeriac, diced
handful of parsley stalks or cleaned roots
30ml/2 tbsp paprika
1 green (bell) pepper, seeded and sliced
5–10ml/1–2 tsp tomato purée (paste)
salt and ground black pepper
90ml/6 tbsp sour cream and 3 cherry peppers (optional), to serve

1 With a sharp knife, skin and fillet the mixed fish, reserving the heads, skin and bones for the stock. Cut the flesh into large chunks, and set aside.

2 Put all the fish heads, skin and bones into a large pan, together with the onions, garlic, celeriac, parsley stalks and paprika, and season with salt and ground black pepper. Cover with water and bring to the boil. Reduce the heat and simmer for 1¼–1½ hours. Strain the stock.

3 Place the fish chunks and green pepper in a large pan and pour over the stock to just cover. Blend the tomato purée with a little stock in a bowl and pour it into the pan. Stir gently to combine the ingredients.

4 Cook the goulash gently but do not stir, or the fish will break up. Cook for about 10–12 minutes, ensuring that the mixture does not reach boiling point, until the fish pieces are tender and flake easily when tested.

5 Check the seasoning, adjusting if necessary. Place half a cherry pepper, if using, in a warmed deep plate or soup bowl. Ladle over the hot goulash and top with a generous spoonful of sour cream, if using.

Octopus Stew Energy 371kcal/1556kJ; Protein 42.5g; Carbohydrate 12.5g, of which sugars 9.9g; Fat 14.5g, of which saturates 2.4g; Cholesterol 108mg; Calcium 113mg; Fibre 2.7g; Sodium 16mg.
Fish Goulash Energy 382kcal/1603kJ; Protein 60.2g; Carbohydrate 9.4g, of which sugars 4.9g; Fat 11.7g, of which saturates 2.4g; Cholesterol 148mg; Calcium 60mg; Fibre 1.9g; Sodium 486mg.

Squid with Black Tagliatelle

This striking dish benefits from the squid being slowly simmered in a tomato sauce. Tagliatelle flavoured and coloured with squid ink looks amazing and tastes deliciously of the sea. Look for it in good Italian delicatessens and some larger supermarkets.

Serves 4

105ml/7 tbsp olive oil
2 shallots, chopped
3 garlic cloves, crushed
45ml/3 tbsp finely chopped fresh parsley
675g/1½lb cleaned squid, cut into rings and rinsed
150ml/¼ pint/⅔ cup dry white wine
400g/14oz can chopped tomatoes
2.5ml/½ tsp dried chilli flakes or powder
450g/1lb squid ink tagliatelle
salt and ground black pepper

1 Heat the olive oil in a large, heavy pan and add the shallots. Cook over medium heat, stirring occasionally, for 4–6 minutes until they have softened and turned pale golden. Add the garlic to the pan and cook for 2–3 minutes until beginning to colour.

2 Add 30ml/2 tbsp of the chopped fresh parsley to the pan, stir, then add the squid and stir again. Cook for 3–4 minutes, then pour in the white wine. Simmer for a few seconds until the wine begins to bubble.

3 Add the chopped tomatoes and dried chilli flakes to the pan and stir well. Season to taste with salt and ground black pepper. Cover the pan with a tight-fitting lid and simmer gently for about 1 hour, until the squid is tender. Stir occasionally during cooking and add more water if necessary.

4 Cook the squid ink tagliatelle in a pan with plenty of boiling, salted water, according to the instructions on the packet, or until the pasta is *al dente*. Drain well and return the tagliatelle to the pan.

5 Add the squid sauce to the pasta and mix well. Spoon into warmed pasta bowls and garnish each serving with the remaining chopped parsley. Serve immediately.

Mediterranean Squid with Olives and Red Wine

Slow cooking in a rich sauce is ideal for squid, resulting in deliciously tender seafood that takes on the flavours of the cooking sauce.

Serves 4

30–45ml/2–3 tbsp olive oil
2 red onions, cut in half lengthways and sliced along the grain
3–4 garlic cloves, chopped
about 750g/1lb 10oz fresh squid, prepared (see Cook's Tip) and cut into thick rings
45–60ml/3–4 tbsp black olives, pitted
5–10ml/1–2 tsp ground cinnamon
5–10ml/1–2 tsp sugar
300ml/½ pint/1¼ cups red wine
2 bay leaves
1 small bunch each of fresh flat leaf parsley and fresh dill, finely chopped
salt and ground black pepper
lemon wedges, to serve

1 Heat the oil in a heavy pan and cook the onions and garlic until golden and soft.

2 Add the squid heads and rings and toss them in the pan for 2–3 minutes, until they begin to colour. Toss in the olives, cinnamon and sugar, pour in the wine and add the bay leaves.

3 Bubble up the liquid, then lower the heat and cover the pan. Cook gently for 35–40 minutes, until most of the liquid has reduced and the squid is tender.

4 Season the squid with salt and pepper to taste and toss in the herbs. Serve immediately, with lemon wedges.

Cook's Tip

To prepare squid, rinse it and peel off the thin film of skin, then sever the head and trim the tentacles. Pull out the backbone and reach down into the body pouch to remove the ink sac and any mushy bits. Rinse the empty pouch and pat dry. Use the pouch and trimmed head for cooking; discard the rest.

Squid with Tagliatelle Energy 738kcal/3112kJ; Protein 40.8g; Carbohydrate 90.2g, of which sugars 8.1g; Fat 24.6g, of which saturates 3.7g; Cholesterol 380mg; Calcium 88mg; Fibre 5.1g; Sodium 204mg.
Mediterranean Squid Energy 304kcal/1275kJ; Protein 30.3g; Carbohydrate 11.4g, of which sugars 6.8g; Fat 10.1g, of which saturates 1.7g; Cholesterol 422mg; Calcium 62mg; Fibre 1.7g; Sodium 468mg.

Simmered Squid and Mooli

This impressive dish features squid slowly simmered in dashi stock, which is an essential ingredient in Japanese cooking. It is a fish stock made from seaweed and dried fish with other flavourings. Look for it in Asian food stores.

Serves 4

450g/1lb squid, cleaned, body and tentacles separated
1kg/2¼lb mooli (daikon), peeled
900ml/1½ pints/3¾ cups dashi stock or the same amount of water and 5ml/1 tsp dashi-no-moto
60ml/4 tbsp shoyu
45ml/3 tbsp sake
15ml/1 tbsp caster (superfine) sugar
30ml/2 tbsp mirin
grated rind of yuzu or lime, to garnish

1 Separate the two triangular flaps from the squid body. Cut the body into 1cm/½in thick rings. Cut the triangular flaps into 1cm/½in strips. Cut off and discard 2.5cm/1in from the thin end of the tentacles. Chop the tentacles into 4cm/1½in lengths.

2 Cut the mooli into 3cm/1¼in thick rounds and shave the edges of the sections with a sharp knife. Plunge the slices into cold water. Drain just before cooking.

3 Put the mooli and squid in a heavy pan and pour over the stock. Bring to the boil, and cook for 5 minutes, skimming constantly. Reduce the heat to low and add the shoyu, sake, sugar and mirin. Cover the surface with a circle of baking parchment cut 2.5cm/1in smaller than the lid of the pan, and simmer for 45 minutes, shaking the pan occasionally.

4 Leave to stand for 5 minutes and serve hot in small bowls with a sprinkle of yuzu or lime rind.

Cook's Tip

When buying mooli look for one that is at least 7.5cm/3in in diameter, with a shiny, undamaged skin, and that sounds dense and heavy when you pat it.

Smoked Mussel and Potato Bake

This slow-baked dish uses smoked mussels, which have a creamy texture and rich flavour, delicious with sour cream and chives. You can easily substitute smoked oysters for the mussels.

Serves 4

2 large maincrop potatoes, cut in half
butter, for greasing
2 shallots, finely diced
2 x 85g/3¼oz cans smoked mussels
1 bunch chives, chopped
300ml/½ pint/1¼ cups sour cream
175g/6oz/1½ cups mature Cheddar cheese, grated
salt and ground black pepper
mixed vegetables, to serve

1 Preheat the oven to 180°C/350°F/Gas 4. Cook the potatoes in a large pan of lightly salted boiling water for 15 minutes until they are just tender. Drain and leave to cool slightly. When cool enough to handle, cut the potatoes into even 3mm/⅛in slices.

2 Grease the base and sides of a 1.2 litre/2 pint/5 cup casserole dish. Lay a few potato slices over the base of the dish. Sprinkle a few shallots over and season well.

3 Drain the oil from the mussels into a bowl. Slice the mussels and add them again to the reserved oil. Stir in the chives and sour cream with half of the cheese. Spoon a little of the sauce over the layer of potatoes.

4 Continue to layer the potatoes, shallots and the sauce in the dish. Finish with a layer of potatoes and sprinkle over the remainder of the cheese.

5 Bake for 30–45 minutes. Remove from the oven and serve while hot with a selection of mixed vegetables.

Cook's Tip

For a dinner party, instead of serving the bake in a large dish, once it has cooked, stamp out rounds using a 5cm/2in cutter and serve on a bed of salad leaves.

Squid and Mooli Energy 159kcal/666kJ; Protein 20.4g; Carbohydrate 11.4g, of which sugars 8.8g; Fat 2.4g, of which saturates 0.7g; Cholesterol 253mg; Calcium 68mg; Fibre 2.3g; Sodium 1011mg.
Mussel Bake Energy 348kcal/1457kJ; Protein 16.7g; Carbohydrate 25.8g, of which sugars 3.4g; Fat 20.6g, of which saturates 3g; Cholesterol 30mg; Calcium 178mg; Fibre 1.8g; Sodium 288mg.

Seafood Pie with Rösti Topping

This oven-baked dish is a mixture of white fish and shellfish with a creamy sauce and finished with a grated potato topping.

Serves 4

750g/1lb 10oz potatoes, unpeeled and scrubbed
50g/2oz/¼ cup butter, melted
350g/12oz cod or haddock fillets, skinned and cut into bitesize pieces
115g/4oz cooked, peeled prawns (shrimp)
115g/4oz cooked, shelled mussels
8–12 shelled queen scallops
50g/2oz/¼ cup butter
1 onion, finely chopped
50g/2oz/½ cup plain (all-purpose) flour
200ml/7fl oz/scant 1 cup dry white wine
300ml/½ pint/1¼ cups fish or vegetable stock
105ml/7 tbsp double (heavy) cream
30ml/2 tbsp chopped fresh dill, plus extra sprigs to garnish
15ml/1 tbsp chopped fresh parsley
60ml/4 tbsp freshly grated Parmesan cheese
salt and ground black pepper

1 Place the potatoes in a large pan. Cover with cold water and bring to the boil. Cook for 10–15 minutes until just tender.

2 Drain the potatoes and set aside until cool enough to handle. Peel and coarsely grate the cooled potatoes into a bowl. Stir in the melted butter and season well with salt and pepper.

3 Preheat the oven to 220°C/425°F/Gas 7. Divide the pieces of cod or haddock and the prawns, mussels and scallops among four individual 18cm/7in rectangular earthenware dishes.

4 Melt the butter in a large pan, add the onion and cook for 6–8 minutes or until softened and light golden. Sprinkle in the flour and stir thoroughly until well blended.

5 Remove the pan from the heat and pour in the wine and stock, stirring until smooth. Bring to the boil, then stir in the cream, herbs and season to taste. Pour the sauce over the fish.

6 Sprinkle the potato evenly over the fish and sauce in the dishes and top with the Parmesan. Bake for 25 minutes until the topping is crisp and the fish is cooked. Serve hot, garnished with dill.

Shellfish Tagine

This slowly simmered stew features a distinctive mix of spices and chillies.

Serves 4

60ml/4 tbsp olive oil
4 garlic cloves, sliced
1–2 green chillies, seeded and chopped
a large handful of flat leaf parsley, roughly chopped
5ml/1 tsp coriander seeds
2.5ml/½ tsp ground allspice
6 cardamom pods, split open
2.5ml/½ tsp ground turmeric
15ml/1 tbsp lemon juice
350g/12oz scorpion fish, red mullet or red snapper fillets, cut into large chunks
225g/8oz squid, cleaned and cut into rings
1 onion, chopped
4 tomatoes, seeded and chopped
300ml/½ pint/1¼ cups warm fish or vegetable stock
225g/8oz large, raw prawns (shrimp)
15ml/1 tbsp chopped fresh coriander (cilantro)
salt and ground black pepper
lemon wedges, to garnish
couscous and crusty bread, to serve

1 Place the olive oil, garlic, chillies, parsley, coriander seeds, allspice and cardamom pods in a mortar and pound to a paste using a pestle. Stir in the turmeric, salt, pepper and lemon juice.

2 Place the fish in a large glass bowl with the squid rings, add the spice paste and mix. Cover and chill for at least 2 hours.

3 Place the onion, seeded and chopped tomatoes and stock in a tagine and cover. Place the tagine in an unheated oven set to 200°C/400°F/Gas 6. Bake for 20 minutes.

4 Remove the fish from the marinade, then drain well. Set aside the squid and any excess marinade, then place the fish in the tagine. Cover and cook in the oven for 5 minutes.

5 Add the prawns, squid rings and the remaining marinade to the tagine and stir to combine. Cover and return to the oven for 5–10 minutes, or until the fish, prawns and squid are tender.

6 Taste and season with salt and pepper if necessary, then stir in the coriander. Serve immediately, garnished with lemon wedges and accompanied by couscous and crusty bread.

Seafood Pie Energy 770kcal/3215kJ; Protein 47.3g; Carbohydrate 44.5g, of which sugars 4.5g; Fat 42.4g, of which saturates 25.5g; Cholesterol 236mg; Calcium 298mg; Fibre 2.7g; Sodium 626mg.
Shellfish Tagine Energy 301kcal/1261kJ; Protein 37.2g; Carbohydrate 7.1g, of which sugars 5.5g; Fat 14g, of which saturates 2.2g; Cholesterol 269mg; Calcium 128mg; Fibre 2.2g; Sodium 251mg.

Seafood Paella

This one-pot Spanish dish involves almost constant attention but the results are well worth the effort.

Serves 4

45ml/3 tbsp olive oil
1 large onion, chopped
2 large garlic cloves, chopped
150g/5oz chorizo, sliced
300g/11oz small squid, cleaned, leave whole if small, or chop into rings and bitesize pieces
1 red (bell) pepper, seeded and sliced
4 tomatoes, peeled, seeded and diced, or 200g/7oz can tomatoes
about 500ml/17fl oz/generous 2 cups chicken stock
105ml/7 tbsp dry white wine
200g/7oz/1 cup short grain Spanish rice or risotto rice
a large pinch of saffron threads
150g/5oz/1¼ cups fresh or frozen peas
12 large cooked prawns (shrimp), in the shell, or 8 langoustines
450g/1lb mussels, scrubbed
450g/1lb clams, scrubbed
salt and ground black pepper

1 Heat the olive oil in a large sauté pan or a paella pan. Cook the onion and garlic until the onion is translucent. Add the chorizo and fry until golden. Add the squid, either whole or in pieces, to the pan and sauté over high heat for 2–3 minutes, stirring occasionally.

2 Stir the pepper slices and the seeded and diced tomatoes into the pan and simmer gently for 5 minutes, until the pepper slices are tender. Pour in the chicken stock and white wine, stir well and bring to the boil.

3 Stir in the rice and saffron and season to taste with salt and ground black pepper. Spread the contents of the pan in an even layer over the base. Bring the liquid back to the boil, then lower the heat and simmer gently for 10 minutes.

4 Add the peas, prawns or langoustines, mussels and clams, stirring them gently into the rice. Cook gently for another 15–20 minutes, until the rice is tender and all the mussels and clams have opened. Discard any that remain closed.

5 If the paella seems dry, add a little more stock or wine. Gently stir everything together and serve piping hot.

Mixed Seafood Risotto

Slow simmering and frequent stirring are essential for this delicious creamy risotto.

Serves 4

1 litre/1¾ pints/4 cups hot fish or shellfish stock
50g/2oz/¼ cup unsalted butter
2 shallots, chopped
2 garlic cloves, chopped
350g/12oz/1¾ cups risotto rice
150ml/¼ pint/⅔ cup dry white wine
2.5ml/ tsp powdered saffron, or a pinch of saffron threads
400g/14oz mixed prepared seafood, thawed if frozen
30ml/2 tbsp freshly grated Parmesan cheese
30ml/2 tbsp chopped fresh flat leaf parsley, to garnish
salt and ground black pepper

1 Pour the stock into a large, heavy pan. Bring to the boil, then pour into a large, heatproof jug (pitcher) or bowl and keep warm.

2 Melt the butter in the rinsed-out pan, add the shallots and garlic and cook over low heat for 3–5 minutes, stirring, until the shallots are soft. Add the rice, stir well to coat the grains with butter, then pour in the wine. Cook over medium heat, stirring occasionally, until the wine has been absorbed.

3 Add a ladleful of hot stock and the saffron, and cook, stirring continuously, until the liquid has been absorbed. Add the seafood and stir well. Continue to add hot stock a ladleful at a time, waiting until each quantity has been absorbed before adding more. Stir the mixture for 20 minutes, or until the rice is swollen and creamy but still with a little 'bite' in the middle.

4 Vigorously mix in the freshly grated Parmesan cheese and season to taste, then sprinkle over the chopped parsley and serve immediately.

Cook's Tip
It is essential to use proper risotto rice, such as arborio or carnaroli for this dish. It has a wonderfully creamy texture when cooked but still retains a 'bite'.

Seafood Paella Energy 613kcal/2566kJ; Protein 43.1g; Carbohydrate 57.7g, of which sugars 10g; Fat 21.8g, of which saturates 5.4g; Cholesterol 313mg; Calcium 246mg; Fibre 4.4g; Sodium 639mg.
Seafood Risotto Energy 547kcal/2284kJ; Protein 27.3g; Carbohydrate 71.3g, of which sugars 1.2g; Fat 13.8g, of which saturates 8.2g; Cholesterol 229mg; Calcium 195mg; Fibre 0.2g; Sodium 350mg.

Turkey and Tomato Hotpot

Often reserved for festive meals, turkey makes a great choice for any occasion. Here the meat is shaped into balls and gently simmered in a slow cooker with rice and a richly flavoured tomato sauce.

Serves 4

white bread loaf, unsliced
30ml/2 tbsp milk
1 garlic clove, crushed
2.5ml/½ tsp caraway seeds
225g/8oz minced (ground) turkey
1 egg white
350ml/12fl oz/1½ cups near-boiling chicken stock
400g/14oz can chopped tomatoes
15ml/1 tbsp tomato purée (paste)
90g/3½oz/½ cup easy-cook (converted) rice
salt and ground black pepper
15ml/1 tbsp chopped fresh basil, to garnish
courgette (zucchini) ribbons, to serve (optional)

1 Using a serrated knife, remove and discard the crusts from the white bread loaf, then cut the bread into cubes.

2 Place the bread cubes in a large mixing bowl and sprinkle with the milk, then leave to soak for about 5 minutes.

3 Add the garlic clove, caraway seeds and turkey to the bread. Season with salt and ground black pepper and mix well to combine all the ingredients.

4 In a bowl, whisk the egg white until stiff peaks form, then fold, half at a time, into the turkey mixture, stirring until well combined. Chill in the refrigerator.

5 Pour the near-boiling chicken stock into the ceramic cooking pot. Add the chopped tomatoes and the tomato purée. Switch the slow cooker to the high setting, cover with the lid and cook for about 1 hour.

6 Meanwhile, shape the turkey mixture into 16 small balls. Stir the rice into the tomato mixture, then add the turkey balls. Cook on high for a further hour, or until the turkey balls and rice are cooked. Serve immediately, allowing four turkey balls per person, and accompanied by courgette ribbons, if using.

Roast Turkey with Mlinces

An oven-baked Croatian recipe for a special occasion. The unusual mlinces are used to soak up the juices.

Serves 10–12

3kg/6½lb turkey, well thawed if frozen
2 garlic cloves, halved
115g/4oz smoked bacon, finely chopped
30ml/2 tbsp chopped fresh rosemary
120ml/4fl oz/½ cup olive oil
250ml/8fl oz/1 cup dry white wine
sprigs of rosemary, to garnish
grilled (broiled) bacon, to serve

For the mlinces
350g/12oz/3 cups plain (all-purpose) flour, sifted
120–150ml/4–5fl oz/½–⅔ cup warm water
30ml/2 tbsp oil
sea salt

1 Preheat the oven to 200°C/400°F/Gas 6. Dry the turkey inside and out using kitchen paper. Rub all over with the halved garlic. Toss the bacon and rosemary together and use to stuff the turkey neck flap. Secure the skin underneath with a cocktail stick (toothpick). Brush with the oil.

2 Place the turkey in a roasting pan and cover loosely with foil. Cook for 45–50 minutes. Remove the foil and reduce the oven temperature to 160°C/325°F/Gas 3.

3 Baste the turkey with the juices then pour over the white wine. Cook for 1 hour, basting occasionally. Reduce the oven to 150°C/300°F/Gas 2, and cook for 45 minutes, basting well.

4 Meanwhile, make the mlinces. Knead the flour with a little salt, the water and oil to make a soft, pliable dough. Divide the dough equally into four pieces.

5 Roll out the dough on a lightly floured surface into 40cm/16in circles. Sprinkle with salt. Bake on baking sheets alongside the turkey for 25 minutes. Break into pieces 6–10cm/2½–4in long.

6 About 6–8 minutes before the turkey is ready, add the mlinces to the meat juices in the pan alongside the turkey. Serve the turkey and mlinces with grilled bacon, garnished with rosemary.

Turkey Hotpot Energy 187kcal/797kJ; Protein 18.2g; Carbohydrate 26.6g, of which sugars 3.9g; Fat 1.7g, of which saturates 0.5g; Cholesterol 32mg; Calcium 44mg; Fibre 1g; Sodium 212mg.
Roast Turkey Energy 377kcal/1585kJ; Protein 42.1g; Carbohydrate 22.7g, of which sugars 0.4g; Fat 13.7g, of which saturates 3.8g; Cholesterol 143mg; Calcium 51mg; Fibre 0.9g; Sodium 274mg.

Traditional Roast Turkey with Pork and Herb Stuffing

Whole roasted turkey is the ultimate slow-cooked food as you can leave it unattended in the oven, only needing to baste it occasionally. This recipe includes stuffing balls, chipolata sausages and gravy.

Serves 8

4.5kg/10lb turkey, with giblets (thawed overnight if frozen)
1 large onion, peeled and stuck with 6 whole cloves
50g/2oz/4 tbsp butter, softened
10 chipolata sausages
salt and ground black pepper

For the stuffing

225g/8oz rindless streaky (fatty) bacon, chopped
1 large onion, finely chopped
450g/1lb pork sausage meat (bulk sausage)
25g/1oz/scant 1/3 cup rolled oats
30ml/2 tbsp chopped fresh parsley
10ml/2 tsp dried mixed herbs
1 large egg, beaten
115g/4oz/1/2 cup ready-to-eat dried apricots, finely chopped

For the gravy

25g/1oz/2 tbsp plain (all-purpose) flour
450ml/3/4 pint/scant 2 cups giblet stock

1 Preheat the oven to 200°C/400°F/Gas 6. To make the stuffing, cook the bacon and onion gently in a pan until the bacon is crisp and the onion tender. Transfer to a large bowl and mix in all the remaining stuffing ingredients. Season to taste.

2 Place the stuffing in the neck end of the turkey, tuck the flap of skin under and secure it with a small skewer or stitch it with thread. Reserve any remaining stuffing.

3 Put the whole onion, studded with cloves, in the body cavity of the turkey and tie the legs together. Weigh the stuffed bird and calculate the cooking time: allow 15 minutes per 450g/1lb plus 15 minutes over. Place the turkey in a large roasting pan.

4 Spread the turkey with the butter and season with salt and pepper. Cover loosely with foil and cook for 30 minutes. Baste the turkey with the pan juices. Then lower the oven to 180°C/350°F/Gas 4 and cook for the remainder of the calculated time (about 3½ hours for a 4.5kg/10lb bird). Baste every 30 minutes or so. Remove the foil for the last hour of cooking.

5 Using wet hands, shape the remaining stuffing into small balls and place in an ovenproof dish. Place the chipolatas in a separate ovenproof dish. About 20 minutes before the end of the turkey cooking time, cook the balls and the chipolatas in the oven.

6 The turkey is cooked when the juices run clear when the thickest part of the thigh is pierced with a skewer or knife. Transfer it to a serving plate, cover with foil and let it stand for 10–15 minutes before carving.

7 Meanwhile, make the gravy. Spoon off the fat from the roasting pan, leaving the meat juices. Blend in the flour and cook for about 2 minutes. Stir in the stock and bring to the boil. Check the seasoning and pour into a gravy boat. Remove the skewer or thread from the bird and pour any juices into the gravy. Serve the turkey with the chipolatas, stuffing balls and gravy.

Turkey Parcels with Rice and Noilly Prat Stuffing

Pretty vine-leaf parcels concealing turkey escalopes are baked in the oven. They also contain a delicious wild rice and pine nut stuffing flavoured with Noilly Prat.

Serves 4

115g/4oz drained vine leaves in brine
4 turkey escalopes, about 115–175g/4–6oz each
300ml/1/2 pint/1 1/4 cups hot chicken stock

For the stuffing

30ml/2 tbsp sunflower oil
3 shallots, chopped
75g/3oz/3/4 cup cooked wild rice
4 tomatoes, peeled and chopped
45ml/3 tbsp Noilly Prat
25g/1oz/1/4 cup pine nuts, chopped
salt and ground black pepper

1 Preheat the oven to 190°C/375°F/Gas 5. Rinse the vine leaves a few times in cold water and drain.

2 To make the stuffing, heat the oil in a frying pan. Add the shallots and fry gently until soft. Remove the pan from the heat and stir in the cooked rice, chopped tomatoes, Noilly Prat and pine nuts. Season with salt and plenty of ground black pepper to taste. Mix well and set aside.

3 Put the turkey escalopes between sheets of clear film (plastic wrap) and flatten with a rolling pin or meat mallet. Top each escalope with a quarter of the stuffing and roll the meat tightly over the filling.

4 Overlap a quarter of the vine leaves to make a rectangle. Centre a turkey roll on top of the vine leaf, roll up and tie securely with raffia or string. Repeat with the remaining leaves and turkey rolls.

5 Pack the rolls snugly in an ovenproof dish, pour over the hot chicken stock and bake in the oven for 40 minutes.

6 Skim any surface fat from the stock and pour into a jug (pitcher). Serve the turkey parcels immediately, with the stock.

Roast Turkey Energy 828kcal/3452kJ; Protein 73.1g; Carbohydrate 19.4g, of which sugars 7g; Fat 51.3g, of which saturates 18.1g; Cholesterol 292mg; Calcium 77mg; Fibre 1.8g; Sodium 1267mg.
Turkey Parcels Energy 389kcal/1639kJ; Protein 55g; Carbohydrate 11.3g, of which sugars 5.2g; Fat 12.9g, of which saturates 2g; Cholesterol 111mg; Calcium 36mg; Fibre 1.7g; Sodium 146mg.

Layered Chicken and Mushroom Bake

This rich, creamy dish is simple to make in the slow cooker and is a hearty supper on a cold winter's day. The sauce combines with juices from the mushrooms and chicken during cooking to make a well-flavoured gravy.

Serves 4

15ml/1 tbsp olive oil
4 large skinless chicken breast fillets, cut into chunks
40g/1½oz/3 tbsp butter
1 leek, finely sliced into rings
25g/1oz/¼ cup plain (all-purpose) flour
550ml/18fl oz/2½ cups milk
5ml/1 tsp Worcestershire sauce (optional)
5ml/1 tsp wholegrain mustard
1 carrot, finely diced
225g/8oz/3 cups button (white) mushrooms, thinly sliced
900g/2lb potatoes, thinly sliced
salt and ground black pepper

1 Heat the olive oil in a large pan. Add the chicken and fry gently until beginning to brown. Remove the chicken from the pan using a slotted spoon, leaving any juices behind. Set aside.

2 Add 25g/1oz/2 tbsp of the butter to the pan and heat gently until melted. Stir in the leek and fry gently for a few minutes. Sprinkle the flour over the leeks, then turn off the heat and gradually blend in the milk until smooth. Slowly bring the mixture to the boil, stirring all the time, until thickened.

3 Remove the pan from the heat and stir in the Worcestershire sauce, if using, mustard, diced carrot, mushrooms and chicken. Season generously.

4 Arrange enough potato slices to cover the base of the ceramic cooking pot. Spoon one-third of the chicken mixture over the top, then cover with another layer of potatoes. Repeat layering, finishing with a layer of potatoes. Dot the remaining butter on top.

5 Cover and cook on high for 4 hours, or until the potatoes are cooked and tender when pierced with a skewer. If you like, place the dish under a moderate grill (broiler) for 5 minutes to brown, then serve immediately.

Apricot and Almond Stuffed Chicken

Couscous makes a light and simple base for this fruity slow-cooker recipe.

Serves 4

50g/2oz/¼ cup ready-to-eat dried apricots
150ml/¼ pint/⅔ cup orange juice
4 skinned chicken breast fillets
50g/2oz/⅓ cup instant couscous
150ml/¼ pint/⅔ cup boiling chicken stock
25g/1oz/¼ cup chopped toasted almonds
1.5ml/¼ tsp dried tarragon
1 egg yolk
30ml/2 tbsp orange marmalade
salt and ground black pepper
boiled or steamed basmati and wild rice, to serve

1 Put the apricots in a bowl and pour over the orange juice. Leave to soak while you prepare the remaining ingredients.

2 Cut a deep pocket horizontally in each chicken breast fillet, taking care not to cut all the way through. Put the fillets between two sheets of oiled clear film (plastic wrap), then gently beat with a rolling pin or mallet until slightly thinner.

3 Put the couscous in a bowl and spoon over 50ml/2fl oz/¼ cup of the stock. Leave to stand until all the stock has been absorbed.

4 Drain the apricots, reserving the juice, then stir them into the couscous along with the almonds and tarragon. Season with salt and pepper, then stir in enough egg yolk to bind the mixture.

5 Divide the stuffing between the chicken fillets, securing with cocktail sticks (toothpicks). Place the stuffed chicken fillets in the base of the ceramic cooking pot.

6 Stir the orange marmalade into the remaining hot stock until dissolved, then stir in the orange juice. Season with salt and pepper and pour over the chicken. Cover the pot and cook on high for 3–5 hours, or until the chicken is tender.

7 Remove the chicken from the sauce and keep warm. Transfer the sauce to a wide pan and boil rapidly until reduced by half. Carve the chicken into slices and arrange on plates. Spoon over the sauce and serve with basmati and wild rice.

Layered Chicken Bake Energy 461kcal/1943kJ; Protein 42.4g; Carbohydrate 43.8g, of which sugars 5.2g; Fat 14.1g, of which saturates 6.4g; Cholesterol 126.3mg; Calcium 49mg; Fibre 4.3g; Sodium 351mg.
Stuffed Chicken Energy 379kcal/1604kJ; Protein 40.2g; Carbohydrate 38g, of which sugars 27g; Fat 8.5g, of which saturates 1.3g; Cholesterol 155mg; Calcium 61mg; Fibre 1.6g; Sodium 117mg.

Hen in a Pot with Parsley Sauce

For this slow-cooker dish, a large chicken could replace the boiling fowl, if you cannot find one.

Serves 6

1.6–1.8kg/3½–4lb boiling fowl (stewing chicken) or whole chicken
½ lemon, sliced
small bunch of parsley and thyme
675g/1½lb carrots, cut into chunks
12 shallots or small onions, whole

For the sauce

50g/2oz/½ cup butter
50g/2oz/½ cup plain (all-purpose) flour
15ml/1 tbsp lemon juice
60ml/4 tbsp chopped flat leaf parsley
150ml/¼ pint/⅔ cup milk
salt and ground black pepper
sprigs of flat leaf parsley, to garnish

1 Remove any string and loose pieces of fat from inside the boiling fowl or chicken, then rinse under cold water and place in the ceramic cooking pot. Add the lemon, parsley and thyme, carrots and onions, and season well. Pour in near-boiling water to just cover the fowl and vegetables. Cover with the lid, switch the slow cooker on to high and cook for 1 hour.

2 Skim off any scum and fat. Re-cover the pot and cook for about 2–2½ hours, or until the fowl is cooked. Carefully lift the fowl on to a warmed serving dish, arrange the vegetables around it and keep warm.

3 Strain the cooking liquid into a pan and boil uncovered to reduce by a third. Strain and leave to settle for 2 minutes, then skim the fat off the surface.

4 For the sauce, melt the butter in a pan, add the flour and cook, stirring, for 1 minute. Gradually stir in the stock (there should be about 600ml/1 pint/2½ cups) and bring to the boil. Add the lemon juice, parsley and milk to the pan. Season with salt and pepper and simmer the sauce for another 1–2 minutes.

5 To serve, pour a little of the sauce over the fowl and vegetables, then garnish with a few sprigs of fresh parsley, and take to the table for carving. Pour the rest of the sauce into a warmed gravy boat or jug (pitcher) and serve separately.

Chicken Fricassée

Large chicken pieces are cooked in a rich, herby sauce for this popular dish, which is made in a slow cooker.

Serves 4

20 small button (pearl) onions or shallots
1.2–1.3kg/2½–3lb chicken, cut into pieces
25g/1oz/2 tbsp butter
30ml/2 tbsp sunflower oil
45ml/3 tbsp plain (all-purpose) flour
250ml/8fl oz/1 cup dry white wine
600ml/1 pint/2½ cups boiling chicken stock
1 bouquet garni
5ml/1 tsp lemon juice
225g/8oz/3 cups button (white) mushrooms
75ml/2½fl oz/⅓ cup double (heavy) cream
45ml/3 tbsp chopped fresh parsley
salt and ground black pepper

1 Put the onions or shallots in a bowl, add just enough boiling water to cover them and leave to soak. Meanwhile, rinse the chicken pieces in cold water and pat dry with kitchen paper.

2 Melt half the butter with the oil in a large pan. Add the chicken pieces and cook, turning occasionally, until lightly browned. Transfer the pieces to the ceramic cooking pot, leaving the juices behind.

3 Stir the flour into the pan juices, then blend in the wine. Stir in the stock and add the bouquet garni and lemon juice. Bring to the boil, stirring, until the sauce has thickened. Season well and pour over the chicken. Cover the pot and switch to high.

4 Drain and peel the onions or shallots. Trim the stalks from the mushrooms. Clean the frying pan, then melt the remaining butter. Add the mushrooms and onions or shallots and cook for 5 minutes, turning frequently until they are lightly browned. Transfer into the ceramic cooking pot with the chicken. Re-cover and cook on high for 3–4 hours, or until the chicken is cooked.

5 Using a slotted spoon, remove the chicken and vegetables to a warmed serving dish. Add the cream and 30ml/2 tbsp of the parsley to the sauce and whisk to combine. Adjust the seasoning if necessary, then pour the sauce over the chicken and vegetables. Sprinkle the fricassée with the remaining parsley and serve.

Hen in a Pot Energy 509kcal/2114kJ; Protein 36.2g; Carbohydrate 20.1g, of which sugars 12.2g; Fat 32g, of which saturates 11.4g; Cholesterol 195mg; Calcium 109mg; Fibre 4g; Sodium 214mg.
Chicken Fricassée Energy 613kcal/2563kJ; Protein 53.1g; Carbohydrate 36.4g, of which sugars 17.9g; Fat 25g, of which saturates 11.1g; Cholesterol 196mg; Calcium 128mg; Fibre 5.3g; Sodium 396mg.

Coq au Vin

This rustic, one-pot casserole contains chunky pieces of chicken, slowly simmered in a rich red wine sauce until tender.

Serves 6

45ml/3 tbsp light olive oil
12 shallots
225g/8oz rindless streaky (fatty) bacon rashers (strips), chopped
3 garlic cloves, finely chopped
225g/8oz small mushrooms, halved
6 boneless chicken thighs
3 chicken breast fillets, halved
1 bottle red wine
salt and ground black pepper
45ml/3 tbsp chopped fresh parsley, to garnish
boiled potatoes, to serve

For the bouquet garni

3 sprigs each parsley, thyme and sage
1 bay leaf
4 peppercorns

For the beurre manié

25g/1oz/2 tbsp butter, softened
25g/1oz/¼ cup plain (all-purpose) flour

1 Heat the oil in a flameproof casserole and cook the shallots for 5 minutes until golden. Increase the heat, then add the bacon, garlic and mushrooms and cook, stirring, for 10 minutes.

2 Transfer the cooked ingredients to a plate, then brown the chicken pieces in the oil remaining in the pan, turning them until golden brown all over. Return the shallots, garlic, mushrooms and bacon to the casserole and pour in the red wine.

3 Tie the ingredients for the bouquet garni in a bundle in a small piece of muslin (cheesecloth) and add to the casserole. Bring to the boil. Reduce the heat, cover and simmer for 30–40 minutes.

4 To make the beurre manié, cream the butter and flour together in a bowl using your fingers to make a smooth paste. Add small lumps of the paste to the casserole, stirring well until each piece has melted. When all the paste has been added, bring the casserole back to the boil and simmer for 5 minutes.

5 Season the casserole to taste with salt and pepper. Serve immediately, garnished with chopped fresh parsley and accompanied by boiled potatoes.

Coq au Vin with Little Onions

This is a famous Burgundian recipe, garnished with little onions and mushrooms.

Serves 4

1 celery stick
1 fresh bay leaf
1 fresh thyme sprig
1 bottle red wine
600ml/1 pint/2½ cups chicken stock
50g/2oz/¼ cup butter
30ml/2 tbsp olive oil
24 small pickling onions
115g/4oz piece of bacon, sliced
45ml/3 tbsp plain (all-purpose) flour
2.25kg/5lb chicken, jointed into 8 pieces
45ml/3 tbsp cognac
2 garlic cloves, chopped
15ml/1 tbsp tomato purée (paste)
250g/9oz button mushrooms
30ml/2 tbsp chopped fresh parsley
salt and ground black pepper
croûtons, to garnish (optional)

1 Tie the celery, bay leaf and thyme together in a bundle and place in a pan. Pour in the wine and stock and simmer, uncovered, for 15 minutes. Melt 15g/½oz/1 tbsp of the butter with half the olive oil in a heavy frying pan and brown 16 of the onions all over. Use a draining spoon to transfer the onions to a plate. Add the bacon and cook, then set aside.

2 Meanwhile, season 30ml/2 tbsp of the flour with salt and pepper. Dust the chicken joints in the flour and fry them in the fat remaining in the pan over medium heat, turning frequently, for about 10 minutes, or until golden brown all over. Pour in the cognac and carefully set it alight using a long match or taper. When the flames have died down, remove the chicken from the pan and set aside.

3 Chop the remaining onions. Add another 15g/½oz/1 tbsp butter to the frying pan and fry the chopped onions with the garlic over a medium heat, stirring for 5 minutes, until softened and just turning brown. Preheat the oven to 190°C/375°F/Gas 5.

4 Add the wine and stock mixture, with the herb bundle, and stir in the tomato purée. Lower the heat, then simmer gently, stirring frequently, for about 20 minutes. Taste and adjust the seasoning, if necessary.

5 Place the chicken pieces and bacon in a flameproof casserole. Pour in the sauce (with the bundle of herbs). Cover and place in the oven. Reduce the temperature to 160°C/325°F/Gas 3 immediately and cook for 1½ hours. Add the whole browned onions and cook for a further 30 minutes.

6 Meanwhile, fry the mushrooms in another 15g/½oz/1 tbsp butter and the remaining oil until browned. Set them aside. Mix the remaining butter and flour to make a paste (known in French as beurre manié).

7 Transfer the chicken and onions to a serving plate. Heat the cooking juices on the stove until simmering. Add the beurre manié in small lumps, whisking to blend the paste into the sauce as it melts. Continue adding small pieces of paste, allowing each to melt completely before adding the next, until the simmering sauce is thickened to taste. Add the mushrooms and cook for a few minutes. Pour the sauce over the chicken and sprinkle with chopped parsley. Garnish with croûtons, if using, and serve.

Coq au Vin Energy 538kcal/2240kJ; Protein 43.5g; Carbohydrate 7g, of which sugars 2.8g; Fat 28.2g, of which saturates 8.9g; Cholesterol 170mg; Calcium 50mg; Fibre 1.1g; Sodium 610mg.
Coq with Onions Energy 630kcal/2618kJ; Protein 42.8g; Carbohydrate 19.3g, of which sugars 7.4g; Fat 41g, of which saturates 17.3g; Cholesterol 209mg; Calcium 67mg; Fibre 2.6g; Sodium 480mg.

Country Cider Hotpot

Root vegetables, chopped bacon and prunes all bring flavour to the wonderful cider gravy in this slow-baked chicken dish.

Serves 4

30ml/2 tbsp plain (all-purpose) flour
4 chicken breast fillets
25g/1oz/2 tbsp butter
15ml/1 tbsp vegetable oil
15 baby onions
4 streaky (fatty) bacon rashers (strips), rinded and chopped
10ml/2 tsp Dijon mustard
450ml/¾ pint/scant 2 cups dry (hard) cider
3 carrots, chopped
2 parsnips, chopped
12 ready-to-eat prunes, pitted
1 fresh rosemary sprig
1 bay leaf
salt and ground black pepper
mashed potatoes, to serve

1 Preheat the oven to 160°C/325°F/Gas 3. Season the flour with salt and pepper and place in a plastic bag. Add the chicken breast fillets to the bag and shake until they are well coated in the seasoned flour. Set aside.

2 Heat the butter and oil in a flameproof casserole. Add the onions and bacon, and fry over a moderate heat for 4 minutes until the onions have started to soften and turn translucent. Remove the onions and bacon from the pan with a slotted spoon and set aside.

3 Add the floured chicken breast fillets to the oil in the casserole and fry, turning occasionally, until they are evenly browned all over. Spread a little of the Dijon mustard over the top of each chicken fillet.

4 Return the onions and bacon to the casserole. Pour in the cider and add the carrots, parsnips, prunes, rosemary sprig and bay leaf. Season well with salt and ground black pepper.

5 Bring to the boil, then cover the casserole with a tight-fitting lid and transfer to the oven. Cook for about 1½ hours until the chicken is tender.

6 Remove the rosemary and bay leaf from the pan, and serve with mashed potatoes.

Chicken, Leek and Bacon Casserole

A whole chicken is slowly braised with leeks and bacon.

Serves 4–6

15ml/1 tbsp vegetable oil
25g/1oz/2 tbsp butter
1.5kg/3½lb chicken
225g/8oz streaky (fatty) bacon, diced
450g/1lb leeks, in 2.5cm/1in pieces
250ml/8fl oz/1 cup chicken stock
250ml/8fl oz/1 cup double (heavy) cream
15ml/1 tbsp chopped fresh tarragon
salt and ground black pepper

1 Preheat the oven to 180°C/350°F/Gas 4. Heat the oil and butter in a flameproof casserole. Add the chicken and cook, breast side down, for 5 minutes until golden. Set aside.

2 Add the bacon to the pan and cook for 4–5 minutes. Add the leeks and cook for 5 minutes until soft. Place the chicken on top, cover the pan and cook in the oven for 1½ hours or until tender.

3 Remove the chicken, bacon and leeks from the pan and keep warm. Skim the fat from the juices. Pour in the stock and cream, and bring to the boil. Cook for 5 minutes until thickened. Stir in the tarragon and season with salt and pepper. Carve the chicken and serve with the bacon, leeks and a little sauce.

Chicken and Pesto Jackets

Baked potatoes with a pesto, chicken and yogurt topping.

Serves 4

4 baking potatoes, pricked
2 chicken breast fillets, skin on
250ml/8fl oz/1 cup plain (natural) yogurt
15ml/1 tbsp pesto sauce
fresh basil sprigs, to garnish

1 Preheat the oven to 200°C/400°F/Gas 6. Bake the potatoes for 1¼ hours until soft. About 20 minutes before the end, place the chicken fillets in an ovenproof dish and bake in the oven.

2 Mix the yogurt and pesto in a bowl. Skin the chicken fillets and cut into slices. Cut open the potatoes and fill with the chicken slices, top with the yogurt sauce, garnish with basil and serve.

Hotpot Energy 544kcal/2279kJ; Protein 41.1g; Carbohydrate 42.9g, of which sugars 32.2g; Fat 21g, of which saturates 8.2g; Cholesterol 136mg; Calcium 129mg; Fibre 8g; Sodium 488mg.
Chicken Casserole Energy 729kcal/3016kJ; Protein 38.3g; Carbohydrate 2.9g, of which sugars 2.4g; Fat 62.6g, of which saturates 27g; Cholesterol 250mg; Calcium 54mg; Fibre 1.7g; Sodium 634mg.
Chicken Jackets Energy 272kcal/1151kJ; Protein 26.1g; Carbohydrate 36.9g, of which sugars 7.3g; Fat 3.3g, of which saturates 1.5g; Cholesterol 57mg; Calcium 180mg; Fibre 2g; Sodium 160mg.

Chicken with Root Vegetables and Lentils

A slow-baked casserole of wonderfully tender chicken, root vegetables and lentils, finished with crème fraîche, mustard and tarragon.

Serves 4

350g/12oz onions
350g/12oz leeks
225g/8oz carrots
450g/1lb swede (rutabaga)
30ml/2 tbsp oil
4 chicken portions, about 900g/2lb total weight
115g/4oz/½ cup green lentils
475ml/16fl oz/2 cups chicken stock
300ml/ ½ pint/1¼ cups apple juice
10ml/2 tsp cornflour (cornstarch)
45ml/3 tbsp crème fraîche
10ml/2 tsp wholegrain mustard
30ml/2 tbsp chopped fresh tarragon
salt and ground black pepper
fresh tarragon sprigs, to garnish

1 Preheat the oven to 190°C/375°F/Gas 5. Roughly chop the onions, leeks, carrots and swede into even pieces.

2 Heat the oil in a large, flameproof casserole. Season the chicken portions with salt and pepper, and fry them until golden. Drain on kitchen paper.

3 Add the onions to the casserole and cook for 5 minutes, stirring, until they begin to soften and colour. Add the leeks, carrots, swede and lentils, and cook, stirring, over medium heat for about 2 minutes.

4 Return the chicken portions to the casserole. Pour in the stock and apple juice, and season with salt and pepper. Bring to the boil and cover with a tight-fitting lid. Cook in the oven for 50 minutes to 1 hour or until the chicken portions are tender.

5 Place the casserole over medium heat. Blend the cornflour with 30ml/2 tbsp water and add to the casserole with the crème fraîche, mustard and tarragon. Adjust the seasoning. Simmer gently for about 2 minutes, stirring. Serve immediately, garnished with tarragon sprigs.

Chicken, Bacon and Leek Pudding

This old-fashioned suet pudding requires long, slow cooking, resulting in a hearty dish bursting with flavour.

Serves 4

200g/7oz unsmoked lean, rindless bacon, preferably in one piece
400g/14oz skinless, boneless chicken, preferably thigh meat
2 leeks, finely chopped
30ml/2 tbsp chopped fresh parsley
175g/6oz/1½ cups self-raising (self-rising) flour
75g/3oz/½ cup shredded suet (US chilled, grated shortening)
120ml/4fl oz/½ cup chicken or vegetable stock, or water
ground black pepper
butter, for greasing

1 Cut the bacon and chicken into bitesize pieces. Place in a large bowl. Add the leeks and half the parsley. Season with pepper.

2 Sift the flour into another large bowl and stir in the suet and the remaining parsley. Stir in sufficient cold water to make a soft dough. Roll out on a lightly floured surface to a circle measuring about 33cm/13in across. Cut out one quarter of the circle (starting from the centre, like a wedge), roll up and reserve.

3 Lightly butter a 1.2 litre/2 pint heatproof bowl and line with the dough. Press the cut edges together to seal them and allow the pastry to overlap the top of the bowl slightly.

4 Spoon the bacon and chicken mixture into the lined bowl, packing it neatly and taking care not to split the pastry. Pour the stock over the mixture, making sure it does not overfill the bowl.

5 Roll out the reserved dough into a circle to form a lid and lay it over the filling, pinching the edges together to seal them well. Cover with baking parchment (pleated in the centre to allow the pudding to rise) and then a large sheet of foil (again, pleated at the centre). Tuck the edges under and press them tightly to the sides of the bowl until well sealed.

6 Steam the pudding over boiling water for about 3½ hours. Check the water level occasionally. Uncover the pudding, slide a knife around the sides and turn out on to a warmed serving plate. Serve immediately.

Chicken Energy 505kcal/2132kJ; Protein 65.2g; Carbohydrate 43.8g, of which sugars 24.7g; Fat 8.9g, of which saturates 3.9g; Cholesterol 170mg; Calcium 181mg; Fibre 9.7g; Sodium 182mg.
Pudding Energy 535kcal/2236kJ; Protein 28.2g; Carbohydrate 39.4g, of which sugars 2.9g; Fat 31.3g, of which saturates 14.8g; Cholesterol 86mg; Calcium 111mg; Fibre 4g; Sodium 999mg.

Chicken Casserole with Onions and Kidney Beans

This hearty, slow-baked casserole is bursting with spicy flavours, rustic textures and appealing colours.

Serves 4–6

275g/10oz/1½ cups dried kidney or other beans, soaked in water overnight
8–12 chicken portions, such as thighs and drumsticks
12 bacon rashers (strips), rinded
2 large onions, thinly sliced
250ml/8fl oz/1 cup dry white wine
2.5ml/½ tsp chopped fresh sage or oregano
2.5ml/½ tsp chopped fresh rosemary
generous pinch of grated nutmeg
150ml/¼ pint/⅔ cup sour cream
15ml/1 tbsp chilli powder or paprika
salt and ground black pepper
fresh rosemary sprigs and lemon wedges, to garnish

1 Preheat the oven to 180°C/350°F/Gas 4. Drain the kidney beans, place in a pan and cover with fresh cold water. Bring to the boil and boil rapidly for 10 minutes, skimming off any scum that rises to the surface. Rinse and drain well. Trim the chicken pieces, and season with salt and pepper.

2 Arrange the bacon rashers around the sides and base of an ovenproof dish. Sprinkle over half of the sliced onions, then half of the beans, followed by the remaining onions and then the remaining beans.

3 In a bowl, mix together the wine with the fresh sage or oregano, the rosemary and nutmeg. Pour the mixture over the onions and beans.

4 In another bowl, mix together the sour cream and the chilli powder or paprika. Toss the chicken in the sour cream mixture and arrange on top of the beans.

5 Cover the dish with foil and bake in the oven for about 1¼–1½ hours, removing the foil for the last 15 minutes of the cooking time. Serve immediately, garnished with rosemary sprigs and lemon wedges.

Chicken in a Pot

This is a traditional way of slowly cooking chicken pieces on top of the stove in their own juices.

Serves 6–8

8 chicken breast fillets
6–8 firm ripe tomatoes, chopped
2 garlic cloves, crushed
3 onions, chopped
60ml/4 tbsp oil
250ml/8fl oz/1 cup chicken stock
2 bay leaves
10ml/2 tsp paprika
10 white peppercorns, bruised
handful of parsley, stalks reserved and leaves finely chopped
salt

1 Put the chicken breast fillets, tomatoes and garlic in a flameproof casserole. Cover and cook gently for 10–15 minutes. Add the remaining ingredients, except the parsley leaves, and stir well.

2 Cover tightly and simmer over very low heat, stirring occasionally, for about 1¾–2 hours or until the chicken is tender. Five minutes before the end of the cooking time, stir in the parsley. Adjust the seasoning as necessary. Place the chicken fillets on serving plates, spoon over the sauce and serve.

Chicken with Apricots

A slowly simmered dish that is deliciously fruity.

Serves 4

4 chicken portions
30ml/2 tbsp seasoned flour
45ml/3 tbsp olive oil
350g/12oz dried apricots, soaked overnight
salt and ground black pepper

1 Coat the chicken in the seasoned flour. Heat the oil and fry the chicken, turning occasionally, until browned on all sides. Remove from the pan and set aside.

2 Add any remaining flour to the pan and cook, stirring, for 1 minute. Gradually stir in the apricot soaking water and bring to the boil, stirring constantly. Return the chicken to the pan and add the apricots. Season to taste with salt and pepper, cover and simmer for 45–50 minutes until tender. Serve hot.

Chicken Casserole Energy 472kcal/1983kJ; Protein 54.3g; Carbohydrate 27.6g, of which sugars 6.1g; Fat 13.9g, of which saturates 6g; Cholesterol 140mg; Calcium 103mg; Fibre 8.1g; Sodium 691mg.
Chicken in a Pot Energy 270kcal/1141kJ; Protein 29g; Carbohydrate 26.9g, of which sugars 8.1g; Fat 5.9g, of which saturates 1.5g; Cholesterol 86mg; Calcium 69mg; Fibre 6.8g; Sodium 125mg.
Chicken with Apricots Energy 345kcal/1456kJ; Protein 33.5g; Carbohydrate 32g, of which sugars 32g; Fat 10.2g, of which saturates 1.6g; Cholesterol 88mg; Calcium 70mg; Fibre 5.5g; Sodium 87mg.

Hunter's Chicken

This slowly simmered dish sometimes has strips of green pepper in the sauce instead of the mushrooms. Creamed potatoes or polenta make a good accompaniment.

Serves 4

15g/½oz/¼ cup dried porcini mushrooms
30ml/2 tbsp olive oil
15g/½oz/1 tbsp butter
4 chicken portions, on the bone, skinned
1 large onion, thinly sliced
400g/14oz can chopped tomatoes
150ml/¼ pint/⅔ cup red wine
1 garlic clove, crushed
leaves of 1 fresh rosemary sprig, finely chopped
115g/4oz/1¾ cups fresh field (portabello) mushrooms, thinly sliced
salt and ground black pepper
fresh rosemary sprigs, to garnish

1 Put the porcini in a bowl, add 250ml/8fl oz/1 cup warm water and soak for 20 minutes. Squeeze the porcini over the bowl, strain the liquid and reserve. Finely chop the porcini.

2 Heat the oil and butter in a large, flameproof casserole until foaming. Add the chicken portions and sauté over medium heat for 5 minutes, or until golden brown. Remove the pieces and drain on kitchen paper.

3 Add the sliced onion and chopped porcini mushrooms to the pan. Cook gently, stirring frequently, for about 3 minutes until the onion has softened but not browned. Stir in the chopped tomatoes, red wine and reserved mushroom soaking liquid, then add the crushed garlic and chopped rosemary, with salt and pepper to taste. Bring to the boil, stirring constantly.

4 Return the chicken portions to the casserole and turn to coat with the sauce. Cover with a tightly fitting lid and simmer gently for 30 minutes.

5 Add the fresh mushrooms to the casserole and stir well to mix into the sauce. Continue simmering gently for 10 minutes, or until the chicken is tender. Taste for seasoning. Serve hot, with creamed potatoes or polenta, if you like. Garnish with the rosemary sprigs.

Chicken in a Salt Crust

Baking food in a casing of salt gives a deliciously moist, tender flavour that, surprisingly, is not too salty. This slow-cooking technique is used in both Italy and France for chicken and whole fish, although chicken is easier to handle.

Serves 6

1.8kg/4lb chicken
about 2.25kg/5lb coarse sea salt

For the garlic purée
450g/1lb onions, quartered
2 large heads of garlic
120ml/4fl oz/½ cup olive oil
salt and ground black pepper

For the tomatoes and peppers
450g/1lb plum tomatoes
3 red (bell) peppers, seeded and quartered
1 red chilli, seeded and chopped
90ml/6 tbsp olive oil
flat leaf parsley, to garnish

1 Preheat the oven to 220°C/425°F/Gas 7. Choose a deep ovenproof dish into which the whole chicken will fit snugly. Line the dish with a double thickness of heavy foil, allowing plenty of excess foil to overhang the top edge of the ovenproof dish.

2 Truss the chicken tightly so that the salt cannot fall into the cavity. Sprinkle a thin layer of salt in the foil-lined dish, then place the chicken on top.

3 Pour the remaining salt all around and over the top of the chicken until it is completely encased. Sprinkle the top with a little water.

4 Cover the chicken tightly with the foil and bake on the lower oven shelf for 1¾ hours.

5 Meanwhile, put the onions in a small heavy pan. Break up the heads of garlic, but leave the skins on. Add to the pan with the olive oil and a little salt and pepper.

6 Cover the pan and cook on top of the stove over the lowest possible heat for about 1 hour or until the garlic heads are completely soft.

7 Plunge the tomatoes into boiling water for 30 seconds, then refresh in cold water. Peel away the skins and quarter.

8 Put the red peppers, tomatoes and chilli in a shallow ovenproof dish and sprinkle with the oil. Bake on the shelf above the chicken for 45 minutes or until the peppers are slightly charred.

9 Squeeze the garlic out of the skins. Process the onions, garlic and pan juices in a blender or food processor until smooth. Return the purée to the clean pan.

10 Open out the foil around the chicken and ease it out of the dish. Transfer it to a large serving platter ready for carving. Place the roasted pepper mixture into a warmed serving dish and garnish with parsley.

11 Reheat the garlic purée. Crack open the salt crust on the chicken and brush away the salt before carving and serving with the garlic purée and pepper mixture.

Hunter's Chicken Energy 310kcal/1299kJ; Protein 38.2g; Carbohydrate 9.2g, of which sugars 7.5g; Fat 10.8g, of which saturates 3.3g; Cholesterol 113mg; Calcium 38mg; Fibre 2.4g; Sodium 128mg.
Chicken in Salt Energy 452kcal/1899kJ; Protein 71.5g; Carbohydrate 8.5g, of which sugars 8.2g; Fat 14.8g, of which saturates 2.6g; Cholesterol 204mg; Calcium 28mg; Fibre 2.3g; Sodium 186mg.

Corn-fed Chicken with Herb Butter

A chicken slowly cooked in a clay pot remains beautifully moist and tender. Flavoured with lemon, parsley and tarragon, serve this as an alternative to a traditional Sunday roast.

Serves 4

3 large carrots, cut into batons
1 celery heart, thickly sliced
2 red onions, quartered
a few sprigs of fresh thyme
1.6kg/3½lb corn-fed chicken
40g/1½oz/3 tbsp butter, softened
15ml/1 tbsp finely chopped fresh parsley
15ml/1 tbsp finely chopped fresh tarragon
1 small lemon, halved
300ml/½ pint/1¼ cups dry white wine or chicken stock
salt and ground black pepper

1 Soak a chicken brick or large clay pot in cold water for 20 minutes, then drain. Place the carrots, celery, red onions and thyme in the pot.

2 Wash the chicken and dry thoroughly. Mix together the butter, parsley and tarragon. Ease up the breast skin of the chicken and spread the butter under it, taking care not to puncture the skin. Place the lemon halves inside the chicken.

3 Rub the chicken with seasoning and nestle it on top of the vegetables. Add the wine or chicken stock and cover. Place the chicken brick or pot in an unheated oven. Set the oven to 200°C/400°F/Gas 6 and cook for about 1¾ hours, or until the chicken is cooked.

4 Remove the lid from the brick or pot and cook for a further 10 minutes, or until the chicken is golden brown. Remove from the pot and leave to stand for 10 minutes before carving and serving with the cooked vegetables.

Cook's Tip
Cook some potatoes in the oven at the same time to accompany the pot-roast – baked potatoes or roast potatoes both go well. Or, if you prefer, serve with creamy mashed potatoes.

Chicken with Potato Dumplings

Slowly poaching chicken pieces in a creamy sauce topped with light herb and potato dumplings makes a delicate yet hearty and warming meal.

Serves 6

1 onion, chopped
300ml/½ pint/1¼ cups vegetable stock
120ml/4fl oz/½ cup white wine
4 large chicken breast fillets
300ml/½ pint/1¼ cups single (light) cream
15ml/1 tbsp chopped fresh tarragon
salt and ground black pepper

For the dumplings
225g/8oz maincrop potatoes, boiled and mashed
175g/6oz/1¼ cups suet (US chilled, grated shortening)
115g/4oz/1 cup self-raising (self-rising) flour
50ml/2fl oz/¼ cup water
30ml/2 tbsp chopped mixed fresh herbs
salt and ground black pepper

1 Place the onion, stock and wine in a deep-sided frying pan. Add the chicken and simmer, covered, for 20 minutes.

2 Remove the chicken from the stock, cut it into chunks and set aside. Strain the stock and discard the onion. Return the stock to the pan and boil until reduced by one-third. Stir in the single cream and tarragon and simmer until just thickened. Stir in the chicken and season with salt and ground black pepper.

3 Spoon the mixture into a 900ml/1½ pint/3¾ cup ovenproof dish. Preheat the oven to 190°C/375°F/Gas 5.

4 Mix together the dumpling ingredients to make a soft dough. Divide into six and shape into balls with floured hands.

5 Place the dumplings on top of the chicken mixture and bake uncovered for 30 minutes until cooked. Serve immediately.

Cook's Tip
Make sure that you do not reduce the sauce too much before cooking in the oven as the dumplings absorb quite a lot of liquid.

Corn-fed Chicken Energy 717kcal/2975kJ; Protein 47.3g; Carbohydrate 13.8g, of which sugars 12.3g; Fat 47.4g, of which saturates 16.6g; Cholesterol 261mg; Calcium 89mg; Fibre 4.1g; Sodium 314mg.
Dumplings Energy 552kcal/2300kJ; Protein 28.2g; Carbohydrate 26.5g, of which sugars 2.6g; Fat 37.4g, of which saturates 21g; Cholesterol 121mg; Calcium 83mg; Fibre 1.3g; Sodium 80mg.

Chicken with Wild Mushrooms and Garlic

This roasted chicken dish has a hint of fresh herbs.

Serves 4

45ml/3 tbsp olive or vegetable oil
1.3kg/3lb chicken
1 large onion, finely chopped
3 celery sticks, chopped
2 garlic cloves, crushed
275g/10oz/4 cups fresh wild mushrooms, sliced if large
5ml/1 tsp chopped fresh thyme
250ml/8fl oz/1 cup chicken stock
250ml/8fl oz/1 cup dry white wine
juice of 1 lemon
30ml/2 tbsp chopped fresh parsley
120ml/4fl oz/½ cup sour cream
salt and ground black pepper
flat leaf parsley, to garnish
fresh green beans, to serve

1 Preheat the oven to 190°C/375°F/Gas 5. Heat the oil in a flameproof roasting pan and brown the chicken all over. Set aside.

2 Add the onion to the pan and fry for about 2 minutes. Add the celery, garlic, mushrooms and thyme and cook for 3 minutes.

3 Pour the chicken stock, wine and lemon juice into the pan. Sprinkle over half of the parsley and season well. Place the chicken back in the pan and cook in the oven for 1½–1¾ hours, or until tender, basting occasionally to prevent it drying out.

4 Remove the chicken from the roasting pan and keep warm. Put the roasting pan on the stove and stir in the sour cream over gentle heat, adding a little extra stock or water if necessary to make the juices into a thick pouring sauce.

5 Arrange the chicken on a warmed serving plate, surrounded by the creamy vegetables. Garnish with the parsley sprigs and serve with the sauce and fresh green beans.

Cook's Tip
Ensure you clean wild mushrooms well to remove any grit, or use cultivated mushrooms instead.

Chicken in White Wine

In Hungary, this one-pot recipe is made with a wine called Badacsonyi Kĕkryalii, which has a full body and distinctive bouquet.

Serves 4

50g/2oz/4 tbsp butter
4 spring onions (scallions), chopped
115g/4oz rindless smoked bacon, diced
2 bay leaves
1 tarragon sprig
1.3kg/3lb cornfed chicken
60ml/4 tbsp sweet sherry or mead
115g/4oz/scant 2 cups button (white) mushrooms, sliced
300ml/½ pint/1¼ cups Badacsonyi or dry white wine
salt and ground black pepper
tarragon and bay leaves, to garnish
fresh steamed rice, to serve

1 Heat the butter in a large, heavy pan or flameproof casserole and sweat the spring onions for 1–2 minutes. Add the bacon, bay leaves and the tarragon, stripping the leaves from the stem. Cook for a further 3–4 minutes.

2 Add the whole chicken to the pan and pour in the sweet sherry or mead. Cover with a tight-fitting lid and cook over very low heat for 15 minutes.

3 Sprinkle the mushrooms into the pan and pour in the wine. Cook, covered, for a further 1 hour. Remove the lid, baste the chicken with the wine mixture and continue to cook, uncovered, for a further 30 minutes, until almost all the liquid has evaporated.

4 Skim any fat from the cooking liquid remaining in the pan. Season to taste with salt and ground black pepper and remove the chicken, vegetables and bacon to a warmed serving dish. Garnish with tarragon and bay leaves and serve the chicken with freshly cooked rice.

Cook's Tip
Traditionally, this recipe also uses a sweet drink with a honeyed caramel flavour called márc. As this can be difficult to find outside of Hungary, it is replaced here with sweet sherry or mead.

Chicken with Garlic Energy 552kcal/2290kJ; Protein 41.8g; Carbohydrate 1.7g, of which sugars 1.5g; Fat 39.8g, of which saturates 13.6g; Cholesterol 226mg; Calcium 54mg; Fibre 0.9g; Sodium 184mg.
Chicken in Wine Energy 671kcal/2783kJ; Protein 45.2g; Carbohydrate 1g, of which sugars 0.9g; Fat 48.7g, of which saturates 18.1g; Cholesterol 250mg; Calcium 32mg; Fibre 0.5g; Sodium 682mg.

Drunken Chicken

Flavoured with a mixture of sherry and tequila, this rich casserole is made in the slow cooker. Serve with bowls of rice to soak up the juices, or with tortillas.

Serves 4

150g/5oz/1 cup raisins
120ml/4fl oz/½ cup sherry
115g/4oz/1 cup plain (all-purpose) flour
2.5ml/½ tsp salt
2.5ml/½ tsp ground black pepper
45ml/3 tbsp vegetable oil
8 skinless chicken thighs
1 onion, halved and thinly sliced
2 garlic cloves, crushed
2 tart eating apples
115g/4oz/1 cup flaked (sliced) almonds
1 slightly under-ripe plantain, peeled and sliced
300ml/½ pint/1¼ cups boiling chicken stock
120ml/4fl oz/½ cup tequila
chopped fresh herbs, to garnish

1 Put the raisins in a bowl and add the sherry. Set aside to soak. Meanwhile, combine the flour, salt and pepper and spread the mixture out on a large plate. Heat 30ml/2 tbsp of the oil in a large frying pan. Coat each chicken thigh in the seasoned flour, then fry, turning, until browned. Drain well on kitchen paper.

2 Heat the remaining oil and fry the onion for 5 minutes, or until soft. Stir in the garlic and cook for 1–2 minutes. Transfer the onions and garlic to the ceramic cooking pot and set to high.

3 Peel, core and dice the apples. Add them to the ceramic cooking pot, then sprinkle over the almonds, plantain slices and raisins. Pour in the sherry, stock and tequila and stir to combine.

4 Add the chicken thighs to the ceramic pot, pressing them down into the stock so they are covered. Cover with the lid and cook for 3 hours, or until the chicken thighs are very tender. Check that the chicken is cooked by piercing the thickest part with a sharp knife or skewer; the juices should run clear. Cook for a little longer, if necessary.

5 Taste the sauce and add a little more salt and ground black pepper if necessary. Serve the chicken piping hot, sprinkled with chopped fresh herbs.

Spring Chicken in Bacon Sauce

This delicious slow-cooker stew is a great alternative to the classic roast.

Serves 4

2 large spring chickens
25g/1oz/2 tbsp unsalted butter
10ml/2 tsp sunflower oil
115g/4oz chopped bacon pieces or smoked streaky (fatty) bacon
2 leeks, sliced
175g/6oz/2¼ cup small button (white) mushrooms, trimmed
120ml/4fl oz/½ cup apple juice, plus a further 15ml/1 tbsp
120ml/4fl oz/½ cup chicken stock
30ml/2 tbsp clear honey
10ml/2 tsp chopped fresh thyme
225g/8oz crisp red apples
10ml/2 tsp cornflour (cornstarch)
salt and ground black pepper
creamy mashed potatoes and steamed baby leeks, to serve

1 Carefully cut the chickens in half to make four portions. Rinse well under cold water, then pat dry using kitchen paper.

2 Heat the butter and oil in a large pan and add the chicken portions. Fry, turning the pieces over, until lightly browned. Transfer to the ceramic cooking pot, leaving the fat in the pan.

3 Add the bacon to the pan and cook for 5 minutes, stirring, until brown. Transfer the bacon to the ceramic cooking pot leaving the fat in the pan. Add the leeks and mushrooms to the pan and cook for a few minutes until beginning to soften.

4 Pour 120ml/4fl oz/½ cup apple juice and the stock into the pan. Stir in the honey and thyme and season with salt and pepper. Bring to a boil, then pour over the chicken and bacon. Cover the ceramic cooking pot, switch to high and cook for 2 hours.

5 Quarter, core and thickly slice the apples. Add them to the cooking pot. Cook for 2 hours, or until the chicken is tender.

6 Remove the chicken and keep warm. Blend the cornflour with the 15ml/1 tbsp apple juice and stir into the cooking liquid until thickened. Taste and adjust the seasoning, if necessary.

7 Serve the chicken on warmed plates with the sauce poured over. Accompany with mashed potatoes and baby leeks.

Drunken Chicken Energy 529kcal/2227kJ; Protein 23.1g; Carbohydrate 63.7g, of which sugars 34.1g; Fat 11.5g, of which saturates 1.8g; Cholesterol 94.5mg; Calcium 76mg; Fibre 2.9g; Sodium 401mg.
Spring Chicken Energy 465kcal/1945kJ; Protein 32.8g; Carbohydrate 25.9g, of which sugars 20.7g; Fat 26.3g, of which saturates 9.5g; Cholesterol 172mg; Calcium 40mg; Fibre 3.3g; Sodium 632mg.

Chicken with Sherry, Tomato and Mushroom Sauce

In this tasty dish, originating from eastern Europe, the chicken is smothered in a rich sauce before being slowly baked in the oven. You can replace the cultivated mushrooms with wild mushrooms, if you like, but do make sure they are well cleaned before using.

Serves 8

1.75kg/4lb chicken, cut into 8 pieces
2.5ml/½ tsp finely chopped fresh thyme
40g/1½oz/3 tbsp butter
45ml/3 tbsp vegetable oil
3–4 garlic cloves, crushed
2 onions, finely chopped
salt and ground white pepper
basil and thyme leaves, to garnish
freshly cooked rice, to serve

For the sauce

120ml/4fl oz/½ cup dry sherry
45ml/3 tbsp tomato purée (paste)
a few fresh basil leaves
30ml/2 tbsp white wine vinegar
pinch of sugar
5ml/1 tsp mild mustard
400g/14oz can chopped tomatoes
225g/8oz/3 cups mushrooms, sliced

1 Preheat the oven to 180°C/350°F/Gas 4. Season the chicken with salt, pepper and thyme. Heat the butter and oil in a large frying pan and gently fry the chicken for 5 minutes, turning occasionally, until golden brown. Remove from the frying pan, place in an ovenproof dish and keep hot.

2 Add the garlic and onion to the frying pan and cook for about 4–5 minutes, or until just soft.

3 For the sauce, mix together the sherry, tomato purée, salt and pepper, basil, vinegar and sugar. Add the mustard and tomatoes. Pour into the frying pan and bring to the boil.

4 Reduce the heat and add the mushrooms. Adjust the seasoning with more sugar or vinegar to taste.

5 Pour the tomato sauce over the chicken. Bake in the oven, covered, for 45–60 minutes, or until cooked and tender. Serve on a bed of rice, garnished with basil and thyme.

Chicken Casserole with Red Pepper, Carrot and Celeriac

A great variety of colourful seasonal vegetables go into this hearty stew, which is then slowly simmered on top of the stove. A selection of herbs such as rosemary, marjoram and thyme are added to flavour the deliciously rich sauce.

Serves 6

60ml/4 tbsp vegetable oil
1 mild onion, thinly sliced
2 garlic cloves, crushed
2 red (bell) peppers, seeded and sliced
1.6kg/3½lb chicken
90ml/6 tbsp tomato purée (paste)
3 potatoes, diced
5ml/1 tsp chopped fresh rosemary
5ml/1 tsp chopped fresh marjoram
5ml/1 tsp chopped fresh thyme
3 carrots, cut into chunks
½ small celeriac, cut into chunks
120ml/4fl oz/½ cup dry white wine
2 courgettes (zucchini), sliced
salt and ground black pepper
chopped fresh rosemary and marjoram, to garnish
dark rye bread, to serve

1 Heat the oil in a flameproof casserole. Add the onion and garlic and cook for 4–5 minutes until soft. Add the sliced peppers and continue to cook for 2–3 minutes.

2 Joint the chicken into six pieces, place in the casserole and brown gently on all sides.

3 After about 15 minutes, add the tomato purée, potatoes, herbs, carrots, celeriac and white wine, and season to taste with salt and pepper. Cook over a gentle heat, covered, for 40–50 minutes.

4 Add the courgette slices 5 minutes before the end of cooking. Adjust the seasoning to taste. Garnish with the chopped herbs and serve with dark rye bread.

Cook's Tip

If fresh herbs are unavailable, you can replace them with 2.5ml/½ tsp dried herbs.

Chicken with Sherry Energy 335kcal/1388kJ; Protein 20g; Carbohydrate 5.7g, of which sugars 4.7g; Fat 24.1g, of which saturates 7.7g; Cholesterol 107mg; Calcium 26mg; Fibre 1.5g; Sodium 127mg.
Casserole Energy 555kcal/2308kJ; Protein 35.2g; Carbohydrate 24.6g, of which sugars 11.5g; Fat 34.2g, of which saturates 8.6g; Cholesterol 160mg; Calcium 87mg; Fibre 4.5g; Sodium 205mg.

Chicken with Tomatoes and Honey

Here, chicken is coated in a thick tomato and honey sauce.

Serves 4

30ml/2 tbsp sunflower oil
25g/1oz/2 tbsp butter
4 chicken quarters
1 onion, grated or finely chopped
1 garlic clove, crushed
5ml/1 tsp ground cinnamon
good pinch of ground ginger
1.3–1.6kg/3–3½lb tomatoes, peeled, cored and chopped
30ml/2 tbsp clear honey
50g/2oz/⅓ cup blanched almonds
15ml/1 tbsp sesame seeds
salt and ground black pepper
chopped flat leaf parsley, to garnish

1 Heat the oil and butter in a flameproof casserole. Cook the chicken until brown. Add the onion, garlic, cinnamon, ginger and tomatoes, and season. Simmer gently, covered, for 1 hour.

2 Transfer the chicken to a serving dish and keep warm. Cook the sauce over high heat until reduced and thickened. Add the honey, cook for 1 minute, then pour over the chicken. Sprinkle with almonds and sesame seeds. Garnish with parsley and serve.

Chicken with Beans and Garlic

A chicken is slowly cooked in the oven with leeks, fennel, garlic and butter beans.

Serves 6

2 leeks, thickly sliced
1 small fennel bulb, chopped
4 garlic cloves, peeled, whole
2 x 400g/14oz cans butter (lima) beans, drained and rinsed
45ml/3 tbsp fresh parsley, chopped
300ml/½ pint/1¼ cups white wine
250ml/8fl oz/1 cup vegetable stock
1.6kg/3½lb chicken
fresh parsley sprigs, to garnish
cooked green vegetables, to serve

1 Preheat the oven to 180°C/350°F/Gas 4. Mix the leeks, fennel, garlic, beans and parsley in a large flameproof casserole. Pour in the wine and stock, and stir well.

2 Place the chicken on top of the vegetables. Bring to the boil, cover, and bake for 1–1½ hours until the chicken is cooked and tender. Garnish with parsley and serve with green vegetables.

Baked Chicken with Mustard and Tarragon

In this recipe, a mild, aromatic wholegrain mustard makes a tasty way of baking a joint of chicken in the oven. Speciality mustards are widely available in delicatessens and wholefood shops. Serve with new potatoes and peas.

Serves 4–6

8–12 chicken joints, or a whole 1kg/2¼lb chicken, jointed
juice of ½ lemon
30–45ml/2–3 tbsp wholegrain whiskey mustard
15ml/1 tbsp chopped fresh tarragon
sea salt and ground black pepper

1 Preheat the oven to 190°C/375°F/Gas 5. Place the chicken joints into a large, shallow baking dish in which the chicken will fit in a single layer.

2 Sprinkle the lemon juice over the chicken joints to flavour the skin. Season the chicken with salt and ground black pepper.

3 Spread the wholegrain whiskey mustard over the chicken joints, rubbing it in a little. Sprinkle over the chopped tarragon.

4 Bake in the preheated oven for about 20–30 minutes, or until the joints are cooked through and tender. Serve immediately, with new potatoes and peas, if you like.

Cook's Tip
The cooking time will depend on the size of the chicken joints. Check them after about 20 minutes.

Variation
A whole chicken can also be baked in this way. Allow about 1½ hours in an oven preheated to 180°C/350°F/Gas 4. When ready, the juices will run clear without any pink colour when the thickest part of the chicken is pierced with a skewer.

Chicken with Tomatoes Energy 579kcal/2413kJ; Protein 33.7g; Carbohydrate 20.7g, of which sugars 19.2g; Fat 40.8g, of which saturates 10.5g; Cholesterol 178mg; Calcium 103mg; Fibre 5.2g; Sodium 192mg.
Chicken with Beans Energy 545kcal/2283kJ; Protein 54g; Carbohydrate 26.7g, of which sugars 6.1g; Fat 22.5g, of which saturates 8.5g; Cholesterol 180mg; Calcium 101mg; Fibre 8.1g; Sodium 713mg.
Baked Chicken Energy 426kcal/1768kJ; Protein 40.3g; Carbohydrate 0g, of which sugars 0g; Fat 29.3g, of which saturates 8.1g; Cholesterol 215mg; Calcium 13mg; Fibre 0g; Sodium 146mg.

Roast Chicken with Herb and Orange Bread Stuffing

Tender roast chicken is slowly baked in the oven and scented with orange and herbs, served with gravy.

Serves 4–6

2 onions
25g/1oz/2 tbsp butter, plus extra
150g/5oz/2½ cups soft white breadcrumbs
30ml/2 tbsp chopped fresh mixed herbs
grated rind of 1 orange
1.6kg/3½lb chicken with giblets
1 carrot, sliced
1 bay leaf
1 fresh thyme sprig
900ml/1½ pints/3¾ cups water
15ml/1 tbsp tomato purée (paste)
10ml/2 tsp cornflour (cornstarch), mixed to a thin paste with 15ml/1 tbsp cold water
salt and ground black pepper
chopped fresh thyme, to garnish

1 Preheat the oven to 200°C/400°F/Gas 6. Finely chop one of the onions. Melt the butter in a pan and add the chopped onion. Cook for 3–4 minutes until soft. Stir in the breadcrumbs, chopped mixed herbs and orange rind. Season well.

2 Remove the giblets and put aside. Wash the neck end of the chicken and dry with kitchen paper. Spoon in the stuffing, then rub a little butter into the breast and season it well. Put the chicken into a roasting pan and cook in the oven for about 20 minutes, then reduce the heat to 180°C/350°F/Gas 4 and cook for a further 1 hour or until the juices run clear when the thickest part of the thigh is pierced with a knife or skewer.

3 Put the giblets, the remaining onion, the carrot, bay leaf, thyme and water into a large pan. Bring to the boil, then simmer while the chicken is roasting.

4 Place the chicken on a warmed serving platter and leave to rest for about 10–15 minutes. Skim the fat off the cooking juices, strain the juices and stock into a pan, and discard the giblets and vegetables. Simmer for about 5 minutes. Whisk in the tomato purée. Whisk the cornflour paste into the gravy and cook for 1 minute. Season and serve with the chicken, garnished with chopped thyme.

Roly Poly Chicken and Chanterelle Pudding

This warming dish is slowly simmered wrapped in muslin.

Serves 4

1 medium onion, chopped
1 celery stick, sliced
10ml/2 tsp chopped fresh thyme
30ml/2 tbsp vegetable oil
2 skinless chicken breast fillets
115g/4oz/1½ cups chanterelles, trimmed and sliced
40g/1½oz/⅓ cup plain (all-purpose) flour
300ml/½ pint/1¼ cups boiling chicken stock
5ml/1 tsp Dijon mustard
10ml/2 tsp wine vinegar
salt and ground black pepper

For the roly poly dough

350g/12oz/3 cups self-raising (self-rising) flour, plus extra
2.5ml/½ tsp salt
150g/5oz/10 tbsp chilled unsalted butter, diced
75ml/5 tbsp cold water

1 Fry the onion, celery and thyme gently in the oil without colouring. Cut the chicken into bitesize pieces, add to the pan with the mushrooms and cook briefly. Stir in the flour, then remove from the heat. Gradually stir in the chicken stock. Return to the heat, simmer to thicken, then add the mustard, vinegar and seasoning. Set aside to cool.

2 To make the dough, sift the flour and salt into a bowl. Add the butter and rub in until the mixture resembles coarse breadcrumbs. Pour in the water all at once and combine without over-mixing.

3 Roll out the dough on a floured surface into a 25 × 30cm/10 × 12in rectangle. Rinse a piece of muslin (cheesecloth), about twice as big as the dough, in a little water and lay it on a clean, flat surface. Spread the chicken filling over the dough and roll up from the short end, using the muslin to help, to make a fat sausage. Enclose the pudding in the muslin and tie the parcel with kitchen string.

4 Lower the pudding into a pan of boiling water, cover and simmer for 1½ hours. Lift out, untie and discard the muslin. Slice the pudding and serve hot.

Roast Chicken Energy 516kcal/2151kJ; Protein 34.4g; Carbohydrate 28.8g, of which sugars 6.9g; Fat 29.9g, of which saturates 9.7g; Cholesterol 169mg; Calcium 71mg; Fibre 2.3g; Sodium 352mg.
Roly Poly Energy 793kcal/3324kJ; Protein 32.4g; Carbohydrate 78.1g, of which sugars 4.2g; Fat 41.3g, of which saturates 22.3g; Cholesterol 135mg; Calcium 350mg; Fibre 4.1g; Sodium 902mg.

Seville Chicken

Oranges and almonds provide a warm, rich flavour to this slow-cooked dish.

Serves 4

1 orange
8 chicken thighs
plain (all-purpose) flour, seasoned with salt and pepper
45ml/3 tbsp olive oil
1 large Spanish (Bermuda) onion, chopped
2 garlic cloves, crushed
1 red (bell) pepper, seeded and sliced
1 yellow (bell) pepper, seeded and sliced
115g/4oz chorizo, sliced
50g/2oz/½ cup flaked (sliced) almonds
225g/8oz/generous 1 cup brown basmati rice
about 600ml/1 pint/2½ cups chicken or vegetable stock
400g/14oz can chopped tomatoes
175ml/6fl oz/¾ cup white wine
generous pinch of dried thyme
salt and ground black pepper
fresh thyme sprigs, to garnish

1 Pare a thin strip of peel from the orange using a vegetable peeler and set it aside. Peel the orange, then cut it into even segments, working over a bowl to catch any excess juice. Dust the chicken thighs with plenty of seasoned flour.

2 Heat the olive oil in a large frying pan and fry the chicken pieces on both sides until nicely brown. Transfer the browned chicken to a plate. Add the onion and crushed garlic to the pan and fry for 4–5 minutes until beginning to brown. Add the sliced peppers and fry, stirring occasionally, until slightly softened.

3 Add the chorizo, stir-fry for a few minutes, then sprinkle over the almonds and rice. Cook, stirring, for 1–2 minutes.

4 Pour in the stock, chopped tomatoes and wine, then add the reserved orange peel and the thyme. Season well. Bring to simmering point, stirring, then return the chicken to the pan.

5 Cover with a tight-fitting lid and cook over very low heat for 1–1¼ hours until the rice and chicken are tender. Just before serving, add the orange segments and juice, and allow to cook briefly to heat through. Season to taste with salt and pepper, garnish with sprigs of fresh thyme and serve.

Roast Chicken with Mediterranean Vegetables and Potatoes

A whole chicken is oven-roasted with a medley of sweet-tasting Mediterranean vegetables.

Serves 4

1.8–2.25kg/4–5lb roasting chicken
150ml/¼ pint/⅔ cup extra virgin olive oil
½ lemon
a few sprigs of fresh thyme
450g/1lb small new potatoes
1 aubergine (eggplant), cut into 2.5cm/1in cubes
1 red or yellow (bell) pepper, seeded and quartered
1 fennel bulb, trimmed and quartered
8 large garlic cloves, unpeeled
coarse sea salt and ground black pepper

1 Preheat the oven to 200°C/400°F/Gas 6. Rub the chicken all over with olive oil and season with pepper. Place the lemon half inside the bird, with a sprig or two of thyme. Put the chicken breast side down in a large roasting pan. Roast for 30 minutes.

2 Remove the chicken from the oven and season with salt. Turn the chicken right side up and baste with juices from the pan.

3 Arrange the potatoes around the chicken and roll them in the cooking juices until they are thoroughly coated. Return the roasting pan to the oven to continue roasting.

4 After 30 minutes, add the aubergine, pepper, fennel and garlic cloves to the pan. Drizzle the vegetables with the remaining oil, and season to taste with salt and pepper.

5 Add the remaining sprigs of thyme to the roasting pan, tucking the sprigs in among the vegetables. Return the chicken and vegetables to the oven and cook for 30–50 minutes more, basting and turning the vegetables occasionally during cooking.

6 To find out if the chicken is cooked, push the tip of a sharp knife between the thigh and breast – if the juices run clear, rather than pink, it is done. The vegetables should be tender and tinged brown. Serve the chicken and vegetables from the pan.

Seville Chicken Energy 861kcal/3598kJ; Protein 65.3g; Carbohydrate 67.1g, of which sugars 17.1g; Fat 34g, of which saturates 5.6g; Cholesterol 155mg; Calcium 172mg; Fibre 6.3g; Sodium 453mg.
Roasted Chicken Energy 798kcal/3310kJ; Protein 43.3g; Carbohydrate 23.7g, of which sugars 6.1g; Fat 59.3g, of which saturates 13.5g; Cholesterol 208mg; Calcium 45mg; Fibre 4.2g; Sodium 183mg.

Chicken with Forty Cloves of Garlic

The smell that emanates from the oven as the chicken and garlic slowly cook is indescribably delicious.

Serves 4–5

5–6 whole heads of garlic
15g/½oz/1 tbsp butter
45ml/3 tbsp olive oil
1.8–2kg/4–4½lb chicken
150g/5oz/1¼ cups plain (all-purpose) flour, plus 5ml/1 tsp
75ml/5 tbsp white port, Pineau de Charentes or other white, fortified wine
2–3 tarragon or rosemary sprigs
30ml/2 tbsp crème fraîche (optional)
few drops of lemon juice (optional)
salt and ground black pepper

1 Separate three of the heads of garlic into cloves and peel them. Remove the first layer of papery skin from the remaining heads of garlic and cut off the tops to expose the cloves, if you like, or leave them whole. Preheat the oven to 180°C/350°F/Gas 4.

2 Heat the butter and 15ml/1 tbsp of the oil in a flameproof casserole that is large enough to take the chicken and garlic. Add the chicken and cook over medium heat, turning it frequently, for 10 minutes, until it is browned all over.

3 Sprinkle in 5ml/1 tsp flour and cook for 1 minute. Add the port or wine. Tuck in the whole heads of garlic and the peeled cloves with the sprigs of tarragon or rosemary. Pour over the remaining oil and season to taste with salt and pepper.

4 Mix the main batch of flour with enough water to make a firm dough. Roll it out into a long sausage and press it around the rim of the casserole, then press on the lid, folding the dough up and over it to create a seal. Cook in the oven for 1½ hours.

5 To serve, lift off the lid to break the seal and remove the chicken and whole garlic to a serving platter and keep warm. Remove and discard the herbs, then place the casserole on the stove and whisk the remaining ingredients to combine the garlic cloves with the juices. Add the crème fraîche, if using, and a little lemon juice to taste, if using. Process the sauce in a food processor or blender until smooth. Reheat the garlic sauce in a clean pan, if necessary, and serve it with the chicken.

Chicken with Shallots, Garlic and Fennel

This is a very simple way to cook chicken slowly in the oven. If you have time, allow the chicken to marinate for a few hours before cooking, for the best flavour.

Serves 4

1.6–1.8kg/3½–4lb chicken, cut into 8 pieces, or 8 chicken joints
250g/9oz shallots, peeled
1 head of garlic, separated into cloves and peeled
60ml/4 tbsp extra virgin olive oil
45ml/3 tbsp tarragon vinegar
45ml/3 tbsp white wine or vermouth (optional)
5ml/1 tsp fennel seeds, crushed
2 bulbs fennel, cut into wedges, feathery tops reserved
150ml/¼ pint/⅔ cup double (heavy) cream
5ml/1 tsp redcurrant jelly
15ml/1 tbsp tarragon mustard
a little sugar (optional)
30ml/2 tbsp chopped fresh flat leaf parsley
salt and ground black pepper

1 Place the chicken pieces, shallots and all but one of the garlic cloves in a large, shallow flameproof dish. Add the olive oil, tarragon vinegar, white wine or vermouth, if using, and the fennel seeds. Season to taste with ground black pepper, then set aside and leave to marinate in a cool place for 2–3 hours.

2 Preheat the oven to 190°C/375°F/Gas 5. Add the wedges of fennel to the chicken, then season with salt and stir well to mix. Transfer the chicken to the oven and cook for 50–60 minutes, stirring once or twice, until the chicken is thoroughly cooked.

3 Transfer the chicken and vegetables to a serving dish and keep them warm. Skim off some of the fat and bring the cooking juices to the boil, then pour in the cream. Stir, scraping up all the juices. Whisk in the redcurrant jelly followed by the mustard. Check the seasoning, adding a little sugar, if necessary.

4 Finely chop the remaining garlic clove with the feathery fennel tops and mix them with the parsley. Pour the sauce over the chicken and then sprinkle the chopped garlic and herb mixture over the top. Serve immediately, with boiled rice or baked potatoes, if you like.

Chicken with Garlic Energy 616kcal/2565kJ; Protein 37.7g; Carbohydrate 31.6g, of which sugars 2.9g; Fat 36.5g, of which saturates 10.4g; Cholesterol 173mg; Calcium 64mg; Fibre 2.6g; Sodium 151mg.
Chicken with Shallots Energy 743kcal/3075kJ; Protein 43.1g; Carbohydrate 5.7g, of which sugars 5.6g; Fat 60.9g, of which saturates 22.2g; Cholesterol 266mg; Calcium 96mg; Fibre 3.9g; Sodium 176mg.

Pot-roast Chicken with Lemon and Garlic

This is a rustic dish that is slowly cooked in one pot in the oven so it is especially easy to prepare. Lardons are thick strips of bacon fat; if you can't get them, use fatty bacon instead. Serve with bread to mop up the juices.

Serves 4

30ml/2 tbsp olive oil
25g/1oz/2 tbsp butter
175g/6oz/1 cup smoked lardons, or roughly chopped streaky (fatty) bacon
8 garlic cloves, peeled
4 onions, quartered
10ml/2 tsp plain (all-purpose) flour
600ml/1 pint/2½ cups hot chicken stock
2 lemons, thickly sliced
45ml/3 tbsp finely chopped fresh thyme
1 chicken, weighing about 1.3–1.6kg/3–3½lb
2 x 400g/14oz cans flageolet, cannellini or haricot (navy) beans, drained and rinsed
salt and ground black pepper

1 Preheat the oven to 190°C/375°F/Gas 5. Heat the oil and butter in a flameproof casserole that is large enough to hold the chicken with a little room around the sides. Add the lardons and cook until golden. Remove with a slotted spoon and drain on kitchen paper.

2 Add the garlic and onions and brown over high heat. Stir in the flour, then the hot chicken stock. Return the lardons to the pan with the sliced lemon and fresh thyme, and season with salt and ground black pepper.

3 Bring the sauce to the boil, stirring constantly until thickened, then place the whole chicken on top. Season well. Transfer the casserole to the oven. Cook for 1 hour, basting the chicken with the cooking juices once or twice during that time to ensure it stays moist.

4 Baste the chicken again. Stir the beans into the casserole and return it to the oven for a further 30 minutes, or until the chicken is cooked through and tender. Carve the chicken into thick slices and serve with the beans.

Stoved Chicken

'Stovies' were originally potatoes cooked slowly on the stove with onions and dripping or butter until falling to pieces. This baked version includes an irresistible layer of bacon and chicken.

Serves 4

1kg/2¼lb baking potatoes, cut into 5mm/¼in slices
butter, for greasing
2 large onions, thinly sliced
15ml/1 tbsp chopped fresh thyme
25g/1oz/2 tbsp butter
15ml/1 tbsp vegetable oil
2 large bacon rashers (strips), chopped
4 large chicken portions, halved
600ml/1 pint/2½ cups hot chicken stock
1 bay leaf
salt and ground black pepper

1 Preheat the oven to 150°C/300°F/Gas 2. Arrange a thick layer of half the potato slices in a large, lightly greased earthenware baking dish, then cover with half the onions. Sprinkle with half the thyme, and season with salt and pepper.

2 Heat the butter and oil in a large, heavy frying pan, add the chopped bacon and chicken pieces and cook, turning them occasionally, until brown on all sides. Using a slotted spoon, transfer the chicken and bacon to the earthenware dish. Reserve the fat in the pan.

3 Sprinkle the remaining chopped thyme over the chicken, season with salt and pepper, then cover with the remaining onion slices, followed by a neat, overlapping layer of the remaining potato slices. Season the top layer of potatoes with more salt and ground black pepper.

4 Pour the chicken stock into the earthenware dish, add the bay leaf and brush the potatoes with the reserved fat from the frying pan. Cover tightly with foil and bake for about 2 hours, or until the chicken is cooked and tender.

5 Preheat the grill (broiler) to medium-hot, then remove the foil from the earthenware dish and place the dish under the grill. Cook until the slices of potato turn golden brown and crisp. Remove the bay leaf and serve immediately.

Pot-roast Chicken Energy 887kcal/3696kJ; Protein 62.5g; Carbohydrate 45.5g, of which sugars 12.9g; Fat 51.7g, of which saturates 16g; Cholesterol 256mg; Calcium 187mg; Fibre 13.9g; Sodium 1519mg.
Stoved Chicken Energy 500kcal/2107kJ; Protein 50g; Carbohydrate 48.2g, of which sugars 8.9g; Fat 13.2g, of which saturates 5.4g; Cholesterol 144mg; Calcium 51mg; Fibre 3.9g; Sodium 405mg.

Shredded Chicken with Walnuts

A whole chicken is slowly simmered in a mildly spiced stock, then shredded and mixed with a creamy walnut and garlic sauce. This dish is ideal when you want a novel recipe for whole chicken.

Serves 6

1.5kg/3lb chicken, trimmed of fat
3 slices of day-old white bread, crusts removed
150ml/¼ pint/⅔ cup milk
175g/6oz/1½ cup shelled walnuts
4–6 garlic cloves
salt and ground black pepper

For the stock

1 onion, quartered
1 carrot, chopped
2 celery sticks, chopped
4–6 cloves
4–6 allspice berries
4–6 black peppercorns
2 bay leaves
5ml/1 tsp coriander seeds
1 bunch of fresh flat leaf parsley, stalks bruised and tied together

For the garnish

30ml/2 tbsp butter
5ml/1 tsp paprika
fresh coriander (cilantro) leaves

1 Put the chicken into a deep pan with all of the ingredients for the stock. Pour in enough water to cover and bring to the boil. Lower the heat, cover and simmer the chicken for 1 hour.

2 Remove the chicken from the pan and leave until cool enough to handle. Meanwhile, boil the stock, uncovered, for 15 minutes until reduced, then strain and season with salt and pepper.

3 When the chicken has cooled a little, pull off the skin and discard it. Tear the chicken flesh into thin strips using two forks or your fingers and put into a large bowl. In a small bowl, soak the bread in the milk for a few minutes.

4 Using a mortar and pestle, pound the walnuts with the garlic to form a paste, or blend them in a food processor. Beat the soaked bread into the paste, then add to the chicken.

5 Beat in spoonfuls of the warm stock to the chicken, bread and walnut mixture to bind the paste until it is light and creamy.

6 Spoon the mixture into a serving dish. Serve immediately, garnished with the butter, paprika and fresh coriander leaves.

Lemon Chicken Thighs Wrapped in Aubergine

Wrapping the meat in strips of fried aubergine may take a little time and effort to prepare, but the result is both impressive and tasty.

Serves 4

juice of 2–3 lemons
2 garlic cloves, crushed
4–6 allspice berries, crushed
8 chicken thighs, skinned and boned
3–4 aubergines (eggplants)
sunflower oil, for deep-frying
30ml/2 tbsp toasted flaked (sliced) almonds
1 lemon, cut into wedges, to serve

1 In a shallow bowl, mix together the lemon juice, garlic and allspice berries. Toss the chicken in the mixture, rolling the pieces over in the juice to coat them thoroughly, then cover and leave to marinate in the refrigerator for about 2 hours.

2 Using a vegetable peeler or a small, sharp knife, peel the aubergines lengthways in stripes like a zebra. Slice the aubergines thinly lengthways – you need 16 strips in total. Soak the slices in a bowl of salted cold water for about 30 minutes.

3 Preheat the oven to 180°C/350°F/Gas 4. Drain the aubergine slices and squeeze out the excess water. Heat the oil for deep-frying in a wok or other deep pan, and deep-fry the slices in batches for 2–3 minutes until golden brown. Remove with a slotted spoon and drain on kitchen paper.

4 On a board or plate, lay two strips of aubergine over one another in a cross shape, then place a chicken thigh in the middle. Tuck the thigh into a bundle and wrap the aubergine around it.

5 Place the aubergine parcel, seam side down, in a lightly greased ovenproof dish and repeat the process with the remaining aubergine strips and chicken.

6 Pour any remaining marinade over the parcels and sprinkle with the almonds. Cover with foil and bake for 40 minutes. Serve hot, with lemon wedges.

Shredded Chicken Energy 222kcal/937kJ; Protein 34.1g; Carbohydrate 7.6g, of which sugars 1.6g; Fat 6.4g, of which saturates 3.3g; Cholesterol 105mg; Calcium 53mg; Fibre 0.2g; Sodium 324mg.
Lemon Chicken Thighs Energy 509kcal/2114kJ; Protein 34.7g; Carbohydrate 2.7g, of which sugars 2.3g; Fat 40g, of which saturates 8.4g; Cholesterol 180mg; Calcium 67mg; Fibre 2.6g; Sodium 108mg.

Chicken with Chickpeas, Almonds and Saffron

The almonds in this tasty, slowly simmered dish are pre-cooked until soft, adding an interesting texture and flavour to the chicken.

Serves 4

75g/3oz/½ cup blanched almonds
75g/3oz/½ cup chickpeas, soaked overnight and drained
4 part-boned chicken breast portions, skinned
50g/2oz/4 tbsp butter
2.5ml/½ tsp saffron threads
2 Spanish (Bermuda) onions, finely sliced
900ml/1½ pints/3¾ cups hot chicken stock
1 small cinnamon stick
60ml/4 tbsp chopped fresh flat leaf parsley, plus extra to garnish
lemon juice, to taste
salt and ground black pepper

1 Place the blanched almonds and the soaked and drained chickpeas in a large flameproof casserole of water and bring to the boil. Boil for 10 minutes, then reduce the heat. Simmer for 1–1½ hours until the chickpeas are soft. Drain the chickpeas and almonds and set aside.

2 Place the skinned chicken pieces in the casserole, together with the butter, half of the saffron, and salt and plenty of black pepper. Heat gently, stirring, until the butter has melted.

3 Add the onions and stock, bring to the boil, then add the reserved cooked almonds, chickpeas and cinnamon stick. Cover with a tightly fitting lid and cook very gently for 45–60 minutes until the chicken is completely tender.

4 Transfer the cooked chicken to a serving plate and keep warm. Bring the sauce in the pan to the boil and cook with the lid off, stirring occasionally, over high heat until it is well reduced and thickened.

5 Add the chopped parsley and remaining saffron to the casserole and cook for a further 2–3 minutes. Sharpen the sauce with a little lemon juice, then pour the sauce over the chicken and serve, garnished with extra fresh parsley.

Tarragon Chicken in Cider

Aromatic tarragon has a distinctive flavour that goes wonderfully with both cream and chicken. This slow-cooker recipe is truly effortless, yet provides an elegant dish for entertaining or a special family meal.

Serves 4

350g/12oz small button (pearl) onions
15ml/1 tbsp sunflower oil
4 garlic cloves, peeled
4 chicken breast fillets, skin on
350ml/12fl oz/1½ cups dry (hard) cider
1 bay leaf
200g/7oz/scant 1 cup crème fraîche or sour cream
30ml/2 tbsp chopped fresh tarragon
15ml/1 tbsp chopped fresh parsley
salt and ground black pepper

1 Put the button onions in a heatproof bowl and pour over enough boiling water to cover. Leave to stand for at least 10 minutes, then drain and peel off the skins. (They should come off very easily after soaking.)

2 Heat the oil in a frying pan, add the onions and cook gently, stirring, for 10 minutes, or until lightly browned. Add the garlic and cook for a further 2–3 minutes. Using a slotted spoon, transfer the onions and garlic to the ceramic cooking pot.

3 Place the chicken breast fillets in the frying pan and cook for 3–4 minutes, turning once or twice until lightly browned on both sides. Transfer the chicken to the ceramic cooking pot.

4 Pour the cider into the pan, add the bay leaf and a little salt and pepper, and bring to the boil. Pour over the chicken. Cover the ceramic cooking pot with the lid and cook on low for 4–5 hours, or until the chicken and onions are cooked and very tender. Lift out the chicken breast fillets. Set aside while you finish preparing the cider sauce.

5 Stir the crème fraîche or sour cream and the herbs into the sauce. Return the chicken breast fillets to the pot and cook for a further 30 minutes on high, or until piping hot. Serve the chicken immediately, with lightly sautéed potatoes and a green vegetable, such as cabbage.

Chicken with Chickpeas Energy 463kcal/1935kJ; Protein 45.2g; Carbohydrate 18.6g, of which sugars 7g; Fat 23.6g, of which saturates 7.9g; Cholesterol 132mg; Calcium 110mg; Fibre 4.8g; Sodium 179mg.
Tarragon Chicken Energy 520kcal/2167kJ; Protein 36.9g; Carbohydrate 12.1g, of which sugars 9.2g; Fat 33.9g, of which saturates 12.9g; Cholesterol 184mg; Calcium 90mg; Fibre 1.5g; Sodium 138mg.

Chicken Tagine with Green Olives and Preserved Lemon

This dish combines two classic Moroccan ingredients, cracked green olives and lemons. Try this recipe when you are looking for a new way to slow-cook a whole chicken instead of the usual roasting method. Serve simply with couscous and a salad or vegetable side dish.

Serves 4

1.3kg/3lb chicken
3 garlic cloves, crushed
small bunch of fresh coriander (cilantro), finely chopped
juice of ½ lemon
5ml/1 tsp coarse salt
45–60ml/3–4 tbsp olive oil
1 large onion, grated
pinch of saffron threads
5ml/1 tsp ground ginger
5ml/1 tsp ground black pepper
1 cinnamon stick
175g/6oz/1½ cups cracked green olives
2 preserved lemons, cut into strips

1 Place the chicken in a deep dish. Rub the garlic, coriander, lemon juice and salt into the body cavity of the chicken. Mix the olive oil with the grated onion, saffron, ginger and pepper and rub this mixture over the outside of the chicken. Cover and leave to stand for about 30 minutes.

2 Transfer the chicken to a tagine or large, heavy flameproof casserole and pour the marinating juices over. Pour in enough water to come halfway up the chicken, add the cinnamon stick and bring the water to the boil. Reduce the heat, cover with a lid and simmer for about 1 hour, turning the chicken occasionally.

3 Preheat the oven to 150°C/300°F/Gas 2. Using two slotted spoons, carefully lift the chicken out of the tagine or casserole and set aside on a plate, covered with foil. Turn up the heat and boil the cooking liquid for 5 minutes to reduce it.

4 Replace the chicken in the tagine or casserole and baste it thoroughly with the juices. Add the green olives and the preserved lemon and place the tagine or casserole in the oven for about 15 minutes. Serve the chicken immediately, with your chosen accompaniments.

Moroccan Roast Chicken

Ideally, this chicken should be slowly cooked whole, Moroccan-style, on a spit over hot charcoal. However, it is still excellent roasted in a hot conventional oven and can be cooked whole, halved or in quarters.

Serves 4–6

1.8kg/4lb chicken
2 small shallots
1 garlic clove
1 fresh parsley sprig
1 fresh coriander (cilantro) sprig
5ml/1 tsp salt
7.5ml/1½ tsp paprika
pinch of cayenne pepper
5–7.5ml/1–1½ tsp ground cumin
about 40g/1½oz/3 tbsp butter
½–1 lemon (optional)
a few sprigs of fresh parsley or coriander (cilantro), to garnish

1 Remove the chicken giblets, if necessary, and rinse out the cavity with cold running water. Pat dry with kitchen paper. Unless cooking it whole, cut the chicken in half or into quarters using poultry shears or a sharp knife.

2 Place the shallots, garlic, herbs, salt and spices in a food processor or blender and process until the shallots are finely chopped. Add the butter and process to make a smooth paste. Thoroughly rub the paste over the skin of the chicken and then allow it to stand for 1–2 hours.

3 Preheat the oven to 200°C/400°F/Gas 6 and place the chicken in a roasting pan. If using, quarter the lemon and place one or two quarters around the chicken pieces (or in the body cavity if the chicken is whole) and squeeze a little juice over the skin.

4 Roast in the oven for 1–1¼ hours (2–2¼ hours for a whole bird) until the juices run clear when the thickest part of the thigh is pierced with a skewer or knife. Baste occasionally with the juices during cooking. If the skin starts to brown too quickly, cover the chicken loosely with foil or baking parchment.

5 When the chicken is cooked, leave it to stand for about 10–15 minutes, covered in foil, before carving. Serve garnished with parsley or coriander.

Tagine Energy 585kcal/2422kJ; Protein 40.4g; Carbohydrate 0.4g, of which sugars 0.3g; Fat 46.7g, of which saturates 11.7g; Cholesterol 208mg; Calcium 68mg; Fibre 1.9g; Sodium 1151mg.
Moroccan Chicken Energy 345kcal/1463kJ; Protein 37.4g; Carbohydrate 40.2g, of which sugars 39.9g; Fat 5g, of which saturates 2.4g; Cholesterol 113mg; Calcium 38mg; Fibre 1.3g; Sodium 147mg.

Roasted Chicken with Grapes and Fresh Root Ginger

Oven-roasted chicken with a delicious blend of spices and sweet fruit.

Serves 4

115–130g/4–4½oz fresh root ginger, grated
6–8 garlic cloves, roughly chopped
juice of 1 lemon
about 30ml/2 tbsp olive oil
2–3 large pinches of ground cinnamon
1–1.6kg/2¼–3½lb chicken
500g/1¼lb seeded red and green grapes
500g/1¼lb seedless green grapes
5–7 shallots, chopped
about 250ml/8fl oz/1 cup chicken stock
salt and ground black pepper

1 Mix together half the ginger, the garlic, half the lemon juice, the oil, cinnamon and seasoning. Rub over the chicken and set aside.

2 Meanwhile, cut the red and green seeded grapes in half, remove the seeds and set aside. Add the whole green seedless grapes to the halved ones.

3 Preheat the oven to 180°C/350°F/Gas 4. Heat a heavy frying pan or flameproof casserole until hot. Remove the chicken from the marinade and cook in the pan until browned on all sides.

4 Put a few shallots into the chicken cavity with the garlic and ginger from the marinade and as many of the red and green grapes as will fit. Roast for 40–60 minutes, or until cooked.

5 Remove the chicken from the pan and keep warm. Pour off any oil from the pan, reserving any sediment in the base. Add the remaining shallots and cook for 5 minutes until softened.

6 Add half the remaining red and green grapes, the remaining ginger, the stock and any juices from the chicken and cook over medium-high heat until the grapes have reduced to a thick sauce. Season with salt, pepper and the remaining lemon juice.

7 Serve the chicken on a warmed serving dish, surrounded by the sauce and the reserved grapes.

Risotto with Chicken

This slowly simmered dish is a classic combination of creamy rice and tender cubes of chicken, flavoured with aromatic saffron, prosciutto, white wine and Parmesan cheese.

Serves 6

30ml/2 tbsp olive oil
225g/8oz boneless chicken breast fillets, cut into bitesize cubes
1 onion, finely chopped
1 garlic clove, finely chopped
450g/1lb/2¼ cups risotto rice
1.5ml/¼ tsp saffron threads
120ml/4fl oz/½ cup dry white wine
1.75 litres/3 pints/7½ cups hot chicken stock
50g/2oz prosciutto, cut into thin strips
30ml/2 tbsp butter, diced
25g/1oz/⅓ cup freshly grated Parmesan cheese, plus extra to serve
salt and ground black pepper
fresh parsley sprigs, to garnish

1 Heat the oil in a large frying pan and fry the cubes of chicken, stirring occasionally, until they start to turn white. Reduce the heat to low and add the chopped onion and garlic. Cook, stirring occasionally, until the onion is soft.

2 Stir in the risotto rice, then cook for 2 minutes, stirring constantly, until all the grains are coated in oil. Add the dry white wine to the rice mixture and cook, stirring constantly, until all the wine has been absorbed. Add the saffron threads to the hot stock, and stir well.

3 Add ladlefuls of the hot saffron stock to the rice mixture, allowing each ladleful to be fully absorbed by the rice before adding the next one.

4 When the rice is about three-quarters cooked, add the strips of prosciutto and stir well to combine. Continue cooking, stirring occasionally, until the rice is just tender and the risotto is creamy.

5 Add the butter and the Parmesan, and stir well. Season with salt and ground black pepper to taste. Serve the risotto hot, sprinkled with a little more Parmesan and garnished with parsley sprigs.

Roast Energy 454kcal/1891kJ; Protein 31.6g; Carbohydrate 19.5g, of which sugars 19.5g; Fat 28.1g, of which saturates 7.1g; Cholesterol 165mg; Calcium 28mg; Fibre 1g; Sodium 116mg.
Risotto Energy 418kcal/1744kJ; Protein 17.9g; Carbohydrate 60.9g, of which sugars 0.8g; Fat 9.5g, of which saturates 3.8g; Cholesterol 44mg; Calcium 72mg; Fibre 0.1g; Sodium 194mg.

Chicken and Split Pea Koresh

This is a Californian version of the traditional Persian koresh, a thick, slow-cooked stew served with rice.

Serves 4–6

50g/2oz/¼ cup green split peas
45–60ml/3–4 tbsp olive oil
1 large or 2 small onions, finely chopped
500g/1¼lb chicken thighs, bones removed
500ml/17fl oz/2¼ cups chicken stock
5ml/1 tsp ground turmeric
2.5ml/½ tsp ground cinnamon
1.5ml/¼ tsp grated nutmeg
2 aubergines (eggplants), diced
8–10 ripe tomatoes, diced
2 garlic cloves, crushed
30ml/2 tbsp dried mint
salt and ground black pepper
fresh mint, to garnish
rice, to serve

1 Put the split peas in a bowl, pour over cold water to cover, then leave to soak for about 4 hours. Drain well.

2 Heat a little of the oil in a pan, add two-thirds of the onions and cook for about 5 minutes. Add the chicken and cook until golden brown on all sides.

3 Add the soaked split peas to the chicken mixture, then the stock, turmeric, cinnamon and nutmeg. Cook over medium-low heat for about 40 minutes, until the split peas are tender.

4 Heat the remaining oil in a pan, add the aubergines and remaining onions and cook until lightly browned and tender. Add the tomatoes, garlic and mint. Season.

5 Just before serving, stir the aubergine mixture into the chicken and split pea stew. Garnish with fresh mint leaves and serve with rice.

Variation
To make a traditional lamb koresh, use 675g/1½lb lamb chunks in place of the chicken. Add to the onions, pour over water to cover and cook for 1½ hours until tender, then proceed as above.

Yogurt Chicken and Rice

An unusual dish in which marinated chicken is layered between flavoured and plain rice and then slowly baked in the oven.

Serves 6

40g/1½oz/3 tbsp butter
1.3–1.6kg/3–3½ lb chicken
1 large onion, chopped
250ml/8fl oz/1 cup chicken stock
2 eggs
475ml/16fl oz/2 cups natural (plain) yogurt
2–3 saffron threads, dissolved in 15ml/1 tbsp boiling water
5ml/1 tsp ground cinnamon
450g/1lb/2¼ cups basmati rice
75g/3oz zereshk or dried cranberries
salt and ground black pepper
herb salad, to serve

1 Melt 25g/1oz/2 tbsp of the butter, and fry the chicken and onion for 4–5 minutes until the onion is softened and the chicken browned. Add the chicken stock, season with salt and pepper, and bring to the boil. Reduce the heat and simmer gently, uncovered, for about 45 minutes or until the chicken is cooked and the stock reduced by half.

2 Remove the chicken and leave until cool enough to handle. Skin and bone the chicken, cut the flesh into large pieces and place in a large bowl. Reserve the stock.

3 In a bowl, beat the eggs and blend with the yogurt. Add the saffron water and cinnamon, and season with salt and pepper. Pour over the chicken and leave to marinate for up to 2 hours.

4 Cook the rice in a large pan of boiling salted water for about 5 minutes, then reduce the heat and simmer very gently for 10 minutes, or until half cooked. Drain, rinse in lukewarm water and drain again.

5 Transfer the chicken from the yogurt mixture to another bowl and mix half the rice into the yogurt mixture. Preheat the oven to 160°C/325°F/Gas 3 and grease a large 10cm/4in deep ovenproof dish.

6 Place the rice and yogurt mixture in the bottom of the dish, arrange the chicken pieces in a layer on top and then add the plain rice. Sprinkle with the zereshk or cranberries.

7 Mix the remaining butter with the reserved chicken stock and pour over the rice. Cover tightly with foil and cook in the oven for 35–45 minutes.

8 Leave the dish to cool for a few minutes. Place on a cold, damp cloth, which will help lift the rice from the bottom of the dish, then run a knife around the edges of the dish. Place a large flat plate over the dish, invert and turn out. You should have a rice 'cake' which can then be cut into wedges. Serve these wedges immediately, with a herb salad.

Cook's Tip
Zereshk is a small sour berry that grows on trees by the water in the warmer part of Iran. It is traditionally served with Persian rice dishes.

Chicken Koresh Energy 208kcal/875kJ; Protein 19.8g; Carbohydrate 14.2g, of which sugars 8.5g; Fat 8.5g, of which saturates 1.6g; Cholesterol 79mg; Calcium 38mg; Fibre 3.8g; Sodium 85mg.
Yogurt Chicken Energy 682kcal/2843kJ; Protein 43.4g; Carbohydrate 69g, of which sugars 8.2g; Fat 25.7g, of which saturates 10.2g; Cholesterol 220mg; Calcium 198mg; Fibre 0.6g; Sodium 250mg.

Chicken Stuffed with Lamb and Rice

Delicious, oven-roasted chickens are stuffed with a blend of meat, nuts and rice.

Serves 6–8

2 x 1kg/2¼lb chickens
about 15g/½oz/1 tbsp butter
natural (plain) yogurt and salad, to serve

For the stuffing

45ml/3 tbsp oil
1 onion, chopped
450g/1lb minced (ground) lamb
75g/3oz/¾ cup almonds, chopped
75g/3oz/¾ cup pine nuts
350g/12oz/1½ cups cooked rice
salt and ground black pepper

1 Preheat the oven to 180°C/350°F/Gas 4. To make the stuffing, heat the oil in a large frying pan and cook the onion over low heat until slightly softened. Add the minced lamb and cook over a moderate heat for 4–8 minutes until well browned, stirring frequently. Set aside.

2 Heat a small, heavy pan over a moderate heat and dry-fry the almonds and pine nuts for about 2–3 minutes until they have turned golden brown. Shake the pan frequently to prevent them from burning.

3 In a large bowl, stir together the meat mixture, almonds, pine nuts and cooked rice until well blended. Season to taste with salt and ground black pepper.

4 Spoon the stuffing mixture into the body cavities of the two chickens. (Any leftover stuffing can be cooked separately in a greased ovenproof dish alongside the chicken. It will take about 30 minutes.) Rub the chickens all over with the butter.

5 Place the chickens in a large roasting pan, cover with foil and bake in the oven for about 45–60 minutes. After they have been in for about 30 minutes, remove the foil and baste the chickens with the cooking juices.

6 Continue roasting without the foil until the chickens are cooked through: the juices will run clear when the thickest part of the thigh is pierced with a skewer or knife. Serve the chickens, cut into portions, with yogurt and a salad.

Chicken Piri-piri

This spicy, slow-baked rice dish features a hot sauce made from Angolan chillies.

Serves 4

4 chicken breast fillets, skin on
30–45ml/2–3 tbsp olive oil
1 large onion, finely sliced
2 carrots, cut into thin strips
1 large parsnip or 2 small parsnips, cut into thin strips
1 red (bell) pepper, seeded and sliced
1 yellow (bell) pepper, seeded and sliced
1 litre/1¾ pints/4 cups chicken or vegetable stock
3 tomatoes, peeled, seeded and chopped
generous dash of piri-piri sauce
15ml/1 tbsp tomato purée (paste)
½ cinnamon stick
1 fresh thyme sprig, plus extra fresh thyme to garnish
1 bay leaf
275g/10oz/1½ cups white long grain rice
15ml/1 tbsp lime or lemon juice
salt and ground black pepper

1 Preheat the oven to 180°C/350°F/Gas 4. Season the chicken skin with salt and pepper. Heat 30ml/2 tbsp oil in a large frying pan, add the chicken fillets and cook, turning occasionally, until browned on all sides. Transfer to a plate, leaving the oil in the pan.

2 Add the onion to the pan and fry for 3 minutes until just soft. Add the carrots, parsnip and peppers and cook for 4 minutes. Cover the pan and cook until the vegetables are quite soft.

3 Pour in the stock, then add the tomatoes, piri-piri sauce, tomato purée and cinnamon. Stir in the thyme and bay leaf. Season to taste and bring to the boil. Using a ladle, spoon off 300ml/½ pint/1¼ cups of the liquid and set aside in a pan.

4 Put the rice into a large ovenproof dish. Transfer the cooked vegetables on to the rice. Top with the chicken fillets and pour over the stock from the frying pan. Cover and cook in the oven for 45 minutes, until the rice and chicken are tender.

5 Meanwhile, heat the reserved chicken stock, adding a few more drops of piri-piri sauce and the lime or lemon juice. Spoon the chicken and rice on to warmed serving plates. Serve the remaining sauce separately or poured over the chicken.

Chicken with Lamb Energy 687kcal/2856kJ; Protein 45.8g; Carbohydrate 15.1g, of which sugars 1.2g; Fat 49.6g, of which saturates 12.4g; Cholesterol 203mg; Calcium 55mg; Fibre 1g; Sodium 166mg.
Chicken Piri-piri Energy 557kcal/2337kJ; Protein 44.3g; Carbohydrate 75.4g, of which sugars 15.5g; Fat 8.8g, of which saturates 1.5g; Cholesterol 105mg; Calcium 73mg; Fibre 5.8g; Sodium 122mg.

Spicy Chicken Stew with Egg

A delicious, mildly spiced stew that is made in the slow cooker. Hard-boiled eggs are added towards the end of the cooking to soak up the flavour of the spices.

Serves 4

30ml/2 tbsp vegetable oil
2 large onions, chopped
3 garlic cloves, chopped
2.5cm/1in piece peeled and finely chopped fresh root ginger
175ml/6fl oz/¾ cup chicken or vegetable stock
250ml/8fl oz/1 cup passata (bottled strained tomatoes) or 400g/14oz can chopped tomatoes
seeds from 5 cardamom pods
2.5ml/½ tsp ground turmeric
large pinch of ground cinnamon
large pinch of ground cloves
large pinch of grated nutmeg
1.3kg/3lb chicken, cut into 8–12 portions
4 hard-boiled eggs
cayenne pepper or hot paprika, to taste
salt and ground black pepper
roughly chopped fresh coriander (cilantro) and onion rings, to garnish
flatbreads or boiled rice, to serve

1 Heat the oil in a large pan, add the onions and cook for 10 minutes until softened. Add the garlic and ginger and cook for 1–2 minutes.

2 Add the stock and the passata or chopped tomatoes to the pan. Bring to the boil and cook, stirring frequently, for about 10 minutes, or until the mixture has thickened, then season.

3 Transfer the mixture to the ceramic cooking pot and stir in the cardamom seeds, turmeric, cinnamon, cloves and grated nutmeg. Add the chicken in a single layer, pushing the pieces down into the sauce. Cover with the lid and cook on the high setting for 3 hours.

4 Remove the shells from the eggs, then prick them a few times with a fork or very fine skewer. Add to the sauce and cook for 30–45 minutes, or until the chicken is cooked through and tender. Season to taste with cayenne pepper or hot paprika. Garnish with coriander and onion rings and serve with flatbread or rice.

East African Roast Chicken

Smothered in a generous layer of butter combined with spices, herbs and coconut milk, this chicken is left to stand overnight to allow the flavours to mingle.

Serves 6

1.8kg/4lb chicken
30ml/2 tbsp softened butter, plus extra for basting
3 garlic cloves, crushed
5ml/1 tsp ground black pepper
5ml/1 tsp ground turmeric
2.5ml/½ tsp ground cumin
5ml/1 tsp dried thyme
15ml/1 tbsp finely chopped fresh coriander (cilantro)
60ml/4 tbsp thick coconut milk
60ml/4 tbsp medium-dry sherry
5ml/1 tsp tomato purée (paste)
salt and chilli powder
fresh coriander (cilantro) leaves, to garnish

1 Remove the giblets from the chicken, if necessary, rinse out the cavity and pat the skin dry. Put the butter and all the remaining ingredients in a bowl and mix together well to form a thick paste.

2 Gently ease the skin of the chicken away from the flesh and rub the flesh generously with the herb and butter mixture. Rub more of the mixture over the skin, legs and wings of the chicken and into the neck cavity.

3 Place the chicken in a roasting pan, cover loosely with foil and leave to marinate overnight in the refrigerator.

4 Preheat the oven to 190°C/375°F/Gas 5. Cover the chicken with clean foil and roast for 1 hour, then turn the chicken over and baste with the pan juices. Cover again with foil and cook for 30 minutes.

5 Remove the foil and place the chicken breast side up. Rub with a little extra butter and roast for a further 10–15 minutes until the juices run clear, rather than pink, when the thickest part of the thigh is pierced with a skewer or knife and the skin is golden brown.

6 Allow the chicken to rest for 10–15 minutes in a warm place before serving, garnished with coriander leaves.

Spicy Chicken Stew Energy 388kcal/1629kJ; Protein 54.6g; Carbohydrate 13g, of which sugars 9.6g; Fat 13.4g, of which saturates 2.8g; Cholesterol 13mg; Calcium 81mg; Fibre 2.5g; Sodium 311mg.
Roast Chicken Energy 449kcal/1862kJ; Protein 36.8g; Carbohydrate 3.4g, of which sugars 1.3g; Fat 30.9g, of which saturates 8.9g; Cholesterol 187mg; Calcium 31mg; Fibre 0.1g; Sodium 172mg.

Spicy Chicken with Horseradish

This oven-baked dish can also be cooked on the barbecue.

Serves 4

45ml/3 tbsp vegetable oil
1 large onion, chopped
175ml/6fl oz/¾ cup tomato ketchup
175ml/6fl oz/¾ cup water
40ml/2½ tbsp fresh lemon juice
25ml/1½ tbsp grated horseradish
15ml/1 tbsp soft light brown sugar
15ml/1 tbsp French mustard
1.3kg/3lb chicken portions
cooked rice, to serve

1 Preheat the oven to 180°C/350°F/Gas 4. Heat 15ml/1 tbsp of oil in a pan. Add the onion and cook for 5 minutes until soft. Stir in the ketchup, water, lemon juice, horseradish, sugar and mustard, and bring to the boil, then simmer for 10 minutes.

2 Heat the remaining oil in a frying pan. Add the chicken portions and brown on all sides. Place in a large ovenproof dish and pour over the sauce. Bake in the oven for 1¼ hours until the chicken is cooked, basting occasionally. Serve on a bed of rice.

Fragrant Chicken Curry

A delicously spicy curry that is ideal for the slow cooker.

Serves 4

75g/3oz/scant ½ cup red lentils, rinsed and drained
30ml/2 tbsp mild curry powder
10ml/2 tsp ground coriander
5ml/1 tsp cumin seeds
350ml/12fl oz/1½ cups boiling vegetable or chicken stock
8 chicken thighs, skinned
225g/8oz fresh shredded spinach
15ml/1 tbsp chopped fresh coriander (cilantro)
salt and ground black pepper
sprigs of fresh coriander, to garnish
rice and poppadums, to serve

1 Place the lentils in the ceramic cooking pot with the curry powder, ground coriander, cumin seeds and stock. Cover and cook on high for 2 hours. Add the chicken to the lentils, cover and cook on high for 3 hours, or until the chicken is just tender.

2 Add the spinach, cover and cook for 30 minutes. Stir in the coriander and season. Garnish with coriander and serve.

Stuffed Roast Masala Chicken

This slow-roasted chicken is smothered in a spicy coating.

Serves 4–6

1 sachet saffron powder
2.5ml/½ tsp grated nutmeg
15ml/1 tbsp warm milk
1.3kg/3lb chicken
90ml/6 tbsp ghee or melted butter
50g/2oz/½ cup desiccated (dry unsweetened shredded) coconut, toasted
steamed carrots, to serve

For the stuffing

3 onions, finely chopped
2 fresh green chillies, chopped
50g/2oz/scant ½ cup sultanas (golden raisins)
50g/2oz/½ cup ground almonds
50g/2oz/¼ cup dried apricots, soaked in water until soft
3 hard-boiled eggs, coarsely chopped
salt

For the masala

4 spring onions (scallions), chopped
2 garlic cloves, crushed
5ml/1 tsp five-spice powder
4–6 green cardamom pods
2.5ml/½ tsp ground turmeric
5ml/1 tsp ground black pepper
30ml/2 tbsp natural (plain) yogurt
75ml/5 tbsp hot water

1 Preheat the oven to 180°C/350°F/Gas 4. Mix the saffron, nutmeg and milk. Brush the inside of the chicken with the mixture and spread some under the skin.

2 Heat 60ml/4 tbsp of the ghee or butter in a frying pan and fry the chicken all over. Remove from the pan and keep warm.

3 To make the stuffing, fry the onions, chillies and sultanas for 2–3 minutes in the same ghee or butter. Remove from the heat, allow to cool, then mix in the ground almonds, apricots, chopped eggs and salt, and use to stuff the chicken.

4 To make the masala, heat the remaining ghee or butter in a pan and gently fry all the ingredients except the water for 2–3 minutes. Add to the water in a roasting pan.

5 Place the chicken on the masala, and roast in the oven for 1 hour. Remove the chicken, set aside and keep warm. Return the masala to the pan and cook until reduced. Pour over the chicken. Sprinkle with the toasted desiccated coconut and serve with steamed carrots.

Spicy Chicken Energy 481kcal/1997kJ; Protein 40.8g; Carbohydrate 1g, of which sugars 0.1g; Fat 34.8g, of which saturates 8.9g; Cholesterol 215mg; Calcium 14mg; Fibre 0.3g; Sodium 147mg.
Fragrant Chicken Energy 591kcal/2490kJ; Protein 75.5g; Carbohydrate 38.2g, of which sugars 3.9g; Fat 16.1g, of which saturates 3.9g; Cholesterol 171mg; Calcium 426mg; Fibre 9.4g; Sodium 880mg.
Masala Chicken Energy 658kcal/2727kJ; Protein 34.1g; Carbohydrate 17.9g, of which sugars 14.9g; Fat 50.5g, of which saturates 19.2g; Cholesterol 234mg; Calcium 95mg; Fibre 3.7g; Sodium 158mg.

Curried Apricot and Chicken Casserole with Almond Rice

A mildly spiced and fruity chicken dish, slowly baked in the oven and served with almond rice.

Serves 4

15ml/1 tbsp oil
8 large chicken thighs, skinned and boned
1 onion, finely chopped
5ml/1 tsp medium curry powder
30ml/2 tbsp plain (all-purpose) flour
450ml/¾ pint/scant 2 cups hot chicken stock
juice of 1 large orange
8 ready-to-eat dried apricots, halved
15ml/1 tbsp sultanas (golden raisins)
salt and ground black pepper

For the almond rice

225g/8oz/1 cup cooked rice
15g/½oz/1 tbsp butter
50g/2oz/½ cup toasted almonds

1 Preheat the oven to 190°C/375°F/Gas 5. Heat the oil in a large frying pan. Cut the chicken into cubes and brown quickly all over in the oil. Add the onion and cook gently until soft and lightly browned.

2 Transfer to a large, flameproof casserole, sprinkle in the curry powder and cook again for a few minutes. Add the flour, and blend in the stock and orange juice. Bring to the boil and season with salt and pepper.

3 Add the apricots and sultanas, cover with a tight-fitting lid and cook in the oven for 1 hour, or until tender. Adjust the seasoning to taste.

4 To make the almond rice, reheat the pre-cooked rice with the butter and season to taste. Stir in the toasted almonds. Serve alongside the chicken.

Variation

This recipe also works well with chicken breast fillets or with diced turkey breast fillets or other boneless turkey meat. Replace the chicken thighs with the same quantity of other meat.

Classic Tandoori Chicken

This is probably the most famous of all the Indian slow-cooked dishes. You need to marinate the chicken well and cook it in an extremely hot oven for a clay-oven-baked taste. If you want authentic 'burnt' spots on the chicken, place the dish under a hot grill for a few minutes after baking.

Serves 4–6

1.5kg/3lb oven-ready chicken
250ml/8fl oz/1 cup natural (plain) yogurt, beaten
60ml/4 tbsp tandoori masala paste
75g/3oz/6 tbsp ghee or butter
salt
salad leaves, to serve
lemon twist and onion slices, to garnish

1 Using a sharp knife or scissors, remove the skin from the chicken and trim off any excess fat. Using a fork, beat the flesh at random.

2 Cut the chicken in half down the centre and through the breast. Cut each piece in half again. Make a few deep gashes diagonally into the flesh. Mix the yogurt with the masala paste and salt. Spread the chicken evenly with the yogurt mixture, spreading some into the gashes. Cover with cling film (plastic wrap) and leave for at least 2 hours, but preferably overnight.

3 Preheat the oven to maximum heat. Place the chicken quarters on a wire rack in a deep baking tray. Spread the chicken with any excess marinade, reserving a little for basting halfway through cooking time.

4 Melt the ghee and pour over the chicken to seal the surface. This helps to keep the centre moist during the roasting period. Cook in the preheated oven for 10 minutes, then remove, leaving the oven on.

5 Baste the chicken pieces with the remaining marinade. Return to the oven and switch off the heat. Leave the chicken in the oven for about 15–20 minutes without opening the door. Serve on a bed of salad leaves and garnish with the lemon twist and onion slices.

Chicken Casserole Energy 500kcal/2105kJ; Protein 54.1g; Carbohydrate 37g, of which sugars 13.2g; Fat 16g, of which saturates 3.6g; Cholesterol 148mg; Calcium 86mg; Fibre 3.1g; Sodium 150mg.
Tandoori Chicken Energy 327kcal/1364kJ; Protein 36g; Carbohydrate 3.9g, of which sugars 1.3g; Fat 18.7g, of which saturates 9.2g; Cholesterol 126mg; Calcium 115mg; Fibre 2.3g; Sodium 287mg.

Chicken in a Cashew Nut Sauce

This mildly spiced, slow-cooker dish has a rich yet delicately flavoured sauce.

Serves 4

1 large onion, roughly chopped
1 clove garlic, crushed
15ml/1 tbsp tomato purée (paste)
50g/2oz/½ cup cashew nuts
7.5ml/1½ tsp garam masala
5ml/1 tsp chilli powder
1.5ml/¼ tsp ground turmeric
5ml/1 tsp salt
15ml/1 tbsp lemon juice
15ml/1 tbsp natural (plain) yogurt
30ml/2 tbsp vegetable oil
450g/1lb chicken breast fillets, skinned and cubed
175g/6oz/2¼ cups button (white) mushrooms
15ml/1 tbsp sultanas (golden raisins)
300ml/½ pint/1¼ cups chicken or vegetable stock
30ml/2 tbsp chopped fresh coriander (cilantro), plus extra to garnish
rice and fruit chutney, to serve

1 Put the onion, garlic, tomato purée, cashew nuts, garam masala, chilli powder, turmeric, salt, lemon juice and yogurt in a food processor and process to a paste.

2 Heat the oil in a large frying pan or wok and fry the cubes of chicken for a few minutes, or until just beginning to brown. Using a slotted spoon, transfer the chicken to the ceramic cooking pot, leaving the oil in the pan.

3 Add the spice paste and mushrooms to the pan, lower the heat and fry gently, stirring frequently, for 3–4 minutes. Transfer the mixture to the ceramic pot.

4 Add the sultanas to the pot and stir in the chicken or vegetable stock. Cover with the lid and switch the slow cooker to high. Cook for 3–4 hours, stirring halfway through the cooking time. The chicken should be cooked through and very tender, and the sauce fairly thick.

5 Stir the chopped coriander into the sauce, then taste and add a little more salt and pepper, if necessary. Serve the curry from the ceramic cooking pot or transfer to a warmed serving dish and garnish with a sprinkling of chopped fresh coriander. Serve with rice and a fruit chutney, such as mango.

Chicken Korma

The use of ground almonds to thicken the sauce gives this mild, slow-cooker curry a beautifully creamy texture.

Serves 4

75g/3oz/¾ cup flaked (sliced) almonds
15ml/1 tbsp ghee or butter
675g/1½lb skinless chicken breast fillets, cut into bitesize pieces
about 15ml/1 tbsp sunflower oil
1 onion, chopped
4 green cardamom pods
2 garlic cloves, crushed
10ml/2 tsp ground cumin
5ml/1 tsp ground coriander
pinch of ground turmeric
1 cinnamon stick
good pinch of chilli powder
250ml/8fl oz/1 cup coconut milk
120ml/4fl oz/½ cup boiling chicken stock
5ml/1 tsp tomato purée (paste) (optional)
75ml/5 tbsp single (light) cream
15–30ml/1–2 tbsp fresh lime or lemon juice
10ml/2 tsp grated lime or lemon rind
5ml/1 tsp garam masala
salt and ground black pepper
saffron rice and poppadums, to serve

1 Dry-fry the almonds in a frying pan until pale golden. Transfer two-thirds of the almonds to a plate and dry-fry the remainder until deeper in colour. Set aside the darker almonds for the garnish. Leave the paler almonds to cool, then grind them until fine in a spice grinder or coffee mill used for the purpose.

2 Heat the ghee or butter in the frying pan and gently fry the chicken pieces until evenly brown. Transfer to a plate. Heat the oil and cook the onion for 8 minutes. Stir in the cardamom pods and garlic and fry for 2 minutes, until the onion is soft.

3 Add the ground almonds, cumin, coriander, turmeric, cinnamon stick and chilli powder to the frying pan and cook for 1 minute. Transfer to the ceramic cooking pot and set to high. Add the coconut milk, stock and tomato purée, if using, to the pot and stir in. Add the chicken and season. Cover with the lid and cook for 3 hours, or until the chicken is cooked and very tender.

4 Stir the cream, citrus juice and rind and garam masala into the curry. Cook on high for 30 minutes. Garnish with the reserved almonds, and serve with saffron rice and poppadums.

Chicken in Cashew Sauce Energy 239kcal/1006kJ; Protein 31.6g; Carbohydrate 10.7g, of which sugars 7.6g; Fat 8.1g, of which saturates 1.7g; Cholesterol 78.9mg; Calcium 39mg; Fibre 1.9g; Sodium 696mg.
Chicken Korma Energy 410kcal/1714kJ; Protein 45.7g; Carbohydrate 7.8g, of which sugars 6.4g; Fat 22g, of which saturates 6g; Cholesterol 136mg; Calcium 98mg; Fibre 1.9g; Sodium 202mg.

Chicken Biriani

Easy to make and very tasty, this is the ideal one-pot dish for a family supper.

Serves 4

10 green cardamom pods
275g/10oz/1½ cups basmati rice, soaked and drained
2.5ml/½ tsp salt
2–3 cloves
5cm/2in cinnamon stick
45ml/3 tbsp vegetable oil
3 onions, sliced
4 skinless chicken breast fillets, each about 175g/6oz, cubed
1.5ml/¼ tsp ground cloves
5ml/1 tsp ground cumin
5ml/1 tsp ground coriander
2.5ml/½ tsp ground black pepper
3 garlic cloves, chopped
5ml/1 tsp finely chopped fresh root ginger
juice of 1 lemon
4 tomatoes, sliced
30ml/2 tbsp chopped fresh coriander (cilantro)
150ml/¼ pint/⅔ cup natural (plain) yogurt
4–5 saffron threads, soaked in 10ml/2 tsp hot milk
150ml/¼ pint/⅔ cup water
toasted flaked (sliced) almonds and fresh coriander (cilantro) sprigs, to garnish
natural (plain) yogurt, to serve

1 Preheat the oven to 190°C/375°F/Gas 5. Remove the seeds from half the cardamom pods and grind them finely, using a mortar and pestle. Set the seeds aside.

2 Bring a flameproof casserole of water to the boil and add the soaked and drained rice, then stir in the salt, the remaining whole cardamom pods, cloves and cinnamon stick. Boil the rice for 2 minutes, then drain, leaving the whole spices in the rice.

3 Heat the oil in the flameproof casserole and fry the onions for 8 minutes, until soft and browned. Add the chicken and the ground spices, including the ground cardamom seeds. Mix well, then add the garlic, ginger and lemon juice. Stir-fry for 5 minutes.

4 Arrange the sliced tomatoes on top. Sprinkle on the coriander, spoon the yogurt on top and cover with the rice.

5 Drizzle the saffron milk over the rice and add the water. Cover and bake for 1 hour. Garnish with the almonds and coriander and serve with the yogurt.

Chicken with Cajun Sauce

Real Cajun sauce is made from a Cajun roux and then slowly simmered to make a richly flavoured coating for the chicken pieces.

Serves 4

115g/4oz/1 cup plain (all-purpose) flour
1.6kg/3½lb chicken, cut into 8 portions
250ml/8fl oz/1 cup buttermilk
vegetable oil, for frying
salt and ground black pepper
fresh parsley sprigs, to garnish

For the sauce

115g/4oz/½ cup lard or white cooking fat, or vegetable oil
65g/2½oz/9 tbsp plain (all-purpose) flour
2 onions, chopped
2–3 celery sticks, chopped
1 large green (bell) pepper, seeded and chopped
2 garlic cloves, finely chopped
250ml/8fl oz/1 cup passata (bottled strained tomatoes)
450ml/¾ pint/scant 2 cups red wine or chicken stock
225g/8oz tomatoes, peeled and chopped
2 bay leaves
15ml/1 tbsp soft light brown sugar
5ml/1 tsp grated orange rind
2.5ml/ ½ tsp cayenne pepper

1 To make the sauce, melt the lard, white cooking fat or oil and stir in the flour. Cook over low heat, stirring, for about 15–20 minutes or until golden brown.

2 Add the onions, celery, green pepper and garlic and cook, stirring, until softened. Stir in the remaining sauce ingredients and season with salt and ground black pepper. Bring the sauce to the boil, then simmer for 1 hour or until the sauce is rich and thick. Stir from time to time.

3 Meanwhile, prepare the chicken. Put the flour in a plastic bag and season with salt and pepper. Dip each portion of chicken in the buttermilk, then place in the bag and shake until coated in the seasoned flour. Set aside for 20 minutes.

4 Heat 2.5cm/1in oil in a frying pan. Gently fry the chicken portions, turning occasionally, for 30 minutes until deep golden and cooked. Drain on kitchen paper. Add them to the sauce, garnish with parsley and serve.

Chicken Biriani Energy 563kcal/2359kJ; Protein 45.4g; Carbohydrate 70g, of which sugars 12.5g; Fat 11.3g, of which saturates 1.7g; Cholesterol 105mg; Calcium 152mg; Fibre 3.2g; Sodium 138mg.
Chicken with Cajun Energy 934kcal/3893kJ; Protein 53.7g; Carbohydrate 49.3g, of which sugars 14.6g; Fat 59.3g, of which saturates 13.8g; Cholesterol 242mg; Calcium 181mg; Fibre 3.3g; Sodium 372mg.

Filipino Chicken Pot

Chicken portions are slowly simmered in a rich stock with pork and chorizo in this nourishing dish, which is served in two courses.

Serves 4–6

3 chicken legs
15ml/1 tbsp vegetable oil
350g/12oz lean pork, diced
1 chorizo sausage, sliced (optional)
1 small carrot, roughly chopped
1 onion, roughly chopped
175g/6oz/1 cup dried haricot (navy) beans, soaked in water overnight
1.75 litres/3 pints/7½ cups water
1 garlic clove, crushed
30ml/2 tbsp tomato purée (paste)
1 bay leaf
2 chicken stock (bouillon) cubes
350g/12oz sweet potatoes or new potatoes, peeled
10ml/2 tsp chilli sauce
30ml/2 tbsp white wine vinegar
3 firm tomatoes, peeled, seeded and chopped
225g/8oz Chinese leaves (Chinese cabbage), shredded
salt and ground black pepper
3 spring onions (scallions), shredded, to garnish
boiled rice, to serve

1 Divide the chicken drumsticks from the thighs. Chop off the narrow end of each drumstick and discard.

2 Heat the oil in a wok or large pan, add the chicken, pork, chorizo, if using, carrot and onion, and brown evenly.

3 Drain and rinse the haricot beans; drain again. Add to the chicken with the water, garlic, tomato purée and bay leaf. Bring to the boil and simmer for 2 hours.

4 Crumble in the chicken stock cubes, add the sweet or new potatoes and the chilli sauce, then simmer for 15–20 minutes until the potatoes are cooked.

5 Add the vinegar, tomatoes and Chinese leaves, and simmer for 2–3 minutes. Season to taste with salt and pepper.

6 The dish is intended to provide enough liquid to be served separately as a first-course soup. This is followed by a main course of the meat and vegetables, sprinkled with the shredded spring onions. Serve with rice as an accompaniment.

Chicken with Chipotle Sauce

Spicy-hot and deliciously rich and smoky, this dish of chicken in a rich chilli sauce is made in the slow cooker. It is great served with rice for a tasty, healthy supper.

Serves 6

6 chipotle chillies
200ml/7fl oz/scant 1 cup boiling water
about 200ml/7fl oz/scant 1 cup chicken stock
45ml/3 tbsp vegetable oil
3 onions
6 chicken breast fillets
salt and ground black pepper
fresh oregano, to garnish

1 Put the dried chillies in a bowl and cover with the boiling water. Leave to stand for about 30 minutes until very soft. Drain, reserving the soaking water in a measuring jug (cup). Cut off the stalk from each chilli, then slit the chilli lengthways and scrape out the seeds with a small, sharp knife.

2 Chop the chillies roughly and put in a food processor or blender. Add enough chicken stock to the soaking water to make it up to 400ml/14fl oz/1⅔ cups, then pour into the food processor or blender. Process until smooth.

3 Heat the oil in a frying pan. Halve and slice the onions and add them to the pan. Cook, stirring, over medium heat for 5 minutes, or until soft but not coloured.

4 Transfer the onions to the ceramic cooking pot and set the slow cooker to the high setting. Sprinkle the onion slices with a little salt and ground black pepper.

5 Remove the skin from the chicken breast fillets and trim off any pieces of fat. Arrange the fillets in a single layer on top of the onion slices in the ceramic cooking pot. Sprinkle with a little salt and several grindings of black pepper.

6 Pour the chilli paste over the chicken fillets, making sure that each piece is evenly coated. Cover the slow cooker with the lid and cook for about 3–4 hours, or until the chicken is cooked through but still moist and tender. Garnish with fresh oregano and serve with rice, if you like.

Filipino Chicken Energy 304kcal/1285kJ; Protein 29.1g; Carbohydrate 31.2g, of which sugars 9.6g; Fat 7.9g, of which saturates 2g; Cholesterol 80mg; Calcium 81mg; Fibre 7.9g; Sodium 132mg.
Chicken with Chipotle Energy 235kcal/989kJ; Protein 36.9g; Carbohydrate 5.9g, of which sugars 4.2g; Fat 7.3g, of which saturates 1.1g; Cholesterol 105mg; Calcium 26mg; Fibre 1.1g; Sodium 92mg.

Spicy Peanut Chicken

Smooth peanut butter adds a special richness to this spicy, slow-cooker rice dish.

Serves 4

4 skinless chicken breast fillets
45ml/3 tbsp groundnut (peanut) or sunflower oil
1 garlic clove, crushed
5ml/1 tsp chopped fresh thyme
15ml/1 tbsp curry powder
juice of ½ lemon
1 onion, finely chopped
2 tomatoes, peeled, seeded and chopped
1 fresh green chilli, seeded and sliced
60ml/4 tbsp smooth peanut butter
750ml/1¼ pints/3 cups boiling chicken stock
300g/11oz/1½ cups easy-cook (converted) white rice
salt and ground black pepper
lemon or lime wedges and sprigs of fresh flat leaf parsley, to garnish

1 Cut the chicken breast fillets into thin strips. In a bowl, mix together 15ml/1 tbsp of the oil with the garlic, thyme, curry powder and lemon juice. Add the chicken strips and stir well to combine. Cover with clear film (plastic wrap) and leave to marinate in the refrigerator for 1½–2 hours.

2 Meanwhile, heat the remaining oil in a frying pan, add the onion and fry for 10 minutes until soft. Transfer to the ceramic cooking pot and switch the slow cooker to high. Add the chopped tomatoes and chilli and stir to combine.

3 Put the peanut butter into a bowl, then blend in the stock, adding a little at a time. Pour the mixture into the ceramic cooking pot, season with salt and pepper and stir. Cover with the lid and cook for 1 hour.

4 About 30 minutes before the end of cooking time, remove the chicken from the refrigerator and leave it to come to room temperature. Add the chicken and the marinade to the ceramic cooking pot and stir to mix. Re-cover and cook for 1 hour.

5 Sprinkle the rice over the casserole, then stir to mix. Cover and cook for a final 45 minutes to 1 hour, or until the chicken and rice are cooked and tender. Serve immediately, garnished with lemon or lime wedges for squeezing over, and fresh parsley.

Jamaican Jerk Chicken

The word 'jerk' refers to the herb and spice seasoning used to marinate meat in Jamaica. This slow-cooker dish is ideal for cooking chicken in this spicy mix.

Serves 4

8 chicken pieces, such as thighs and legs
15ml/1 tbsp sunflower oil
15g/½ oz/1 tbsp unsalted butter

For the sauce

1 bunch of spring onions (scallions), trimmed and finely chopped
2 garlic cloves, crushed
1 hot red chilli pepper, halved, seeded and finely chopped
5ml/1 tsp ground allspice
2.5ml/½ tsp ground cinnamon
5ml/1 tsp dried thyme
1.5ml/¼ tsp freshly grated nutmeg
10ml/2 tsp demerara (raw) sugar
15ml/1 tbsp plain (all-purpose) flour
300ml/½ pint/1¼ cups hot chicken stock
15ml/1 tbsp red wine or white wine vinegar
15ml/1 tbsp lime juice
10ml/2 tsp tomato purée (paste)
salt and ground black pepper
salad leaves or rice, to serve

1 Wipe the chicken pieces, then pat dry on kitchen paper. Heat the oil and butter in a frying pan, then add the chicken, in batches if necessary, and cook until browned on all sides. Remove with a slotted spoon, leaving the fat in the pan, and transfer to the ceramic cooking pot. Switch the slow cooker to high.

2 Add the spring onions, garlic and chilli to the frying pan and cook gently for 4–5 minutes, or until softened, stirring frequently. Stir in the allspice, cinnamon, thyme, nutmeg and sugar. Sprinkle in the flour and stir to mix, then gradually add the chicken stock, stirring until the mixture bubbles and thickens. Remove the pan from the heat.

3 Stir the vinegar, lime juice, tomato purée and some salt and ground black pepper into the sauce. Pour over the chicken pieces, cover with the lid and cook on high for 3–4 hours, or until the chicken is cooked and very tender.

4 Remove the chicken from the sauce and place on a serving dish. Taste the sauce and adjust the seasoning, then serve separately, with salad leaves or rice as an accompaniment.

Spicy Peanut Chicken Energy 635kcal/2677kJ; Protein 45.8g; Carbohydrate 70.7g, of which sugars 4.4g; Fat 20.8g, of which saturates 4.1g; Cholesterol 105mg; Calcium 65mg; Fibre 2.1g; Sodium 354mg.
Jamaican Jerk Chicken Energy 189kcal/794kJ; Protein 21g; Carbohydrate 7g, of which sugars 3.1g; Fat 8.8g, of which saturates 3.1g; Cholesterol 107mg; Calcium 24mg; Fibre 0.5g; Sodium 238mg.

Spicy Chicken Jambalaya

This classic dish is great for a family supper, and perfect for making in a slow cooker.

Serves 6

225g/8oz skinless chicken breast fillets
175g/6oz piece raw smoked gammon (smoked or cured ham) or bacon
30ml/2 tbsp olive oil
1 large onion, peeled and chopped
2 garlic cloves, crushed
2 sticks celery, diced
5ml/1 tsp chopped fresh thyme or 2.5ml/½ tsp dried thyme
5ml/1 tsp mild chilli powder
2.5ml/½ tsp ground ginger
10ml/2 tsp tomato purée (paste)
2 dashes of Tabasco sauce
750ml/1¼ pints/3 cups boiling chicken stock
300g/11oz/1½ cups easy-cook (converted) rice
115g/4oz chorizo sausage, sliced
30ml/2 tbsp chopped fresh flat leaf parsley, plus extra, to garnish
salt and ground black pepper

1 Cut the chicken into 2.5cm/1in cubes and season. Trim any fat off the gammon or bacon, then cut the meat into 1cm/½in cubes.

2 Heat 15ml/1 tbsp of the olive oil in a pan, add the onion and fry gently for 5 minutes, until beginning to colour. Add the garlic, celery, thyme, chilli powder and ginger and cook for 1 minute. Transfer to the ceramic cooking pot and set to high.

3 Heat the remaining 15ml/1 tbsp olive oil in the pan, add the chicken pieces and fry briefly until lightly browned. Add to the ceramic cooking pot with the gammon or bacon cubes.

4 Add the tomato purée and Tabasco sauce to the stock and stir well. Pour into the pot, cover and cook on high for 1½ hours.

5 Sprinkle the rice into the pot and stir to mix. Cover and cook on high for 45 minutes to 1 hour, or until the rice is almost tender and most of the stock has been absorbed. Add a little extra hot stock or water if the mixture is dry.

6 Stir in the chorizo and cook on high for a further 15 minutes, or until heated through. Stir in the parsley, then taste and adjust the seasoning. Turn off the slow cooker and leave to stand for 10 minutes. Serve garnished with chopped fresh parsley.

Chicken Gumbo with Okra, Ham, Tomatoes and Prawns

A hearty, spicy stew that is ideal for slow baking in the oven in a clay pot.

Serves 4

30ml/2 tbsp olive oil
1 onion, chopped
225g/8oz skinless chicken breast fillets, cut into small chunks
25g/1oz/¼ cup plain (all-purpose) flour
5ml/1 tsp paprika
30ml/2 tbsp tomato purée (paste)
600ml/1 pint/2½ cups hot, well-flavoured chicken stock
400g/14oz can chopped tomatoes with herbs
a few drops of Tabasco
175g/6oz okra
1 red, orange or yellow (bell) pepper, seeded and chopped
2 celery sticks, sliced
225g/8oz/1⅓ cups diced lean cooked ham
225g/8oz large prawns (shrimp), peeled, deveined and heads removed, but with tails intact
salt and ground black pepper
boiled rice, to serve

1 Soak a clay pot or chicken brick in cold water for 20 minutes, then drain. Heat the oil in a large frying pan, add the onion and cook for 5 minutes until soft and golden. Add the chicken to the pan and fry for 1–2 minutes to seal. Stir in the flour, paprika and tomato purée and cook, stirring constantly, for 1–2 minutes.

2 Gradually add the stock, stirring constantly, then bring to the boil. Add the tomatoes, then remove the pan from the heat. Add a few drops of Tabasco and season with salt and pepper.

3 Cut the okra in half if large, then add to the clay pot or chicken brick with the pepper and the sliced celery. Add the chicken and tomato mixture and stir well to mix. Cover the clay pot or chicken brick and place it in an unheated oven. Set the oven to 200°C/400°F/Gas 6 and cook for 30 minutes.

4 Remove the pot or brick from the oven, then add the ham and the prawns and stir well. Cover again and return to the oven for 10 minutes, or until the ham is heated through and the prawns are just cooked. To serve, spoon some boiled rice into warmed plates or bowls and ladle over the gumbo.

Spicy Jambalaya Energy 384kcal/1617kJ; Protein 21.2g; Carbohydrate 48.6g, of which sugars 2.9g; Fat 13g, of which saturates 3.6g; Cholesterol 43mg; Calcium 57mg; Fibre 1.1g; Sodium 630mg.
Chicken Gumbo Energy 290kcal/1221kJ; Protein 37.3g; Carbohydrate 15g, of which sugars 9.6g; Fat 9.4g, of which saturates 1.9g; Cholesterol 182mg; Calcium 153mg; Fibre 4.2g; Sodium 858mg.

Chicken and Prawn Jambalaya

A colourful mixture of rice, peppers and tomatoes with chicken, gammon and prawns is slowly simmered on the stove in one pot.

Serves 10

2 chickens, each about 1.3–1.6kg/3–3½lb
450g/1lb piece raw smoked gammon (smoked or cured ham)
50g/2oz/⅓ cup lard or white cooking fat
50g/2oz/½ cup plain (all-purpose) flour
3 onions, finely sliced
2 green (bell) peppers, seeded and sliced
675g/1½lb tomatoes, peeled and chopped
2–3 garlic cloves, crushed
10ml/2 tsp chopped fresh thyme or 5ml/1 tsp dried thyme
24 raw Mediterranean prawns (jumbo shrimp), peeled with tails intact
500g/1¼lb/2½ cups white long grain rice
1.2 litres/2 pints/5 cups water
2–3 dashes Tabasco sauce
45ml/3 tbsp chopped fresh flat leaf parsley, plus tiny fresh parsley sprigs, to garnish
salt and ground black pepper

1 Cut each chicken into ten pieces and season well with salt and pepper. Dice the gammon, discarding the rind and fat.

2 Melt the lard or white cooking fat in a large, heavy frying pan. Add the chicken in batches and cook until golden brown all over. Lift out with a slotted spoon and set aside. Reduce the heat and sprinkle the flour into the fat in the pan. Stir until the roux turns a golden brown colour. Return the chicken to the pan.

3 Add the gammon, onions, peppers, tomatoes, garlic and thyme and stir well. Cook, stirring regularly, for 10 minutes, then add the prawns and mix lightly. Stir in the rice and pour in the water. Season well with salt, black pepper and Tabasco sauce.

4 Bring to the boil, then cook gently, stirring occasionally, until the rice is tender and the liquid has been absorbed. Add a little extra hot water if it becomes dry. Check the seasoning.

5 Mix the parsley into the finished dish, garnish with sprigs of parsley and serve the jambalaya with plenty of crusty bread.

Fragrant Rice with Chicken, Mint and Nuoc Cham

This refreshing dish greatly benefits from slowly simmering the chicken in a spiced stock, which provides an unforgettably rich and fragrant flavour.

Serves 4

350g/12oz/1¾ cups long grain rice, rinsed and drained
2–3 shallots, halved and sliced
1 bunch of fresh mint, stalks removed, leaves finely shredded
2 spring onions (scallions), finely sliced, to garnish
nuoc cham, to serve

For the stock

2 meaty chicken legs
1 onion, peeled and quartered
4cm/1½in fresh root ginger, peeled and coarsely chopped
15ml/1 tbsp nuoc mam
3 black peppercorns
1 bunch of fresh mint
sea salt

1 To make the stock, put the chicken legs into a deep pan. Add all the other ingredients, except the salt, and pour in 1 litre/1¾ pints/4 cups water. Bring the water to the boil, skim off any foam that rises to the top, then reduce the heat and simmer gently with the lid on for 1 hour.

2 Remove the lid, increase the heat and simmer for a further 30 minutes to reduce the stock. Skim off any fat, strain the stock and season with salt. Measure out 750ml/1¼ pints/3 cups of stock. Remove the chicken meat from the bone and shred.

3 Put the rice in a heavy pan and stir in the stock. When the rice settles, check that the stock sits roughly 2.5cm/1in above the rice; if not, top it up. Bring the liquid to the boil, cover the pan and cook for about 25 minutes, or until all the water has been absorbed by the rice.

4 Remove the pan from the heat and add the shredded chicken, shallots and most of the mint. Cover the pan again and leave the flavours to mingle for about 10 minutes. Transfer the rice to warmed bowls, or a serving dish, garnish with the remaining mint and the sliced spring onions, and serve with nuoc cham.

Chicken Jambalaya Energy 740kcal/3079kJ; Protein 50.6g; Carbohydrate 52.9g, of which sugars 7.7g; Fat 36.1g, of which saturates 11.1g; Cholesterol 240mg; Calcium 79mg; Fibre 2.2g; Sodium 593mg.
Fragrant Rice Energy 370kcal/1569kJ; Protein 12g; Carbohydrate 79g, of which sugars 1g; Fat 3g, of which saturates 0g; Cholesterol 26mg; Calcium 41mg; Fibre 0.8g; Sodium 200mg.

Poussin and New Potato Pot-roast

Slow-cooked pot-roasts are traditionally associated with the colder months. But this delicious version is a simple summer dish, cooked in a clay chicken brick, that uses new-season potatoes.

Serves 4

2 poussins, about 500g/1¼lb each
25g/1oz/2 tbsp butter
15ml/1 tbsp clear honey
500g/1¼lb small new potatoes
1 red onion, halved lengthways and cut into thin wedges
4–5 small rosemary sprigs
2 bay leaves
1 lemon, cut into wedges
450ml/¾ pint/scant 2 cups hot chicken stock
salt and ground black pepper

1 Soak a clay chicken brick in cold water for 20 minutes, then drain. Cut the poussins in half, along the breast bone. Melt the butter, mix it together with the honey and brush over the poussins. Season with salt and pepper.

2 Place the small new potatoes and onion wedges in the base of the chicken brick. Tuck the rosemary sprigs, bay leaves and lemon wedges in among the vegetables. Pour over the hot chicken stock (see Cook's Tips).

3 Place the halved poussins on top of the vegetables. Cover the chicken brick and place it in an unheated oven. Set the oven to 200°C/400°F/Gas 6 and cook for 50–60 minutes, or until the poussin juices run clear and the vegetables are tender.

4 Uncover the chicken brick for the last 10 minutes of cooking time to add more colour to the poussins, if necessary. Serve a poussin half per person, accompanied by the cooked vegetables.

Cook's Tips

- *Make sure the stock is hot, but not boiling, when it is added to the chicken brick otherwise the chicken brick may crack.*
- *A poussin is a baby chicken, around 4–6 weeks old. Poussins can be cooked by grilling (broiling), roasting or pot-roasting, but are especially tender and moist cooked in a chicken brick.*

Poussins with Bulgur Wheat and Vermouth

These oven-roasted birds are filled with a bulgur wheat and nut stuffing laced with vermouth, and served with a medley of roast vegetables finished with an unusual vermouth glaze.

Serves 4

50g/2oz/⅓ cup bulgur wheat
150ml/¼ pint/⅔ cup dry white vermouth
60ml/4 tbsp olive oil
1 large onion, finely chopped
2 carrots, finely chopped
75g/3oz/¾ cup pine nuts, chopped
5ml/1 tsp celery seeds
4 poussins
3 red onions, quartered
4 baby aubergines (eggplants), halved
4 patty pan squashes
12 baby carrots
45ml/3 tbsp corn syrup
salt and ground black pepper

1 Preheat the oven to 200°C/400°F/Gas 6. Put the bulgur wheat in a heatproof bowl, pour over half the vermouth and cover with boiling water. Set aside.

2 Heat half the oil in a large frying pan. Add the onion and carrots, and fry for 10 minutes, then remove the pan from the heat and stir in the pine nuts, celery seeds and the well-drained bulgur wheat.

3 Stuff the poussins with the bulgur wheat mixture. Place them in a roasting pan, brush with oil and sprinkle with salt and pepper. Roast for 45–55 minutes until the juices run clear when the thickest part of the thigh is pierced with a skewer or knife.

4 Meanwhile, spread out the red onions, aubergines, patty pans and baby carrots in a single layer on a baking sheet.

5 Mix the corn syrup with the remaining vermouth and oil in a bowl. Season with salt and pepper. Brush the corn syrup mixture over the vegetables and roast for 35–45 minutes until golden.

6 Cut each poussin in half and serve immediately, with the roasted vegetables.

Poussin Pot-roast Energy 443kcal/1852kJ; Protein 30.1g; Carbohydrate 24.2g, of which sugars 5.4g; Fat 25.8g, of which saturates 8.9g; Cholesterol 158mg; Calcium 23mg; Fibre 1.5g; Sodium 153mg.
Poussins with Bulgur Energy 582kcal/2419kJ; Protein 23.7g; Carbohydrate 37.5g, of which sugars 27.5g; Fat 34.4g, of which saturates 5.4g; Cholesterol 87mg; Calcium 91mg; Fibre 6.5g; Sodium 126mg.

Poussins with Raisin-walnut Stuffing

This slow-cooked dish is easy to prepare and offers something different for a midweek supper.

Serves 4
250ml/8fl oz/1 cup port
90g/3½oz/⅔ cup raisins
15ml/1 tbsp walnut oil
75g/3oz/1 cup mushrooms, finely chopped
1 large celery stick, finely chopped
1 small onion, chopped
50g/2oz/1 cup fresh breadcrumbs
50g/2oz/½ cup chopped walnuts
15ml/1 tbsp each chopped fresh basil and parsley or 30ml/2 tbsp chopped fresh parsley
2.5ml/½ tsp dried thyme
75g/3oz/6 tbsp butter, melted
4 poussins
salt and ground black pepper
salad and vegetables, to serve

1 Preheat the oven to 180°C/350°F/Gas 4. In a small bowl, combine the port and raisins, and leave to soak for 20 minutes.

2 Meanwhile, heat the oil in a non-stick frying pan. Add the mushrooms, celery and onion, and cook over low heat for 8–10 minutes until softened. Allow to cool slightly.

3 Drain the raisins, reserving the port. Combine the raisins, breadcrumbs, walnuts, basil (if using), parsley and thyme in a bowl. Stir in the onion mixture and 60ml/4 tbsp of the melted butter. Add salt and pepper to taste.

4 Fill the cavity of each bird with the stuffing mixture. Do not pack too tightly. Tie the legs together, looping the tail with string to enclose the stuffing securely.

5 Brush the birds with the remaining butter and place in a roasting pan just large enough to hold them comfortably. Pour over the reserved port. Roast, basting occasionally, for about 1 hour or until the juices run clear when the thickest part of the thigh is pierced with a skewer or knife.

6 Leave the birds to stand for 10 minutes before serving. Cut each poussin in half and pour some of the pan juices over each portion. Serve the poussin halves accompanied by salad and vegetables of your choice.

Marinated Pigeon in Red Wine

The time taken to marinate and cook this casserole is well rewarded by the fabulous rich flavour of the finished dish. Stir-fried green cabbage and celeriac purée would make good accompaniments to this hearty casserole.

Serves 4
4 pigeons (US squabs), about 225g/8oz each
30ml/2 tbsp olive oil
1 onion, coarsely chopped
225g/8oz/3¼ cups chestnut mushrooms, sliced
15ml/1 tbsp plain (all-purpose) flour
300ml/½ pint/1¼ cups hot game stock
30ml/2 tbsp chopped fresh parsley
salt and ground black pepper
flat leaf parsley, to garnish

For the marinade
15ml/1 tbsp light olive oil
1 onion, chopped
1 carrot, chopped
1 celery stick, chopped
3 garlic cloves, sliced
6 allspice berries, bruised
2 bay leaves
8 black peppercorns, bruised
150ml/¼ pint/⅔ cup red wine vinegar
150ml/¼ pint/⅔ cup red wine
45ml/3 tbsp redcurrant jelly

1 Mix together all the ingredients for the marinade in a large bowl. Add the pigeons and turn them in the marinade, then cover the bowl and chill for about 12 hours, turning the pigeons frequently.

2 Preheat the oven to 150°C/300°F/Gas 2. Heat the oil in a large, flameproof casserole and cook the onion and mushrooms for about 5 minutes, or until the onion has softened.

3 Meanwhile, drain the pigeons and strain the marinade into a jug (pitcher), then set both aside separately.

4 Sprinkle the flour over the pigeons and add them to the casserole, breast side down. Pour in the marinade and stock, and add the chopped parsley and seasoning. Cover and cook in the oven for 2½ hours.

5 Check the seasoning, then serve the pigeons on warmed plates and ladle the sauce over them. Garnish with parsley.

Poussins Energy 820kcal/3410kJ; Protein 38.3g; Carbohydrate 35g, of which sugars 25.1g; Fat 51.7g, of which saturates 17.4g; Cholesterol 215mg; Calcium 90mg; Fibre 2.3g; Sodium 358mg.
Marinated Pigeon Energy 428kcal/1785kJ; Protein 32.8g; Carbohydrate 16.7g, of which sugars 12.4g; Fat 23.3g, of which saturates 1.3g; Cholesterol 0mg; Calcium 51mg; Fibre 2g; Sodium 135mg.

Pigeon and Stout Casserole

The flesh on pigeon breasts is dark and, like most small birds, can be quite dry, so slow cooking them in a casserole with stout is an ideal way to keep them moist. When buying the pigeon breasts, ask your butcher for the carcasses for stock, if possible. Serve with spiced rice and a watercress or rocket salad.

Serves 6

175g/6oz thick streaky (fatty) bacon, cut into strips
2 medium onions, finely chopped
2 or 3 garlic cloves, crushed
6 pigeon (US squab) breast fillets
seasoned flour, for coating
50g/2oz/¼ cup butter
15ml/1 tbsp olive oil
30ml/2 tbsp Irish whiskey (optional)
600ml/1 pint/2½ cups hot chicken stock
300ml/½ pint/1¼ cups stout
175g/6oz button (white) mushrooms
beurre manié, if needed
15–30ml/1–2 tbsp rowan jelly
sea salt and ground black pepper

1 Preheat the oven to 150°C/300°F/Gas 2. Cook the streaky bacon strips gently in a large, flameproof casserole until the fat runs out. Add the onion and crushed garlic and cook until they are soft. Remove from the casserole and set aside.

2 Coat the breast fillets thickly with seasoned flour. Add the butter and oil to the pan, heat until the butter is foaming, then add the meat and brown well on all sides. Pour in the Irish whiskey, if using. Carefully set it alight and shake the pan until the flames go out – this improves the flavour.

3 Stir in the hot chicken stock, stout and the mushrooms, and bring the mixture slowly to the boil. Cover with a tight-fitting lid and cook in the preheated oven for 1½–2 hours, or until the pigeon breast fillets are tender.

4 Remove from the oven and lift the pigeon breast fillets on to a serving dish. Thicken the gravy, if necessary, by adding small pieces of beurre manié, stirring until the sauce thickens. Stir in rowan jelly to taste and check the seasoning, adding salt and pepper, if necessary. Serve the pigeon breast fillets with the gravy while hot.

Pigeons with Pancetta

Mild, succulent pigeon breast fillets are delicious with a slowly cooked stock made from the pigeon bones.

Serves 4

4 whole pigeons (US squabs)
2 large onions
2 carrots, roughly chopped
1 celery stick, roughly chopped
25g/1oz dried porcini mushrooms
25g/1oz/2 tbsp butter
30ml/2 tbsp olive oil
50g/2oz pancetta, diced
2 garlic cloves, crushed
150ml/¼ pint/⅔ cup red wine
salt and ground black pepper
flat leaf parsley, to garnish
cooked oyster mushrooms, to serve

1 To prepare a pigeon, cut down the length of the bird, just to one side of the breastbone. Gradually scrape away the meat from the breastbone until the breast fillet comes away. Do the same on the other side, then repeat with the other pigeons.

2 Put the pigeon carcasses in a large pan. Halve one of the onions, leaving the skin on. Add to the pan with the carrots and celery and just cover with water. Bring to the boil, reduce the heat and simmer very gently, uncovered, for 1½ hours to make a dark, rich stock. Leave to cool slightly, then strain into a bowl.

3 Cover the dried mushrooms with 150ml/¼ pint/⅔ cup hot water and soak for 30 minutes. Peel and finely chop the remaining onion. Melt half the butter with the oil in a frying pan. Add the onion and pancetta and fry gently for 3 minutes. Add the breast fillets, skin side down, and fry for 2 minutes each side.

4 Add the mushrooms, with the soaking liquid, garlic, wine and 250ml/8fl oz/1 cup of the stock. Bring to the boil, then simmer gently for 5 minutes until the fillets are tender, but still a little pink.

5 Lift out the fillets and keep hot. Return the sauce to the boil and boil rapidly to reduce slightly. Gradually whisk in all the remaining butter and season with salt and pepper to taste.

6 Transfer the fillets to warmed serving plates and pour over the sauce. Serve immediately, garnished with sprigs of parsley and accompanied by oyster mushrooms.

Pigeon Casserole Energy 436kcal/1817kJ; Protein 38.7g; Carbohydrate 6.7g, of which sugars 5.3g; Fat 27.2g, of which saturates 6.2g; Cholesterol 33mg; Calcium 48mg; Fibre 1.7g; Sodium 639mg.
Pigeons with Pancetta Energy 372kcal/1549kJ; Protein 37.5g; Carbohydrate 10.1g, of which sugars 7.6g; Fat 17.6g, of which saturates 4.3g; Cholesterol 21mg; Calcium 76mg; Fibre 2.1g; Sodium 319mg.

Moroccan Pigeon Pie

An unusual pie, filled with a flavoursome mixture of pigeon, eggs, spices and nuts.

Serves 6

3 pigeons (US squabs), washed
50g/2oz/4 tbsp butter
1 onion, chopped
1 cinnamon stick
2.5ml/½ tsp ground ginger
30ml/2 tbsp chopped fresh coriander (cilantro)
45ml/3 tbsp chopped fresh parsley
pinch of ground turmeric
15ml/1 tbsp caster (superfine) sugar
1.5ml/¼ tsp ground cinnamon
115g/4oz/1 cup toasted almonds, finely chopped
6 eggs, beaten
salt and ground black pepper
ground cinnamon and icing (confectioners') sugar, to garnish

For the pastry

175g/6oz/¾ cup butter, melted
16 sheets filo pastry
1 egg yolk

1 Place the pigeons in a pan with the butter, onion, cinnamon stick, ginger, coriander, parsley and turmeric. Season and cover with water. Bring to the boil, then cover and simmer for 1 hour.

2 Strain the stock and reserve. Skin and bone the pigeons. Chop the flesh into chunks. Preheat the oven to 180°C/350°F/Gas 4. Mix together the sugar, cinnamon and almonds, and set aside.

3 Measure 150ml/¼ pint/⅔ cup of the reserved stock into a pan. Add the eggs and mix well. Stir over low heat until creamy and very thick and almost set. Season with salt and pepper.

4 Brush a large ovenproof dish with melted butter and lay in the first sheet of pastry. Brush with butter and continue with five more sheets of pastry. Cover with the almond mixture, then half the egg mixture. Moisten with a little stock.

5 Layer on four sheets of pastry, brushing with butter. Add the pigeon meat, then the remaining egg mixture and more stock. Cover with the remaining pastry, and tuck in any overlap.

6 Brush with egg yolk and bake for 40 minutes. Raise the oven to 200°C/400°F/Gas 6, and bake for 15 minutes until crisp and golden. Garnish with a lattice of cinnamon and sugar, and serve.

Braised Farm Pigeon with Elderberry Wine

Elderberry wine is a deep, rich, almost port-like wine, and is perfect for using in this traditional and simple slow-cooked casserole.

Serves 4

4 pigeons (US squabs)
15ml/1 tbsp plain (all-purpose) flour
30ml/2 tbsp olive oil, plus extra if needed
1 onion, chopped
225g/8oz button (white) mushrooms, sliced
250ml/8fl oz/1 cup dark stock
100ml/3½fl oz/scant ½ cup elderberry wine
salt and ground black pepper
kale, to serve (optional)

1 Preheat the oven to 170°C/325°F/Gas 3. Season the pigeons inside and out with salt and ground black pepper and roll liberally in the flour. Heat a heavy pan over medium heat, add the olive oil and wait for it to bubble slightly. Cook the pigeons until lightly browned all over, then transfer them to a large casserole dish.

2 Brown the onion in the pan used for the pigeons and then add the sliced mushrooms and cook briefly, still over medium heat, adding more oil if necessary. Add the vegetables to the casserole with the pigeons and mix around well.

3 Pour in the stock, elderberry wine and just enough water to cover. Bring to the boil, cover tightly with a lid and cook in the preheated oven for 2 hours, until the pigeons are tender.

4 Remove the birds from the casserole and keep warm. Boil the cooking liquor rapidly to thicken slightly. Return the pigeons to the pan and heat through. Serve with kale, if you like.

Variation

This recipe suits most game birds, so if you can't find pigeon, or it is the wrong season, you can use partridge, woodcock, pheasant or even wild duck or goose instead.

Pigeon Pie Energy 628kcal/2607kJ; Protein 27.1g; Carbohydrate 15.1g, of which sugars 1.6g; Fat 51.7g, of which saturates 6.6g; Cholesterol 224mg; Calcium 113mg; Fibre 2.1g; Sodium 130mg.
Braised Farm Pigeon Energy 296kcal/1237kJ; Protein 31g; Carbohydrate 6.8g, of which sugars 2.5g; Fat 14.3g, of which saturates 0.1g; Cholesterol 0mg; Calcium 35mg; Fibre 1g; Sodium 117mg.

Braised Guinea Fowl with Red Cabbage

The slightly gamey flavour of guinea fowl is complemented in this slow-cooker dish by the sweet, fruity flavour of red cabbage, braised in apple juice and scented with juniper berries.

Serves 4

15ml/1 tbsp unsalted butter
½ red cabbage, weighing about 450g/1lb, cut into wedges
1.3kg/3lb oven-ready guinea fowl, jointed
15ml/1 tbsp sunflower oil
3 shallots, very finely chopped
15ml/1 tbsp plain (all-purpose) flour
120ml/4fl oz/½ cup chicken stock
150ml/¼ pint/⅔ cup apple juice
15ml/1 tbsp soft light brown sugar
15ml/1 tbsp red wine vinegar
4 juniper berries, lightly crushed
salt and ground black pepper

1 Use half the butter to grease the ceramic cooking pot. Shred the cabbage finely, then place in the cooking pot, packing it down tightly.

2 Rinse the guinea fowl portions and pat dry with kitchen paper. Heat the remaining butter and the oil in a pan and brown the guinea fowl on all sides. Lift from the pan, leaving the fat behind, and place on top of the red cabbage.

3 Add the shallots to the frying pan and cook for 5 minutes. Sprinkle with the flour, cook for a few seconds, then gradually stir in the stock and the apple juice. Bring to the boil, stirring continuously, until thickened. Remove from the heat, stir in the sugar, vinegar and juniper berries, and season.

4 Pour the sauce over the guinea fowl, cover and cook on high for 4 hours, or until the meat and cabbage are tender. Check the seasoning and serve.

Variation
Other mild-tasting poultry or game such as chicken or pheasant can be used in place of the guinea fowl, if preferred.

Guinea Fowl and Vegetable Stew

This slow-cooker stew of guinea fowl cooked with spring vegetables and flavoured with mustard and herbs is a real winner.

Serves 4

1.6kg/3½lb guinea fowl
45ml/3 tbsp plain (all-purpose) flour
45ml/3 tbsp olive oil
115g/4oz pancetta, diced
1 onion, chopped
3 cloves garlic, chopped
200ml/7fl oz/scant 1 cup white wine
225g/8oz baby carrots
225g/8oz baby turnips
6 baby leeks, cut into large pieces
sprig of fresh thyme
1 bay leaf
10ml/2 tsp Dijon mustard
150ml/¼ pint/⅔ cup boiling chicken or vegetable stock
225g/8oz shelled peas
30ml/2 tbsp chopped fresh parsley
15ml/1 tbsp chopped fresh mint
salt and ground black pepper

1 Joint the guinea fowl into eight pieces. Rinse them, then pat dry on kitchen paper. Season the flour with salt and pepper and toss the guinea fowl portions into it. Set aside any leftover flour.

2 Heat 30ml/2 tbsp of the oil in a large frying pan. Cook the pancetta until lightly browned. Using a slotted spoon, transfer the pancetta to the ceramic cooking pot, leaving any fat in the pan.

3 Add the guinea fowl portions to the pan and fry, turning, until browned on all sides. Arrange the guinea fowl portions in a single layer in the cooking pot on top of the pancetta.

4 Add the remaining oil to the frying pan. Cook the onion for 3–4 minutes, until just soft. Add the garlic and cook for about 1 minute, then stir in the reserved flour. Gradually stir in the wine and bring to the boil. Pour over the guinea fowl.

5 Add the carrots, turnips and leeks to the cooking pot with the thyme and bay leaf. Blend the mustard with the stock, season with salt and pepper and pour over. Cover and cook on high for 3–4 hours, or until the guinea fowl and vegetables are tender.

6 Add the peas to the pot and cook for 45 minutes. Stir in most of the herbs. Ladle into warmed serving plates, sprinkle over the remaining fresh herbs and serve immediately.

Braised Guinea Fowl Energy 456kcal/1907kJ; Protein 44.5g; Carbohydrate 20g, of which sugars 15g; Fat 22.5g, of which saturates 6.7g; Cholesterol 225mg; Calcium 96mg; Fibre 3.1g; Sodium 15mg.
Guinea Fowl Stew Energy 581kcal/2425kJ; Protein 50.5g; Carbohydrate 29.1g, of which sugars 11.2g; Fat 26.5g, of which saturates 7.4g; Cholesterol 224mg; Calcium 109mg; Fibre 6.9g; Sodium 668mg.

Guinea Fowl with Beans and Kale

Slowly cooking guinea fowl in a clay pot or chicken brick gives a delicious, moist result. Here, the guinea fowl is cooked on a colourful bed of herb-flavoured beans and vegetables.

Serves 4

1.3kg/3lb guinea fowl
45ml/3 tbsp olive oil
4 shallots, chopped
1 garlic clove, crushed
3 celery sticks, sliced
400g/14oz can chopped tomatoes
2 x 400g/14oz cans mixed beans, drained
5 fresh thyme sprigs
2 bay leaves
150ml/¼ pint/⅔ cup white wine
300ml/½ pint/1¼ cups well-flavoured chicken stock
175g/6oz curly kale
salt and ground black pepper

1 Soak a clay pot or chicken brick in cold water for about 20 minutes, then drain. Rub the guinea fowl with 15ml/1 tbsp of the olive oil and season with salt and pepper. Place the remaining oil in a frying pan, add the shallots, garlic and celery and sauté for 4–5 minutes.

2 Remove the shallots, garlic and celery with a slotted spoon and place in the clay pot or chicken brick. Add the tomatoes and beans and stir throughout. Tuck in the fresh thyme sprigs and bay leaves.

3 Put the guinea fowl in the frying pan and brown on all sides, then pour in the wine and stock and bring to the boil. Lift the bird out of the pan and place on top of the vegetables in the pot or brick and then pour the liquid over. Cover and place in an unheated oven set to 200°C/400°F/Gas 6. Cook for 1 hour.

4 Add the curly kale to the pot or brick, nestling it among the beans. Cover and cook for 10–15 minutes, or until the guinea fowl is tender. Season the bean mixture and serve.

Variation
Use chard, spring greens (collards) or Savoy cabbage in place of curly kale, if you prefer.

Braised Pheasant with Bacon

In winter, at the end of their season, pheasant is not suitable for roasting, so this slow casserole enriched with bacon and wild mushrooms and chestnuts is ideal.

Serves 4

2 mature pheasants
50g/2oz/¼ cup butter
75ml/5 tbsp brandy
12 baby (pearl) onions, peeled
1 celery stick, chopped
50g/2oz unsmoked rindless bacon, cut into strips
45ml/3 tbsp plain (all-purpose) flour
550ml/18fl oz/2½ cups chicken stock, boiling
175g/6oz peeled, cooked chestnuts
350g/12oz/4 cups fresh ceps, trimmed and sliced, or 15g/½oz/¼ cup dried porcini mushrooms, soaked in warm water for 20 minutes
15ml/1 tbsp lemon juice
salt and ground black pepper
watercress or fresh parsley sprigs, to garnish

1 Preheat the oven to 160°C/325°F/Gas 3. Season the pheasants with salt and black pepper. Melt half of the butter in a large flameproof casserole and brown the pheasants on all sides over medium heat. Transfer the pheasants to a shallow dish and pour off the cooking fat.

2 Return the casserole to the heat and brown the sediment. Add the brandy, stir well with a wooden spoon to loosen the sediment, then pour all the cooking juices over the pheasant.

3 Wipe out the casserole and melt the remaining butter. Add the onions, celery and bacon and brown lightly. Stir in the flour. Remove from the heat.

4 Stir in the stock gradually so that it is completely absorbed by the flour. Add the chestnuts, mushrooms, the pheasants and their juices. Bring back to a gentle simmer, then cover and cook in the oven for 1½ hours.

5 Transfer the cooked pheasants and vegetables to a warmed serving plate. Bring the sauce back to the boil, add the lemon juice and season to taste. Pour the sauce into a jug (pitcher) or gravy boat and garnish the birds with watercress or parsley.

Guinea Fowl Energy 617kcal/2585kJ; Protein 53.1g; Carbohydrate 32.9g, of which sugars 8.7g; Fat 28.6g, of which saturates 1.5g; Cholesterol 0mg; Calcium 98mg; Fibre 11.6g; Sodium 1017mg.
Braised Pheasant Energy 883kcal/3699kJ; Protein 86.8g; Carbohydrate 32.3g, of which sugars 6.9g; Fat 41.6g, of which saturates 15.8g; Cholesterol 35mg; Calcium 205mg; Fibre 2.9g; Sodium 920mg.

Pheasant with Oatmeal Stuffing

Like most game, pheasant tends to be dry, so offset this by laying slices of fatty unsalted bacon over the breast while they are being slowly roasted in the oven.

Serves 4–6

2 oven-ready pheasants
6 unsmoked streaky (fatty) bacon rashers (strips)
50g/2oz/¼ cup softened butter
15g/½oz/2 tbsp seasoned flour
450ml/¾ pint/scant 2 cups chicken stock
salt and ground black pepper
watercress or rocket (arugula), to garnish

For the stuffing

1 small onion, finely chopped
pheasant livers, finely chopped
115g/4oz/1 cup pinhead oatmeal
50g/2oz/¼ cup butter, melted

1 To prepare the stuffing, put the onion and the pheasant livers into a mixing bowl with the oatmeal and butter. Mix well and season with salt and pepper. Add cold water to moisten slightly.

2 Preheat the oven to 200°C/400°F/Gas 6. Wipe the birds inside and out and divide the stuffing between the two birds, spooning in loosely to allow the stuffing to expand during cooking.

3 Use kitchen string to truss the birds for cooking, and lay the bacon rashers over the breasts. Spread half the butter over the birds and lay them in a roasting pan with the remaining butter.

4 Roast for 45–50 minutes, basting often. Ten minutes before the end, remove the rashers, baste the birds and then dredge with a little seasoned flour. Baste again and return to the oven to brown.

5 When cooked, remove the string and put the pheasants on to a heated serving dish. Keep warm while you make the gravy.

6 Pour all but 30ml/2 tbsp of the fat out of the roasting pan and sprinkle in the remaining flour, stirring well to blend and dislodge any sediment. Blend in the stock, season and bring to the boil. Simmer for a few minutes, stirring, then pour into a gravy boat.

7 To serve, garnish the pheasant breasts with the bacon pieces and watercress or rocket. Hand the gravy round separately.

Roast Pheasant with Port

Slowly roasting young pheasant in foil keeps the flesh tender and moist.

Serves 4

oil, for brushing
2 hen pheasants, about 675g/1½lb each
50g/2oz/4 tbsp unsalted butter, softened
8 fresh thyme sprigs
2 bay leaves
6 streaky (fatty) bacon rashers (strips)
15ml/1 tbsp plain (all-purpose) flour
175ml/6fl oz/¾ cup game or chicken stock, plus extra
15ml/1 tbsp redcurrant jelly
45–60ml/3–4 tbsp port
ground black pepper

1 Preheat the oven to 230°C/450°F/Gas 8. Line a large roasting pan with a sheet of strong foil large enough to enclose the pheasants. Lightly brush the foil with oil.

2 Wipe the pheasants with damp kitchen paper and remove any extra fat or skin. Using your fingertips, carefully loosen the skin of the breasts. Spread the butter between the skin and breast meat of each bird. Tie the legs securely with string, then lay the thyme sprigs and a bay leaf over the breast of each bird. Lay bacon rashers over the breasts, place the birds in the foil-lined tin and season with pepper. Bring together the long ends of the foil, fold over securely to enclose, then seal the ends.

3 Roast the birds for 20 minutes, then reduce the oven temperature to 190°C/375°F/Gas 5 and cook for a further 40 minutes. Uncover the birds and roast for 10–15 minutes more or until they are browned and the juices run clear when the thickest part of the thigh is pierced with a knife or skewer. Transfer the birds to a board and leave to stand, covered with clean foil, for 10–15 minutes before carving.

4 Pour the juices from the foil into the roasting pan and skim off any fat. Sprinkle in the flour and cook over medium heat, stirring, until smooth. Whisk in the game or chicken stock and redcurrant jelly, and bring to the boil. Reduce the heat and simmer until the sauce thickens slightly, adding more stock if needed, then stir in the port and adjust the seasoning to taste. Strain and serve with the pheasants.

Pheasant with Oatmeal Energy 847kcal/3529kJ; Protein 69.7g; Carbohydrate 25.2g, of which sugars 1.1g; Fat 52.5g, of which saturates 23.1g; Cholesterol 598mg; Calcium 92mg; Fibre 2.3g; Sodium 697mg.
Roast Pheasant Energy 526kcal/2195kJ; Protein 50.1g; Carbohydrate 6.4g, of which sugars 4.5g; Fat 29g, of which saturates 8.2g; Cholesterol 25mg; Calcium 104mg; Fibre 2g; Sodium 798mg.

Pheasant in Green Pipian Sauce

An unusual and delicious way of roasting pheasant, Mexican-style, that keeps it wonderfully moist.

Serves 4

2 pheasants
30ml/2 tbsp corn oil
175g/6oz/generous 1 cup pepitas (Mexican pumpkin seeds)
15ml/1 tbsp achiote (annatto) seeds
1 onion, finely chopped
2 garlic cloves, chopped
275g/10oz can tomatillos (Mexican green tomatoes)
475ml/16fl oz/2 cups hot chicken stock
salt and ground black pepper
fresh coriander (cilantro), to garnish

1 Preheat the oven to 180°C/350°F/Gas 4. Using a large, sharp knife or poultry shears, cut the pheasants in half lengthways and season well with salt and pepper.

2 Heat the oil in a large frying pan and cook the pheasant pieces until lightly browned on all sides. Lift out of the pan, drain and arrange, skin side up, in a single layer in a roasting pan. Set aside.

3 Grind the pepitas finely in a nut grinder or a food processor. Shake through a sieve (strainer) into a bowl. Grind the achiote seeds, add them to the bowl and set to one side.

4 Place the onion, garlic, tomatillos and their juice into a food processor and purée. Pour into a pan. Add the pepita mixture, stir in the stock and simmer over very low heat for 10 minutes. Do not let the mixture boil as it will separate. Remove from the heat and leave to cool.

5 Pour the sauce over the pheasant halves. Bake for 40 minutes or until tender, basting from time to time with the sauce. Garnish with coriander and serve.

Cook's Tip
Achiote, also called annatto, is a musky-flavoured seed, common in Mexican cooking. There is no substitute. Look out for it in Caribbean and Latin American markets.

Pheasant Pie

This popular country dish can be made with whatever game birds are available.

Serves 8–10

4 pheasant and/or pigeon (US squab) breast portions, skinned
225g/8oz lean stewing beef
115g/4oz streaky (fatty) bacon
butter, for frying
2 onions, finely chopped
1 large garlic clove, crushed
15ml/1 tbsp plain (all-purpose) flour
300ml/½ pint/¼ cup pigeon or pheasant stock
15ml/1 tbsp tomato purée (paste)
15ml/1 tbsp chopped fresh parsley
a little grated lemon rind
15ml/1 tbsp rowan or redcurrant jelly
50–115g/2–4oz button (white) mushrooms, halved or quartered
a small pinch of grated nutmeg or ground cloves (optional)
milk or beaten egg, to glaze
sea salt and ground black pepper

For the rough-puff pastry
225g/8oz/2 cups plain (all-purpose) flour, sifted
2.5ml/½ tsp salt
5ml/1 tsp lemon juice
115g/4oz/½ cup butter, in walnut-sized pieces

1 Make the pastry. Mix the flour and salt in a large bowl. Add the lemon juice and the butter and just enough cold water to bind the ingredients together. Turn the dough on to a floured board and roll the pastry into a long strip. Fold it into three and press the edges together. Half-turn the pastry, rib it with the rolling pin to equalize the air in it and roll it into a strip once again. Repeat this folding and rolling process three more times.

2 Slice the pheasant or pigeon breast portions from the bone and cut the meat into thin strips. Trim away any fat from the stewing beef and slice into strips. Cut the streaky bacon into thin strips, and then cook it very gently in a heavy frying pan until the fat runs. Add some butter and brown the sliced pigeon or pheasant and stewing steak in it, a little at a time.

3 Remove the meats from the pan and set aside. Cook the onions and garlic in the fat for 2–3 minutes over medium heat. Remove and set aside with the meats, then stir the flour into the remaining fat. Cook for 1–2 minutes, and then gradually stir in enough stock to make a fairly thin gravy. Add the tomato purée, parsley, lemon rind and jelly and the mushrooms. Season to taste and add the nutmeg or cloves, if using.

4 Return the browned meats, chopped onion and garlic to the pan containing the gravy, and mix well before turning into a deep 1.75 litre/3 pint/7¼ cup pie dish. Leave to cool. Meanwhile, preheat the oven to 220°C/425°F/Gas 7.

5 Roll the pastry out to make a circle 2.5cm/1in larger than the pie dish, and cut out to make a lid for the pie. Wet the rim of the pie dish and line with the remaining pastry strip. Dampen the strip and cover with the lid, pressing down well to seal.

6 Trim away any excess pastry and knock up the edges. Make a hole in the centre for the steam and use trimmings to decorate. Glaze the top with milk or beaten egg. Bake in the oven for about 20 minutes, until the pastry is well risen, then reduce the oven to 150°C/300°F/Gas 2 for another 1½ hours, until cooked. Protect the pastry from over-browning, if necessary, by covering with a double layer of wet baking parchment. Serve.

Pheasant in Sauce Energy 807kcal/3379kJ; Protein 90.5g; Carbohydrate 11.5g, of which sugars 3.7g; Fat 44.6g, of which saturates 10g; Cholesterol 0mg; Calcium 181mg; Fibre 3.5g; Sodium 272mg.
Pheasent Pie Energy 448kcal/1871kJ; Protein 28.3g; Carbohydrate 29.5g, of which sugars 5.3g; Fat 24.9g, of which saturates 9.5g; Cholesterol 55mg; Calcium 67mg; Fibre 1.5g; Sodium 393mg.

Grouse with Orchard Fruit Stuffing

Tart apples, plums and pears make a fabulous orchard fruit stuffing that perfectly complements the rich, gamey flavour of grouse.

Serves 2

juice of ½ lemon
2 young grouse
50g/2oz/¼ cup butter
4 Swiss chard leaves
50ml/2fl oz/¼ cup Marsala
salt and ground black pepper

For the stuffing

2 shallots, finely chopped
1 tart cooking apple, peeled, cored and chopped
1 pear, peeled, cored and chopped
2 plums, halved, stoned (pitted) and chopped
pinch of mixed (apple pie) spice

1 Sprinkle the lemon juice over the grouse and season well. Melt half the butter in a flameproof casserole, add the grouse and cook for 10 minutes, or until browned. Use tongs to remove the grouse from the casserole and set aside.

2 Add the shallots to the fat remaining in the casserole and cook until just softened. Add the apple, pear, plums and mixed spice, and cook for about 5 minutes, or until the fruits are just beginning to soften. Remove the casserole from the heat and spoon the hot fruit mixture into the body cavities of the birds.

3 Truss the birds neatly with string. Smear the remaining butter over the birds and wrap them in the chard leaves, then return them to the casserole.

4 Pour in the Marsala and heat until simmering. Cover tightly and simmer for 20 minutes, or until the birds are tender, taking care not to overcook them. Leave to rest in a warm place for about 10 minutes before serving.

Cook's Tip

There isn't much liquid in the pan for cooking the birds – they are steamed rather than boiled, so it is important that the casserole has a heavy base and a tight-fitting lid, otherwise the liquid may evaporate and the chard will burn on the base.

Michaelmas Goose with Stuffing

This traditional roast goose with apple stuffing is perfect for an autumnal feast.

Serves 6–8

4.5kg/10lb goose, with giblets
1 onion, sliced
2 carrots, sliced
2 celery sticks, sliced
small bunch of parsley and thyme
450g/1lb black pudding (blood sausage), crumbled or chopped
1 large garlic clove, crushed
2 large cooking apples, peeled, cored and finely chopped
250ml/8fl oz/1 cup dry (hard) cider
15ml/1 tbsp plain (all-purpose) flour
salt and ground black pepper
watercress or parsley, to garnish

1 Remove the goose liver from the giblets and put the remainder into a pan with the onion, carrots, celery and herbs. Cover with cold water, season and simmer for 30–45 minutes to make a stock for the gravy. Preheat the oven to 200°C/400°F/Gas 6.

2 Meanwhile, chop the liver finely and mix it with the black pudding, garlic and apples. Add salt and ground pepper, and then sprinkle in 75ml/2½fl oz/⅓ cup cider to bind. Wipe out the goose and stuff it loosely with this mixture. Prick the skin all over with a fork, sprinkle with salt and pepper and rub in well.

3 Calculate the cooking time at 15 minutes per 450g/1lb plus 15 minutes. Put the goose on a rack in a roasting pan, cover with foil and put in the oven. After 1 hour, pour off the hot fat from the pan and reserve. Pour the remaining cider over and return to the oven. Baste the goose occasionally and remove the foil 30 minutes before the end to allow the bird to brown. Transfer to a serving dish and put it in a warm place to rest.

4 Meanwhile, make the gravy. Pour off any fat from the roasting pan, leaving 30ml/2 tbsp, then sprinkle in enough flour to absorb it. Cook over medium heat for 1 minute, scraping the pan. Strain the giblet stock and stir in enough to make a gravy. Bring to the boil and simmer, stirring, for a few minutes. Add any juices from the goose, season and pour into a gravy boat.

5 Garnish the goose with parsley or watercress. Carve into slices and serve with the gravy, potatoes and seasonal vegetables.

Grouse with Stuffing Energy 508kcal/2121kJ; Protein 46.9g; Carbohydrate 19.5g, of which sugars 18.7g; Fat 24.3g, of which saturates 13.8g; Cholesterol 53mg; Calcium 185mg; Fibre 4.2g; Sodium 406mg.
Michaelmas Goose Energy 795kcal/3297kJ; Protein 32.8g; Carbohydrate 17.1g, of which sugars 2.3g; Fat 65.4g, of which saturates 20.6g; Cholesterol 171mg; Calcium 109mg; Fibre 0.4g; Sodium 800mg.

Roast Goose with Apples

This roast dish is served on Christmas Day in Germany. Here it is served with stuffed apples.

Serves 6

115g/4oz/scant 1 cup raisins
finely grated rind and juice of 1 orange
25g/1oz/2 tbsp butter
1 onion, finely chopped
75g/3oz/¾ cup hazelnuts, chopped
175g/6oz/3 cups fresh white breadcrumbs
15ml/1 tbsp clear honey
15ml/1 tbsp chopped fresh marjoram
30ml/2 tbsp chopped fresh parsley
6 red eating apples
15ml/1 tbsp lemon juice
4.5/10lb oven-ready young goose
salt and ground black pepper
fresh herbs, to garnish
orange wedges, red cabbage and green beans, to serve

1 Preheat the oven to 220°C/425°F/Gas 7. Put the raisins in a bowl and pour over the orange juice. Melt the butter in a frying pan and gently cook the onion for 5 minutes. Add the chopped nuts to the pan and cook for a further 4–5 minutes, or until beginning to brown.

2 Mix the onion and nuts into the raisins with 50g/2oz/1 cup of breadcrumbs, the orange rind, honey, herbs and seasoning.

3 Wash the apples and remove the cores to leave a 2cm/¾in hole. Make a shallow cut around the middle of each apple. Brush the cut and the cavity with the lemon juice to prevent it from browning. Pack the centre with the nut and raisin stuffing.

4 Mix the remaining breadcrumbs into the stuffing and stuff the bird's tail end. Close with a small skewer. Place the goose in a roasting pan, then prick the skin all over with a skewer. Roast for 30 minutes, then reduce the oven temperature to 180°C/350°F/Gas 4 and cook for a further 3 hours, pouring the excess fat out of the pan several times.

5 Arrange the apples around the goose and bake for 30–40 minutes. Rest the goose in a warm place for 15 minutes, before carving. Garnish with fresh herbs, and serve with stuffed apples and orange wedges, red cabbage and green beans.

Duck Stew with Olives

The sweetness of the onions in this slow-cooker recipe balances the saltiness of the olives beautifully. Creamy mashed potatoes make the perfect accompaniment.

Serves 4

4 duck quarters or breast portions
225g/8oz baby (pearl) onions
2.5ml/½ tsp caster (superfine) sugar
30ml/2 tbsp plain (all-purpose) flour
250ml/8fl oz/1 cup dry red wine
250ml/8fl oz/1 cup duck or chicken stock
1 bouquet garni
115g/4oz/1 cup pitted green or black olives, or a combination of the two
salt and ground black pepper

1 Put the duck, skin side down, in a large frying pan and cook for 10–12 minutes, turning to colour evenly, until browned on both sides. Lift out with a slotted spoon and place, skin side up, in the ceramic cooking pot. Switch the slow cooker to high.

2 Pour off most of the fat from the pan, leaving about 15ml/1 tbsp behind. Add the onions and cook over medium-low heat until beginning to colour. Sprinkle over the sugar and cook for 5 minutes until golden, stirring frequently. Sprinkle with the flour and cook, uncovered, for 2 minutes, stirring frequently.

3 Gradually stir the wine into the onions, followed by the stock. Bring to the boil, then pour over the duck. Add the bouquet garni to the pot, cover with the lid and cook on high for 1 hour.

4 Turn the slow cooker to the low setting and cook for a further 4–5 hours, or until the duck and onions are very tender.

5 Put the olives in a heatproof bowl and pour over very hot water to cover. Leave to stand for 1 minute, then drain. Add the olives to the pot, re-cover and cook for a further 30 minutes.

6 Transfer the duck, onions and olives to a warmed serving dish or individual plates. Skim all the fat from the cooking liquid and discard the bouquet garni. Season the sauce to taste with black pepper and a little salt, if needed, then spoon over the duck and serve immediately.

Roast Goose Energy 822kcal/3437kJ; Protein 54.8g; Carbohydrate 44.1g, of which sugars 21.8g; Fat 48.7g, of which saturates 0.9g; Cholesterol 0mg; Calcium 87mg; Fibre 3.1g; Sodium 486mg.
Duck Stew with Olives Energy 414kcal/1736kJ; Protein 47.3g; Carbohydrate 8.2g, of which sugars 2.3g; Fat 18.5g, of which saturates 5.2g; Cholesterol 257mg; Calcium 67mg; Fibre 1.6g; Sodium 917mg.

Roast Mallard

This oven-roasted mallard is especially tasty served on a potato-cake bed. Traditional accompaniments include game chips and apple sauce or rowan jelly. Puréed Jerusalem artichokes would also go very well with game birds.

Serves 2–3
1 oven-ready mallard
1 small onion, studded with cloves
a few apple slices
25g/1oz/2 tbsp butter, softened
salt and ground black pepper
5 streaky (fatty) bacon rashers (strips)

1 Thoroughly wash the bird inside and out under cold running water and wipe dry on kitchen paper.

2 Weigh the mallard and calculate the necessary cooking time at 15 minutes per 450g/1lb for rare meat, or 20 minutes per 450g/1lb if you prefer the meat well done. Preheat the oven to 200°C/400°F/Gas 6.

3 Put the clove-studded onion and a few apple slices inside the bird. Spread the butter all over the skin, and season.

4 Cover with the bacon rashers and put the duck into a roasting pan with 30ml/2 tbsp water. Roast in the preheated oven for the time estimated, removing the rashers for the last 10 minutes to allow the skin to brown.

5 To serve, carve the meat and arrange on warmed serving plates, leaving the legs whole.

Cook's Tips
- *Wildfowl from coastal areas can have a fishy flavour. To offset this, put the oven-ready bird into a pan of cold, salted water and bring to the boil. Reduce the heat and leave to simmer for 15–20 minutes, then remove the bird and wash and dry both inside and out before proceeding.*
- *Wildfowl are often served rare. The meat is lean and will be dry unless slowly cooked to retain moisture.*

Roast Farmyard Duck with Cider

Cooking apples are used to offset the richness of duck in this oven-roasted dish. Serve with vegetables, including roast potatoes and, perhaps, some red cabbage.

Serves 4
2kg/4½lb oven-ready duck or duckling
300ml/½ pint/1¼ cups dry (hard) cider
60ml/4 tbsp double (heavy) cream
sea salt and ground black pepper

For the stuffing
75g/3oz/6 tbsp butter
115g/4oz/2 cups fresh white breadcrumbs
450g/1lb cooking apples, peeled, cored and diced
15ml/1 tbsp sugar, or to taste
freshly grated nutmeg

1 Preheat the oven to 200°C/400°F/Gas 6. To make the stuffing, melt the butter in a pan and fry the breadcrumbs until golden brown. Add the apples to the breadcrumbs with salt, pepper, sugar and a pinch of nutmeg. Mix well.

2 Wipe the duck inside and out and remove any obvious excess fat. Rub the skin with salt. Stuff the duck with the prepared mixture, then secure the vent with a small skewer.

3 Weigh the stuffed duck and calculate the cooking time, allowing 20 minutes per 450g/1lb. Prick the skin all over with a fork to allow the fat to run out during the cooking time, then lay it on top of a wire rack in a roasting pan, sprinkle with ground black pepper and put it into the oven to roast.

4 About 20 minutes before the end of the estimated cooking time, remove the duck from the oven and pour off all the fat that has accumulated under the rack (reserve it for frying). Slide the duck off the rack into the roasting pan and pour the cider over. Return to the oven and finish cooking, basting occasionally.

5 Transfer the duck to a serving dish and keep warm while you make the sauce. Set the roasting pan over medium heat and boil the cider to reduce it by half. Stir in the cream, heat through and season. Remove the stuffing from the duck. Carve the duck into slices or joint it. Serve with stuffing and the cider sauce.

Roast Mallard Energy 486kcal/2028kJ; Protein 49.6g; Carbohydrate 0.1g, of which sugars 0.1g; Fat 32g, of which saturates 14.1g; Cholesterol 278mg; Calcium 28mg; Fibre 0g; Sodium 1.08g.
Roast Duck Energy 572kcal/2397kJ; Protein 31.5g; Carbohydrate 34.6g, of which sugars 13.1g; Fat 33.1g, of which saturates 17.8g; Cholesterol 211mg; Calcium 74mg; Fibre 2.4g; Sodium 498mg.

Spiced Duck with Pears

This delicious, slow-cooked casserole includes sautéed pears, which are added towards the end of cooking. The sauce is a pounded pine nut and garlic paste, which both flavours and thickens.

Serves 6

6 duck portions, either breast or leg pieces
15ml/1 tbsp olive oil
1 large onion, thinly sliced
1 cinnamon stick, halved
2 thyme sprigs
475ml/16fl oz/2 cups hot chicken stock

To finish

3 firm ripe pears
30ml/2 tbsp olive oil
2 garlic cloves, sliced
25g/1oz/⅓ cup pine nuts
2.5ml/½ tsp saffron threads
25g/1oz/2 tbsp raisins
salt and ground black pepper
young thyme sprigs or parsley, to garnish

1 Preheat the oven to 180°C/ 350°F/Gas 4. Fry the duck portions in the oil for about 5 minutes until golden. Transfer the duck to an ovenproof dish and drain off all but 15ml/1 tbsp of the fat left in the pan.

2 Add the onion to the pan and fry for 5 minutes. Add the cinnamon stick, thyme and stock and bring to the boil. Pour over the duck and bake in the oven for 1¼ hours.

3 Meanwhile, peel, core and halve the pears and fry quickly in the oil on the cut sides until golden. Pound the garlic, pine nuts and saffron in a mortar, with a pestle, to make a smooth paste.

4 Add the paste to the casserole along with the raisins and pears. Bake for a further 15 minutes until the pears are tender. Season to taste with salt and pepper and garnish with thyme or parsley. Serve with mashed potatoes and a green vegetable, if you like.

Cook's Tip

A good stock is essential for this dish. Buy a large duck (plus two breast portions if you want to be generous) and joint it yourself, using the giblets and carcass for stock.

Roast Duckling with Honey

A sweet and sour orange sauce is the perfect foil for the richness of the duck in this oven-roasted recipe. Frying the orange rind first helps to intensify its sharp, tangy flavour.

Serves 4

2.25kg/5lb oven-ready duckling
2.5ml/½ tsp ground allspice
1 orange
15ml/1 tbsp sunflower oil
30ml/2 tbsp plain (all-purpose) flour
150ml/¼ pint/⅔ cup chicken or duck stock
10ml/2 tsp red wine vinegar
15ml/1 tbsp clear honey
salt and ground black pepper
watercress or rocket (arugula) and thinly pared orange rind, to serve

1 Preheat the oven to 220°C/425°F/Gas 7. Using a fork, pierce the duckling all over, except the breast, so that the fat runs out during cooking.

2 Using your hands, rub the ground allspice all over the skin of the duckling and sprinkle with salt and plenty of black pepper.

3 Put the duckling on a rack over a roasting pan and cook in the preheated oven for about 20 minutes. Then reduce the oven temperature to 190°C/375°F/Gas 5 and cook for a further 2 hours. Baste the duckling occasionally during cooking with the juices from the pan.

4 Meanwhile, thinly pare the rind from the orange and cut into very fine strips. Heat the oil in a pan and gently fry the orange rind for 2–3 minutes. Squeeze the juice from the orange and set aside.

5 Transfer the duckling to a warmed serving dish and keep warm. Drain off all but 30ml/2 tbsp fat from the pan, sprinkle in the flour and stir well.

6 Stir in the stock, vinegar, honey, orange juice and rind. Bring to the boil, stirring all the time. Simmer for 2–3 minutes. Season the sauce with salt and pepper. Serve the duckling with watercress or rocket and thinly pared orange rind.

Spiced Duck Energy 296kcal/1235kJ; Protein 21.5g; Carbohydrate 14.7g, of which sugars 11.3g; Fat 18.8g, of which saturates 2.8g; Cholesterol 110mg; Calcium 40mg; Fibre 2.3g; Sodium 147mg.
Roast Duckling Energy 381kcal/1590kJ; Protein 33.7g; Carbohydrate 5.8g, of which sugars 2.9g; Fat 25g, of which saturates 7.1g; Cholesterol 203mg; Calcium 24mg; Fibre 0.1g; Sodium 188mg.

Duckling Jubilee

This roasted dish partners duck with an apricot sauce.

Serves 4
2kg/4½lb duckling
60ml/4 tbsp chopped fresh parsley
1 lemon, quartered
3 carrots, sliced
2 celery sticks, sliced
1 onion, roughly chopped
salt and ground black pepper
apricots and sage flowers, to garnish

For the sauce
425g/15oz can apricots in syrup
50g/2oz/¼ cup sugar
10ml/2 tsp English (hot) mustard
60ml/4 tbsp apricot jam
15ml/1 tbsp lemon juice
10ml/2 tsp grated lemon rind
50ml/2fl oz/¼ cup orange juice
1.5ml/¼ tsp each ground ginger and ground coriander
60–75ml/4–5 tbsp brandy

1 Preheat the oven to 220°C/425°F/Gas 7. Clean the duck well and pat dry with kitchen paper. Season the skin liberally. Mix together the parsley, lemon, carrots, celery and onion in a bowl, then spoon this mixture into the cavity of the duck.

2 Cook the duck for 45 minutes on a rack set over a roasting pan. Baste the duck occasionally with its juices. Remove the duck from the oven and prick the skin all over with a fork. Return it to the oven, reduce the temperature to 180°C/350°F/Gas 4 and cook for a further 1–1½ hours or until golden brown, tender and crisp.

3 Meanwhile, to make the sauce, put the apricots and their syrup, the sugar and mustard in a food processor or blender. Add the jam and process until smooth.

4 Pour the apricot mixture into a pan and stir in the lemon juice and rind, orange juice and spices. Bring to the boil, add the brandy and cook for a further 1–2 minutes. Remove from the heat and check the seasoning, adding salt and pepper if necessary. Pour into a jug (pitcher) or gravy boat.

5 Discard the fruit, vegetables and herbs from inside the duck and arrange the bird on a serving platter. Garnish with fresh apricots and sage flowers. Serve the sauce separately.

Mediterranean Duck with Harissa and Saffron

Harissa is a fiery chilli sauce from north Africa. Mixed with cinnamon, saffron and preserved lemon, it gives this slow-cooked casserole an unforgettable flavour.

Serves 4
15ml/1 tbsp olive oil
1.8–2kg/4–4½lb duck, quartered
1 large onion, thinly sliced
1 garlic clove, crushed
2.5ml/½ tsp ground cumin
400ml/14fl oz/1⅔ cups duck or chicken stock
juice of ½ lemon
5–10ml/1–2 tsp harissa
1 cinnamon stick
5ml/1 tsp saffron threads
50g/2oz/⅓ cup black olives
50g/2oz/⅓ cup green olives
peel of 1 preserved lemon, rinsed, drained and cut into fine strips
2–3 lemon slices
30ml/2 tbsp chopped fresh coriander (cilantro), plus extra leaves to garnish
salt and ground black pepper

1 Heat the oil in a flameproof casserole. Add the duck quarters and cook until browned. Remove with a slotted spoon and set aside. Cook the onion and garlic in the oil remaining in the pan for 5 minutes until soft. Add the cumin and cook for 2 minutes.

2 Pour in the stock and lemon juice, then add the harissa, cinnamon and saffron. Bring to the boil. Return the duck to the casserole and add the olives, preserved lemon peel and lemon slices. Season with salt and pepper.

3 Lower the heat, partially cover the casserole and simmer gently for about 45 minutes, or until the duck is cooked through. Discard the cinnamon stick. Stir in the chopped coriander and garnish with the coriander leaves.

Cook's Tip
The rich flavour of duck is best appreciated when a duck reaches its full-grown size. Look for duck with supple, waxy skin with a dry appearance, a long body and tender, meaty breasts.

Duckling Jubilee Energy 352kcal/1491kJ; Protein 28.3g; Carbohydrate 33.5g, of which sugars 33.5g; Fat 9.1g, of which saturates 3g; Cholesterol 150mg; Calcium 47mg; Fibre 1g; Sodium 167mg.
Mediterranean Duck Energy 262kcal/1095kJ; Protein 26.6g; Carbohydrate 8.3g, of which sugars 5.9g; Fat 14g, of which saturates 3.5g; Cholesterol 135mg; Calcium 79mg; Fibre 2.8g; Sodium 709mg.

Duck and Chestnut Casserole

Serve this slow-cooked casserole with a mixture of mashed potatoes and celeriac to soak up the rich juices from the duck.

Serves 4–6

2kg/4½lb duck
45ml/3 tbsp olive oil
175g/6oz baby (pearl) onions
50g/2oz field (portabello) mushrooms, sliced
50g/2oz/1 cup shiitake mushrooms, sliced
300ml/½ pint/1¼ cups red wine
300ml/½ pint/1¼ cups hot beef stock
225g/8oz canned, peeled, unsweetened chestnuts, drained
salt and ground black pepper
fresh parsley, to garnish
mashed potatoes and celeriac, to serve

1 Joint the duck into eight pieces. Heat the oil in a large frying pan and cook the duck pieces until lightly browned all over. Remove the duck pieces from the frying pan using a slotted spoon and set aside.

2 Add the baby onions to the pan and cook for 10 minutes, until they have softened and are well browned.

3 Add the mushrooms to the pan and cook for a few minutes more. Deglaze the pan with the red wine. Bring to the boil and let it bubble until reduced by half. Meanwhile, preheat the oven to 180°C/350°F/Gas 4.

4 Pour the contents of the frying pan into a casserole and stir in the stock. Add the browned duck and the chestnuts, season well with salt and pepper and cook in the oven for 1½ hours. Garnish with parsley and serve with mashed potatoes and celeriac.

Cook's Tip
Unlike some poultry, duck freezes well because its high fat content ensures that it retains its flavour and moisture when it is thawed. However, the flesh can easily be damaged, so check the packaging carefully before buying. Fresh duck is also available all year round.

Wild Duck Roasted with Morels and Madeira

The deliciously rich flavour of wild duck combines well with the stronger, earthy taste of the various mushrooms in this recipe.

Serves 4

2 x 1kg/2¼lb mallards (dressed and barded weight)
50g/2oz/4 tbsp unsalted butter
75ml/5 tbsp Madeira or sherry
1 onion, halved and sliced
½ celery stick, chopped
1 small carrot, chopped
10 large dried morel mushrooms
225g/8oz/3 cups blewits, parasol and field (portabello) mushrooms, trimmed and sliced
600ml/1 pint/2½ cups chicken stock, boiling
1 fresh thyme sprig
10ml/2 tsp wine vinegar
salt and ground black pepper
fresh parsley sprigs and carrot juliennes, to garnish
game chips, to serve

1 Preheat the oven to 190°C/375°F/Gas 5 and season the ducks with salt and pepper. Melt half of the butter in a large frying pan. Add the ducks and cook until lightly browned on all sides. Transfer them to a shallow dish, leaving the butter and juices in the pan.

2 Heat the sediment in the pan, pour in the Madeira or sherry and bring to the boil, stirring constantly and scraping the base to deglaze the pan. Pour this liquid over the birds and set the dish aside.

3 Heat the remaining butter in a large, flameproof casserole and add the onion, celery and carrot. Place the birds on top, reserve the Madeira or sherry, and cook in the oven for about 40 minutes.

4 Tie all the mushrooms in a 45cm/18in square of muslin (cheesecloth). Add the hot chicken stock, the Madeira or sherry from the frying pan, the thyme and the muslin bag of mushrooms to the casserole. Cover and return to the oven for 40 minutes.

5 Transfer the birds to a warmed serving platter, remove and discard the thyme and set the mushrooms aside.

6 Process the braising liquid in a food processor or blender and pour it back into the casserole. Break open the muslin bag and stir the mushrooms into the sauce. Add the wine vinegar, season to taste with salt and ground black pepper. Gently heat the sauce for 1 minute until hot.

7 Garnish the ducks with parsley and carrot. Serve with game chips and hand the Madeira or sherry sauce separately in a jug (pitcher) or gravy boat.

Cook's Tip
Mallard is the most popular wild duck, although widgeon and teal are good substitutes. A widgeon will serve two, but allow one teal per person.

Casserole Energy 405kcal/1689kJ; Protein 22.2g; Carbohydrate 16.2g, of which sugars 4.4g; Fat 24.7g, of which saturates 6.4g; Cholesterol 134mg; Calcium 41mg; Fibre 2.1g; Sodium 125mg.
Wild Duck Energy 1444kcal/5961kJ; Protein 33.3g; Carbohydrate 2.6g, of which sugars 2.1g; Fat 142.5g, of which saturates 81.1g; Cholesterol 499mg; Calcium 55mg; Fibre 0.9g; Sodium 1032mg.

Duck Cassoulet

Based on the traditional, slow-cooked French dish, this favourite recipe is full of flavours and makes a hearty and warming meal.

Serves 6

3–4 duck breast fillets, 450g/1lb total weight
225g/8oz thick-cut streaky (fatty) pork or unsmoked streaky (fatty) bacon rashers (strips)
450g/1lb Toulouse or garlic sausages
45ml/3 tbsp vegetable oil
450g/1lb onions, chopped
2 garlic cloves, crushed
2 x 425g/15oz cans cannellini beans, rinsed and drained
225g/8oz carrots, roughly chopped
400g/14oz can chopped tomatoes
15ml/1 tbsp tomato purée (paste)
1 bouquet garni
30ml/2 tbsp chopped fresh thyme or 15ml/1 tbsp dried
475ml/16fl oz/2 cups well-flavoured chicken stock
115g/4oz/2 cups fresh white or wholemeal (whole-wheat) breadcrumbs
salt and ground black pepper
fresh thyme sprigs, to garnish
warm crusty bread, to serve

1 Preheat the oven to 160°C/325°F/Gas 3. Cut the duck fillets and pork or bacon rashers into large pieces. Twist the sausages to shorten them and then cut them into short lengths.

2 Heat the oil in a large flameproof casserole. Cook the meat in batches, until well browned. Remove from the pan with a slotted spoon and drain on kitchen paper. Add the onions and garlic to the pan and cook for 3–4 minutes until just soft.

3 Stir in the beans, carrots, tomatoes, tomato purée, bouquet garni, thyme and seasoning. Return the meat to the casserole and mix well. Add just enough stock to cover the meat and beans. Bring to the boil. Cover and cook in the oven for 1 hour. Add extra water if it starts to dry out during cooking.

4 Remove the bouquet garni. Sprinkle the breadcrumbs in an even layer over the top of the cassoulet and return to the oven, uncovered, for a further 40 minutes, or until the meat is tender and the top crisp and lightly brown. Garnish with fresh thyme sprigs and serve immediately, with plenty of warm crusty bread to mop up the juices.

Anita Wong's Duck

This slowly simmered dish is packed with Asian flavours. Serve on its own or with fragrant rice for a more substantial meal.

Serves 4–6

60ml/4 tbsp vegetable oil
2 garlic cloves, chopped
2.25kg/5lb duck, with giblets (if making your own stock)
2.5cm/1in piece fresh root ginger, thinly sliced
45ml/3 tbsp bean paste
30ml/2 tbsp light soy sauce
15ml/1 tbsp dark soy sauce
15ml/1 tbsp sugar
2.5ml/½ tsp Chinese five-spice powder
3 pieces star anise
450ml/¾ pint/scant 2 cups duck stock (see Cook's Tip)
salt
shredded spring onions (scallions), to garnish

1 Heat the oil in a large pan. Fry the garlic without browning for 1 minute, then add the duck. Turn frequently in the pan until the outside is slightly brown all over. Transfer to a plate and keep warm.

2 Add the ginger to the pan, then stir in the bean paste. Cook for 1 minute, then add both soy sauces, the sugar and the five-spice powder. Return the duck to the pan and fry, turning, until the outside is coated.

3 Add the star anise and stock, and season to taste. Cover tightly and simmer gently for 2–2½ hours, or until the duck is tender. Skim off any excess fat. Leave the bird in the sauce to cool.

4 Cut the duck into serving portions and pour over the sauce. Garnish with shredded spring onions and serve cold.

Cook's Tip

To make stock, put the duck giblets in a pan with a small onion and a piece of bruised fresh root ginger. Cover with 600ml/1 pint/2½ cups water, bring to the boil and then simmer, covered, for 20 minutes. Strain and blot with kitchen paper to remove the excess fat.

Duck Cassoulet Energy 739kcal/3085kJ; Protein 40.2g; Carbohydrate 49.6g, of which sugars 11.6g; Fat 44.8g, of which saturates 14.2g; Cholesterol 142mg; Calcium 118mg; Fibre 9.4g; Sodium 1848mg.
Anita Wong's Energy 233kcal/977kJ; Protein 22.7g; Carbohydrate 4.2g, of which sugars 1g; Fat 14.2g, of which saturates 3.1g; Cholesterol 113mg; Calcium 23mg; Fibre 1.3g; Sodium 652mg.

Steak and Kidney Pie

Chunks of succulent beef and kidney are gently simmered in a slow cooker.

Serves 4

225g/8oz ox or lamb's kidney
45ml/3 tbsp oil
675g/1½lb stewing steak, cubed
15g/½ oz/1 tbsp unsalted butter
2 onions, chopped
30ml/2 tbsp plain (all-purpose) flour
300ml/½ pint/1¼ cups beef stock
15ml/1 tbsp tomato purée (paste)
10ml/2 tsp English (hot) mustard
2 bay leaves
375g/13oz puff pastry
beaten egg, to glaze
15ml/1 tbsp chopped fresh parsley
salt and ground black pepper

1 Remove all fat and skin from the kidney and cut into cubes or thick slices. Heat 30ml/2 tbsp of the oil in a frying pan and brown the beef on all sides. Transfer from the pan with a slotted spoon to the ceramic cooking pot. Set the slow cooker to high.

2 Add the kidney to the pan and brown for 1–2 minutes, then add to the beef. Heat the remaining oil and the butter in the pan. Cook the onions for 5 minutes, until just coloured. Sprinkle with the flour and stir in, then remove the pan from the heat.

3 Gradually stir the stock into the pan, followed by the tomato purée and mustard. Bring to the boil, stirring constantly, until thickened. Pour the gravy over the meat, then add the bay leaves and season. Stir well and cover with the lid. Reduce the cooker to low and cook for 5–7 hours, or until the meat is tender.

4 Meanwhile, roll out the pastry and cut out a 25cm/10in round. Transfer the pastry round to a baking sheet lined with baking parchment. Mark the pastry into quarters, cutting almost but not quite through it. Decorate with pastry trimmings, then flute the edge. Cover with clear film (plastic wrap) and chill until needed.

5 Towards the end of the meat's cooking time, preheat the oven to 200°C/400°F/Gas 6. Brush the pastry with beaten egg, then bake for 25 minutes, or until well risen and golden brown.

6 Stir the parsley into the stew and spoon on to plates. Quarter the crust and use to top each portion. Serve immediately.

Beef and Mushroom Pudding

This slow-cooker pudding features beef and mushrooms in a rich gravy inside a light pastry crust.

Serves 4

25g/1oz/½ cup dried porcini mushrooms
475ml/16fl oz/2 cups hot beef stock
675g/1½lb stewing steak
60ml/4 tbsp plain (all-purpose) flour
45ml/3 tbsp sunflower oil
1 large onion, finely chopped
225g/8oz chestnut or flat mushrooms, thickly sliced
1 bay leaf
15ml/1 tbsp Worcestershire sauce
75ml/2½fl oz/⅓ cup port or red wine
salt and ground black pepper

For the pastry

275g/10oz/2½ cups self-raising (self-rising) flour
2.5ml/½ tsp baking powder
2.5ml/½ tsp salt
15ml/1 tbsp each chopped parsley and fresh thyme
75g/3oz/½ cup beef or vegetable suet (US chilled, grated shortening)
50g/2oz/¼ cup butter, frozen and grated
1 egg, lightly beaten
150ml/¼ pint/⅔ cup cold water

1 Put the dried mushrooms in a bowl and pour over the stock. Leave for 20 minutes. Meanwhile, trim the meat and cut into 2cm/¾in pieces. Place the flour in a bowl, season, then toss in the meat to coat. Heat the oil in a frying pan and fry the meat in batches until browned. Transfer to the ceramic cooking pot. Add the onion to the pan and cook gently for 10 minutes. Add to the beef, then add the chestnut mushrooms and the bay leaf.

2 In a bowl, combine the Worcestershire sauce with the port or wine, then pour into the cooking pot. Drain and chop the soaked mushrooms, then add to the pot with the stock. Stir well, then cover and cook on high or auto for 1 hour. Reduce to low and cook for 5–6 hours until the meat and onions are tender. Remove the bay leaf, then leave the mixture to cool completely.

3 To make the pastry, butter a deep 1.75 litre/3 pint/7½ cup heatproof bowl. Sift the flour, baking powder and salt into a mixing bowl and stir in the herbs, then the suet and butter. Add the egg and enough cold water to mix, and gather into a soft dough. Knead until smooth, then cut off a quarter. Shape the rest into a ball and roll out into a round large enough to line the bowl. Lift up the pastry and press into the bowl, allowing the excess to fall over the sides. Roll out the reserved pastry to make a round large enough to use as a lid for the pudding.

4 Spoon in the cooled filling and enough gravy to come within 1cm/½in of the rim. (Reserve the remaining gravy to serve with the pudding.) Brush the top edge of the pastry with water and place the lid on top. Press the edges together and trim off any excess. Cover the bowl with a pleated, double thickness layer of baking parchment and secure under the rim using string. Cover with pleated foil to allow the pudding to rise. Put an inverted saucer or metal pastry ring in the base of the cleaned cooking pot and place the bowl on top. Pour in enough near-boiling water to come just over halfway up the sides of the bowl. Cover and cook on high for 3 hours.

5 Carefully remove the bowl from the slow cooker, then take off the foil, string and baking parchment. Loosen the edges of the pudding and invert on to a warmed serving plate.

Steak and Kidney Pie Energy 637kcal/2652kJ; Protein 18.7g; Carbohydrate 46.2g, of which sugars 5.2g; Fat 43.4g, of which saturates 13.1g; Cholesterol 259mg; Calcium 99mg; Fibre 2.7g; Sodium 578mg.
Beef Pudding Energy 1061kcal/4444kJ; Protein 70g; Carbohydrate 75.1g, of which sugars 4.8g; Fat 54.3g, of which saturates 24.5g; Cholesterol 265mg; Calcium 319mg; Fibre 4.4g; Sodium 941mg.

Braised Beef with Horseradish

This dark, rich beef with a spicy kick makes an ideal alternative to a meat roast. The meat slowly tenderizes in the slow cooker and all the flavours blend together.

Serves 4

30ml/2 tbsp plain (all-purpose) flour
4 x 175g/6oz braising steaks
30ml/2 tbsp sunflower oil
12 small shallots, peeled and halved
1 garlic clove, crushed
1.5ml/¼ tsp ground ginger
5ml/1 tsp curry powder
10ml/2 tsp dark muscovado (molasses) sugar
475ml/16fl oz/2 cups near-boiling beef stock
15ml/1 tbsp Worcestershire sauce
30ml/2 tbsp creamed horseradish
225g/8oz baby carrots, trimmed
1 bay leaf
salt and ground black pepper
30ml/2 tbsp chopped fresh chives, to garnish
roast vegetables, to serve

1 Place the flour in a large, flat dish and season with salt and black pepper. Toss the steaks in the flour to coat. Heat the oil in a pan and quickly brown the steaks on both sides. Transfer them to the ceramic cooking pot.

2 Add the halved shallots to the pan and cook gently for 10 minutes, or until golden and beginning to soften. Stir in the garlic, ginger and curry powder and cook for 1 minute more, then remove the pan from the heat.

3 Transfer the shallot mixture to the ceramic cooking pot, spreading it over the meat, and sprinkle with the sugar.

4 Pour the beef stock over the shallots and meat, then add the Worcestershire sauce, horseradish, baby carrots and bay leaf. Stir to combine, then season with salt and black pepper. Cover with the lid and cook on high or auto for 1 hour.

5 Reduce the slow cooker to low, or leave on auto, and continue to cook the stew for a further 5–6 hours, or until the beef and vegetables are very tender.

6 Remove the bay leaf from the stew and sprinkle with the chopped chives before serving with roast vegetables.

Spiced Beef

This is not a recipe to rush. The meat is first cured for three or four days and then simmered for hours in the slow cooker until tender. Serve on bread, with chutney.

Serves 6

15ml/1 tbsp coarsely ground black pepper
10ml/2 tsp ground ginger
15ml/1 tbsp juniper berries, crushed
15ml/1 tbsp coriander seeds, crushed
5ml/1 tsp ground cloves
15ml/1 tbsp ground allspice
45ml/3 tbsp soft dark brown sugar
2 bay leaves, crushed
1 small onion, finely chopped
1.8kg/4lb corned beef, silverside (pot roast) or tail end
300ml/½ pint/1¼ cups Guinness
fruit chutney and brown bread, to serve

1 First, spice the beef: blend the pepper, spices and sugar thoroughly, then mix in the bay leaves and onion. Rub the mixture into the meat, then put it into a suitable lidded container and refrigerate for 3–4 days, turning and rubbing with the mixture daily.

2 Put the meat into the ceramic cooking pot and add enough cold water to just cover the meat. Cover with the lid and switch on to auto or high. Cook for 3 hours, then leave on auto or reduce to low and cook for a further 3–4 hours, until the meat is very tender. For the last hour of cooking time, pour in the Guinness.

3 When the joint is cooked, leave it to cool in the cooking liquid. Wrap in foil and keep in the refrigerator until required, then slice thinly to serve. It will keep for about 1 week.

Cook's Tips

- *As a first course, serve the beef thinly sliced with home-made brown bread and a fruit chutney, such as apple and sultana (golden raisin).*
- *Spiced beef is excellent as finger food for parties, sliced thinly and served with sour cream lightly flavoured with horseradish and black pepper.*

Braised Beef Energy 478kcal/2010kJ; Protein 62.5g; Carbohydrate 17.7g, of which sugars 9.6g; Fat 18.1g, of which saturates 7.4g; Cholesterol 176mg; Calcium 65mg; Fibre 2.5g; Sodium 423mg.
Spiced Beef Energy 309kcal/1301kJ; Protein 53.6g; Carbohydrate 2g, of which sugars 2g; Fat 9.7g, of which saturates 3.6g; Cholesterol 137mg; Calcium 15mg; Fibre 0g; Sodium 140mg.

Pot-roast Beef with Guinness

This heart-warming, rich pot roast is ideal for slow cooking in the oven for a winter supper. Brisket of beef has the best flavour but this dish works equally well with rolled silverside or topside.

Serves 6

30ml/2 tbsp vegetable oil
900g/2lb rolled brisket of beef
275g/10oz onions, roughly chopped
2 celery sticks, thickly sliced
450g/1lb carrots, cut into chunks
675g/1½ lb potatoes, cut into large chunks
30ml/2 tbsp plain (all-purpose) flour
475ml/16fl oz/2 cups beef stock
300ml/½ pint/1¼ cups Guinness
1 bay leaf
45ml/3 tbsp chopped fresh thyme
5ml/1 tsp soft light brown sugar
30ml/2 tbsp wholegrain mustard
15ml/1 tbsp tomato purée (paste)
salt and ground black pepper

1 Preheat the oven to 180°C/350°F/Gas 4. Heat the oil in a large flameproof casserole and brown the meat all over.

2 Remove the meat from the pan and drain it on a double layer of kitchen paper. Add the chopped onions to the pan and cook for about 4 minutes, or until they are just beginning to soften and turn brown, stirring all the time.

3 Add the celery, carrot and potato to the casserole and cook over medium heat for 2–3 minutes, or until they are just beginning to colour.

4 Stir in the flour and cook for a further 1 minute, stirring continuously. Pour in the beef stock and the Guinness and stir until well combined. Bring the sauce to the boil, stirring continuously with a wooden spoon.

5 Add the bay leaf, thyme, sugar, mustard, tomato purée and plenty of seasoning. Place the meat on top, cover tightly and transfer to the oven.

6 Cook for about 2½ hours, or until the vegetables and meat are tender. Adjust the seasoning and add another pinch of sugar, if necessary. To serve, remove the meat and carve into thick slices. Serve with the vegetables and plenty of gravy.

Beef Hotpot with Herb Dumplings

This hotpot is flavoured with shallots and mushrooms, and finished with herby dumplings.

Serves 4

40g/1½oz/3 tbsp butter
30ml/2 tbsp sunflower oil
115g/4oz/⅔ cup lardons or pancetta, diced
900g/2lb lean braising steak, cut into chunks
45ml/3 tbsp plain (all-purpose) flour
450ml/¾ pint/scant 2 cups beer
450ml/¾ pint/scant 2 cups beef stock
20g/¾oz/⅓ cup dried porcini mushrooms, soaked in 60ml/4 tbsp warm water for 20 minutes
1 bouquet garni
8 shallots
175g/6oz/2 cups button (white) mushrooms
salt and ground black pepper
sprigs of thyme, to garnish

For the herb dumplings

115g/4oz/1 cup self-raising (self-rising) flour
50g/2oz/scant ½ cup shredded suet (US chilled, grated shortening)
2.5ml/½ tsp salt
2.5ml/½ tsp mustard powder
15ml/1 tbsp chopped fresh parsley
15ml/1 tbsp chopped fresh thyme

1 Soak a clay pot in cold water for 20 minutes, then drain. In a frying pan, melt half the butter with half the oil, and brown the lardons or pancetta. Remove with a slotted spoon and transfer to the clay pot. Add the beef to the pan and brown, then add to the clay pot. Sprinkle the flour into the fat in the pan and stir.

2 Stir the beer and stock into the pan and bring to the boil. Add the mushroom soaking liquid to the pan with the porcini. Season well. Pour the sauce over the meat in the clay pot, then add the bouquet garni. Cover the pot and place in an unheated oven, set to 200°C/400°F/Gas 6, and cook for 30 minutes, then reduce to 160°C/325°F/Gas 3 and cook for a further 1 hour.

3 Heat the remaining butter and oil in the pan. Cook the shallots until golden. Set aside. Add the button mushrooms and sauté for 2 minutes. Add both into the pot and cook for 30 minutes.

4 Mix together the dumpling ingredients. Add cold water to bind to a sticky dough. Divide into 12 balls and place on top of the hotpot. Cover and cook for 25 minutes. Serve immediately.

Pot-roast Beef Energy 402kcal/1691kJ; Protein 35.5g; Carbohydrate 33.8g, of which sugars 11.9g; Fat 13.6g, of which saturates 4.4g; Cholesterol 81mg; Calcium 58mg; Fibre 4g; Sodium 142mg.
Beef Hotpot Energy 527kcal/2194kJ; Protein 10.3g; Carbohydrate 39.1g, of which sugars 6.4g; Fat 35.5g, of which saturates 14.9g; Cholesterol 50mg; Calcium 169mg; Fibre 3.1g; Sodium 789mg.

Beef and Guinness Casserole

Stout and beef make natural partners in this richly flavoured version of a popular dish, which is slowly simmered on top of the stove. It is suitable for any occasion, including informal entertaining, because it is simple to prepare and can be left to cook. Serve with creamy, well-buttered mashed potatoes.

Serves 4

30ml/2 tbsp olive oil
900g/2lb stewing beef (such as rib steak or shoulder), cut into thin slices
1 onion, chopped
2 leeks, sliced
2 carrots, sliced
2 celery sticks, sliced
2 garlic cloves, finely chopped
300ml/½ pint/1¼ cups well-reduced beef stock
150ml/¼ pint/⅔ cup Guinness
50g/2oz/¼ cup butter
75g/3oz streaky (fatty) bacon, trimmed and diced
115g/4oz wild or cultivated mushrooms, quartered or sliced
50g/2oz shallots or small onions, left whole
25g/1oz/¼ cup plain (all-purpose) flour
salt and ground black pepper

1 Heat the olive oil in a large pan and fry the meat, in batches, for a few minutes until evenly browned. Transfer to a flameproof casserole. Sauté the vegetables for 5 minutes in the pan.

2 Add the vegetables to the meat, and add the chopped garlic. Pour in the stock and the Guinness and stir well. Season with salt and pepper. Cover the casserole and bring to the boil, then reduce the heat and simmer gently for about 1½ hours.

3 Remove the meat from the casserole and strain the cooking liquid and reserve. Discard the vegetables.

4 Clean the casserole and sauté the bacon, mushrooms and shallots or onions in the butter for 5–10 minutes. When the vegetables are tender, sprinkle in the flour and cook, stirring, over low heat for 2–3 minutes, then slowly blend in the reserved cooking liquid, and cook, stirring, until it thickens.

5 Return the meat to the casserole, and reheat, stirring until well combined. Serve with mashed potatoes.

Corned Beef with Dumplings

Slowly simmered corned beef tends to be associated with St Patrick's Day. If lightly cured, the meat may need to be soaked before cooking, but check with the butcher when buying; if in doubt, soak in cold water overnight.

Serves 6

1.3kg/3lb corned silverside (pot roast) or brisket
4 cloves
1 onion
2 bay leaves
8–10 whole black peppercorns
1 small cabbage

For the dumplings

1 small onion, finely chopped
small bunch of fresh parsley, chopped
115g/4oz/1 cup self-raising (self-rising) flour
50g/2oz/scant ½ cup shredded beef suet (US chilled, grated shortening)
salt and ground black pepper

1 Soak the meat in cold water, if necessary, for several hours or overnight. When ready to cook, drain the meat and place in a large pan or flameproof casserole. Cover with fresh cold water.

2 Stick the cloves into the onion and add it to the pan with the bay leaves and peppercorns. Bring slowly to the boil, cover and simmer for 2 hours, or until the meat is tender.

3 Meanwhile, make the dumplings. Mix the onion and chopped parsley with the flour and suet, and season with salt and pepper. Add just enough water to make a soft, but not too sticky, dough. Dust your hands with a little flour and shape the dough into 12 dumplings.

4 When the meat is cooked, remove it from the pan and keep warm. Bring the cooking liquid to a brisk boil, put in the dumplings and bring back to the boil. Cover tightly and cook the dumplings briskly for 15 minutes.

5 Meanwhile, slice the cabbage leaves finely and cook lightly in a little of the beef stock (keep the remaining stock for making soup). Serve the beef thinly sliced with the dumplings and shredded cabbage. Boiled potatoes and parsley sauce are traditional accompaniments.

Beef Casserole Energy 670kcal/2786kJ; Protein 57.5g; Carbohydrate 14g, of which sugars 7.3g; Fat 42g, of which saturates 17.5g; Cholesterol 169mg; Calcium 71mg; Fibre 3.7g; Sodium 478mg.
Corned Beef Energy 451kcal/1895kJ; Protein 54.6g; Carbohydrate 21g, of which sugars 4.5g; Fat 17.4g, of which saturates 7.7g; Cholesterol 139mg; Calcium 86mg; Fibre 2.4g; Sodium 142mg.

Beef with Stout and Potatoes

Braising beef in stout results in beautifully succulent meat. Bake it in a moderate oven for long, slow tenderizing, if you prefer.

Serves 4

675g/1½lb stewing beef
15ml/1 tbsp vegetable oil
25g/1oz/2 tbsp butter
225g/8oz tiny white onions
175ml/6fl oz/¾ cup stout or dark beer
300ml/½ pint/1¼ cups beef stock
1 bouquet garni
675g/1½lb firm, waxy potatoes, cut into thick slices
225g/8oz/3 cups mushrooms, sliced
15ml/1 tbsp plain (all-purpose) flour
2.5ml/½ tsp mild mustard
salt and ground black pepper
chopped thyme sprigs, to garnish

1 Trim any excess fat from the beef and cut into four pieces. Season both sides of the meat. Heat the oil and 10g/¼oz/1½ tsp of the butter in a large, heavy pan.

2 Add the beef and brown on both sides, taking care not to burn the butter. Remove from the pan and set aside.

3 Add the onions to the pan and cook for 3–4 minutes until lightly browned all over. Return the beef to the pan with the onions. Pour on the stout or beer and stock and season to taste.

4 Next, add the bouquet garni to the pan and top with the potato slices, distributing them evenly over the surface to cover the beef. Bring the ingredients to a boil, then reduce the heat, cover with a tight-fitting lid and simmer gently for 1 hour.

5 Add the sliced mushrooms over the potatoes. Cover again and simmer for a further 30 minutes. Remove the beef and vegetables with a slotted spoon and arrange on a platter.

6 Mix the remaining butter with the flour to make a roux. Whisk a little at a time into the cooking liquid in the pan. Stir in the mustard. Cook over medium heat for 2–3 minutes, stirring all the while, until thickened.

7 Season the sauce and pour over the beef. Garnish with plenty of thyme sprigs and serve immediately.

Braised Beef with Vegetables

One-pot stews are not only great family dishes but are perfect for informal entertaining. The food can be prepared ahead and left to cook in the oven while you spend time with your guests, and there is little fear of anything overcooking or burning. This slow-cooked casserole features deliciously tender beef with carrots, leeks and potatoes.

Serves 4–6

1kg/2¼lb lean stewing beef, cut into 5cm/2in cubes
45ml/3 tbsp plain (all-purpose) flour
45ml/3 tbsp oil
1 large onion, thinly sliced
1 large carrot, thickly sliced
2 celery sticks, finely chopped
300ml/½ pint/¼ cup hot beef stock
30ml/2 tbsp tomato purée (paste)
5ml/1 tsp dried mixed herbs
15ml/1 tbsp dark muscovado (molasses) sugar
225g/8oz baby potatoes, halved
2 leeks, thinly sliced
salt and ground black pepper

1 Preheat the oven to 150°C/300°F/Gas 2. Season the flour and use to coat the beef cubes.

2 Heat the oil in a large, flameproof casserole. Add a small batch of meat, cook quickly until browned on all sides and, with a slotted spoon, lift out. Repeat with the remaining beef.

3 Add the onion, carrot and celery to the casserole. Cook over medium heat for about 10 minutes, stirring frequently, until they begin to soften and brown slightly at the edges.

4 Return the meat to the casserole and add the stock, tomato purée, herbs and sugar, at the same time scraping up any sediment that has stuck to the casserole. Heat until the liquid nearly comes to the boil.

5 Cover with a tight-fitting lid and put into the hot oven. Cook for 2–2½ hours, or until the beef is tender.

6 Stir in the potatoes and leeks, cover and cook for a further 30 minutes or until the potatoes are soft. Serve immediately.

Beef with Stout Energy 538kcal/2253kJ; Protein 43.4g; Carbohydrate 35.5g, of which sugars 6.2g; Fat 24.5g, of which saturates 10.2g; Cholesterol 111mg; Calcium 44mg; Fibre 3.2g; Sodium 172mg.
Braised Beef Energy 450kcal/1880kJ; Protein 41.3g; Carbohydrate 23.6g, of which sugars 10.3g; Fat 21.7g, of which saturates 7.3g; Cholesterol 97mg; Calcium 63mg; Fibre 3.5g; Sodium 137mg.

Dundee Beef Stew

Dundee is famously known as the home of marmalade, and this oven-cooked stew is flavoured with it. The red wine quite possibly also came into Dundee's busy port even though the majority must have come into Leith, the larger port for Edinburgh, farther south. This stew is excellent served with warming, creamy mashed potatoes.

Serves 4

900g/2lb stewing beef
50g/2oz/½ cup plain (all-purpose) flour
2.5ml/½ tsp paprika
30ml/2 tbsp vegetable oil
225g/8oz onions, peeled and chopped
50g/2oz/¼ cup butter
100g/3¾oz button (white) mushrooms, quartered
2 garlic cloves, crushed with a little salt
15ml/1 tbsp bitter marmalade
300ml/½ pint/1¼ cups red wine
150ml/¼ pint/⅔ cup beef stock
salt and ground black pepper
creamy mashed potatoes, to serve

1 Preheat the oven to 180°C/350°F/Gas 4. Cut the meat into 2.5cm/1in cubes. Season the flour with salt, black pepper and the paprika, spread it on a tray and coat the meat in it.

2 Heat the vegetable oil in a large, heavy pan. Add the beef and lightly brown on all sides. Do this in a few batches if your pan is small.

3 Transfer the meat to a casserole. Brown the onions in the original pan, turning occasionally and adding a little extra oil or some butter, if necessary. Add to the casserole.

4 Keeping the pan hot, add the rest of the butter and brown the mushrooms, then transfer to the casserole.

5 Add the rest of the ingredients to the casserole and bring to the boil, stirring to combine the marmalade and evenly distribute the meat and mushrooms.

6 Cover the casserole with a tight-fitting lid and place in the preheated oven for about 3 hours, until the meat is tender. Serve with creamy mashed potatoes.

One-pot Beef Stew

This recipe harks back to the idea of cooking everything in one pot over a fire in the hearth, the traditional way of preparing food in many rural farms and cottages across the Western world. It makes a superb alternative to a Sunday roast and is more forgiving as the beef, being slowly braised in stock, can sit and wait until you are ready to eat.

Serves 8

25g/1oz/2 tbsp butter, softened
25g/1oz/¼ cup plain (all-purpose) flour
1.6kg/3½lb silverside (pot roast), boned and rolled
450g/1lb small whole onions, peeled
450g/1lb small carrots, cut into two
8 celery sticks, cut into four
12 small potatoes
30ml/2 tbsp chopped fresh parsley

1 Make a beurre manié by combining the softened butter and the flour thoroughly. This will be used later to thicken the sauce for the stew.

2 Put the beef in a large pan, pour in cold water to just cover and cover with a tight-fitting lid. Bring to the boil, then simmer gently for 2 hours, topping up with boiling water.

3 After 2 hours, add the prepared vegetables to the pan and simmer the stew for a further 30 minutes, until all the vegetables are just cooked.

4 Remove the beef and vegetables from the pan, arrange on a serving dish and keep warm. Ladle about 350ml/12fl oz/1½ cups of the cooking liquor into a clean pan and bring to the boil. Whisk in the beurre manié to thicken it, adding a small spoonful at a time. Add the chopped fresh parsley to the sauce and stir in until well combined.

5 When ready to eat, pour the sauce over the beef and vegetables, retaining some to pass round the table in a warmed gravy boat or jug (pitcher) for diners to help themselves. Cut the meat in thick slices and serve, accompanied by a healthy portion of the vegetables.

Dundee Beef Stew Energy 544kcal/2276kJ; Protein 53.3g; Carbohydrate 17.1g, of which sugars 6.2g; Fat 24.1g, of which saturates 10.4g; Cholesterol 177mg; Calcium 53mg; Fibre 1.5g; Sodium 242mg.
One-pot Beef Stew Energy 875kcal/3656kJ; Protein 89.8g; Carbohydrate 38.5g, of which sugars 16.7g; Fat 41.1g, of which saturates 17.7g; Cholesterol 231mg; Calcium 121mg; Fibre 6.3g; Sodium 358mg.

Boeuf Bourguignon

This is a classic French dish of beef cooked Burgundy-style, with red wine, small pieces of bacon, shallots and mushrooms. It is baked in the oven for several hours at a low temperature until the meat is deliciously tender and succulent.

Serves 6

175g/6oz rindless streaky (fatty) bacon rashers (strips), chopped
900g/2lb lean braising steak, such as top rump (round) steak
30ml/2 tbsp plain (all-purpose) flour
45ml/3 tbsp sunflower oil
25g/1oz/2 tbsp butter
12 shallots
2 garlic cloves, crushed
175g/6oz/2⅓ cups mushrooms, sliced
450ml/¾ pint/scant 2 cups robust red wine
150ml/¼ pint/⅔ cup beef stock or consommé
1 bay leaf
2 sprigs each of fresh thyme, parsley and marjoram
salt and ground black pepper

1 Preheat the oven to 160°C/325°F/Gas 3. Heat a large flameproof casserole, then add the chopped bacon and cook, stirring occasionally, until the pieces are crisp and golden brown.

2 Meanwhile, cut the beef into 2.5cm/1in cubes. Season the flour and use to coat the meat. Use a slotted spoon to remove the bacon from the casserole and set aside. Add the oil and then fry the beef in batches until lightly browned all over. Set aside with the bacon.

3 Add the butter to the fat remaining in the casserole. Cook the shallots and garlic until they are just beginning to colour, then add the mushrooms and cook for a further 5 minutes.

4 Return the bacon and beef to the casserole, and stir in the red wine and the beef stock or consommé. Tie the herbs together to create a bouquet garni and add to the casserole.

5 Cover with a tight-fitting lid and cook in the oven for about 1½–2 hours, or until the meat is tender, stirring once or twice during the cooking time. Season to taste with salt and pepper and serve the casserole with creamy mashed root vegetables, such as celeriac and potatoes.

Beef Carbonade

This rich stew of beef, cooked slowly with onions, garlic and beer, is a favourite French dish.

Serves 6

45ml/3 tbsp vegetable oil
3 onions, sliced
45ml/3 tbsp plain (all-purpose) flour
2.5ml/½ tsp mustard powder
1kg/2¼lb stewing beef (shin, shank or chuck), cut into large cubes
2–3 garlic cloves, finely chopped
300ml/½ pint/1¼ cups dark beer or ale
150ml/¼ pint/⅔ cup water
5ml/1 tsp soft dark brown sugar
1 fresh thyme sprig
1 fresh bay leaf
1 celery stick
salt and ground black pepper

For the topping

50g/2oz/¼ cup butter
1 garlic clove, crushed
15ml/1 tbsp Dijon mustard
45ml/3 tbsp chopped fresh parsley
6–12 slices of French baguette

1 Preheat the oven to 160°C/325°F/Gas 3. Heat 30ml/2 tbsp of the oil in a pan and cook the onions over low heat until softened. Remove from the pan and set aside.

2 Mix together the flour and mustard and season. Toss the beef in the flour. Heat the remaining oil in the pan and brown the beef all over, then transfer it to a deep, earthenware baking dish.

3 Reduce the heat and return the onions to the pan. Add the garlic, cook briefly, then add the beer or ale, water and sugar. Tie the thyme and bay leaf together and add to the pan with the celery. Bring to the boil, stirring, then season with salt and pepper.

4 Pour the sauce over the beef and mix well. Cover tightly, then place in the oven for 2½ hours, or until the meat is tender.

5 To make the topping, beat together the butter, crushed garlic, Dijon mustard and 30ml/2 tbsp of the chopped fresh parsley. Spread the flavoured butter thickly over the bread. Increase the oven temperature to 190°C/375°F/Gas 5. Taste and season the stew, then arrange the prepared bread slices, buttered side up, on top. Bake for 20 minutes, or until the bread is browned and crisp. Sprinkle the remaining chopped fresh parsley over the top to garnish and serve immediately.

Boeuf Bourguignon Energy 459kcal/1913kJ; Protein 39g; Carbohydrate 8.1g, of which sugars 3.1g; Fat 24.7g, of which saturates 8.9g; Cholesterol 122mg; Calcium 37mg; Fibre 1.2g; Sodium 497mg.
Beef Carbonade Energy 532kcal/2234kJ; Protein 41.1g; Carbohydrate 40g, of which sugars 10.7g; Fat 21.8g, of which saturates 9.1g; Cholesterol 108mg; Calcium 102mg; Fibre 2.7g; Sodium 409mg.

Provençal Beef Stew

This rich, fruity stew from France is ideal for the slow cooker. Serve with mashed or boiled potatoes and vegetables.

Serves 4

45ml/3 tbsp olive oil
115g/4oz lean salt pork or thick-cut bacon, diced
900g/2lb stewing beef, cut into 4cm/1½ in pieces
250ml/8fl oz/1 cup fruity red wine
150ml/¼ pint/⅔ cup beef stock
1 bouquet garni
1 small onion, studded with 2 cloves
1 large onion, chopped
2 carrots, sliced
2 ripe tomatoes, peeled, seeded and chopped
10ml/2 tsp tomato purée (paste)
2 garlic cloves, very finely chopped
grated rind and juice of ½ unwaxed orange
15ml/1 tbsp chopped fresh parsley
salt and ground black pepper

1 Heat 15ml/1 tbsp of the oil in a large frying pan, then add the salt pork or bacon and cook over a medium heat for 4–5 minutes, stirring frequently, until browned and the fat is rendered. Using a slotted spoon, transfer the pork or bacon to the ceramic cooking pot and switch the slow cooker to high.

2 Working in batches, add the beef to the pan in a single layer. Fry for 6–8 minutes, turning occasionally, until evenly browned on all sides. Transfer the beef to the ceramic cooking pot and continue browning the rest of the meat in the same way, adding more oil when needed.

3 Pour the wine and stock over the beef in the ceramic cooking pot, then add the bouquet garni and the clove-studded onion. Add the remaining oil and the chopped onion to the frying pan and cook gently for 5 minutes. Stir in the sliced carrots and cook for a further 5 minutes, until just softened. Stir in the tomatoes, tomato purée and garlic, then transfer to the ceramic cooking pot.

4 Cover with the lid and switch the slow cooker to low. Cook for about 5–7 hours, or until the beef and vegetables are very tender. Uncover the cooker and skim off any fat from the surface. Season with salt and pepper, discard the bouquet garni and the clove-studded onion, and stir in the orange rind and juice and the chopped parsley. Serve immediately.

Slow-baked Beef with a Potato Crust

This recipe makes the most of braising beef by marinating it in red wine and topping it with a cheesy, grated potato crust that bakes to a golden, crunchy consistency.

Serves 4

675g/1½lb stewing beef, diced
300ml/½ pint/1¼ cups red wine
3 juniper berries, crushed
pared strip of orange peel
30ml/2 tbsp olive oil
2 onions, cut into chunks
2 carrots, cut into chunks
1 garlic clove, crushed
225g/8oz/3 cups button (white) mushrooms
150ml/¼ pint/⅔ cup beef stock
30ml/2 tbsp cornflour (cornstarch)
salt and ground black pepper

For the crust

450g/1lb potatoes, grated
15ml/1 tbsp olive oil
30ml/2 tbsp creamed horseradish
50g/2oz/½ cup grated mature (sharp) Cheddar cheese
salt and ground black pepper

1 Place the beef in a non-metallic bowl. Add the wine, juniper berries and orange peel and season with pepper. Mix well, then cover and leave to marinate for 4 hours or overnight if possible.

2 Preheat the oven to 160°C/325°F/Gas 3. Drain the beef, reserving the marinade. Heat the oil in a large flameproof casserole and fry the meat in batches for 5 minutes to brown and seal. Add the onions, carrots and garlic and cook for 5 minutes. Stir in the mushrooms, marinade and beef stock.

3 Mix the cornflour with water to make a smooth paste and stir into the beef mixture. Season with salt and pepper, cover and cook in the oven for 1½ hours.

4 Prepare the crust about 45 minutes before the end of the cooking time. Blanch the grated potatoes in boiling water for 5 minutes. Drain well and then squeeze out all the extra liquid. Stir in the olive oil, horseradish, grated cheese and seasoning, then sprinkle the mixture evenly over the surface of the beef.

5 Increase the oven temperature to 200°C/400°F/Gas 6 and cook for a further 30 minutes until the potato crust is crisp and lightly browned. Serve immediately.

Provençal Beef Stew Energy 547kcal/2286kJ; Protein 55.8g; Carbohydrate 8.7g, of which sugars 7.2g; Fat 27.8g, of which saturates 8.9g; Cholesterol 170mg; Calcium 43mg; Fibre 2g; Sodium 682mg.
Slow-baked Beef Energy 641kcal/2678kJ; Protein 45.9g; Carbohydrate 36.6g, of which sugars 10.8g; Fat 29.6g, of which saturates 10.6g; Cholesterol 111mg; Calcium 152mg; Fibre 4.2g; Sodium 306mg.

Clay-pot Beef with Red Peppers

Using a clay pot to cook lean meat keeps it moist and juicy. Here, it is cooked with sweet peppers and onion in a rich red wine sauce.

Serves 6

1.2kg/2½lb top rump (round) steak or silverside (pot roast) of beef, neatly tied
2 garlic cloves
30ml/2 tbsp sunflower oil
1 large onion, chopped
300ml/½ pint/1¼ cups beef stock
15ml/1 tbsp tomato purée (paste)
150ml/¼ pint/⅔ cup red wine
1 bouquet garni
4 sweet romano red (bell) peppers, halved lengthways and seeded
15ml/1 tbsp butter, softened
15ml/1 tbsp plain (all-purpose) flour
salt and ground black pepper

1 Soak the clay pot in cold water for 20 minutes, then drain. Using a sharp knife, make about 20 small incisions in the beef. Cut the garlic cloves into thin slivers and insert into the cuts.

2 Season the beef with salt and pepper. Heat the sunflower oil in a large frying pan, add the beef and cook, stirring frequently with a wooden spoon until browned on all sides. Remove the beef from the pan and set aside.

3 Add the onion to the pan and fry gently for 5–8 minutes, stirring occasionally, until light golden. Transfer the onion to the clay pot. Place the beef on top of the onion in the pot, then mix the stock, tomato purée and wine, and pour over the beef.

4 Add the bouquet garni to the pot, then cover and place it in an unheated oven. Set the oven to 200°C/ 400°F/Gas 6 and cook for 1 hour. Uncover, baste the meat and add the pepper halves, arranging them around the meat. Cook, uncovered, for a further 45 minutes until the beef is tender, basting occasionally.

5 Transfer the beef to a warmed serving dish with the peppers and onion. Drain the juices from the clay pot into a pan and heat gently. Blend together the butter and flour to make a smooth paste, then add small pieces of the paste to the sauce, whisking until blended. Bring the sauce to the boil and simmer gently for 1 minute, whisking, until thickened slightly. Pour into a gravy boat and serve with the beef and vegetables.

Beef Stew with Macaroni

Pasta is served with a thick beef stew, which has been simmered slowly on top of the stove in a rich sauce until the meat is very tender.

Serves 4

25g/1oz dried mushrooms (ceps or porcini)
6 garlic cloves
900g/2lb stewing beef, cut into 5cm/2in cubes
115g/4oz lardons, or thick streaky (fatty) bacon, cut into strips
45ml/3 tbsp olive oil
2 onions, sliced
300ml/½ pint/1¼ cups dry white wine
30ml/2 tbsp passata (bottled strained tomatoes)
pinch of ground cinnamon
sprig of rosemary
1 bay leaf
225g/8oz/2 cups large macaroni
50g/2oz/⅔ cup freshly grated Parmesan cheese
salt and ground black pepper

1 Soak the dried mushrooms in warm water for 30 minutes. Drain, set the mushrooms aside and reserve the liquid.

2 Cut three of the garlic cloves into thin strips and insert into the pieces of beef by making little slits with a sharp knife. Push the lardons or pieces of bacon into the beef with the garlic. Season the meat with salt and pepper.

3 Heat the oil in a heavy pan and brown the beef, in batches, on all sides. Transfer to a plate. Add the sliced onions to the pan and cook until lightly browned. Crush the remaining garlic and add to the onions with the meat.

4 Stir in the white wine, passata, mushrooms, cinnamon, rosemary and bay leaf and season with salt and pepper. Cook gently for 30 minutes, stirring often. Strain the mushroom liquid and add to the stew with enough water to cover. Bring to the boil, cover and simmer gently for 3 hours, until the meat is very tender.

5 Cook the macaroni in a large pan of boiling, salted water for 10 minutes, or until *al dente*. Lift the pieces of meat out of the gravy and transfer to a warmed serving platter. Drain the pasta and layer in a serving bowl with the gravy and cheese. Serve with the meat.

Clay-pot Beef Energy 420kcal/1760kJ; Protein 44.7g; Carbohydrate 15.5g, of which sugars 11.7g; Fat 18.6g, of which saturates 6.9g; Cholesterol 113mg; Calcium 42mg; Fibre 3g; Sodium 154mg.
Beef Stew Energy 892kcal/3728kJ; Protein 68.9g; Carbohydrate 52.2g, of which sugars 9.5g; Fat 41.3g, of which saturates 14.8g; Cholesterol 162mg; Calcium 216mg; Fibre 3.4g; Sodium 668mg.

Meat Loaf

This classic dish of minced pork and beef with bacon and fresh herbs is quick and simple to prepare. The results are delicious, thanks to the long, slow baking time in the oven, allowing all the flavours to combine.

Serves 4–6

8 smoked streaky (fatty), rindless bacon rashers (strips)
2 lean bacon rashers (strips), diced
1 onion, finely chopped
2 garlic cloves, crushed
115g/4oz/2 cups fresh breadcrumbs
90ml/6 tbsp milk
450g/1lb lean minced (ground) beef
450g/1lb lean minced (ground) pork
2.5ml/½ tsp chopped fresh thyme
30ml/2 tbsp chopped fresh parsley
2 eggs, beaten
salt and ground black pepper
herby mashed potatoes and steamed carrots, to serve

1 Preheat the oven to 200°C/400°F/Gas 6. Line a 1.75 litre/3 pint/7½ cup buttered loaf tin (pan) with the rashers of streaky bacon. Stretch the rashers using the back of a knife, if necessary, to completely fill the tin.

2 In a large, heavy frying pan, fry the diced bacon, without any extra oil, until almost crisp. Stir in the chopped onion and garlic and fry for a further 2–3 minutes until they are soft and have turned a pale golden brown.

3 Place the fresh breadcrumbs in a large bowl. Pour in the milk and mix well. Set aside for about 5 minutes to allow the breadcrumbs to soak up all the millk.

4 Add the minced meats, the cooked bacon, onion and garlic mixture to the bowl and mix until thoroughly combined. Add the fresh herbs and beaten eggs to the mixture. Season with salt and pepper and mix well.

5 Spoon the mixture into the loaf tin. Level the top and cover the tin with foil. Bake for about 1½ hours in the preheated oven. Turn out on to a warmed serving dish and leave to stand for 5 minutes before serving in slices, with herby mashed potatoes and steamed carrots.

Beef Rolls with Garlic and Tomato Sauce

Thin slices of beef are wrapped around a richly flavoured stuffing. They are then slowly baked in the oven with a garlic, tomato and red wine sauce.

Serves 4

4 thin slices of rump (round) steak, about 115g/4oz each
4 slices smoked ham
150g/5oz Pecorino cheese, grated
2 garlic cloves, crushed
75ml/5 tbsp chopped fresh parsley
2 eggs, soft-boiled and shelled
45ml/3 tbsp olive oil
1 large onion, finely chopped
150ml/¼ pint/⅔ cup passata (bottled strained tomatoes)
75ml/2½fl oz/⅓ cup red wine
2 bay leaves
150ml/¼ pint/⅔ cup beef stock
salt and ground black pepper
flat leaf parsley, to garnish

1 Preheat the oven to 160°C/325°F/Gas 3. Lay the beef slices on a sheet of baking parchment. Cover the beef with another sheet of parchment or clear film (plastic wrap) and beat with a mallet or rolling pin until very thin. Lay a ham slice over each.

2 Mix the cheese in a bowl with the garlic, parsley, eggs and a little salt and pepper. Stir well until all the ingredients are evenly mixed. Spoon the stuffing on to the ham and beef slices. Fold two opposite sides of the meat over the stuffing, then roll up the meat to form neat parcels. Secure with kitchen string.

3 Heat the oil in a frying pan. Add the parcels and fry quickly on all sides to brown. Transfer to an ovenproof dish.

4 Add the onion to the frying pan and fry for 3 minutes. Stir in the passata, wine, bay leaves and stock, and season with salt and black pepper. Bring to the boil, then pour the sauce over the meat in the dish.

5 Cover the dish and bake in the oven for 1 hour. Remove the meat and take off the string. Spoon on to warmed serving plates. Taste the sauce, adding extra salt and pepper if necessary, and spoon it over the meat. Serve immediately, garnished with flat leaf parsley.

Beef Rolls Energy 488kcal/2036kJ; Protein 51.3g; Carbohydrate 7.8g, of which sugars 6g; Fat 26.8g, of which saturates 11.6g; Cholesterol 219mg; Calcium 532mg; Fibre 2.2g; Sodium 885mg.
Meat Loaf Energy 441kcal/1840kJ; Protein 36.8g; Carbohydrate 16.4g, of which sugars 1.8g; Fat 25.9g, of which saturates 10g; Cholesterol 170mg; Calcium 68mg; Fibre 0.6g; Sodium 495mg.

Sauerbraten

This German dish, meaning 'sour roast', is marinaded before being simmered on the stove, resulting in a sweet and sour flavour.

Serves 6

1kg/2¼lb silverside (pot roast)
30ml/2 tbsp sunflower oil
1 onion, sliced
115g/4oz smoked streaky (fatty) bacon, diced
15ml/1 tbsp cornflour (cornstarch)
50g/2oz/1 cup crushed ginger nut biscuits (gingersnaps)
flat leaf parsley, to garnish
buttered noodles, to serve

For the marinade

2 onions, sliced
1 carrot, sliced
2 celery sticks, sliced
600ml/1 pint/2½ cups water
150ml/¼ pint/⅔ cup red vinegar
1 bay leaf
6 cloves
6 whole black peppercorns
15ml/1 tbsp soft dark brown sugar
10ml/2 tsp salt

1 Make the marinade. Put the onions, carrot and celery into a pan with the water. Bring to the boil and simmer for 5 minutes. Add the remaining marinade ingredients and simmer for a further 5 minutes. Cover and leave to cool.

2 Put the beef in a flameproof casserole into which it just fits. Pour over the marinade, cover and leave to marinate in the refrigerator for 3 days if possible, turning daily.

3 Dry the beef thoroughly using kitchen paper. Heat the oil in a large frying pan and brown the beef. Remove and set aside. Add the onion to the pan and fry for 5 minutes. Add the bacon and cook for a further 5 minutes, or until lightly browned.

4 Strain the marinade, reserving the liquid. Put the onion and bacon in a large flameproof casserole or pan, then put the beef on top. Pour over the marinade. Bring to the boil, cover, then simmer gently for 1½–2 hours, or until the beef is very tender.

5 Remove the beef and keep warm. Blend the cornflour with a little cold water. Add to the cooking liquid with the biscuit crumbs and cook, stirring, until thickened. Slice the beef and serve with the noodles. Garnish with parsley and serve the gravy separately.

Roast Beef Marinated in Vegetables

A whole fillet of beef is marinated, then slowly roasted and served with potato dumplings.

Serves 6

900g/2lb fillet (tenderloin) or sirloin
2 rindless bacon rashers (strips), finely shredded
2 onions, finely chopped
2 carrots, finely chopped
2 parsnips, finely chopped
225g/8oz/1 cup celeriac or 4 celery sticks, finely diced
2 bay leaves
2.5ml/½ tsp allspice
5ml/1 tsp dried thyme
30ml/2 tbsp chopped fresh flat leaf parsley
250ml/8fl oz/1 cup red wine vinegar
60ml/4 tbsp olive oil
50g/2oz/4 tbsp butter
2.5ml/½ tsp sugar
120ml/4fl oz/½ cup sour cream
salt and ground black pepper
flat leaf parsley, to garnish

For the dumplings

6 large potatoes, peeled and quartered
115g/4oz/1 cup plain (all-purpose) flour
2 eggs, beaten

1 The day before, lard the beef with strips of bacon and season well. Place the beef in a non-metallic bowl and sprinkle around the vegetables and bay leaves.

2 In another bowl, mix together the allspice, thyme, parsley, vinegar and half of the olive oil. Pour this over the beef. Cover with clear film (plastic wrap) and place in the refrigerator. Leave for 2–3 hours, or longer if possible. Baste the beef occasionally with the marinade.

3 Preheat the oven to 180°C/350°F/Gas 4. Heat the remaining olive oil in a pan, add the beef and brown all over. Transfer the joint to a large roasting pan. Pour a little water into the pan to deglaze, stir well, then pour over the meat.

4 Spoon the vegetable marinade around the joint in the roasting pan and dot the top of the meat with the butter. Sprinkle on the sugar. Roast for 1¼–1½ hours, basting occasionally.

5 Meanwhile, make the dumplings. Cook the potatoes for 15–20 minutes, drain, then mash well. Sprinkle the flour over the potatoes with half the egg and stir well. When all the flour is incorporated, add the remaining egg.

6 Turn the potato mixture on to a lightly floured surface and shape into two evenly sized oblongs. Bring a pan of salted water to the boil and cook for about 20 minutes. Leave to cool a little before slicing into portions.

7 While the dumplings are cooking, remove the joint from the roasting pan and leave to stand for about 10–15 minutes before carving. Remove a spoonful of the cooked vegetables from the pan and reserve for garnishing. Carefully process the remaining vegetables and meat juices in a food processor or blender until smooth.

8 Reheat the vegetable purée in a pan and season to taste. Add a little extra water if the sauce is too thick. Stir in the sour cream. Serve the beef in slices with the sauce and dumplings and garnish with reserved vegetables and parsley sprigs.

Sauerbraten Energy 296kcal/1244kJ; Protein 40.3g; Carbohydrate 7.4g, of which sugars 3.6g; Fat 11.9g, of which saturates 3.6g; Cholesterol 102mg; Calcium 23mg; Fibre 0.3g; Sodium 131mg.
Roast Beef Energy 711kcal/2970kJ; Protein 44.4g; Carbohydrate 53.9g, of which sugars 12.8g; Fat 36.7g, of which saturates 14.9g; Cholesterol 185mg; Calcium 127mg; Fibre 5.9g; Sodium 354mg.

Hungarian Goulash

Paprika is a distinctive feature of Hungarian cookery. It is a spicy seasoning ground from a variety of sweet red pepper, which has been grown in this area since the end of the 16th century. It adds a delicious depth of flavour to this famous slow-cooked beef stew.

Serves 4–6

30ml/2 tbsp vegetable oil, melted lard or white cooking fat
2 onions, chopped
900g/2lb braising or stewing steak, trimmed and cubed
1 garlic clove, crushed
generous pinch of caraway seeds
30ml/2 tbsp paprika
1 firm ripe tomato, chopped
2.4 litres/4 pints/10 cups hot beef stock
2 green (bell) peppers, seeded and sliced
450g/1lb potatoes, diced
salt

For the dumplings
2 eggs, beaten
90ml/6 tbsp plain (all-purpose) flour, sifted

1 Heat the oil, lard or white cooking fat in a large, heavy pan. Add the onion and cook until soft.

2 Add the beef cubes to the pan and cook for 10 minutes, browning gently, stirring frequently to prevent the meat from sticking to the pan.

3 Add the garlic, caraway seeds and a little salt to the pan. Remove from the heat and stir in the paprika and tomato. Pour in the beef stock and cook, covered, over low heat for about 1–1½ hours, or until tender.

4 Add the peppers and potatoes to the pan and cook for a further 20–25 minutes, stirring occasionally.

5 Meanwhile, make the dumplings by mixing the beaten eggs together with the flour and a little salt. With lightly floured hands, roll out the dumplings and drop them into the simmering stew for 2–3 minutes, or until they rise to the surface. Adjust the seasoning and serve the goulash in warm dishes.

Hungarian Cholent

Cholent is an ideal dish to make in the slow cooker. It contains beans, grains, meat and vegetables, and the addition of whole boiled eggs is a classic feature.

Serves 4

250g/9oz/1⅓ cups dried haricot (navy) beans
30ml/2 tbsp olive oil
1 onion, chopped
4 garlic cloves, finely chopped
50g/2oz pearl barley
15ml/1 tbsp ground paprika
pinch of cayenne pepper
1 celery stick, chopped
400g/14oz can chopped tomatoes
3 carrots, sliced
1 small turnip, diced
2 baking potatoes, peeled and cut into chunks
675g/1½lb mixture of beef brisket, stewing beef and smoked beef, cut into cubes
1 litre/1¾ pints/4 cups boiling beef stock
30ml/2 tbsp easy-cook (converted) white rice
4 eggs, at room temperature
salt and ground black pepper

1 Place the beans in a large bowl. Pour over cold water to cover and leave to soak for at least 8 hours, or overnight, if you like.

2 Drain the beans well, then place them in a large pan, cover with fresh cold water and bring to the boil. Boil them steadily for about 10 minutes, skimming off any froth that rises to the surface, then drain well and set aside.

3 Meanwhile, heat the oil in a pan, add the onion and cook gently for about 10 minutes, or until soft. Transfer the onions to the ceramic cooking pot. Add the garlic, beans, barley, paprika, cayenne pepper, celery, tomatoes, carrots, turnip, potatoes, beef and stock to the onions and stir to combine.

4 Cover the pot with the lid and cook on low for 5–6 hours, or until the meat and vegetables are tender. Add the rice, stir, and season with salt and pepper.

5 Rinse the eggs in tepid water, then lower them, one at a time, into the hot stock. Cover and cook for a further 45 minutes, or until the rice is cooked. Serve hot, making sure each portion contains a whole egg.

Hungarian Goulash Energy 371kcal/1562kJ; Protein 39.5g; Carbohydrate 29.2g, of which sugars 6.1g; Fat 11.5g, of which saturates 3.2g; Cholesterol 164mg; Calcium 52mg; Fibre 2.5g; Sodium 140mg.
Hungarian Cholent Energy 860kcal/3607kJ; Protein 58.9g; Carbohydrate 74.2g, of which sugars 13.7g; Fat 38.8g, of which saturates 12.7g; Cholesterol 341mg; Calcium 164mg; Fibre 10.9g; Sodium 639mg.

Holishkes

This is a traditional Jewish dish. The cabbage leaves are stuffed with a delicious beef filling and then slowly baked in a tomato sauce.

Serves 6–8

1kg/2¼lb lean minced (ground) beef
75g/3oz/scant ½ cup long grain rice
4 onions, 2 chopped and 2 sliced
5–8 garlic cloves, chopped
2 eggs
45ml/3 tbsp water
1 large head of white or green cabbage
2 x 400g/14oz cans chopped tomatoes
45ml/3 tbsp demerara (raw) sugar
45ml/3 tbsp white wine vinegar, cider vinegar or lemon juice
pinch of ground cinnamon
salt and ground black pepper
lemon wedges, to serve

1 Put the beef, rice, 5ml/1 tsp salt, pepper, chopped onions and garlic in a bowl. Beat the eggs with the water, and combine with the meat mixture. Chill in the refrigerator until needed.

2 Cut the core from the cabbage in a cone shape and discard. Bring a large pan of water to the boil, lower the cabbage into the water and blanch for 1–2 minutes, then remove from the pan. Peel one or two layers of leaves off, then re-submerge the cabbage. Repeat until all the leaves are removed.

3 Preheat the oven to 150°C/300°F/Gas 2. Form the beef mixture into ovals, the size of small lemons, and wrap each in one or two cabbage leaves, folding and overlapping the leaves so that the mixture is completely enclosed.

4 Lay the cabbage rolls in the base of a large ovenproof dish, alternating with the sliced onions. Pour the tomatoes over and add the sugar, vinegar or lemon juice, salt, pepper and cinnamon. Cover and bake for 2 hours.

5 During cooking, remove the holishkes from the oven and baste them with the tomato juices two or three times. After 2 hours, uncover the dish and cook for a further 30–60 minutes, or until the tomato sauce has thickened and is lightly browned on top. Serve hot with wedges of lemon.

Sweet and Sour Tongue

Tongue has rather gone out of fashion these days but it is wonderful when slowly simmered in a tasty stock until very tender. Here it is served hot with a sweet-and-sour sauce. Any leftovers would be delicious served cold, without the sauce, thinly sliced for sandwiches or a salad.

Serves 8

1kg/2¼lb fresh ox tongue
2–3 onions, 1 sliced and 1–2 chopped
3 bay leaves
½–1 beef or vegetable stock (bouillon) cube or a small amount of stock powder or bouillon
45ml/3 tbsp vegetable oil
60ml/4 tbsp potato flour
120ml/4fl oz/½ cup honey
150g/5oz/1 cup raisins
2.5ml/½ tsp salt
2.5ml/½ tsp ground ginger
1 lemon, sliced
fresh rosemary sprigs, to garnish

1 Put the tongue, sliced onion and bay leaves in a large pan. Pour over cold water to cover and add the beef or vegetable stock cube, powder or bouillon. Bring to the boil, reduce the heat, cover with a tight-fitting lid and simmer gently for about 2–3 hours. Leave to cool.

2 In a small frying pan, heat the vegetable oil, add the chopped onion and cook for about 5–6 minutes, until softened and beginning to turn a pale golden colour.

3 Stir the potato flour into the cooked onions in the pan and gradually add about 500ml/17fl oz/generous 2 cups of the stock, stirring constantly to prevent lumps forming.

4 Stir the honey, raisins, salt and ground ginger into the sauce. Continue to cook, stirring constantly, until the sauce has thickened and is smooth. Add the lemon slices and set the sauce aside.

5 Slice the tongue thinly and serve on warmed serving plates. Generously coat the slices with the sweet-and-sour sauce. Garnish with the rosemary sprigs.

Holishkes Energy 425kcal/1773kJ; Protein 29.7g; Carbohydrate 27.5g, of which sugars 17.6g; Fat 22.3g, of which saturates 9.2g; Cholesterol 123mg; Calcium 86mg; Fibre 3.7g; Sodium 134mg.
Tongue Energy 446kcal/1864kJ; Protein 21g; Carbohydrate 30.6g, of which sugars 28.1g; Fat 27.6g, of which saturates 0.7g; Cholesterol 98mg; Calcium 34mg; Fibre 1.3g; Sodium 1528mg.

Pot-roasted Brisket

This big, pot-roasted beef dish includes a heavy, sausage-shaped dumpling, which is added to the pot and cooked with the meat.

Serves 6–8

5 onions, sliced
3 bay leaves
1–1.6kg/2¼–3½lb beef brisket
1 garlic head, broken into cloves
4 carrots, thickly sliced
5–10ml/1–2 tsp paprika
500ml/17fl oz/generous 2 cups beef stock
3–4 potatoes, peeled and quartered
salt and ground black pepper

For the dumpling

about 90cm/36in sausage casing
250g/9oz/2¼ cups plain (all-purpose) flour
120ml/4fl oz/½ cup semolina or couscous
10–15ml/2–3 tsp paprika
1 carrot, grated and 2 carrots, diced (optional)
250ml/8fl oz/1 cup rendered chicken fat
30ml/2 tbsp crisp, fried onions
½ onion, grated and 3 onions, thinly sliced
3 garlic cloves, chopped
salt and ground black pepper

1 Preheat the oven to 180°C/350°F/Gas 4. Put one-third of the onions and a bay leaf in an ovenproof dish, then top with the beef. Sprinkle over the garlic, carrots and the remaining bay leaves. Add salt, pepper and paprika, then top with the remaining onions. Pour in enough stock to fill the dish to about 5–7.5cm/2–3in and cover with foil. Cook in the oven for 2 hours.

2 Meanwhile, make the dumpling. In a bowl, combine all the ingredients and stuff the mixture into the casing, leaving enough space for the mixture to expand. Tie into sausage-shaped lengths.

3 When the meat has cooked for about 2 hours, add the dumpling and potatoes to the pan, re-cover and cook for a further 1 hour, or until the meat and potatoes are tender.

4 Remove the foil from the dish and increase the oven temperature to 190–200°C/375–400°F/Gas 5–6. Move the onions away from the top of the meat to the side of the dish and return to the oven for a further 30 minutes, or until the meat, onions and potatoes are beginning to brown and become crisp. Serve hot or cold.

Tagine of Beef with Peas and Saffron

This slow-cooked tagine is a great dish to serve for a midweek meal. It can be made with beef or lamb and is quick and easy to prepare. Saffron imparts a pungent taste and delicate colour. The peas, tomatoes and tangy lemon added towards the end of cooking enliven the rich, gingery beef mixture and the brown olives finish it off.

Serves 6

1.2kg/2½lb chuck steak or braising steak, trimmed and cubed
30ml/2 tbsp olive oil
1 onion, chopped
25g/1oz fresh root ginger, peeled and chopped
5ml/1 tsp ground ginger
pinch of cayenne pepper
pinch of saffron threads
1.2kg/2½lb shelled fresh peas
2 tomatoes, peeled, seeded and chopped
1 preserved lemon, chopped
a handful of brown kalamata olives
salt and ground black pepper
crusty bread or plain couscous, to serve

1 Put the cubed chuck or braising steak in a tagine, flameproof casserole or heavy pan with the olive oil, chopped onion, fresh and ground ginger, cayenne pepper and saffron, and season with salt and ground black pepper.

2 Pour in enough water to cover the meat completely and bring to the boil. Reduce the heat, cover the pan with a tight-fitting lid and simmer for about 1½ hours, or until the meat is very tender. Continue to cook the meat for an extra 30–45 minutes, if necessary.

3 Add the peas, tomatoes, preserved lemon and olives to the pan. Stir well and cook on a slightly higher heat, with the lid off, for about 10 minutes, or until the peas are tender and the sauce has reduced slightly.

4 Taste the sauce to check the seasoning, adding more salt or pepper if necessary. Spoon into warmed serving bowls and serve with crusty bread or plain couscous.

Pot-roasted Brisket Energy 586kcal/2453kJ; Protein 33.2g; Carbohydrate 55.5g, of which sugars 9.6g; Fat 27.3g, of which saturates 10.8g; Cholesterol 85mg; Calcium 93mg; Fibre 3.8g; Sodium 93mg.
Tagine of Beef Energy 492kcal/2049kJ; Protein 57.9g; Carbohydrate 25.6g, of which sugars 7g; Fat 18.2g, of which saturates 6g; Cholesterol 126mg; Calcium 61mg; Fibre 10.1g; Sodium 134mg.

Stewed Beef Curry

This deliciously aromatic curry uses stewing beef, which is succulent and tender after long, slow simmering in the spicy, fragrant sauce.

Serves 4

900g/2lb lean stewing beef
15ml/1 tbsp oil
1 large onion, finely chopped
4 cloves
4 green cardamom pods
2 green chillies, finely chopped
2.5cm/1in piece fresh root ginger, finely chopped
2 garlic cloves, crushed
2 dried red chillies
15ml/1 tbsp curry paste
10ml/2 tsp ground coriander
5ml/1 tsp ground cumin
2.5ml/½ tsp salt
150ml/¼ pint/⅔ cup hot beef stock
handful of fresh coriander (cilantro) sprigs, to garnish
boiled rice, to serve

1 Trim any visible fat from the beef and cut the meat into 2.5cm/1in cubes.

2 Heat the oil in a large, heavy frying pan and stir-fry the onion, cloves and cardamom pods for about 5 minutes. Add the fresh green chillies, ginger, garlic and dried red chillies and fry for a further 2 minutes until the spices release their fragrances and the fresh chilli has softened a little.

3 Add the curry paste to the pan and fry for 2 minutes until fragrant. Add the cubed beef and fry for 5–8 minutes until all the meat pieces are lightly browned.

4 Add the coriander, cumin, salt and stock. Cover and simmer gently for 1–1½ hours or until the meat is tender. Garnish with fresh coriander sprigs and serve immediately, accompanied by boiled rice.

Cook's Tip
When whole cardamom pods are used as a flavouring in curries, they are not meant to be eaten. In India, they are left on the side of the plate, along with any bones from the meat in the dish.

Beef Vindaloo

A fiery, slow-cooked dish originally from Goa. A vindaloo is made using a unique blend of hot aromatic spices and vinegar to give it a distinctive flavour.

Serves 6

15ml/1 tbsp cumin seeds
4 dried red chillies
5ml/1 tsp black peppercorns
seeds from 5 green cardamom pods
5ml/1 tsp fenugreek seeds
5ml/1 tsp black mustard seeds
2.5ml/½ tsp salt
2.5ml/½ tsp demerara (raw) sugar
60ml/4 tbsp white wine vinegar
30ml/2 tbsp oil
1 large onion, finely chopped
900g/2lb lean stewing beef, cut into 2.5cm/1in cubes
2.5cm/1in piece fresh root ginger, finely chopped
1 garlic clove, crushed
10ml/2 tsp ground coriander
2.5ml/½ tsp ground turmeric
plain and yellow basmati rice, to serve

1 Put the cumin seeds, chillies, peppercorns, cardamom seeds, fenugreek seeds and mustard seeds into a spice grinder (or a mortar and pestle) and grind to a fine powder.

2 Spoon into a bowl, add the salt, sugar and white wine vinegar and mix to a thin paste. Heat 15ml/1 tbsp of the oil in a large, heavy pan and fry the onion, stirring, for 5 minutes until soft.

3 Put the onion and the spice paste into a food processor or blender and process to a coarse paste.

4 Heat the remaining oil in the frying pan and fry the meat cubes for about 10 minutes until lightly browned all over. Remove with a slotted spoon.

5 Add the ginger and garlic to the oil remaining in the pan and fry for about 2 minutes. Stir in the ground coriander and the turmeric and fry for a further 2 minutes. Add the spice and onion paste to the pan and fry, stirring frequently, for about 5 minutes until fragrant.

6 Return the beef cubes to the pan with 300ml/½ pint/1¼ cups water. Cover and simmer for about 1–1½ hours or until the meat is tender. Serve with plain and yellow basmati rice.

Stewed Beef Curry Energy 442kcal/1840kJ; Protein 52.2g; Carbohydrate 2.8g, of which sugars 0.1g; Fat 24.7g, of which saturates 9g; Cholesterol 131mg; Calcium 25mg; Fibre 0g; Sodium 147mg.
Beef Vindaloo Energy 352kcal/1468kJ; Protein 36.5g; Carbohydrate 9.5g, of which sugars 4.2g; Fat 19.2g, of which saturates 6.3g; Cholesterol 87mg; Calcium 44mg; Fibre 0.9g; Sodium 102mg.

Beef with Green Beans

Green beans slowly cooked with beef is a variation on the traditional recipe which uses lamb. The sliced red pepper provides a contrast to the colour of the beans and chillies, and adds extra flavour.

Serves 4

275g/10oz fine green beans, cut into 2.5cm/1in pieces
15ml/1 tbsp oil
1 onion, sliced
5ml/1 tsp grated fresh root ginger
5ml/1 tsp crushed garlic
5ml/1 tsp chilli powder
6.5ml/1¼ tsp salt
1.5ml/¼ tsp ground turmeric
2 tomatoes, chopped
450g/1lb lean beef, cubed
475ml/16fl oz/2 cups water
1 red (bell) pepper, seeded and sliced
15ml/1 tbsp chopped fresh coriander (cilantro)
2 fresh green chillies, chopped
warm chapatis, to serve (optional)

1 Blanch the beans in boiling water for 3–4 minutes, then rinse under cold running water, drain and set aside.

2 Heat the oil in a large, heavy pan and gently fry the onion slices, stirring frequently, until golden brown.

3 In a bowl, mix the ginger, garlic, chilli powder, salt, turmeric and chopped tomatoes. Spoon the mixture into the pan and stir-fry with the onion for 5–7 minutes.

4 Add the cubed beef and stir-fry for a further 3 minutes. Pour in the water, bring to the boil and lower the heat. Half-cover the pan and cook for 1–1¼ hours until most of the water has evaporated and the meat is tender. Add a little more water if the mixture looks like it is drying out during cooking.

5 Add the green beans to the pan and mix everything together well. Finally, add the red pepper, chopped fresh coriander and green chillies. Cook the mixture with the lid removed, stirring occasionally, for a further 7–10 minutes, or until the green beans and pepper are tender.

6 Spoon into a large bowl or individual plates. Serve the beef hot, with warm chapatis, if you like.

Beef Rendang

This spicy dish is slowly simmered on top of the stove and is usually served with the meat quite dry. If you prefer more sauce, add a little more water.

Serves 6–8

2 onions or 5–6 shallots, chopped
4 garlic cloves, chopped
2.5cm/1in piece fresh galangal, peeled and sliced, or 15ml/1 tbsp galangal paste
2.5cm/1in piece fresh root ginger, peeled and sliced
4–6 fresh red chillies, seeded and roughly chopped
lower part only of 1 lemon grass stalk, sliced
2.5cm/1in piece fresh turmeric, peeled and sliced, or 5ml/1 tsp ground turmeric
1kg/2¼lb prime beef, in one piece
5ml/1 tsp coriander seeds, dry-fried
5ml/1 tsp cumin seeds, dry-fried
2 kaffir lime leaves, torn into small pieces
2 x 400ml/14fl oz cans coconut milk
300ml/½ pint/1¼ cups water
30ml/2 tbsp dark soy sauce
5ml/1 tsp tamarind pulp, soaked in 60ml/4 tbsp warm water
8–10 small new potatoes, scrubbed
salt and ground black pepper
deep-fried onions, sliced fresh red chillies and spring onions (scallions), to garnish

1 Put the onions or shallots in a food processor. Add the garlic, galangal, ginger, chillies, sliced lemon grass and turmeric. Process to a fine paste or grind in a mortar, using a pestle.

2 Cut the meat into cubes using a large, sharp knife, then place the cubes in a bowl. Grind the dry-fried coriander and cumin seeds, then add to the meat with the onion and chilli paste and kaffir lime leaves; stir well. Cover and leave in a cool place to marinate.

3 Pour the coconut milk and water into a wok or large pan, then stir in the spiced meat and the soy sauce. Strain the tamarind water and add to the wok or pan. Stir over medium heat until the liquid boils, then simmer gently, half-covered, for about 1½ hours.

4 Add the potatoes to the pan and simmer for 20–25 minutes, or until the meat and potatoes are tender. Season and serve, garnished with deep-fried onions, chillies and spring onions.

Beef with Green Beans Energy 309kcal/1289kJ; Protein 29.7g; Carbohydrate 15.1g, of which sugars 10g; Fat 15g, of which saturates 4.9g; Cholesterol 65mg; Calcium 70mg; Fibre 3.8g; Sodium 83mg.
Beef Rendang Energy 289kcal/1210kJ; Protein 30.2g; Carbohydrate 15.4g, of which sugars 8.6g; Fat 12.2g, of which saturates 5g; Cholesterol 73mg; Calcium 63mg; Fibre 1.4g; Sodium 465mg.

Vietnamese Beef Fondue

A long-simmered stock is essential for this dish.

Serves 4–6

30ml/2 tbsp sesame oil
1 garlic clove, crushed
2 shallots, finely chopped
2.5cm/1in piece fresh root ginger, peeled and finely sliced
1 lemon grass stalk, cut into several pieces and bruised
30ml/2 tbsp sugar
250ml/8fl oz/1 cup white rice vinegar
700g/1lb 10oz beef fillet, thinly sliced into rectangular strips
salt and ground black pepper
chopped or sliced salad vegetables, herbs and rice wrappers, to serve

For the beef stock

450g/1lb meaty beef bones
15ml/1 tbsp soy sauce
15ml/1 tbsp nuoc mam
1 onion, peeled and quartered
2.5cm/1in piece fresh root ginger, peeled and chopped
3 cloves
1 star anise
1 cinnamon stick

For the dipping sauce

15ml/1 tbsp white rice vinegar
juice of 1 lime
5ml/1 tsp sugar
1 garlic clove, peeled and chopped
2 Thai chillies, seeded and chopped
12 canned anchovy fillets, drained
2 slices of pineapple, centre removed and flesh chopped

1 Make the stock. Put the bones into a pan with the other ingredients and cover with water. Bring to the boil, then simmer, covered, for 1–2 hours. Then cook, uncovered, for 30 minutes until reduced. Strain out 300ml/½ pint/1¼ cups and set aside.

2 Make the dipping sauce. Mix the vinegar and lime juice with the sugar. Using a mortar and pestle, crush the garlic and chillies together. Add the anchovy fillets and pineapple and pound to a paste. Stir in the lime juice mixture and set aside in a serving bowl.

3 When ready to eat, heat 15ml/1 tbsp of the sesame oil in a heavy pan, wok or fondue pot. Stir-fry the garlic, shallots, ginger and lemon grass, then add the sugar, vinegar, beef stock and the remaining sesame oil. Bring to the boil, then season to taste.

4 Transfer the pan to a burner at the table. Lay the beef on a serving dish. Each person cooks a beef strip in the broth and dips it into the sauce. Serve with salad, herbs and rice wrappers.

Braised Beef in a Rich Peanut Sauce

This slow-cooker dish features tender beef in a rich, sweet, glossy sauce.

Serves 4

900g/2lb stewing, chuck, shin or blade steak
45ml/3 tbsp vegetable oil
2 onions, chopped
2 cloves garlic, crushed
5ml/1 tsp paprika
pinch of ground turmeric
225g/8oz celeriac or swede (rutabaga), in 2cm/¾in chunks
425ml/15fl oz/1¾ cups boiling beef stock
15ml/1 tbsp fish or anchovy sauce
30ml/2 tbsp tamarind sauce (optional)
10ml/2 tsp soft light brown sugar
1 bay leaf
1 sprig of thyme
30ml/2 tbsp smooth peanut butter
45ml/3 tbsp easy-cook (converted) white rice
5ml/1 tsp white wine vinegar
salt and ground black pepper

1 Using a sharp knife, cut the beef into 2.5cm/1in cubes. Heat 30ml/2 tbsp of the oil in a pan and fry the beef, turning until well browned all over. Transfer the meat and any juices to the ceramic cooking pot and switch the slow cooker to high.

2 Add the remaining 15ml/1 tbsp oil to the frying pan, add the onions and fry gently for 10 minutes until softened. Add the garlic, paprika and turmeric to the pan and cook for 1 minute. Transfer the mixture to the ceramic pot and add the diced celeriac or swede.

3 Pour in the stock, fish or anchovy sauce and taramind sauce, if using, and add the sugar, bay leaf and thyme. Cover with the lid, then reduce the heat to low and cook for 4 hours, or until the beef and vegetables are just tender.

4 Turn the slow cooker up to high, then remove about 60ml/4 tbsp of the cooking juices to a bowl and blend with the peanut butter. Stir the mixture into the casserole, sprinkle with the rice, and stir again to combine.

5 Cover the pot and cook for about 45 minutes, or until the rice is cooked and the sauce has thickened slightly. Stir in the wine vinegar and season to taste. Serve immediately.

Vietnamese Fondue Energy 412kcal/1712kJ; Protein 41g; Carbohydrate 17g, of which sugars 15g; Fat 19g, of which saturates 6g; Cholesterol 112mg; Calcium 54mg; Fibre 0.8g; Sodium 1000mg.
Braised Beef Energy 577kcal/2408kJ; Protein 48.9g; Carbohydrate 14.1g, of which sugars 8.9g; Fat 36.8g, of which saturates 12.2g; Cholesterol 141mg; Calcium 70mg; Fibre 2.4g; Sodium 561mg.

Black Bean Chilli Con Carne

Fresh green and dried red chillies add plenty of fire to this classic one-pot dish of tender beef slowly cooked in a spicy tomato sauce.

Serves 6

225g/8oz/1 ¼ cups dried black beans
500g/1 ¼lb braising steak
30ml/2 tbsp vegetable oil
2 onions, chopped
1 garlic clove, crushed
1 green chilli, seeded and chopped
15ml/1 tbsp paprika
10ml/2 tsp ground cumin
10ml/2 tsp ground coriander
400g/14oz can chopped tomatoes
300ml/½ pint/1 ¼ cups beef stock
1 dried red chilli, crumbled
5ml/1 tsp hot pepper sauce
1 fresh red (bell) pepper, seeded and chopped
salt
fresh coriander (cilantro), to garnish
boiled rice, to serve

1 Put the beans in a large pan. Add enough cold water to cover them, bring to the boil and boil vigorously for about 10 minutes. Drain, transfer to a clean bowl, cover with cold water and leave to soak for about 8 hours or overnight.

2 Preheat the oven to 150°C/300°F/Gas 2. Cut the braising steak into small dice. Heat the vegetable oil in a large, flameproof casserole. Add the chopped onion, crushed garlic and chopped green chilli and cook them gently for 5 minutes until soft, using a slotted spoon to transfer the mixture to a plate.

3 Increase the heat to high, add the meat to the casserole and brown on all sides, then stir in the paprika, ground cumin and ground coriander.

4 Add the tomatoes, beef stock, dried chilli and hot pepper sauce. Drain the beans and add them to the casserole, with enough water to cover. Bring to simmering point, cover and cook in the oven for 2 hours. Stir occasionally and add extra water, if necessary.

5 Season the casserole with salt and add the chopped red pepper. Replace the lid, return the casserole to the oven and cook for 30 minutes more, or until the meat and beans are tender. Sprinkle over the fresh coriander and serve with rice.

Osso Bucco with Risotto Milanese

Two one-pot dishes in one recipe. Osso bucco is a slow-cooked veal stew that is traditionally accompanied by this saffron-scented risotto.

Serves 4

50g/2oz/¼ cup butter
15ml/1 tbsp olive oil
1 large onion, chopped
1 leek, finely chopped
45ml/3 tbsp plain (all-purpose) flour
4 large pieces of veal shin, hind cut
600ml/1 pint/2½ cups dry white wine
salt and ground black pepper

For the risotto

25g/1oz/2 tbsp butter
1 onion, finely chopped
350g/12oz/1¾ cups risotto rice
1 litre/1¾ pints/4 cups hot chicken stock
2.5ml/½ tsp saffron threads
60ml/4 tbsp white wine
50g/2oz/⅔ cup freshly grated Parmesan cheese

For the gremolata

grated rind of 1 lemon
30ml/2 tbsp chopped fresh parsley
1 garlic clove, finely chopped

1 Heat the butter and oil in a large, heavy frying pan. Add the onion and leek, and cook for 5 minutes. Season the flour and toss the veal in it, then add to the pan and cook until it browns.

2 Gradually stir in the wine and heat until simmering. Cover the pan and simmer for 1½ hours, stirring occasionally. Use a slotted spoon to transfer the veal to a warmed serving dish, then boil the sauce until it is reduced and thickened.

3 Make the risotto 30 minutes before the end of the cooking time for the stew. Melt the butter in a large pan and cook the onion until soft. Stir in the rice to coat all the grains in butter. Add a ladleful of boiling chicken stock and mix well. Continue adding the stock a ladleful at a time, allowing each portion to be completely absorbed before adding the next.

4 Pound the saffron threads in a mortar, then stir in the wine. Add to the risotto and cook for 5 minutes. Stir in the Parmesan.

5 Mix the rind, parsley and garlic together for the gremolata. Spoon some risotto on to each plate, then add the veal. Sprinkle each with a little gremolata and serve immediately.

Black Bean Chilli Energy 289kcal/1216kJ; Protein 27.3g; Carbohydrate 24.7g, of which sugars 7.8g; Fat 9.7g, of which saturates 2.8g; Cholesterol 45mg; Calcium 61mg; Fibre 7.8g; Sodium 65mg.
Osso Bucco Energy 899kcal/3754kJ; Protein 46.3g; Carbohydrate 90.6g, of which sugars 7.1g; Fat 27.4g, of which saturates 14.2g; Cholesterol 178mg; Calcium 249mg; Fibre 2.4g; Sodium 427mg.

Rolled Veal Roast

Veal is flattened then layered or rolled around a filling before being slowly roasted.

Serves 4–6

1.6kg/3lb shoulder of veal or lean pork, cut into 2cm/¾in slices
225g/8oz smoked bacon rashers (strips)
175g/6oz sliced ham
4 eggs, beaten
45ml/3 tbsp milk
3 dill pickles, finely diced
115g/4oz/½ cup butter
45ml/3 tbsp plain (all-purpose) flour
350ml/12fl oz/1½ cups water or chicken stock
salt and ground black pepper
baby carrots, runner beans and dill pickle slices, to serve

1 Preheat the oven to 180°C/350°F/Gas 4. Place the veal or pork between two pieces of clear film (plastic wrap) and pound or flatten into a regular shape using a meat mallet or rolling pin. Season well.

2 Top each slice of veal or pork with a layer of bacon and ham. Beat the eggs in a small pan with the milk and stir until the mixture is softly scrambled. Leave to cool a little.

3 Place a layer of the scrambled egg on top of each slice and spread with a knife, then sprinkle on the finely diced dill pickle. Carefully roll up each slice. Tie the rolls securely at regular intervals with kitchen string.

4 Heat the butter in a large flameproof casserole. Add the meat rolls and brown on all sides. Take the pan off the heat. Remove the rolls and set aside. Sprinkle the flour into the pan and stir well.

5 Return the pan to the heat and cook the flour mixture until pale brown, then slowly add half of the water. Return the meat rolls to the pan and bring to the boil, then put the casserole in the oven for 1¾–2 hours to roast slowly, adding the remaining water during cooking, if necessary, to prevent the veal rolls from drying out.

6 When cooked, leave the rolls to stand for 10 minutes before serving in slices with the gravy and baby carrots, runner beans and dill pickle slices.

Veal Stew with Tomatoes

This slow-cooker dish is traditionally made with lean and mildly flavoured veal. If you prefer, pork fillet can be used instead and makes an excellent, and more economical, alternative.

Serves 4

30ml/2 tbsp plain (all-purpose) flour
675g/1½lb boneless veal shoulder, trimmed and cut into cubes
30ml/2 tbsp sunflower oil
4 shallots, very finely chopped
300ml/½ pint/1¼ cups boiling vegetable or chicken stock
150ml/¼ pint/⅔ cup dry white wine
15ml/1 tbsp tomato purée (paste)
225g/8oz tomatoes, peeled, seeded and chopped
115g/4oz mushrooms, quartered
grated rind and juice of 1 small unwaxed orange
1 bouquet garni
salt and ground black pepper
30ml/2 tbsp chopped fresh parsley, to garnish

1 Put the flour in a small plastic bag and season with salt and pepper. Drop the pieces of meat into the bag a few at a time and shake to coat with the flour.

2 Heat 15ml/1 tbsp of the oil in a pan, add the shallots and cook gently for 5 minutes. Transfer to the ceramic cooking pot and switch to high or auto.

3 Add the remaining 15ml/1 tbsp oil to the pan and fry the meat in batches until well browned on all sides, then transfer to the ceramic cooking pot.

4 Pour the stock and white wine into the pan. Add the tomato purée and bring to the boil, stirring. Pour the sauce over the meat. Add the tomatoes, mushrooms, orange rind and juice, and bouquet garni to the pot and stir briefly to mix the ingredients. Cover with the lid and cook for about 1 hour.

5 Reduce the temperature to low or leave on auto and cook for about 3–4 hours, or until the meat and mushrooms are very tender. Remove the bouquet garni from the stew. Taste the sauce to check the seasoning and add more salt and ground black pepper if necessary. Garnish with chopped fresh parsley and serve immediately.

Veal Roast Energy 495kcal/2062kJ; Protein 45.3g; Carbohydrate 6.6g, of which sugars 0.9g; Fat 32.2g, of which saturates 15.6g; Cholesterol 289mg; Calcium 55mg; Fibre 0.2g; Sodium 1187mg.
Veal Stew Energy 323kcal/1358kJ; Protein 38.2g; Carbohydrate 13.8g, of which sugars 5.4g; Fat 10.6g, of which saturates 2.3g; Cholesterol 141mg; Calcium 47mg; Fibre 1.7g; Sodium 314mg.

Spiced Pork Roast with Apple and Thyme Cream Sauce

Belly of pork is ideal for slow cooking. In this unusual dish, the pork is boned and skinned for stuffing and rolling. Serve with mashed potato, carrots and sprouting broccoli.

Serves 6

1 onion, finely chopped
3 garlic cloves, crushed
75g/3oz/6 tbsp butter
bunch of mixed fresh herbs, leaves finely chopped
225g/8oz/4 cups fresh breadcrumbs
1 egg, beaten
1.3kg/3lb piece of pork belly
15ml/1 tbsp oil
salt and ground black pepper

For the spicy paste
25g/1oz/2 tbsp butter, melted
30ml/2 tbsp chutney
15ml/1 tbsp lemon juice
2 garlic cloves, crushed
30ml/2 tbsp mild Irish mustard, with Guinness or whiskey

For the sauce
2 large cooking apples, peeled, cored and chopped
1 onion, chopped
2 garlic cloves, crushed
1 or 2 thyme sprigs
150ml/¼ pint/⅔ cup medium cider
150ml/¼ pint/⅔ cup chicken stock
300ml/½ pint/1¼ cups single (light) cream

1 Cook the onion and garlic in the butter until soft, then add the herbs and breadcrumbs. Mix in the egg, and season with salt and pepper. Preheat the oven to 150°C/300°F/Gas 2.

2 Meanwhile, trim off any fat from the meat and prick the centre with a fork. Mix all the spicy paste ingredients together and rub over the meat. Spread the breadcrumb stuffing over the meat, then roll it up and tie it with kitchen string.

3 Brown the meat in the oil in a roasting pan on the stove, then cook in the oven for 3 hours. Halfway through cooking, brush with more paste. Turn over and return to the oven.

4 Meanwhile, make the sauce. Put the apples, onion and garlic in a pan and add the thyme, cider and stock. Bring to the boil and simmer for 15 minutes, then discard the thyme. Add the cream. Process the mixture in a blender, strain and season to taste. Slice the roast meat and serve with the sauce.

Roast Belly of Pork with Root Vegetables

Nothing quite compares with the rich flavour of belly of pork, particularly when it is slowly roasted in the oven until tender with a crisp layer of crackling.

Serves 4–6

1 small swede (rutabaga), weighing about 500g/1lb 2oz
1 onion
1 parsnip
2 carrots
15ml/1 tbsp olive oil
1.5kg/3lb 6oz piece pork belly, well scored
15ml/1 tbsp fresh thyme leaves or 5ml/1 tsp dried thyme
sea salt flakes and ground black pepper

1 Preheat the oven to 220°C/425°F/Gas 7. Cut the vegetables into 2cm/¾in cubes and stir them with the oil in a roasting pan until evenly coated. Pour in 300ml/½ pint/1¼ cups water.

2 Sprinkle the pork rind with thyme, salt and pepper, rubbing them well into the scored slashes. Place the pork on top of the vegetables with the skin side uppermost.

3 Put the pork and vegetables into the hot oven and cook for 30 minutes, by which time the liquid will have almost evaporated to leave a golden crust in the bottom of the pan.

4 Add 600ml/1 pint/2½ cups cold water to the vegetables in the pan. Reduce the oven to 180°C/350°F/Gas 4, and cook for 1½ hours, or until the pork is tender and the juices run clear when the centre of the meat is pierced with a sharp knife. Check during the final 30 minutes to make sure the liquid does not dry up completely, adding a little extra water if necessary.

5 If the crackling is not yet crisp enough, increase the oven temperature to 220°C/425°F/Gas 7 and continue cooking for another 10–20 minutes, adding extra water if necessary.

6 With a sharp knife, slice off the crackling. Serve it with thick slices of the pork, some vegetables and the golden juices spooned over.

Spiced Pork Roast Energy 814kcal/3409kJ; Protein 73.2g; Carbohydrate 41.9g, of which sugars 12.6g; Fat 39.8g, of which saturates 20.2g; Cholesterol 264mg; Calcium 145mg; Fibre 2.4g; Sodium 581mg.
Roast Belly Energy 1014kcal/4194kJ; Protein 39.5g; Carbohydrate 9.4g, of which sugars 7.3g; Fat 91.2g, of which saturates 33.1g; Cholesterol 180mg; Calcium 81mg; Fibre 3.3g; Sodium 202mg.

Loin of Pork with Prune Stuffing

Pork is stuffed with dried fruit and then slowly roasted until tender. Crushed ginger biscuits are used as a thickening ingredient and add colour and flavour to the sauce.

Serves 4

1.3kg/3lb cured or smoked loin of pork
15ml/1 tbsp sunflower oil
1 onion, chopped
250ml/8fl oz/1 cup dry red wine
15ml/1 tbsp soft dark brown sugar

For the stuffing

75g/3oz ready-to-eat prunes, finely chopped
45ml/3 tbsp apple juice or water
75g/3oz/1½ cups day-old ginger nut biscuit (gingersnap) crumbs
seeds from 3 cardamom pods, crushed
salt and ground black pepper

1 Preheat the oven to 230°C/450°F/Gas 8. Put the pork, fat side down, on a board. Make a cut about 3cm/1¼in deep along the length to within 1cm/½in of the ends, then make two deep cuts to the left and right, to create two pockets in the meat.

2 To make the stuffing, put the prunes in a bowl. Spoon over the apple juice or water, then add the biscuit crumbs and crushed cardamon seeds. Season with salt and pepper and mix well.

3 Fill the pockets in the meat with the stuffing. Tie the joint at regular intervals with string. Heat the oil in a roasting pan set on the stove and brown the joint over high heat. Set aside.

4 Add the onion to the pan and fry for 10 minutes, until soft. Return the joint to the pan. Add the wine, sugar and seasoning. Roast for 10 minutes, then reduce the oven temperature to 180°C/350°F/Gas 4 and roast, uncovered, for a further 1 hour and 50 minutes, or until cooked and golden brown.

5 Remove the joint from the pan and keep warm. Pour the meat juices through a sieve (strainer) into a pan and simmer for 10 minutes, until slightly reduced. Carve the pork joint and serve with the sauce separately in a gravy boat or jug (pitcher).

Roast Loin of Pork with Apricot and Spinach

This is an updated variation on the traditional pork and fruit theme. The pork joint is packed with a tangy apricot stuffing before being slowly roasted in the oven until deliciously tender.

Serves 6–8

1.6–1.8kg/3½–4lb loin of pork, boned and skinned
1 onion, sliced
juice of 1 orange
30ml/2 tbsp wholegrain mustard
30ml/2 tbsp demerara (raw) sugar
salt and ground black pepper

For the stuffing

50g/2oz/¼ cup ready-to-eat dried apricots, chopped
50g/2oz spinach, blanched and chopped
50g/2oz mature (sharp) Cheddar cheese, grated
1 cooking apple, peeled and grated
grated rind of ½ orange

1 To make the stuffing, put all the stuffing ingredients into a large mixing bowl and stir until well combined. Preheat the oven to 180°C/350°F/Gas 4.

2 Place the loin of pork, fat side down, on a board and place the stuffing down the centre. Roll the meat up and tie with kitchen string. Season with salt and ground black pepper and put in a roasting pan with the onion and 60ml/4 tbsp water. Cook uncovered for about 35 minutes per 450g/1lb.

3 About 40 minutes before the end of the estimated cooking time, pour off the cooking juices from the roasting pan into a small pan and discard the onion. Stir the orange juice into the cooking juices.

4 Spread the surface of the joint all over with the mustard and sprinkle with the demerara sugar. Return it to the oven and increase the temperature to 200°C/400°F/Gas 6 for 15 minutes or until the pork has turned crisp.

5 Meanwhile, boil up the juices and simmer on high heat until reduced to make a thin sauce. Serve with the sliced meat.

Loin of Pork Energy 688kcal/2870kJ; Protein 40.6g; Carbohydrate 25.3g, of which sugars 17.1g; Fat 43.3g, of which saturates 15.5g; Cholesterol 123mg; Calcium 57mg; Fibre 1.3g; Sodium 179mg.
Roast Loin Energy 330kcal/1385kJ; Protein 49.4g; Carbohydrate 6.9g, of which sugars 6.3g; Fat 11.6g, of which saturates 4.9g; Cholesterol 145mg; Calcium 105mg; Fibre 1.2g; Sodium 227mg.

Cider-glazed Gammon

This is a classic buffet centrepiece, which is ideal for making in the slow cooker. A fresh cranberry sauce provides the perfect foil to the richness of the meat. Soaking smoked gammon overnight helps to remove the excess salts.

Serves 8

2kg/4½lb middle gammon (smoked or cured ham) joint, soaked overnight, if smoked
2 small onions
about 30 whole cloves
3 bay leaves
10 black peppercorns
150ml/¼ pint/⅔ cup medium cider
45ml/3 tbsp soft light brown sugar

For the cranberry sauce

350g/12oz/3 cups cranberries
175g/6oz/scant 1 cup caster (superfine) sugar
grated rind and juice of 2 clementines
30ml/2 tbsp port

1 Drain the gammon joint, if soaked overnight, then place it in the ceramic cooking pot. Stud the onions with six of the cloves and add to the cooking pot with the bay leaves and peppercorns.

2 Pour over enough cold water to just cover the gammon. Switch the slow cooker to high, cover with the lid and cook for 1 hour. Skim off any scum from the surface, re-cover and cook for a further 4–5 hours. Check once during cooking and skim the surface, if necessary.

3 Carefully lift the gammon joint out of the slow cooker using large forks or slotted spoons, and place in a roasting pan or ovenproof dish. Leave to stand for about 15 minutes until cool enough to handle.

4 Meanwhile, make the glaze. Pour the cider into a small pan, add the soft brown sugar and heat gently, stirring, until dissolved. Simmer for 5 minutes to make a sticky glaze, then remove from the heat and leave to cool for a few minutes so that it thickens slightly.

5 Preheat the oven to 220°C/425°F/Gas 7. Using a pair of scissors, snip the string off the gammon, then carefully slice off the rind, leaving a thin, even layer of fat over the meat.

6 Using a sharp knife, score the fat into a neat diamond pattern. Press a clove into the centre of each diamond, then spoon over the glaze. Bake for about 25 minutes, or until the fat is brown, glistening and crisp. Remove from the oven and set aside until ready to serve.

7 Meanwhile, make the cranberry sauce. Wash the ceramic cooking pot, then add all the ingredients for the cranberry sauce to it. Switch the slow cooker to high and cook, uncovered, for 20 minutes, stirring continuously, until the sugar has dissolved completely.

8 Cover the pot with the lid and cook on the high setting for 1½–2 hours, or until the cranberries are tender. Transfer the sauce to a jug (pitcher) or bowl, or keep warm in the slow cooker until ready to serve with the gammon. (The sauce can be served either hot or cold.)

Pot-roast Loin of Pork with Apple

Slow-roasted pork loin with crisp crackling and a spiced apple and raisin stuffing makes a wonderful main course for a Sunday feast.

Serves 6–8

1.8kg/4lb boned loin of pork
300ml/½ pint/1¼ cups dry (hard) cider
150ml/¼ pint/⅔ cup sour cream
7.5ml/1½ tsp salt

For the stuffing

25g/1oz/2 tbsp butter
1 small onion, chopped
50g/2oz/1 cup fresh white breadcrumbs
2 apples, cored, peeled and chopped
50g/2oz/scant ½ cup raisins
finely grated rind of 1 orange
pinch of ground cloves
salt and ground black pepper

1 Preheat the oven to 220°C/425°F/Gas 7. To make the stuffing, melt the butter in a frying pan and gently fry the onion for 10 minutes until soft. Stir in the remaining stuffing ingredients.

2 Put the pork, rind side down, on a board. Make a horizontal cut between the meat and outer layer of fat, cutting to within 2.5cm/1in of the edges to make a pocket. Push the stuffing into the pocket. Roll up the pork lengthways and tie firmly with string. Score the rind at 2cm/¾in intervals with a sharp knife.

3 Pour the cider and sour cream into a large casserole. Stir to combine, then add the pork, rind-side down. Transfer to the oven and cook, uncovered, for 30 minutes.

4 Turn the joint over so that the rind is on top. Baste with the juices from the pan, then sprinkle the rind with salt. Cook for a further 1 hour, basting after 30 minutes. Reduce the oven to 180°C/350°F/Gas 4. Cook for 1½ hours, then remove the casserole from the oven and leave the joint to stand for about 20 minutes before carving and serving.

Cook's Tip

Do not baste during the final 1½ hours of roasting otherwise the crackling will not become crisp.

Cider-glazed Gammon Energy 404kcal/1689kJ; Protein 44.1g; Carbohydrate 15.2g, of which sugars 14.8g; Fat 18.8g, of which saturates 6.3g; Cholesterol 57mg; Calcium 25mg; Fibre 1g; Sodium 220mg.
Pot-roast Loin Energy 398kcal/1667kJ; Protein 49.7g; Carbohydrate 13g, of which sugars 8.2g; Fat 15.5g, of which saturates 7.1g; Cholesterol 160mg; Calcium 50mg; Fibre 0.7g; Sodium 239mg.

Bacon with Parsley Sauce

Slowly simmering a piece of bacon in a well-flavoured stock results in a beautifully tender dish. In the old days, bacon was extremely salty and required soaking in several changes of cold water before cooking. Today, however, the meat can be brought to the boil in cold water and then drained.

Serves 6–8

piece of bacon, such as corner or collar, weighing about 1.3kg/3lb
1 large onion, thickly sliced
1 large carrot, thickly sliced
2 celery sticks, roughly chopped
6 black peppercorns
4 whole cloves
2 bay leaves

For the parsley sauce
600ml/1 pint/2½ cups milk
25g/1oz/2 tbsp butter
25g/1oz/¼ cup plain (all-purpose) flour
handful of fresh parsley, finely chopped
salt and ground black pepper

1 Put the bacon in a large pan and cover it with cold water. Bring the water slowly to the boil, then drain off and discard the water. If necessary, rinse out the pan. Place the rinsed bacon back in the pan.

2 Add the onion, carrot, celery, peppercorns, cloves and bay leaves to the pan with the bacon. Pour in just enough cold water to cover the bacon by about 2.5cm/1in or slightly more, if necessary.

3 Bring the stock slowly to the boil and, if necessary, skim off any scum that rises to the surface. Cover the pan and simmer very gently for about 1 hour 20 minutes.

4 To make the parsley sauce, put the milk, butter and flour into a pan. Stirring continuously with a whisk, cook over medium heat until the sauce thickens and comes to the boil. Stir in the parsley and let the sauce bubble gently for 1–2 minutes before seasoning to taste with salt and pepper.

5 Lift the bacon on to a warmed serving plate, cover with foil and leave to rest for 15 minutes before slicing and serving with the parsley sauce.

Boston Baked Beans

The slow cooker was actually invented for making baked beans. Molasses gives the beans a very rich flavour and dark colour, but you can replace it with maple syrup, if you prefer.

Serves 8

450g/1lb/2½ cups dried haricot (navy) beans
4 whole cloves
2 onions, peeled
1 bay leaf
90ml/6 tbsp tomato ketchup
30ml/2 tbsp molasses
30ml/2 tbsp soft dark brown sugar
15ml/1 tbsp Dijon-style mustard
475ml/16fl oz/2 cups unsalted vegetable stock
225g/8oz piece of salt pork
salt and ground black pepper

1 Rinse the beans, then place in a large bowl. Cover with cold water and leave to soak for at least 8 hours or overnight.

2 Drain and rinse the beans. Place in a large pan, cover with cold water and bring to the boil. Boil for 10 minutes, then drain and transfer into the ceramic cooking pot. Stick two cloves in each onion. Add them to the pot with the bay leaf.

3 In a bowl, blend together the ketchup, molasses, sugar, mustard and stock, and pour over the beans. Add more stock, or water, if necessary, so that the beans are almost covered with liquid. Cover with the lid and switch the slow cooker to low. Cook for 3 hours.

4 Towards the end of the cooking time, place the salt pork in a pan of boiling water and cook for 3 minutes. Using a sharp knife, score the pork rind in deep 1.5cm/½ in cuts. Add the salt pork to the ceramic cooking pot, pushing it down just below the surface of the beans, skin side up. Cover the pot with the lid and cook for a further 5–6 hours, until the beans are tender.

5 Remove the pork from the beans and set aside until cool enough to handle, Using a sharp knife, slice off the rind and fat and finely slice the meat.

6 Using a spoon, skim off any fat from the top of the beans, then stir in the pieces of meat. Season to taste with salt and black pepper, and serve hot.

Bacon Energy 467kcal/1937kJ; Protein 32.7g; Carbohydrate 5.7g, of which sugars 3.7g; Fat 34.8g, of which saturates 14.4g; Cholesterol 87mg; Calcium 118mg; Fibre 0.4g; Sodium 2045mg.
Boston Baked Beans Energy 228kcal/968kJ; Protein 13.4g; Carbohydrate 43.9g, of which sugars 19.4g; Fat 1g, of which saturates 0.1g; Cholesterol 0mg; Calcium 140mg; Fibre 9.5g; Sodium 334mg.

Prosciutto-wrapped Pork Fillets

The smokey flavour of Italian ham goes well with pork.

Serves 4

2 x 225g/8oz pork fillets (tenderloins), trimmed
6 slices Parma ham or prosciutto
15ml/1 tbsp olive oil
150ml/¼ pint/⅔ cup white wine
mashed root vegetables and wilted pak choi (bok choy), to serve

For the stuffing

15g/½oz/1 tbsp butter
1 shallot, very finely chopped
1 stick celery, very finely chopped
finely grated rind of ½ orange
115g/4oz/½ cup stoned (pitted), ready-to-eat prunes, chopped
25g/1oz/½ cup fresh breadcrumbs
30ml/2 tbsp chopped fresh parsley
pinch of grated nutmeg
salt and ground black pepper

1 Melt the butter in a frying pan. Fry the shallot and celery until soft. Transfer to a bowl and stir in the orange rind, prunes, breadcrumbs, parsley and nutmeg. Season and leave to cool.

2 Slice down the length of each fillet, cutting three-quarters of the way through. Open out each fillet and lay it out on a board. Cover the meat with a piece of oiled clear film (plastic wrap). Gently bash with a rolling pin until the meat is 5mm/¼in thick.

3 Arrange three slices of the ham on a board and place one pork fillet on top. Repeat with the remaining ham and fillet. Divide the stuffing between the fillets, then fold over to enclose the filling. Wrap the ham around the fillets, and secure with one or two wooden cocktail sticks (toothpicks).

4 Heat the oil in the clean frying pan and quickly brown the wrapped fillets all over, taking care not to dislodge the cocktail sticks, before transferring them to the ceramic cooking pot. Pour the wine into the frying pan and heat, then pour over the pork.

5 Cover the cooker with the lid and cook on high for 1 hour, then reduce the temperature to low and cook for 2–3 hours, or until the pork is cooked completely through and tender.

6 Remove the sticks and cut the pork into slices. Arrange on warmed plates and spoon over some of the cooking juices. Serve with mashed root vegetables and wilted pak choi leaves.

Pork and Potato Hotpot

Long simmering in the slow cooker makes this pork meltingly tender and allows the potato slices to soak up all the delicious juices. It is perfect for a family meal or a casual supper with friends.

Serves 4

25g/1oz/2 tbsp butter
15ml/1 tbsp oil
1 large onion, very thinly sliced
1 garlic clove, crushed
225g/8oz/generous 3 cups button (white) mushrooms, sliced
1.5ml/¼ tsp dried mixed herbs
900g/2lb potatoes, thinly sliced
4 thick pork chops
750ml/1¼ pints/3 cups vegetable or chicken stock
salt and ground black pepper

1 Use 15g/½ oz/1 tbsp of the butter to grease the base and halfway up the sides of the ceramic cooking pot.

2 Heat the oil in a frying pan, add the sliced onion and cook gently for about 5 minutes, until softened. Add the garlic and mushrooms to the pan and cook for a further 5 minutes until softened. Remove the pan from the heat and stir in the herbs.

3 Spoon half the mushroom mixture into the base of the ceramic cooking pot, then arrange half the potato slices on top and season with salt and ground black pepper.

4 Using a sharp knife, trim as much fat as possible from the pork chops, then place them on top of the potatoes in a single layer. Pour about half the stock over the top to cover the potatoes and prevent them discolouring.

5 Repeat the layers of the mushroom mixture and potatoes, finishing with a layer of neatly overlapping potatoes. Pour over the remaining stock; it should just cover the potatoes, so use a little more or less if necessary. Dot the remaining butter on top of the potatoes and cover with the lid.

6 Cook the stew on high for 4–5 hours, or until the potatoes and meat are tender when pierced with a thin skewer. If you like, place the hotpot under a medium grill (broiler) for 5–10 minutes to brown before serving.

Pork Fillets Energy 245kcal/1027kJ; Protein 17.3g; Carbohydrate 14.6g, of which sugars 11.3g; Fat 10.8g, of which saturates 4g; Cholesterol 59mg; Calcium 34mg; Fibre 2g; Sodium 378mg.
Pork Hotpot Energy 511kcal/2132kJ; Protein 17.9g; Carbohydrate 41.5g, of which sugars 6.5g; Fat 31.5g, of which saturates 12.1g; Cholesterol 67mg; Calcium 40mg; Fibre 3.7g; Sodium 529mg.

Pork in Cider with Dumplings

Pork and fruit are a perfect combination in this slowly baked one-pot dish.

Serves 6

115g/4oz/½ cup pitted prunes, roughly chopped
115g/4oz/½ cup ready-to-eat dried apricots, roughly chopped
300ml/½ pint/1¼ cups dry (hard) cider
30ml/2 tbsp plain (all-purpose) flour
675g/1½lb lean boneless pork, cut into cubes
30ml/2 tbsp vegetable oil
350g/12oz onions, roughly chopped
2 garlic cloves, crushed
6 celery sticks, roughly chopped
475ml/16fl oz/2 cups stock
12 juniper berries, lightly crushed
30ml/2 tbsp chopped fresh thyme
425g/15oz can black-eyed beans (peas), drained
salt and ground black pepper

For the dumplings

115g/4oz/1 cup self-raising (self-rising) flour
50g/2oz/scant ½ cup vegetable suet (US chilled, grated shortening)
45ml/3 tbsp chopped fresh parsley
90ml/6 tbsp water

1 Preheat the oven to 180°C/350°F/Gas 4. Place the prunes and apricots in a bowl. Pour in the cider and leave for 20 minutes. Season the flour, then toss the pork in it to coat. Reserve any that is left over. Heat the oil in a flameproof casserole and brown the meat. Remove with a slotted spoon and drain on kitchen paper.

2 Add the onions, garlic and celery to the casserole and cook for 5 minutes. Add any reserved flour and cook for a further 1 minute. Blend in the stock until smooth. Add the cider and fruit, juniper berries, thyme and seasoning. Bring to the boil, add the pork, cover tightly and then cook in the oven for 50 minutes.

3 Just before the end of the cooking time, make the dumplings. Sift the flour into a large bowl, add a pinch of salt, then stir in the suet and parsley. Add the water gradually and mix all the ingredients together to form a smooth, slightly sticky dough.

4 Remove the casserole from the oven and add the beans. Divide the dumpling mixture into six, form into rough rounds and place on top of the stew. Return the casserole to the oven, then cover and cook for a further 20–25 minutes, or until the dumplings are cooked and the pork is tender.

Pork Fillet with Spinach and Lentils

Lean pork fillet, wrapped in spinach and cooked in a clay pot on a bed of Puy lentils.

Serves 4

500–675g/1¼–1½lb pork fillet (tenderloin)
15ml/1 tbsp sunflower oil
15g/½oz/1 tbsp butter
8–12 large spinach leaves
1 onion, chopped
1 garlic clove, finely chopped
2.5cm/1in piece fresh root ginger, finely grated
1 red chilli, finely chopped (optional)
250g/9oz/generous 1 cup Puy lentils
750ml/1¼ pints/3 cups chicken or vegetable stock
200ml/7fl oz/scant 1 cup coconut cream
salt and ground black pepper

1 Soak a small clay pot in cold water for about 15 minutes, then drain. Cut the pork fillet widthways into two equal pieces. Season the pork well with salt and ground black pepper.

2 Heat the sunflower oil and butter in a frying pan. Cook the pork fillet until browned on all sides. Remove the meat from the pan using a slotted spoon and set aside.

3 Meanwhile, add the spinach to a pan of boiling water and cook for 1 minute, or until just wilted. Drain in a colander and refresh under cold running water. Drain well. Lay the spinach leaves on a board, overlapping them slightly to form a rectangle. Place the fillets on top and wrap the leaves around to enclose.

4 Cook the onion in the frying pan for 5 minutes, stirring, until soft. Add the garlic, ginger and chilli, if using, and fry for 1 minute. Add the lentils and then stir in the stock. Bring to the boil, then boil rapidly for 10 minutes. Remove the pan from the heat and stir in the coconut cream. Transfer the mixture to the clay pot and arrange the fillets on top.

5 Cover the clay pot and place it in an unheated oven. Set the oven to 190°C/375°F/Gas 5 and cook for 45 minutes, or until the lentils and pork are cooked. Cut the meat into slices.

6 To serve, spoon the lentils and some cooking juice on to serving plates and top each portion with slices of the pork.

Pork in Cider Energy 468kcal/1968kJ; Protein 32.6g; Carbohydrate 46.9g, of which sugars 21g; Fat 16.5g, of which saturates 5.9g; Cholesterol 71mg; Calcium 174mg; Fibre 8.2g; Sodium 437mg.
Pork Fillet Energy 399kcal/1683kJ; Protein 42.3g; Carbohydrate 39.1g, of which sugars 5g; Fat 9.2g, of which saturates 4g; Cholesterol 87mg; Calcium 81mg; Fibre 3.5g; Sodium 206mg.

Pork Stew with Coriander and Red Wine

This lightly spiced stew is slowly baked in a low oven until the meat is meltingly tender and the rich sauce is thick and full of flavour.

Serves 4

675g/1½lb pork fillet (tenderloin), boneless leg or chump steaks
20ml/4 tsp coriander seeds
2.5ml/½ tsp caster (superfine) sugar
45ml/3 tbsp olive oil
2 large onions, sliced
300ml/½ pint/1¼ cups red wine
salt and ground black pepper
fresh coriander (cilantro), to garnish
salad and olives, to serve

1 Cut the pork into small chunks, discarding any excess fat. Crush the coriander seeds with a mortar and pestle until fairly finely ground.

2 In a bowl, mix the coriander seeds with the caster sugar, and season with salt and ground black pepper. Rub this mixture all over the meat with your hands. Leave to marinate for up to 4 hours.

3 Preheat the oven to 160°C/325°F/Gas 3. Heat 30ml/2 tbsp of the oil in a frying pan over high heat. Brown the meat quickly, then transfer to an ovenproof dish.

4 Add the remaining oil to the pan and fry the onions until beginning to soften and colour. Stir in the red wine and a little salt and pepper and bring just to the boil.

5 Pour the onion and wine mixture over the meat and cover with a tight-fitting lid. Bake for 1 hour, or until the meat is very tender. Serve immediately, garnished with fresh coriander and accompanied by a leafy salad and olives.

Cook's Tip
A coffee grinder can also be used to grind the coriander seeds. Alternatively, use 15ml/1 tbsp ground coriander.

Black Bean Stew

This simple, slow-cooked stew uses a few robust ingredients to create a wonderfully intense flavour.

Serves 5–6

275g/10oz/1⅓ cups black beans
675g/1½lb boneless belly pork, cut into thick rashers (strips)
60ml/4 tbsp olive oil
350g/12oz baby (pearl) onions
2 celery sticks, thickly sliced
10ml/2 tsp paprika
150g/5oz chorizo sausage, cut into chunks
600ml/1 pint/2½ cups light chicken or vegetable stock
2 green (bell) peppers, seeded and cut into large pieces
salt and ground black pepper

1 Put the beans in a bowl and cover with plenty of cold water. Leave to soak overnight. Drain the beans into a pan and cover with fresh cold water. Bring to the boil and boil rapidly for about 10 minutes. Drain thoroughly.

2 Preheat the oven to 160°C/325°F/Gas 3. Cut away any rind from the pork belly rashers and cut the meat into large chunks.

3 Heat the oil in a large frying pan and fry the onions and celery for 3 minutes until beginning to turn soft. Add the pork to the pan and fry for 5–10 minutes, stirring occasionally, until the pork is browned.

4 Add the paprika and chorizo and fry for a further 2 minutes. Transfer to an ovenproof dish with the beans and mix together.

5 Add the stock to the pan and bring to the boil. Season lightly, then pour over the meat and beans. Cover and bake for 1 hour.

6 Stir the green peppers into the stew and return to the oven for a further 15 minutes. Serve hot.

Cook's Tip
This is the sort of stew to which you can add a variety of winter vegetables, such as chunks of leek, turnip, celeriac and even small whole potatoes.

Pork Stew Energy 393kcal/1640kJ; Protein 38.4g; Carbohydrate 12.4g, of which sugars 7.8g; Fat 15.9g, of which saturates 3.6g; Cholesterol 106mg; Calcium 58mg; Fibre 1.8g; Sodium 129mg.
Black Bean Energy 760kcal/3159kJ; Protein 32.1g; Carbohydrate 37.3g, of which sugars 9.2g; Fat 54.7g, of which saturates 18.6g; Cholesterol 91mg; Calcium 85mg; Fibre 5.9g; Sodium 303mg.

Pork Casserole with Madeira

Lean pork is slowly cooked with a variety of meats and vegetables in a richly flavoured Madeira sauce.

Serves 8

15g/½oz/¼ cup dried mushrooms
225g/8oz/1 cup pitted prunes
225g/8oz lean boneless pork
225g/8oz lean boneless venison
225g/8oz chuck steak
225g/8oz kielbasa (see Cook's Tip)
25g/1oz/¼ cup plain (all-purpose) flour
2 onions, sliced
45ml/3 tbsp olive oil
60ml/4 tbsp dry Madeira
900g/2lb can or packet sauerkraut, rinsed
4 tomatoes, peeled and chopped
4 cloves
5cm/2in cinnamon stick
1 bay leaf
2.5ml/½ tsp dill seeds
600ml/1 pint/2½ cups stock
salt and ground black pepper
handful of chopped fresh parsley, to garnish

1 Pour boiling water to completely cover the dried mushrooms and prunes in a bowl. Leave for 30 minutes, then drain well.

2 Cut the pork, venison, chuck steak and kielbasa sausage into 2.5cm/1in cubes, then toss together in the flour. Gently fry the onions in the oil for 10 minutes. Transfer to a plate, then brown the meat in the pan in several batches for 5 minutes or until well browned. Remove and set aside.

3 Add the Madeira to the pan and simmer for 2–3 minutes, stirring. Return the meat to the pan with the onion, sauerkraut, tomatoes, cloves, cinnamon, bay leaf, dill seeds, mushrooms and prunes. Pour in the stock and season with salt and pepper.

4 Bring to the boil, cover and simmer gently for 1¾–2 hours, or until the meat is very tender. Uncover for the last 20 minutes to let the sauce reduce and thicken. Garnish with chopped parsley and serve immediately.

Cook's Tip
Kielbasa is a garlic-flavoured pork and beef sausage, but any similar type of continental sausage can be used.

Pork Stew with Sauerkraut

This slow-cooked dish contains lots of robust flavours common to many traditional eastern European recipes. The sauerkraut is a perfect partner for the deliciously tender chunks of pork, which is braised on the stove in a rich sauce flavoured with paprika and dill.

Serves 4–6

30ml/2 tbsp vegetable oil, lard or white cooking fat
2 onions, finely chopped
2 garlic cloves, crushed
900g/2lb lean pork, cut into 5cm/2in cubes
5ml/1 tsp caraway seeds (optional)
15ml/1 tbsp chopped fresh dill
900ml/1½ pints/3¾ cups hot pork or vegetable stock
900g/2lb/4 cups sauerkraut, drained
15ml/1 tbsp paprika
salt and ground black pepper
dill, to garnish
sour cream, sprinkled with paprika, and pickled chillies (optional), to serve

1 Heat the oil, lard or white cooking fat in a large, heavy pan and cook the onion for 3–4 minutes until beginning to soften. Add the crushed garlic and continue to cook for a further 3 minutes, stirring frequently.

2 Add the pork cubes to the pan and fry, stirring occasionally, until evenly browned on all sides. Stir in the caraway seeds, if using, and the chopped fresh dill.

3 Pour the pork or vegetable stock into the pan and mix until all the ingredients are well combined. Season with salt and ground black pepper to taste.

4 Cover the pan with a tight-fitting lid and simmer over a gentle heat for about 1 hour.

5 Stir the drained sauerkraut into the stew. Add the paprika and mix well. Leave to simmer gently for a further 45 minutes, or until the pork is tender.

6 Garnish the stew with a little more chopped dill. Spoon into warmed individual bowls and serve with sour cream sprinkled with paprika and pickled chillies, if you like.

Pork Casserole Energy 327kcal/1367kJ; Protein 24.5g; Carbohydrate 21.7g, of which sugars 15.4g; Fat 15.6g, of which saturates 5.1g; Cholesterol 59mg; Calcium 104mg; Fibre 5.4g; Sodium 954mg.
Pork Stew Energy 273kcal/1140kJ; Protein 35.7g; Carbohydrate 10.2g, of which sugars 6.4g; Fat 10.2g, of which saturates 2.6g; Cholesterol 95mg; Calcium 112mg; Fibre 4.7g; Sodium 994mg.

Pork and Garlic Sausage Casserole with Apple

This hearty and filling slow-cooked casserole contains a variety of pork cuts. The light ale helps to tenderize the meat, and adds a robust flavour to the sauce.

Serves 6

45ml/3 tbsp sunflower oil
225g/8oz lean, smoked bacon, rinded and diced
450g/1lb lean shoulder of pork, trimmed and cut into 2.5cm/1in cubes
1 large onion, sliced
900g/2lb potatoes, thickly sliced
250ml/8fl oz/1 cup light ale
225g/8oz/2 cups German garlic sausage, skinned and sliced
500g/1¼lb/2¼ cups sauerkraut, drained
2 red eating apples, cored and sliced
5ml/1 tsp caraway seeds
salt and ground black pepper

1 Preheat the oven to 180°C/350°F/Gas 4. Heat 30ml/2 tbsp of the sunflower oil in a flameproof casserole. Fry the bacon for 2–3 minutes, stirring frequently until beginning to colour.

2 Add the cubes of pork and cook for 4–5 minutes until lightly browned on all sides. Remove the bacon and pork cubes from the pan and set aside.

3 Add the remaining oil to the pan and gently cook the onion for 6–8 minutes, until soft. Return the meat to the pan and add the sliced potatoes, stirring to mix.

4 Pour the ale into the pan and stir gently to mix. Bring the mixture to the boil, then reduce the heat. Cover the pan with a tight-fitting lid and cook in the preheated oven for 45 minutes.

5 Stir the garlic sausage, drained sauerkraut, sliced apple and caraway seeds into the pan. Season with salt and ground black pepper to taste.

6 Return the casserole to the oven and cook for a further 30 minutes, or until the meat is tender. Serve immediately.

Pork with Sauerkraut and Chillies

A traditional, slowly simmered stew with the classic partnership of pork and sauerkraut. The tender meat is cooked in a mildly spiced sauce with added kick thanks to the presence of chillies. Use veal in place of the pork, if you prefer.

Serves 4

60ml/4 tbsp vegetable oil, lard or white cooking fat
450g/1lb lean pork or veal, cut into bitesize cubes
2.5ml/½ tsp paprika
400g/14oz shredded sauerkraut, drained and well rinsed
2 fresh red chillies
90ml/6 tbsp pork stock
salt and ground black pepper
50ml/2fl oz/¼ cup sour cream
coarse grain mustard, paprika and sage leaves, to garnish
crusty bread, to serve

1 Heat the oil, lard or white cooking fat in a heavy frying pan. Add the pork or veal and cook, stirring occasionally, until evenly browned on all sides.

2 Add the paprika and the shredded sauerkraut to the pan. Cook, stirring, for 2–3 minutes to incorporate the paprika. Transfer to a flameproof casserole.

3 Halve the chillies and remove the seeds before burying the chillies in the middle of the casserole. If you want a slightly hotter dish, you can leave the seeds in or stir a few of them into the casserole.

4 Add the pork stock to the casserole. Cover the pan with a tight-fitting lid and bring the mixture to the boil. Reduce the heat and simmer gently for 1–1½ hours, or until the meat is tender. Stir occasionally to prevent the contents sticking to the base of the pan.

5 Remove the chillies, if you prefer, and season to taste with salt and ground black pepper. Spoon the casserole on to four warmed serving plates. Add a dollop of the sour cream on to each serving and spoon on a little of the coarse grain mustard. Sprinkle with paprika and garnish with sage leaves. Serve with crusty bread to mop up the juices.

Pork Sausage Energy 472kcal/1976kJ; Protein 32g; Carbohydrate 37.7g, of which sugars 11.7g; Fat 21.6g, of which saturates 6.2g; Cholesterol 110mg; Calcium 91mg; Fibre 5.3g; Sodium 1449mg.
Pork with Chillies Energy 273kcal/1132kJ; Protein 25.6g; Carbohydrate 1.8g, of which sugars 1.6g; Fat 18.1g, of which saturates 4.4g; Cholesterol 78mg; Calcium 71mg; Fibre 2.2g; Sodium 674mg.

Portuguese Pork

The Portuguese expanded their empire during the 15th century, establishing outposts in India and Malaysia. One of the lasting results of this expansion was the influence of Portuguese cooking on Indian cuisine, as shown with this fiery pork curry recipe. To ensure maximum flavour, the pieces of pork from the spare ribs should be marinated for at least two hours in the spicy paste – longer if possible – before being slowly simmered on the stove.

Serves 4–6

115g/4oz deep-fried onions, crushed
4 fresh red chillies, chopped
60ml/4 tbsp vindaloo curry paste
90ml/6 tbsp white wine vinegar
90ml/6 tbsp tomato purée (paste)
2.5ml/½ tsp fenugreek seeds
5ml/1 tsp ground turmeric
5ml/1 tsp crushed mustard seeds, or 2.5ml/½ tsp mustard powder
7.5ml/1½ tsp sugar
900g/2lb boneless pork spare ribs, cubed
250ml/8fl oz/1 cup water
salt
plain boiled rice, to serve

1 Place the crushed onions, red chillies, curry paste, vinegar, tomato purée, fenugreek seeds, ground turmeric and mustard seeds or powder in a large bowl. Mix well until thoroughly combined. Add in the sugar and season with a little salt to taste.

2 Add the pork cubes to the spicy paste and mix well until they are evenly coated. Cover the bowl with clear film (plastic wrap) and leave to marinate in the refrigerator for 2 hours, or longer if possible.

3 Transfer the meat and the marinade to a heavy pan. Stir in the water. Bring to the boil and then simmer gently for 2 hours, until the pork is tender. Serve immediately, with the rice.

Cook's Tip
When preparing fresh chillies, it is a good idea to wear rubber gloves, especially if using the hotter varieties. Never touch your eyes, nose or mouth while handling them, and wash both the gloves and your hands with soap and warm water afterwards.

Pork Casserole with Dried Fruit

A spicy paste is added to this oven-baked casserole of pork, onions and fruit.

Serves 6

1kg/2¼lb shoulder or leg of pork, cut into 5cm/2in cubes
25ml/1½ tbsp plain (all-purpose) flour, seasoned
45–60ml/3–4 tbsp olive oil
2 large onions, chopped
2 garlic cloves, finely chopped
600ml/1 pint/2½ cups white wine
105ml/7 tbsp water
115g/4oz/½ cup ready-to-eat dried apricots
115g/4oz/½ cup ready-to-eat prunes
grated rind and juice of 1 orange
pinch of muscovado (brown) sugar
30ml/2 tbsp chopped fresh parsley
½–1 fresh green chilli, seeded and finely chopped
salt and ground black pepper

For the paste

3 ancho and 2 pasilla chillies (or 5 large dried red chillies)
30ml/2 tbsp olive oil
2 shallots, chopped
2 garlic cloves, chopped
1 green chilli, seeded and chopped
10ml/2 tsp ground coriander
5ml/1 tsp mild Spanish paprika
50g/2oz/½ cup blanched almonds, toasted
15ml/1 tbsp chopped fresh oregano

1 To make the paste, cook the dried chillies in a dry frying pan over low heat for 1–2 minutes. Soak them in warm water for 30 minutes. Drain, reserving the soaking water, and discard their stalks and seeds. Preheat the oven to 160°C/325°F/Gas 3.

2 Heat the oil in a frying pan. Cook the shallots, garlic, green chilli and coriander for 5 minutes. Transfer to a food processor or blender. Add the drained chillies, paprika, almonds and oregano. Process, adding enough chilli soaking liquid to make a paste.

3 Toss the pork in the flour. Heat 45ml/3 tbsp of the oil in a frying pan and brown the pork. Transfer to a flameproof casserole. Cook the onions and garlic in the pan until just soft. Add the wine, water and half the paste and cook for 2 minutes. Stir into the pork. Cover the casserole and cook in the oven for 1½ hours.

4 Increase the oven to 180°C/350°F/Gas 4. Add the apricots, prunes, orange juice and sugar. Cook for 30–45 minutes. Transfer to the stove, stir in the remaining paste and simmer for 5 minutes. Sprinkle with the orange rind, parsley and chilli, and serve.

Portuguese Pork Energy 267kcal/1119kJ; Protein 34.6g; Carbohydrate 11.3g, of which sugars 7.3g; Fat 9.6g, of which saturates 2.5g; Cholesterol 95mg; Calcium 68mg; Fibre 2.2g; Sodium 166mg.
Pork Casserole Energy 477kcal/1999kJ; Protein 40.7g; Carbohydrate 25.6g, of which sugars 21g; Fat 19.1g, of which saturates 3.8g; Cholesterol 105mg; Calcium 86mg; Fibre 4.1g; Sodium 149mg.

Spicy Pork and Rice Casserole

This is a hearty, slow-cooked dish of marinated pork, vegetables and rice.

Serves 4–6

500g/1¼lb lean pork, such as fillet (tenderloin), cut into strips
60ml/4 tbsp vegetable oil
1 onion, chopped
1 garlic clove, crushed
1 green (bell) pepper, cut into pieces
about 300ml/½ pint/1¼ cups chicken or vegetable stock
225g/8oz/generous 1 cup white long grain rice
150ml/¼ pint/⅔ cup single (light) cream
150g/5oz/1½ cups freshly grated Parmesan cheese
salt and ground black pepper

For the marinade

120ml/4fl oz/½ cup dry white wine
30ml/2 tbsp lemon juice
1 onion, chopped
4 juniper berries, lightly crushed
3 cloves
1 fresh red chilli, seeded and finely sliced

1 Mix the marinade ingredients in a bowl, add the pork and marinate for 3–4 hours. Transfer the pork to a plate using a slotted spoon and pat dry. Strain the marinade and set aside.

2 Heat the oil in a heavy pan, and cook the pork strips until evenly brown. Transfer to a plate using a slotted spoon. Cook the onion and garlic in the pan for 3–4 minutes, then add the pepper for 3–4 minutes. Return the pork to the pan. Pour in the marinade and the stock. Bring to the boil and season, then cover and simmer for 10 minutes, or until the meat is nearly tender.

3 Preheat the oven to 160°C/325°F/Gas 3. Cook the rice in salted boiling water for 8 minutes or until three-quarters cooked. Drain well. Spread half the rice over the base of a buttered, earthenware dish. Using a slotted spoon, top with a neat layer of meat and vegetables, then spread over the remaining rice.

4 Stir the cream and 30ml/2 tbsp of the Parmesan into the liquid in which the pork was cooked. Transfer to a jug (pitcher) and then carefully pour the cream mixture over the rice and sprinkle with the remaining Parmesan. Cover with foil and bake for 20 minutes, then remove the foil and cook for 5 minutes more, until the top is lightly brown. Serve immediately.

Hot and Sour Pork

This slow-cooker dish has all the flavours of a stir-fry without the hassle. Using lean pork fillet and reducing the temperature to low after an hour means that the meat remains moist and tender, while the vegetables retain their crunch.

Serves 4

15ml/1 tbsp dried Chinese mushrooms
150ml/¼ pint/⅔ cup boiling vegetable stock
350g/12oz pork fillet (tenderloin)
115g/4oz baby corn kernels
1 green (bell) pepper
225g/8oz pineapple chunks in natural juice
20ml/4 tsp cornflour (cornstarch)
15ml/1 tbsp sunflower oil
115g/4oz water chestnuts
2.5cm/1in piece fresh root ginger, grated
1 fresh red chilli, seeded and finely chopped
5ml/1tsp Chinese five-spice powder
15ml/1 tbsp sherry vinegar
15ml/1 tbsp dark soy sauce
15ml/1 tbsp hoisin sauce
plain boiled or fried rice, to serve

1 Put the mushrooms in a heatproof bowl, then pour over the stock and leave for 15–20 minutes. Trim any fat from the pork and cut into 1cm/½in slices. Slice the corn kernels lengthways. Halve, seed and slice the pepper. Drain the pineapple chunks, reserving the juice. Drain the mushrooms, reserving the stock, and slice any large ones. In a bowl, blend the cornflour with a little of the reserved pineapple juice, then stir in the remainder.

2 Heat the oil in a frying pan. Sear the pork for 30 seconds on each side, or until lightly browned. Transfer to the ceramic cooking pot and add the vegetables, pineapple chunks and water chestnuts.

3 In a bowl, combine the ginger, chilli and five-spice powder with the vinegar, soy sauce, hoisin sauce and reserved stock. Pour in the pineapple juice mixture, then pour into the frying pan and bring to the boil, stirring constantly. As soon as the mixture thickens, pour over the pork and vegetables.

4 Cover the slow cooker with the lid and switch to high. Cook for 1 hour, then reduce the temperature to low and cook for 1–2 hours, or until the pork is tender. Serve with the rice.

Spicy Pork Energy 490kcal/2040kJ; Protein 31.7g; Carbohydrate 33.3g, of which sugars 3g; Fat 23.9g, of which saturates 10.2g; Cholesterol 91mg; Calcium 342mg; Fibre 0.6g; Sodium 340mg.
Hot and Sour Pork Energy 358kcal/1509kJ; Protein 19.9g; Carbohydrate 49.4g, of which sugars 36.3g; Fat 10.3g, of which saturates 2.8g; Cholesterol 60.4mg; Calcium 43mg; Fibre 2.7g; Sodium 405mg.

Pork Rib Stew with Cabbage

This substantial stew makes the most of cheap ingredients, combining flavoursome ribs with a simple broth and some fresh green cabbage. Slow simmering makes the ribs meltingly tender and allows them to release their flavour into the rest of the dish. It makes a simple and easy midweek meal, served with new potatoes.

Serves 4–6

40g/1½oz/¼ cup bacon dripping or 40ml/2½ tbsp vegetable oil
1.8kg/4lb pork spare ribs
900ml/1½ pints/3¾ cups hot beef stock
6 black peppercorns
4 bay leaves
5ml/1 tsp caraway seeds
5ml/1 tsp paprika
2 large onions, roughly chopped
2–3 carrots, roughly chopped
3–4 garlic cloves, roughly chopped
175ml/6fl oz/¾ cup dry white wine
1 cabbage, quartered and core removed
chopped fresh parsley or dill, to garnish
boiled new potatoes, to serve

1 Heat the bacon dripping or oil in a heavy pan. Add the spare ribs and cook over high heat for 5 minutes, turning occasionally, until they are evenly browned all over.

2 Pour in the beef stock, stir to combine and scrape up any sediment from the bottom of the pan. Add the peppercorns, bay leaves, caraway seeds, paprika, onions, carrots, garlic and white wine, and mix well.

3 Bring to the boil, then reduce the heat. Cover the pan with a tight-fitting lid and simmer over low heat for about 1½ hours. Stir the mixture a couple of times during cooking.

4 Add the cabbage to the pan and mix well. Continue to simmer gently for a further 30 minutes, until the ribs are tender and the cabbage is cooked.

5 Ladle the stew on to warmed, deep serving plates or wide bowls. Garnish with the chopped parsley or dill and serve immediately, with boiled new potatoes.

Braised Spicy Spare Ribs

Choose really meaty ribs for slow roasting in this dish, as the juices are turned into a tasty sauce.

Serves 6

25g/1oz/¼ cup plain (all-purpose) flour
5ml/1 tsp salt
5ml/1 tsp ground black pepper
1.6kg/3½lb pork spare ribs, cut into individual pieces
30ml/2 tbsp sunflower oil
1 onion, finely chopped
1 garlic clove, crushed
45ml/3 tbsp tomato purée (paste)
30ml/2 tbsp chilli sauce
30ml/2 tbsp red wine vinegar
pinch of ground cloves
600ml/1 pint/2½ cups beef stock
15ml/1 tbsp cornflour (cornstarch)
flat leaf parsley, to garnish
sauerkraut and crusty bread, to serve

1 Preheat the oven to 180°C/350°F/Gas 4. Combine the flour, salt and pepper in a dish. Add the ribs and toss to coat.

2 Heat the oil in a large frying pan and cook the ribs, turning them until well browned. Transfer to a roasting pan and sprinkle over the chopped onion.

3 In a bowl, mix together the garlic, tomato purée, chilli sauce, vinegar, cloves and stock. Pour over the ribs, then cover with foil. Roast for 1½ hours, or until tender, removing the foil for the last 30 minutes.

4 Transfer the juices from the roasting pan into a small pan. Blend the cornflour in a cup with a little water and stir in. Bring to the boil, stirring, then simmer for 2–3 minutes until thickened.

5 Arrange the ribs on a bed of sauerkraut, then pour over a little sauce. Serve the remaining sauce separately in a warmed jug (pitcher). Garnish with flat leaf parsley and serve with sauerkraut and crusty bread.

Cook's Tip
If time allows, first marinate the ribs for a couple of hours in sunflower oil mixed with red wine vinegar.

Pork Rib Stew Energy 539kcal/2241kJ; Protein 45g; Carbohydrate 6.1g, of which sugars 5.9g; Fat 35.1g, of which saturates 11.2g; Cholesterol 159mg; Calcium 62mg; Fibre 2.2g; Sodium 161mg.
Spare Ribs Energy 327kcal/1357kJ; Protein 24.2g; Carbohydrate 13.3g, of which sugars 6.2g; Fat 19.9g, of which saturates 6.7g; Cholesterol 78mg; Calcium 44mg; Fibre 1.3g; Sodium 218mg.

Pork Ribs with Ginger and Chilli

Ginger, garlic and chilli are used to flavour the sweet-and-sour sauce that coats these ribs. First cook the pork ribs in a covered clay pot to tenderize the meat, then uncover the dish so that the ribs become sticky and brown.

Serves 4

16–20 small meaty pork ribs, about 900g/2lb total weight
1 onion, finely chopped
5cm/2in piece fresh root ginger, peeled and grated
2 garlic cloves, crushed
2.5–5ml/½–1 tsp chilli powder
60ml/4 tbsp soy sauce
45ml/3 tbsp tomato purée (paste)
45ml/3 tbsp clear honey
30ml/2 tbsp red wine vinegar
45ml/3 tbsp dry sherry
60ml/4 tbsp water
salt and ground black pepper
rice or baked potatoes, to serve

1 Soak the clay pot in cold water for 20 minutes, then drain. Place the ribs in the pot, arranging them evenly.

2 Mix together the onion, ginger, garlic, chilli powder, soy sauce, tomato purée, honey, wine vinegar, sherry and water.

3 Pour the sauce over the ribs and toss to coat them. Cover the clay pot and place in an unheated oven. Set the oven to 220°C/425°F/Gas 7. Cook for 1 hour.

4 Remove the lid, baste the ribs and season with salt and pepper. Cook, uncovered, for 15–20 minutes, basting the ribs two to three times during cooking. Serve with rice or baked potatoes.

Cook's Tips

- *For a stronger flavour, place the ribs in a shallow dish, coat them evenly with the sauce and leave to marinate in a cool place for 1–2 hours before cooking in the clay pot.*
- *If you cannot get hold of fresh root ginger, ginger in sunflower oil (sold in small jars) is available from major supermarkets. It is in a paste form and can simply be added whenever the flavour of fresh root ginger is required. Use 10ml/2 tsp instead of the 5cm/2in piece of fresh ginger.*

Potato and Sausage Casserole

This slow-cooker version of the traditional and popular dish means that it is easy to prepare, and you can simply leave it alone to simmer gently to perfection.

Serves 4

15ml/1 tbsp vegetable oil
8 large pork sausages
4 bacon rashers (slices), cut into 2.5cm/1in pieces
1 large onion, chopped
2 garlic cloves, crushed
4 large baking potatoes, thinly sliced
1.5ml/¼ tsp fresh sage
300ml/½ pint/1¼ cups hot vegetable stock
salt and ground black pepper

1 Heat the oil in a frying pan. Gently fry the sausages for about 5 minutes, turning frequently until they are golden but not cooked through. Remove from the frying pan and set aside. Pour away all but about 10ml/2 tsp of fat from the pan.

2 Add the bacon to the pan and fry for 2 minutes. Add the onion and fry for about 8 minutes, stirring frequently until beginning to soften and turn golden. Add the garlic and fry for a further 1 minute, then turn off the heat.

3 Arrange half the potato slices in the base of the ceramic cooking pot. Spoon the bacon and onion mixture on top. Season well with salt and ground black pepper, and sprinkle with the fresh sage. Cover with the remaining potato slices.

4 Pour the stock over the potatoes and top with the sausages. Cover with the lid and cook on high for 3–4 hours, or until the potatoes are tender and the sausages cooked through. Serve hot.

Cook's Tips

- *For a traditionally Irish accompaniment, serve this delicious, hearty casserole with braised green cabbage.*
- *Choose good-quality sausages because it will make all the difference to the final result. Many Irish artisan butchers export quality Irish sausages, and it is well worth keeping an eye out for them if you have a butcher nearby.*

Pork Ribs Energy 633kcal/2637kJ; Protein 42.9g; Carbohydrate 11.5g, of which sugars 11.2g; Fat 45.2g, of which saturates 14.1g; Cholesterol 149mg; Calcium 43mg; Fibre 0.5g; Sodium 250mg.
Potato and Sausage Energy 717kcal/2984kJ; Protein 20.5g; Carbohydrate 49.9g, of which sugars 6.1g; Fat 49.8g, of which saturates 18.1g; Cholesterol 78.1mg; Calcium 73mg; Fibre 4g; Sodium 1322mg.

Toulouse Cassoulet

This slow-baked French speciality features the famous garlic and herb sausages.

Serves 6–8

450g/1lb dried haricot (navy) or cannellini beans, soaked overnight in cold water, then rinsed and drained
675g/1½lb Toulouse sausages
550g/1¼lb each boneless lamb and pork shoulder, cut into 5cm/2in pieces
1 large onion, finely chopped
3 or 4 garlic cloves, finely chopped
4 tomatoes, peeled, seeded and chopped
300ml/½ pint/1¼ cups hot chicken stock
1 bouquet garni
60ml/4 tbsp fresh breadcrumbs
salt and ground black pepper

1 Put the beans in a pan with water to cover. Boil for 10 minutes and drain, then return to a clean pan, cover with water and bring to the boil. Reduce the heat and simmer for 45 minutes, or until tender. Add a little salt and leave to soak in the cooking water.

2 Preheat the oven to 180°C/ 350°F/Gas 4. Place the sausages in a frying pan and cook for 20–25 minutes until brown all over. Drain on kitchen paper and pour off all but 15ml/1 tbsp of the fat.

3 Season the lamb and pork and fry, in batches, on high heat until browned, then transfer to a large dish. Add the onion and garlic to the pan and cook, stirring, for 5 minutes until soft. Add the tomatoes for 2–3 minutes, then transfer to the meat dish. Add the stock and bring to the boil, then skim off the fat.

4 Spoon a quarter of the beans into a large casserole, and top with a third of the sausages, meat and vegetables. Continue to layer, ending with a layer of beans. Add the bouquet garni, pour over the stock and top up with enough of the bean cooking liquid to just cover. Bake the casserole, covered, for 2 hours.

5 Uncover the casserole, sprinkle over the breadcrumbs and press with the back of a spoon to moisten them. Continue cooking the cassoulet, uncovered, for about 20 minutes more until browned. Serve immediately.

Italian Pork Sausage Stew

This hearty, slow-cooker casserole, made with spicy sausages and haricot beans, is flavoured with fragrant fresh herbs and dry Italian wine.

Serves 4

225g/8oz/1¼ cups dried haricot (navy) beans
2 sprigs fresh thyme
30ml/2 tsp olive oil
450g/1lb fresh Italian pork sausages
1 onion, finely chopped
2 sticks celery, finely diced
300ml/½ pint/1¼ cups dry red or white wine, preferably Italian
1 sprig of fresh rosemary
1 bay leaf
300ml/½ pint/1¼ cups boiling vegetable stock
200g/7oz can chopped tomatoes
¼ head dark green cabbage such as cavolo nero or Savoy, finely shredded
salt and ground black pepper
chopped fresh thyme, to garnish
crusty Italian bread, to serve

1 Put the haricot beans in a large bowl and cover with cold water. Leave to soak for at least 8 hours, or overnight.

2 Drain the beans and place in a pan with the thyme sprigs and at least twice their volume of cold water. Bring to the boil and boil steadily for 10 minutes, then drain and place in the ceramic cooking pot, discarding the thyme.

3 Meanwhile, heat the oil in a pan and cook the sausages until browned all over. Transfer to the ceramic cooking pot and pour away all but 15ml/1 tbsp of the fat in the frying pan.

4 Add the onion and celery to the pan and cook gently for 5 minutes until softened but not coloured. Add the wine, rosemary and bay leaf and bring to the boil. Pour over the sausages, add the stock and season with salt and pepper. Cover with the lid, switch the slow cooker to high and cook for 5–6 hours, until the beans are tender.

5 Stir the chopped tomatoes and the shredded cabbage into the stew. Cover and cook for 30–45 minutes, or until the cabbage is tender but not overcooked. Divide between warmed plates, garnish with a little chopped fresh thyme and serve with crusty Italian bread.

Toulouse Cassoulet Energy 378kcal/1586kJ; Protein 31.1g; Carbohydrate 28.5g, of which sugars 6.7g; Fat 16.5g, of which saturates 5.6g; Cholesterol 93mg; Calcium 92mg; Fibre 6.6g; Sodium 581mg.
Italian Pork Sausage Stew Energy 620kcal/2593kJ; Protein 28.4g; Carbohydrate 47.4g, of which sugars 9.9g; Fat 30.9g, of which saturates 10.8g; Cholesterol 67.5mg; Calcium 205mg; Fibre 7.6g; Sodium 1139mg.

Sauerkraut with Pork and Sausages

Strasbourg is renowned for its pork and beef sausages – use them to get the best from this casserole from the Alsace region of France.

Serves 8

30ml/2 tbsp vegetable oil
1 onion, sliced
120g/4oz smoked rindless streaky (fatty) bacon rashers (strips), chopped
900g/2lb bottled sauerkraut, well rinsed and drained
1 apple, peeled and sliced
1 or 2 bay leaves
2.5ml/½ tsp dried thyme
4–5 juniper berries
250ml/8fl oz/1 cup dry white wine
125ml/4fl oz/½ cup apple juice or water
6 Strasbourg sausages, knackwurst or frankfurters
6 spare ribs
900g/2lb small potatoes, peeled
4 smoked gammon (smoked or cured ham) chops or steaks

1 Preheat the oven to 150°C/300°F/Gas 2. Heat half the oil in a large, flameproof casserole over medium heat, then add the sliced onion and chopped bacon and cook, stirring occasionally, for about 5 minutes until the onion has softened and the bacon has just coloured.

2 Tilt the pan and spoon off as much fat as possible, then stir in the sauerkraut, apple, bay leaves, dried thyme, juniper berries, white wine and apple juice or water. Cover the casserole with a tight-fitting lid, place in the preheated oven and cook for about 30 minutes.

3 In a second large, flameproof casserole, heat the remaining oil over medium heat and add the spare ribs. Cook, turning frequently, until browned on all sides. Add the spare ribs to the casserole with the sausages and cook, still covered, for 1¼ hours, stirring occasionally.

4 Bring a large pan of lightly salted water to the boil over medium heat. Add the potatoes, cook for 10 minutes until almost tender, drain and add to the casserole with the gammon chops. Push them into the sauerkraut and continue cooking, covered, for 30–45 minutes more. Season with salt, if needed, and pepper before serving.

Toad-in-the-hole

This oven-baked dish is classic comfort food – perfect for lifting the spirits on cold winter days. Use only the best sausages for this grown-up version, which includes chives.

Serves 4–6

175g/6oz/1½ cups plain (all-purpose) flour
30ml/2 tbsp chopped fresh chives
2 eggs
300ml/½ pint/1¼ cups milk
50g/2oz/⅓ cup white vegetable fat or lard
450g/1lb Cumberland sausages or good-quality pork sausages
salt and ground black pepper

1 Preheat the oven to 220°C/425°F/Gas 7. Sift the flour into a bowl with a pinch of salt and pepper. Make a well in the centre of the flour.

2 Whisk the chives with the eggs and milk, then pour this into the well in the flour. Gradually whisk the flour into the liquid to make a smooth batter. Cover and leave to stand for at least 30 minutes.

3 Put the vegetable fat or lard into a small roasting pan and place in the oven for 3–5 minutes until very hot.

4 Add the sausages to the pan and cook in the oven for about 15 minutes. Turn the sausages twice during cooking.

5 Pour the batter over the sausages, ensuring it is spread out evenly, and cook for about 20 minutes, or until the batter is risen and turned golden. Serve immediately.

Variation
For a young children's supper, make small individual toad-in-the-holes: omit the chopped fresh chives from the batter and cook small cocktail sausages in patty tins (muffin pans) until golden. Add the batter and cook for 10–15 minutes, or until puffed and golden brown.

Sauerkraut Energy 454kcal/1896kJ; Protein 32.1g; Carbohydrate 26.5g, of which sugars 8.2g; Fat 22.9g, of which saturates 7.4g; Cholesterol 74mg; Calcium 90mg; Fibre 4.4g; Sodium 1662mg.
Toad-in-the-hole Energy 448kcal/1871kJ; Protein 15.6g; Carbohydrate 33.1g, of which sugars 4.9g; Fat 29.2g, of which saturates 11.7g; Cholesterol 111mg; Calcium 188mg; Fibre 1.7g; Sodium 692mg.

Braised Shoulder of Lamb with Dulse

Dulse is a sea vegetable or seaweed and is good for flavouring dishes, especially lamb. It is ideal in this slow-cooked dish, which can be simmered on the stove or baked in the oven.

Serves 4

1.8kg/4lb shoulder of lamb, bone in and well trimmed of fat
30ml/2 tbsp vegetable oil
250g/9oz onions
25g/1oz/2 tbsp butter
pinch of caster (superfine) sugar
500ml/17fl oz/generous 2 cups water
50g/2oz dried dulse
1 bay leaf
salt and ground black pepper

1 Preheat the oven to 180°C/350°F/Gas 4, if necessary (see Step 5). Season the lamb all over.

2 Heat a pan, big enough to hold the lamb and with a lid, on the stove. When hot, add the oil and brown the lamb all over. (This can be a little difficult, as there are bits you really can't reach with the bone in, but brown as much as you can.)

3 Remove the lamb from the pan and drain off the excess fat, reserving it in case you need extra for the sauce. Peel the onions, cut in half and slice – not too finely – into half rounds.

4 Return the pan to a medium heat and add the butter. Add the sliced onions with the sugar and a little salt and pepper. Stir to coat with the butter, then cook for 8 minutes until coloured.

5 Place the lamb on top of the onions, add the water, dulse and bay leaf, and season again. Cover and bring to the boil. Cook for 2 hours either over very low heat or in the oven, if the pan will fit and has ovenproof handles.

6 Remove the lamb from the pan, set aside and keep warm. Check the sauce for consistency, adding some of the reserved fat if necessary. Strain and adjust the seasoning. Slice the lamb and serve with the sauce.

Shoulder of Lamb with Pearl Barley and Baby Vegetables

In this wonderful, slow-cooked stew, the pearl barley absorbs all the rich meat juices and stock to become full-flavoured and nutty in texture.

Serves 4

60ml/4 tbsp olive oil
1 large onion, chopped
2 garlic cloves, chopped
2 celery sticks, sliced
a little plain (all-purpose) flour
675g/1½lb boned shoulder of lamb, cut into cubes
900ml–1 litre/1½–1¾ pints/3¾–4 cups lamb stock
115g/4oz/⅔ cup pearl barley
225g/8oz baby carrots
225g/8oz baby turnips
salt and ground black pepper
30ml/2 tbsp chopped fresh marjoram, to garnish
crusty bread, to serve

1 Heat 45ml/3 tbsp of the oil in a flameproof casserole. Cook the onion and garlic until softened, add the celery, then cook until the vegetables brown.

2 Season the flour with salt and pepper and toss the lamb in it. Use a slotted spoon to remove the vegetables from the casserole and set aside.

3 Add and heat the remaining oil with the juices in the casserole. Brown the lamb in batches until golden. When all the meat is evenly browned, return it to the casserole with the onion mixture.

4 Stir in 900ml/1½ pints/3¾ cups of the stock. Add the pearl barley. Cover the casserole, then bring to the boil, reduce the heat and simmer for about 1 hour, or until the pearl barley and the lamb are tender.

5 Add the baby carrots and turnips to the casserole for the final 15 minutes of cooking. Stir the meat occasionally during cooking and add the remaining stock, if it is becoming a little dry. Stir in seasoning to taste, and serve piping hot, garnished with marjoram. Warm, crusty bread for mopping up the juices would make a good accompaniment.

Braised Lamb Energy 677kcal/2808kJ; Protein 43.5g; Carbohydrate 5.2g, of which sugars 3.7g; Fat 53.7g, of which saturates 23.7g; Cholesterol 194mg; Calcium 48mg; Fibre 1.3g; Sodium 188mg.
Shoulder of Lamb Energy 565kcal/2364kJ; Protein 37.2g; Carbohydrate 37.2g, of which sugars 11g; Fat 30.9g, of which saturates 10.4g; Cholesterol 128mg; Calcium 85mg; Fibre 3.9g; Sodium 180mg.

Roast Lamb with Beans and Green Peppercorns

Roasting the lamb slowly on a bed of beans results in a dish that combines meltingly tender meat with vegetables all in one pot.

Serves 6

8–10 garlic cloves, peeled
1.8–2kg/4–4½lb leg of lamb
30ml/2 tbsp olive oil
400g/14oz spinach leaves
400g/14oz can flageolet, cannellini or haricot (navy) beans, drained
400g/14oz can butter (lima) beans, drained
2 large, fresh rosemary sprigs, plus extra to garnish
15–30ml/1–2 tbsp drained, bottled green peppercorns

1 Preheat the oven to 150°C/300°F/Gas 2. Set four garlic cloves aside and slice the rest lengthways into three or four pieces. Make shallow slits in the skin of the lamb with a sharp knife and insert pieces of garlic in each.

2 Heat the olive oil in a heavy, shallow flameproof casserole or a roasting pan that is large enough to hold the leg of lamb. Add the reserved garlic cloves and the fresh spinach leaves to the casserole or pan and cook over medium heat, stirring occasionally, for 4–5 minutes, or until the spinach is wilted.

3 Add the mixed beans to the casserole and tuck the rosemary sprigs and peppercorns among them. Place the lamb on top, then cover the casserole or roasting pan with foil or a tight-fitting lid. Roast the lamb for 3–4 hours until it is cooked to your taste. Serve the lamb and beans hot, garnished with the remaining fresh rosemary sprigs.

Cook's Tip
Green peppercorns are the underripe berry of the pepper plant. They are usually preserved in brine and have a fresh flavour that is less pungent than the berry in its dried, black form. They are available in brine in jars and cans. They should be refrigerated once opened, and can be kept for 1 month.

Tuscan Pot-roasted Shoulder of Lamb

This boned and rolled shoulder of lamb makes the perfect alternative to a traditional roast. Check that the lamb will fit in the slow cooker before you start.

Serves 6

15ml/1 tbsp olive oil
1.3kg/3lb lamb shoulder, trimmed, boned and tied
3 large garlic cloves, quartered
12 small fresh rosemary sprigs
115g/4oz lean rinded smoked bacon, chopped
1 onion, chopped
3 carrots, finely chopped
3 celery sticks, finely chopped
1 leek, finely chopped
150ml/¼ pint/⅔ cup red wine
300ml/½ pint/1¼ cups lamb or vegetable stock
400g/14oz can chopped tomatoes
3 sprigs of fresh thyme
2 bay leaves
400g/14oz can flageolet (small cannellini) beans, drained and rinsed
salt and ground black pepper
potatoes or crusty bread, to serve

1 Heat the oil in a large frying pan and brown the lamb on all sides. Remove from the pan and leave to cool slightly. Make 12 deep incisions all over the meat. Push garlic quarters and a small sprig of rosemary into each incision.

2 Add the bacon, onion, carrot, celery and leek to the pan and cook for 10 minutes until soft. Transfer to the ceramic cooking pot, followed by the wine, stock and chopped tomatoes, then season with salt and pepper. Stir in the thyme and bay leaves. Place the lamb on top, cover and cook on high for 4 hours.

3 Lift the lamb out of the pot and stir the beans into the vegetable mixture. Return the lamb, re-cover and cook for a further 1–2 hours, or until the lamb is cooked and tender.

4 Remove the lamb from the cooking pot using slotted spoons, cover with foil to keep warm, and set aside for 10 minutes.

5 Remove the string from the lamb and carve into thick slices. Remove the thyme and bay leaves from the pot and carefully skim off any fat from the surface. Spoon the vegetables on to warmed serving plates and arrange the sliced lamb on top. Serve with potatoes or warm crusty bread.

Roast Lamb Energy 705kcal/2945kJ; Protein 74.3g; Carbohydrate 22.2g, of which sugars 4.2g; Fat 35.9g, of which saturates 15.4g; Cholesterol 246mg; Calcium 186mg; Fibre 8.7g; Sodium 775mg.
Tuscan Shoulder Energy 710kcal/2958kJ; Protein 60.2g; Carbohydrate 13.7g, of which sugars 4.8g; Fat 44.6g, of which saturates 19.4g; Cholesterol 229mg; Calcium 58mg; Fibre 4.7g; Sodium 864mg.

Lamb Pot-roasted with Tomatoes, Beans and Onions

This slow-braised dish of lamb and tomatoes, spiced with cinnamon and stewed with green beans, shows a Greek influence. It is also good made with courgettes instead of beans.

Serves 8

8 garlic cloves, chopped
2.5–5ml/½–1 tsp ground cumin
45ml/3 tbsp olive oil
juice of 1 lemon
1kg/2¼lb lamb on the bone
2 onions, thinly sliced
500ml/17fl oz/generous 2 cups lamb, beef or vegetable stock
75–90ml/5–6 tbsp tomato purée (paste)
1 cinnamon stick
2–3 large pinches of ground allspice or ground cloves
15–30ml/1–2 tbsp sugar
400g/14oz/scant 3 cups runner (green) beans
salt and ground black pepper
15–30ml/1–2 tbsp chopped fresh parsley, to garnish

1 Preheat the oven to 160°C/325°F/Gas 3. In a bowl, mix together the garlic, ground cumin, olive oil and lemon juice, and season with salt and ground black pepper. Using your hands, rub the mixture all over the piece of lamb.

2 Heat a flameproof casserole that is big enough to hold the lamb. Add the lamb to the casserole and quickly brown all over, turning until evenly coloured.

3 Add the onions to the casserole and pour in the stock until it just covers the meat. Stir in the tomato purée, cinnamon stick, ground allspice or cloves and sugar. Cover and cook in the oven for 2–3 hours.

4 Remove the casserole from the oven and pour the stock into a separate pan. Move the onions to the side of the dish and return to the oven, uncovered, for 20 minutes.

5 Meanwhile, add the green beans to the hot stock and cook until they are tender and the sauce has thickened slightly. Leave the meat to rest for 5–10 minutes before slicing and serving with sauce and beans. Garnish with parsley.

Middle-eastern Roast Lamb and Potatoes

The delicious smell of garlic and saffron will come wafting out of the oven as this fabulous aromatic dish slowly cooks. Serve as an alternative to the traditional roast for a Sunday dinner, or for a hassle-free main course at a dinner party.

Serves 6–8

2.75kg/6lb leg of lamb
4 garlic cloves
60ml/4 tbsp olive oil
juice of 1 lemon
2–3 saffron threads, soaked in 15ml/1 tbsp boiling water
5ml/1 tsp mixed dried herbs, oregano or marjoram
450g/1lb small baking potatoes, thickly sliced
2 large or 4 small onions, thickly sliced
salt and ground black pepper
fresh thyme, to garnish

1 Make eight incisions in the leg of lamb using a sharp knife. Chop the garlic cloves in half and press the pieces into the slits. Place the lamb in a large, non-metallic dish.

2 Mix together the olive oil, lemon juice, saffron mixture and mixed dried herbs. Using your hands, rub the mixture all over the leg of lamb. Cover loosely with foil and leave in a cool place to marinate for 2 hours, or longer if possible.

3 Preheat the oven to 180°C/350°F/Gas 4. Place the potato and onion slices in a large roasting pan, roughly placing them in overlapping layers.

4 Lift the leg of lamb out of the marinade and place it on top of the sliced potato and onions in the roasting pan, fat side up. Season well with plenty of salt and ground black pepper.

5 Pour the marinade over the lamb and vegetables, then roast for 2 hours in the preheated oven. Baste the meat occasionally with the pan juices during the cooking time.

6 Remove from the oven and cover with foil, then leave to rest for 10 minutes before carving. Garnish with fresh thyme.

Lamb Pot-roasted Energy 371kcal/1544kJ; Protein 26.3g; Carbohydrate 7.9g, of which sugars 6.5g; Fat 26.4g, of which saturates 10.9g; Cholesterol 104mg; Calcium 40mg; Fibre 1.9g; Sodium 103mg.
Middle-eastern Lamb Energy 719kcal/2997kJ; Protein 74.4g; Carbohydrate 13g, of which sugars 3.5g; Fat 41.2g, of which saturates 17.7g; Cholesterol 282mg; Calcium 33mg; Fibre 1.3g; Sodium 169mg.

Lamb with Globe Artichokes

A garlic-studded leg of lamb is slowly cooked with red wine and artichoke hearts.

Serves 6–8

1 leg of lamb, about 2kg/4½lb
1–2 garlic heads, divided into cloves, thinly sliced, leaving 5–6 whole
handful of fresh rosemary, stalks removed
475ml/16fl oz/2 cups dry red wine
30–60ml/2–4 tbsp olive oil
4 globe artichokes
a little lemon juice
5 shallots, chopped
250ml/8fl oz/1 cup beef stock
salt and ground black pepper
green salad with garlic-rubbed croûtons, to serve (optional)

1 Make incisions all over the lamb. Put a sliver of garlic and as many rosemary leaves as you can into each incision. Season with salt and plenty of black pepper. Put the lamb in a non-metallic dish and pour half the wine and all of the oil over the top. Set aside and leave to marinate until ready to roast.

2 Preheat the oven to 230°C/450°F/Gas 8. Put the meat and its juices in a roasting pan and surround with the remaining whole garlic cloves. Roast for 10–15 minutes, then reduce the oven to 160°C/325°F/Gas 3 and cook for a further 1 hour.

3 Meanwhile, prepare the artichokes. Snap off the tough leaves and trim the ends off the base. Quarter and cut out the inside thistle heart. Place into a bowl of water with the lemon juice.

4 About 20 minutes before the lamb is cooked, drain the globe artichokes and place them around the meat. When the lamb is cooked, transfer the meat and artichokes to a serving dish. Pour the meat juices and roasted garlic into a pan.

5 Spoon off the fat from the pan juices and add the chopped shallots and the remaining red wine to the pan. Cook over a high heat until the liquid has reduced, then add the stock and cook, stirring constantly, until the pan juices are rich and flavourful.

6 Coat the lamb and artichokes with the roasted garlic and red wine sauce and garnish with extra rosemary. Serve with a green salad and garlic croûtons, if you like.

Leg of Lamb with Pickle Sauce

The sourness of the pickle sauce makes a sharp contrast to the rich roasted lamb.

Serves 6–8

1.8kg/4lb lean leg of lamb
30–45ml/2–3 tbsp salt
finely grated rind of 1 lemon
50g/2oz/4 tbsp butter
4 rosemary sprigs
handful of flat leaf parsley
extra sprigs of rosemary and flat leaf parsley, to garnish
braised red cabbage, to serve

For the pickle sauce
25g/1oz/2 tbsp butter
8–10 gherkins, chopped
50g/2oz/½ cup plain (all-purpose) flour
250ml/8fl oz/1 cup lamb stock
generous pinch of saffron
30ml/2 tbsp sour cream
5–10ml/1–2 tsp white wine vinegar
salt and ground black pepper

1 Preheat the oven to 180°C/350°F/Gas 4. Flatten the lamb with a rolling pin, rub with salt and leave for 30 minutes. Mix the lemon rind and butter together.

2 Place the lamb in a roasting pan and spread the lemon butter over. Add the fresh herbs to the pan and roast for 1½–1¾ hours, basting occasionally. Strain the meat juices.

3 Meanwhile, make the pickle sauce. Heat the butter in a small pan and cook the gherkins for 5 minutes, stirring occasionally. Remove from the heat. Sprinkle in the flour and stir for a further 2–3 minutes. Pour the stock into the pan and bring to the boil. Stir in the saffron and simmer for 15 minutes.

4 Off the heat, stir the sour cream, vinegar and the strained meat juices into the sauce. Season to taste. Garnish the lamb with herbs and serve with the sauce and red cabbage.

Cook's Tip
Leave the leg of lamb to stand for 10–20 minutes after cooking to allow the fibres in the meat to relax, making it more tender, firmer and easier to carve.

Lamb Energy 595kcal/2487kJ; Protein 72.4g; Carbohydrate 2.2g, of which sugars 1.6g; Fat 28.3g, of which saturates 11.4g; Cholesterol 275mg; Calcium 53mg; Fibre 0.5g; Sodium 217mg.
Leg of Lamb Energy 412kcal/1715kJ; Protein 34.1g; Carbohydrate 6.2g, of which sugars 1.4g; Fat 28g, of which saturates 10.4g; Cholesterol 137mg; Calcium 34mg; Fibre 0.7g; Sodium 120mg.

Bulgarian Lamb in Pastry

This is an impressive dish to serve on special occasions. Skim the meat juices, bring them back to the boil and serve as a gravy with the tender lamb.

Serves 6–8
1.5kg/3½lb leg of lamb, boned
40g/1½oz/3 tbsp butter
2.5ml/½ tsp each dried thyme, basil and oregano
2 garlic cloves, crushed
45ml/3tbsp lemon juice
salt, for sprinkling
1 egg, beaten, for sealing and glazing
1 oregano or marjoram sprig, to garnish

For the pastry
450g/1lb/4 cups plain (all-purpose) flour, sifted
250g/9oz/generous 1 cup chilled butter, diced
150–250ml/¼–½ pint/⅔–1 cup iced water

1 Preheat the oven to 190°/375°F/Gas 5. To make the pastry, place the flour and butter in a food processor or blender and process until the mixture resembles fine breadcrumbs. Add enough iced water to make a soft, but not sticky, dough. Knead gently and form into a ball. Wrap in clear film (plastic wrap) and refrigerate for 1–2 hours.

2 Meanwhile, put the lamb in a roasting pan, tie the joint with kitchen string and cut 20 small holes in the meat, with a sharp knife. Cream together the butter, dried herbs, garlic and lemon juice and use to fill the small cuts in the lamb.

3 Sprinkle the whole joint with salt. Place the lamb in a roasting pan and cook for 1 hour, then allow to cool. Remove the string.

4 Roll out the pastry on a lightly floured surface until large enough to wrap around the lamb in one piece. Seal the pastry edges with a little of the egg and place in a clean roasting pan.

5 With any remaining scraps of pastry, make leaves or other shapes as decorations. Brush with more of the egg. Return to the oven and bake for a further 30–45 minutes. Serve hot, in slices, accompanied by the gravy from the meat juices, and garnished with a sprig of oregano or marjoram.

Lamb Stew

This slowly simmered dish is traditionally known as a broth. It makes a warming and nourishing meal on a cold winter's day.

Serves 4
30ml/2 tbsp olive oil
2 onions, roughly chopped
2 celery sticks, thickly sliced
2 carrots, thickly sliced
2 parsnips, roughly chopped
1 small swede (rutabaga), roughly chopped
800g/1¾lb lamb, such as boned shoulder, trimmed and cut into bitesize pieces
lamb or vegetable stock
30ml/2 tbsp chopped fresh thyme leaves or 10ml/2 tsp dried thyme
3 potatoes
2 leeks, trimmed
handful of chopped fresh parsley
salt and ground black pepper

1 Heat a large pan, add half the olive oil and stir in the onions, celery, carrots, parsnips and swede. Cook all the vegetables quickly, stirring occasionally, until golden brown and then lift them out and set aside.

2 Add the remaining oil to the pan. Quickly fry the lamb pieces in batches, turning occasionally, until evenly browned on all sides.

3 Return the browned vegetables to the pan with the lamb and pour over enough stock to just cover the ingredients. Add the fresh or dried thyme and season with a little salt and ground black pepper.

4 Bring to the boil and skim off any surface scum. Cover with a tight-fitting lid and cook gently, so that the liquid barely bubbles, for about 1½ hours, until the lamb is tender.

5 Peel and cut the potatoes into cubes and add to the pan. Cover and cook gently for 15–20 minutes until just soft.

6 Thinly slice the white part of the leeks and add to the pan, adjust the seasoning to taste and cook for 5 minutes.

7 Before serving, thinly slice the green parts of the leeks and add to the broth with the parsley. Cook for a few minutes until the leeks soften, and serve immediately.

Bulgarian Energy 768kcal/3201kJ; Protein 33.8g; Carbohydrate 44.1g, of which sugars 1.2g; Fat 51.9g, of which saturates 26.3g; Cholesterol 187mg; Calcium 104mg; Fibre 2.1g; Sodium 310mg.
Lamb Stew Energy 594kcal/2488kJ; Protein 45.2g; Carbohydrate 39.4g, of which sugars 17.9g; Fat 29.6g, of which saturates 11.5g; Cholesterol 152mg; Calcium 151mg; Fibre 8.5g; Sodium 224mg.

Mutton Hotpot

This slow-baked mutton hotpot would have been a Sunday treat in bygone days. Mutton is worth looking out for – try your local farmers' market or ask your butcher if he could get it. It often has a superior flavour to lamb, although it requires longer, slower cooking.

Serves 6
6 mutton chops
6 lamb's kidneys
1 large onion, sliced
450g/1lb potatoes, sliced
600ml/1 pint/2½ cups lamb stock
salt and ground black pepper

1 Preheat the oven to 180°C/350°F/Gas 4. Trim the mutton chops, leaving a little fat on them but no bone. Slice the kidneys in two horizontally and remove the fat and core with sharp scissors.

2 Place three of the mutton chops in a deep casserole and season well with salt and ground black pepper. Add a layer of half the kidneys in the casserole on top of the chops, followed by half the sliced onion and, finally, half the potatoes. Season lightly with salt and pepper. Repeat the layering process, seasoning as you go. Make sure that you finish with an even layer of potatoes.

3 Heat the stock in a separate pan until bubbling. Pour it into the casserole, just about covering everything but leaving the potatoes just showing at the top. Cover with a tight-fitting lid and cook in the preheated oven for 2 hours.

4 Remove the lid for the last 30 minutes to allow the potatoes to brown. Serve immediately, placing a mutton chop and two kidney halves on each plate, with plenty of onions and potatoes.

Variation
If you prefer, you can use lamb chops instead. Use two chops per person and reduce the cooking time by about 30 minutes as lamb does not need the full 2 hours.

Lancashire Hotpot

This dish is traditionally made without browning the lamb or vegetables, and relies on long, slow cooking to develop the flavour. You can brown the top under the grill, if you like, once it has finished simmering in the slow cooker.

Serves 4
8 middle neck or loin lamb chops, about 900g/2lb in total weight
900g/2lb potatoes, thinly sliced
2 onions, sliced
2 carrots, sliced
1 stick celery, trimmed and sliced
1 leek, sliced
225g/8oz/generous 3 cups button (white) mushrooms, sliced
5ml/1 tsp dried mixed herbs
small sprig of rosemary
475ml/16fl oz/2 cups lamb or beef stock
15g/½oz/1 tbsp butter, melted
salt and ground black pepper

1 Trim the lamb chops of excess fat. Place a layer of sliced potatoes in the base of the ceramic cooking pot, and top with some sliced vegetables and a sprinkling of dried herbs. Season with salt and ground black pepper. Place four of the lamb chops in an even layer on top of the vegetables.

2 Repeat the layers of sliced potato, vegetables, dried mixed herbs and lamb chops, tucking the rosemary sprig down the side of the ceramic cooking pot. Continue layering up the remaining vegetables, finishing with a neat layer of potato slices on the top.

3 Pour the lamb or beef stock into the ceramic cooking pot to just come up to the top layer of potatoes. Cover with the lid and switch the slow cooker to the high or auto setting. Cook for 1 hour.

4 Reduce the slow cooker temperature to the low setting or leave on auto and cook for a further 6–8 hours, or until all the meat and vegetables are tender.

5 Brush the top layer of potatoes with the melted butter. Place the cooking pot, uncovered, under a preheated grill (broiler) and cook for 5 minutes, until the potatoes are lightly browned. Spoon on to warmed plates and serve.

Mutton Hotpot Energy 626kcal/2629kJ; Protein 76.9g; Carbohydrate 23.1g, of which sugars 5g; Fat 25.8g, of which saturates 11.6g; Cholesterol 374mg; Calcium 76mg; Fibre 2g; Sodium 269mg.
Lancashire Hotpot Energy 850kcal/3544kJ; Protein 44.7g; Carbohydrate 45.3g, of which sugars 10.1g; Fat 55.8g, of which saturates 26.5g; Cholesterol 186mg; Calcium 72mg; Fibre 4.3g; Sodium 274mg.

Lamb and Carrot Casserole with Barley

Barley and carrots make natural partners for lamb. In this slow-cooker casserole, the barley extends the meat and adds to the flavour and texture, as well as thickening and enriching the sauce.

Serves 6

675g/1½lb stewing lamb
15ml/1 tbsp vegetable oil
2 onions
675g/1½lb carrots, thickly sliced
4–6 celery sticks, sliced
45ml/3 tbsp pearl barley, rinsed and drained
600ml/1 pint/2½ cups near-boiling lamb or vegetable stock
5ml/1 tsp fresh thyme leaves or pinch of dried mixed herbs
salt and ground black pepper
steamed spring cabbage and jacket potatoes, to serve

1 Trim all excess fat from the lamb, then cut the meat into 3cm/1¼in pieces. Heat the oil in a frying pan, add the lamb and fry until browned. Remove with a slotted spoon and set aside.

2 Slice the onions and add to the pan. Fry gently for 5 minutes until golden. Add the carrots and celery and cook for a further 3–4 minutes or until beginning to soften.

3 Transfer the cooked vegetables to the ceramic cooking pot and switch the slow cooker to high. Sprinkle the pearl barley over the vegetables, then arrange the lamb pieces on top. Lightly season with salt and ground black pepper, then sprinkle with the fresh or dried herbs.

4 Pour the lamb or vegetable stock into the cooking pot, so that all of the ingredients are covered. Cover the slow cooker with the lid and cook on auto or high for 2 hours.

5 Lift the lid and, using a large spoon, skim off any scum that has risen to the surface of the casserole. Re-cover the cooker and leave on the auto setting or switch to low and cook for a further 4–6 hours or until the meat, vegetables and barley are tender. Serve immediately, accompanied by spring cabbage and jacket potatoes.

Irish Stew

Simple and delicious, this is the quintessential Irish main course. Traditionally, mutton chops are used, but as they are harder to find these days you can use lamb instead. Do try to seek out some mutton, however, as it has a deeper flavour than lamb and is ideal for slow cooking.

Serves 4

1.3kg/3lb boneless lamb chops, cut into large chunks
15ml/1 tbsp vegetable oil
3 onions
4 large carrots
900ml/1½ pints/3¾ cups water
4 large floury potatoes, cut into large chunks
1 large fresh thyme sprig
15g/½ oz/1 tbsp unsalted butter
15ml/1 tbsp finely chopped fresh parsley
salt and ground black pepper

1 Trim any fat from the lamb. Heat the vegetable oil in a large, flameproof casserole and cook the lamb chunks until evenly browned on all sides. Remove from the casserole with a slotted spoon and set aside.

2 Cut the onions into quarters and thickly slice the carrots. Add them to the oil remaining in the casserole and cook, stirring, for 5 minutes, or until the onions are browned and beginning to soften.

3 Return the browned lamb chunks to the casserole and pour in the measured water. Bring to the boil, reduce the heat, cover the casserole with a tight-fitting lid and simmer over low heat for 1 hour.

4 Add the potato chunks to the pan with the thyme sprig and mix until well combined. Continue to simmer gently, with the lid on, for a further 1 hour. Stir the stew occasionally during the cooking time.

5 When the meat and vegetables are tender, remove the stew and leave it to settle for a few minutes. Remove the fat from the liquid by skimming it with a spoon. Stir in the butter and chopped parsley. Season well before serving.

Lamb Casserole Energy 304kcal/1263kJ; Protein 23.2g; Carbohydrate 13g, of which sugars 11.3g; Fat 18g, of which saturates 7.5g; Cholesterol 84mg; Calcium 53mg; Fibre 3.6g; Sodium 110mg.
Irish Stew Energy 898kcal/3763kJ; Protein 70.4g; Carbohydrate 60g, of which sugars 19.1g; Fat 43.6g, of which saturates 19.5g; Cholesterol 255mg; Calcium 104mg; Fibre 7g; Sodium 359mg.

Lamb in Dill Sauce

In this slow-cooker recipe, lamb is simmered with vegetables to make a clear broth, which is thickened with an egg and cream mixture to make a sauce.

Serves 6

1.3kg/3lb lean boneless lamb
1 small onion, trimmed and quartered
1 carrot, thickly sliced
1 bay leaf
4 sprigs of fresh dill, plus 45ml/3 tbsp chopped
1 thinly pared strip of lemon rind
750ml/1 1/4 pints/3 cups near-boiling lamb or vegetable stock
15ml/1 tbsp olive oil
15g/1/2 oz/1 tbsp unsalted butter
225g/8oz small shallots, peeled
15ml/1 tbsp plain (all-purpose) flour
115g/4oz frozen petits pois (baby peas), defrosted
1 egg yolk
75ml/2 1/2fl oz/1/3 cup single (light) cream, at room temperature
salt and ground black pepper
new potatoes and carrots, to serve

1 Trim the lamb and cut into 2.5cm/1in pieces. Place in the ceramic cooking pot with the onion, carrot, bay leaf, sprigs of dill and lemon rind. Pour over the stock, cover and cook on high for 1 hour. Skim off any scum, then re-cover and cook for 2 hours on high or 4 hours on low, until the lamb is fairly tender.

2 Remove the meat from the pot. Strain the stock, discarding the vegetables and herbs. Clean the pot. Return the meat and half the stock (reserving the rest), cover and switch to high.

3 Heat the oil and butter in a pan, add the shallots and cook gently for 10–15 minutes, or until tender. Turn off the heat, then transfer the shallots to the cooking pot, using a slotted spoon.

4 Sprinkle the flour over the fat remaining in the pan, then stir in the reserved stock, a little at a time. Bring to the boil, stirring, until thickened, then stir into the cooking pot. Stir in the peas and season. Cook on high for 30 minutes until piping hot.

5 Blend the egg yolk and the cream together, then stir in a few spoonfuls of the hot stock. Add to the casserole in a thin stream, stirring until slightly thickened. Stir in the chopped dill and serve immediately, with steamed new potatoes and carrots.

Lamb Pie with Mustard Thatch

Here, a traditional shepherd's pie is made in the slow cooker and given a contemporary twist with a tangy topping of mashed potato flavoured with peppery mustard. Steamed green vegetables make a delicious accompaniment.

Serves 4

450g/1lb lean minced (ground) lamb
1 onion, very finely chopped
2 celery sticks, thinly sliced
2 carrots, finely diced
15ml/1 tbsp cornflour (cornstarch) blended into 150ml/1/4 pint/2/3 cup lamb stock
15ml/1 tbsp Worcestershire sauce
30ml/2 tbsp chopped fresh rosemary, or 10ml/2 tsp dried
800g/1 3/4lb floury potatoes, diced
60ml/4 tbsp milk
15ml/1 tbsp wholegrain mustard
25g/1oz/2 tbsp butter
salt and ground black pepper

1 Heat a large frying pan, then add the minced lamb, breaking it up with a wooden spoon, and cook until lightly browned all over. Add the onion, celery and carrots to the pan and cook for 2–3 minutes, stirring frequently.

2 Stir the stock and cornflour mixture into the pan. Bring the mixture to the boil, stirring constantly, then remove from the heat. Stir in the Worcestershire sauce and the fresh or dried rosemary, and season well with salt and ground black pepper.

3 Transfer the mixture to the ceramic cooking pot and switch the slow cooker to the high setting. Cover with the lid and cook for 3 hours.

4 Towards the end of the cooking time, bring a large pan of salted water to the boil and add the potatoes. Cook for about 10–12 minutes until tender. Drain well, mash, and stir in the milk, mustard and butter. Season to taste.

5 Spoon the mashed potatoes on top of the lamb in the cooking pot, spreading the mixture out evenly. Cook for a further 45 minutes. Draw a fork through the topping to create lines and brown under a preheated grill (broiler) for a few minutes, if you like, then serve immediately.

Lamb in Dill Sauce Energy 631kcal/2629kJ; Protein 60.9g; Carbohydrate 7g, of which sugars 3.5g; Fat 40g, of which saturates 17.5g; Cholesterol 249mg; Calcium 123mg; Fibre 1.9g; Sodium 566mg.
Lamb Pie Energy 458kcal/1920kJ; Protein 26.5g; Carbohydrate 42.2g, of which sugars 8.1g; Fat 21.5g, of which saturates 10.6g; Cholesterol 101mg; Calcium 84mg; Fibre 3.5g; Sodium 264mg.

Lamb with Shallots and Potatoes

This lamb casserole is finished with a topping of garlic, parsley and lemon rind.

Serves 6

1kg/2¼lb boneless shoulder of lamb, trimmed of fat and cut into 5cm/2in cubes
1 garlic clove, finely chopped
finely grated rind of ½ lemon and juice of 1 lemon
90ml/6 tbsp olive oil
45ml/3 tbsp plain (all-purpose) flour, seasoned
1 large onion, sliced
5 anchovy fillets in olive oil, drained
2.5ml/½ tsp caster (superfine) sugar
300ml/½ pint/1¼ cups white wine
475ml/16fl oz/2 cups lamb stock or half stock and half water
1 bouquet garni, made from 1 fresh bay leaf, 1 fresh thyme sprig and 1 fresh parsley sprig
500g/1¼lb small new potatoes
250g/9oz shallots, peeled but whole
45ml/3 tbsp double (heavy) cream (optional)
salt and ground black pepper

For the topping

shredded rind of ½ lemon
45ml/3 tbsp chopped fresh flat leaf parsley
1 garlic clove, chopped

1 Mix the lamb, garlic, rind and half the lemon juice. Season, then add 15ml/1 tbsp olive oil and marinate for 12–24 hours. When ready to cook, chop the topping ingredients together. Set aside.

2 Drain the lamb, reserving the marinade. Preheat the oven to 180°C/350°F/Gas 4. Heat the oil in a frying pan, toss the lamb in the seasoned flour, then brown in the pan. Transfer to a flameproof casserole. Fry the onion for 10 minutes. Add the anchovies and sugar, mashing the fish well. Add the marinade, wine and stock. Bring to the boil, then simmer for 5 minutes. Pour over the lamb.

3 Add the bouquet garni to the casserole and season. Cover and cook in the oven for 1 hour. Add the potatoes, re-cover, and cook for 20 minutes. Brown the shallots in the frying pan and add to the casserole. Cover and cook for 30–40 minutes. Transfer the lamb and vegetables to a serving dish. Discard the herbs.

4 Boil the cooking juices on the stove to reduce them. Add the cream, if using, and heat through. Season and add lemon juice to taste. Pour over the lamb, sprinkle on the topping and serve.

Lamb Stewed with Tomatoes and Garlic

This delicious, rustic stew is easy to make in the slow cooker. Serve simply, with fresh crusty bread and a green leaf salad.

Serves 4

1.2kg/2½lb stewing lamb
30ml/2 tbsp plain (all-purpose) flour, seasoned with ground black pepper
60ml/4 tbsp olive oil
2 large cloves garlic, finely chopped
1 sprig fresh rosemary
150ml/¼ pint/⅔ cup dry white wine
150ml/¼ pint/⅔ cup lamb or beef stock
2.5ml/½ tsp salt
450g/1lb fresh tomatoes, peeled and chopped, or 400g/14oz can chopped tomatoes
salt and ground black pepper

1 Trim all fat and gristle from the lamb and cut into 2.5cm/1in cubes. Toss in the flour to coat. Set aside any excess flour. Heat the oil in a pan and brown the lamb, in two batches, for about 5 minutes. Transfer to the ceramic cooking pot.

2 Add the garlic and cook for a few seconds before adding the rosemary, wine and stock. Bring almost to the boil, stirring. Pour over the lamb. Season and stir in the tomatoes. Cover the cooking pot with the lid and switch the slow cooker to high or auto. Cook for 1 hour.

3 Reduce the heat to low or leave on auto and cook for a further 6–8 hours, or until the lamb is tender. Taste and adjust the seasoning before serving.

Variation
For Lamb with Butternut Squash, sauté 675g/1½lb cubed lamb fillet in 15ml/1 tbsp oil, then transfer to the ceramic cooking pot. Fry 1 chopped onion and 2 crushed garlic cloves until soft, and add to the lamb with 1 cubed butternut squash, 400g/14oz can chopped tomatoes, 150ml/¼ pint/⅔ cup lamb stock and 5ml/1 tsp dried marjoram. Cover and cook on low for 5–6 hours.

Lamb with Shallots Energy 553kcal/2311kJ; Protein 37g; Carbohydrate 26.2g, of which sugars 5.3g; Fat 30.6g, of which saturates 10.4g; Cholesterol 128mg; Calcium 79mg; Fibre 2.7g; Sodium 261mg.
Lamb with Tomatoes Energy 636kcal/2656kJ; Protein 62.4g; Carbohydrate 11.5g, of which sugars 3.9g; Fat 35.5g, of which saturates 12.2g; Cholesterol 222mg; Calcium 62mg; Fibre 1.4g; Sodium 508mg.

Lamb Shanks with Beans and Herbs

For this hearty winter meal, the lamb shanks are cooked slowly in a clay pot on a bed of tasty beans and vegetables, until tender.

Serves 4

175g/6oz/1 cup dried cannellini beans, soaked overnight in cold water
150ml/¼ pint/⅔ cup water
45ml/3 tbsp olive oil
4 large lamb shanks, about 225g/8oz each
1 large onion, chopped
450g/1lb carrots, cut into thick chunks
2 celery sticks, cut into thick chunks
450g/1lb tomatoes, quartered
250ml/8fl oz/1 cup vegetable stock
4 fresh rosemary sprigs
2 bay leaves
salt and ground black pepper

1 Soak a large clay pot in cold water for 20 minutes, then drain. Drain and rinse the cannellini beans and place in a large pan of unsalted boiling water and boil rapidly for 10 minutes, then drain. Place the measured water in the clay pot, then add the beans.

2 Heat 30ml/2 tbsp of the olive oil in a large frying pan, add the lamb shanks and cook over high heat, turning the shanks occasionally, until brown on all sides. Remove them with a slotted spoon and set aside. Heat the remaining oil in the pan, then add the onion and sauté for 5 minutes, until turning soft and translucent.

3 Add the carrots and celery to the pan and cook for 2–3 minutes. Stir in the tomatoes and stock and mix well. Transfer the vegetable mixture to the clay pot and season well with salt and pepper. Stir in the rosemary and bay leaves.

4 Place the lamb shanks on top of the beans and vegetables. Cover the clay pot and place it in an unheated oven. Set the oven to 220°C/425°F/Gas 7 and cook for 30 minutes, or until the liquid is bubbling.

5 Reduce the oven temperature to 160°C/325°F/Gas 3 and cook for about 1½ hours, or until the meat is tender. Check the seasoning and serve on warmed plates, placing each lamb shank on a bed of beans and vegetables.

Lamb Goulash with Tomatoes and Peppers

Goulash is a dish that has travelled across Europe from Hungary and is popular in many places, such as the Czech Republic and Germany. This slowly simmered version is not a true goulash, however, because of the addition of flour. Nevertheless, it has a wonderful infusion of tomatoes, paprika, green peppers and marjoram.

Serves 4–6

30ml/2 tbsp vegetable oil, melted lard or white cooking fat (optional)
900g/2lb lean lamb, trimmed and cut into cubes
1 large onion, roughly chopped
2 garlic cloves, crushed
3 green (bell) peppers, seeded and diced
30ml/2 tbsp paprika
2 x 400g/14oz cans chopped plum tomatoes
15ml/1tbsp chopped fresh flat leaf parsley
5ml/1 tsp chopped fresh marjoram
30ml/2 tbsp plain (all-purpose) flour
60ml/4 tbsp cold water
salt and ground black pepper
green salad, to serve

1 Heat the oil, lard or white cooking fat, if using, in a frying pan. Dry fry or fry the pieces of lamb for 5–8 minutes, or until browned on all sides. Season well.

2 Add the onion and garlic and cook for a further 2 minutes before adding the green peppers and paprika.

3 Pour in the tomatoes and enough water, if needed, to cover the meat in the pan. Stir in the herbs. Bring to the boil, turn down the heat, cover and simmer very gently for 1½ hours, or until the lamb is tender.

4 Blend the flour with the cold water and pour into the stew. Bring back to the boil, then reduce the heat to a simmer and cook until the sauce has thickened.

5 Taste and adjust the seasoning, if necessary, and serve the lamb goulash with a crisp and refreshing green salad.

Lamb Shanks Energy 743kcal/3121kJ; Protein 79.2g; Carbohydrate 39.7g, of which sugars 18.7g; Fat 30.9g, of which saturates 10.1g; Cholesterol 225mg; Calcium 127mg; Fibre 12.3g; Sodium 200mg.
Lamb Goulash Energy 396kcal/1656kJ; Protein 32.6g; Carbohydrate 19.4g, of which sugars 13.8g; Fat 21.5g, of which saturates 8.5g; Cholesterol 114mg; Calcium 53mg; Fibre 4g; Sodium 147mg.

Lamb Casserole with Garlic and Broad Beans

This dish is slowly simmered on top of the stove until the chunks of stewing lamb are meltingly tender. The casserole is flavoured with a large amount of garlic, and plenty of dry sherry adds richness to the sauce. The addition of broad beans adds attractive colour.

Serves 6

45ml/3 tbsp olive oil
1.3kg–1.6kg/3–3½lb lamb fillet, cut into 5cm/2in cubes
1 large onion, chopped
6 large garlic cloves, unpeeled
1 bay leaf
5ml/1 tsp paprika
120ml/4fl oz/½ cup dry sherry
115g/4oz shelled fresh or frozen broad (fava) beans
30ml/2 tbsp chopped fresh parsley
salt and ground black pepper
mashed or boiled potatoes, to serve (optional)

1 Heat 30ml/2 tbsp of the oil in a large flameproof casserole. Add half the lamb cubes to the pan and cook for 45 minutes until evenly browned on all sides. Transfer to a plate and set aside. Brown the rest of the meat in the same way and remove from the casserole.

2 Heat the remaining oil in the pan, add the onion and cook for about 5 minutes until softened and just beginning to turn brown. Return the browned lamb cubes to the casserole and stir in with the onion.

3 Add the garlic cloves, bay leaf, paprika and sherry to the casserole. Season with salt and ground black pepper. Bring the mixture to the boil, then reduce the heat. Cover the pan with a tight-fitting lid and simmer very gently for 1½–2 hours, until the meat is tender.

4 About 10 minutes before the end of the cooking time, stir in the broad beans. Re-cover the pan and place back in the oven until the meat and beans are tender.

5 Stir in the chopped parsley just before serving. Accompany the casserole with mashed or boiled potatoes, if you like.

Braised Lamb with Apricots and Herb Dumplings

A fruity, oven-cooked lamb casserole, topped with light, herby dumplings.

Serves 6

30ml/2 tbsp sunflower oil
675g/1½lb lean lamb fillet, cut into 2.5cm/1in cubes
350g/12oz baby (pearl) onions, peeled
1 garlic clove, crushed
225g/8oz/3 cups button (white) mushrooms
175g/6oz/¾ cup small ready-to-eat dried apricots
about 250ml/8fl oz/1 cup well-flavoured lamb or beef stock
250ml/8fl oz/1 cup red wine
15ml/1 tbsp tomato purée (paste)
salt and ground black pepper
fresh herb sprigs, to garnish

For the dumplings

115g/4oz/1 cup self-raising (self-rising) flour
50g/2oz/scant ½ cup shredded vegetable suet (US chilled, grated shortening)
15–30ml/1–2 tbsp chopped fresh mixed herbs

1 Preheat the oven to 160°C/325°F/Gas 3. Heat the oil in a large, flameproof casserole, add the lamb and cook over high heat until browned. Remove the meat from the casserole using a slotted spoon, then set aside and keep warm.

2 Add the onions, garlic and mushrooms to the pan and cook gently for 5 minutes. Return the meat to the casserole, then add the apricots, stock, wine and tomato purée, and season to taste. Bring to the boil, stirring, then transfer to the oven and cook, covered, for 1½–2 hours, until the lamb is tender.

3 Meanwhile, make the dumplings. Mix the flour, suet, herbs and seasoning in a bowl. Add enough cold water to make a soft, elastic dough. Divide the dough into small, marble-size pieces and, using floured hands, roll each piece into a small ball.

4 Remove the lid from the casserole and place the dumplings on top. Increase the oven temperature to 190°C/375°F/Gas 5. Return the casserole to the oven and cook for a further 20–25 minutes until the herb dumplings are cooked. Serve garnished with the fresh herb sprigs.

Lamb Casserole Energy 541kcal/2258kJ; Protein 50.8g; Carbohydrate 3.5g, of which sugars 1.2g; Fat 33.7g, of which saturates 13.8g; Cholesterol 190mg; Calcium 45mg; Fibre 1.6g; Sodium 221mg.
Braised Lamb Energy 499kcal/2091kJ; Protein 28.5g; Carbohydrate 36.7g, of which sugars 20.2g; Fat 24.4g, of which saturates 10.1g; Cholesterol 86mg; Calcium 132mg; Fibre 4.8g; Sodium 277mg.

Baked Meatballs with Chilli Tomato Sauce

These piquant meatballs are first browned before being immersed in the sauce and slowly simmered in a clay pot in the oven. Serve with pasta.

Serves 4

450g/1lb lean minced (ground) lamb
1 large onion, grated
1 garlic clove, crushed
50g/2oz/1 cup fresh white breadcrumbs
15ml/1 tbsp chopped fresh parsley
1 small egg, lightly beaten
30ml/2 tbsp olive oil
salt and ground black pepper
60ml/4 tbsp finely grated Parmesan cheese and rocket (arugula) leaves, to serve

For the sauce

1 onion, finely chopped
400g/14oz can chopped tomatoes
200ml/7fl oz/scant 1 cup passata (bottled strained tomatoes)
5ml/1 tsp sugar
2 green chillies, seeded and finely chopped
30ml/2 tbsp chopped fresh oregano
salt and ground black pepper

1 Soak a small clay pot in cold water for 15 minutes, then drain. Mix the lamb, onion, garlic, breadcrumbs, parsley and seasoning in a bowl. Add the egg and stir to bind the mixture.

2 Shape the mixture into 20 small even balls. Heat the olive oil in a frying pan, add the meatballs and cook over high heat, stirring occasionally, until they are browned all over.

3 Meanwhile, to make the sauce, mix together the onion, tomatoes, passata, sugar, seeded and chopped chillies and oregano. Season well and pour the sauce into the clay pot.

4 Place the meatballs in the sauce, then cover and place in an unheated oven set to 200°C/400°F/Gas 6 and cook for 1 hour, stirring after 30 minutes. Serve with Parmesan cheese and rocket.

Variation
Minced (ground) beef or sausage meat (bulk sausage) can be used in place of the minced lamb in this dish, if you prefer.

Lamb Meatballs in Rich Tomato Sauce

The slow cooker is ideal for simmering these lamb meatballs in a delicious tomato sauce.

Serves 4

50g/2oz/1 cup fresh white breadcrumbs
1 egg, lightly beaten
finely grated rind of ½ small orange
2.5ml/½ tsp dried oregano
450g/1lb minced (ground) lamb
1 small onion, grated
2 cloves garlic, crushed
15ml/1 tbsp plain (all-purpose) flour
30ml/2 tbsp olive oil
salt and ground black pepper
flat leaf parsley, to garnish

For the sauce

1 onion, very finely chopped
400g/14oz can chopped tomatoes
150ml/¼ pint/⅔ cup hot lamb or beef stock
1 bay leaf

1 Mix the breadcrumbs, beaten egg, orange rind and oregano in a bowl. Add the lamb, onion and garlic and season with salt and pepper. Mix together until thoroughly combined.

2 Using dampened hands, press the meat mixture into small sausage-shapes, about 5cm/2in long, and roll them in flour. Place in the refrigerator for 30 minutes to firm up slightly.

3 Heat the oil in a large frying pan and add the meatballs, working in batches, if necessary. Cook for 5–8 minutes, turning the meatballs until evenly browned all over. Transfer to a plate and set aside, leaving the fat and juices in the pan.

4 To make the sauce, add the onion to the pan and cook for 3–4 minutes, until beginning to soften. Pour in the tomatoes, bring to the boil and cook for 1 minute. Transfer to the ceramic cooking pot and stir in the stock. Add the bay leaf, and season.

5 Place the meatballs in a single layer in the sauce. Cover and cook on high or auto for 1 hour. Reduce the temperature to low or leave on auto and cook for a further 4–5 hours. Serve garnished with fresh parsley.

Baked Meatballs Energy 443kcal/1853kJ; Protein 33.1g; Carbohydrate 22.5g, of which sugars 11.1g; Fat 25.3g, of which saturates 10.3g; Cholesterol 148mg; Calcium 246mg; Fibre 3g; Sodium 389mg.
Lamb Meatballs Energy 363kcal/1515kJ; Protein 26.1g; Carbohydrate 15g, of which sugars 5.3g; Fat 22.5g, of which saturates 8.3g; Cholesterol 141mg; Calcium 68mg; Fibre 1.5g; Sodium 239mg.

Kleftiko

For this Greek recipe, marinated lamb steaks or chops are braised slowly in the oven to become meltingly tender. The dish is sealed, like a pie, with a flour dough lid to trap succulence and flavour. A tight-fitting foil cover will serve equally well, although it will not look quite as impressive when the dish is served.

Serves 4

juice of 1 lemon
15ml/1 tbsp chopped fresh oregano
4 lamb leg steaks or chump chops with bones
30ml/2 tbsp olive oil
2 large onions, thinly sliced
2 bay leaves
150ml/¼ pint/⅔ cup dry white wine
225g/8oz/2 cups plain (all-purpose) flour
salt and ground black pepper

1 Mix together the lemon juice, oregano and salt and pepper, and brush over both sides of the steaks or chops. Leave to marinate for at least 4 hours or overnight.

2 Preheat the oven to 160°C/325°F/Gas 3. Drain the lamb, reserving the marinade, and dry with kitchen paper. Heat the olive oil in a large frying pan and cook the lamb over high heat until browned on both sides.

3 Transfer the lamb to a shallow, ovenproof pie dish. Sprinkle the sliced onions and bay leaves around the lamb, then pour over the white wine and the reserved marinade.

4 Mix the flour with enough water to make a firm dough. Moisten the rim of the pie dish. Roll out the dough on a floured surface and use to cover the dish so it is tightly sealed.

5 Bake for 2 hours, then break away the dough crust and serve the lamb hot with boiled potatoes, if you like.

Cook's Tip

They are not absolutely essential for this dish, but lamb steaks or chops with bones will provide lots of additional flavour. Boiled potatoes make a delicious accompaniment.

Moussaka

This slow-cooker classic is delicious in summer or winter, served with a salad.

Serves 6

900g/2lb small or medium aubergines (eggplant), thinly sliced
60ml/4 tbsp olive oil
1 onion, finely chopped
2 garlic cloves, crushed
450g/1lb lean minced (ground) lamb
400g/14oz can chopped tomatoes
5ml/1 tsp dried oregano
pinch of ground cinnamon
salt and ground black pepper

For the topping
50g/2oz/¼ cup butter
50g/2oz/½ cup plain (all-purpose) flour
600ml/1 pint/2½ cups milk
pinch of freshly grated nutmeg
75g/3oz/¾ cup grated mature (sharp) Cheddar cheese
1 egg yolk
30ml/2 tbsp white breadcrumbs

1 Layer the aubergine slices in a colander, sprinkling each layer with salt. Place the colander over a bowl for 20 minutes. Rinse the slices under cold running water and dry with kitchen paper.

2 Brush the slices with oil, then arrange on a baking sheet. Place under a grill (broiler) and cook, turning once, until softened and golden brown. Arrange half the slices in the bottom of the ceramic cooking pot and switch to high. Set aside the remaining slices.

3 Heat the remaining oil in a heavy pan. Cook the onion for 10 minutes, then add the garlic and lamb and cook, stirring, until the meat is browned. Stir the tomatoes, oregano and cinnamon into the pan, season and bring to the boil. Spoon into the slow cooker over the aubergine. Arrange the remaining slices on top, cover and cook for 2 hours.

4 Meanwhile, make the topping. Melt the butter in a pan, stir in the flour and cook for 1 minute. Stir in the milk, bring to the boil and stir until thickened. Season, then stir in the nutmeg and two-thirds of the cheese. Leave to cool for 5 minutes, then beat in the egg. Pour over the aubergine. Cover and cook for 2 hours.

5 Sprinkle the remaining cheese and the breadcrumbs over the top and cook under a grill (broiler) until golden brown. Leave to stand for 5–10 minutes before serving.

Kleftiko Energy 658kcal/2760kJ; Protein 57.9g; Carbohydrate 53.8g, of which sugars 8.1g; Fat 22.2g, of which saturates 7.2g; Cholesterol 184mg; Calcium 148mg; Fibre 3.5g; Sodium 130mg.
Moussaka Energy 444kcal/1850kJ; Protein 24.1g; Carbohydrate 1.5g, of which sugars 11.2g; Fat 31g, of which saturates 14g; Cholesterol 93.5mg; Calcium 268mg; Fibre 4.1g; Sodium 266mg.

Lamb with Honey, Saffron and Prunes

The spicy, fruity flavours in this dish are allowed to mingle over many hours in the slow cooker.

Serves 6

115g/4oz/½ cup pitted prunes
350ml/12fl oz/1½ cups hot tea
1kg/2¼lb stewing lamb, such as shoulder
30ml/2 tbsp olive oil
1 onion, chopped
2.5ml/½ tsp ground ginger
2.5ml/½ tsp curry powder
pinch of freshly grated nutmeg
10ml/2 tsp ground cinnamon
1.5ml/¼ tsp saffron threads
30ml/2 tbsp hot water
75ml/5 tbsp clear honey
200ml/7fl oz/scant 1 cup near-boiling lamb or beef stock
salt and ground black pepper
115g/4oz/1 cup blanched almonds, toasted, 30ml/2 tbsp chopped fresh coriander (cilantro) and 3 hard-boiled eggs, cut into wedges, to garnish

1 Put the prunes in a heatproof bowl, then pour over the tea and leave to soak. Meanwhile, trim the lamb and cut into chunky pieces, no larger than 2.5cm/1in. Heat the oil in a frying pan and sauté the lamb in batches for 5 minutes, stirring frequently, until browned. Remove with a slotted spoon and transfer to the ceramic cooking pot.

2 Add the onion to the frying pan and cook for 5 minutes, until starting to soften. Stir in the ginger, curry powder, nutmeg, cinnamon, salt and a large pinch of black pepper, and cook for 1 minute. Add to the ceramic cooking pot with the meat and their juices. Drain the prunes, adding the soaking liquid to the lamb. Cover the prunes.

3 Soak the saffron in the hot water for 1 minute, then add to the cooking pot with the honey and stock. Cover with the lid and cook on high or auto for 1 hour. Reduce the temperature to low and cook for a further 5–7 hours, or until the lamb is very tender.

4 Add the prunes to the cooking pot and stir to mix. Cook for 30 minutes, or until warmed through. Serve sprinkled with the almonds and coriander, and topped with the hard-boiled egg.

Lamb and Pumpkin Couscous

Slow simmering on top of the stove produces beautifully tender pieces of lamb enlivened by spices, fruit and chunky vegetables.

Serves 4–6

75g/3oz/½ cup chickpeas, soaked overnight and drained
675g/1½lb lean lamb
2 large onions, sliced
pinch of saffron threads
1.5ml/¼ tsp ground ginger
2.5ml/½ tsp ground turmeric
5ml/1 tsp ground black pepper
1.2 litres/2 pints/5 cups water
450g/1lb carrots
675g/1½lb pumpkin
75g/3oz/⅔ cup raisins
400g/14oz/2¼ cups couscous
salt
sprigs of fresh parsley, to garnish

1 Place the chickpeas in a large pan of boiling water. Boil for 10 minutes, then reduce the heat and cook for 1–1½ hours until tender. Place in cold water and remove the skins by rubbing with your fingers. Discard the skins and drain.

2 Cut the lamb into bitesize pieces and place in the pan with the sliced onions. Add the saffron, ginger and turmeric, and season with the pepper and salt. Pour in the water and stir well, then slowly bring to the boil. Cover the pan with a tight-fitting lid and simmer for about 1 hour, or until the lamb pieces are cooked and tender.

3 Peel or scrape the carrots and cut them into large chunks. Cut the pumpkin into 2.5cm/1in cubes, discarding the skin, seeds and pith.

4 Stir the carrots, pumpkin and raisins into the meat mixture with the chickpeas, cover the pan and simmer for 30–35 minutes more, stirring occasionally, until the vegetables and meat are completely tender.

5 Meanwhile, prepare the couscous according to the instructions on the packet and steam on top of the stew, then fork lightly to fluff up. Spoon the couscous on to a warmed serving plate, add the stew and stir the stew into the couscous. Extra gravy can be served separately. Sprinkle some tiny sprigs of fresh parsley over the top and serve immediately.

Lamb with Honey Energy 490kcal/2051kJ; Protein 43.6g; Carbohydrate 23.8g, of which sugars 23.4g; Fat 25.2g, of which saturates 10.3g; Cholesterol 279mg; Calcium 41mg; Fibre 1.4g; Sodium 197mg.
Couscous Energy 725kcal/3034kJ; Protein 34.8g; Carbohydrate 115.4g, of which sugars 69.5g; Fat 16.6g, of which saturates 6.8g; Cholesterol 86mg; Calcium 282mg; Fibre 21.5g; Sodium 297mg.

Fragrant Lamb Curry with Rice

Lamb and rice are slowly cooked together in a clay pot.

Serves 4

1 large onion, quartered
2 garlic cloves
1 green chilli, halved and seeded
5cm/2in piece fresh root ginger
15ml/1 tbsp ghee or butter
15ml/1 tbsp vegetable oil
675g/1½lb boned shoulder or leg of lamb, cut into chunks
15ml/1 tbsp ground coriander
10ml/2 tsp ground cumin
1 cinnamon stick, in 3 pieces
150ml/¼ pint/⅔ cup thick natural (plain) yogurt
150ml/¼ pint/⅔ cup water
75g/3oz/⅓ cup ready-to-eat dried apricots, cut into chunks
salt and ground black pepper
1 onion, sliced and fried, and sprigs of coriander (cilantro), to garnish

For the rice

250g/9oz/1¼ cups basmati rice
6 cardamom pods, split open
25g/1oz/2 tbsp butter
45ml/3 tbsp toasted cashew nuts or flaked (sliced) almonds

1 Soak a large clay pot in cold water for 20 minutes, then drain. Place the onion, garlic, chilli and ginger in a food processor or blender and process with 15ml/1 tbsp water to a smooth paste.

2 Heat the ghee and oil in a frying pan. Fry the lamb in batches until brown. Remove from the pan using a slotted spoon and set aside. Add the paste to the pan, stir in the coriander and cumin, add the cinnamon stick and fry for 1–2 minutes. Return the meat to the pan. Stir in the yogurt and the water, and season. Transfer to the clay pot, cover and place in an unheated oven. Set the oven to 180°C/350°F/Gas 4 and cook for 45 minutes.

3 Meanwhile, place the rice in a bowl, cover with cold water and soak for 20 minutes. Drain and cook in a pan of boiling salted water for 10 minutes. Drain and stir in the cardamom pods.

4 Remove the pot from the oven and stir in the apricots. Pile the rice on top and dot with the butter. Drizzle over 60ml/4 tbsp water, then sprinkle the cashew nuts or almonds on top. Cover, reduce the oven to 150°C/300°F/Gas 2 and cook for 30 minutes.

5 Remove the pot and fluff up the rice with a fork. Serve sprinkled with fried onion slices and sprigs of fresh coriander.

Roast Lamb Shanks in Barley Broth

Succulent slow-roasted lamb shanks studded with garlic and rosemary make a fabulous meal when served in a hearty vegetable, barley and tomato broth.

Serves 4

4 small lamb shanks
4 garlic cloves, cut into slivers
handful of fresh rosemary sprigs
30ml/2 tbsp olive oil
2 carrots, diced
2 celery sticks, diced
1 large onion, chopped
1 bay leaf
few sprigs of fresh thyme
1.2 litres/2 pints/5 cups lamb stock
50g/2oz pearl barley
450g/1lb tomatoes, peeled and roughly chopped
grated rind of 1 large lemon
30ml/2 tbsp chopped fresh parsley
salt and ground black pepper

1 Preheat the oven to 150°C/300°F/Gas 2. Make small cuts all over the lamb and insert slivers of garlic and sprigs of rosemary into them. Heat the oil in a flameproof casserole and brown the shanks two at a time. Remove and set aside.

2 Add the carrots, celery and onion in batches and cook until lightly browned. Put all the vegetables in the casserole with the bay leaf and thyme. Pour in stock to cover, place the lamb shanks on top and roast for 2 hours.

3 Meanwhile, pour the remaining stock into a large pan. Add the pearl barley, then bring to the boil. Reduce the heat, cover the pan and simmer gently for about 1 hour, or until the barley is tender.

4 Remove the shanks from the casserole using a slotted spoon. Skim the fat from the surface of the vegetables, then add to the barley broth. Stir in the tomatoes, lemon rind and parsley.

5 Bring the soup back to the boil. Reduce the heat and simmer for about 5 minutes. Add the shanks and heat through, then season with salt and pepper.

6 Place a lamb shank into each of four large bowls, then ladle the barley broth over the meat and serve immediately.

Fragrant Curry Energy 769kcal/3208kJ; Protein 43.6g; Carbohydrate 67.6g, of which sugars 14.5g; Fat 36.2g, of which saturates 15g; Cholesterol 142mg; Calcium 134mg; Fibre 2.6g; Sodium 252mg.
Roast Shanks in Broth Energy 287kcal/1199kJ; Protein 22.5g; Carbohydrate 19.5g, of which sugars 7.6g; Fat 13.7g, of which saturates 0.9g; Cholesterol 0mg; Calcium 35mg; Fibre 2.3g; Sodium 24mg.

Tagine of Lamb with Crunchy Country Salad

Morocco's hearty tagines are well known for their tender meat slowly cooked in a combination of honey and warm spices. This delicious recipe is for one of the most traditional and popular tagines, which is best served with a crunchy salad, spiked with chilli to balance the sweetness of the main dish. Offer lots of fresh bread for mopping up the thick, syrupy sauce.

Serves 6

1kg/2¼lb boneless shoulder of lamb, trimmed and cubed
30–45ml/2–3 tbsp sunflower oil
25g/1oz fresh root ginger, peeled and chopped
pinch of saffron threads
10ml/2 tsp ground cinnamon
1 onion, finely chopped
2–3 garlic cloves, chopped
350g/12oz/1½ cups pitted prunes, soaked for 1 hour
30ml/2 tbsp clear honey
salt and ground black pepper

For the salad

2 onions, chopped
1 red (bell) pepper, seeded and chopped
1 green (bell) pepper, seeded and chopped
2–3 celery sticks, chopped
2–3 green chillies, seeded and chopped
2 garlic cloves, chopped
30ml/2 tbsp olive oil
juice of ½ lemon
small bunch of parsley, chopped
a little mint, chopped

1 Put the meat in a flameproof casserole or heavy pan. Add the oil, ginger, saffron, cinnamon, onion, garlic and seasoning, then pour in enough water to cover. Heat until just simmering, cover with a lid and simmer gently for about 2 hours, topping up the water, if necessary, until the meat is very tender.

2 Drain the prunes and add them to the tagine. Stir in the honey and simmer for a further 30 minutes, or until the sauce has reduced.

3 To make the salad, mix the onions, peppers, celery, chillies and garlic in a bowl. Pour the olive oil and lemon juice over the vegetables and toss to coat. Season with salt and add the parsley and mint. Serve the hot lamb tagine with the chilli-laced salad.

Moroccan Lamb Stew

A spicy, fruity stew with slow-cooked lamb pieces, served with couscous.

Serves 6–8

225g/8oz/1¼ cups dried chickpeas soaked in water overnight, drained
60ml/4 tbsp olive oil
10ml/2 tsp sugar
10ml/2 tsp ground cumin
5ml/1 tsp ground cinnamon
5ml/1 tsp ground ginger
2.5ml/½ tsp ground turmeric
2.5ml/½ tsp powdered saffron or paprika
1.3kg/3lb lamb shoulder, trimmed and cut into 5cm/2in pieces
2 onions, coarsely chopped
3 garlic cloves, finely chopped
2 tomatoes, peeled, seeded and chopped
75g/3oz/⅔ cup raisins, soaked in warm water
10–24 pitted black olives
2 preserved lemons, thinly sliced, or grated rind of 1 unwaxed lemon
60–90ml/4–6 tbsp chopped fresh coriander (cilantro)
salt and ground black pepper
450g/1lb couscous, to serve

1 Place the chickpeas in a large pan, cover with water and boil for 10 minutes. Drain and return to a clean pan. Cover with fresh cold water and bring to the boil, then simmer, covered, for 1–1½ hours until tender. Add a little salt and set aside.

2 In a large bowl, combine half the olive oil with the sugar, cumin, cinnamon, ginger, turmeric, saffron or paprika, pepper and 5ml/1 tsp salt. Mix in the lamb and set aside for 20 minutes.

3 In a large frying pan, heat the remaining oil and brown the lamb in batches for 4–5 minutes. Transfer to a large flameproof casserole. Add the onions to the pan and cook until soft. Stir in the garlic and tomatoes with 250ml/8fl oz/1 cup water. Pour into the casserole and cover with water. Bring to the boil, then simmer for 1 hour, or until the meat is tender.

4 Add the chickpeas to the casserole with 250ml/8fl oz/1 cup of the chickpea cooking liquid. Add the raisins and the soaking liquid and simmer for 30 minutes. Add the olives and preserved lemons or rind. Simmer for 20–30 minutes, then add half the coriander.

5 Just before serving, prepare the couscous according to the packet instructions. Serve with the stew, garnished with coriander.

Tagine of Lamb Energy 600kcal/2504kJ; Protein 42g; Carbohydrate 28.2g, of which sugars 25.8g; Fat 36.3g, of which saturates 10.9g; Cholesterol 222mg; Calcium 112mg; Fibre 4.9g; Sodium 199mg.
Moroccan Stew Energy 517kcal/2163kJ; Protein 40.1g; Carbohydrate 29g, of which sugars 12.8g; Fat 27.7g, of which saturates 9.7g; Cholesterol 124mg; Calcium 120mg; Fibre 5.3g; Sodium 448mg.

Spicy Lamb and Potato Stew

Indian spices transform this simple, slow-cooked lamb and potato stew into a mouthwatering dish. Serve with naan breads, if you like.

Serves 6

675g/1½lb lean lamb fillet
15ml/1 tbsp oil
1 onion, finely chopped
2 bay leaves
1 fresh green chilli, seeded and finely chopped
2 garlic cloves, finely chopped
10ml/2 tsp ground coriander
5ml/1 tsp ground cumin
2.5ml/½ tsp ground turmeric
2.5ml/½ tsp chilli powder
2.5ml/½ tsp salt
2 tomatoes, peeled and chopped
600ml/1 pint/2½ cups hot chicken stock
2 large potatoes, cut into bitesize chunks
chopped fresh coriander (cilantro), to garnish

1 Remove any visible fat from the lamb and cut the meat into neat 2.5cm/1in cubes.

2 Heat the oil in a large, heavy pan and fry the onion, bay leaves, chilli and garlic for about 5 minutes, stirring frequently, until the onion is beginning to soften.

3 Add the cubes of lamb to the pan and cook, stirring them occasionally, for about 6–8 minutes until they are lightly and evenly browned on all sides.

4 Add the ground coriander, ground cumin, ground turmeric, chilli powder and salt and cook gently for 3–4 minutes, stirring all the time to prevent the spices from sticking to the bottom of the pan.

5 Stir the tomatoes and chicken stock into the pan and simmer for 5 minutes. Bring to the boil, cover with a tight-fitting lid and then simmer for 1 hour.

6 Add the bitesize chunks of potato to the simmering mixture, stir in, and cook for a further 30–40 minutes, or until the meat is tender and much of the excess juice has been absorbed, leaving a thick but minimal sauce. Garnish with chopped fresh coriander and serve piping hot.

Rogan Josh

This is one of the most popular lamb dishes. Traditionally, fatty meat on the bone is slow-cooked until most of the fat is separated from the meat. The fat that escapes from the meat is known as rogan, and josh refers to the red colour. This recipe, however, uses lean lamb, which is slowly simmered in the sauce until it is meltingly tender.

Serves 4–6

45ml/3 tbsp lemon juice
250ml/8fl oz/1 cup natural (plain) yogurt
5ml/1 tsp salt
2 garlic cloves, crushed
2.5cm/1in piece fresh root ginger, finely grated
900g/2lb lean lamb fillet, cubed
60ml/4 tbsp vegetable oil
2.5ml/½ tsp cumin seeds
2 bay leaves
4 green cardamom pods
1 onion, finely chopped
10ml/2 tsp ground coriander
10ml/2 tsp ground cumin
5ml/1 tsp chilli powder
400g/14oz can chopped tomatoes
30ml/2 tbsp tomato purée (paste)
150ml/¼ pint/⅔ cup water
toasted cumin seeds and bay leaves, to garnish
plain boiled rice, to serve

1 In a large bowl, mix together the lemon juice, yogurt, salt, half the crushed garlic and the ginger. Add the lamb, cover and marinate in the refrigerator overnight.

2 Heat the oil in a karahi, wok or large pan and fry the cumin seeds for 2 minutes. Add the bay leaves and cardamom pods and fry for a further 2 minutes.

3 Add the onion and remaining garlic and fry, stirring frequently, for 5 minutes until the onion is soft. Add the coriander, cumin and chilli powder. Fry for 2 minutes.

4 Add the marinated lamb to the pan and cook for a further 5 minutes, stirring occasionally to prevent the mixture from sticking to the base of the pan and starting to burn.

5 Stir in the tomatoes, tomato purée and water. Cover and simmer for 1–1½ hours, until the meat is tender. Garnish with cumin seeds and bay leaves, and serve with the rice.

Spicy Lamb Stew Energy 284kcal/1192kJ; Protein 24g; Carbohydrate 14.1g, of which sugars 3.1g; Fat 15.1g, of which saturates 6.3g; Cholesterol 86mg; Calcium 23mg; Fibre 1.3g; Sodium 109mg.
Rogan Josh Energy 557kcal/2335kJ; Protein 54.2g; Carbohydrate 20.4g, of which sugars 18.7g; Fat 29.5g, of which saturates 13.5g; Cholesterol 190mg; Calcium 139mg; Fibre 4.6g; Sodium 277mg.

Rezala

This delectable lamb recipe uses whole lamb chops, which are slowly simmered in a rich, spicy sauce until they are falling off the bone. Serve with naan breads and boiled basmati rice.

Serves 4

1 large onion, roughly chopped
10ml/2 tsp grated fresh root ginger
10ml/2 tsp crushed garlic
4 or 5 cloves
2.5ml/½ tsp black peppercorns
6 green cardamom pods
5cm/2in piece cinnamon stick, cut into 2 pieces
8 lamb rib chops
60ml/4 tbsp vegetable oil
1 large onion, finely sliced
175ml/6fl oz/¾ cup natural (plain) yogurt
50g/2oz/¼ cup butter
2.5ml/1 tsp salt
2.5ml/½ tsp ground cumin
2.5ml/½ tsp hot chilli powder
whole nutmeg
2.5ml/½ tsp sugar
15ml/1 tbsp lime juice
pinch of saffron, soaked in 15ml/1 tbsp hot water for 10–15 minutes
15ml/1 tbsp rose water
rose petals, to garnish
naan bread or boiled basmati rice, to serve (optional)

1 Process the onion in a blender or food processor. Add a little water if necessary to form a smooth paste. Put the paste into a glass bowl and add the grated ginger, crushed garlic, cloves, peppercorns, cardamom pods and cinnamon. Mix well.

2 Put the lamb chops in a large shallow glass dish and add the spice paste. Mix thoroughly, cover the bowl and leave the lamb to marinate for 3–4 hours or overnight in the refrigerator. Bring back to room temperature before cooking.

3 In a karahi, wok or large, heavy frying pan, heat the vegetable oil over medium heat and fry the sliced onion for about 6–7 minutes, until golden brown and softened. Remove the onion slices with a slotted spoon, squeezing out as much oil as possible on the side of the pan. Drain the onions on a piece of kitchen paper.

4 In the remaining oil in the pan, fry the marinated lamb chops for 4–5 minutes, turning occasionally until lightly browned on all sides. Reduce the heat to low, cover the pan and cook for a further 5–7 minutes.

5 Meanwhile, mix the yogurt and butter together in a small pan and place over low heat. Cook for 5–6 minutes, stirring constantly, then stir into the lamb chops along with the salt. Add the cumin and chilli powder and cover the pan. Gently simmer for about 45–50 minutes until the lamb chops are cooked and very tender.

6 Using a nutmeg grater, or the finest cutting surface on a large, stainless steel grater, grate about 2.5ml/½ tsp of fresh nutmeg and add to the pan containing the lamb. Stir in the sugar and cook for 1–2 minutes.

7 Add the lime juice, saffron and rose water to the lamb. Stir and mix well, then simmer for 2–3 minutes and remove from the heat. Spoon into a dish and garnish with the fried onion and rose petals. Serve immediately with naan bread or boiled basmati rice, if you like.

Lamb with Apricots

Dried apricots are a useful ingredient to have in your kitchen as they can really transform a curry or stew. Here, they are combined with cinnamon, cardamom, cumin and coriander to make a delicious sauce with a hint of sweetness for slow-cooked lamb.

Serves 6

900g/2lb lean stewing lamb
15ml/1 tbsp oil
2.5cm/1in piece cinnamon stick
4 green cardamom pods
1 onion, chopped
15ml/1 tbsp curry paste
5ml/1 tsp ground cumin
5ml/1 tsp ground coriander
1.5ml/¼ tsp salt
175g/6oz/¾ cup ready-to-eat dried apricots
350ml/12fl oz/1½ cups hot lamb stock
fresh coriander (cilantro), to garnish
saffron rice and mango chutney, to serve

1 Remove all the visible fat from the stewing lamb and cut the meat into 2.5cm/1in cubes.

2 Heat the oil in a large, heavy pan and fry the cinnamon stick and cardamoms for 2 minutes. Add the onion and gently fry for about 6–8 minutes, stirring occasionally.

3 Add the curry paste and fry for 2 minutes. Stir in the ground cumin and coriander and the salt, and stir-fry for a further 2–3 minutes.

4 Add the meat, apricots and the stock. Cover and cook for 1–1½ hours. Serve, garnished with fresh coriander, on yellow saffron rice, with mango chutney in a separate bowl.

Cook's Tip

It is best to buy green cardamom pods from an Indian grocer or health food store, as the cardamoms sold in supermarkets are often bleached and do not have as full a flavour. Cardamom is a versatile spice in Indian cuisine, used in many savoury and sweet dishes.

Rezala Energy 545kcal/2263kJ; Protein 33.8g; Carbohydrate 15.5g, of which sugars 11g; Fat 39.3g, of which saturates 15.9g; Cholesterol 141mg; Calcium 134mg; Fibre 2g; Sodium 244mg.
Lamb with Apricots Energy 462kcal/1931kJ; Protein 28.5g; Carbohydrate 23.2g, of which sugars 17.6g; Fat 29.1g, of which saturates 7.8g; Cholesterol 86mg; Calcium 77mg; Fibre 5.8g; Sodium 114mg.

Spicy Spring Lamb Roast

Coating a leg of lamb with a spicy, fruity rub before slowy roasting it in the oven gives it a wonderful flavour.

Serves 6

1.6kg/3½lb lean leg of spring lamb
5ml/1 tsp chilli powder
5ml/1 tsp crushed garlic
5ml/1 tsp ground coriander
5ml/1 tsp ground cumin
5ml/1 tsp salt
15ml/1 tbsp dried breadcrumbs
45ml/3 tbsp natural (plain) low-fat yogurt
30ml/2 tbsp lemon juice
30ml/2 tbsp sultanas (golden raisins)
15ml/1 tbsp oil

For the garnish

mixed salad leaves
fresh coriander (cilantro)
2 tomatoes, quartered
1 large carrot, shredded
lemon wedges

1 Preheat the oven to 180°C/350°F/Gas 4. Trim any excess fat from the lamb. Rinse the joint, pat it dry and set aside on a sheet of foil large enough to enclose it completely.

2 In a medium bowl, mix together the chilli powder, garlic, ground coriander, ground cumin and salt.

3 Mix together the breadcrumbs, yogurt, lemon juice and sultanas in a food processor or blender.

4 Add the contents of the food processor to the spice mixture, together with the oil, and mix well. Pour this on to the leg of lamb and rub all over the meat.

5 Enclose the meat in the foil and place in an ovenproof dish. Cook in the oven for about 1½ hours.

6 Remove the lamb from the oven, open the foil and, using the back of a spoon, spread the mixture evenly over the meat. Return the lamb, uncovered, to the oven for another 45 minutes or until it is cooked right through and tender.

7 Slice the meat and serve with the mixed salad leaves, fresh coriander, tomatoes, carrot and lemon wedges.

Lamb and New Potato Curry

This dish makes the most of an economical cut of meat by cooking it slowly until the meat is falling from the bone. Chillies and coconut cream give it lots of flavour.

Serves 4

25g/1oz/2 tbsp butter
2 onions, sliced into rings
4 garlic cloves, crushed
2.5ml/½ tsp ground cumin
2.5ml/½ tsp ground coriander
2.5ml/½ tsp turmeric
2.5ml/½ tsp cayenne pepper
2–3 red chillies, seeded and finely chopped
300ml/½ pint/1¼ cups hot chicken stock
200ml/7fl oz/scant 1 cup coconut cream
4 lamb shanks, excess fat removed
450g/1lb new potatoes, halved
6 ripe tomatoes, quartered
salt and ground black pepper
fresh coriander (cilantro) leaves, to garnish
spicy rice, to serve

1 Preheat the oven to 160°C/325°F/Gas 3. Melt the butter in a large flameproof casserole, add the onions and cook, stirring frequently, over low heat for 6–8 minutes, until beginning to soften. Add the garlic for 3–4 minutes. Stir in the spices and chillies, then cook for a further 2 minutes.

2 Stir in the hot stock and coconut cream. Place the lamb shanks in the liquid and cover the casserole with foil. Cook in the oven for about 2 hours, turning the shanks twice in the cooking liquid, first after about 1 hour and again about 30 minutes later.

3 Par-boil the potatoes for about 10 minutes until barely tender, drain and add to the casserole with the tomatoes, then cook uncovered in the oven for a further 35 minutes. Season to taste with salt and pepper. Serve garnished with coriander leaves and accompanied by the spicy rice.

Cook's Tip
Make this dish a day in advance, if possible. Cool and chill overnight, then skim off the excess fat that has risen to the surface. Reheat thoroughly before you serve it.

Lamb Roast Energy 478kcal/1987kJ; Protein 39.1g; Carbohydrate 3.5g, of which sugars 0.6g; Fat 34.4g, of which saturates 10.1g; Cholesterol 145mg; Calcium 37mg; Fibre 0g; Sodium 119mg.
Lamb Curry Energy 364kcal/1528kJ; Protein 23.5g; Carbohydrate 30.5g, of which sugars 12.1g; Fat 17.4g, of which saturates 8.8g; Cholesterol 89mg; Calcium 58mg; Fibre 3.5g; Sodium 205mg.

Rabbit with Pappardelle

This rich-tasting dish is ideal for entertaining as the sauce can be kept warm in the slow cooker until needed.

Serves 4

15g/½oz dried porcini mushrooms
150ml/¼ pint/⅔ cup warm water
1 small onion
½ carrot
½ celery stick
2 bay leaves
25g/1oz/2 tbsp butter or 15ml/1 tbsp olive oil
40g/1½oz pancetta or rindless streaky (fatty) bacon, chopped
15ml/1 tbsp roughly chopped fresh flat leaf parsley, plus extra to garnish
250g/9oz boneless rabbit meat
60ml/4 tbsp dry white wine
200g/7oz can chopped plum tomatoes or 200ml/7fl oz/scant 1 cup passata (bottled strained tomatoes)
300g/11oz fresh or dried pappardelle
salt and ground black pepper

1 Put the dried mushrooms in a bowl, pour over the warm water and leave to soak for 15 minutes. Finely chop the vegetables, either in a food processor or by hand. Tear each bay leaf, so they will release their flavour when added to the sauce.

2 Heat the butter or oil in a large frying pan until just sizzling. Add the vegetables, pancetta or bacon and the parsley and cook for 5 minutes. Add the rabbit and fry on both sides for 3–4 minutes. Transfer the mixture to the ceramic cooking pot and switch to high or auto. Add the wine and tomatoes or passata.

3 Drain the mushrooms and add the soaking liquid to the slow cooker. Chop the mushrooms and add to the mixture with the bay leaves. Season to taste and stir well, cover with the lid and cook for 1 hour. Reduce the setting to low or leave on auto, and cook for a further 2 hours, or until the meat is tender.

4 Lift out the rabbit pieces, cut them into bitesize chunks and stir them back into the sauce. Remove and discard the bay leaves. Taste the sauce and season as necessary. The sauce is now ready to serve, but can be kept hot in the cooker for 1–2 hours.

5 Cook the pasta according to the packet instructions. Drain and mix into the sauce. Serve immediately, sprinkled with parsley.

Rabbit Casserole with Juniper

Simmering rabbit in the slow cooker is ideal for this lean meat because it helps to keep it moist and juicy.

Serves 4

900g/2lb prepared rabbit pieces
1 onion, roughly chopped
2 garlic cloves, crushed
1 bay leaf
350ml/12fl oz/1½ cups fruity red wine
2 sprigs of fresh thyme
1 sprig of fresh rosemary
15ml/1 tbsp juniper berries
30ml/2 tbsp olive oil
15g/½oz dried porcini mushrooms
30ml/2 tbsp chopped fresh parsley
25g/1oz/2 tbsp chilled butter
salt and ground black pepper

1 Put the rabbit in a glass or ceramic dish with the onion, garlic, bay leaf and wine. Bruise the thyme and rosemary and lightly crush the juniper berries and stir into the dish. Cover and chill for 4 hours or overnight, turning the pieces once or twice.

2 Remove the rabbit from the dish, reserving the marinade, and pat dry with kitchen paper. Heat the oil in a frying pan, add the rabbit pieces and fry for 3–5 minutes, turning to brown all over. Transfer the meat to the ceramic cooking pot.

3 Pour the marinade into the frying pan and bring to boiling point. Pour over the rabbit, cover the cooking pot with the lid and switch the slow cooker to high. Cook for about 1 hour.

4 Meanwhile, put the mushrooms in a bowl and pour over 150ml/¼ pint/⅔ cup boiling water. Leave to soak for 1 hour, then drain, reserving the soaking liquid. Chop the mushrooms and put them in a small bowl and cover with clear film (plastic wrap).

5 Pour the mushroom soaking liquid into the cooking pot and cook for 2 hours. Lift out the rabbit pieces and strain the liquid, discarding the vegetables, herbs and berries. Wipe the pot, then return the rabbit and liquid. Add the mushrooms and season.

6 Cover and cook for 1 hour, or until the meat is tender. Stir in the parsley, then lift out the rabbit pieces and arrange on a serving dish. Cut the butter into cubes and gradually whisk into the sauce to thicken it. Spoon over the rabbit and serve.

Rabbit with Pappardelle Energy 393kcal/1653kJ; Protein 23g; Carbohydrate 46g, of which sugars 4.9g; Fat 13.3g, of which saturates 5g; Cholesterol 46mg; Calcium 80mg; Fibre 1.1g; Sodium 128mg.
Rabbit Casserole Energy 356kcal/1483kJ; Protein 32g; Carbohydrate 3.2g, of which sugars 2.3g; Fat 17.5g, of which saturates 6.3g; Cholesterol 163mg; Calcium 30mg; Fibre 0.6g; Sodium 66mg.

Rabbit with Red Wine and Prunes

This dish of casseroled rabbit pieces has a wonderfully rich flavour and the prunes add a distinctive sweetness to the sauce. Serve with crisp, golden sautéed potatoes.

Serves 4

8 rabbit portions
30ml/2 tbsp vegetable oil
2 onions, finely chopped
2 garlic cloves, finely chopped
60ml/4 tbsp Armagnac or brandy
300ml/½ pint/1¼ cups dry red wine
5ml/1 tsp soft light brown sugar
16 ready-to-eat prunes
150ml/¼ pint/⅔ cup double (heavy) cream
salt and ground black pepper

1 Season the rabbit portions liberally with salt and ground black pepper. Heat the vegetable oil in a large, flameproof casserole and cook the rabbit portions in batches, turning occasionally, until they are evenly browned on all sides.

2 Remove the browned rabbit portions from the casserole, add the onion and garlic, and cook, stirring occasionally, for about 6–8 minutes until the onion has softened.

3 Return the rabbit to the casserole, add the Armagnac or brandy and ignite it. When the flames have died down, pour in the wine. Stir in the sugar and prunes, cover and simmer for 30 minutes.

4 Remove the rabbit portions from the casserole and transfer to a warmed serving dish. Add the cream to the sauce and simmer for 3–5 minutes, then season to taste with salt and pepper, and serve immediately.

Variations

- *Chicken can also be cooked in this way. Use 4 chicken drumsticks and 4 thighs in place of the rabbit portions.*
- *The prunes can be replaced with ready-to-eat dried apricots if you prefer – these go well with the rabbit and particularly well with chicken.*

Braised Rabbit

Rabbit now features frequently on restaurant menus. It is delicious slowly braised in this rich sauce, made with stock and cider or stout. Serve with potatoes boiled in their skins and a lightly cooked green vegetable.

Serves 4–6

1 rabbit, prepared and jointed by the butcher
30ml/2 tbsp seasoned flour
30ml/2 tbsp olive oil or vegetable oil
25g/1oz/2 tbsp butter
115g/4oz streaky (fatty) bacon
1 onion, roughly chopped
2 or 3 carrots, sliced
1 or 2 celery sticks, trimmed and sliced
300ml/½ pint/1¼ cups hot chicken stock
300ml/½ pint/1¼ cups dry (hard) cider or stout
a small bunch of parsley leaves, chopped
salt and ground black pepper

1 Soak the joints in cold salted water for at least 2 hours, then pat them dry with kitchen paper and toss them in seasoned flour. Preheat the oven to 200°C/400°F/Gas 6.

2 Heat the oil and butter together in a large flameproof casserole. Shake off and reserve any excess flour from the rabbit joints. Cook the meat until evenly browned on all sides. Lift out and set aside.

3 Add the bacon to the casserole and cook for 3–4 minutes, then remove and set aside with the rabbit pieces. Add the vegetables to the casserole and cook gently, stirring occasionally, until just colouring, then sprinkle over any remaining seasoned flour to absorb the fats in the casserole. Stir over low heat for 1 minute to cook the flour. Add the stock and cider or stout, stirring, to make a smooth sauce.

4 Return the rabbit and bacon to the casserole, and add half of the chopped parsley and a light seasoning of salt and black pepper. Mix gently together, then cover with a tight-fitting lid and put into the preheated oven. Cook for 15–20 minutes, then reduce the oven temperature to 150°C/300°F/Gas 2 for about 1½ hours, or until the rabbit is tender. Add the remaining parsley and serve immediately.

Rabbit Energy 543kcal/2259kJ; Protein 29.3g; Carbohydrate 19.4g, of which sugars 18.2g; Fat 29.9g, of which saturates 15.3g; Cholesterol 156mg; Calcium 99mg; Fibre 3g; Sodium 81mg.
Braised Rabbit Energy 368kcal/1535kJ; Protein 32.9g; Carbohydrate 10.5g, of which sugars 5.8g; Fat 19.7g, of which saturates 8g; Cholesterol 133mg; Calcium 88mg; Fibre 1.4g; Sodium 567mg.

Rabbit Salmorejo

Small pieces of jointed rabbit make an interesting alternative to chicken in this spicy, slow-cooked dish from Spain. Serve with a simple dressed salad.

Serves 4

675g/1½lb rabbit portions
300ml/½ pint/1¼ cups dry white wine
15ml/1 tbsp sherry vinegar
several oregano sprigs
2 bay leaves
90ml/6 tbsp olive oil
175g/6oz baby (pearl) onions, peeled and left whole
1 fresh red chilli, seeded and finely chopped
4 garlic cloves, sliced
10ml/2 tsp paprika
150ml/¼ pint/⅔ cup chicken stock
salt and ground black pepper
flat leaf parsley sprigs, to garnish

1 Put the rabbit in a bowl. Add the wine, vinegar, oregano and bay leaves and toss together lightly. Cover and leave to marinate for several hours or overnight.

2 Drain the rabbit, reserving the marinade, and pat dry on kitchen paper. Heat the oil in a large frying pan. Add the rabbit and cook on all sides until golden, then remove with a slotted spoon. Fry the onions until beginning to colour.

3 Remove the onions from the pan and add the chilli, garlic and paprika. Cook, stirring, for about 1 minute. Add the reserved marinade with the stock. Season lightly.

4 Return the rabbit to the pan with the onions. Bring to the boil, then reduce the heat and cover with a lid. Simmer very gently for about 45 minutes until the rabbit is tender. Serve garnished with a few sprigs of flat leaf parsley, if you like.

Cook's Tip

If more convenient, rather than cooking on the stove, transfer the stew to an ovenproof dish and bake in the oven at 180°C/350°F/Gas 4 for about 50 minutes.

Hare Pot Pies

The pie filling is simmered in the slow cooker until tender before being topped with pastry and baked in the oven.

Serves 4

45ml/3 tbsp olive oil
1 leek, sliced
225g/8oz parsnips, sliced
225g/8oz carrots, sliced
1 fennel bulb, sliced
675g/1½lb boneless hare, diced
30ml/2 tbsp plain (all-purpose) flour
60ml/4 tbsp Madeira
300ml/½ pint/1¼ cups game or chicken stock
45ml/3 tbsp chopped fresh parsley
450g/1lb puff pastry, thawed if frozen
beaten egg yolk, to glaze

1 Heat 30ml/2 tbsp of the oil in a large pan. Add the leek, parsnips, carrots and fennel and cook for 10 minutes until soft. Using a slotted spoon, transfer the vegetables to the ceramic cooking pot. Cover and switch the slow cooker to high or auto.

2 Heat the remaining oil in the pan and fry the hare in batches until well browned. When all the meat is browned, return it to the pan. Add the flour and cook, stirring, for a few seconds, then gradually add the Madeira and stock and bring to the boil.

3 Transfer the hare mixture to the ceramic cooking pot and cook for 1 hour. Switch the slow cooker to low or leave on auto and cook for a further 5–6 hours, until the meat and vegetables are tender. Stir in the chopped parsley, then set aside to cool.

4 To make the pies, preheat the oven to 220°C/425°F/Gas 7. Spoon the filling into four small pie dishes. Cut the pastry into quarters and roll out to make the lids, making them larger than the dishes. Trim any excess pastry and use to line the dish rims.

5 Dampen the pastry rims with cold water and cover with the lids. Pinch the edges together to seal. Brush with beaten egg yolk and make a small hole in the top of each one.

6 Stand the pies on a baking tray and bake for 25 minutes, or until the pastry is golden. If necessary, cover the pies with foil to prevent them becoming too brown. Serve immediately.

Rabbit Salmorejo Energy 311kcal/1294kJ; Protein 23.2g; Carbohydrate 9.5g, of which sugars 2.6g; Fat 20.4g, of which saturates 4.1g; Cholesterol 83mg; Calcium 65mg; Fibre 0.9g; Sodium 52mg.
Hare Pot Pies Energy 906kcal/3784kJ; Protein 45g; Carbohydrate 60.4g, of which sugars 10g; Fat 53.7g, of which saturates 15.9g; Cholesterol 107mg; Calcium 180mg; Fibre 7.6g; Sodium 553mg.

Spicy Venison Casserole

Being low in fat but high in flavour, venison is an excellent choice for healthy, yet rich, slow-cooked casseroles. Cranberries and orange bring a fruitiness to this spicy recipe.

Serves 4

15ml/1 tbsp olive oil
1 onion, chopped
2 celery sticks, sliced
10ml/2 tsp ground allspice
15ml/1 tbsp plain (all-purpose) flour
675g/1 ½lb stewing venison, cubed
225g/8oz fresh or frozen cranberries
grated rind and juice of 1 orange
900ml/1 ½ pints/3¾ cups beef or venison stock
salt and ground black pepper

1 Heat the oil in a flameproof casserole. Add the onion and celery and fry for about 5 minutes, or until softened.

2 Meanwhile, mix the allspice with the flour and spread the mixture out on a large plate. Toss a few pieces of venison at a time in the flour mixture until they are all lightly coated. Spread the floured venison out on a large plate until ready to cook.

3 When the onion and celery are just softened, remove them from the casserole using a slotted spoon and set aside. Add the venison pieces to the casserole, in batches, and cook until well browned and sealed on all sides.

4 Add the cranberries and the orange rind and juice to the casserole, along with the stock, and stir well. Return the vegetables and the browned venison to the casserole and heat until simmering. Cover tightly and reduce the heat.

5 Simmer for about 45 minutes, or until the venison is tender, stirring occasionally. Season the venison casserole to taste with salt and pepper before serving.

Cook's Tip
Freshly made stock is always best but if you are short of time, look for cartons or tubs of fresh stock in the chilled food cabinets of larger supermarkets.

Casseroled Venison with Stout

Venison, both wild and farmed, is readily available and makes an interesting alternative to more common meats. Serve this oven-cooked dish with boiled potatoes and red cabbage.

Serves 6

900g/2lb stewing venison, such as shoulder, cut into 5cm/2in pieces
45ml/3 tbsp seasoned flour
30ml/2 tbsp olive oil
2 or 3 large onions, sliced
5 or 6 juniper berries, crushed
3 allspice berries
rind of ½ lemon or orange
25g/1oz/2 tbsp butter
about 300ml/½ pint/1 ¼ cups chicken or beef stock
150ml/¼ pint/⅔ cup red wine vinegar or cider vinegar
300ml/½ pint/1 ¼ cups stout or red wine
salt and ground black pepper

1 Preheat the oven to 180°C/350°F/Gas 4. Toss the meat cubes in the seasoned flour. Shake off and reserve the excess flour.

2 Heat the oil in a heavy frying pan and fry the meat until well browned all over. Lift out the pieces with a slotted spoon and put them into a flameproof casserole. Add the onions to the casserole with the juniper berries and allspice, a little salt and black pepper and the lemon or orange rind.

3 Melt the butter in the pan in which the meat was browned, add the reserved flour, and stir and cook for 1 minute. Mix the stock, vinegar and stout or red wine together and gradually add to the pan, stirring until it boils and thickens.

4 Pour the sauce over the meat in the casserole, cover closely and cook in the oven for 1 hour. Reduce the temperature to 150°C/300°F/Gas 2 and cook for a further 2 hours, or until the venison is tender. Check the casserole occasionally and add a little extra stock or water, if required. Serve piping hot.

Cook's Tip
Venison, like other game, is lean, so marinating, basting and braising all help to offset any tendency to dryness.

Spicy Venison Energy 242kcal/1025kJ; Protein 38.3g; Carbohydrate 10.4g, of which sugars 7.1g; Fat 6.6g, of which saturates 1.8g; Cholesterol 84mg; Calcium 27mg; Fibre 1.4g; Sodium 105mg.
Venison with Stout Energy 294kcal/1233kJ; Protein 34.7g; Carbohydrate 9.3g, of which sugars 4.9g; Fat 10.6g, of which saturates 3.9g; Cholesterol 84mg; Calcium 37mg; Fibre 1.3g; Sodium 114mg.

Venison Stew

This simple yet deeply flavoured stew makes a wonderful supper dish, incorporating rich red wine and sweet redcurrant jelly with the depth of the bacon.

Serves 4

1.3kg/3lb stewing venison (shoulder or topside), trimmed and diced
50g/2oz/¼ cup butter
225g/8oz piece of streaky (fatty) bacon, cut into 2cm/¾in lardons
2 large onions, chopped
1 large carrot, diced
1 large garlic clove, crushed
30ml/2 tbsp plain (all-purpose) flour
½ bottle red wine
about 300ml/½ pint/1¼ cups dark stock
1 bay leaf
sprig of fresh thyme
200g/7oz button (white) mushrooms, sliced
30ml/2 tbsp redcurrant jelly
salt and ground black pepper

1 Pat dry the diced venison pieces thoroughly using kitchen paper. Set to one side.

2 Melt the butter in a large heavy pan, then brown the bacon lardons over medium heat, stirring occasionally. Reduce the heat slightly and add the onions and carrot. Stir in until lightly browned.

3 Add the venison to the pan, along with the garlic, and stir into the mixture. Sprinkle on the flour and mix well.

4 Pour in the wine and dark stock to cover, along with the herbs, mushrooms and redcurrant jelly.

5 Cover the pan and simmer over low heat until the meat is cooked, approximately 1½–2 hours. Serve immediately, with creamy mashed potato and green vegetables, if you like.

Cook's Tip

This dish can be cooked and then left until required – a couple of days if need be. The flavours will be enhanced if it has been left for a while. Simply reheat and serve when needed.

Venison in Guinness

Mustard, juniper berries and bay leaves combine with lean venison and stout to create a slowly baked casserole with a vibrant flavour and a wonderful aroma.

Serves 6

15ml/1 tbsp olive oil
675g/1½lb stewing venison, cut into cubes
3 onions, sliced
2 garlic cloves, crushed
15ml/1 tbsp plain (all-purpose) flour
5ml1 tsp mustard powder
6 juniper berries, lightly crushed
2 bay leaves
400ml/14fl oz/1⅔ cups Guinness
10ml/2 tsp soft light brown sugar
30ml/2 tbsp balsamic vinegar
salt and ground black pepper

For the dumplings

175g/6oz/1½ cups self-raising (self-rising) flour
5ml/1 tsp mustard powder
75g/3oz/generous ½ cup shredded beef suet (US chilled, grated shortening)
10ml/2 tsp horseradish sauce

1 Preheat the oven to 180°C/350°F/Gas 4. Heat the oil in a flameproof casserole. Fry the meat, in batches, until browned. As each batch browns, remove it to a plate. Add the onions, with a little more oil, if necessary. Cook, stirring, for 5 minutes until soft. Add the garlic, then return the venison to the pan.

2 Mix the flour and mustard in a bowl, sprinkle into the pan and stir until the flour has been absorbed. Add the juniper berries and bay leaves and stir in the Guinness, sugar and vinegar.

3 Pour over enough water to cover the meat. Season with salt and pepper and bring to simmering point. Cover and cook in the oven for 2–2½ hours, until the venison is tender. Stir occasionally and add a little more water, if needed.

4 About 20 minutes before the end of the cooking time, make the dumplings. Sift the flour and mustard into a bowl. Season with salt and pepper and mix in the suet. Stir in the horseradish sauce and enough water to make a soft dough. With floured hands, form into six dumplings. Place these gently on top of the venison. Return the casserole to the oven and cook for about 15 minutes more, until the dumplings are well risen and cooked. Serve immediately.

Venison Stew Energy 727kcal/3045kJ; Protein 83.8g; Carbohydrate 17.5g, of which sugars 14.4g; Fat 31.3g, of which saturates 13.8g; Cholesterol 226mg; Calcium 70mg; Fibre 2.9g; Sodium 985mg.
Guinness Energy 393kcal/1651kJ; Protein 29.1g; Carbohydrate 33.4g, of which sugars 6.4g; Fat 16.3g, of which saturates 7.5g; Cholesterol 67mg; Calcium 136mg; Fibre 2.3g; Sodium 189mg.

Stuffed Braised Venison

Slow braising is an ideal method for cooking venison.

Serves 6–8

2.5–3kg/5½–6½lb leg of venison, boned
7.5ml/1½ tsp unsalted butter
15ml/1 tbsp vegetable oil
1 carrot, halved lengthways
1 onion, halved
120ml/4fl oz/½ cup beef or venison stock
4–5 black peppercorns
salt

For the stuffing

40g/1½oz/3 tbsp unsalted butter
5 shallots, chopped, drained
10g/¼oz dried wild mushrooms, soaked in warm water for 15 minutes and chopped
150g/5oz/2 cups mushrooms, sliced
10ml/2 tsp juniper berries, crushed
5ml/1 tsp chopped fresh marjoram
salt and ground black pepper

For the sauce

475ml/16fl oz/2 cups venison or beef stock
90ml/3½fl oz/scant ½ cup medium white wine
300ml/½ pint/1¼ cups whipping cream
10ml/2 tsp arrowroot

1 Make the stuffing. Melt the butter in a pan and fry the shallots for 3 minutes. Add the mushrooms and cook for 5–7 minutes until tender. Add the juniper berries and marjoram, and season.

2 Preheat the oven to 180°C/350°F/Gas 4. Put the stuffing inside the venison and tie with string. Heat the butter and the oil in a flameproof casserole, and fry the meat until browned. Add the carrot, onion, stock, peppercorns and salt to season. Cover the casserole and cook in the oven for 1½ hours, or until tender.

3 Remove the venison from the casserole and keep warm. Strain the juices into a pan. Add the stock and wine, bring to the boil and cook until reduced slightly. Add the cream and reduce further.

4 Blend the arrowroot with a little water to form a paste, then add a little of the hot sauce. Stir into the pan and boil until thickened. Serve the venison with the sauce and vegetables.

Venison Pie

This is a variation on beef cottage pie using rich, slowly simmered minced venison. The resulting dish is particularly tasty. Serve with lightly steamed green vegetables of your choice.

Serves 6

30ml/2 tbsp olive oil
2 leeks, trimmed and chopped
1kg/2¼lb minced (ground) venison
30ml/2 tbsp chopped fresh parsley
300ml/½ pint/1¼ cups game consommé
salt and ground black pepper

For the topping

1.5kg/3¼lb mixed root vegetables, such as sweet potatoes, parsnips and swede (rutabaga), coarsely chopped
15ml/1 tbsp horseradish sauce
25g/1oz/2 tbsp butter

1 Heat the oil in a heavy frying pan. Add the leeks and cook, stirring occasionally, for about 8 minutes, or until softened and beginning to brown.

2 Add the minced venison to the pan and cook for about 10 minutes, stirring frequently, or until the meat is well browned. Stir in the chopped parsley, game consommé and seasoning, then bring to the boil. Cover the pan, reduce the heat and simmer for about 20 minutes, stirring occasionally.

3 Meanwhile, preheat the oven to 200°C/400°F/Gas 6 and prepare the topping. Cook the vegetables in boiling, salted water to cover for 15–20 minutes. Drain well and mash the vegetables together with the horseradish sauce and butter, and season with salt and pepper.

4 Spoon the venison mixture into an ovenproof dish and top with the mashed vegetables. Bake for 20 minutes, or until piping hot and beginning to brown. Serve immediately.

Variation
This pie can be made with other minced (ground) meats, such as beef, lamb or pork. If leeks aren't available, then use a large onion and chop coarsely.

Stuffed Venison Energy 459kcal/1919kJ; Protein 44.8g; Carbohydrate 15.2g, of which sugars 10.7g; Fat 25.1g, of which saturates 14.2g; Cholesterol 146mg; Calcium 98mg; Fibre 4.4g; Sodium 195mg.
Venison Pie Energy 307kcal/1291kJ; Protein 39.8g; Carbohydrate 13.2g, of which sugars 12.5g; Fat 12g, of which saturates 4.1g; Cholesterol 93mg; Calcium 154mg; Fibre 5.8g; Sodium 176mg.

Braised Sausages with Onions, Celeriac and Apple

This full-flavoured casserole is slow-cooked comfort food at its best – serve with mashed potatoes and a glass or two of full-bodied red wine on a cold winter's night.

Serves 4

45ml/3 tbsp sunflower oil
450g/1lb venison sausages
2 onions, sliced
15ml/1 tbsp plain (all-purpose) flour
400ml/14fl oz/1⅔ cups dry (hard) cider
350g/12oz celeriac, cut into large chunks
15ml/1 tbsp Worcestershire sauce
15ml/1 tbsp chopped fresh sage
2 small tart cooking apples, cored and sliced
salt and ground black pepper

1 Preheat the oven to 180°C/350°F/Gas 4. Heat the oil in a heavy frying pan, add the sausages and fry until evenly browned all over, for about 5–7 minutes. Transfer the browned sausages to a earthenware casserole dish.

2 Drain off any excess oil from the frying pan, leaving about 15ml/1 tbsp. Add the onions and cook for a few minutes, stirring frequently, until softened and golden.

3 Stir in the flour, then gradually add the cider and bring to the boil, stirring. Add the celeriac and cook for 2 minutes. Stir in the Worcestershire sauce and sage. Season well with salt and ground black pepper.

4 Pour the cider and celeriac mixture over the sausages in the casserole dish, then cover and cook in the oven for 30 minutes. Add the apples and cook for 10–15 minutes, or until the apples are just tender. Serve immediately.

Variation
Try good-quality pork and herb or duck sausages in this recipe instead of the venison sausages, if you like.

Venison Sausages with Red Wine Gravy

Strongly flavoured, meaty sausages are delicious slowly simmered in a red wine gravy flavoured with shiitake mushrooms. Serve with polenta or mashed potatoes.

Serves 4

15ml/1 tbsp sunflower oil (optional)
12 venison or wild boar sausages
2 leeks, sliced
2 plump garlic cloves, sliced
225g/8oz/3 cups shiitake mushrooms, quartered
15ml/1 tbsp plain (all-purpose) flour
600ml/1 pint/2½ cups red wine
30ml/2 tbsp chopped mixed fresh herbs, such as flat leaf parsley and marjoram
salt and ground black pepper

1 Pour the sunflower oil, if using, into a large, heavy frying pan, add the venison or wild boar sausages and cook over medium heat for about 10–15 minutes, turning occasionally, until evenly browned all over.

2 Add the leeks, garlic and mushrooms to the pan, and mix well. Cook the vegetables for 10–15 minutes, or until the leeks are soft and beginning to brown.

3 Sprinkle in the flour and gradually pour in the red wine, stirring with a wooden spoon and pushing the sausages around to mix the flour and the liquid smoothly with the leeks.

4 Bring slowly to the boil, reduce the heat and simmer for 10–15 minutes, stirring occasionally, or until the gravy is smooth and glossy. Season the gravy with salt and pepper to taste and then sprinkle the mixed herbs over the sausages. Serve immediately, with polenta or mashed potatoes, if you like.

Cook's Tip
Shiitake mushrooms have a slightly floury-looking medium to dark grey-brown cap. They have a firm and meaty texture that becomes silky when cooked. The stalks can be tough so discard, if necessary, before cooking.

Braised Sausages Energy 538kcal/2240kJ; Protein 43.5g; Carbohydrate 7g, of which sugars 2.8g; Fat 28.2g, of which saturates 8.9g; Cholesterol 170mg; Calcium 50mg; Fibre 1.1g; Sodium 610mg.
Venison Sausages Energy 246kcal/1026kJ; Protein 7.8g; Carbohydrate 11.7g, of which sugars 2.9g; Fat 7.8g, of which saturates 3g; Cholesterol 15mg; Calcium 71mg; Fibre 3g; Sodium 447mg.

Baked Tomato Casserole

This is a beautifully fresh-tasting tomato dish. Slow baking in the oven helps to intensify the flavour of the tomatoes and the spices add a subtle piquancy.

Serves 4

40ml/2½ tbsp olive oil
45ml/3 tbsp chopped fresh flat leaf parsley
1kg/2¼lb firm ripe tomatoes
5ml/1 tsp caster (superfine) sugar
40g/1½oz/scant 1 cup day-old breadcrumbs
2.5ml/½ tsp chilli powder or paprika
salt
chopped parsley, to garnish
rye bread, to serve

1 Preheat the oven to 200°C/400°F/Gas 6. Brush a large baking dish with 15ml/1 tbsp of the oil.

2 Sprinkle the chopped flat leaf parsley over the base of the dish. Cut the tomatoes into even slices, discarding the two end slices of each. Arrange the slices of tomato in the dish so that they overlap slightly. Sprinkle them with a little salt and the caster sugar.

3 In a mixing bowl, stir together the breadcrumbs, the remaining oil and chilli powder or paprika. Sprinkle this mixture over the top of the tomatoes.

4 Place the dish in the preheated oven and bake for about 40–50 minutes until the tomatoes are tender and the breadcrumb topping is golden brown and crisp. If the topping is getting too brown during cooking, loosely cover the dish with foil. Serve hot or cold, garnished with chopped parsley and accompanied by rye bread.

Variation
To vary this recipe, replace half the quantity of tomatoes with 450g/1lb courgettes (zucchini). Slice the courgettes evenly and arrange alternate slices of courgette and tomato in the dish, overlapping the slices as before.

New Potato and Vegetable Casserole

Here is a simple one-pot meal that is ideal for feeding large numbers of people. It is packed with nutritious vegetables that are lightly spiced and has lots of garlic.

Serves 4

60ml/4 tbsp olive oil
1 large onion, chopped
2 small aubergines (eggplants), cut into small cubes
4 courgettes (zucchini), cut into small chunks
1 green (bell) pepper, seeded and chopped
1 red or yellow (bell) pepper, seeded and chopped
115g/4oz/1 cup fresh or frozen peas
115g/4oz green beans
450g/1lb new or salad potatoes, cubed
2.5ml/½ tsp cinnamon
2.5ml/½ tsp ground cumin
5ml/1 tsp paprika
4–5 tomatoes, skinned
400g/14oz can chopped tomatoes
30ml/2 tbsp chopped fresh parsley
3–4 garlic cloves, crushed
350ml/12fl oz/1½ cups hot vegetable stock
salt and ground black pepper
black olives, to garnish
fresh parsley sprigs, to garnish

1 Preheat the oven to 190°C/375°F/Gas 5. Heat 45ml/3 tbsp of the oil in a heavy frying pan, add the onion and cook until softened and golden. Add the aubergines and cook, stirring, for about 3 minutes.

2 Add the courgettes, green and red or yellow peppers, peas, beans and potatoes, together with the spices and seasoning. Continue to cook the mixture for about 3 minutes, stirring all the time. Transfer to a shallow ovenproof dish.

3 Halve, seed and chop the fresh tomatoes and mix with the canned tomatoes, chopped fresh parsley, garlic and the remaining olive oil in a bowl.

4 Pour the hot vegetable stock over the vegetable mixture and then spoon over the prepared tomato mixture.

5 Cover the dish with the lid and bake in the preheated oven for 30–45 minutes until the vegetables are tender. Serve hot, garnished with black olives and parsley.

Baked Tomato Casserole Energy 155kcal/649kJ; Protein 3.1g; Carbohydrate 15.7g, of which sugars 8.2g; Fat 9.3g, of which saturates 1.4g; Cholesterol 0mg; Calcium 46mg; Fibre 3.1g; Sodium 101mg.
Potato Casserole Energy 307kcal/1282kJ; Protein 9.4g; Carbohydrate 39.9g, of which sugars 17.8g; Fat 13.3g, of which saturates 2.1g; Cholesterol 0mg; Calcium 92mg; Fibre 8.7g; Sodium 30mg.

Harvest Vegetable and Lentil Bake

This oven-baked dish is easy to prepare and is delicious served with warm garlic bread. Try adding a few sun-dried tomatoes with the lentils, if you like.

Serves 6

15ml/1 tbsp sunflower or olive oil
2 leeks, sliced
1 garlic clove, crushed
4 celery sticks, chopped
2 carrots, sliced
2 parsnips, diced
1 sweet potato, diced
225g/8oz swede (rutabaga), diced
175g/6oz/¾ cup whole brown or green lentils
450g/1lb tomatoes, peeled, seeded and chopped
15ml/1 tbsp chopped fresh thyme
15ml/1 tbsp chopped fresh marjoram
900ml/1½ pints/3¾ cups hot vegetable stock
15ml/1 tbsp cornflour (cornstarch)
45ml/3 tbsp water
salt and ground black pepper
warm garlic bread, to serve

1 Preheat the oven to 180°C/350°F/Gas 4. Heat the oil in a large, flameproof casserole. Add the leeks, garlic and celery, and cook over low heat, stirring occasionally, for about 3 minutes, until the leeks are just beginning to soften.

2 Add the carrots, parsnips, sweet potato, swede, brown or green lentils, tomatoes, thyme, marjoram and vegetable stock and season to taste with salt and pepper. Stir the vegetables well to combine. Bring to the boil, stirring occasionally, to make sure that the vegetables do not stick to the base of the pan.

3 Cover and bake for about 50 minutes, until the vegetables and lentils are cooked through and tender, removing the casserole from the oven and gently stirring the vegetable mixture once or twice during the cooking time.

4 Remove the casserole from the oven. Mix the cornflour with 45ml/3 tbsp cold water in a small bowl to make a smooth paste. Stir the mixture into the casserole and heat on top of the stove, stirring until the mixture comes to the boil and thickens, then simmer gently for 2 minutes, stirring constantly. Taste and adjust the seasoning, if necessary, then serve in warmed bowls. Hand around garlic bread.

Tagine of Yam, Carrots and Prunes

A tagine featuring tender caramelized vegetables.

Serves 4–6

45ml/3 tbsp olive oil
25–30 button (pearl) onions, blanched and peeled
900g/2lb yam, cut into chunks
2–3 carrots, cut into chunks
150g/5oz ready-to-eat pitted prunes
5ml/1 tsp ground cinnamon
2.5ml/½ tsp ground ginger
10ml/2 tsp clear honey
450ml/¾ pint/scant 2 cups vegetable stock
small bunch of fresh coriander (cilantro), finely chopped
small bunch of mint, finely chopped
salt and ground black pepper

1 Preheat the oven to 200°C/400°F/Gas 6. Heat the oil in a flameproof casserole. Cook the onions for 5 minutes, then set aside half of them. Cook the yam and carrots until browned. Stir in the prunes, cinnamon, ginger, honey and stock. Season well.

2 Cover and bake for 45 minutes. Stir in the reserved onions and bake for 10 minutes. Stir in the coriander and mint, and serve.

Mixed Vegetable Casserole

A gloriously simple and nutritious dish.

Serves 4

1 aubergine (eggplant), diced
115g/4oz/½ cup okra, halved
225g/8oz/2 cups frozen peas
225g/8oz/1½ cups green beans
4 courgettes (zucchini), diced
2 onions, finely chopped
450g/1lb old potatoes, diced
1 red (bell) pepper, sliced
400g/14oz can chopped tomatoes
150ml/¼ pint/⅔ cup vegetable stock
60ml/4 tbsp olive oil
75ml/5 tbsp chopped fresh parsley
5ml/1 tsp paprika
salt
3 tomatoes, sliced and 1 courgette (zucchini), sliced, for the topping

1 Preheat the oven to 190°C/375°F/Gas 5. Add the vegetables to a flameproof casserole. Stir in the tomatoes, stock, oil, parsley, paprika and salt. Top with slices of tomatoes and courgette.

2 Cover and cook for 1 hour, until tender. Serve hot or cold.

Harvest Bake Energy 202kcal/857kJ; Protein 9.4g; Carbohydrate 36.2g, of which sugars 10.3g; Fat 3.2g, of which saturates 0.5g; Cholesterol 0mg; Calcium 70mg; Fibre 6.4g; Sodium 60mg.
Tagine of Yam Energy 431kcal/1825kJ; Protein 5.6g; Carbohydrate 86.4g, of which sugars 23g; Fat 9.5g, of which saturates 1.5g; Cholesterol 0mg; Calcium 97mg; Fibre 7.6g; Sodium 27mg.
Casserole Energy 573kcal/2416kJ; Protein 32.5g; Carbohydrate 81.5g, of which sugars 19.5g; Fat 15.3g, of which saturates 2.5g; Cholesterol 0mg; Calcium 250mg; Fibre 25.7g; Sodium 60mg.

Tagine of Butter Beans, Cherry Tomatoes and Olives

Serve this slow-cooked bean dish with grills or roasts. It is also delicious served on its own, with a leafy salad and fresh, crusty bread.

Serves 4

115g/4oz/⅔ cup butter (lima) beans, soaked overnight
30–45ml/2–3 tbsp olive oil
1 onion, chopped
2–3 garlic cloves, crushed
25g/1oz fresh root ginger, peeled and chopped
pinch of saffron threads
16 cherry tomatoes
generous pinch of sugar
handful of fleshy black olives, pitted
5ml/1 tsp ground cinnamon
5ml/1 tsp paprika
small bunch of flat leaf parsley
salt and ground black pepper

1 Rinse the soaked beans and place them in a large pan with plenty of water. Bring to the boil and boil for about 10 minutes, skimming off any foam that rises to the surface. Reduce the heat and simmer gently for 1–1½ hours until tender. Drain the beans and refresh under cold water.

2 Heat the olive oil in a heavy pan. Add the onion and cook, stirring frequently, for about 6–7 minutes or until beginning to soften, but do not let it brown. Add the garlic and ginger, and cook for about 4 minutes. Stir in the saffron threads, followed by the cherry tomatoes and a sprinkling of sugar.

3 As the tomatoes begin to soften in the pan, stir in the butter beans. When the tomatoes have heated through, stir in the black olives, ground cinnamon and paprika. Season to taste with salt and ground black pepper and sprinkle over the parsley. Serve immediately.

Cook's Tip

If you forget to soak the dried beans the night before, you could use two 400g/14oz cans of pre-cooked butter beans instead. Make sure you rinse the beans well before adding as canned beans tend to be salty.

Mushroom and Fennel Hotpot

Hearty and richly flavoured, this tasty stew is ideal for making in the slow cooker. It is a marvellous vegetarian main dish in itself, but is also a good accompaniment to meat dishes. The dried mushrooms swell up a great deal after soaking, so a little goes a long way in terms of both flavour and quantity.

Serves 4

25g/1oz/½ cup dried shiitake mushrooms
1 small head of fennel
30ml/2 tbsp olive oil
12 shallots, peeled
225g/8oz/3 cups button (white) mushrooms, trimmed and halved
250ml/8fl oz/1 cup dry (hard) cider
25g/1oz/½ cup sun-dried tomatoes
30ml/2 tbsp/½ cup sun-dried tomato paste
1 bay leaf
salt and ground black pepper
chopped fresh parsley, to garnish

1 Place the dried shiitake mushrooms in a heatproof bowl. Pour over just enough hot water to cover them and leave to soak for about 15–20 minutes. Meanwhile, trim and slice the head of fennel.

2 Heat the oil in a heavy pan. Add the shallots and fennel, then cook for about 10 minutes over medium heat, until the vegetables are soft and just beginning to brown. Add the button mushrooms to the pan and cook for a further 2–3 minutes, stirring occasionally.

3 Transfer the vegetable mixture to the ceramic cooking pot. Drain the shiitake mushrooms, adding 30ml/2 tbsp of the soaking liquid to the pot. Chop them and add to the pot.

4 Pour the dry cider into the pot and stir in the sun-dried tomatoes and tomato paste. Add the bay leaf. Cover the cooker with the lid and cook on high for 3–4 hours, or until the vegetables are tender.

5 Remove the bay leaf and season to taste with salt and ground black pepper. Serve sprinkled with plenty of chopped fresh parsley.

Tagine Energy 138kcal/578kJ; Protein 5.5g; Carbohydrate 12.8g, of which sugars 3.5g; Fat 7.6g, of which saturates 1.1g; Cholesterol 0mg; Calcium 51mg; Fibre 5.2g; Sodium 605mg.
Mushroom Hotpot Energy 94kcal/394kJ; Protein 2.1g; Carbohydrate 4.2g, of which sugars 4g; Fat 6g, of which saturates 0.9g; Cholesterol 0mg; Calcium 28mg; Fibre 2.4g; Sodium 17mg.

Root Vegetable Casserole with Caraway Dumplings

Soft cheese gives this slow-cooker casserole a creamy richness.

Serves 3

300ml/½ pint/1¼ cups dry (hard) cider
175ml/6fl oz/¾ cup boiling vegetable stock
2 leeks
2 carrots
2 small parsnips
225g/8oz potatoes
1 sweet potato, about 175g/6oz
1 bay leaf
7.5ml/1½ tsp cornflour (cornstarch)
115g/4oz full-fat soft cheese with garlic and herbs
salt and ground black pepper

For the dumplings

115g/4oz/1 cup self-raising (self-rising) flour
5ml/1 tsp caraway seeds
50g/2oz/scant ½ cup shredded vegetable suet (US chilled, grated shortening)
1 courgette (zucchini), grated
about 75ml/5 tbsp cold water

1 Reserve 15ml/1 tbsp of the cider and pour the rest into the ceramic cooking pot with the stock. Cover and switch to high.

2 Meanwhile, prepare the vegetables. Trim the leeks and cut into 2cm/¾in slices. Peel the carrots, parsnips, potatoes and sweet potato and cut into 2cm/¾in chunks. Add to the ceramic cooking pot with the bay leaf. Cover and cook for 3 hours.

3 In a bowl, blend the cornflour with the reserved cider. Add the cheese and mix together, then blend in a few spoonfuls of the cooking liquid. Stir into the vegetables. Season with salt and pepper. Cover and cook for 1–2 hours, or until almost tender.

4 Towards the end of the cooking time, make the dumplings. Sift the flour into a bowl and stir in the caraway seeds, suet, courgettes, salt and pepper. Stir in enough water to make a soft dough. Shape the mixture into 12 walnut-size dumplings.

5 Place the dumplings on top of the casserole, cover and cook for a further hour, or until the vegetables and dumplings are cooked. Serve in warmed deep soup plates.

Spicy Root Vegetable Gratin

Subtly spiced, this rich gratin is slowly baked in the oven and is substantial enough to serve on its own for lunch or supper. It is also perfect as a tasty side dish to accompany grilled meats.

Serves 4

2 large potatoes, total weight about 450g/1lb
2 sweet potatoes, total weight about 275g/10oz
175g/6oz celeriac
15ml/1 tbsp unsalted butter
5ml/1 tsp curry powder
5ml/1 tsp ground turmeric
2.5ml/½ tsp ground coriander
5ml/1 tsp mild chilli powder
3 shallots, chopped
150ml/¼ pint/⅔ cup single (light) cream
150ml/¼ pint/⅔ cup milk
salt and ground black pepper
chopped fresh flat leaf parsley, to garnish

1 Peel the potatoes, sweet potatoes and celeriac and cut into thin, even slices using a sharp knife or the slicing attachment on a food processor. Immediately place the vegetables in a bowl of cold water to prevent them from discolouring.

2 Preheat the oven to 180°C/350°F/Gas 4. Heat half the butter in a heavy pan, add the curry powder, ground turmeric and coriander and half the chilli powder. Cook for 2 minutes, then leave to cool slightly.

3 Drain the vegetables, then pat them dry with kitchen paper. Place in a bowl, add the spice mixture and the shallots, and mix well. Arrange the vegetables in a shallow baking dish, seasoning well with salt and pepper between the layers.

4 In a bowl, mix together the cream and milk until well blended. Pour the mixture over the vegetables in the dish, then sprinkle the remaining chilli powder on top.

5 Cover the dish with baking parchment and bake for about 45 minutes. Remove the baking parchment, dot the vegetables with the remaining butter and bake for a further 50 minutes, or until the top is golden brown. Serve the gratin garnished with chopped parsley.

Root Casserole Energy 616kcal/2584kJ; Protein 11.9g; Carbohydrate 74.9g, of which sugars 17.1g; Fat 28.9g, of which saturates 15.9g; Cholesterol 35mg; Calcium 256mg; Fibre 9.5g; Sodium 369mg.
Spicy Gratin Energy 268kcal/1129kJ; Protein 5.8g; Carbohydrate 37.7g, of which sugars 9.8g; Fat 11.6g, of which saturates 7.1g; Cholesterol 31mg; Calcium 127mg; Fibre 3.6g; Sodium 117mg.

Mixed-bean Hotpot

This impressive slow-cooker dish has a deliciously rich and tangy tomato sauce.

Serves 6

40g/1½oz/3 tbsp butter
4 shallots, peeled and finely chopped
40g/1½oz/⅓ cup plain (all-purpose) or wholemeal (whole-wheat) flour
300ml/½ pint/1¼ cups passata (bottled strained tomatoes)
120ml/4fl oz/½ cup unsweetened apple juice
60ml/4 tbsp soft light brown sugar
60ml/4 tbsp tomato ketchup
60ml/4 tbsp dry sherry
60ml/4 tbsp cider vinegar
60ml/4 tbsp light soy sauce
400g/14oz can butter (lima) beans
400g/14oz can flageolet (small cannellini) beans
400g/14oz can chickpeas
175g/6oz green beans, cut into 2.5cm/1in lengths
225g/8oz/3 cups mushrooms, sliced
450g/1lb unpeeled potatoes
15ml/1 tbsp olive oil
15ml/1 tbsp chopped fresh thyme
15ml/1 tbsp fresh marjoram
salt and ground black pepper
fresh herbs, to garnish

1 Melt the butter in a pan, add the shallots and fry gently for 5–6 minutes, until softened. Add the flour and cook for 1 minute, stirring all the time, then gradually stir in the passata. Stir in the apple juice, sugar, ketchup, sherry, vinegar and soy sauce. Bring the mixture to the boil, stirring constantly until it thickens.

2 Rinse the beans and chickpeas and drain well. Place them in the ceramic cooking pot with the green beans and mushrooms and pour over the sauce. Stir well, then cover with the lid and cook on high for 3 hours.

3 Meanwhile, thinly slice the potatoes and par-boil them for about 4 minutes. Drain, then toss them in the oil to lightly coat.

4 Stir the fresh herbs into the bean mixture and season with salt and pepper. Arrange the potato slices on top of the beans, overlapping them slightly so that they completely cover the beans. Cover and cook for 2 hours, or until the potatoes are tender.

5 Place the ceramic cooking pot under a medium grill (broiler) and cook for 4–5 minutes to brown the potato topping. Serve garnished with herbs.

Spicy Bean Chilli with Cornbread

This slow-cooker chilli has a tasty cornbread topping.

Serves 4

115g/4oz/generous ½ cup dried red kidney beans, soaked for 6 hours or overnight
115g/4oz/generous ½ cup dried black-eyed beans (peas), soaked for 6 hours or overnight
1 bay leaf
15ml/1 tbsp vegetable oil
1 large onion, finely chopped
1 garlic clove, crushed
5ml/1 tsp ground cumin
5ml/1 tsp chilli powder
5ml/1 tsp mild paprika
2.5ml/½ tsp dried marjoram
450g/1lb mixed vegetables such as potatoes, carrots, aubergines (eggplants), parsnips and celery
1 vegetable stock (bouillon) cube
400g/14oz can chopped tomatoes
15ml/1 tbsp tomato purée (paste)
salt and ground black pepper

For the cornbread topping

250g/9oz/2¼ cups fine cornmeal
30ml/2 tbsp wholemeal (whole-wheat) flour
7.5ml/1½ tsp baking powder
1 egg, plus 1 egg yolk lightly beaten
300ml/½ pint/1¼ cups milk

1 Drain the beans and rinse well. Place in a pan with 600ml/1 pint/2½ cups of cold water and the bay leaf. Bring to the boil and boil rapidly for 10 minutes. Turn off the heat, leave to cool slightly, then add to the ceramic cooking pot and switch to high.

2 Heat the oil in a pan, add the onion and cook for 7–8 minutes. Add the garlic, cumin, chilli powder, paprika and marjoram and cook for 1 minute. Transfer to the ceramic cooking pot and stir.

3 Peel or trim the vegetables as necessary, then cut into 2cm/¾in chunks. Add to the pot, submerging those that may discolour. Cover and cook for 3 hours, until the beans are tender.

4 Add the stock cube and tomatoes to the pot, then stir in the tomato purée and season with salt and pepper. Replace the lid and cook for 30 minutes until the mixture is at boiling point.

5 Make the topping. Combine the cornmeal, flour, baking powder and a pinch of salt in a bowl. Make a well in the centre and add the egg, egg yolk and milk. Mix, then spoon over the bean mixture. Cover and cook for 1 hour, or until the topping is firm. Serve.

Mixed-bean Hotpot Energy 483kcal/2042kJ; Protein 18.5g; Carbohydrate 73.3g, of which sugars 24.8g; Fat 13.8g, of which saturates 4.5g; Cholesterol 14mg; Calcium 134mg; Fibre 10.9g; Sodium 826mg.
Spicy Chilli Energy 613kcal/2595kJ; Protein 29.6g; Carbohydrate 97.4g, of which sugars 15.8g; Fat 14.5g, of which saturates 3.4g; Cholesterol 112mg; Calcium 257mg; Fibre 13.4g; Sodium 413mg.

Mushroom and Courgette Lasagne

This dish can be prepared in the slow cooker early in the day, then left to cook.

Serves 6

30ml/2 tbsp olive oil
50g/2oz/¼ cup butter
450g/1lb courgettes (zucchini), thinly sliced
1 onion, finely chopped
450g/1lb/6 cups chestnut mushrooms, thinly sliced
2 garlic cloves, crushed
6–8 non-pre-cook lasagne sheets
50g/2oz/½ cup freshly grated Parmesan cheese
salt and ground black pepper
fresh oregano leaves, to garnish

For the tomato sauce

15g/½oz dried porcini mushrooms
120ml/4fl oz/½ cup hot water
1 onion
1 carrot
1 celery stick
30ml/2 tbsp olive oil
2 x 400g/14oz cans chopped tomatoes
15ml/1 tbsp sun-dried tomato paste
5ml/1 tsp sugar
5ml/1 tsp dried basil or mixed herbs

For the white sauce

40g/1½oz/3 tbsp butter
40g/1½oz/⅓ cup plain (all-purpose) flour
900ml/1½ pints/3¾ cups milk
freshly grated nutmeg

1 Make the tomato sauce. Put the dried porcini mushrooms in a bowl. Pour over the hot water and leave to soak for 15 minutes. Transfer the porcini and liquid to a sieve (strainer) set over a bowl and squeeze the mushrooms with your hands to release as much liquid as possible. Chop the mushrooms finely and set aside. Strain the soaking liquid through a fine sieve and reserve.

2 Chop the onion, carrot and celery finely. Heat the olive oil in a pan and fry the vegetables until softened. Place in a food processor with the tomatoes, tomato paste, sugar, herbs, porcini and soaking liquid, and blend to a purée.

3 For the lasagne, heat the olive oil and half the butter in a large, heavy pan. Cook the courgette slices in batches, turning frequently, for 5–8 minutes, until lightly coloured on both sides. Remove from the pan with a slotted spoon and transfer to a bowl. Melt the remaining butter in the pan, and cook the onion for about 3 minutes, stirring. Add the mushrooms and garlic and cook for 5 minutes. Add to the courgettes and season with salt and pepper.

4 For the white sauce, melt the butter in a large pan, then add the flour and cook, stirring, for 1 minute. Turn off the heat and gradually whisk in the milk. Bring to the boil and cook, stirring, until the sauce is smooth and thick. Season with salt, black pepper and nutmeg.

5 Ladle half of the tomato sauce into the ceramic cooking pot and spread out to cover the base. Add half the vegetable mixture, spreading it evenly. Top with about one-third of the white sauce, then about half the lasagne sheets, breaking them to fit the cooking pot. Repeat these layers, then top with the remaining white sauce and sprinkle with grated Parmesan.

6 Cover the ceramic cooking pot with the lid and cook on low for 2–2½ hours or until the lasagne is tender. If you like, brown the top under a medium grill (broiler). Garnish with the fresh oregano leaves, and serve immediately.

Pasta with Mushrooms

The slow cooker is ideal for making this pasta sauce of mushrooms, garlic and sun-dried tomatoes, together with white wine and stock.

Serves 4

15g/½oz dried porcini mushrooms
120ml/4fl oz/½ cup hot water
2 cloves garlic, finely chopped
2 large pieces sun-dried tomato in olive oil, drained, sliced into strips
120ml/4fl oz/½ cup dry white wine
120ml/4fl oz/½ cup hot vegetable stock
225g/8oz/2 cups chestnut mushrooms, thinly sliced
1 handful fresh flat leaf parsley, roughly chopped
450g/1lb/4 cups dried short pasta shapes, such as ruote, penne, fusilli or eliche
salt and ground black pepper
rocket (arugula) and/or fresh flat leaf parsley, to garnish

1 Put the dried porcini mushrooms in a large bowl. Pour over the hot water and leave to soak for 15 minutes.

2 While the mushrooms are soaking, put the garlic, tomatoes, wine, stock and chestnut mushrooms into the ceramic cooking pot and switch the slow cooker to high.

3 Transfer the porcini mushrooms to a sieve (strainer) set over a bowl, then squeeze them with your hands to release as much liquid as possible. Reserve the soaking liquid. Chop the porcini finely. Add the liquid and the chopped porcini to the ceramic cooking pot, and cover the slow cooker with the lid. Cook on high for 1 hour, stirring halfway through the cooking time to make sure the mushrooms cook evenly.

4 Switch the slow cooker to the low setting and cook for a further 1–2 hours, until the mushrooms are tender.

5 Cook the pasta in boiling salted water for about 10 minutes, or according to the instructions on the packet. Drain the pasta and transfer it to a large warmed bowl. Stir the chopped parsley into the sauce in the cooking pot and season to taste with salt and ground black pepper. Add the sauce to the pasta in the bowl and toss well. Serve immediately, garnished with rocket and/or parsley.

Lasagne Energy 421kcal/1757kJ; Protein 15.5g; Carbohydrate 32.9g, of which sugars 15g; Fat 26.2g, of which saturates 12.4g; Cholesterol 49mg; Calcium 346mg; Fibre 3.8g; Sodium 310mg.
Pasta with Mushrooms Energy 420kcal/1787kJ; Protein 15.1g; Carbohydrate 84.9g, of which sugars 5.1g; Fat 2.6g, of which saturates 0.3g; Cholesterol 0 mg; Calcium 61mg; Fibre 4.8g; Sodium 14mg.

Courgettes with Rice

This slow-cooked rice dish is first simmered on the stove and then finished in the oven.

Serves 4 as a main course
8 as a side dish
1kg/2¼lb courgettes (zucchini)
60ml/4 tbsp olive oil
3 onions, finely chopped
3 garlic cloves, crushed
5ml/1 tsp chilli powder
400g/14oz can chopped tomatoes
200g/7oz/1 cup risotto or short grain rice
600–750ml/1–1¼ pints/2½–3 cups vegetable or chicken stock
30ml/2 tbsp chopped fresh parsley
30ml/2 tbsp chopped fresh dill
salt and ground white pepper
sprigs of dill and olives, to garnish
thick natural (plain) yogurt, to serve

1 Preheat the oven to 190°C/375°F/Gas 5. Top and tail the courgettes and slice into large chunks.

2 Heat half the olive oil in a large pan and gently fry the onions and garlic until just soft. Stir in the chilli powder and tomatoes and simmer for about 5–8 minutes before adding the courgettes. Add salt to taste.

3 Cook over low to medium heat for 10–15 minutes, before stirring the rice into the pan.

4 Add the stock to the pan, cover and simmer for 45 minutes, or until the rice is tender. Stir the mixture occasionally.

5 Season with pepper, and stir in the parsley and dill. Transfer to an ovenproof dish and bake in the oven for about 45 minutes.

6 Halfway through cooking, brush the remaining oil over the courgette mixture. Garnish with the dill sprigs and olives. Serve with the natural yogurt.

Cook's Tip
Add extra liquid, as necessary, while simmering the rice on the stove to prevent the mixture from sticking to the pan.

Rosemary Risotto with Borlotti Beans

The low, constant heat of the slow cooker produces a delicious risotto. Easy-cook rice means that all the liquid can be added at the same time, rather than gradually, as with a traditional risotto.

Serves 3
400g/14oz can borlotti beans
15g/½oz/1 tbsp butter
15ml/1 tbsp olive oil
1 onion, finely chopped
2 garlic cloves, crushed
120ml/4fl oz/½ cup dry white wine
225g/8oz/generous 1 cup easy-cook (converted) Italian rice
750ml/1¼ pints/3 cups boiling vegetable stock
60ml/4 tbsp mascarpone cheese
5ml/1 tsp chopped fresh rosemary
65g/2½oz/¾ cup freshly grated Parmesan cheese, plus extra to serve (optional)
salt and ground black pepper

1 Rinse the beans well and drain. Place two-thirds of the beans in a food processor or blender and process to a coarse paste. Transfer the remaining beans to a bowl and set aside.

2 Heat the butter and oil in a pan, add the onion and garlic and fry gently for 7–8 minutes until soft. Transfer the mixture to the ceramic cooking pot and stir in the wine and the bean paste. Cover with the lid and cook on high for 1 hour.

3 Add the rice to the pot, then stir in the stock. Re-cover with the lid and cook for about 45 minutes, stirring once halfway through cooking. The rice should be almost tender and most of the stock should have been absorbed.

4 Stir the reserved beans, mascarpone and rosemary into the risotto. Cover again with the lid and cook for a further 15 minutes, until the rice is tender but still has a little bite.

5 Stir the Parmesan cheese into the risotto and season to taste with salt and ground black pepper. Turn off the slow cooker, cover and leave to stand for 5 minutes, so that the risotto absorbs the flavours fully and the rice completes cooking.

6 Spoon the rice into warmed serving bowls and serve immediately, sprinkled with extra Parmesan, if you like.

Courgettes with Rice Energy 201kcal/837kJ; Protein 5.6g; Carbohydrate 30.1g, of which sugars 8g; Fat 6.6g, of which saturates 1g; Cholesterol 0mg; Calcium 72mg; Fibre 3g; Sodium 10mg.
Rosemary Risotto Energy 651kcal/2740kJ; Protein 25g; Carbohydrate 87g, of which sugars 4.6g; Fat 22.2g, of which saturates 10.5g; Cholesterol 41.9mg; Calcium 357mg; Fibre 7.1g; Sodium 1462mg.

Clay-pot Saffron Risotto with Spinach

Rice cooks to perfection in the moist environment of a clay pot. This risotto can be made without the constant checking usually needed.

Serves 4

a few saffron threads
30ml/2 tbsp boiling water
15ml/1 tbsp olive oil
50g/2oz/¼ cup butter
1 onion, finely chopped
350g/12oz/1¾ cups risotto rice
900ml/1½ pints/3¾ cups warm vegetable stock
150ml/¼ pint/⅔ cup dry white wine
225g/8oz baby spinach leaves
300ml/½ pint/1¼ cups hot vegetable stock
40g/1½oz/¼ cup shelled walnuts, chopped
75g/3oz Parmesan cheese, shaved
salt and ground black pepper

1 Soak a large clay pot in cold water for 20 minutes, then drain. Meanwhile, place the saffron in a bowl, cover with the boiling water and set aside.

2 Heat the oil and half the butter in a large, heavy pan. Add the onion and cook gently for 5 minutes, or until soft, stirring occasionally. Add the rice and stir for about 3 minutes, until the grains are thoroughly coated in oil and butter.

3 Pour the stock into the clay pot, add the saffron water, wine and the rice mixture, and stir together. Cover and place in an unheated oven. Set the oven to 190°C/375°F/Gas 5 and cook for 50 minutes, stirring after 30 minutes.

4 Stir in the spinach, add the stock, then cover and cook for 10 minutes, or until the rice is tender. Stir in the walnuts, the remaining butter and half the Parmesan cheese. Season and serve sprinkled with the remaining Parmesan shavings.

Cook's Tip

Risotto is made from Italian short grain rice, of which there are several varieties. Arborio rice is widely available, but you may also find carnaroli and vialone nano. When cooked, risotto rice has a creamy consistency but the grains retain a slight 'bite'.

Vegetable Paella

A colourful assortment of vegetables is slowly baked with rice to make this dish.

Serves 4

1 large aubergine (eggplant)
45ml/3 tbsp extra virgin olive or sunflower oil
2 onions, quartered and sliced
2 garlic cloves, crushed
300g/11oz/1½ cups short grain Spanish or risotto rice
1.2–1.5 litres/2–2½ pints/5–6¼ cups vegetable stock
1 red (bell) pepper, halved, seeded and sliced
1 yellow (bell) pepper, halved, seeded and sliced
200g/7oz fine green beans, halved
115g/4oz/scant 2 cups chestnut mushrooms, quartered, or brown cap (cremini) or button (white) mushrooms, halved
1 dried chilli, crushed
115g/4oz/1 cup frozen peas
salt and ground black pepper
fresh coriander (cilantro) leaves, to garnish

1 Soak a clay pot or Chinese sand pot in cold water for 20 minutes, then drain. Cut the aubergine in half lengthways, then cut it crossways into thin slices.

2 Heat 30ml/2 tbsp of the oil in a large frying pan, add the aubergine slices and cook until golden. Transfer to the clay pot. Add the remaining oil, and cook the onion, stirring occasionally, for a few minutes until golden.

3 Add the garlic and rice and cook for 1–2 minutes, stirring, until the rice becomes transparent. Pour 900ml/1½ pints/3¾ cups of the stock into the clay pot, then add the rice mixture.

4 Stir in the peppers, green beans, mushrooms, chilli and seasoning. Cover the pot and place in an unheated oven.

5 Set the oven to 200°C/400°F/Gas 6 and cook for 1 hour, or until the rice is almost tender. After 40 minutes, remove the pot from the oven and add a little more stock to moisten the paella. Stir well, re-cover and return to the oven.

6 Add the peas and a little more stock to the paella and cook for a further 10 minutes. Adjust the seasoning and sprinkle over the coriander. Lightly stir through and then serve.

Clay-pot Risotto Energy 630kcal/2618kJ; Protein 17.2g; Carbohydrate 72.6g, of which sugars 2.3g; Fat 26.9g, of which saturates 11.4g; Cholesterol 45mg; Calcium 356mg; Fibre 1.8g; Sodium 362mg.
Vegetable Paella Energy 458kcal/1911kJ; Protein 11.8g; Carbohydrate 80g, of which sugars 14.3g; Fat 10.3g, of which saturates 1.5g; Cholesterol 0mg; Calcium 80mg; Fibre 7.1g; Sodium 10mg

Savoury Nut Loaf

Ideal as an alternative to the traditional meat roast, this wholesome, slow-cooker dish is perfect for special occasions. It is also good with a fresh tomato sauce.

Serves 4

30ml/2 tbsp olive oil, plus extra for greasing
1 onion, finely chopped
1 leek, finely chopped
2 celery sticks, finely chopped
225g/8oz/3 cups mushrooms, chopped
2 garlic cloves, crushed
425g/15oz can lentils, rinsed and drained
115g/4oz/1 cup mixed nuts, such as hazelnuts, cashew nuts and almonds, finely chopped
50g/2oz/½ cup plain (all-purpose) flour
50g/2oz/½ cup grated mature (sharp) Cheddar cheese
1 egg, beaten
45–60ml/3–4 tbsp chopped fresh mixed herbs
salt and ground black pepper
chives and sprigs of fresh flat leaf parsley, to garnish

1 Place an upturned saucer or metal pastry ring in the base of the ceramic cooking pot. Pour in about 2.5cm/1in hot water and switch the slow cooker to high. Lightly grease the base and sides of a 900g/2lb loaf tin (pan) or terrine that will fit in the cooker. Line the base and sides with baking parchment.

2 Heat the oil in a large pan, add the onion, leek, celery, mushrooms and garlic, then cook for 10 minutes until softened. Remove the pan from the heat, then stir in the lentils, nuts and flour, cheese, egg and herbs. Season with salt and pepper.

3 Spoon the nut mixture into the prepared loaf tin or terrine, pressing right into the corners. Level the surface, then cover the tin with a piece of foil. Place in the ceramic cooking pot and pour in enough near-boiling water to come just over halfway up the side of the dish. Cover the slow cooker with the lid and cook for 3–4 hours, or until the loaf is firm to the touch.

4 Leave the loaf to cool in the tin for about 15 minutes, then turn out on to a serving plate. Serve the loaf hot or cold, cut into thick slices and garnished with fresh chives and sprigs of flat leaf parsley.

Beetroot Casserole

This slowly simmered casserole can be served as a light meal in itself or with a simple salad. It has a wonderful sweet and sour flavour.

Serves 4

50g/2oz/4 tbsp butter
1 onion, chopped
2 garlic cloves, crushed
675g/1½lb uncooked beetroot, peeled
2 large carrots, peeled
½ lemon
115g/4oz/1½ cups button (white) mushrooms
300ml/½ pint/1¼ cups hot vegetable stock
2 bay leaves
15ml/1 tbsp chopped fresh mint, plus sprigs to garnish (optional)
salt and ground black pepper

For the hot dressing

150ml/¼ pint/⅔ cup sour cream
2.5ml/½ tsp paprika, plus extra to garnish

1 Melt the butter in a pan and fry the onion and garlic for 5 minutes. Meanwhile, dice the beetroot and carrot. Grate the rind and squeeze the juice of the ½ lemon. Add the beetroot, carrots and mushrooms and fry for 5 minutes.

2 Pour in the stock with the lemon rind and bay leaves. Season with salt and pepper. Bring to the boil, turn down the heat, cover and simmer for 1 hour, or until the vegetables are soft.

3 Turn off the heat and stir in the lemon juice and chopped mint, if using. Leave the pan to stand, covered, for 5 minutes, to develop the flavours.

4 Meanwhile, for the dressing, gently heat the sour cream and paprika in a pan, stirring all the time, until bubbling. Transfer the beetroot mixture to a serving bowl, then spoon over the dressing. Serve garnished with mint and extra paprika, if you like.

Cook's Tip
Wear clean rubber or plastic gloves to avoid staining your hands when preparing beetroot.

Savoury Nut Loaf Energy 484kcal/2019kJ; Protein 23.7g; Carbohydrate 34.1g, of which sugars 5.1g; Fat 29g, of which saturates 5.4g; Cholesterol 69mg; Calcium 238mg; Fibre 8.7g; Sodium 128mg.
Beetroot Energy 256kcal/1064kJ; Protein 5.3g; Carbohydrate 18.5g, of which sugars 16.1g; Fat 18.5g, of which saturates 11.3g; Cholesterol 49mg; Calcium 87mg; Fibre 4.3g; Sodium 212mg.

Mixed Bean and Aubergine Tagine

A bean pot or tagine is used for slowly cooking this dish.

Serves 4

115g/4oz/generous ½ cup dried red kidney beans, soaked overnight and drained
115g/4oz/generous ½ cup dried black-eyed beans (peas) or cannellini beans, soaked overnight and drained
600ml/1 pint/2½ cups water
2 bay leaves
2 celery sticks, cut into 8 pieces
75ml/5 tbsp olive oil
1 aubergine (eggplant), about 350g/12oz, cut into chunks
1 onion, thinly sliced
3 garlic cloves, crushed
1–2 fresh red chillies, seeded and finely chopped
30ml/2 tbsp tomato purée (paste)
5ml/1 tsp paprika
2 large tomatoes, roughly chopped
300ml/½ pint/1¼ cups hot vegetable stock
15ml/1 tbsp each chopped mint, parsley and coriander (cilantro)
salt and ground black pepper
fresh herb sprigs, to garnish

For the mint yogurt

150ml/¼ pint/⅔ cup natural (plain) yogurt
30ml/2 tbsp chopped fresh mint
2 spring onions (scallions), chopped

1 Place the kidney beans in a large pan of boiling water. Bring back to the boil and boil rapidly for 10 minutes, then drain. Place the black-eyed or cannellini beans in a separate pan of boiling water and boil rapidly for 10 minutes, then drain.

2 Place the measured water in a soaked bean pot or tagine, add the bay leaves, celery and beans. Cover and place in an unheated oven set to 190°C/375°F/Gas 5. Cook for 1–1½ hours. Drain well.

3 Heat the oil in a frying pan. Cook the aubergine until browned. Set aside. Cook the onion for 5 minutes, then add the garlic and chillies for 5 minutes. Stir the tomato purée and paprika into the pan for 1–2 minutes. Reduce the oven to 160°C/325°F/Gas 3.

4 Transfer the contents of the pan to the bean pot or tagine. Add the tomatoes, cooked aubergine, drained beans and stock. Cook in the oven for 1 hour.

5 Mix together the mint yogurt ingredients. Stir the herbs into the tagine and season. Serve garnished with the herb sprigs.

Baked Stuffed Apples

Tangy apples are stuffed with an aromatic pilaff, then slowly baked in the oven.

Serves 4

4 cooking apples, or any firm, sour apple of your choice
30ml/2 tbsp olive oil
juice of ½ lemon
10ml/2 tsp sugar
salt and ground black pepper

For the filling

30ml/2 tbsp olive oil
a little butter
1 onion, finely chopped
2 garlic cloves
30ml/2 tbsp pine nuts
30ml/2 tbsp currants, soaked in warm water for 5–10 minutes and drained
5–10ml/1–2 tsp ground cinnamon
5–10ml/1–2 tsp ground allspice
5ml/1 tsp sugar
175g/6oz/scant 1 cup short grain rice, thoroughly rinsed and drained
1 bunch each of fresh flat leaf parsley and dill, finely chopped

To serve

1 tomato
1 lemon
a few fresh mint or basil leaves

1 Make the filling. Heat the oil and butter in a heavy pan, stir in the onion and garlic and cook until soft. Add the pine nuts and currants and cook until the nuts turn golden. Stir in the spices, sugar and rice, and pour in water to just cover. Bring to the boil.

2 Season with salt and pepper. Lower the heat and simmer for 10–12 minutes, until almost all the water has been absorbed. Stir in the herbs and turn off the heat. Cover the pan with a dish towel and the lid, and leave the rice to steam for 5 minutes.

3 Preheat the oven to 200°C/400°F/Gas 6. Using a knife, cut the stalk ends off the apples and keep to use as lids. Core each apple, removing some of the flesh to create a cavity for stuffing. Pack spoonfuls of the filling into the apples. Replace the lids and stand the apples, tightly packed, in a small baking dish.

4 In a bowl, mix together 120ml/4fl oz/½ cup water with the oil, lemon juice and sugar. Pour over and around the apples, then bake for 30–40 minutes, until tender and the juices are caramelized. Serve immediately, with a tomato and lemon garnish and a sprinkling of mint or basil leaves.

Mixed Bean Tagine Energy 328kcal/1377kJ; Protein 14.9g; Carbohydrate 35.2g, of which sugars 9.3g; Fat 15.3g, of which saturates 2.2g; Cholesterol 0mg; Calcium 96mg; Fibre 12.8g; Sodium 28mg.
Baked Stuffed Apples Energy 382kcal/1595kJ; Protein 5g; Carbohydrate 54.1g, of which sugars 18.8g; Fat 16.5g, of which saturates 1.9g; Cholesterol 0mg; Calcium 26mg; Fibre 2.1g; Sodium 4mg.

Onions Stuffed with Goat's Cheese and Sun-dried Tomatoes

Long, gentle cooking is the best way to get maximum flavour from onions, so the slow cooker is the natural choice for this delicious stuffed-onion dish.

Serves 4

2 large onions, unpeeled
30ml/2 tbsp olive oil (or use oil from the sun-dried tomatoes)
150g/5oz/⅔ cup firm goat's cheese, crumbled or cubed
50g/2oz/1 cup fresh white breadcrumbs
8 sun-dried tomatoes in olive oil, drained and chopped
1 garlic clove, finely chopped
2.5ml/½ tsp fresh thyme
30ml/2 tbsp chopped fresh parsley
1 small egg, beaten
45ml/3 tbsp pine nuts
150ml/¼ pint/⅔ cup near-boiling vegetable stock
salt and ground black pepper
chopped fresh parsley, to garnish

1 Bring a large pan of water to the boil. Add the whole onions in their skins and boil for 10 minutes.

2 Drain the onions and leave until cool enough to handle, then cut each onion in half horizontally and peel. Using a teaspoon, remove the centre of each onion, leaving a thick shell.

3 Very finely chop the flesh from one of the scooped-out onion halves and place in a bowl. Stir in 5ml/1 tsp of the olive oil or oil from the sun-dried tomatoes, then add the goat's cheese, breadcrumbs, sun-dried tomatoes, garlic, thyme, parsley, egg and pine nuts. Season with salt and pepper and mix well.

4 Divide the stuffing among the onions and cover each one with a piece of oiled foil. Brush the base of the ceramic cooking pot with 15ml/1 tbsp of oil, then pour in the stock. Put the onions in the base of the cooking pot, cover and cook on high for 4 hours, or until the onions are tender but still hold their shape.

5 Remove the onions from the slow cooker and transfer them to a grill (broiler) pan. Remove the foil and drizzle with the remaining oil. Brown under the grill for 3–4 minutes, taking care not to burn the nuts. Serve immediately, garnished with parsley.

Pumpkin Stuffed with Apricot Pilaff

An oven-baked pumpkin filled with a fruity pilaff makes a great centrepiece.

Serves 4–6

1 pumpkin, weighing about 1.2kg/2½lb
225g/8oz/generous 1 cup long grain rice, well rinsed
30–45ml/2–3 tbsp olive oil
15ml/1 tbsp butter
a few saffron threads
5ml/1 tsp coriander seeds
2–3 strips of orange peel, pith removed and finely sliced
45–60ml/3–4 tbsp shelled pistachio nuts
30–45ml/2–3 tbsp dried cranberries, soaked in boiling water for 5 minutes and drained
175g/6oz/¾ cup ready-to-eat dried apricots, sliced or chopped
1 bunch of fresh basil, leaves torn
1 bunch each of fresh coriander (cilantro), mint and flat leaf parsley, coarsely chopped
salt and ground black pepper
lemon wedges and thick natural (plain) yogurt, to serve

1 Preheat the oven to 200°C/400°F/Gas 6. Wash the pumpkin and cut off the stalk end to use as a lid. Scoop all the seeds out of the middle with a spoon, and pull out the stringy bits. Replace the lid, put the pumpkin on a baking tray and bake for 1 hour.

2 Meanwhile, put the rice in a pan and pour in enough water to cover. Add a pinch of salt and bring to the boil, then partially cover the pan and simmer for 10–12 minutes, until the water has been absorbed and the rice is cooked but still has a bite.

3 Heat the oil and butter in a heavy pan. Stir in the saffron, coriander seeds, orange peel, pistachios, cranberries and apricots, then stir in the cooked rice. Season with salt and pepper. Turn off the heat, cover the pan with a dish towel and the lid and leave the pilaff to steam for 10 minutes, then toss in the herbs.

4 Spoon the pilaff into the cavity in the pumpkin. Put the lid back on and bake in the oven for a further 20 minutes.

5 To serve, remove the lid and slice a round off the top of the pumpkin. Place the ring on a plate and spoon some pilaff in the middle. Prepare the rest in the same way. Serve with lemon wedges and a bowl of yogurt.

Onions with Cheese Energy 330kcal/1370kJ; Protein 13.8g; Carbohydrate 14.3g, of which sugars 11.3g; Fat 24.7g, of which saturates 8.4g; Cholesterol 83.7mg; Calcium 98mg; Fibre 1.9g; Sodium 349mg.
Pumpkin Energy 345kcal/1443kJ; Protein 9.9g; Carbohydrate 50.1g, of which sugars 18.6g; Fat 12g, of which saturates 2.6g; Cholesterol 5mg; Calcium 299mg; Fibre 9.6g; Sodium 93mg.

Couscous-stuffed Sweet Peppers

This slow-cooker recipe for stuffed peppers couldn't be easier. The peppers are softened in boiling water before filling to ensure really tender results. Choose red, yellow or orange peppers for this dish, but avoid green ones because they tend to discolour after a couple of hours of cooking.

Serves 4

4 (bell) peppers
75g/3oz/½ cup instant couscous
75ml/2½fl oz/⅓ cup boiling vegetable stock
15ml/1 tbsp olive oil
10ml/2 tsp white wine vinegar
50g/2oz ready-to-eat dried apricots, finely chopped
75g/3oz feta cheese, cut into tiny cubes
3 ripe tomatoes, skinned, seeded and chopped
45ml/3 tbsp toasted pine nuts
30ml/2 tbsp finely chopped fresh parsley
salt and ground black pepper
flat leaf parsley, to garnish

1 Halve the peppers lengthways, then remove the cores and seeds. Place the peppers in a large heatproof bowl and pour over boiling water to cover. Leave to stand for about 3 minutes, then drain thoroughly and set aside.

2 Meanwhile, put the couscous in a small bowl and pour over the stock. Leave to stand for about 5 minutes, until all the water has been absorbed.

3 Using a fork, fluff up the couscous, then stir in the oil, vinegar, apricots, feta cheese, tomatoes, pine nuts and parsley, and season to taste with salt and ground black pepper.

4 Place spoonfuls of the couscous mixture into the pepper halves, gently packing it down using the back of the spoon.

5 Place the peppers, filling side up, in the ceramic cooking pot, then pour 150ml/¼ pint/⅔ cup near-boiling water around them.

6 Cover the cooker with the lid, switch to the high setting and cook for 2–3 hours, or until the peppers are tender. Brown them under a hot grill (broiler) for 2 minutes, if you like, and serve garnished with fresh parsley.

Stuffed Onions, Potatoes and Courgettes

The vegetarian filling of these oven-roasted vegetables is mildly spiced and has the sharp tang of lemon juice. They are also excellent cold and are good served as an appetizer, as well as a main course.

Serves 4

4 potatoes, peeled
4 onions, skinned
4 courgettes (zucchini), halved widthways
2–4 garlic cloves, chopped
45–60ml/3–4 tbsp olive oil
45–60ml/3–4 tbsp tomato purée (paste)
1.5ml/¼ tsp ras curry powder
large pinch of ground allspice
seeds of 2–3 cardamom pods
juice of ½ lemon
30–45ml/2–3 tbsp chopped fresh parsley
90–120ml/6–8 tbsp hot vegetable stock
salt and ground black pepper
salad, to serve (optional)

1 Bring a large pan of salted water to the boil. Starting with the potatoes, then the onions and finally the courgettes, add to the boiling water and cook until they become almost tender but not cooked through. Allow about 10 minutes for the potatoes, 8 minutes for the onions and 4–6 minutes for the courgettes. Remove the vegetables from the pan and leave to cool.

2 When the vegetables are cool enough to handle, hollow them out using a knife and spoon. Preheat the oven to 190°C/375°F/Gas 5.

3 Finely chop the cut-out vegetable flesh and put it in a bowl. Add the garlic, half the olive oil, the tomato purée, curry powder, allspice, cardamom seeds, lemon juice, parsley, salt and pepper and mix well together. Use the stuffing mixture to fill the hollowed vegetables.

4 Arrange the stuffed vegetables in a roasting pan and drizzle with the vegetable stock and the remaining oil. Roast for about 35–40 minutes, or until they are golden brown. Serve warm or cold, with a salad, if you like.

Sweet Peppers Energy 303kcal/1266kJ; Protein 33.7g; Carbohydrate 33.6g, of which sugars 17g; Fat 15.8g, of which saturates 3.9g; Cholesterol 13mg; Calcium 105mg; Fibre 4.3g; Sodium 285mg.
Stuffed Onions Energy 347kcal/1452kJ; Protein 10.2g; Carbohydrate 56.7g, of which sugars 22.1g; Fat 10.3g, of which saturates 1.6g; Cholesterol 0mg; Calcium 135mg; Fibre 8.2g; Sodium 62mg.

Spicy Parsnip and Chickpea Stew

Sweet parsnips go very well with the spices in this Indian-style vegetable stew, made in the slow cooker.

Serves 4

5 garlic cloves, finely chopped
1 small onion, chopped
5cm/2in piece fresh root ginger, finely chopped
2 green chillies, seeded and chopped
75ml/5 tbsp cold water
60ml/4 tbsp groundnut (peanut) oil
5ml/1 tsp cumin seeds
10ml/2 tsp coriander seeds
5ml/1 tsp ground turmeric
2.5ml/½ tsp chilli powder or mild paprika
50g/2oz/½ cup cashew nuts, toasted and ground
225g/8oz tomatoes, peeled and chopped
400g/14oz can chickpeas, drained and rinsed
900g/2lb parsnips, cut into chunks
350ml/12fl oz/1½ cups boiling vegetable stock
juice of 1 lime, to taste
salt and ground black pepper
chopped fresh coriander (cilantro) leaves, toasted cashew nuts and natural (plain) yogurt, to serve

1 Reserve 10ml/2 tsp of the garlic, then place the remainder in a food processor or blender with the onion, ginger and half the chilli. Add the water and process to a smooth paste.

2 Heat the oil in a large frying pan, add the cumin seeds and cook for 30 seconds. Stir in the coriander seeds, turmeric, chilli powder or paprika and the ground cashew nuts. Add the ginger and chilli paste and cook, stirring frequently, until the paste bubbles and the water starts to evaporate.

3 Add the tomatoes to the pan and cook for 1 minute. Transfer the mixture to the ceramic cooking pot and switch the slow cooker to high. Add the chickpeas and parsnips to the pot and stir to coat in the spicy tomato mixture, then stir in the stock and season with salt and pepper. Cover with the lid and cook on high for 4 hours, or until the parsnips are tender.

4 Stir half the lime juice, the reserved garlic and green chilli into the stew. Re-cover and cook for 30 minutes more, then taste and add more lime juice if needed. Spoon on to plates and sprinkle with fresh coriander leaves and toasted cashew nuts. Serve immediately, with a generous spoonful of natural yogurt.

Spiced Clay-pot Chickpeas

This sweet and spicy dish has a well-developed flavour after long, slow cooking in a clay pot. Serve it hot as a main course with rice or couscous, or serve cold as a salad, drizzled with olive oil and lemon juice.

Serves 4

250g/9oz/1½ cups dried chickpeas, soaked overnight in cold water
30ml/2 tbsp olive oil
2 onions, cut into wedges
10ml/2 tsp ground cumin
1.5ml/¼ tsp ground turmeric
1.5ml/¼ tsp cayenne pepper
15ml/1 tbsp ground coriander
5ml/1 tsp ground cinnamon
300ml/½ pint/1¼ cups hot vegetable stock
2 carrots, sliced
115g/4oz/½ cup ready-to-eat dried apricots, halved
50g/2oz/scant ½ cup raisins
25g/1oz/¼ cup flaked (sliced) almonds
30ml/2 tbsp chopped fresh coriander (cilantro)
30ml/2 tbsp chopped fresh flat leaf parsley
salt and ground black pepper

1 Soak a bean clay pot in cold water for 20 minutes, then drain. Place the chickpeas in a pan with plenty of cold water. Bring to the boil and boil rapidly for 10 minutes, then place the chickpeas in the bean pot, pour in lukewarm water and cover.

2 Place in an unheated oven and set the temperature to 200°C/400°F/Gas 6. Cook for 1 hour, then reduce the oven temperature to 160°C/325°/Gas 3. Cook for another hour, or until the chickpeas are tender.

3 Meanwhile, place the olive oil and onions in a frying pan and cook for 6–8 minutes, or until softened. Add the cumin, turmeric, cayenne, coriander and cinnamon and cook for 2–3 minutes. Stir in the stock, carrots, apricots, raisins and almonds and bring the mixture to the boil.

4 Drain the chickpeas, add the spicy vegetable mixture to the clay pot and stir. Cover and return to the oven for 30 minutes.

5 Season with salt and pepper, stir in half the fresh coriander and parsley, and serve sprinkled with the remainder.

Spicy Parsnip Stew Energy 453kcal/1899kJ; Protein 14.8g; Carbohydrate 50.1g, of which sugars 16.6g; Fat 23g, of which saturates 4.3g; Cholesterol 0mg; Calcium 148mg; Fibre 15.8g; Sodium 394mg.
Spiced Chickpeas Energy 403kcal/1696kJ; Protein 17.1g; Carbohydrate 58.5g, of which sugars 27.1g; Fat 12.8g, of which saturates 1.4g; Cholesterol 0mg; Calcium 167mg; Fibre 10.9g; Sodium 45mg.

Spicy Chickpea and Aubergine Stew

Aubergines and chickpeas go particularly well with the warm spices in this substantial stew. Serve with boiled rice, or on its own with some Indian breads, if you prefer.

Serves 4

3 garlic cloves
2 large onions
3 large aubergines (eggplants)
200g/7oz/1 cup chickpeas, soaked overnight
60ml/4 tbsp olive oil
2.5ml/½ tsp ground cumin
2.5ml/½ tsp ground cinnamon
2.5ml/½ tsp ground coriander
3 x 400g/14oz cans chopped tomatoes
salt and ground black pepper
boiled rice (optional), to serve

For the garnish

30ml/2 tbsp olive oil
1 onion, sliced
1 garlic clove, sliced
sprigs of fresh coriander (cilantro)

1 Chop the garlic and onions and set aside. Cut the aubergines into bitesize cubes. Place the aubergine cubes in a colander and sprinkle them with salt. Sit the colander in a bowl and leave for 30 minutes, to allow the bitter juices to escape. Rinse the aubergine with cold water and dry on kitchen paper. Set aside.

2 Drain the chickpeas and put in a pan with enough water to cover. Bring to the boil and boil vigorously for 10 minutes, skimming off any foam that rises to the surface. Reduce the heat and simmer for 1–1½ hours, or until tender. Drain.

3 Heat the oil in a large pan. Add the garlic and onion, and cook until soft. Add the spices and cook, stirring, for a few seconds. Add the aubergine and stir. Cook for 5 minutes.

4 Add the tomatoes and chickpeas and season with salt and pepper. Cover and simmer for 20 minutes.

5 To make the garnish, heat the olive oil in a frying pan and, when very hot, add the sliced onion and garlic. Fry, stirring constantly, until golden and crisp.

6 Serve the stew with boiled rice, if using, topped with onion and garlic and garnished with fresh coriander.

Saffron and Pickled Walnut Pilaff

Fragrant saffron gives this lovely slow-cooker dish a warm, spiced flavour and a glorious colour.

Serves 4

5ml/1 tsp saffron threads
50g/2oz/½ cup pine nuts
45ml/3 tbsp olive oil
1 large onion, finely chopped
3 garlic cloves, crushed
1.5ml/¼ tsp ground allspice
4cm/1½in piece fresh root ginger, grated
750ml/1¼ pints/3 cups boiling vegetable stock
300g/10oz/generous 1½ cups easy-cook (converted) rice
50g/2oz/½ cup pickled walnuts, drained and roughly chopped
40g/1½2oz/¼ cup raisins
45ml/3 tbsp roughly chopped fresh parsley or coriander (cilantro)
salt and ground black pepper
parsley or coriander (cilantro) leaves, to garnish
natural (plain) yogurt, to serve

1 Put the saffron threads in a heatproof bowl with 15ml/1 tbsp boiling water and leave to stand. Meanwhile, heat a large frying pan and dry-fry the pine nuts until golden. Set them aside.

2 Heat the oil in a pan, add the onion and fry for 8 minutes. Stir in the garlic, allspice and ginger and cook for 2 minutes, stirring constantly. Transfer to the ceramic cooking pot. Pour the stock into the cooking pot and stir to combine, then cover with the lid and switch to high. Cook for 1 hour.

3 Sprinkle the rice into the cooking pot, then stir to mix thoroughly. Re-cover with the lid and cook for 1 hour, or until the rice is almost tender and most of the stock has been absorbed. Add a little extra stock or water to the pot if the mixture is already becoming dry.

4 Stir the saffron and soaking liquid into the rice, then add the pine nuts, walnuts, raisins and parsley or coriander, and stir well to combine. Season to taste with salt and ground black pepper.

5 Re-cover the pot with the lid and cook for 15 minutes, until the rice is very tender and all the ingredients are completely warmed through. Garnish with fresh parsley or coriander leaves and serve with a bowl of natural yogurt.

Chickpea Stew Energy 201kcal/843kJ; Protein 7.1g; Carbohydrate 22.3g, of which sugars 10.4g; Fat 10g, of which saturates 1.4g; Cholesterol 0mg; Calcium 57mg; Fibre 5.9g; Sodium 175mg.
Pilaff Energy 585kcal/2456kJ; Protein 10.2g; Carbohydrate 77.1g, of which sugars 11.1g; Fat 28.5g, of which saturates 3.1g; Cholesterol 0mg; Calcium 72mg; Fibre 2g; Sodium 222mg.

Spiced Indian Rice with Spinach, Tomatoes and Cashew Nuts

This all-in-one rice dish is simple to prepare in the slow cooker and makes a delicious, nutritious meal for all the family. It can also be served as a tasty accompaniment to a spicy meat curry.

Serves 4

30ml/2 tbsp sunflower oil
15ml/1 tbsp ghee or unsalted butter
1 onion, finely chopped
2 garlic cloves, crushed
3 tomatoes, peeled, seeded and chopped
275g/10oz/1½ cups easy-cook (converted) brown rice
5ml/1 tsp each ground coriander and ground cumin, or 10ml/2 tsp dhana jeera powder
2 carrots, coarsely grated
750ml/1¼ pints/3 cups boiling vegetable stock
175g/6oz baby spinach leaves, washed
50g/2oz/½ cup unsalted cashew nuts, toasted
salt and ground black pepper

1 Heat the oil and ghee or butter in a heavy pan, add the onion and fry gently for 6–7 minutes, until soft. Add the garlic and chopped tomatoes and cook for a further 2 minutes.

2 Rinse the rice in a sieve (strainer) under cold running water, drain well and transfer to the pan. Add the coriander and cumin or dhana jeera powder and stir for a few seconds. Turn off the heat and transfer the mixture from the pan to the ceramic cooking pot.

3 Stir the carrots into the cooking pot, then pour in the stock, season with salt and pepper, and stir to mix. Switch the slow cooker on to high. Cover and cook for 1 hour.

4 Lay the spinach on the surface of the rice, replace the lid and cook for a further 30–40 minutes, or until the spinach has wilted and the rice is cooked and tender.

5 Stir the spinach into the rice in the pot and check the seasoning, adding a little more salt and pepper, if necessary. Sprinkle the cashew nuts over the rice and serve immediately.

Vegetable Kashmiri

Tender vegetables simmered in the slow cooker in a spicy and aromatic yogurt sauce make a lovely vegetarian main meal.

Serves 4

10ml/2 tsp cumin seeds
8 black peppercorns
2 green cardamom pods, seeds only
5cm/2in cinnamon stick
2.5ml/½ tsp grated nutmeg
45ml/3 tbsp vegetable oil
1 fresh green chilli, seeded and chopped
2.5cm/1in piece fresh root ginger, grated
5ml/1 tsp chilli powder
2.5ml/½ tsp salt
2 large potatoes, cut into 2.5cm/1in chunks
225g/8oz cauliflower florets
400ml/14fl oz/1⅔ cups boiling vegetable stock
150ml/¼ pint/⅔ cup Greek (US strained plain) yogurt
225g/8oz okra, thickly sliced
toasted flaked (sliced) almonds and sprigs of fresh coriander (cilantro), to garnish

1 Put the cumin seeds, peppercorns, cardamom seeds, cinnamon stick and nutmeg in a mortar or spice grinder, and grind to a fine powder.

2 Heat the oil in a frying pan, add the chilli and ginger and fry for 2 minutes, stirring all the time. Add the chilli powder, salt and ground spice mixture to the pan, and fry gently for 2–3 minutes, stirring constantly to prevent the spices from sticking to the pan.

3 Transfer the mixture to the ceramic cooking pot and stir in the potatoes and cauliflower. Pour in all but a few spoonfuls of the stock, cover with the lid, and cook on high for 2 hours.

4 In a bowl, stir the remaining hot stock into the yogurt, then pour over the vegetable mixture in the cooking pot, and stir until thoroughly combined.

5 Add the okra to the pot, stir, cover and cook for a further 1½–2 hours, or until all the vegetables are very tender. Serve the curry straight from the ceramic cooking pot, or spoon into a warmed serving dish. Sprinkle with toasted almonds and fresh coriander sprigs, to garnish.

Spiced Indian Rice Energy 473kcal/1989kJ; Protein 10.1g; Carbohydrate 72.1g, of which sugars 9.2g; Fat 18g, of which saturates 4.5g; Cholesterol 8mg; Calcium 111mg; Fibre 4.8g; Sodium 349mg.
Vegetable Kashmiri Energy 294kcal/1231kJ; Protein 9g; Carbohydrate 35.5g, of which sugars 7g; Fat 13.8g, of which saturates 4g; Cholesterol 6mg; Calcium 161mg; Fibre 5.1g; Sodium 427mg.

Vegetable and Cashew Nut Biriani

This hearty slow-cooker dish is full of Indian flavours.

Serves 4

1 small aubergine (eggplant), sliced
3 onions, 1 chopped, 2 finely sliced
2 garlic cloves
2.5cm/1in piece fresh root ginger, peeled
about 60ml/4 tbsp sunflower oil
3 parsnips, cut into 2cm/¾in pieces
5ml/1 tsp ground cumin
5ml/1 tsp ground coriander
2.5ml/½ tsp chilli powder
750ml/1¼ pints/3 cups boiling vegetable stock
1 red (bell) pepper, sliced
275g/10oz/generous 1½ cups easy-cook (converted) basmati or white rice
175g/6oz/1½ cup unsalted cashew nuts
40g/1½oz/¼ cup sultanas (golden raisins)
salt and ground black pepper
2 hard-boiled eggs, quartered, and sprigs of fresh coriander (cilantro), to garnish

1 Sprinkle the aubergine slices with salt in a colander. Leave for 30 minutes, then rinse thoroughly, pat dry and cut into bitesize pieces. Add the chopped onion to a food processor with the garlic and ginger. Add enough cold water to process to a paste.

2 Heat 30ml/2 tbsp of the oil in a frying pan, and cook the sliced onions for 10 minutes. Add the aubergine and parsnips and cook for 4 minutes. Transfer to the ceramic cooking pot and set to high.

3 Add 15ml/1 tbsp oil to the pan, and fry the onion paste with the cumin, coriander and chilli powder for 3–4 minutes. Stir in one-third of the stock, then transfer the mixture to the pot. Add the remaining stock and the pepper to the pot, then season and cover. Cook for 2–3 hours. Spoon the rice over the vegetables, then re-cover and cook for 45–55 minutes, until the rice is tender.

4 Meanwhile, heat the remaining oil in a clean frying pan, add the nuts and stir-fry for 2 minutes. Add the sultanas and fry for a few seconds. Drain the nuts and sultanas on kitchen paper.

5 Stir half the cashew nuts and sultanas into the vegetable rice. Turn off the slow cooker, cover and leave to stand for 5 minutes. Spoon the biriani on to a serving dish. Top with the remaining nuts and sultanas. Serve garnished with eggs and coriander.

Rice with Lime and Lemon Grass

The nutty flavour of brown rice is enhanced by the fragrance of limes and lemon grass in this tasty slow-cooker dish.

Serves 4

2 limes
1 lemon grass stalk
15ml/1 tbsp sunflower oil
1 onion, chopped
2.5cm/1in piece fresh root ginger, peeled and very finely chopped
7.5ml/1½ tsp coriander seeds
7.5ml/1½ tsp cumin seeds
750ml/1¼ pints/3 cups boiling vegetable stock
275g/10oz/1½ cups easy-cook (converted) brown rice
60ml/4 tbsp chopped fresh coriander (cilantro)
salt and ground black pepper
spring onions (scallions), toasted coconut strips and lime wedges, to garnish

1 Using a cannelle knife (zester) or fine grater, pare the rind from the limes, taking care not to remove any of the bitter white pith. Set the rind aside.

2 Cut off the lower portion of the lemon grass stalk, discarding the papery top end of the stalk. Finely chop the lemon grass and set aside.

3 Heat the oil in a large pan. Add the onion and cook over low heat for 5 minutes. Stir in the ginger, coriander and cumin seeds, lemon grass and lime rind, and cook for 2–3 minutes. Transfer the mixture to the ceramic cooking pot.

4 Pour the vegetable stock into the cooking pot, briefly stir to combine, then cover with the lid and switch the slow cooker to high. Cook for 1 hour.

5 Rinse the rice in cold running water until the water runs clear, then drain and add to the ceramic cooking pot. Cook for 45 minutes to 1½ hours, or until the rice is tender and has absorbed all the stock.

6 Stir the fresh coriander into the rice and season with salt and pepper. Fluff up the grains with a fork and serve garnished with strips of spring onion, toasted coconut and lime wedges.

Vegetable Biriani Energy 801kcal/3360kJ; Protein 18.7g; Carbohydrate 103.4g, of which sugars 25.7g; Fat 37.6g, of which saturates 6.7g; Cholesterol 0mg; Calcium 129mg; Fibre 9.2g; Sodium 230mg.
Rice with Lime Energy 308kcal/1304kJ; Protein 5.6g; Carbohydrate 64g, of which sugars 5.1g; Fat 5.1g, of which saturates 0.9g; Cholesterol 0mg; Calcium 17mg; Fibre 2g; Sodium 129mg.

Sweet Pumpkin and Peanut Curry

Rich, sweet, spicy and fragrant, the flavours of this Thai-style curry really come together during the long simmering in the slow cooker. Serve with plain boiled rice or noodles for a substantial supper dish.

Serves 4

30ml/2 tbsp vegetable oil
4 garlic cloves, crushed
4 shallots, finely chopped
30ml/2 tbsp yellow curry paste
2 kaffir lime leaves, torn
15ml/1 tbsp chopped fresh galangal
450g/1lb pumpkin, peeled, seeded and diced
225g/8oz sweet potatoes, diced
400ml/14fl oz/1⅔ cups near-boiling vegetable stock
300ml/½ pint/1¼ cups coconut milk
90g/3½oz/1½ cups chestnut mushrooms, sliced
15ml/1 tbsp soy sauce
90g/3½oz/scant 1 cup peanuts, roasted and chopped
50g/2oz/⅓ cup pumpkin seeds, toasted, and fresh green chilli flowers, to garnish

1 Heat the oil in a frying pan. Add the garlic and shallots and cook over medium heat, stirring occasionally, for 10 minutes, until softened and beginning to turn golden.

2 Add the yellow curry paste to the pan and stir-fry over medium heat for 30 seconds, until fragrant. Transfer the mixture to the ceramic cooking pot.

3 Add the lime leaves, galangal, pumpkin and sweet potatoes to the cooking pot. Pour the hot vegetable stock and about 150ml/¼ pint/⅔ cup of the coconut milk over the vegetables, and stir to combine. Cover with the lid and cook on the high setting for 1½ hours.

4 Stir the mushrooms and soy sauce into the curry, then add the chopped peanuts and pour in the remaining coconut milk. Cover and cook on high for a further 3 hours, or until the vegetables are very tender.

5 Spoon the curry into warmed serving bowls, garnish with the pumpkin seeds and chillies, and serve immediately.

Kidney Bean Curry

This is a delicious dish packed with spicy flavours. You can replace the dried beans with a can of pre-cooked beans if you do not have time for the long simmering. Other pulses also work well in this dish.

Serves 4

225g/8oz/scant 1 cup dried red kidney beans, soaked overnight and drained
30ml/2 tbsp vegetable oil
2.5ml/½ tsp cumin seeds
1 onion, thinly sliced
1 fresh green chilli, finely chopped
2 garlic cloves, crushed
2.5cm/1in piece fresh root ginger, grated
30ml/2 tbsp curry paste
5ml/1 tsp ground cumin
5ml/1 tsp ground coriander
2.5ml/½ tsp chilli powder
2.5ml/½ tsp salt
400g/14oz can chopped tomatoes
30ml/2 tbsp chopped fresh coriander (cilantro)

1 Put the soaked kidney beans in a large pan with double the volume of water. Boil vigorously for 10 minutes. Skim off any scum that rises to the surface. Cover and cook for 1–1½ hours or until the beans are soft. If you want to reduce the cooking time, cook the beans in a pressure cooker for 20–25 minutes. Alternatively, replace the dried beans with canned beans. Use a 400g/14oz can and drain it very thoroughly.

2 Meanwhile, heat the vegetable oil in a large, heavy frying pan. Add the cumin seeds and fry for 2–3 minutes, until they begin to splutter.

3 Add the onion, chilli, garlic and ginger, and fry, stirring frequently, for 5 minutes until the onion has softened. Stir in the curry paste, cumin, ground coriander, chilli powder and salt, and cook for 5 minutes, stirring constantly.

4 Add the chopped tomatoes to the pan and simmer for about 5 minutes. Drain the beans and stir them in with the fresh coriander, reserving a little of the herb for the garnish.

5 Cover the pan with a tight-fitting lid and simmer for about 20–25 minutes, adding a little water if necessary. Serve garnished with the reserved fresh coriander.

Sweet Pumpkin Curry Energy 337kcal/1404kJ; Protein 10.3g; Carbohydrate 21.7g, of which sugars 10.8g; Fat 23.8g, of which saturates 4g; Cholesterol 0mg; Calcium 168mg; Fibre 5.1g; Sodium 554mg.
Kidney Bean Curry Energy 156kcal/653kJ; Protein 6.4g; Carbohydrate 17g, of which sugars 5.4g; Fat 7.6g, of which saturates 1g; Cholesterol 0mg; Calcium 90mg; Fibre 5.1g; Sodium 236mg.

Masala Chana

Chickpeas are cooked in a variety of ways all over India. Tamarind adds a sharp, tangy flavour to this slowly simmered curry.

Serves 4

225g/8oz/1¼ cups dried chickpeas, soaked overnight and drained
50g/2oz tamarind stick
120ml/4fl oz/½ cup boiling water
30ml/2 tbsp oil
2.5ml/½ tsp cumin seeds
1 onion, finely chopped
2 garlic cloves, crushed
2.5cm/1in piece fresh root ginger, grated
1 fresh green chilli, finely chopped
5ml/1 tsp ground cumin
5ml/1 tsp ground coriander
1.5ml/¼ tsp ground turmeric
2.5ml/½ tsp salt
225g/8oz tomatoes, peeled and finely chopped
2.5ml/½ tsp garam masala
chopped fresh chillies and chopped onion, to garnish

1 Place the chickpeas in a large pan with double the volume of cold water. Bring to the boil and boil vigorously for 10 minutes. Skim off any scum that has risen to the surface of the liquid, using a slotted spoon. Lower the heat, cover the pan with a tight-fitting lid and simmer for 1½–2 hours or until the chickpeas are tender.

2 Meanwhile, break up the tamarind and soak in the boiling water for about 15–20 minutes. Rub the tamarind through a sieve (strainer) into a bowl, discarding any stones and fibre left behind in the sieve.

3 Heat the oil in a large, heavy pan and fry the cumin seeds for 2 minutes until they splutter. Add the onion, garlic, ginger and chilli, and fry for 5 minutes.

4 Stir in the cumin and coriander, with the turmeric and salt and fry for 3–4 minutes. Add the chopped tomatoes. Bring to the boil and then simmer for 5 minutes.

5 Drain the chickpeas and add to the tomato mixture together with the garam masala and tamarind pulp. Cover and simmer gently for about 25–30 minutes. Garnish with the chopped chillies and onion before serving.

Black Bean Hotpot

Molasses imparts a rich treacly flavour to the spicy sauce, which incorporates a stunning mix of black beans, vibrant red and yellow peppers and orange butternut squash. The hotpot is baked in the oven to help the flavours mingle.

Serves 4

225g/8oz/1¼ cups dried black beans, soaked overnight
1 bay leaf
30ml/2 tbsp vegetable oil
1 large onion, chopped
1 garlic clove, chopped
5ml/1 tsp mustard powder
15ml/1 tbsp molasses or black treacle
30ml/2 tbsp soft dark brown sugar
5ml/1 tsp dried thyme
2.5ml/½ tsp dried chilli flakes
5ml/1 tsp vegetable bouillon powder
1 red (bell) pepper, seeded and diced
1 yellow (bell) pepper, seeded and diced
675g/1½lb butternut squash or pumpkin, seeded and cut into 1cm/½in dice
salt and ground black pepper
sprigs of thyme, to garnish
cornbread or plain boiled rice, to serve

1 Drain the soaked black beans and rinse well. Place in a large pan, cover with fresh water and add the bay leaf. Bring to the boil, then boil rapidly for 10 minutes, skimming off any scum that rises to the surface. Reduce the heat, cover the pan and simmer for about 30 minutes, until tender. Drain, reserving the cooking water. Preheat the oven to 180°C/350°F/Gas 4.

2 Heat the oil in a flameproof casserole, add the onion and garlic and cook, stirring frequently, for 5 minutes until softened and turning golden. Stir in the mustard powder, molasses or treacle, sugar, dried thyme, chilli flakes and seasoning. Cook for about 1 minute, stirring, then stir in the black beans.

3 Add enough water to the reserved liquid to make 400ml/14fl oz/1⅔ cups, mix in the bouillon powder and pour into the casserole. Cover and cook in the oven for 25 minutes.

4 Stir in the peppers and the squash or pumpkin. Cover, then bake for a further 45 minutes until the vegetables are tender. Garnish with thyme sprigs and serve with cornbread or rice.

Masala Chana Energy 256kcal/1075kJ; Protein 13.1g; Carbohydrate 32.2g, of which sugars 4.1g; Fat 9.2g, of which saturates 1.1g; Cholesterol 0mg; Calcium 105mg; Fibre 6.8g; Sodium 285mg.
Black Bean Hotpot Energy 297kcal/1252kJ; Protein 15.1g; Carbohydrate 45.9g, of which sugars 20.3g; Fat 7.1g, of which saturates 1g; Cholesterol 0mg; Calcium 129mg; Fibre 12.6g; Sodium 16mg.

Roasted Squash with Rice Stuffing

Gem squash has a sweet, subtle taste that contrasts well with the olives and sun-dried tomatoes in this slow-baked recipe. The rice adds substance without changing any of the flavour.

Serves 4 as a side dish

4 whole gem squashes
225g/8oz cooked white long grain rice (about 90g/3½ oz/½ cup raw weight)
75g/3oz sun-dried tomatoes in oil, drained and chopped
50g/2oz/½ cup pitted black olives, chopped
60ml/4 tbsp soft goat's cheese
30ml/2 tbsp olive oil
15ml/1 tbsp chopped fresh basil leaves, plus basil sprigs, to garnish
yogurt and mint dressing and green salad, to serve

1 Preheat the oven to 180°C/350°F/Gas 4. Using a sharp knife, trim the base of each squash, slice off the top of each and scoop out and discard the seeds.

2 In a large bowl, mix together the cooked rice, chopped sun-dried tomatoes, black olives, soft cheese, half the oil and the basil. Stir until well combined.

3 Lightly oil a shallow baking dish with the remaining olive oil. The dish should be just large enough to hold the squash side by side. Divide the rice mixture among the squash, packing it down, and place them in the dish.

4 Cover the dish with a piece of foil and bake in the oven for about 45–50 minutes, until the squash are tender when pierced with a skewer.

5 Garnish with basil sprigs and serve the stuffed squash with a yogurt and mint dressing and a green salad.

Variation
You could try using ricotta cheese or cream cheese containing garlic and herbs in place of the soft goat's cheese in this recipe.

Stuffed Vine Leaves with Garlic Yogurt

These vine leaves are stuffed with rice that is deliciously flavoured with fresh herbs, lemon and a little chilli, before being slowly simmered.

Serves 6

225g/8oz packet preserved vine leaves
1 onion, finely chopped
½ bunch of spring onions (scallions), trimmed and finely chopped
60ml/4 tbsp chopped fresh parsley
10 large mint sprigs, chopped
finely grated rind of 1 lemon
2.5ml/½ tsp crushed dried chillies
7.5ml/1½ tsp fennel seeds, crushed
175g/6oz/scant 1 cup cooked long grain rice
120ml/4fl oz/½ cup olive oil
150ml/¼ pint/⅔ cup thick natural (plain) yogurt
2 garlic cloves, crushed
salt
lemon wedges and mint leaves, to garnish (optional)

1 Rinse the vine leaves in plenty of cold water. Put in a bowl, cover with boiling water and leave for 10 minutes. Drain thoroughly. Mix together the onion, spring onions, parsley, mint, lemon, chilli, fennel, rice and 25ml/1½ tbsp of the oil. Season with salt.

2 Place a vine leaf, veined side facing upwards, on a work surface and cut off the stalk. Place a heaped teaspoonful of the rice mixture near the stalk end of the leaf. Fold the stalk end over the rice filling, then fold over the sides and carefully roll up into a neat cigar shape.

3 Repeat with the remaining filling to make about 28 stuffed leaves. If some of the vine leaves are quite small, use two and patch them together to make parcels of the same size.

4 Place any remaining leaves in the base of a large, heavy pan. Pack the stuffed leaves in a single layer in the pan. Spoon over the remaining oil, then add 300ml/½ pint/1¼ cups boiling water. Place a plate over the leaves to keep them submerged. Cover the pan and cook over very low heat for 45 minutes.

5 Mix together the yogurt and garlic in a bowl and transfer to a small serving dish. Transfer the stuffed leaves to a serving plate and garnish with lemon wedges and mint, if you like. Serve with the garlic yogurt.

Roasted Squash Energy 208kcal/870kJ; Protein 6.3g; Carbohydrate 23.1g, of which sugars 4.6g; Fat 10.6g, of which saturates 3.9g; Cholesterol 14mg; Calcium 97mg; Fibre 2.5g; Sodium 93mg.
Stuffed Vine Leaves Energy 339kcal/1407kJ; Protein 5.8g; Carbohydrate 32.2g, of which sugars 7.3g; Fat 20.9g, of which saturates 2.7g; Cholesterol 0mg; Calcium 95mg; Fibre 3.4g; Sodium 14mg.

Braised Vine Leaves

These popular stuffed vine leaves keep deliciously moist when cooked slowly in a clay pot. The rice filling is flavoured with pine nuts, tomatoes and fresh mint.

Serves 4

12 fresh vine leaves
30ml/2 tbsp olive oil
1 small onion, chopped
30ml/2 tbsp pine nuts
1 garlic clove, crushed
115g/4oz cooked long grain rice
2 tomatoes, skinned, seeded and finely chopped
15ml/1 tbsp chopped fresh mint
1 lemon, sliced
150ml/¼ pint/⅔ cup dry white wine
200ml/7fl oz/scant 1 cup hot vegetable stock
salt and ground black pepper
lemon wedges, to serve

1 Soak the clay pot in cold water for 20 minutes, then drain. Blanch the vine leaves in a pan of boiling water for about 2 minutes or until they darken and soften. Rinse the leaves under cold running water and leave to drain.

2 Heat the oil in a frying pan, add the onion and cook for about 5–6 minutes, stirring frequently, until softened and turning golden. Add the pine nuts and crushed garlic to the pan and cook, stirring continuously, until the onions and pine nuts are a golden brown colour.

3 Transfer the contents of the pan to a bowl with the cooked rice. Add the tomatoes and mint and mix together. Season with salt and pepper to taste.

4 Place a spoonful of the rice mixture at the stalk end of each vine leaf. Fold the sides over the filling and roll up tightly.

5 Place the stuffed vine leaves close together, seam side down, in the clay pot. Place the lemon slices on top. Pour over the wine and sufficient stock to just cover the lemon slices.

6 Cover with the lid and place in an unheated oven. Set the oven to 200°C/400°F/Gas 6 and cook for 30 minutes. Reduce to 160°C/325°F/Gas 3 and cook for a further 30 minutes. Serve hot or cold, with lemon wedges.

Vine Leaves with Cumin, Lemon and Herbs

Fresh herbs and spices give the brown rice filling its zest and unique taste.

Serves 6–8

250g/9oz/1¼ cups brown rice
30–45ml/2–3 tbsp natural (plain) yogurt
3 garlic cloves, chopped
1 egg, lightly beaten
5–10ml/1–2 tsp ground cumin
2.5ml/½ tsp ground cinnamon
several handfuls of raisins
3–4 spring onions (scallions), thinly sliced
½ bunch fresh mint or 10ml/2 tsp dried mint, plus extra to garnish
25 preserved or fresh vine leaves
salt, if necessary

For cooking
8–10 unpeeled garlic cloves
juice of ½–1 lemon
90ml/6 tbsp olive oil

For serving
1 lemon, cut into wedges
15–25 Greek black olives
150ml/¼ pint/⅔ cup natural (plain) yogurt

1 Put the rice in a pan with 300ml/½ pint/1¼ cups water. Bring to the boil, reduce the heat, cover and simmer for 30 minutes, or until just tender. Drain well and leave to cool slightly.

2 Put the rice in a bowl, and mix in the yogurt, garlic, egg, ground cumin and cinnamon, raisins, spring onions and mint. If you are using preserved leaves, rinse them well. If using fresh leaves, blanch in salted boiling water for 2 minutes, then rinse and drain.

3 Lay the leaves on a board, shiny side down. Place a generous tablespoon of the mixture near the stalk. Fold up, starting at the bottom, then the sides, and finally rolling up towards the top.

4 Layer the rolls in a steamer and stud with the whole garlic cloves. Fill the base of the steamer with water and drizzle the lemon juice and olive oil evenly over the rolls. Cover the steamer tightly and steam for 40 minutes, adding more water if necessary.

5 Set aside the rolls to cool slightly. Arrange on a serving dish and serve hot or leave to cool further. Garnish and serve with lemon wedges, olives, and a bowl of yogurt, for dipping.

Braised Vine Leaves Energy 258kcal/1072kJ; Protein 4.6g; Carbohydrate 28.8g, of which sugars 5.5g; Fat 11.1g, of which saturates 1.2g; Cholesterol 0mg; Calcium 49mg; Fibre 2.1g; Sodium 11mg.
Vine Leaves Energy 220kcal/924kJ; Protein 3.5g; Carbohydrate 31.1g, of which sugars 6g; Fat 9.9g, of which saturates 1.6g; Cholesterol 24mg; Calcium 27mg; Fibre 1.2g; Sodium 18mg.

Spicy Tamarind Chickpeas

Chickpeas make a good base for many vegetarian dishes. In this slow-cooker recipe they are tossed with sharp tamarind and spices to make a light vegetarian lunch or side dish.

Serves 4

225g/8oz/1 ¼ cups dried chickpeas, soaked overnight
50g/2oz tamarind pulp
45ml/3 tbsp vegetable oil
2.5ml/½ tsp cumin seeds
1 onion, very finely chopped
2 garlic cloves, crushed
2.5cm/1in piece fresh root ginger, peeled and grated
1 fresh green chilli, finely chopped
5ml/1 tsp ground cumin
5ml/1 tsp ground coriander
1.5ml/¼ tsp ground turmeric
2.5ml/½ tsp salt
225g/8oz tomatoes, skinned and finely chopped
2.5ml/½ tsp garam masala
chopped fresh chillies and chopped onion, to garnish

1 Drain the chickpeas and place in a pan with double the volume of cold water. Bring to the boil and boil vigorously for 10 minutes. Skim off any scum, then drain the chickpeas and transfer to the ceramic cooking pot.

2 Pour 750ml/1 ¼ pints/3 cups of near-boiling water over the chickpeas and switch the slow cooker to high. Cover with the lid and cook for 4–5 hours, or until the chickpeas are just tender.

3 Towards the end of the cooking time, put the tamarind in a bowl and break up with a fork. Pour over 120ml/4fl oz/½ cup of boiling water and leave to soak for about 15 minutes.

4 Transfer the tamarind to a sieve (strainer) and discard the water. Rub the pulp through, discarding any stones and fibre.

5 Heat the oil in a large pan. Fry the cumin seeds for 2 minutes, until they splutter. Add the onion, garlic and ginger and fry for 5 minutes. Add the chilli, cumin, coriander, turmeric and salt, and fry for 3–4 minutes. Add the tomatoes, garam masala and tamarind pulp and bring to the boil. Add to the chickpeas.

6 Cover and cook for a further 1 hour. Serve straight from the ceramic cooking pot, and garnish with chopped chilli and onion.

Coconut, Tomato and Lentil Dhal with Toasted Almonds

Richly flavoured and utterly moreish, this lentil dish makes a filling supper served straight from the slow cooker with warm naan bread and plain yogurt.

Serves 4

30ml/2 tbsp vegetable oil
1 large onion, very finely chopped
3 garlic cloves, chopped
1 carrot, diced
10ml/2 tsp cumin seeds
10ml/2 tsp yellow mustard seeds
2.5cm/1in piece fresh root ginger, grated
10ml/2 tsp ground turmeric
5ml/1 tsp mild chilli powder
5ml/1 tsp garam masala
225g/8oz/1 cup split red lentils
400ml/14fl oz/1⅔ cup boiling vegetable stock
400ml/14fl oz/1⅔ cups coconut milk
5 tomatoes, peeled, seeded and chopped
juice of 2 limes
60ml/4 tbsp chopped fresh coriander (cilantro)
salt and ground black pepper
25g/1oz/¼ cup flaked (sliced) almonds, toasted, to garnish

1 Heat the oil in a pan. Add the onion and cook for 5 minutes, until softened, stirring occasionally. Add the garlic, carrot, cumin, mustard seeds and ginger to the pan. Cook for 3–4 minutes, stirring, until the seeds begin to pop, the aromas are released and the carrot softens slightly.

2 Add the turmeric, chilli powder and garam masala to the pan and cook, stirring, for 1 minute until the flavours begin to mingle.

3 Transfer the mixture to the ceramic cooking pot. Add the lentils, stock, coconut milk and tomatoes and season with salt and pepper. Stir well and cover the pot with the lid.

4 Cook on high for 2 hours, or until the lentils are soft, stirring halfway through the cooking time. Stir the lime juice and about 45ml/3 tbsp of fresh coriander into the dhal.

5 Check the seasoning and cook for a further 30 minutes. To serve, sprinkle with the remaining fresh coriander and the toasted almonds.

Spicy Chickpeas Energy 277kcal/1164kJ; Protein 12.8g; Carbohydrate 32.6g, of which sugars 5.3g; Fat 11.5g, of which saturates 1.3g; Cholesterol 0mg; Calcium 103mg; Fibre 7.1g; Sodium 274mg.
Coconut and Lentil Dhal Energy 335kcal/1421kJ; Protein 16.6g; Carbohydrate 46.3g, of which sugars 14.3g; Fat 10.6g, of which saturates 1.4g; Cholesterol 0mg; Calcium 99mg; Fibre 5.5g; Sodium 230mg.

Lentil Dhal with Roasted Garlic and Whole Spices

This slowly simmered lentil dish is topped with a garnish of onion and spices.

Serves 4–6

40g/1 ½oz/3 tbsp ghee or butter
1 onion, chopped
2 fresh green chillies, seeded and chopped
15ml/1 tbsp chopped fresh root ginger
225g/8oz/1 cup yellow or red lentils
900ml/1 ½ pints/3¾ cups water
45ml/3 tbsp roasted garlic purée
5ml/1 tsp ground cumin
5ml/1 tsp ground coriander
200g/7oz tomatoes, peeled and diced
a little lemon juice
salt and ground black pepper
30–45ml/2–3 tbsp coriander (cilantro) sprigs, to garnish

For the spicy garnish

30ml/2 tbsp groundnut (peanut) oil
4–5 shallots, sliced
2 garlic cloves, thinly sliced
15g/½oz/1 tbsp ghee or butter
5ml/1 tsp cumin seeds
5ml/1 tsp mustard seeds
3–4 small dried red chillies
8–10 fresh curry leaves

1 For the spicy garnish, heat the oil in a heavy pan. Add the shallots and fry them, stirring occasionally, until they are crisp and browned. Add the garlic and cook, stirring frequently, for 2 minutes until it colours. Remove from the pan and reserve.

2 For the dhal, melt the ghee or butter in the pan and cook the onion, chillies and ginger for 10 minutes. Stir in the lentils and water. Bring to the boil, reduce the heat and part-cover the pan. Simmer, stirring occasionally, for 50–60 minutes.

3 Stir in the roasted garlic purée, cumin and ground coriander, then season with salt and pepper. Cook for 10 minutes, uncovered, stirring frequently. Stir in the tomatoes and then adjust the seasoning, adding lemon juice to taste if necessary.

4 To finish the garnish, melt the ghee or butter in a frying pan. Add the cumin and mustard seeds and fry until the seeds pop. Stir in the chillies, curry leaves and the shallot mixture, then swirl the mixture into the dhal. Garnish with coriander sprigs, the reserved spicy fried shallots and garlic, and serve.

Baked Eggs with Creamy Leeks

These deliciously creamy eggs are gently steamed in the slow cooker. Enjoy them for a light lunch or supper with fresh bread and a salad. You can use other vegetables in place of the leeks, if you prefer, such as puréed spinach or ratatouille.

Serves 4

15g/½oz/1 tbsp butter, plus extra for greasing
225g/8oz small leeks, thinly sliced
60–90ml/4–6 tbsp whipping or double (heavy) cream
freshly grated nutmeg
4 eggs
salt and ground black pepper

1 Pour about 2.5cm/1in hot water into the ceramic cooking pot and switch the slow cooker to high.

2 Using a pastry brush, lightly butter the base and insides of four 175ml/6fl oz/¾ cup ramekins or use small individual soufflé dishes.

3 Melt the butter in a small frying pan and cook the leeks over medium heat, stirring frequently, until softened.

4 Add 45ml/3 tbsp of the cream and cook gently for about 5 minutes, or until the leeks are very soft and the cream has thickened a little. Season with salt, black pepper and nutmeg.

5 Spoon the leeks into the ramekins or soufflé dishes, dividing the mixture equally. Using the back of the spoon, make a hollow in the centre of each pile of leeks, then break an egg into the hollow.

6 Spoon 5–10ml/1–2 tsp of the remaining cream over each egg and season lightly with salt and ground black pepper.

7 Cover each dish with clear film (plastic wrap) and place in the slow cooker. If necessary, pour in a little more boiling water to come halfway up the sides of the dishes.

8 Cover with the lid and cook for 30 minutes, or until the egg whites are set and the yolks are still soft, or a little longer if you prefer the eggs firmer. Serve immediately.

Lentil Dhal Energy 233kcal/978kJ; Protein 9.5g; Carbohydrate 23.8g, of which sugars 3.1g; Fat 11.8g, of which saturates 5.3g; Cholesterol 20mg; Calcium 28mg; Fibre 2.5g; Sodium 73mg.
Baked Eggs Energy 149kcal/614kJ; Protein 4.4g; Carbohydrate 2.2g, of which sugars 1.8g; Fat 13.7g, of which saturates 7.5g; Cholesterol 123mg; Calcium 39mg; Fibre 1.3g; Sodium 64mg.

Slow-cooked Spiced Onions

Onions marinated and then slowly baked in a spicy sauce are fabulous with grilled or roasted meats.

Serves 4

675g/1½lb Spanish (Bermuda) or red onions
90ml/6 tbsp olive or sunflower oil or a mixture of both
pinch of saffron threads
2.5ml/½ tsp ground ginger
5ml/1 tsp ground black pepper
5ml/1 tsp ground cinnamon
15ml/1 tbsp sugar

1 Slice the onions very thinly and place them in a shallow dish. In a bowl, blend together the olive and/or sunflower oil, saffron, ground ginger, black pepper, cinnamon and sugar, and pour over the onions. Stir gently to mix, then set the onions aside for about 2 hours.

2 Preheat the oven to 160°C/325°F/Gas 3 and pour the onions and the marinade into a casserole or ovenproof dish.

3 Fold a large piece of foil into three and place over the top of the casserole or ovenproof dish, securing it with a lid.

4 Cook in the oven for about 45 minutes, or until the onions are very soft, then increase the oven temperature to 200°C/400°F/ Gas 6. Remove the lid and foil and cook for a further 5–10 minutes, or until the onions are lightly glazed. Serve immediately.

Cook's Tips

- *Onions that are grown in warmer climates are milder than those from cooler regions. Consequently, Spanish onions, also known as Bermuda onions, have a mild, sweet flavour. Their skins are a rich golden colour and they are one of the largest varieties available.*
- *When slicing onions, chop off the neck and just a little of the base to help the onion stay together. Score a line with a knife down the side of the onion and peel away the outer skin and the first layer of flesh.*

Oven-roasted Red Onions

The wonderful taste of these slow-cooked red onions is enhanced still further with the powerful flavours of fresh rosemary and juniper berries, and the added tangy sweetness of balsamic vinegar.

Serves 4

4 large or 8 small red onions
45ml/3 tbsp olive oil
6 juniper berries, crushed
8 small rosemary sprigs
30ml/2 tbsp balsamic vinegar
salt and ground black pepper

1 Soak a clay onion baker in cold water for 15 minutes, then drain. If the base of the baker is glazed, only the lid will need to be soaked.

2 Trim the roots from the onions and remove the skins, if you like. Cut the onions from the tip to the root, cutting the large onions into quarters and the small onions in half.

3 Rub the onions with olive oil, salt and black pepper and the juniper berries. Place the onions in the baker, inserting the rosemary in among the onions. Pour the remaining olive oil and vinegar over.

4 Cover and place in an unheated oven. Set the oven to 200°C/400°F/Gas 6 and cook for 40 minutes. Remove the lid and cook for a further 10 minutes. Serve immediately.

Variation

Add a similar quantity of long, thin potato wedges to the onion. Use a larger dish so that the vegetables are still in one layer.

Cook's Tip

To help hold back the tears during preparation, chill the onions first for about 30 minutes and then remove the root end last. The root contains the largest concentration of the sulphuric compounds that make the eyes water.

Slow-cooked Onions Energy 224kcal/926kJ; Protein 2.1g; Carbohydrate 17.3g, of which sugars 13.4g; Fat 16.9g, of which saturates 2.4g; Cholesterol 0mg; Calcium 60mg; Fibre 2.4g; Sodium 6mg.
Oven-roasted Red Onions Energy 128kcal/530kJ; Protein 1.8g; Carbohydrate 11.9g, of which sugars 8.4g; Fat 8.6g, of which saturates 1.2g; Cholesterol 0mg; Calcium 38mg; Fibre 2.1g; Sodium 5mg.

Baked Onions

Onions deserve to be used more as a vegetable in their own right. They become deliciously sweet and mildly flavoured when boiled or slowly baked, and can be cooked very conveniently in the oven when baking potatoes or parsnips.

Serves 4

4 large onions

1 Preheat the oven to 180°C/350°F/Gas 4. Put a little cold water into a roasting pan in which the onions will fit in a single layer. Arrange the unpeeled onions in the pan.

2 Bake the onions in the preheated oven for about 1 hour. The onions are ready when they feel soft and tender when squeezed at the sides. Peel the skins and serve immediately.

Sweet and Sour Onion Salad

This recipe features whole baby onions that are slowly simmered in a tasty, tangy stock until tender. It makes a great side dish for a summer salad or at a barbecue with hot or cold meats.

Serves 6

450g/1lb baby (pearl) onions, peeled
50ml/2fl oz/¼ cup wine vinegar
45ml/3 tbsp olive oil
40g/1½oz/3 tbsp caster (superfine) sugar
45ml/3 tbsp tomato purée (paste)
1 bay leaf
2 parsley sprigs
65g/2½oz/½ cup raisins
salt and ground black pepper

1 Put all the ingredients into a large, heavy pan with about 300ml/½ pint/1¼ cups water and stir well. Bring to the boil and simmer gently, uncovered, for 45 minutes, or until the onions are tender and most of the liquid has evaporated.

2 Remove the bay leaf and parsley from the pan. Check the seasoning, adding salt and pepper if necessary. Transfer the onions to a serving dish. Serve at room temperature.

Baked Fennel with a Crumb Crust

The aniseed flavour of baked fennel makes it a good accompaniment to all kinds of dishes – it goes very well with pasta.

Serves 4

3 fennel bulbs, cut lengthways into quarters
30ml/2 tbsp olive oil
1 garlic clove, chopped
50g/2oz/1 cup day-old wholemeal (whole-wheat) breadcrumbs
30ml/2 tbsp chopped fresh flat leaf parsley
salt and ground black pepper
a few fronds of fennel leaves, to garnish (optional)

1 Cook the fennel in a pan of boiling salted water for about 10 minutes. Preheat the oven to 190°C/375°F/Gas 5.

2 Drain the fennel and place in a large earthenware baking dish or baking tray, then brush with half the olive oil.

3 In a bowl, mix together the garlic, breadcrumbs and chopped parsley, then stir in the rest of the oil. Sprinkle the mixture evenly over the fennel, then season well with salt and pepper.

4 Bake the fennel for 30 minutes or until it is tender and the breadcrumb topping is crisp and golden. Serve hot, garnished with a few fronds of fennel leaves, if you like.

Variation

For a cheese-topped version, add 60ml/4 tbsp finely grated strong-flavoured cheese, such as mature (sharp) Cheddar, Red Leicester or Parmesan, to the breadcrumb mixture in step 3.

Cook's Tips

- *Fennel has a distinctive liquorice flavour, which particularly complements fish dishes. All parts of the plant are edible.*
- *When buying fennel, look for compact, unblemished white-green bulbs. The leaves should look fresh and green. Tougher specimens will have bulbs that spread at the top.*

Baked Onions Energy 90kcal/375kJ; Protein 3g; Carbohydrate 19.8g, of which sugars 14g; Fat 0.5g, of which saturates 0g; Cholesterol 0mg; Calcium 63mg; Fibre 3.5g; Sodium 8mg.
Onion Salad Energy 138kcal/578kJ; Protein 1.5g; Carbohydrate 21.5g, of which sugars 19.7g; Fat 5.7g, of which saturates 0.8g; Cholesterol 0mg; Calcium 30mg; Fibre 1.5g; Sodium 27mg.
Baked Fennel Energy 114kcal/477kJ; Protein 3g; Carbohydrate 12.6g, of which sugars 3.1g; Fat 6.1g, of which saturates 0.8g; Cholesterol 0mg; Calcium 67mg; Fibre 4.3g; Sodium 114mg.

Baked Mushrooms with Hazelnuts

Large mushrooms, full of texture and flavour, are topped with crunchy hazelnut pieces, fresh parsley, and garlic-flavoured oil, before being slowly baked in the oven.

Serves 4

2 garlic cloves
grated rind of 1 lemon
90ml/6 tbsp olive oil
8 large field (portabello) mushrooms
50g/2oz/½ cup hazelnuts, coarsely chopped
30ml/2 tbsp chopped fresh parsley
salt and ground black pepper

1 Crush the garlic cloves with a little salt, using a mortar and pestle or on a chopping board. Place the crushed garlic in a small bowl and stir in the grated lemon rind and the olive oil. Leave the mixture to stand for at least 30 minutes to allow all the flavours to develop.

2 Preheat the oven to 200°C/400°F/Gas 6. Arrange the mushrooms, stalk side up, in a single layer in a large, ovenproof earthenware dish. Drizzle about 60ml/4 tbsp of the garlic and lemon oil over them and bake in the preheated oven for about 10 minutes.

3 Remove the mushrooms from the oven, and baste them with the remaining garlic and lemon oil, then sprinkle the chopped hazelnuts evenly over the top. Bake in the oven for about 10–15 minutes more, until the mushrooms are tender. Season with salt and pepper and sprinkle with the chopped parsley. Serve immediately.

Cook's Tips

- *Almost any unsalted nuts can be used in this recipe in place of the hazelnuts. Try pine nuts, cashew nuts, almonds or walnuts.*
- *Nuts can go rancid quickly, so for the freshest flavour buy in small quantities, or buy them in shells and remove the shells just before using.*

Baked Aubergines with Cheese

This wonderful slow-baked dish of aubergines is cloaked in a thick cheese sauce, which, when cooked, has a topping like a soufflé. It is delicious hot but even better cold and, although it takes a while to prepare, is the perfect dish to make ahead of time for barbecues or a picnic lunch.

Serves 4–6

2 large aubergines (eggplants), cut into 5mm/¼in thick slices
about 60ml/4 tbsp olive oil
25g/1oz/2 tbsp butter
30ml/2 tbsp plain (all-purpose) flour
500ml/17fl oz/2¼ cups hot milk
about ⅛ of a whole nutmeg, freshly grated
cayenne pepper
4 large (US extra large) eggs, lightly beaten
400g/14oz/3½ cups grated cheese, such as Gruyère, or a mixture of Parmesan and Cheddar
salt and ground black pepper

1 Layer the aubergine slices in a bowl or colander, sprinkling each layer with salt, and leave to drain for at least 30 minutes. Rinse well, then pat dry with kitchen paper.

2 Heat the oil in a large frying pan, then fry the aubergine slices until golden brown on both sides. Remove from the pan and set aside.

3 Melt the butter in a heavy pan, then add the flour and cook for 1 minute, stirring. Remove from the heat and gradually stir in the hot milk. Return to the heat and slowly bring to the boil, stirring constantly, until the sauce thickens and becomes smooth. Season with nutmeg, cayenne pepper, salt and black pepper and leave to cool.

4 When the sauce is cool, beat in the eggs, then mix in the grated cheese, reserving a little to sprinkle on top of the dish. Preheat the oven to 180°C/350°F/Gas 4.

5 In an ovenproof dish, arrange a layer of the aubergine, then pour over some sauce. Repeat, ending with sauce. Sprinkle with the cheese. Bake for about 35–40 minutes, until golden and firm. Serve hot or leave to cool before eating.

Baked Mushrooms Energy 255kcal/1052kJ; Protein 5.2g; Carbohydrate 1.7g, of which sugars 1g; Fat 25.4g, of which saturates 3.1g; Cholesterol 0mg; Calcium 43mg; Fibre 3.1g; Sodium 12mg.
Aubergines Energy 296kcal/1228kJ; Protein 14.7g; Carbohydrate 6.6g, of which sugars 5.1g; Fat 23.6g, of which saturates 10.6g; Cholesterol 39mg; Calcium 297mg; Fibre 3.4g; Sodium 297mg.

Three Vegetable Kugel

Grated seasonal vegetables are baked until crisp on top and creamy and tender inside. This version of the classic Jewish casserole combines the traditional flavours and method but uses a more contemporary combination of vegetables.

Serves 4

2 courgettes (zucchini), coarsely grated
2 carrots, coarsely grated
2 potatoes, peeled and coarsely grated
1 onion, grated
3 eggs, lightly beaten
3 garlic cloves, chopped
pinch of sugar
15ml/1 tbsp finely chopped fresh parsley
2–3 pinches of dried basil
30–45ml/2–3 tbsp matzo meal
105ml/7 tbsp olive oil or vegetable oil
salt and ground black pepper

1 Preheat the oven to 180°C/350°F/Gas 4. Put the courgettes, carrots, potatoes, onion, eggs, garlic, sugar, parsley, basil, salt and pepper in a bowl and combine.

2 Add the matzo meal to the bowl and stir together until the mixture forms a thick batter.

3 Pour half the olive or vegetable oil into an ovenproof dish. Spoon in the vegetable mixture, then evenly pour over the remaining oil.

4 Bake in the preheated oven for 40–60 minutes, or until the vegetables are tender and the kugel top is golden brown. Serve immediately.

Cook's Tip
Matzo is a thin, brittle unleavened bread, rather like a cracker. It is usually made with only plain (all-purpose) flour and water, although some have additional flavourings, like onion. Matzo is traditionally eaten during the Jewish Passover festival in place of the forbidden bread. Matzo meal is made by grinding matzos, and comes in fine or medium texture.

Mediterranean Baked Vegetables

This colourful selection of vegetables is baked in the oven in a shallow clay pot. It makes an excellent vegetarian meal.

Serves 4–6

75ml/5 tbsp olive oil
2 onions, halved and sliced
1 garlic clove, crushed
15ml/1 tbsp finely chopped fresh sage
4 large, well-flavoured tomatoes, quartered
3 courgettes (zucchini), thickly sliced
2 small yellow (bell) peppers, quartered and seeded
2 small red (bell) peppers, quartered and seeded
60ml/4 tbsp fresh white or wholemeal (whole-wheat) breadcrumbs
60ml/4 tbsp freshly grated Parmesan cheese
8–10 pitted black olives
salt and ground black pepper
sage leaves, to garnish

1 Heat 30ml/2 tbsp of the olive oil in a heavy frying pan, add the onions and cook, stirring occasionally, for 6–8 minutes until softened and beginning to colour.

2 Add the garlic to the pan and continue cooking until the onions are really soft and golden. Stir in the sage and season well with salt and pepper.

3 Transfer the onions to a large earthenware baking dish. Spread them out evenly in the base, then arrange the tomatoes, courgettes and peppers on top.

4 Preheat the oven to 200°F/400°C/Gas 6. Drizzle the remaining oil over the mixed vegetables and season well. Bake in the oven for 30 minutes.

5 Sprinkle the fresh white or wholemeal breadcrumbs and Parmesan cheese over the vegetables and arrange the black olives on top.

6 Return to the oven for a further 10–15 minutes, or until the vegetables are tender. Serve garnished with sage leaves.

Vegetable Kugel Energy 358kcal/1488kJ; Protein 9.2g; Carbohydrate 26.6g, of which sugars 5.7g; Fat 24.5g, of which saturates 4.2g; Cholesterol 143mg; Calcium 63mg; Fibre 2.9g; Sodium 71mg.
Baked Vegetables Energy 260kcal/1083kJ; Protein 9.5g; Carbohydrate 24.9g, of which sugars 15.4g; Fat 14.2g, of which saturates 3.7g; Cholesterol 10mg; Calcium 192mg; Fibre 4.9g; Sodium 275mg.

Cheese-topped Roast Baby Vegetables

A simple way of serving baby vegetables. Slow roasting really helps to bring out their flavour, and the cheese topping turns it into a dish that can be enjoyed on its own for supper.

Serves 4

1kg/2¼lb mixed baby vegetables, such as aubergines (eggplants), onions or shallots, courgettes (zucchini), corn on the cob and mushrooms
1 red (bell) pepper, seeded and cut into large pieces
1–2 garlic cloves, finely chopped
15–30ml/1–2 tbsp olive oil
30ml/2 tbsp chopped fresh mixed herbs
225g/8oz cherry tomatoes
115g/4oz/1 cup coarsely grated mozzarella cheese
salt and ground black pepper
black olives, to serve (optional)

1 Preheat the oven to 220°C/425°F/Gas 7. Cut all the vegetables in half lengthways.

2 Place the halved baby vegetables and pepper pieces in an ovenproof dish with the finely chopped garlic and plenty of salt and ground black pepper. Drizzle the oil over and toss the vegetables to coat them. Bake the vegetables for 20 minutes, or until they are tinged brown at the edges, stirring once during the cooking time.

3 Remove the ovenproof dish from the oven and stir in the chopped fresh mixed herbs. Sprinkle the cherry tomatoes over the surface and top with the coarsely grated mozzarella cheese.

4 Return to the oven and bake for a further 5–10 minutes until the cheese has melted and is bubbling. Serve immediately, with black olives, if you like.

Variation
This dish can also be made with a mixture of regular-sized vegetables. Simply chop them all into bitesize pieces and continue from Step 2.

Roasted Tomatoes and Garlic

This recipe is so simple to prepare, yet tastes absolutely wonderful. Use a large, shallow earthenware dish that will allow the tomatoes to sear and char in a very hot oven.

Serves 4

8 well-flavoured tomatoes (see Cook's Tip), halved
12 garlic cloves, unpeeled
60ml/4 tbsp extra virgin olive oil
3–4 bay leaves
salt and ground black pepper
45ml/3 tbsp fresh oregano leaves, to garnish

1 Preheat the oven to 230°C/450°F/Gas 8. Select a large, shallow ovenproof dish that will hold all the tomato halves snugly in a single layer.

2 Arrange the halved tomatoes in the dish and tuck the whole, unpeeled garlic cloves evenly in among the tomatoes.

3 Brush the tomatoes all over with the extra virgin olive oil, and tuck in the bay leaves. Sprinkle plenty of ground black pepper over the top.

4 Bake in the preheated oven for about 30–40 minutes, or until the tomatoes have softened and are sizzling in the dish with the edges tinged a golden brown colour.

5 Season with a little salt and more black pepper, if needed. Garnish with oregano leaves and serve immediately.

Cook's Tips
• *If possible, try to find ripe plum tomatoes to use for this recipe as they not only keep their shape better than other varieties, but they have a more intense flavour. In addition, they do not tend to fall apart when roasted in the oven at such a high temperature.*
• *Leave the stalks on the tomatoes, if you like, for a more interesting-looking dish.*

Cheese-topped Vegetables Energy 212kcal/883kJ; Protein 9.2g; Carbohydrate 24.3g, of which sugars 18.4g; Fat 9.4g, of which saturates 4.5g; Cholesterol 17mg; Calcium 174mg; Fibre 4.8g; Sodium 128mg.
Roasted Tomatoes Energy 138kcal/571kJ; Protein 2g; Carbohydrate 6.6g, of which sugars 5.6g; Fat 11.7g, of which saturates 1.8g; Cholesterol 0mg; Calcium 36mg; Fibre 2.5g; Sodium 19mg.

Braised Red Cabbage with Beetroot

The moist, gentle cooking of the clay pot finishes this vegetable side dish to perfection. Serve with casseroles and roast meats – it is especially good with roast pork.

Serves 6–8

675g/1½lb red cabbage
30ml/2 tbsp olive oil
1 Spanish (Bermuda) onion, sliced
30ml/2 tbsp light muscovado (brown) sugar
2 tart eating apples, peeled, cored and sliced
300ml/½ pint/1¼ cups hot vegetable stock
60ml/4 tbsp red wine vinegar
375g/13oz raw beetroot (beet), peeled and coarsely grated
salt and ground black pepper

1 Soak a large clay pot or bean pot in cold water for 20 minutes, then drain. Finely shred the red cabbage and place in the clay pot.

2 Heat the olive oil in a frying pan and cook the onion for about 6–8 minutes, stirring frequently, until soft and transparent. Stir in the sugar and fry the onion gently until it is caramelized and golden. Take care not to overcook.

3 Stir in the apple slices, vegetable stock and red wine vinegar, then transfer the mixture to the clay pot. Season with salt and ground black pepper.

4 Cover and place in an unheated oven. Set the oven temperature to 190°C/375°F/Gas 5 and cook for 1 hour.

5 Stir in the beetroot, re-cover the pot and cook for a further 20–30 minutes, or until the cabbage and beetroot are tender. Serve immediately.

Cook's Tip
When buying cabbage, choose one that is firm and heavy for its size. The leaves should look healthy – avoid any with curling leaves or blemishes. These guidelines apply to any type of cabbage – red, green or white.

New Potatoes with Thyme and Lemon

These tasty potatoes are oven-roasted in a clay pot. They are the perfect accompaniment to grilled or roasted meat or poultry, and are ideal for serving as an alternative to traditional roast potatoes.

Serves 4

675g/1½lb small new potatoes
4 garlic cloves, sliced
8 thyme sprigs
4 strips finely pared lemon rind
75ml/5 tbsp olive oil
coarsely ground black pepper
coarse sea salt

1 Soak a clay pot in cold water for 20 minutes, then drain. Scrub the new potatoes and rinse thoroughly in cold water. Place the potatoes in the pot.

2 Add the sliced garlic cloves, fresh thyme sprigs and pared lemon rind to the pot, tucking them in among the potatoes. Sprinkle over plenty of coarsely ground black pepper and coarse sea salt.

3 Drizzle the olive oil all over the potatoes. Cover the pot with the lid and place in an unheated oven. Set the oven to 200°C/400°F/Gas 6 and cook for 1 hour, or until just tender.

4 If you wish, remove the lid and bake in the oven for a further 15–20 minutes, until slightly golden. If you prefer to keep the skins soft, remove the potatoes from the oven and leave to stand for 10 minutes before serving.

Cook's Tips
• *Thyme is an aromatic, woody herb that goes particularly well with lemon. It has a strong aroma and pungent flavour and grows wild in most warm climates. Thyme is often associated with dishes from the Mediterranean.*
• *You could easily make this dish with older potatoes – simply peel them, if you like, then cut into even chunks or wedges before adding to the pot.*

Braised Cabbage Energy 99kcal/415kJ; Protein 2.5g; Carbohydrate 16.2g, of which sugars 15g; Fat 3.1g, of which saturates 0.4g; Cholesterol 0mg; Calcium 63mg; Fibre 3.5g; Sodium 39mg.
New Potatoes Energy 242kcal/1011kJ; Protein 2.9g; Carbohydrate 27.2g, of which sugars 2.2g; Fat 14.3g, of which saturates 2.1g; Cholesterol 0mg; Calcium 10mg; Fibre 1.7g; Sodium 19mg.

Potato Wedges with Tomato and Chilli Salsa

This is a healthier version of traditionally baked potato skins; the clay pot keeps the potato flesh wonderfully moist and fluffy.

Serves 4

6 potatoes, about 115g/4oz each
45ml/3 tbsp olive oil
salt and ground black pepper

For the tomato and chilli salsa

4 juicy ripe tomatoes
1 sun-dried tomato in olive oil, drained
3 spring onions (scallions)
1–2 red or green chillies, halved and seeded
15ml/1 tbsp extra virgin olive oil
10ml/2 tsp lemon juice

1 Soak a clay pot or a potato pot in cold water for 20 minutes, then drain. Scrub the potatoes and dry with kitchen paper. Cut each potato lengthways into four wedges. Brush with a little of the oil and sprinkle with salt and pepper.

2 Place the potatoes in the clay pot and cover with the lid. Place the pot in an unheated oven, set the temperature to 200°C/400°F/Gas 6 and cook for 55–60 minutes, or until the potatoes are tender.

3 Meanwhile, finely chop the tomatoes, sun-dried tomato, spring onions and chilli and mix together with the olive oil and lemon juice. Cover and leave to stand for about 30 minutes to allow the flavours to mingle.

4 Uncover the potatoes, brush with the remaining olive oil and bake, uncovered, for a further 15 minutes until slightly golden. Divide the potato wedges and salsa among four serving bowls and plates, and serve immediately.

Cook's Tip

Varieties of floury potatoes that produce a fluffy texture when baked are best for these wedges. Good types to use include Maris Piper, Désirée, King Edward and Pentland Squire.

Potatoes with Roasted Garlic

Potatoes slowly roasted in their skins retain a deep, earthy taste, and, as a bonus, they absorb less fat too. The whole garlic cloves will mellow during the cooking to give a deliciously pungent and sweet but not overly-strong taste. They can be served alongside the potatoes, or squeeze the soft flesh out of the skins and use as a garnish.

Serves 4

1kg/2¼lb small floury potatoes
60–75ml/4–5 tbsp sunflower oil
10ml/2 tsp walnut oil
2 whole garlic bulbs, unpeeled
salt and ground black pepper

1 Preheat the oven to 240°C/475°F/Gas 9. Gently scrub the potatoes, place in a large pan of cold water and bring to the boil. Boil vigorously for a couple of minutes, then drain and leave to dry.

2 Combine the sunflower and walnut oils in a roasting pan and place in the oven to get really hot. Add the potatoes and garlic to the pan and coat evenly in the oil.

3 Sprinkle the potatoes and garlic with plenty of salt and ground black pepper. Place the pan in the oven and cook for about 10 minutes.

4 Reduce the oven temperature to 200°C/400°F/Gas 6. Continue cooking, basting occasionally with the oil, for a further 30–40 minutes.

5 Serve immediately. Accompany each portion of the potatoes with several cloves of the roasted garlic for eating whole or squeezing over the potatoes.

Cook's Tip

Some people are fearful of whole roasted garlic cloves, but they do lose much of their strength and become soft and sweet during cooking. If anyone really does not want the garlic paste, you can save the cloves for your next soup or mashed potato.

Potato Wedges Energy 238kcal/1001kJ; Protein 4g; Carbohydrate 30.8g, of which sugars 4.9g; Fat 11.9g, of which saturates 1.8g; Cholesterol 0mg; Calcium 23mg; Fibre 2.6g; Sodium 28mg.
Potatoes with Garlic Energy 312kcal/1310kJ; Protein 6.2g; Carbohydrate 44.3g, of which sugars 3.7g; Fat 13.4g, of which saturates 1.7g; Cholesterol 0mg; Calcium 20mg; Fibre 3.5g; Sodium 29mg.

Berrichonne Potatoes

A French potato dish with a difference. The potatoes on top will be crispy and golden brown, while underneath they will be tender. Omit the bacon for a vegetarian dish.

Serves 4

900g/2lb maincrop potatoes
25g/1oz/2 tbsp butter
1 onion, finely chopped
115g/4oz unsmoked streaky (fatty) bacon, rinds removed (optional)
350ml/12fl oz/1½ cups hot vegetable stock
coarse sea salt and ground black pepper
15ml/1 tbsp chopped fresh parsley, to garnish

1 Preheat the oven to 200°C/400°F/Gas 6. Peel the potatoes and trim them into barrel shapes. Leave the potatoes to stand in a bowl of cold water.

2 Melt the butter in a heavy frying pan. Add the onions, stir and cover with a lid. Cook for 5–6 minutes, until they are soft but not browned.

3 Chop the bacon into pieces and stir into the onions in the pan. Cover the pan and cook for 2 minutes.

4 Spoon the onion mixture into the base of a 1.5 litre/ 2½ pint/6¼ cup rectangular shallow ovenproof dish. Lay the potatoes over the onion mixture and pour the stock over, making sure it comes halfway up the sides of the dish.

5 Season with a little salt and plenty of ground black pepper. Place in the preheated oven and cook for 1 hour, until the potatoes are tender. Garnish with chopped parsley.

Cook's Tip
Use the best stock you can find for this dish. If you do not have any home-made stock, then try to find tubs of fresh stock available in supermarkets. If you use a stock (bouillon) cube, you may not need to add any more salt.

Potatoes, Peppers and Shallots Roasted with Rosemary

These luscious roasted potatoes soak up both the taste and wonderful aromas of the shallots and rosemary.

Serves 4

500g/1¼lb waxy potatoes
12 shallots
2 yellow (bell) peppers
45–60ml/3–4 tbsp olive oil
2 rosemary sprigs
salt and ground black pepper
crushed peppercorns, to garnish

1 Preheat the oven to 200°C/400°F/Gas 6. Par-boil the potatoes in their skins in a pan of boiling salted water for about 5 minutes. Drain and, when they are cool enough to handle, peel and halve each one lengthways.

2 Peel the shallots, allowing them to fall into their natural segments. Cut each sweet pepper lengthways into eight strips, discarding the seeds and pith.

3 Oil a shallow ovenproof dish thoroughly with 15ml/1 tbsp olive oil. Arrange the potatoes and peppers in alternating rows and stud with the shallots.

4 Cut the rosemary sprigs into 5cm/2in lengths and tuck them in among the vegetables. Season with salt and pepper, and pour over the remaining oil, tossing the vegetables to coat evenly.

5 Place in the oven, uncovered, for 30–40 minutes until all the vegetables are tender. Turn the vegetables occasionally to cook and brown evenly. Serve hot or at room temperature, garnished with crushed peppercorns.

Cook's Tip
This dish is excellent served with a simple dish of roast or grilled lamb, beef or chicken. It also makes a delicious light meal in itself and is the perfect comfort food.

Berrichonne Energy 289kcal/1213kJ; Protein 8.6g; Carbohydrate 37.5g, of which sugars 3.8g; Fat 12.6g, of which saturates 5.9g; Cholesterol 32mg; Calcium 20mg; Fibre 2.5g; Sodium 425mg.
Potatoes with Rosemary Energy 176kcal/742kJ; Protein 4.2g; Carbohydrate 33.6g, of which sugars 12.6g; Fat 3.7g, of which saturates 0.6g; Cholesterol 0mg; Calcium 40mg; Fibre 4.1g; Sodium 20mg.

Potatoes Baked with Fennel, Onions, Garlic and Saffron

Vegetables are gently braised in a delicious stock in the oven. This dish makes a very sophisticated and attractive accompaniment to egg-based vegetarian meals, grilled fish and chicken.

Serves 4–6

500g/1¼lb small waxy potatoes, cut into chunks or wedges
good pinch of saffron threads (12–15 threads)
1 garlic bulb, separated into cloves
12 small red or yellow onions, peeled but left whole
3 fennel bulbs, cut into wedges, feathery tops reserved for garnish (optional)
4–6 fresh bay leaves
6–9 fresh thyme sprigs
175ml/6fl oz/¾ cup vegetable stock
30ml/2 tbsp sherry or balsamic vinegar
2.5ml/½ tsp sugar
5ml/1 tsp fennel seeds, crushed
2.5ml/½ tsp paprika
45ml/3 tbsp olive oil
salt and ground black pepper

1 Boil the potato chunks or wedges in a large pan of boiling salted water for 8–10 minutes. Drain. Preheat the oven to 190°C/375°F/Gas 5. Soak the saffron threads in 30ml/2 tbsp warm water for 10 minutes.

2 Peel and finely chop two of the garlic cloves and set aside. Place the potatoes, whole red or yellow onions, remaining unpeeled garlic cloves, fennel wedges, fresh bay leaves and thyme sprigs in a large roasting pan or dish. Mix together the stock and the saffron and its soaking liquid in a jug (pitcher) or measuring cup.

3 Add the vinegar and sugar to the stock mixture, then pour the liquid over the vegetables. Stir in the fennel seeds, paprika, chopped garlic and oil, and season with salt and pepper.

4 Cook the vegetables in the oven for 1–1¼ hours, stirring occasionally, until they are just tender. Chop the reserved fennel tops, if using, and sprinkle them over the vegetables to garnish. Season with more salt and pepper and serve immediately.

Tomato and Potato Bake

This recipe is a great way for livening up potatoes to serve on their own or to accompany a roast. The ingredients are first fried together on the stove before being slowly baked in the oven.

Serves 4

4 large ripe tomatoes
120ml/4fl oz/½ cup olive oil
1 large onion, finely chopped
3 garlic cloves, crushed
1kg/2¼lb maincrop waxy potatoes
coarse sea salt and ground black pepper
15ml/1 tbsp fresh flat leaf parsley, to garnish

1 Prepare the tomatoes. Place them in a large heatproof bowl and cover with near-boiling water. Leave submerged for about 2–3 minutes, then remove and leave to cool slightly.

2 The skin of the tomatoes should have loosened enough to peel off easily. Cut into wedges and remove the seeds and discard. Chop the flesh.

3 Preheat the oven to 180°C/350°F/Gas 4. Heat the oil in a flameproof casserole. Fry the onion, stirring frequently, for about 5 minutes until softened and just starting to brown. Add the garlic to the pan and cook for 2–3 minutes.

4 Add the tomatoes to the pan, season with salt and pepper and cook, stirring, for 1 minute. Cut the potatoes into wedges and add to the pan. Cook for 10 minutes.

5 Season the mixture again and cover the casserole with a tight-fitting lid. Place on the middle shelf of the oven and cook for 45 minutes to 1 hour. Garnish with fresh parsley and serve.

Cook's Tip
Make sure that the potatoes are completely and evenly coated in the oil for even cooking.

Potatoes with Fennel Energy 162kcal/676kJ; Protein 4.4g; Carbohydrate 23.6g, of which sugars 7.1g; Fat 6.2g, of which saturates 0.9g; Cholesterol 0mg; Calcium 49mg; Fibre 4.9g; Sodium 23mg.
Tomato Bake Energy 399kcal/1670kJ; Protein 5.9g; Carbohydrate 49.3g, of which sugars 10.6g; Fat 21.2g, of which saturates 3.2g; Cholesterol 0mg; Calcium 41mg; Fibre 4.6g; Sodium 39mg.

Herby Potato Bake

Wonderfully creamy potatoes, well flavoured with lots of fresh herbs, are gently baked in the oven until beautifully tender. The dish is topped with a sprinkling of cheese to make a golden, crunchy topping.

Serves 4

675g/1½lb waxy potatoes
25g/1oz/2 tbsp butter
1 onion, finely chopped
1 garlic clove, crushed
2 eggs
300ml/½ pint/1¼ cups crème fraîche or double (heavy) cream
115g/4oz/1 cup Gruyère, grated
60ml/4 tbsp chopped mixed fresh herbs, such as chervil, thyme, chives and parsley
freshly grated nutmeg
salt and ground black pepper

1 Preheat the oven to 190°C/375°F/Gas 5 and place a baking sheet in the oven to heat up. Lightly butter an ovenproof dish.

2 Peel the potatoes and cut them into matchsticks. Set aside while you make up the sauce mixture.

3 Melt the butter in a heavy frying pan and cook the onions, stirring frequently, for 4–5 minutes until beginning to soften.

4 Add the garlic to the pan and cook for a further 2–3 minutes. Remove the pan from the heat to cool slightly.

5 In a large mixing bowl, add the eggs, crème fraîche or double cream and about half of the grated Gruyère cheese. Whisk together until well combined.

6 Stir the onion mixture, chopped fresh herbs and sliced potatoes into the mixing bowl. Season with salt, ground black pepper and grated nutmeg. Mix until well combined. Spoon the mixture into the prepared dish and sprinkle over the remaining Gruyère cheese.

7 Place the dish on the hot baking sheet and cook in the oven for 50 minutes to 1 hour, until the top is golden brown and the potatoes are tender. Serve immediately, straight from the dish, as this will ensure that the potatoes stay really hot.

Drachena

A cross between an omelette and a pancake, this is a savoury dish, which is slowly baked in the oven. It is popular in Russia and other European countries.

Serves 2–3

4 tomatoes
15ml/1 tbsp olive oil
1 bunch spring onions (scallions), finely sliced
1 garlic clove, crushed
45ml/3 tbsp wholemeal (whole-wheat) rye flour
60ml/4 tbsp milk
150ml/¼ pint/⅔ cup sour cream
4 eggs, beaten
30ml/2 tbsp chopped fresh parsley
25g/1oz/2 tbsp butter, melted
salt and ground black pepper
green salad, to serve

1 Place the tomatoes in a large heatproof bowl and cover with near-boiling water. Leave them submerged for 2–3 minutes, then remove and leave to cool slightly. The skin should have loosened enough to peel off easily. Cut into wedges, discard the seeds and chop the flesh.

2 Preheat the oven to 180°C/350°F/Gas 4. Heat the oil in a frying pan and gently cook the spring onions for 3–5 minutes. Add the garlic and cook for 1 minute more, or until the spring onions are soft.

3 Sprinkle the spring onions and garlic into the base of a lightly greased shallow 20cm/8in ovenproof dish, and sprinkle over the chopped tomatoes.

4 Mix the flour to a smooth paste in a bowl with the milk. Gradually add the sour cream, then mix with the beaten eggs. Stir in the fresh parsley and melted butter. Season with salt and black pepper.

5 Pour the egg mixture over the vegetables. Bake in the oven for 40–45 minutes, or until hardly any liquid seeps out when a knife is pushed into the middle.

6 Run a knife around the edge of the dish to loosen, then cut into wedges and serve immediately, with a fresh green salad.

Potato Bake Energy 614kcal/2550kJ; Protein 15.6g; Carbohydrate 30.6g, of which sugars 5g; Fat 48g, of which saturates 30.8g; Cholesterol 221mg; Calcium 310mg; Fibre 2.5g; Sodium 321mg.
Drachena Energy 384kcal/1598kJ; Protein 13.4g; Carbohydrate 19.4g, of which sugars 7.9g; Fat 28.9g, of which saturates 13.5g; Cholesterol 302mg; Calcium 155mg; Fibre 2.4g; Sodium 187mg.

Baked Potatoes with a Creamy Cheese Filling

In this recipe, potatoes are cooked in the oven, then filled with a rich cream and cheese filling before being browned under the grill. They make a tasty meal.

Serves 6
3 baking potatoes
115g/4oz/1 cup mature (sharp) Cheddar cheese, grated
90ml/6 tbsp single (light) cream
sea salt and ground black pepper

1 Preheat the oven to 200°C/400°F/Gas 6. Scrub the potatoes and pat dry. Prick each one with a fork and cook directly on the middle shelf of the oven for 1¼–1½ hours until cooked through and tender.

2 Remove the potatoes from the oven and cut each one in half. Place the halves on a baking sheet and make shallow dips in the centre of each half, raising the potato up at the edges.

3 In a bowl, mix together the grated cheese and cream until well combined. Divide the mixture between the potato halves, packing it into the dips. Preheat the grill (broiler).

4 Grill (broil) the potatoes for 5 minutes until the cheese has melted and bubbles. Serve hot, sprinkled with salt and pepper.

Variation
Non-vegetarians could add other ingredients to the cheese and cream mixture, such as chopped ham or cooked bacon.

Cook's Tip
You can speed up this recipe by starting the potatoes off in the microwave. Prick the scrubbed potatoes well and place in a covered microwave dish. Cook on high until starting to soften – test after 2 minutes, then every minute. Place in the oven to crisp the skins and finish cooking for about 45 minutes.

Braised Potatoes and Onions

Layers of thinly sliced potato and onions are gently braised in the oven in butter and stock. This savoury potato dish makes a tasty accompaniment to both meat and fish.

Serves 6
450g/1lb maincrop potatoes
2 onions
2 garlic cloves, crushed
50g/2oz/4 tbsp butter, softened and diced
300ml/½ pint/1¼ cups hot vegetable stock
coarse sea salt and ground black pepper
15ml/1 tbsp finely chopped fresh parsley, to garnish

1 Preheat the oven to 180°C/350°F/Gas 4. Grease the base and sides of a 1.5 litre/2½ pint/6¼ cup ovenproof dish.

2 Scrub the potatoes and slice them as thinly as possible. Slice the onions to about the same thickness.

3 Line the dish with some of the sliced potatoes. Sprinkle some onions and garlic on top. Layer up the remaining potatoes and onions, seasoning between each layer.

4 Push the vegetables down into the dish and dot the top with the butter. Pour the stock over and bake in the oven for about 1½ hours, covering with foil if the top starts to over brown. Serve with parsley and plenty of salt and pepper.

Variation
If you want to make this dish more substantial, sprinkle some grated cheese over the top for the last 30 minutes of cooking.

Cook's Tip
A mandolin is a handy kitchen utensil that would be useful for preparing the potatoes and onions in this recipe. The vegetables are sliced by rubbing them across an adjustable blade.

Baked Potatoes Energy 179kcal/748kJ; Protein 7.1g; Carbohydrate 16.5g, of which sugars 1.7g; Fat 9.4g, of which saturates 6.1g; Cholesterol 27mg; Calcium 161mg; Fibre 1g; Sodium 154mg.
Braised Potatoes Energy 118kcal/494kJ; Protein 1.5g; Carbohydrate 12.9g, of which sugars 1.6g; Fat 7.1g, of which saturates 4.4g; Cholesterol 18mg; Calcium 9mg; Fibre 0.9g; Sodium 59mg.

Truffade

Baked until meltingly soft, this warming cheese and potato supper is the perfect slow bake to come home to. In France, where it originated, it would be made with a Tomme or Cantal cheese – look for them in good cheese stores.

Serves 4–6

1 large onion, thinly sliced
675g/1½lb baking potatoes, very thinly sliced
150g/5oz/1¼ cups grated hard cheese, such as Tomme, Cantal or mature (sharp) Cheddar
freshly grated nutmeg
coarse sea salt and ground black pepper
mixed salad leaves, to serve

1 Preheat the oven to 180°C/350°F/Gas 4. Lightly grease the base of a shallow baking dish or roasting pan with the oil or melted butter.

2 Arrange a layer of sliced onion over the base of the dish, then add a layer of sliced potatoes and about half of the grated cheese. Finish with the remaining onions and top with a layer of sliced potatoes.

3 Brush the top layer of potatoes with oil or melted butter and season with nutmeg, salt and pepper.

4 Sprinkle the remaining grated cheese over the top and bake for about 1 hour, or until the vegetables are tender and the top is golden brown.

5 Leave the dish to stand for about 5 minutes, then cut into wedges and serve with a salad.

Variation
In France, they also make a non-vegetarian version of this dish, which is cooked with finely diced fatty bacon, and the cheese is chopped, not grated. The ingredients are mixed and cooked slowly in a little lard or white cooking fat in a heavy frying pan on top of the stove.

Baked Scalloped Potatoes with Feta Cheese and Olives

Thinly sliced potatoes are slowly baked with Greek feta cheese, black and green olives and olive oil. This dish is excellent served with toasted pitta bread.

Serves 4

4–6 large, unpeeled potatoes, total weight about 900g/2lb
150ml/¼ pint/⅔ cup extra virgin olive oil
leaves from a sprig of rosemary
275g/10oz/2½ cups feta cheese, coarsely crumbled
115g/4oz/1 cup pitted, mixed black and green olives
300ml/½ pint/1¼ cups hot vegetable stock
salt and ground black pepper
toasted pitta bread, to serve

1 Preheat the oven to 200°C/400°F/Gas 6. Bring a large pan of salted water to the boil and cook the potatoes for 15 minutes until only just tender.

2 Drain the potatoes and set them aside until they are cool enough to handle. Carefully remove the peel from the potatoes using a small sharp knife, and cut them into thin slices.

3 Brush the base and sides of a 1.5 litre/2½ pint/6¼ cup rectangular ovenproof dish with some of the olive oil.

4 Arrange half the potatoes in the dish in an even layer. Top with half of the rosemary, cheese and olives, and season with salt and pepper. Arrange the rest of the potatoes in an even layer on top.

5 Add the remaining rosemary leaves, crumbled cheese and olives, and drizzle with the remaining olive oil. Pour the hot vegetable stock over the top and season the top layer with salt and plenty of ground black pepper.

6 Bake for 35 minutes, covering the dish loosely with foil after about 20 minutes to prevent the top from getting too brown. Serve hot, straight from the dish, with the toasted pitta bread.

Truffade Energy 117kcal/494kJ; Protein 3.2g; Carbohydrate 20.8g, of which sugars 3.4g; Fat 2.9g, of which saturates 1.7g; Cholesterol 7mg; Calcium 40mg; Fibre 1.6g; Sodium 48mg.
Scalloped Potatoes Energy 584kcal/2429kJ; Protein 14.8g; Carbohydrate 37.3g, of which sugars 4g; Fat 42.7g, of which saturates 13.7g; Cholesterol 48mg; Calcium 279mg; Fibre 3.1g; Sodium 1662mg.

Potatoes and Parsnips Baked with Garlic and Cream

As the potatoes and parsnips cook, they gradually absorb the garlic-flavoured cream, while the cheese on top browns to a crispy finish.

Serves 4–6

3 large potatoes, total weight about 675g/1½lb
350g/12oz parsnips
200ml/7fl oz/scant 1 cup single (light) cream
105ml/7 tbsp milk
2 garlic cloves, crushed
5ml/1 tsp freshly grated nutmeg
75g/3oz/¾ cup coarsely grated Gruyère cheese
salt and ground black pepper

1 Peel the potatoes and parsnips and cut them into thin slices, using a sharp knife. Place them in a pan of salted boiling water and cook for 5 minutes. Drain and leave to cool slightly.

2 Meanwhile, pour the cream and milk into a heavy pan, add the garlic and bring to the boil. Remove the pan from the heat and leave to stand for about 10 minutes.

3 Lightly grease a 25cm/10in rectangular earthenware baking dish. Preheat the oven to 180°C/350°F/Gas 4.

4 Layer the potatoes and parsnips in the prepared dish, seasoning each layer with salt, pepper and a little grated nutmeg.

5 Pour the garlic-flavoured cream and milk mixture into the dish and press the sliced potatoes and parsnips down into the liquid. The liquid should come to just underneath the top layer. Cover with lightly buttered foil and bake for 45 minutes.

6 Remove the dish from the oven and remove the foil from the dish. Sprinkle the grated Gruyère cheese over the vegetables in an even layer.

7 Return the dish to the oven and bake, uncovered, for a further 20–30 minutes, or until the potatoes and parsnips are tender and the topping is golden brown. Serve immediately.

Potato Gratin

Potatoes, layered with mustard butter and slowly baked until golden, are perfect to serve with a green salad, or as an accompaniment to a vegetable or nut roast.

Serves 4

4 large potatoes, total weight about 900g/2lb
30ml/2 tbsp butter
15ml/1 tbsp olive oil
2 large garlic cloves, crushed
30ml/2 tbsp Dijon mustard
15ml/1 tbsp lemon juice
15ml/1 tbsp fresh thyme leaves, plus extra to garnish
50ml/2fl oz/¼ cup hot vegetable stock
salt and ground black pepper

1 Thinly slice the potatoes using a knife, mandolin or the slicing attachment on a food processor. Place the potato slices in a bowl of cold water to prevent them from discolouring.

2 Preheat the oven to 200°C/400°F/Gas 6. Heat the butter and oil in a deep frying pan. Add the garlic and cook gently for 2–3 minutes until light golden, stirring constantly. Stir in the mustard, lemon juice and thyme. Remove from the heat and pour the mixture into a jug (pitcher).

3 Drain the potatoes and pat dry with kitchen paper. Place a layer of potatoes in the frying pan, season and pour over one-third of the butter mixture. Arrange another layer of potatoes on top, pour over half of the remaining butter mixture and season. Arrange a final layer of potatoes on top, pour over the remainder of the butter mixture and the stock. Season and sprinkle with the reserved thyme.

4 Cover the potatoes with baking parchment and bake for 1 hour, then remove the paper, return to the oven and cook for 15 minutes or until golden.

Variation
Any root vegetables can be used for this recipe: try using sweet potatoes, parsnips, swede (rutabaga) or turnips.

Potatoes and Parsnips Energy 241kcal/1009kJ; Protein 7.8g; Carbohydrate 27g, of which sugars 6.4g; Fat 11.7g, of which saturates 7.2g; Cholesterol 31mg; Calcium 174mg; Fibre 3.8g; Sodium 126mg.
Potato Gratin Energy 238kcal/1002kJ; Protein 3.9g; Carbohydrate 36.3g, of which sugars 3g; Fat 9.6g, of which saturates 4.5g; Cholesterol 16mg; Calcium 15mg; Fibre 2.3g; Sodium 70mg.

Cheesy Potato Cake

This unusual dish is made from a layered ring of potatoes, cheese and fresh herbs. Slow baking gives the ingredients a rich flavour.

Serves 4

3 large potatoes
1 small onion, finely sliced into rings
200g/7oz/1¾ cups red Leicester or mature (sharp) Cheddar cheese, grated
fresh thyme sprigs
150ml/¼ pint/⅔ cup single (light) cream
salt and ground black pepper
salad leaves, to serve

1 Preheat the oven to 200°C/400°F/Gas 6. Peel the potatoes and cook in boiling water for 10 minutes, until they are just starting to soften. Remove from the water and pat dry.

2 Finely slice the potatoes, using the straight edge of a grater or a mandolin. Grease the base and sides of an 18cm/7in cake tin (pan) with butter and lay some of the potatoes on the base to cover it completely. Season with salt and pepper.

3 Sprinkle some of the sliced onion rings over the potato slices and top with a little of the cheese. Sprinkle over some fresh thyme and then continue to layer the ingredients, finishing with cheese and a little more seasoning.

4 Press the potato layers right down with your hand into the cake tin. (The mixture may seem quite high at this point but it will cook down.)

5 Pour the cream over and give the tin a shake to distribute it evenly. Cook in the oven for 50–55 minutes, until the potatoes are tender. Remove from the oven and cool. Invert on to a plate and cut into wedges. Serve with a few salad leaves.

Variation
Make this dish more substantial by toping the wedges with slices of grilled (broiled) bacon or roasted red (bell) peppers.

Pan Haggerty

This Northumberland dish of potatoes, onions and cheese is slowly simmered on the stove. Use a firm-fleshed potato, such as Romano or Maris Piper, which will hold its shape.

Serves 2

1 large onion
450g/1lb potatoes
30ml/2 tbsp olive oil
25g/1oz/2 tbsp butter
2 garlic cloves, crushed
115g/4oz/1 cup grated mature (sharp) Cheddar cheese
45ml/3 tbsp chopped fresh chives, plus extra to garnish
coarse sea salt and ground black pepper

1 Halve and thinly slice the onion, using a sharp knife or a mandolin. Peel and thinly slice the potatoes.

2 Heat the oil and butter in a large heavy frying pan. Remove from the heat and cover the base with a layer of potatoes, followed by layers of onion slices, garlic, cheese and chives, and plenty of salt and ground black pepper.

3 Continue layering the vegetables and cheese, ending with grated cheese. Cover the pan with a tight-fitting lid or foil, and cook the pan haggerty over low heat on the stove for about 30–40 minutes, or until the potatoes and onion are tender when tested with a knife.

4 Preheat the grill (broiler) to hot. Uncover the pan, cover the pan handle with foil to protect it, if necessary, and brown the top under the grill. Serve the pan haggerty straight from the pan, sprinkled with extra chives to garnish.

Variations
• *Other hard cheeses such as Red Leicester or Monterey Jack work well in this recipe.*
• *For a slightly sweeter flavour and extra colour, use 1 sliced red onion in place of the brown-skinned variety.*
• *Add some slices of ham or salami into the layers, if you like.*

Potato Cake Energy 408kcal/1706kJ; Protein 17.1g; Carbohydrate 30.2g, of which sugars 4g; Fat 24.1g, of which saturates 15.6g; Cholesterol 69mg; Calcium 417mg; Fibre 2g; Sodium 392mg.
Pan Haggerty Energy 542kcal/2257kJ; Protein 19.6g; Carbohydrate 42.2g, of which sugars 7.2g; Fat 33.9g, of which saturates 15g; Cholesterol 60mg; Calcium 429mg; Fibre 3.3g; Sodium 413mg.

Potato, Onion and Garlic Gratin

This tasty slow-cooker dish makes the perfect accompaniment to roasts, stews and grilled meat or fish. Slowly cooking the potatoes in stock with onions and garlic gives them a deep, rich flavour.

Serves 4

40g/1½oz/3 tbsp butter
1 large onion, finely sliced into rings
2–4 garlic cloves, finely chopped
2.5ml/½ tsp dried thyme
900g/2lb waxy potatoes, very finely sliced
450ml/¾ pint/scant 2 cups boiling vegetable stock
coarse sea salt and ground black pepper

1 Lightly grease the inside of the ceramic cooking pot with 15g/½oz/1 tbsp of the butter. Spoon a layer of onions into the pot, then sprinkle over a little garlic, thyme, salt and pepper.

2 Carefully arrange an overlapping layer of potato slices on top of the onion mixture. Continue to layer the ingredients in the pot, finishing with a layer of sliced potatoes.

3 Pour just enough of the stock into the pot to cover the potatoes. Cover with the lid and cook on low for 8–10 hours, or on high for 4–5 hours, until the potatoes are tender.

4 If you like, brown the potatoes under a hot grill (broiler) for 3–4 minutes. Serve sprinkled with a little salt and pepper.

Variations

• To make this dish more substantial, sprinkle 115g/4oz/1 cup of grated Gruyère cheese over the top of the cooked potatoes and brown under a preheated grill (broiler) for 3–4 minutes until golden-brown and bubbling.
• Alternatively, crumble 165g/5½oz/scant 1 cup soft goat's cheese on to the gratin 30 minutes before the end of cooking.
• To vary the flavour, try using chopped rosemary or sage in place of the thyme, or use crushed juniper berries instead.

Orange Candied Sweet Potatoes

This dish is the classic accompaniment to a traditional Thanksgiving dinner. Long simmering in orange juice and maple syrup in the slow cooker results in deliciously sweet and tender potatoes. For a really fresh, festive look, serve this dish with extra orange segments.

Serves 8

900g/2lb sweet potatoes
150ml/¼ pint/⅔ cup orange juice
30ml/2 tbsp maple syrup
5ml/1 tsp freshly grated ginger
2.5ml/½ tsp ground cinnamon
2.5ml/½ tsp ground cardamom
5ml/1 tsp salt
ground black pepper
orange segments, to serve (optional)

1 Peel the sweet potatoes and cut them into 2cm/¾in cubes. Put the cubes into a large heatproof bowl and pour over just enough near-boiling water to cover. Leave them to stand for about 5 minutes.

2 Meanwhile, put the orange juice, maple syrup, ginger, cinnamon and cardamom in the ceramic cooking pot. Season with the salt and stir the mixture until well combined. Switch the slow cooker to high.

3 Drain the sweet potato cubes and add them to the ceramic cooking pot. Gently stir to coat the pieces in the spicy orange mixture. Cover and cook for 4–5 hours, until tender, stirring twice during cooking.

4 Stir the orange segments, if using, into the sweet potatoes, and season to taste with plenty of ground black pepper. Serve immediately.

Variation

You can serve this rich vegetable dish as a purée, if you prefer (but omit the orange segments). Transfer the cooked candied sweet potatoes to a food processor, adding a little of the sauce, and blend until smooth. You may need to add a little more of the sauce to make a soft, creamy, spoonable purée.

Potato Gratin Energy 260kcal/1092kJ; Protein 5.1g; Carbohydrate 41.9g, of which sugars 6.4g; Fat 9.1g, of which saturates 5.4g; Cholesterol 21mg; Calcium 31mg; Fibre 3.3g; Sodium 171mg.
Orange Candied Potatoes Energy 53kcal/226kJ; Protein 2.9g; Carbohydrate 13.7g, of which sugars 11.8g; Fat 0g, of which saturates 0g; Cholesterol 0mg; Calcium 5mg; Fibre 0.2g; Sodium 158mg.

Roasted Sweet Potatoes, Onions and Beetroot in Coconut Paste

Sweet potatoes and beetroot become wonderfully sweet when slowly roasted. They work well with savoury onions and an aromatic coconut, ginger and garlic paste.

Serves 4

30ml/2 tbsp groundnut (peanut) or mild olive oil
450g/1lb sweet potatoes, peeled and cut into strips or chunks
4 beetroot (beets), cooked, peeled and cut into wedges
450g/1lb small onions, halved
5ml/1 tsp coriander seeds, crushed
3–4 small whole fresh red chillies
salt and ground black pepper
chopped fresh coriander (cilantro), to garnish

For the paste

2 large garlic cloves, chopped
1–2 green chillies, seeded and chopped
15ml/1 tbsp chopped fresh root ginger
45ml/3 tbsp chopped fresh coriander (cilantro)
75ml/5 tbsp coconut milk
30ml/2 tbsp groundnut (peanut) or mild olive oil
grated rind of ½ lime
2.5ml/½ tsp soft light brown sugar

1 To make the paste, process the garlic, chillies, ginger, coriander and coconut milk in a food processor or blender. Transfer the paste into a small bowl and beat in the oil, grated lime rind and light brown sugar. Preheat the oven to 200°C/400°F/Gas 6.

2 Heat the oil in a large roasting pan in the oven for 5 minutes. Add the sweet potatoes, beetroot, onions and coriander seeds, tossing them in the hot oil. Roast the vegetables for 10 minutes.

3 Stir in the paste and the whole red chillies. Season well with salt and pepper, and shake the pan to toss the vegetables and coat them thoroughly with the paste.

4 Return the vegetables to the oven and cook for a further 25–35 minutes, or until the vegetables are tender. During cooking, stir the mixture two or three times to prevent the coconut and ginger paste from sticking to the roasting pan. Serve the vegetables immediately, garnished with a little chopped fresh coriander.

Spinach Braised with Sweet Potatoes

Sweet potatoes make an interesting alternative to the ordinary variety. Here, the garlic and ginger subtly complement the slow-cooked potatoes and spinach.

Serves 4

30ml/2 tbsp sunflower oil
1 onion, chopped
1 garlic clove, finely chopped
2.5cm/1in piece fresh root ginger, peeled and grated
2.5ml/½ tsp cayenne pepper
675g/1½lb sweet potatoes
150ml/¼ pint/⅔ cup vegetable stock
225g/8oz spinach
45ml/3 tbsp pine nuts, toasted
salt and ground black pepper

1 Soak a clay potato pot in cold water for 20 minutes, then drain. Heat the oil in a large frying pan, add the onion, garlic, ginger and cayenne pepper and fry gently, stirring occasionally, for about 8 minutes or until the onion is softened.

2 Peel the sweet potatoes and cut them into 2.5cm/1in chunks. Add the chunks to the frying pan and stir to coat them in the oil and spices.

3 Transfer the potato mixture to the clay pot and add the vegetable stock. Cover the pot and place in an unheated oven. Set the oven to 220°C/425°F/Gas 7 and cook for 50–60 minutes, or until the potatoes are just tender, stirring halfway through cooking.

4 Wash the spinach and shred roughly. Stir into the potatoes with the toasted pine nuts, re-cover the clay pot and cook for a further 5 minutes in the oven until the spinach is wilted. Remove from the oven and leave to stand for 5 minutes. Adjust the seasoning and serve immediately.

Cook's Tip

To toast pine nuts, heat a heavy frying pan and add the nuts. Cook them for 3–4 minutes or until they turn a golden brown colour, stirring occasionally. Watch the nuts carefully – they will scorch and burn quickly if toasted for too long.

Sweet Potatoes Energy 272kcal/1143kJ; Protein 4.4g; Carbohydrate 39.8g, of which sugars 19.2g; Fat 11.8g, of which saturates 1.7g; Cholesterol 0mg; Calcium 98mg; Fibre 6.3g; Sodium 122mg.
Spinach Energy 293kcal/1231kJ; Protein 5.4g; Carbohydrate 38.5g, of which sugars 11.8g; Fat 14.2g, of which saturates 1.4g; Cholesterol 0mg; Calcium 141mg; Fibre 5.7g; Sodium 147mg.

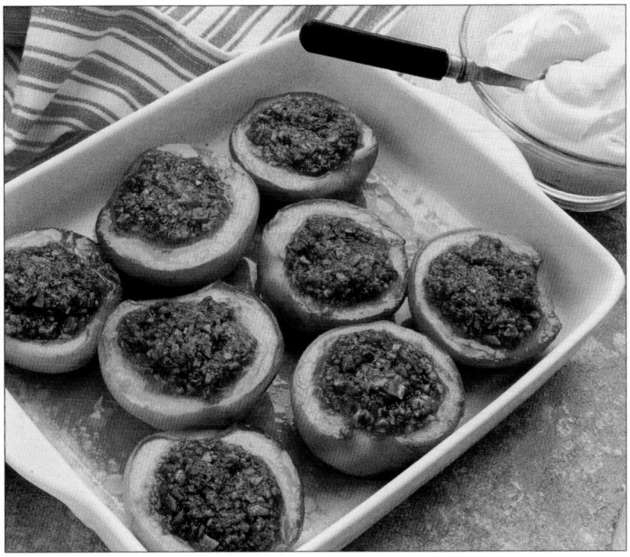

Stuffed Peaches with Mascarpone Cream

These peaches are packed with an amaretti and almond filling and then slowly baked in the oven.

Serves 4

4 large peaches, halved and stoned (pitted)
40g/1½oz amaretti, crumbled
30ml/2 tbsp ground almonds
45ml/3 tbsp sugar
15ml/1 tbsp unsweetened cocoa powder
150ml/¼ pint/⅔ cup sweet wine
25g/1oz/2 tbsp butter

For the mascarpone cream
30ml/2 tbsp caster (superfine) sugar
3 egg yolks
15ml/1 tbsp sweet wine
225g/8oz/1 cup mascarpone cheese
150ml/¼ pint/⅔ cup double (heavy) cream

1 Preheat the oven to 200°C/ 400°F/Gas 6. Using a teaspoon, scoop some of the flesh from the cavities in the peaches, to make a space for stuffing. Chop the scooped-out flesh.

2 Mix together the amaretti, almonds, sugar, cocoa and peach flesh. Add enough wine to make the mixture into a thick paste.

3 Place the peaches in a buttered ovenproof dish and fill them with the stuffing. Dot with the butter, then pour the remaining wine into the dish. Bake for 35 minutes.

4 To make the mascarpone cream, beat the sugar and egg yolks until thick and pale. Stir in the wine, then fold in the mascarpone. Whip the double cream until it forms soft peaks and fold into the mixture. Remove the peaches from the oven and leave to cool. Serve at room temperature, with the mascarpone cream passed round separately.

Cook's Tip
Mascarpone is a thick, velvety Italian cream cheese, made from cow's milk. It is often used in desserts, or eaten with fresh fruit.

Poached Pears in Red Wine

In this recipe, the pears take on a red blush from the wine and make a very pretty dessert. For best results, use a small slow cooker, which ensures that the pears stay submerged during cooking.

Serves 4

1 bottle fruity red wine
150g/5oz/¾ cup caster (superfine) sugar
45ml/3 tbsp clear honey
1 cinnamon stick
1 vanilla pod (bean), split lengthways
large strip of lemon or orange rind
2 whole cloves
2 black peppercorns
4 firm ripe pears
juice of ½ lemon
mint leaves, to decorate
whipped cream or sour cream, to serve

1 Pour the red wine into the ceramic cooking pot. Add the sugar, honey, cinnamon stick, vanilla pod, lemon or orange rind, cloves and peppercorns. Cover with the lid and cook on high for 30 minutes, stirring occasionally.

2 Meanwhile, peel the pears using a vegetable peeler, leaving the stem intact. Take a very thin slice off the base of each pear so it will stand square and upright. As each pear is peeled, toss it in the lemon juice to prevent the flesh browning when exposed to the air.

3 Place the pears in the spiced wine mixture in the cooking pot. Cover with the lid and cook for 2–4 hours, turning the pears occasionally, until they are just tender; be careful not to overcook them.

4 Transfer the pears to a bowl, using a slotted spoon. Continue to cook the wine mixture, uncovered, for a further hour, until reduced and thickened a little, then turn off the slow cooker and leave to cool. Alternatively, to save time, pour the cooking liquor into a pan and boil briskly for 10–15 minutes.

5 Strain the cooled liquid over the pears and chill for at least 3 hours. Divide the pears between four individual serving dishes and spoon a little of the wine syrup over each one. Garnish with fresh mint and serve with whipped or sour cream.

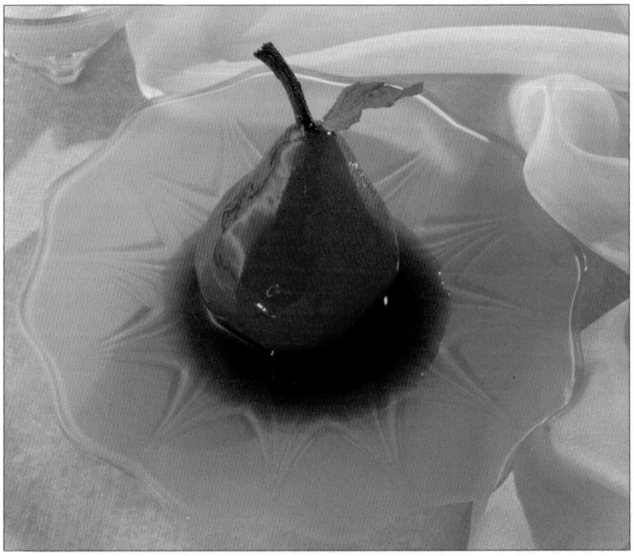

Stuffed Peaches Energy 626kcal/2607kJ; Protein 12g; Carbohydrate 40.9g, of which sugars 36g; Fat 44g, of which saturates 23.5g; Cholesterol 240mg; Calcium 96mg; Fibre 2.7g; Sodium 130mg.
Poached Pears in Red Wine Energy 87kcal/367kJ; Protein 0.5g; Carbohydrate 16.6g, of which sugars 16.6g; Fat 0.2g, of which saturates 0g; Cholesterol 0mg; Calcium 19mg; Fibre 3.3g; Sodium 7mg.

Coconut Custard

This slow-cooker dessert, made with rich, creamy coconut milk, is delicious served with a selection of fresh fruit.

Serves 4

4 eggs
75g/3oz/generous ⅓ cup soft light brown sugar
250ml/8fl oz/1 cup coconut milk
5ml/1 tsp vanilla, rose or jasmine extract
icing (confectioners') sugar, to decorate
sliced fresh fruit, to serve

1 Pour about 2.5cm/1in of hot water into the base of the ceramic cooking pot and switch the slow cooker on to the low setting. Whisk the eggs and sugar in a bowl until smooth. Gradually add the coconut milk and flavoured extract, and whisk well.

2 Strain the mixture into a jug (pitcher), then pour into four individual heatproof glasses, ramekins or one single ovenproof dish. Cover the containers with clear film (plastic wrap).

3 Place the dishes in the slow cooker and, if necessary, pour a little more boiling water around them to reach just over halfway up their sides.

4 Cover the ceramic cooking pot with the lid, then cook for 3 hours, or until the custards are lightly set. Test with a fine skewer or cocktail stick (toothpick); it should come out clean.

5 Carefully lift the dishes out of the slow cooker and leave to cool. Once cool, chill in the refrigerator until ready to serve. Decorate the custards with a light dusting of icing sugar, and serve with sliced fruit.

Cook's Tip
Line the bases of individual ramekins with rounds of baking parchment, then lightly oil the sides. After cooking and chilling, run a knife around the insides of the custards and turn out on to individual dessert plates.

Coconut Crème Caramel

This is a version of the classic French dessert made with coconut milk.

Serves 4–6

4 large (US extra large) eggs
4 egg yolks
50g/2oz/¼ cup caster (superfine) sugar
600ml/1 pint/2½ cups coconut milk
toasted slivers of coconut, to decorate

For the caramel
150g/5oz/¾ cup caster (superfine) sugar

1 Preheat the oven to 160°C/325°F/Gas 3. To make the caramel, heat the sugar and 75ml/5 tbsp water in a heavy pan, stirring until the sugar dissolves. Bring to the boil and, without stirring, let the mixture bubble until dark golden and almost like treacle.

2 Pour the caramel into an ovenproof dish, tilting the dish to swirl it around so that it covers the bottom and sides – you will need to do this quickly. Set aside and leave the caramel to set.

3 In a bowl, beat the eggs and egg yolks with the caster sugar. Heat the coconut milk in a small pan, but don't allow it to boil. Then gradually pour it on to the egg mixture, while beating constantly. Pour the mixture through a sieve (strainer) over the caramel in the dish.

4 Set the dish in a bain-marie. You can use a roasting pan or wide oven dish half-filled with water. Place it in the oven for 50 minutes, or until the custard has just set, but still feels soft when touched. Leave the dish to cool, then chill in the refrigerator for at least 6 hours, or overnight.

5 To serve, loosen the custard around the sides using a thin knife. Place a flat serving plate over the top and invert the custard, holding on to the dish and plate at the same time. Shake it a little before removing the inverted dish, then carefully lift it off as the caramel drizzles down the sides.

6 Decorate the custard with freshly grated coconut and serve immediately.

Coconut Custard Energy 175kcal/738kJ; Protein 7.5g; Carbohydrate 22.7g, of which sugars 22.7g; Fat 6.7g, of which saturates 2g; Cholesterol 227mg; Calcium 57mg; Fibre 0g; Sodium 151mg.
Coconut Caramel Energy 256kcal/1078kJ; Protein 9g; Carbohydrate 31g, of which sugars 31g; Fat 11g, of which saturates 4g; Cholesterol 338mg; Calcium 79mg; Fibre 0.4g; Sodium 200mg.

Citrus and Caramel Custards

These baked custards, made rich with cream and egg yolks, are delicately scented with tangy citrus flavours and aromatic cinnamon.

Serves 4

450ml/¾ pint/scant 2 cups milk
150ml/¼ pint/⅔ cup single (light) cream
1 cinnamon stick, broken in half
thinly pared rind of ½ lemon
thinly pared rind of ½ orange
4 egg yolks
5ml/1 tsp cornflour (cornstarch)
40g/1½oz/3 tbsp caster (superfine) sugar
grated rind of ½ lemon
grated rind of ½ orange
a little icing (confectioner's) sugar, to decorate

1 Place the milk and cream in a pan. Add the cinnamon stick and the strips of pared citrus rind. Bring to the boil, then simmer for 10 minutes.

2 Preheat the oven to 160°C/325°F/Gas 3. Whisk the egg yolks, cornflour and caster sugar together. Remove the rinds and cinnamon from the hot milk and cream and discard. Whisk the hot milk and cream into the egg yolk mixture.

3 Stir the grated citrus rind into the custard mixture. Pour into four individual cazuelas, or earthenware oven dishes, each about 13cm/5in in diameter. Place in a roasting pan and pour warm water into the pan to reach three-quarters of the way up their sides. Bake for 25–30 minutes, or until the custards are just set. Remove the dishes from the water; leave to cool, then chill.

4 Preheat the grill (broiler) to high. Sprinkle the custards liberally with icing sugar and place under the grill until the tops turn golden brown and caramelize. Serve immediately.

Cook's Tips

- *Prepare the grated rind first, then cut strips of rind from the ungrated side of the citrus fruits using a vegetable peeler.*
- *You can use a special cook's gas-gun or salamander to caramelize the tops instead of grilling (broiling) them.*

Petits Pots de Crème au Mocha

The name of these lovely slow-cooker custards comes from the baking cups they are traditionally made in, called pots de crème. The addition of coffee gives the dessert an even richer, more luxurious flavour.

Serves 4

5ml/1 tsp instant coffee powder
15ml/1 tbsp soft light brown sugar
300ml/½ pint/1¼ cups milk
150ml/¼ pint/⅔ cup double (heavy) cream
115g/4oz plain (semisweet) chocolate
15ml/1 tbsp coffee liqueur (optional)
4 egg yolks
whipped cream and candied cake decorations, to decorate (optional)

1 Put the instant coffee and brown sugar in a pan and stir in the milk and cream. Bring the mixture to the boil over medium heat, stirring constantly, until the coffee and sugar have dissolved completely.

2 Remove the pan from the heat and add the plain chocolate. Stir until the chocolate has melted, then stir in the coffee liqueur, if using.

3 In a bowl, whisk the egg yolks, then slowly whisk in the chocolate mixture until well blended. Strain the custard mixture into a large jug (pitcher) and divide equally among pots de crème or ramekins – first checking that they will all fit inside the ceramic cooking pot.

4 Cover each pot de crème or ramekin with a piece of foil, then transfer to the ceramic cooking pot. Pour enough hot water around the dishes to come just over halfway up their sides. Cover the slow cooker with the lid and cook on high for 2½–3 hours, or until the custards are just set and a knife inserted into the middle comes out clean.

5 Carefully remove the pots or ramekins from the cooker and leave to cool. Cover and chill in the refrigerator until ready to serve, then decorate with whipped cream and candied cake decorations, if you like.

Citrus Custards Energy 225kcal/939kJ; Protein 8g; Carbohydrate 16.6g, of which sugars 16.6g; Fat 14.6g, of which saturates 7.3g; Cholesterol 229mg; Calcium 197mg; Fibre 0g; Sodium 69mg.
Petits Pots Energy 443kcal/1840kJ; Protein 8.3g; Carbohydrate 23.7g, of which sugars 23.7g; Fat 35.7g, of which saturates 20.2g; Cholesterol 264mg; Calcium 196mg; Fibre 0.2g; Sodium 74mg.

Maple Custards

Maple syrup has a really distinctive flavour and gives these little slow-cooker desserts a wonderfully rich and indulgent taste. Try to find pure maple syrup – it will make all the difference to these custards.

Serves 6

3 eggs
120ml/4fl oz/½ cup maple syrup
250ml/8fl oz/1 cup warm milk
150ml/¼ pint/⅔ cup warm single (light) cream
5ml/1 tsp vanilla extract
whole nutmeg, to grate

1 Beat the eggs in a large mixing bowl, then whisk in the maple syrup, followed by the warm milk, warm cream and the vanilla extract. Grate in a little fresh nutmeg.

2 Strain the custard mixture into six individual ramekins – first checking that the dishes will all fit inside the ceramic cooking pot of the slow cooker in a single layer. Carefully cover each ramekin with a piece of kitchen foil, then place them in the ceramic cooking pot.

3 Pour very hot water around the dishes to come about three-quarters of the way up their sides. Cover with the lid and cook on low for 2½–3 hours, or until set. To test, insert a skewer in the middle; it should come out clean.

4 Transfer the custards to a wire rack. Leave for 5 minutes and serve warm, or leave to cool completely, then chill. Remove from the refrigerator about 30 minutes before serving.

Cook's Tip

Warming the milk and cream until tepid will help the custard cook and set more quickly. You can do this in a pan on the stove, or more simply, pour the milk and cream into a heatproof bowl or jug (pitcher) and place in the slow cooker filled with near-boiling water to a depth of about 5cm/2in. Switch the slow cooker to high and leave for 30 minutes. Remove the milk, then turn the slow cooker to low and use the hot water in the ceramic cooking pot to cook the custards.

Baked Coffee Custards

These delightfully rich custards are flavoured with coffee. They are ideal for a dinner party as you can bake them in the oven before the guests arrive and then chill until needed.

Serves 4

25g/1oz/6 tbsp finely ground fresh coffee
300ml/½ pint/1¼ cups milk
150ml/¼ pint/⅔ cup single (light) cream
2 eggs, beaten
30ml/2 tbsp caster (superfine) sugar
whipped cream and unsweetened cocoa powder, to decorate

1 Preheat the oven to 190°C/375°F/Gas 5. Put the ground coffee in a heatproof jug (pitcher). Heat the milk in a pan until it is nearly boiling. Pour the milk over the coffee and leave to stand for 5 minutes.

2 Strain the coffee-flavoured milk back into the pan through a fine sieve (strainer). Add the single cream and heat again until nearly boiling.

3 Beat the eggs and sugar in a large bowl. Pour the heated coffee-flavoured cream into the bowl, whisking all the time. Strain into the rinsed jug.

4 Carefully pour the egg and cream mixture into four 150ml/¼ pint/⅔ cup ramekins. Cover each with a piece of foil or baking parchment.

5 Stand the ramekins in a roasting pan and pour enough hot water into the roasting pan to come halfway up the sides of the ramekins. Bake in the preheated oven for 40 minutes, or until lightly set.

6 Remove the ramekins from the roasting pan and allow to cool. When cold, chill the custards in the refrigerator for about 2 hours. Decorate each custard with a swirl of whipped cream and a sprinkling of unsweetened cocoa powder, if you like, before serving.

Maple Custard Energy 174kcal/735kJ; Protein 8.6g; Carbohydrate 24.5g, of which sugars 18.7g; Fat 5.3g, of which saturates 1.6g; Cholesterol 116mg; Calcium 97mg; Fibre 9.1g; Sodium 120mg.
Coffee Custards Energy 207kcal/860kJ; Protein 8.4g; Carbohydrate 12.1g, of which sugars 12.1g; Fat 14.3g, of which saturates 7.6g; Cholesterol 174mg; Calcium 147mg; Fibre 0g; Sodium 96mg.

Caramel Custard with Fresh Fruit

A creamy caramel dessert is a wonderful way to end a meal. It is light and delicious, and easy to make.

Serves 6
6 eggs
4 drops vanilla extract
115g/4oz/generous ½ cup sugar
750ml/1¼ pints/3 cups semi-skimmed (low-fat) milk
fresh fruit, such as strawberries, blueberries, orange and banana slices, and raspberries, to serve

For the caramel
30ml/2 tbsp sugar
30ml/2 tbsp water

1 To make the caramel, place the sugar and water in a heavy pan and heat until the sugar has completely dissolved and the mixture is bubbling and pale gold in colour. Watch the sugar carefully, as it can quickly burn once it begins to caramelize. Pour carefully into a 1.2 litre/2 pint/5 cup soufflé dish. Leave the caramel to cool.

2 Preheat the oven to 180°C/350°F/Gas 4. To make the custard, break the eggs one at a time into a mixing bowl and whisk until frothy.

3 Stir the vanilla extract into the whisked eggs and gradually add the sugar. Add the milk in a steady stream, whisking constantly as you pour.

4 Carefully pour the custard over the top of the caramel in the base of the soufflé dish.

5 Cook the custard in the oven for 35–40 minutes. Remove from the oven and leave to cool for 30 minutes or until the mixture is set.

6 Loosen the custard from the sides of the dish with a knife. Place a serving dish upside-down on top of the soufflé dish and invert, giving a gentle shake if necessary to turn out the custard on to the serving dish.

7 Arrange fresh fruit of your choice around the custard on the serving dish and serve immediately.

Rice Condé Sundae

Slowly cooking rice pudding on top of the hob instead of in the oven gives it a light, creamy texture, especially if you remember to stir it frequently. It is particularly good served cold with a topping of fruit and toasted nuts or a trickle of hot chocolate sauce.

Serves 4
50g/2oz/generous ¼ cup short grain pudding rice
5ml/1 tsp vanilla extract
2.5ml/½ tsp ground cinnamon
45ml/3 tbsp sugar
600ml/1 pint/2½ cups milk

For the toppings
soft berry fruits, such as strawberries, raspberries and cherries
chocolate sauce and flaked (sliced) toasted almonds (optional)

1 Mix the rice, vanilla extract, ground cinnamon and sugar in a pan. Pour in the milk and slowly bring the mixture to the boil, stirring constantly. Reduce the heat to low so that the mixture is barely simmering.

2 Cook the rice over low heat for about 30–40 minutes, stirring frequently to release the starch from the grains. Add extra milk to the rice if it begins to dry out a little during the cooking process.

3 When the rice grains are soft, remove the pan from the heat. Allow the rice to cool completely, stirring it occasionally, then chill in the refrigerator.

4 Before serving, stir the rice pudding and spoon it into four sundae dishes. Top with soft berry fruits, and with chocolate sauce and toasted almonds, if using.

Variation
For a special occasion, use single cream instead of milk, and glaze the fruit with a little melted redcurrant jelly. (Add a splash of port to the jelly, if you like.)

Custard Energy 197kcal/830kJ; Protein 10.6g; Carbohydrate 23.3g, of which sugars 23.3g; Fat 7.7g, of which saturates 2.9g; Cholesterol 198mg; Calcium 187mg; Fibre 0g; Sodium 125mg.
Rice Condé Energy 185kcal/782kJ; Protein 6.9g; Carbohydrate 34.8g, of which sugars 24.8g; Fat 2.7g, of which saturates 1.6g; Cholesterol 9mg; Calcium 204mg; Fibre 1.1g; Sodium 71mg.

Winter Fruit Poached in Mulled Wine

Poaching fresh apples and pears with dried apricots and figs in a spicy wine syrup in the slow cooker makes a seasonal winter dessert. Serve on its own or with a generous spoonful of thick cream.

Serves 4

300ml/½ pint/1¼ cups fruity red wine
300ml/½ pint/1¼ cups fresh apple or orange juice
thinly pared strip of orange or lemon peel
45ml/3 tbsp clear honey
1 small cinnamon stick
4 whole cloves
4 cardamom pods, split
2 pears, such as Comice or William
8 ready-to-eat figs
12 ready-to-eat dried apricots
2 eating apples, peeled, cored and thickly sliced

1 Pour the wine and apple or orange juice into the ceramic cooking pot. Add the citrus peel, honey, cinnamon stick, cloves and cardamom pods. Cover with the lid and cook on high for 1 hour.

2 Peel, core and halve the pears, keeping the stalk intact if possible. Place in the slow cooker with the figs and apricots. Cook for 1 hour. Gently turn the pears, then add the sliced apples and cook for a further 1½–2 hours, or until all the fruit is tender.

3 Using a slotted spoon, remove the fruit from the cooking pot and place in a serving dish. Set aside while you finish the syrup.

4 Strain the syrup into a pan, discarding the spices, then bring to the boil. Boil vigorously for about 10 minutes, until reduced by about one-third. Pour over the fruit and serve hot or cold.

Cook's Tip
Choose tart, well-tasting apples such as Cox's Orange Pippin, Braeburn or Granny Smith. They stand up particularly well against the sweet dried fruits and spicy, robust red wine syrup.

Baked Stuffed Apples

Using Italian amaretti to stuff the apples in this slow-cooker dessert gives a lovely almondy flavour. Dried cranberries and glacé fruit add sweetness and colour. Choose apples that will stay firm during cooking.

Serves 4

75g/3oz/6 tbsp butter, softened
45ml/3 tbsp orange or apple juice
75g/3oz/scant ½ cup light muscovado (brown) sugar
grated rind and juice of ½ orange
1.5ml/¼ tsp ground cinnamon
30ml/2 tbsp crushed amaretti
25g/1oz/¼ cup pecan nuts, chopped
25g/1oz/¼ cup dried cranberries or sour cherries
25g/1oz/¼ cup luxury mixed glacé (candied) fruit, chopped
4 large cooking apples, such as Bramleys
cream, crème fraîche or vanilla ice cream, to serve

1 Grease the ceramic cooking pot with 15g/½oz/1 tbsp of the butter, then pour in the fruit juice and switch the slow cooker to the high setting.

2 Put the remaining butter, the sugar, orange rind and juice, cinnamon and amaretti crumbs in a bowl and mix well.

3 Add the nuts and dried cranberries or sour cherries and glacé fruit to the bowl and mix well, then set aside the filling while you prepare the apples.

4 Wash and dry the apples. Remove the cores using an apple corer, then carefully enlarge each core cavity to twice its size, using the corer to shave out more flesh. Using a sharp knife, score each apple around its equator.

5 Divide the filling among the apples, packing it into the hole, then piling it on top. Stand the apples in the cooking pot and cover with the lid. Reduce the temperature to low and cook for 4 hours, or until tender.

6 Transfer the apples to warmed serving plates and spoon the sauce over the top. Serve immediately, with cream, crème fraîche or vanilla ice cream.

Winter Fruit Energy 347kcal/1476kJ; Protein 5g; Carbohydrate 78.1g, of which sugars 78.1g; Fat 1.9g, of which saturates 0g; Cholesterol 0mg; Calcium 284mg; Fibre 11.4g; Sodium 72mg.
Baked Stuffed Apples Energy 347kcal/1457kJ; Protein 1.6g; Carbohydrate 42.4g, of which sugars 41.3g; Fat 20.3g, of which saturates 10.3g; Cholesterol 40mg; Calcium 27mg; Fibre 3g; Sodium 131mg.

Papaya Cooked with Ginger

Spicy ginger enhances the delicate flavour of papaya perfectly. This slow-cooker recipe is excellent for busy people because it takes no more than 10 minutes to prepare and can then be left to cook gently. Be careful not to overcook the papaya or the flesh will become watery.

Serves 4

150ml/¼ pint/⅔ cup hot water
45ml/3 tbsp raisins
shredded finely pared rind and juice of 1 lime
2 ripe papayas
2 pieces stem ginger in syrup, drained, plus 15ml/1 tbsp syrup from the jar
8 amaretti or other dessert biscuits (cookies), coarsely crushed
25g/1oz/¼ cup pistachio nuts, chopped
15ml/1 tbsp light muscovado (brown) sugar
60ml/4 tbsp crème fraîche, plus extra to serve

1 Pour the water into the base of the ceramic cooking pot and switch the slow cooker to high. Put the raisins in a small bowl and pour over the lime juice. Stir until well combined, then leave to soak for at least 5 minutes, while preparing the remaining ingredients.

2 Cut the papayas in half and scoop out and discard their seeds using a teaspoon.

3 Finely chop the stem ginger and combine with the biscuits, raisins and lime juice, lime rind, two-thirds of the nuts, the sugar and crème fraîche.

4 Fill the papayas with the mixture and place in the cooking pot. Cover and cook for 1–1½ hours. Drizzle with the ginger syrup, sprinkle with the remaining nuts and serve immediately, with crème fraîche.

Variation
Try using chopped almonds and Greek (US strained plain) yogurt in place of the pistachio nuts and crème fraîche.

Hot Bananas with Rum and Raisins

These sticky, sweet bananas are made in the slow cooker and are utterly moreish. The rich sauce becomes almost toffee-like during the long cooking, and is irresistible.

Serves 4

30ml/2 tbsp seedless raisins
45ml/3 tbsp dark rum
40g/1½oz/3 tbsp unsalted (sweet) butter
50g/2oz/¼ cup soft light brown sugar
4 slightly under-ripe bananas, peeled and halved lengthways
1.5ml/¼ tsp grated nutmeg
1.5ml/¼ tsp ground cinnamon
25g/1oz/¼ cup flaked (sliced) almonds, toasted (optional)
whipped cream or vanilla ice cream, to serve

1 Put the raisins in a bowl and spoon over 30ml/2 tbsp of the rum. Set aside and leave to soak.

2 Cut the butter into small cubes and place in the ceramic cooking pot with the sugar and remaining 15ml/1 tbsp rum. Switch the slow cooker to high and leave uncovered for 15 minutes, until the butter and sugar have melted.

3 Add the bananas to the butter and sugar mixture, cover with the lid and cook for 30 minutes, or until the fruit is almost tender, turning over the bananas halfway through cooking time.

4 Sprinkle the nutmeg and cinnamon over the bananas, then stir in the rum and raisins. Re-cover and cook for 10 minutes.

5 Carefully lift the bananas out of the ceramic cooking pot and arrange on a serving dish or individual plates. Spoon over the sauce, then sprinkle with almonds, if using. Serve hot with whipped cream or vanilla ice cream.

Variation
If you don't like the taste of rum, try using an orange liqueur, such as Cointreau, instead. It makes a very good alternative and is a little less overpowering.

Papaya Energy 302kcal/1272kJ; Protein 4.1g; Carbohydrate 45.6g, of which sugars 36.6g; Fat 12.8g, of which saturates 5.7g; Cholesterol 17mg; Calcium 70mg; Fibre 5.7g; Sodium 136mg.
Hot Bananas Energy 323kcal/1355kJ; Protein 3g; Carbohydrate 47.1g, of which sugars 44.7g; Fat 12.1g, of which saturates 5.6g; Cholesterol 21mg; Calcium 33mg; Fibre 1.9g; Sodium 72mg.

Baked Peaches

This recipe uses fresh ripe peaches with a hint of cloves to give them a lovely aromatic, spicy flavour. The fruits are slowly baked in the oven until deliciously tender. This is a great dish to make the most of peaches when they are in season.

Serves 6

40g/1½oz/3 tbsp unsalted (sweet) butter
6 firm ripe peaches, washed
12 whole cloves
90g/3½oz/½ cup vanilla sugar
45ml/3 tbsp brandy or dry white wine (optional)
fresh mint leaves and a little sifted icing (confectioners') sugar, to decorate
shelled pistachio nuts and whipped cream or crème fraîche, to serve

1 Preheat the oven to 180°C/350°F/Gas 4. Spread half the unsalted butter around an ovenproof dish, making sure both the sides and base are well coated.

2 Halve the peaches and remove the stones (pits) using a sharp knife. Place the peach halves, skin side down, in the prepared dish. Push a whole clove into the centre of each peach half.

3 Sprinkle the vanilla sugar over the peaches and dot the remaining butter into each peach half. Drizzle over the brandy or dry white wine, if using. Bake for 30–40 minutes, or until the peaches are tender.

4 Decorate with sprigs of fresh mint, and sprinkle over a little of the icing sugar. Serve the baked peaches hot or cold, with freshly whipped cream or crème fraîche and a few shelled pistachio nuts.

Cook's Tip
The cooking time will depend on the size and ripeness of the peaches. Small, ripe peaches will cook quicker than larger, less ripe peaches. Check them with a skewer after 30 minutes.

Cassava Sweet

This sweet and sticky baked dessert is made with cassava root and coconut milk with a hint of aniseed. It is perfect with jasmine tea.

Serves 6–8

350ml/12fl oz/1½ cups coconut milk
115g/4oz/generous ½ cup palm sugar (jaggery)
2.5ml/½ tsp ground aniseed
salt
675g/1½lb cassava root, peeled and coarsely grated

1 Preheat the oven to 190°C/375°F/Gas 5. Grease a baking dish with butter.

2 In a mixing bowl, whisk the coconut milk with the palm sugar, ground aniseed and a pinch of salt, until the palm sugar has completely dissolved.

3 Beat the grated cassava root into the coconut mixture until well combined. Pour into the greased baking dish.

4 Place the dish in the oven and bake for about 1 hour, or until cooked through and golden brown on top.

5 Leave the sweet to cool a little in the dish before serving warm or at room temperature.

Variation
This dessert can also be made using sweet potatoes or yams in place of the cassava root.

Cook's Tip
To prepare the cassava root for grating, use a sharp knife to split the whole length of the root and then carefully peel off the skin using a vegetable peeler or knife. Simply grate the peeled root using a coarse grater.

Baked Peaches Energy 70kcal/299kJ; Protein 1.1g; Carbohydrate 17.3g, of which sugars 17.3g; Fat 0.1g, of which saturates 0g; Cholesterol 0mg; Calcium 8mg; Fibre 1.5g; Sodium 3mg.
Cassava Sweet Energy 254kcal/1086kJ; Protein 1g; Carbohydrate 64g, of which sugars 25g; Fat 1g, of which saturates 1g; Cholesterol 2mg; Calcium 39mg; Fibre 1.8g; Sodium 0.2g.

Tapioca Pudding

This slow-cooker version of the classic tapioca pudding is made from large pearl tapioca and coconut milk and is served warm. It is very good served with fresh tropical fruits such as lychees.

Serves 4

115g/4oz/⅔ cup large pearl tapioca
475ml/16fl oz/2 cups very hot water
115g/4oz/generous ½ cup caster (superfine) sugar
pinch of salt
250ml/8fl oz/1 cup coconut milk
250g/9oz prepared tropical fruits
shredded lime rind and shaved fresh coconut, to decorate (optional)

1 Put the tapioca in a bowl and pour over enough warm water to cover generously. Leave the tapioca to soak for 1 hour until the grains swell, then drain well and set aside.

2 Pour the measured hot water into the ceramic cooking pot and switch the slow cooker to the high setting. Add the sugar and salt and stir until dissolved.

3 Cover the slow cooker with the lid and cook for about 30 minutes, until the water inside the cooking pot reaches boiling point.

4 Add the tapioca and coconut milk to the ceramic cooking pot and stir until well combined. Cover again with the lid and cook for a further 1–1½ hours, or until the tapioca grains have all turned transparent.

5 Spoon into one large dish or four individual bowls and serve warm with tropical fruits, decorated with the lime rind and coconut shavings, if using.

Cook's Tip
This dish includes a considerable amount of sugar but you may prefer to reduce the quantity according to taste.

Souffléed Rice Pudding

Using skimmed milk to make this baked pudding is a healthy option, but you could use whole milk if you prefer a creamier taste.

Serves 4

65g/2½oz/⅓ cup short grain pudding rice
45ml/3 tbsp clear honey
750ml/1¼ pints/3 cups skimmed milk
1 vanilla pod (bean) or 2.5ml/½ tsp vanilla extract
2 egg whites
5ml/1 tsp freshly grated nutmeg
wafer biscuits, to serve (optional)

1 Place the rice, honey and milk in a heavy or non-stick pan, and bring the milk to just below boiling point, watching it closely to prevent it from boiling over. Add the vanilla pod (but do not add vanilla extract at this stage, if using).

2 Reduce the heat to the lowest setting and cover the pan with a tight-fitting lid. Leave to cook for about 1–1¼ hours, stirring occasionally to prevent sticking, until most of the liquid has been absorbed.

3 Remove the vanilla pod or, if using vanilla extract, add this to the rice mixture now. Preheat the oven to 220°C/425°F/Gas 7. Grease a 1 litre/1¾ pint/4 cup baking dish with butter.

4 Place the egg whites in a large grease-free bowl and whisk them until they hold soft peaks. Using either a large metal spoon or a spatula, carefully fold the egg whites evenly into the rice and milk mixture. Transfer to the baking dish.

5 Sprinkle with grated nutmeg and bake in the oven for about 15–20 minutes, until the rice pudding has risen well and the surface is golden brown. Serve the pudding hot, with wafer biscuits, if you like.

Cook's Tip
This pudding is also delicious if served with a topping of stewed dried fruit, such as apricots, prunes or dates.

Tapioca Pudding Energy 273kcal/1164kJ; Protein 2.7g; Carbohydrate 66.7g, of which sugars 41.9g; Fat 1.3g, of which saturates 0.4g; Cholesterol 0mg; Calcium 43mg; Fibre 1.7g; Sodium 73mg.
Rice Pudding Energy 183kcal/773kJ; Protein 9.1g; Carbohydrate 30.4g, of which sugars 17.4g; Fat 3.3g, of which saturates 2g; Cholesterol 11mg; Calcium 230mg; Fibre 0g; Sodium 112mg.

Traditional Rice Pudding

This classic, slow-baked dessert is delectably smooth and creamy with just a hint of fragrant spices, thanks to the vanilla pod and a little fresh nutmeg.

Serves 4

600ml/1 pint/2½ cups creamy milk
1 vanilla pod (bean)
50g/2oz/generous ¼ cup short grain pudding rice
45ml/3 tbsp caster (superfine) sugar
25g/1oz/2 tbsp butter
freshly grated nutmeg

1 Pour the creamy milk into a pan and add the vanilla pod. Bring to simmering point, then remove from the heat, cover and leave the flavour of the vanilla to mingle with the milk for about 1 hour.

2 Preheat the oven to 150°C/300°F/Gas 2. Put the rice and sugar in an ovenproof dish. Strain the vanilla-flavoured milk over the rice, discarding the vanilla pod. Stir to mix, then dot the surface with the butter.

3 Bake, uncovered, in the preheated oven for about 2 hours. After about 40 minutes, stir the pudding, gently folding the surface skin into the rice.

4 Stir the rice pudding again after a further 40 minutes. At this stage, sprinkle the surface of the pudding with the freshly grated nutmeg. Allow the pudding to finish cooking in the oven without any further stirring. Spoon into a warmed bowl and serve immediately.

Cook's Tips

- *Always use a non-stick pan when heating milk, if you have one. Otherwise the milk is likely to stick to the bottom of the pan and will easily burn.*
- *Serve the rice pudding with a spoonful of thick cherry or raspberry jam, if you like.*

Rice Pudding with Lemon and Cinnamon

There are many versions of rice pudding to choose from, but the presence here of pistachios, lemon, cinnamon and rose petals, makes this version a distinctly unusual one.

Serves 4–6

75g/3oz/scant ½ cup short grain pudding rice
45ml/3 tbsp sugar
900ml/1½ pints/3¾ cups full-fat (whole) milk
25g/1oz/2 tbsp unsalted (sweet) butter
1 cinnamon stick
strip of lemon rind
halved pistachios and rose petals, to decorate (optional)

1 Put the rice, sugar, full-fat milk, unsalted butter, cinnamon stick and lemon rind into a large heavy pan. Gently stir until all the ingredients are well combined.

2 Cover the pan with a tight-fitting lid and cook the rice over very low heat, stirring occasionally, for about 1½ hours. Add a little extra milk or water if the mixture looks like it is becoming a little dry.

3 When the rice has absorbed the liquid and become thick and creamy, remove and discard the cinnamon stick and the lemon rind.

4 Spoon the rice pudding into warmed, individual serving bowls. Sprinkle each serving with halved pistachios and rose petals, to decorate, if you like.

Variations

- *For an extra creamy version of this rice pudding, fold in 150ml/¼ pint/⅔ cup lightly whipped double (heavy) cream, just before serving.*
- *Instead of rose petals, try decorating with some other edible flowers or leaves.*

Rice Pudding Energy 433kcal/1829kJ; Protein 5.8g; Carbohydrate 85.6g, of which sugars 65.7g; Fat 6.9g, of which saturates 3.3g; Cholesterol 112mg; Calcium 113mg; Fibre 0.5g; Sodium 68mg.
Pudding with Lemon Energy 205kcal/852kJ; Protein 5.9g; Carbohydrate 24.6g, of which sugars 14.6g; Fat 9.3g, of which saturates 5.9g; Cholesterol 30mg; Calcium 184mg; Fibre 0g; Sodium 90mg.

Caramel Rice Pudding with Fresh Fruits

This slowly baked rice pudding is finished with a crunchy caramelized topping. It is a family favourite served with plenty of fresh fruit.

Serves 4

15g/½oz/1 tbsp butter
50g/2oz/generous ¼ cup short grain pudding rice
75ml/5 tbsp demerara (raw) sugar
400g/14oz can evaporated milk made up to about 600ml/1 pint/2½ cups with water
2 fresh baby pineapples
2 figs
1 crisp eating apple
10ml/2 tsp lemon juice
salt

1 Preheat the oven to 150°C/300°F/Gas 2. Grease a soufflé dish lightly with a little of the butter.

2 Put the rice in a sieve (strainer) and wash it thoroughly under cold running water. Drain well and place it into the prepared soufflé dish.

3 Add 30ml/2 tbsp of the demerara sugar to the soufflé dish, with a pinch of salt. Pour on the diluted evaporated milk and stir gently to combine.

4 Dot the surface of the rice with the remaining butter. Bake in the preheated oven for about 2 hours, then leave to cool for 30 minutes.

5 Meanwhile, quarter the baby pineapples and the figs. Cut the apple into segments and toss the pieces in a bowl with the lemon juice. Preheat the grill (broiler).

6 Sprinkle the remaining sugar evenly over the rice. Cook under the grill for 5 minutes or until the sugar has caramelized.

7 Leave the rice to stand for 5 minutes to allow the caramel to harden, then serve with the fresh fruit.

Coconut Rice Pudding

A delicious adaptation of the classic creamy rice pudding. This dessert is baked in a clay pot and flavoured with coconut milk, finished off with a crispy coconut crust.

Serves 4

75g/3oz/scant ½ cup short grain pudding rice
40g/1½oz/3 tbsp caster (superfine) sugar
2.5ml/½ tsp vanilla extract
300ml/½ pint/1¼ cups milk
400ml/14fl oz/1⅔ cups coconut milk
105ml/7 tbsp single (light) cream
30ml/2 tbsp desiccated (dry unsweetened shredded) coconut or slivers of fresh coconut, to decorate

1 Soak a small clay pot in cold water for 15 minutes, then drain well. Add the rice, sugar, vanilla extract, milk, coconut milk and cream to the pot and mix thoroughly until all the ingredients are well combined.

2 Cover the clay pot with the lid and place in a cold oven. Set the oven temperature to 180°C/350°F/Gas 4 and cook the rice for about 1 hour.

3 Remove the lid from the clay pot, stir the pudding gently, then re-cover and cook for a further 30–45 minutes, or until the rice is tender.

4 Remove the lid, stir the pudding again, then sprinkle with desiccated coconut or slivers of fresh coconut.

5 Return the pot to the oven and bake, uncovered, for about 10–15 minutes, until the topping is just brown and crisp.

Variation
If you prefer, this rice pudding can be made with extra milk instead of the single cream to reduce the fat content of the dessert. However, use full-cream (whole) milk, for a richer, creamier flavour.

Caramel Pudding Energy 313kcal/1321kJ; Protein 9.6g; Carbohydrate 54.3g, of which sugars 44.3g; Fat 7.6g, of which saturates 4.5g; Cholesterol 25mg; Calcium 312mg; Fibre 1.9g; Sodium 147mg.
Coconut Pudding Energy 259kcal/1087kJ; Protein 5.8g; Carbohydrate 34g, of which sugars 19.9g; Fat 11.6g, of which saturates 8.2g; Cholesterol 19mg; Calcium 153mg; Fibre 1g; Sodium 153mg.

Baked Coconut Rice Pudding with Pineapple and Ginger

This rice pudding needs long, slow cooking in a low oven but it is well worth the wait.

Serves 4–6

90g/3½oz/½ cup short grain pudding rice
600ml/1 pint/2½ cups coconut milk
300ml/½ pint/1¼ cups full-fat (whole) milk
75g/2¾oz/scant ½ cup caster (superfine) sugar
25g/1oz/2 tbsp butter, plus extra for greasing
45ml/3 tbsp grated fresh or desiccated (dry unsweetened shredded) coconut, toasted
1 small, ripe pineapple
30ml/2 tbsp sesame oil
5cm/2in piece fresh root ginger, peeled and grated
shavings of toasted coconut, to decorate

1 Preheat the oven to 150°C/300°F/Gas 2. Grease an ovenproof dish. In a bowl, mix the rice with the coconut milk, milk and 50g/2oz/¼ cup of the sugar and pour it into the ovenproof dish. Dot pieces of butter over the top and place the dish in the oven.

2 After 30 minutes, take the dish out and gently stir in the toasted coconut. Return it to the oven for a further 1½ hours, or until almost all the milk is absorbed and a golden skin has formed on top of the pudding.

3 Meanwhile, using a sharp knife, peel the pineapple and remove the core, then cut the flesh into bitesize cubes.

4 Towards the end of the cooking time, heat the oil in a large wok or heavy pan. Stir in the ginger, stir-fry until the aroma is released, then add the pineapple cubes, turning them over to sear on both sides. Sprinkle with the remaining sugar and continue to cook until the pineapple is slightly caramelized.

5 Serve the pudding spooned into bowls and topped with the hot, caramelized pineapple and toasted coconut.

Chocolate Chip and Banana Pudding

Rich, dense and sticky, this pudding is steamed in the slow cooker.

Serves 4

200g/7oz/1¾ cups self-raising (self-rising) flour
75g/3oz/6 tbsp unsalted (sweet) butter
2 ripe bananas, mashed
75g/3oz/6 tbsp caster (superfine) sugar
50ml/2fl oz/1¼ cups milk
1 egg, lightly beaten
75g/3oz/⅔ cup chocolate chips or chopped unsweetened chocolate

For the chocolate sauce

90g/3½oz/½ cup caster (superfine) sugar
50ml/2fl oz/¼ cup water
175g/6oz/1¼ cups plain (semisweet) chocolate chips or chopped unsweetened chocolate
25g/1oz/2 tbsp unsalted butter
30ml/2 tbsp brandy or orange juice

1 Grease and line the base of a 1 litre/1¾ pint/4 cup heatproof bowl with baking parchment. Put an inverted saucer in the base of the ceramic cooking pot and pour in 2.5cm/1in of hot water.

2 Turn the slow cooker to high. Sift the flour into a large bowl and rub in the butter until it resembles coarse breadcrumbs. Stir in the mashed bananas and the sugar and mix well.

3 In a clean bowl, whisk together the milk and egg, then beat into the banana mixture. Stir in the chocolate chips or chopped chocolate and spoon into the lined bowl. Cover with a double thickness of buttered foil and place in the cooking pot. Pour in boiling water to come just over halfway up the side of the bowl.

4 Cover and cook on high for 3–4 hours, or until well risen and a skewer comes out clean. Turn off the slow cooker and leave the pudding in the water while you make the sauce.

5 Heat the sugar and water in a pan, stirring, until the sugar has dissolved. Take off the heat and stir in the chocolate. Add the butter in the same way. Stir in the brandy or orange juice.

6 Run a knife around the inside of the bowl to loosen the pudding. Turn it out and serve hot, with the sauce poured over.

Baked Coconut Pudding Energy 414kcal/1735kJ; Protein 6g; Carbohydrate 56g, of which sugars 39g; Fat 19g, of which saturates 9g; Cholesterol 24mg; Calcium 156mg; Fibre 1.6g; Sodium 200mg.
Chocolate Pudding Energy 926kcal/3890kJ; Protein 11.1g; Carbohydrate 131.9g, of which sugars 93.2g; Fat 41.1g, of which saturates 24.6g; Cholesterol 118mg; Calcium 266mg; Fibre 3.3g; Sodium 378mg.

Sticky Coffee and Pear Pudding

This dark and moist fruity pudding is simple to make in the slow cooker.

Serves 6

115g/4oz/½ cup butter, softened, plus extra for greasing
30ml/2 tbsp ground coffee
15ml/1 tbsp near-boiling water
4 ripe pears, peeled, cored, halved and thinly sliced across each half part of the way through
juice of ½ orange
115g/4oz/generous ½ cup golden caster (superfine) sugar, plus 15ml/1 tbsp for baking
2 eggs, beaten
50g/2oz/½ cup self-raising (self-rising) flour, sifted
50g/2oz/½ cup toasted skinned hazelnuts, finely ground
45ml/3 tbsp maple syrup
fine strips of orange rind, to decorate

For the orange cream

300ml/½ pint/1¼ cups whipping cream
15ml/1 tbsp icing (confectioners') sugar, sifted
finely grated rind of ½ orange

1 Pour 2.5cm/1in of hot water into the ceramic cooking pot. Place an upturned saucer in the base, then turn on to high. Grease and line the base of a deep 18cm/7in cake tin (pan). Put the coffee in a bowl and pour the water over. Stir until dissolved. Brush the pears with the orange juice.

2 Beat the butter and the 115g/4oz sugar together in a bowl until light and fluffy, then beat in the eggs. Fold in the flour, then add the hazelnuts and coffee. Spoon into the tin, and level the surface. Pat the pears dry on kitchen paper and arrange in a circle in the sponge mixture. Brush them with some maple syrup, then sprinkle with the 15ml/1 tbsp caster sugar.

3 Cover the top of the tin with foil and place in the ceramic cooking pot. Pour in boiling water to come just over halfway up the sides of the tin. Cover and cook for 3–3½ hours, until firm.

4 Make the orange cream. Whip the cream, sugar and orange rind until soft peaks form. Spoon into a bowl and chill until needed. Leave the sponge to cool in the tin for 10 minutes, then turn over on to a serving plate. Brush with the remaining maple syrup and decorate with orange rind. Serve with the orange cream.

Steamed Chocolate Puddings

Drenched in a thick chocolate syrup and packed with fruit, this slow-cooker pudding is pure indulgence.

Serves 4

1 apple, peeled and cored, diced
25g/1oz/¼ cup cranberries, thawed if frozen
175g/6oz/¾ cup soft dark brown sugar
115g/4oz/½ cup soft margarine
2 eggs, lightly beaten
50g/2oz/½ cup self-raising (self-rising) flour, sifted
45ml/3 tbsp unsweetened cocoa powder

For the syrup

115g/4oz plain (semisweet) chocolate, chopped
30ml/2 tbsp clear honey
15g/½oz/1 tbsp unsalted butter
2.5ml/½ tsp vanilla extract

1 Pour 2.5cm/1in of hot water into the cooking pot and switch the slow cooker to high. Grease four individual heatproof bowls with oil, then line with baking parchment.

2 Place the diced apple in a bowl, then add the cranberries and 15ml/1 tbsp of the sugar. Mix well, then divide among the four bowls, gently patting it down into the base of each one.

3 Place the remaining sugar in a clean mixing bowl and add the margarine, eggs, flour and cocoa. Beat together until smooth. Spoon into the bowls and cover each with a double thickness of greased foil. Place the bowls in the cooking pot and pour in hot water to come two-thirds of the way up the sides of the bowls.

4 Cover with the lid and cook on high for 1½–2 hours, or until the puddings are well-risen and firm. Carefully remove from the slow cooker and leave to stand for 10 minutes.

5 Meanwhile, make the chocolate syrup. Put the chocolate, honey, butter and vanilla extract in a heatproof bowl and place in the hot water in the slow cooker. Leave for 10 minutes, until the butter has melted, then stir until smooth.

6 Run a knife around the edge of the puddings to loosen, then turn over on to plates. Serve immediately, with the syrup.

Coffee Pudding Energy 852kcal/3571kJ; Protein 12.5g; Carbohydrate 107g, of which sugars 45g; Fat 44.5g, of which saturates 23.8g; Cholesterol 169mg; Calcium 362mg; Fibre 5.3g; Sodium 493mg.
Steamed Puddings Energy 739kcal/3094kJ; Protein 9.1g; Carbohydrate 88.3g, of which sugars 77.2g; Fat 41.3g, of which saturates 14.4g; Cholesterol 124mg; Calcium 103mg; Fibre 3.1g; Sodium 438mg.

Date Puddings with Toffee Sauce

Fresh dates make this slow-cooker dessert an utterly irresistible treat.

Serves 6

50g/2oz/¼ cup butter, softened, plus extra for greasing
175g/6oz/generous 1 cup fresh dates, peeled, stoned (pitted) and chopped
75ml/5 tbsp boiling water
75g/3oz/½ cup light muscovado (brown) sugar
2 eggs, beaten
115g/4oz/1 cup self-raising (self-rising) flour
2.5ml/½ tsp bicarbonate of soda (baking soda)

For the sauce
50g/2oz/¼ cup butter, at room temperature
75g/3oz/½ cup light muscovado (brown) sugar
60ml/4 tbsp double (heavy) cream
30ml/2 tbsp brandy

1 Grease six individual pudding moulds or tins (pans) that will fit in the slow cooker. Pour very hot water into the ceramic cooking pot to a depth of 2cm/¾in. Switch the cooker to high.

2 Put the dates in a heatproof bowl with the boiling water and mash well with a potato masher to make a fairly smooth paste.

3 Put the butter and sugar in a mixing bowl and beat until pale and fluffy. Gradually beat in the eggs. Fold in the flour and bicarbonate of soda. Add the date paste and gently fold in.

4 Spoon the mixture into the greased moulds or tins. Cover each with a piece of foil. Place in the ceramic cooking pot and pour enough boiling water around the puddings to come just over halfway up the sides. Cover with the lid and cook on high for 1½–2 hours, or until well risen and firm. Remove the puddings from the slow cooker.

5 Meanwhile, make the sauce. Put the butter, sugar, cream and brandy in a pan and heat very gently, stirring occasionally, until the mixture is smooth. Increase the heat and boil for 1 minute.

6 Turn the warm puddings out on to individual dessert plates. Spoon the sauce over each one and serve immediately.

Blueberry Muffin Pudding

You can't cook traditional muffins in a slow cooker but this delicious alternative will satisfy your cravings.

Serves 4

75g/3oz/6 tbsp butter, plus extra for greasing
75g/3oz/6 tbsp soft light brown sugar
105ml/7 tbsp buttermilk, at room temperature
2 eggs, lightly beaten, at room temperature
225g/8oz/2 cups self-raising (self-rising) flour
pinch of salt
5ml/1 tsp ground cinnamon
150g/5oz/¼ cup fresh blueberries
10ml/2 tsp demerara (raw) sugar, for sprinkling
custard or crème fraîche, to serve

1 Place an upturned saucer or metal pastry ring in the base of the slow cooker. Pour in about 5cm/2in of very hot water, then switch the slow cooker to high. Lightly grease a 1.5 litre/2½ pint/6¼ cup heatproof dish with butter – first making sure that it will fit the inside of your slow cooker.

2 Put the butter and sugar in a heatproof jug (pitcher) and place in the ceramic cooking pot. Leave uncovered for 20 minutes, stirring, until melted.

3 Remove the jug from the slow cooker and leave to cool until tepid, then stir in the buttermilk and mix in the beaten egg.

4 Sift the flour, salt and cinnamon into a mixing bowl. Stir in the blueberries, then make a hollow in the middle. Pour in the buttermilk mixture and stir until just combined. Do not overmix.

5 Spoon the mixture into the prepared dish, then sprinkle the top with the demerara sugar. Cover with a piece of buttered foil and place in the ceramic cooking pot. Pour in more boiling water around the dish, if necessary, to come halfway up the sides.

6 Cover the slow cooker with the lid and cook for 3–4 hours, until a skewer inserted in the middle comes out clean. Remove from the slow cooker and let the pudding cool slightly before serving with custard or crème fraîche.

Date Puddings Energy 462kcal/1932kJ; Protein 5.1g; Carbohydrate 50.3g, of which sugars 35.9g; Fat 26.9g, of which saturates 16g; Cholesterol 138mg; Calcium 109mg; Fibre 1.1g; Sodium 244mg.
Blueberry Pudding Energy 499kcal/2101kJ; Protein 10.1g; Carbohydrate 76.2g, of which sugars 34.4g; Fat 19.2g, of which saturates 10.7g; Cholesterol 153mg; Calcium 262mg; Fibre 2.2g; Sodium 367mg.

Bread Pudding

This baked dessert is spicy, rich and filling – and is an ideal winter food. Serve the pudding warm with custard or cream or, if you prefer, it is just as nice left until cold.

Makes 9 squares

225g/8oz/4 cups stale bread, weighed after removing crusts
300ml/½ pint/1¼ cups milk
50g/1¾oz/4 tbsp dark muscovado (molasses) sugar
85g/3oz/½ cup shredded suet (US chilled, grated shortening) or grated chilled butter
225g/8oz/1⅓ cups mixed dried fruit, including currants, sultanas (golden raisins), finely chopped citrus peel
15ml/1 tbsp mixed (apple pie) spice
2.5ml/½ tsp freshly grated nutmeg
finely grated rind of 1 small orange and 1 small lemon, plus a little orange or lemon juice
1 egg, lightly beaten
caster (superfine) sugar, for sprinkling

1 Break the bread into small pieces. Place in a large mixing bowl, pour the milk over and leave for about 30 minutes.

2 Preheat the oven to 180°C/350°F/Gas 4. Butter an 18cm/7in square and 5cm/2in deep ovenproof dish.

3 Break up the bread before stirring in the sugar, suet or butter, dried fruit, spices and citrus rinds. Beat in the egg, adding some orange or lemon juice to make a soft mixture.

4 Spread the mixture into the dish and level the surface. Bake for 1¼ hours, or until the top is brown and firm to the touch.

5 Sprinkle caster sugar over the surface and cool before cutting into squares.

Cook's Tip
Although the shredded suet is traditional in this recipe, you may prefer to use grated chilled butter.

Fresh Currant Bread and Butter Pudding

Fresh mixed red- and blackcurrants add a tart touch to this scrumptious baked pudding in which layers of custard-soaked bread are cooked to a crisp golden crust.

Serves 6

8 slices day-old white bread, crusts removed
50g/2oz/¼ cup butter, softened
115g/4oz/1 cup redcurrants
115g/4oz/1 cup blackcurrants
4 eggs, beaten
75g/3oz/6 tbsp caster (superfine) sugar
475ml/16fl oz/2 cups creamy milk
5ml/1 tsp vanilla extract
freshly grated nutmeg
30ml/2 tbsp demerara (raw) sugar
single (light) cream, to serve

1 Preheat the oven to 160°C/325°F/Gas 3. Generously butter a 1.2 litre/2 pint/5 cup ovenproof earthenware dish.

2 Spread the slices of bread generously with the butter, then cut them in half diagonally. Layer the slices in the dish, buttered side up, sprinkling the currants between the layers.

3 Beat the eggs and caster sugar lightly together in a large mixing bowl, then gradually whisk in the creamy milk and vanilla extract, along with a large pinch of freshly grated nutmeg.

4 Pour the milk mixture over the bread, pushing the slices down into the liquid. Sprinkle the demerara sugar and a little more nutmeg over the top. Place the dish in a roasting pan and fill with hot water to come halfway up the sides of the dish.

5 Bake for 40 minutes, then increase the oven temperature to 180°C/350°F/Gas 4 and bake for about 20 minutes more, or until the top is golden. Serve warm, with single cream.

Variation
A mixture of blueberries and raspberries would work just as well as the currants in this recipe.

Bread Pudding Energy 254kcal/1072kJ; Protein 4.3g; Carbohydrate 39.7g, of which sugars 27g; Fat 10.2g, of which saturates 5.3g; Cholesterol 31mg; Calcium 103mg; Fibre 1.4g; Sodium 147mg.
Currant Pudding Energy 328kcal/1377kJ; Protein 10.3g; Carbohydrate 42.2g, of which sugars 25.4g; Fat 14.3g, of which saturates 7.4g; Cholesterol 156mg; Calcium 186mg; Fibre 1.9g; Sodium 321mg.

Fruity Bread and Butter Pudding

Fresh currants add a tart touch to this scrumptious slow-cooker pudding.

Serves 4

40g/1½oz/3 tbsp butter, softened, plus extra for greasing
6 slices of day-old bread, crusts removed
115g/4oz/1 cup prepared redcurrants and raspberries
3 eggs, beaten
50g/2oz/¼ cup golden caster (superfine) sugar
300ml/½ pint/1¼ cups creamy milk
5ml/1 tsp vanilla extract
freshly grated nutmeg
30ml/2 tbsp demerara (raw) sugar
single (light) cream, to serve

1 Butter a 1 litre/1¾ pints/4 cup round or oval baking dish – first checking that it fits in the slow cooker. Pour 2.5cm/1in of very hot water into the ceramic cooking pot. Place an upturned saucer in the base and switch the cooker to high.

2 Spread the slices of bread with the butter, then cut them in half diagonally. Arrange the triangles in the dish in neat layers, overlapping the slices, with the buttered side facing up. Sprinkle the currants and berries over the bread and between the slices.

3 Place the eggs and caster sugar in a large mixing bowl and briefly beat together. Gradually whisk in the milk, vanilla extract and a large pinch of freshly grated nutmeg until well mixed.

4 Place the baking dish in the ceramic cooking pot, then slowly pour the egg and milk mixture over the bread, pushing the bread slices down to submerge them. Sprinkle the sugar and a little nutmeg over the top, then cover the dish with foil.

5 Pour near-boiling water around the dish, so that the water level comes just over halfway up the sides of the dish. Cover with the lid and cook on high for 3–4 hours, or until a skewer inserted into the centre comes out clean.

6 Carefully remove the dish from the slow cooker and, if you like, briefly brown the top of the pudding under a hot grill (broiler). Cool slightly, then serve with the single cream.

Maple and Pecan Croissant Pudding

Croissants give this tasty, oven-baked dessert a light and fluffy texture.

Serves 4

75g/3oz/generous ½ cup sultanas (golden raisins)
45ml/3 tbsp brandy
50g/2oz/¼ cup butter, plus extra for greasing
4 large croissants
40g/1½oz/⅓ cup pecan nuts, roughly chopped
3 eggs, lightly beaten
300ml/½ pint/1¼ cups milk
150ml/¼ pint/⅔ cup single (light) cream
120ml/4fl oz/½ cup maple syrup
25g/1oz/2 tbsp demerara (raw) sugar
maple syrup and pouring (half-and-half) cream, to serve (optional)

1 Place the sultanas and brandy in a small pan and heat gently, until warm. Leave to stand for 1 hour. Soak a small clay pot in cold water for 15 minutes, then drain. Leave for 2–3 minutes, then lightly grease the base and sides.

2 Cut the croissants into thick slices, and spread with butter on one side. Arrange the slices, butter side up and slightly overlapping, in the soaked clay pot. Sprinkle the brandy-soaked sultanas and the roughly chopped pecan nuts over the buttered croissant slices.

3 In a large bowl, beat the eggs and milk together, then gradually beat in the single cream and maple syrup.

4 Pour the egg custard through a sieve (strainer) over the croissants, fruit and nuts in the dish. Leave the uncooked pudding to stand for 30 minutes, so that some of the egg custard liquid is absorbed by the croissants.

5 Sprinkle the sugar evenly over the top, then cover the dish and place in a cold oven. Set the oven to 180°C/350°F/Gas 4 and bake for 40 minutes. Remove the lid and continue to cook for 20 minutes, or until the custard is set and the top is golden.

6 Leave the pudding to cool for about 15 minutes before serving warm, with extra maple syrup and a little pouring cream, if you like.

Fruity Pudding Energy 405Kcal/1700kJ; Protein 12.6g; Carbohydrate 53.7g, of which sugars 30.7g; Fat 16.9g, of which saturates 8.6g; Cholesterol 202mg; Calcium 234mg; Fibre 2.1g; Sodium 405mg.
Croissant Pudding Energy 731kcal/3056kJ; Protein 15g; Carbohydrate 72.3g, of which sugars 49.4g; Fat 45.6g, of which saturates 19.5g; Cholesterol 226mg; Calcium 217mg; Fibre 1.8g; Sodium 507mg.

Bread and Butter Pudding with Whiskey Sauce

This slowly baked dessert is the ultimate comfort food. The whiskey sauce is heavenly, but the pudding can also be served with chilled cream or vanilla ice cream – the contrast between the hot and cold is utterly mouthwatering.

Serves 6

8 slices of white bread, buttered
115–150g/4–5oz/⅔–¾ cup sultanas (golden raisins), or mixed dried fruit
2.5ml/½ tsp grated nutmeg
150g/5oz/¾ cup caster (superfine) sugar
2 large (US extra large) eggs
300ml/½ pint/1¼ cups single (light) cream
450ml/¾ pint/scant 2 cups milk
5ml/1 tsp of vanilla extract
light muscovado (brown) sugar, for sprinkling (optional)

For the whiskey sauce

150g/5oz/10 tbsp butter
115g/4oz/generous ½ cup caster (superfine) sugar
1 egg
45ml/3 tbsp Irish whiskey

1 Preheat the oven to 180°C/350°F/Gas 4. Remove the crusts from the bread and put four slices, buttered side down, in the base of an ovenproof dish. Sprinkle with the fruit, some of the nutmeg and 15ml/1 tbsp sugar.

2 Place the remaining four slices of bread on top, buttered side down, and sprinkle again with nutmeg and 15ml/1 tbsp sugar.

3 Beat the eggs lightly, add the cream, milk, vanilla extract and the remaining sugar, and mix well to make a custard. Pour this mixture over the bread, and sprinkle light muscovado sugar over the top, if you like to have a crispy crust. Bake in the preheated oven for 1 hour, or until all the liquid has been absorbed and the pudding is risen and browned.

4 Meanwhile, make the whiskey sauce. Melt the butter in a heavy pan, add the caster sugar and dissolve over low heat. Remove from the heat and add the egg, whisking vigorously, and then add the whiskey. Serve the pudding on warmed plates, with the whiskey sauce poured over the top.

Apricot Panettone Pudding

Panettone and pecan nuts make a rich addition to this 'no-butter' version of a traditional, oven-baked bread and butter pudding.

Serves 6

sunflower oil, for greasing
350g/12oz panettone, sliced into triangles
25g/1oz/¼ cup pecan nuts
75g/3oz/⅓ cup ready-to-eat dried apricots, chopped
500ml/17fl oz/generous 2 cups full-cream (whole) milk
5ml/1 tsp vanilla extract
1 large (US extra large) egg, beaten
30ml/2 tbsp maple syrup
freshly grated nutmeg
demerara (raw) sugar, for sprinkling

1 Lightly grease a 1 litre/1¾ pint/4 cup ovenproof earthenware dish. Arrange half of the panettone triangles in the dish, sprinkle over half the pecan nuts and all of the chopped, dried apricots, then add another layer of panettone on top.

2 Heat the milk and vanilla extract in a small pan until the milk just simmers. Put the egg and maple syrup in a large bowl, grate in about 2.5ml/½ tsp nutmeg, then whisk in the hot milk.

3 Preheat the oven to 200°C/400°F/Gas 6. Pour the egg mixture over the panettone, lightly pressing down the bread. Leave the pudding to stand for about 10 minutes, to allow the panettone slices to soak up a little of the liquid.

4 Sprinkle over the reserved pecan nuts and sprinkle a little demerara sugar and freshly grated nutmeg over the top. Bake for 40–45 minutes, until the pudding is risen and golden brown. Serve immediately.

Cook's Tip

Panettone is a light fruit cake, originally from northern Italy but now popular all over the world. It is traditionally eaten at festivals such as Christmas or Easter. Panettone is baked in cylindrical moulds, giving it a distinctive shape. You can now find panettone in different flavours.

Bread Pudding Energy 757kcal/3168kJ; Protein 11.7g; Carbohydrate 82g, of which sugars 65.2g; Fat 40.8g, of which saturates 24.3g; Cholesterol 207mg; Calcium 232mg; Fibre 0.9g; Sodium 472mg.
Apricot Pudding Energy 294kcal/1237kJ; Protein 9.4g; Carbohydrate 43.2g, of which sugars 21.8g; Fat 10.4g, of which saturates 3.7g; Cholesterol 44mg; Calcium 180mg; Fibre 2.3g; Sodium 248mg.

Cherry Batter Pudding

This batter pudding – or 'clafoutis' – originated in the Limousin area of central France, where batters play an important role in the hearty cuisine. Similar fruit and custard desserts are found in Alsace.

Serves 4

450g/1lb ripe cherries
30ml/2 tbsp Kirsch or fruit brandy or 15ml/1 tbsp lemon juice
15ml/1 tbsp icing (confectioners') sugar
30g/1oz/3 tbsp plain (all-purpose) flour
45ml/3 tbsp sugar
175ml/6fl oz/¾ cup milk or single (light) cream
2 eggs
grated rind of ½ lemon
pinch of freshly grated nutmeg
1.5ml/¼ tsp vanilla extract

1 Remove the pits from the cherries, if you like, then mix them with the Kirsch, brandy or lemon juice and icing sugar and set aside for 1–2 hours.

2 Preheat the oven to 190°C/375°F/Gas 5. Generously butter a 28cm/11in oval gratin dish or other shallow ovenproof dish.

3 Sift the flour into a bowl, add the sugar and slowly whisk in the milk until smoothly blended.

4 Add the eggs, lemon rind, nutmeg and vanilla extract into the flour mixture and whisk until well combined and smooth.

5 Sprinkle the cherries evenly in the baking dish. Pour over the batter, ensuring it is distributed evenly around the cherries.

6 Bake in the oven for 45 minutes, or until set and puffed around the edges – a knife inserted in the centre should come out clean. Serve warm or at room temperature.

Cook's Tip
Serve this dish with whipped double (heavy) cream, custard or vanilla ice cream, if you like.

Black Cherry Batter Pudding

This version of the traditional French cherry batter pudding is made with slightly tart black cherries. It can be made with cream in place of milk, and is excellent served with ice cream.

Serves 6

450g/1lb/2 cups fresh black cherries, pitted
25g/1oz/¼ cup plain (all-purpose) flour
50g/2oz/½ cup icing (confectioner's) sugar, plus extra for dusting
4 eggs, beaten
250ml/8fl oz/1 cup full-cream (whole) milk
30ml/2 tbsp cherry liqueur, such as Kirsch or maraschino
vanilla ice cream, to serve

1 Preheat the oven to 180°C/350°F/Gas 4. Grease a 1.2 litre/2 pint/5 cup baking dish and add the cherries.

2 Sift the flour and icing sugar into a large mixing bowl, then gradually whisk in the beaten eggs until the mixture is smooth. Whisk in the milk until well blended, then stir in the cherry liqueur.

3 Pour the batter into the baking dish and then stir gently to ensure that the cherries are evenly distributed. Transfer to the oven and bake for about 40 minutes, or until just set and light golden brown. Insert a small knife into the centre of the pudding to test if it is cooked in the middle; the blade should come out clean.

4 Allow the pudding to cool for at least 15 minutes, then dust liberally with icing sugar just before serving, either warm or at room temperature. Vanilla ice cream is a good accompaniment.

Variation
Try other fruit or nut liqueurs in this dessert. Almond-flavoured liqueur is delicious teamed with cherries, while hazelnut, raspberry or orange liqueurs will also work well. Other fruits that can be used in this pudding include blackberries, blueberries, plums, peaches, nectarines and apricots.

Cherry Energy 357kcal/1493kJ; Protein 8.1g; Carbohydrate 39.4g, of which sugars 29.8g; Fat 19.7g, of which saturates 11.4g; Cholesterol 140mg; Calcium 147mg; Fibre 1.4g; Sodium 183mg.
Black Cherry Energy 167kcal/704kJ; Protein 6.7g; Carbohydrate 23.8g, of which sugars 20.6g; Fat 4.5g, of which saturates 1.5g; Cholesterol 129mg; Calcium 89mg; Fibre 0.8g; Sodium 66mg.

Lemon Surprise Pudding

This is a much-loved dessert that many people remember from childhood. The surprise is the unexpected sauce concealed beneath the delectable sponge in this slowly baked dish.

Serves 4

50g/2oz/¼ cup butter, plus extra for greasing
grated rind and juice of 2 lemons
115g/4oz/½ cup caster (superfine) sugar
50g/2oz/½ cup self-raising (self-rising) flour
2 eggs, separated
300ml/½ pint/1¼ cups milk

1 Preheat the oven to 190°C/375°F/Gas 5. Use a little butter to grease a 1.2 litre/2 pint/5 cup baking dish.

2 Beat the lemon rind, remaining butter and caster sugar in a large mixing bowl until pale and fluffy. Sift in the self-raising flour and fold into the creamed butter.

3 Add the egg yolks and beat into the mixture. Gradually whisk in the lemon juice and the milk (don't be alarmed – the mixture will curdle horribly).

4 Place the egg whites in a grease-free bowl and whisk until they form stiff peaks.

5 Fold the egg whites lightly into the lemon mixture using a metal spoon, then pour into the prepared baking dish.

6 Place the dish in a roasting pan and pour in hot water to come halfway up the side of the dish. Bake for 45 minutes, until golden. Serve immediately.

Cook's Tip
Lemons are often waxed before packing. If a recipe uses the rind of the lemons either buy unwaxed lemons or scrub the peel thoroughly to remove the wax.

Apple Pudding

This delectable, oven-baked dessert features tender apples topped with a light, airy sponge.

Serves 4

4 crisp eating apples
a little lemon juice
300ml/½ pint/1¼ cups milk
40g/1½oz/3 tbsp butter
40g/1½oz/⅓ cup plain (all-purpose) flour
25g/1oz/2 tbsp caster (superfine) sugar
2.5ml/½ tsp vanilla extract
2 eggs, separated

1 Preheat the oven to 200°C/400°F/ Gas 6. Butter an ovenproof dish measuring 20–23cm/8–9in diameter and 5cm/2in deep. Peel, core and slice the apples and place in an even layer in the base of the dish. Pour over the lemon juice.

2 Put the milk, butter and flour in a pan. Stirring continuously with a whisk, cook over medium heat until the sauce thickens and comes to the boil. Let it bubble gently for 1–2 minutes, stirring well to make sure it does not stick and burn on the bottom of the pan. Pour into a bowl, add the sugar and vanilla extract, and then stir in the egg yolks.

3 In a separate bowl, whisk the egg whites until stiff peaks form. With a large metal spoon, fold the egg whites into the custard. Pour the custard mixture evenly over the apple slices in the dish.

4 Put into the hot oven and cook for about 40 minutes, until puffed up, deep golden brown and firm to the touch.

5 Serve the pudding immediately once it comes out of the oven, before the soufflé-like topping begins to fall.

Variation
Stewed fruit, such as cooking apples, plums, rhubarb or gooseberries sweetened with honey or sugar, would also make a good base for this pudding, as would fresh summer berries (blackberries, raspberries, redcurrants and blackcurrants).

Lemon Pudding Energy 319kcal/1341kJ; Protein 7g; Carbohydrate 43.1g, of which sugars 33.8g; Fat 14.5g, of which saturates 8.1g; Cholesterol 126mg; Calcium 166mg; Fibre 0.4g; Sodium 190mg.
Apple Pudding Energy 240kcal/1006kJ; Protein 7g; Carbohydrate 26.8g, of which sugars 19.2g; Fat 12.5g, of which saturates 6.8g; Cholesterol 121mg; Calcium 127mg; Fibre 1.9g; Sodium 131mg.

Steamed Raisin Pudding

This light pudding is slowly steamed in a pan on top of the stove. Use the softest, juiciest raisins you can find.

Serves 6

15–25g/½–1oz/1–2 tbsp butter, softened
100g/3½oz/⅔ cup raisins
175g/6oz/3 cups fresh white breadcrumbs
75g/3oz/½ cup shredded suet (US chilled, grated shortening)
75g/3oz/6 tbsp soft brown sugar
25g/1oz/¼ cup cornflour (cornstarch)
finely grated rind of 1 lemon
2 eggs
60ml/4 tbsp orange marmalade
30ml/2 tbsp fresh lemon juice

For the sauce

1 lemon
25g/1oz/¼ cup cornflour (cornstarch)
300ml/½ pint/1¼ cups milk
50g/2oz/¼ cup caster (superfine) sugar
25g/1oz/2 tbsp butter

1 Smear the butter on the inside of a 1.2 litre/2 pint heatproof bowl and press half the raisins on the buttered surface.

2 Mix together the breadcrumbs, suet, brown sugar, cornflour, lemon rind and the remaining raisins. Beat the eggs with the marmalade and lemon juice and stir into the dry ingredients.

3 Carefully spoon the mixture into the bowl, being careful not to disturb the raisins. Cover the bowl with pleated baking parchment and then a large sheet of foil, also pleated. Tuck the edges under and press tightly to the sides. Steam over a pan of boiling water for 1¾ hours.

4 Pare two or three large strips of lemon rind and put into a pan with 150ml/¼ pint/⅔ cup water. Bring to the boil and simmer for 10 minutes. Discard the rind. Blend the cornflour with the milk and stir into the pan. Squeeze the juice from half the lemon and add to the pan with the sugar and butter. Heat until the sauce thickens and comes to the boil.

5 Turn the pudding out on to a warmed serving plate, spooning a little sauce over the top. Serve immediately.

Christmas Pudding

This rich, slowly steamed pudding is a must for any Christmas feast. Serve with a traditional hot white sauce, flavoured with whiskey, brandy or rum, or simply offer a jug of cream liqueur, to be poured over the pudding as a sauce.

Makes 2 puddings, each serving 6–8

275g/10oz/5 cups fresh breadcrumbs
225g/8oz/1 cup light muscovado (brown) sugar
225g/8oz/1 cup currants
275g/10oz/2 cups raisins
225g/8oz/1⅓ cups sultanas (golden raisins)
50g/2oz/⅓ cup chopped (candied) peel
115g/4oz/½ cup glacé (candied) cherries
225g/8oz shredded suet (US chilled, grated shortening), or vegetarian equivalent
2.5ml/½ tsp salt
10–20ml/2–4 tsp mixed (apple pie) spice
1 carrot, coarsely grated
1 apple, peeled, cored and finely chopped
grated rind and juice of 1 small orange
2 large (US extra large) eggs, lightly whisked
450ml/¾ pint/scant 2 cups stout

1 Mix the breadcrumbs, sugar, dried fruit and peel in a bowl. Shred and add the suet, salt, mixed spice, carrot, apple and orange rind. Mix until well combined. Stir in the orange juice, eggs and stout. Leave the mixture overnight, giving it a stir occasionally, if convenient.

2 Well grease and line two 1.2 litre/2 pint/5 cup heatproof bowls with baking parchment. Stir the mixture and turn into the bowls. Cover with buttered circles of baking parchment, then tie pudding cloths over the top, or tightly cover them with several layers of baking parchment and foil, tied under the rim.

3 Steam for about 6–7 hours. Ensure the puddings do not go off the boil, and top up with more water as needed.

4 When cool, re-cover the puddings with paper or foil and store in a cool, dry place for at least a month. When required, steam for another 2–3 hours. Serve hot, with a traditional white sauce.

Raisin Pudding Energy 456kcal/1922kJ; Protein 7.7g; Carbohydrate 74.4g, of which sugars 43.4g; Fat 16.8g, of which saturates 8.6g; Cholesterol 82mg; Calcium 131mg; Fibre 1.1g; Sodium 304mg.
Christmas Energy 7171kcal/30,432kJ; Protein 38.8g; Carbohydrate 1596.3g, of which sugars 1479.8g; Fat 112.9g, of which saturates 58g; Cholesterol 321mg; Calcium 1071mg; Fibre 13.8g; Sodium 1965mg.

Fruit Slice

A dried fruit filling is packed between shortcrust pastry and then baked in the oven in this tasty treat.

Makes 24 slices

8 slices of stale bread, or plain cake
75g/3oz/⅔ cup plain (all-purpose) flour
pinch of salt
2.5ml/½ tsp baking powder
10ml/2 tsp mixed (apple pie) spice
115g/4oz/generous ½ cup sugar, plus extra for sprinkling
175g/6oz/¾ cup currants or mixed dried fruit
50g/2oz/¼ cup butter, melted
1 egg, lightly beaten
milk, to mix

For the shortcrust pastry

225g/8oz/2 cups plain (all-purpose) flour
2.5ml/½ tsp salt
115g/4oz/½ cup butter

1 To make the shortcrust pastry, mix together the flour, salt and the butter in a large bowl. Using the fingertips, rub the mixture until it resembles fine breadcrumbs. Mix in 30–45ml/2–3 tbsp cold water and knead lightly to form a firm dough. Wrap in clear film (plastic wrap) and chill for 30 minutes.

2 Preheat the oven to 190°C/375°F/Gas 5 and grease and flour a square baking tin (pan).

3 Remove the crusts from the bread and make the remainder into crumbs, or make the cake into crumbs. Put the crumbs into a mixing bowl with the flour, salt, baking powder, mixed spice, sugar and dried fruit. Mix well to combine.

4 Add the butter and egg to the dry ingredients with enough milk to make a fairly stiff, spreadable mixture.

5 Roll out the pastry and, using the baking tin as a guide, cut out one piece to make the lid. Use the rest, re-rolled as necessary, to line the base of the tin. Spread the pastry with the mixture, then cover with the pastry lid.

6 Make diagonal slashes across the top. Bake in the oven for 50–60 minutes, or until golden. Sprinkle with sugar and leave to cool in the tin. Cut into slices.

Classic Cheesecake

This popular cake has many variations but it is hard to beat this simple and plain version. A crushed biscuit base is topped with cream cheese, before being slowly baked in the oven.

Serves 8

50g/2oz/1 cup digestive biscuits (graham crackers), crushed
900g/2lb/4 cups cream cheese, at room temperature
240g/8¾oz/scant 1¼ cups caster (superfine) sugar
grated rind of 1 lemon
45ml/3 tbsp lemon juice
5ml/1 tsp vanilla extract
4 eggs, at room temperature

1 Preheat the oven to 160°C/325°F/Gas 3. Grease a 20cm/8in springform cake tin (pan). Place the tin on a round of foil 10–13cm/4–5in larger than the diameter of the tin. Press it up the sides to seal tightly.

2 Sprinkle the crushed digestive biscuits in the base of the tin. Press down gently to form an even layer.

3 In a large bowl, beat the cream cheese with a wooden spoon or an electric mixer until smooth.

4 Add the sugar, lemon rind and juice, and vanilla extract to the cream cheese, and beat until blended.

5 Beat the eggs into the cheese mixture, one at a time. Beat the mixture just enough to blend thoroughly, being careful not to overmix.

6 Pour the mixture into the prepared tin. Set the tin in a roasting pan and pour enough hot water into the roasting pan to come 2.5cm/1in up the side of the cake tin. Place in the oven.

7 Bake for about 1½ hours, or until the top of the cake is golden brown. Leave to cool in the tin.

8 Run a knife around the edge to loosen, then remove the rim of the tin. Chill for at least 4 hours before serving.

Fruit Slice Energy 156kcal/656kJ; Protein 2.4g; Carbohydrate 24.2g, of which sugars 10.5g; Fat 6.2g, of which saturates 3.7g; Cholesterol 23mg; Calcium 43mg; Fibre 0.8g; Sodium 128mg.
Cheesecake Energy 668kcal/2772kJ; Protein 7g; Carbohydrate 34.8g, of which sugars 33.1g; Fat 56.9g, of which saturates 34.5g; Cholesterol 203mg; Calcium 144mg; Fibre 0.1g; Sodium 393mg.

Chocolate Cheesecake Brownies

A very dense chocolate brownie mixture that is made in the slow cooker. It is swirled with creamy cheese to give it an attractive marbled effect.

Makes 9

50g/2oz dark (bittersweet) chocolate (minimum 70 per cent cocoa solids), chopped
50g/2oz/¼ cup unsalted butter
65g/2½oz/5 tbsp light muscovado (brown) sugar
1 egg, beaten
25g/1oz/¼ cup plain (all-purpose) flour

For the cheesecake mixture
115g/4oz/½ cup full-fat cream cheese
25g/1oz/2 tbsp caster (superfine) sugar
5ml/1 tsp vanilla extract
½ beaten egg

1 Line the base and sides of a 15cm/6in square fixed-base cake tin (pan) with baking parchment. Pour about 5cm/2in of very hot water into the ceramic cooking pot and switch to high. Put the chocolate and butter in a heatproof bowl and place in the slow cooker. Leave to stand for 10 minutes.

2 Meanwhile, make the cheesecake mixture. Put the cream cheese, sugar and vanilla extract in a clean mixing bowl and beat together. Gradually beat in the egg until the mixture is very smooth and creamy. Set aside.

3 Stir the chocolate and butter mixture until completely melted and smooth, then remove the bowl from the slow cooker. Add the muscovado sugar and stir to combine. Place an upturned saucer in the base of the cooking pot.

4 Mix the beaten egg into the melted chocolate mixture a little at a time, then sift over the flour and gently fold in. Spoon the chocolate mixture into the tin. Drop small spoonfuls of the cheesecake mixture on top and swirl the mixtures together.

5 Cover the tin with foil and place in the pot. Pour in more boiling water around the tin to come just over halfway up the sides. Cook for 2 hours, or until just set. Remove the tin from the pot and place on a wire rack to cool. Cut into squares.

Chocolate Chip Walnut Cake

The tangy flavour of orange works well in this chocolate and nut slow-cooker loaf.

Serves 8

115g/4oz/1 cup plain (all-purpose) flour
25g/1oz/¼ cup cornflour (cornstarch)
5ml/1 tsp baking powder
115g/4oz/½ cup butter, at room temperature
115g/4oz/½ cup golden caster (superfine) sugar
2 eggs, lightly beaten
75g/3oz/½ cup plain (semisweet), milk or white chocolate chips
50g/2oz/½ cup chopped walnuts
finely grated rind of ½ orange

For the topping
115g/4oz/1 cup icing (confectioners') sugar, sifted, plus 5ml/1 tsp for dusting
20–30ml/4 tsp–2 tbsp freshly squeezed orange juice
walnut halves, to decorate

1 Grease and line a 450g/1lb loaf tin (pan) with baking parchment. Place an upturned saucer in the ceramic cooking pot and pour in 2.5cm/1in very hot water. Switch the cooker to high.

2 Sift the flour, cornflour and baking powder together twice, then set aside. Place the butter in a large bowl and beat until creamy. Add the golden sugar and beat until light and fluffy. Beat in the eggs.

3 Fold half of the flour mixture into the bowl, then add the rest with the chocolate chips, walnuts and orange rind. Fold in until just blended. Spoon into the loaf tin and loosely cover with foil. Put the tin on the saucer inside the pot. Pour in enough boiling water to come two-thirds of the way up the sides of the tin.

4 Cover the cooker with the lid and cook for 2½–3 hours, or until a fine skewer inserted into the cake comes out clean. Remove the cake from the cooker and stand it on a wire rack for 10 minutes, then turn out and leave to cool on the rack.

5 To decorate the cake, place 115g/4oz/1 cup icing sugar in a bowl. Stir in 20ml/4 tsp orange juice, adding a little more if needed to make it the consistency of thick cream. Drizzle the mixture over the cake, then decorate with walnut halves dusted with the 5ml/1 tsp icing sugar. Leave to set before serving.

Brownies Energy 174kcal/727kJ; Protein 2.9g; Carbohydrate 16.2g, of which sugars 14g; Fat 11.3g, of which saturates 6.8g; Cholesterol 65mg; Calcium 25mg; Fibre 0.2g; Sodium 86mg.
Chocolate Chip Cake Energy 395kcal/1655kJ; Protein 4.7g; Carbohydrate 51g, of which sugars 36.9g; Fat 20.5g, of which saturates 9.9g; Cholesterol 87mg; Calcium 49mg; Fibre 0.9g; Sodium 171mg.

Rich Chocolate Cake

A rich, dense chocolate cake made in the slow cooker.

Serves 8

115g/4oz plain (semisweet) chocolate, cut into small pieces
45ml/3 tbsp milk
150g/5oz/10 tbsp butter, at room temperature
200g/7oz/scant 1 cup soft light brown sugar
3 eggs, lightly beaten
200g/7oz/1¾ cups self-raising (self-rising) flour
15ml/1 tbsp unsweetened cocoa powder
icing (confectioners') sugar and unsweetened cocoa powder, for dusting

For the chocolate buttercream
75g/3oz/6 tbsp butter, at room temperature
115g/4oz/1 cup icing (confectioners') sugar
15ml/1 tbsp (unsweetened) cocoa powder
2.5ml/½ tsp vanilla extract

1 Grease and line a deep 18cm/7in cake tin (pan) with baking parchment. Pour about 5cm/2in very hot water into the ceramic cooking pot, then turn the cooker to high. Put the chocolate and milk into a heatproof bowl and place in the pot. Leave for 10 minutes, then stir until smooth. Remove and set aside to cool.

2 Place the butter and sugar in a bowl and beat together until fluffy. Beat in the eggs, then stir in the chocolate mixture. Fold in the flour and cocoa. Spoon into the prepared tin and cover with a piece of foil. Put a saucer in the bottom of the cooking pot, then rest the tin on top. If necessary, pour in more boiling water to come just over halfway up the tin.

3 Cover and cook for 3–3½ hours, or until firm and a skewer comes out clean. Lift the tin out and leave on a wire rack for 10 minutes. Turn out and leave to cool. Remove the lining paper.

4 To make the buttercream, put the butter in a bowl and beat until soft. Sift over the icing sugar and cocoa powder, then stir together. Add the vanilla extract and beat until light and fluffy.

5 Cut the cake in half horizontally and spread a thick layer of the buttercream on one of the halves. Sandwich the cakes back together, then dust with a mix of sugar and cocoa, and serve.

Chocolate Potato Cake

This is a very rich, moist chocolate cake, topped with a thin layer of chocolate icing. Use a good-quality dark chocolate for best results and serve with whipped cream.

Makes a 23cm/9in cake

200g/7oz/1 cup sugar
250g/9oz/1 cup and 2 tbsp butter
4 eggs, separated
275g/10oz dark (bittersweet) chocolate
75g/3oz/¾ cup ground almonds
165g/5½oz mashed potato
225g/8oz/2 cups self-raising (self-rising) flour
5ml/1 tsp cinnamon
45ml/3 tbsp milk
white and dark (bittersweet) chocolate shavings, to garnish
whipped cream, to serve

1 Preheat the oven to 180°C/350°F/Gas 4. Grease and base-line a 23cm/9in round cake tin with a circle of baking parchment. In a large bowl, cream together the sugar and 225g/8oz/1 cup of the butter until light and fluffy. Then beat the egg yolks into the creamed mixture, one at a time, until it is smooth and creamy.

2 Finely chop 175g/6oz of the chocolate and stir it into the creamed mixture with the almonds. Pass the potato through a sieve (strainer) or ricer and stir it into the creamed chocolate mixture. Sift together the flour and cinnamon and fold into the mixture with the milk. Whisk the egg whites until they hold stiff but not dry peaks, and fold into the cake mixture.

3 Spoon into the tin, level the top and make a slight hollow in the middle to keep it level during cooking. Bake for 1¼ hours, until a skewer inserted in the centre comes out clean. Leave to cool slightly in the tin, then turn out and cool on a wire rack.

4 Meanwhile, break the remaining chocolate into a heatproof bowl over a pan of hot water. Add the remaining butter in small pieces and stir until the mixture is smooth and glossy.

5 Peel off the lining paper and trim the top of the cake so that it is level. Smooth over the chocolate icing and allow to set. Decorate with white and dark chocolate shavings and serve with lashings of whipped cream.

Chocolate Cake Energy 564kcal/2363kJ; Protein 6.6g; Carbohydrate 70g, of which sugars 51g; Fat 30.5g, of which saturates 18.2g; Cholesterol 146mg; Calcium 129mg; Fibre 1.5g; Sodium 321mg.
Potato Energy 5707kcal/23853kJ; Protein 82.6g; Carbohydrate 593.8g, of which sugars 393.4g; Fat 350.7g, of which saturates 187g; Cholesterol 1313mg; Calcium 915mg; Fibre 21.1g; Sodium 1878mg.

Frosted Carrot and Parsnip Cake

This slow-cooker cake, decorated with sugared rind, is very light and crumbly.

Serves 8

1 orange or lemon
10ml/2 tsp caster (superfine) sugar
175g/6oz/¾ cup butter or margarine
175g/6oz/¾ cup soft light brown sugar
3 eggs, lightly beaten
175g/6oz carrots and parsnips, coarsely grated
50g/2oz/⅓ cup sultanas (golden raisins)
115g/4oz/1 cup self-raising (self-rising) flour
50g/2oz/½ cup self-raising (self-rising) wholemeal (whole-wheat) flour
5ml/1 tsp baking powder

For the topping

50g/2oz/¼ cup caster (superfine) sugar
1 egg white
pinch of salt

1 Put an upturned saucer or metal pastry cutter in the base of the ceramic cooking pot and pour in about 2.5cm/1in hot water. Turn the slow cooker to high. Lightly grease a deep 18cm/7in round fixed-based cake tin (pan) or soufflé dish with oil and line the base with baking parchment.

2 Finely grate the orange or lemon rind. Selecting the longest shreds, put about half the rind in a bowl and mix with the caster sugar. Arrange the sugar-coated rind on a sheet of baking parchment and leave in a warm place to dry.

3 Put the butter or margarine and brown sugar in a large bowl and beat together until pale and fluffy. Add the eggs a little at a time, beating well after each addition. Stir in the unsugared orange or lemon rind, grated carrots, parsnips and sultanas.

4 Sift the flours and baking powder together, adding any bran left in the sieve (strainer), then gradually fold into the carrot and parsnip mixture. Transfer the mixture to the tin and level the surface. Cover loosely with greased foil, then place in the cooking pot, on top of the saucer or pastry cutter. Pour enough boiling water around the tin to come just over halfway up the sides.

5 Cover the cooker with the lid and cook for 3–5 hours, or until a skewer inserted in the centre of the cake comes out clean. Lift the tin out of the cooker and leave to stand for 5 minutes. Turn the cake out on to a wire rack and leave until cool.

6 To make the topping, place the caster sugar in a bowl over the near-simmering water in the slow cooker. Squeeze the juice from the orange or lemon and add 30ml/2 tbsp of the juice to the sugar. Stir over the heat until the sugar dissolves. Remove from the heat, add the egg white and salt, and whisk for 1 minute with an electric beater.

7 Return the bowl to the heat and whisk for about 6 minutes until the mixture becomes stiff and glossy, holding a good shape. Remove from the heat and allow to cool for about 5 minutes, whisking frequently.

8 Swirl the meringue topping over the cake and leave for about 1 hour to firm up. To serve, sprinkle the cake with the sugared orange or lemon rind.

Pumpkin and Banana Cake

This slow-cooker cake is like a cross between a carrot cake and banana bread.

Serves 12

225g/8oz/2 cups self-raising (self-rising) flour
7.5ml/1½ tsp baking powder
2.5ml/½ tsp ground cinnamon
2.5ml/½ tsp ground ginger
pinch of salt
125g/5oz/10 tbsp soft light brown sugar
75g/3oz/¾ cup pecans or walnuts, chopped
115g/4oz pumpkin flesh, coarsely grated
2 small bananas, mashed
2 eggs, lightly beaten
150ml/¼ pint/⅔ cup sunflower oil

For the topping

50g/2oz/¼ cup butter, at room temperature
150g/5oz/⅔ cup soft cheese
1.5ml/¼ tsp vanilla extract
115g/4oz/1 cup icing (confectioners') sugar
pecan halves, to decorate

1 Line the base and sides of a deep 20cm/8in round fixed-base cake tin (pan) with baking parchment. Place an upturned saucer in the base of the ceramic cooking pot, then pour in about 2.5cm/1in of very hot water. Switch the slow cooker to high.

2 Sift the flour, baking powder, cinnamon, ginger and salt into a large bowl. Stir in the sugar, chopped pecans or walnuts and grated pumpkin. Make a hollow in the middle. In another bowl, combine the bananas, eggs and oil. Stir into the dry ingredients.

3 Spoon the mixture into the tin.Cover with buttered foil and place in the pot. Pour in boiling water to come just over halfway up the sides of the tin. Cover and cook for 4–4½ hours, or until the cake is firm and a skewer inserted into it comes out clean.

4 Remove the cake from the cooker and stand the tin on a wire rack to cool for 15 minutes. Turn out and leave to cool completely, then peel off the lining paper.

5 To make the topping, put the butter, soft cheese and vanilla extract in a bowl and beat until smooth. Sift in the sugar and beat until creamy. Spread the topping over the top of the cake and decorate with pecan halves. Chill for 1 hour before serving.

Frosted Cake Energy 410kcal/1718kJ; Protein 5.9g; Carbohydrate 53g, of which sugars 38.2g; Fat 20.8g, of which saturates 12.2g; Cholesterol 132mg; Calcium 98mg; Fibre 1.9g; Sodium 290mg.
Pumpkin Cake Energy 374kcal/1567kJ; Protein 5.1g; Carbohydrate 43.2g, of which sugars 28.7g; Fat 21.3g, of which saturates 6.5g; Cholesterol 58mg; Calcium 101.7mg; Fibre 1g; Sodium 203mg.

Light Fruit Cake

This incredibly easy all-in-one fruit cake is made in the slow cooker. It is deliciously light and crumbly, and the combination of wholemeal flour and long cooking ensures that it stays beautifully moist.

Serves 12

2 eggs
130g/4½oz/generous ½ cup butter, at room temperature
225g/8oz/1 cup light muscovado (brown) sugar
150g/5oz/1¼ cups self-raising (self-rising) flour
150g/5oz/1¼ cups wholemeal (whole-wheat) self-raising (self-rising) flour
pinch of salt
5ml/1 tsp mixed (apple pie) spice
450g/1lb/2½ cups luxury mixed dried fruit

1 Line the base and sides of a deep 18cm/7in round or 15cm/6in square fixed-base cake tin (pan) with baking parchment. Place an upturned saucer or metal pastry ring in the base of the ceramic cooking pot, then pour in about 2.5cm/1in of very hot water. Switch the slow cooker to high.

2 Crack the eggs into a large mixing bowl. Add the butter and sugar, then sift over the flours, salt and spice, adding any bran left in the sieve (strainer). Stir together until mixed, then add the dried fruit and beat for 2 minutes until the mixture is smooth and glossy.

3 Spoon the mixture into the prepared cake tin and level the surface. Cover the tin with a piece of buttered foil.

4 Put the tin in the slow cooker and pour in enough boiling water to come just over halfway up the sides of the tin. Cover with the lid and cook for 4–5 hours, or until a skewer inserted into the middle of the cake comes out clean.

5 Remove the cake from the slow cooker and place on a wire rack. Leave the cake to cool in the tin for about 15 minutes, then turn out and leave to cool completely before serving. To store, wrap the cake in baking parchment and then kitchen foil, and keep in a cool, dry place.

Marbled Spice Cake

This slow-cooker cake can be made in a ring-shaped cake mould, called a kugelhupf, or in a plain ring-shaped cake tin. It looks spectacular with smooth, drizzled icing.

Serves 8

75g/3oz/6 tbsp butter, softened, plus extra for greasing
115g/4oz/½ cup soft light brown sugar
2 eggs
few drops of vanilla extract
130g/4½oz/generous 1 cup plain (all-purpose) flour, plus extra for dusting
7.5ml/1½ tsp baking powder
45ml/3 tbsp milk
30ml/2 tbsp malt extract or black treacle (molasses)
5ml/1 tsp mixed (apple pie) spice
2.5ml/½ tsp ground ginger
75g/3oz/¾ cup icing (confectioners') sugar, sifted, to decorate

1 Grease and flour a 1.2 litre/2 pint/5 cup kugelhupf mould or ring-shaped cake tin (pan). Put an upturned saucer in the base of the cooking pot and pour in 5cm/2in hot water. Switch to high.

2 Put the butter and sugar in a bowl and beat until fluffy. In a separate bowl, beat the eggs and vanilla extract, then gradually beat into the butter. Sift together the flour and baking powder, then fold into the butter, adding a little milk between each addition. Spoon one-third of the mixture into a bowl and stir in the malt extract or treacle, mixed spice and ginger.

3 Drop a large spoonful of the light mixture into the cake tin, followed by a spoonful of the dark mixture. Continue in this way until all the mixture has been used. Run a knife or skewer through the mixtures to give a marbled effect.

4 Cover the tin with foil and place in the ceramic cooking pot. Pour boiling water around the tin to come just over halfway up the sides. Cover and cook for 3–4 hours, until a skewer inserted into the cake comes out clean. Lift the cake on to a wire rack and leave in the tin for 10 minutes before turning out to cool.

5 To decorate, place the icing sugar in a bowl and add warm water to make a smooth icing. Drizzle the mixture over the cake, then leave to set before serving in thick slices.

Light Fruit Cake Energy 351kcal/1482kJ; Protein 4.9g; Carbohydrate 63g, of which sugars 46g; Fat 10.6g, of which saturates 6g; Cholesterol 60.8mg; Calcium 78.6mg; Fibre 2.3g; Sodium 148mg.
Marbled Spice Cake Energy 215kcal/902kJ; Protein 2.8g; Carbohydrate 33g, of which sugars 20.3g; Fat 8.8g, of which saturates 5.2g; Cholesterol 49mg; Calcium 84mg; Fibre 0.5g; Sodium 172mg.

Apple Cake

This deliciously fruity cake is perhaps best in autumn, when home-grown apples are in season. It is slowly baked in the oven, which helps to keep the inside lovely and moist, and gives the cake a satisfyingly crunchy top.

Makes 1 cake

225g/8oz/2 cups self-raising (self-rising) flour
good pinch of salt
pinch of ground cloves
115g/4oz/½ cup butter, at room temperature
3 or 4 cooking apples, such as Bramley's Seedling
115g/4oz/generous ½ cup caster (superfine) sugar
2 eggs, beaten
a little milk, to mix
granulated (white) sugar, for sprinkling

1 Preheat the oven to 190°C/375°F/Gas 5 and butter a 20cm/8in cake tin (pan).

2 Sift the flour, salt and ground cloves into a bowl. Cut in the butter and, using your fingertips, rub in until the mixture resembles fine breadcrumbs.

3 Peel and core the apples. Slice the flesh thinly and add to the rubbed-in mixture with the caster sugar.

4 Mix in the eggs and enough milk to make a fairly stiff dough, then turn the mixture into the prepared tin and sprinkle with granulated sugar.

5 Bake the cake in the preheated oven for 30–40 minutes, or until springy to the touch and a skewer inserted in the centre of the cake comes out clean. Leave to cool slightly on a wire rack. When cold, turn out and store in an airtight container until ready to serve.

Cook's Tip
Serve either cold as a cake or warm, with a spoonful of chilled cream or custard, as a dessert.

Apple Ring Cake

This attractive fruit and nut cake is slowly baked in a ring-shaped cake tin.

Serves 12

7 eating apples, such as Cox's or Granny Smith
350ml/12fl oz/1½ cups vegetable oil
450g/1lb/2¼ cups caster (superfine) sugar
3 eggs
425g/15oz/3 1/2 cups plain (all-purpose) flour
5ml/1 tsp salt
5ml/1 tsp bicarbonate of soda (baking soda)
5ml/1 tsp ground cinnamon
5ml/1 tsp vanilla extract
115g/4oz/1 cup chopped walnuts
175g/6oz/generous 1 cup raisins
icing (confectioners') sugar, for dusting

1 Preheat the oven to 180°C/350°F/Gas 4. Lightly grease a 23cm/9in ring mould.

2 Quarter, peel and core the apples. Thinly slice the apple flesh and place into a bowl. Set aside.

3 With an electric mixer, beat the oil and sugar together in a large mixing bowl until blended. Gradually add the eggs and continue beating until the mixture is creamy.

4 In a separate bowl, sift together the flour, salt, bicarbonate of soda and cinnamon.

5 Fold the flour mixture into the egg mixture, along with the vanilla extract. Stir in the apples, walnuts and raisins.

6 Pour the mixture into the mould and bake until the cake springs back when touched lightly, about 1¼ hours. Leave to stand for 15 minutes, then turn out and transfer to a cooling rack. Dust with a layer of icing sugar before serving.

Variation
The fruit and nuts in this cake can be varied: use sultanas (golden raisins) glacé cherries, pecans or walnuts, if you prefer.

Apple Cake Energy 2315kcal/9717kJ; Protein 37g; Carbohydrate 312.5g, of which sugars 145.3g; Fat 110.9g, of which saturates 64.1g; Cholesterol 702mg; Calcium 948mg; Fibre 10.7g; Sodium 1.68g.
Ring Cake Energy 603kcal/2532kJ; Protein 7g; Carbohydrate 83.1g, of which sugars 56g; Fat 29.4g, of which saturates 3.4g; Cholesterol 48mg; Calcium 95mg; Fibre 2.8g; Sodium 32mg.

Citrus Sponge

This light sponge cake is made with matzo and potato flour. The addition of orange juice and citrus rind gives it a wonderful tangy taste.

Serves 6–8

12 eggs, separated
300g/11oz/1½ cups caster (superfine) sugar
120ml/4fl oz/½ cup fresh orange juice
grated rind of 1 orange
grated rind of 1 lemon
50g/2oz/½ cup potato flour, sifted
90g/3½oz/¾ cup fine matzo meal or matzo meal flour, sifted
large pinch of salt
icing (confectioners') sugar, for dusting (optional)
fresh orange or grapefruit pieces, to serve (optional)

1 Preheat the oven to 160°C/325°F/Gas 3. In a large mixing bowl, whisk the egg yolks until they are pale and frothy. Whisk the caster sugar, fresh orange juice, orange rind and lemon rind into the eggs.

2 Fold the two sifted flours into the egg mixture. In a clean, grease-free bowl, whisk the egg whites with the salt until stiff, then fold into the egg yolk mixture.

3 Pour the cake mixture into a deep, ungreased 25cm/10in cake tin (pan) and bake for about 1 hour, or until a cocktail stick (toothpick), inserted in the centre, comes out clean. Leave to cool in the tin.

4 When the cake is cold, turn it out and invert it on to a serving plate. Liberally dust the top of the cake with some icing sugar before serving, if you wish. Serve with pieces of fresh orange or grapefruit, if you like.

Cook's Tip
When testing to see if the cake is cooked, if you don't have a cocktail stick (toothpick) to hand, use a strand of raw dried spaghetti instead – it will work just as well.

Tangy Apple Cake

This cake is beautifully firm and moist, with pieces of apple peeking through the top. Using fresh orange juice gives the cake a delicious flavour and the cinnamon is the perfect partner for the apple slices.

Serves 6–8

375g/13oz/3¼ cups self-raising (self-rising) flour
3–4 large cooking apples, or cooking and eating apples
10ml/2 tsp ground cinnamon
500g/1¼lb/2½ cups caster (superfine) sugar
4 eggs, lightly beaten
250ml/8fl oz/1 cup vegetable oil
120ml/4fl oz/½ cup orange juice
10ml/2 tsp vanilla extract
2.5ml/½ tsp salt

1 Preheat the oven to 180°C/350°F/Gas 4. Lightly grease a 30 × 38cm/12 × 15in square cake tin (pan) and dust with a little of the flour. Core and thinly slice the apples, but do not peel them.

2 Put the sliced apples in a bowl and mix with the cinnamon and 75ml/5 tbsp of the sugar.

3 In a separate bowl, beat together the eggs, remaining sugar, vegetable oil, orange juice and vanilla extract until well combined. Sift in the remaining flour and salt, then stir into the mixture until combined.

4 Pour two-thirds of the cake mixture into the prepared tin, top with one-third of the apples, then pour over the remaining cake mixture and top with the remaining apples. Bake for about 1 hour, or until golden brown.

5 Leave the cake to cool in the tin to allow the juices to soak in. Serve while still warm, cut into squares.

Cook's Tip
This sturdy little cake is perfect served with with a cup of tea or coffee for an afternoon break.

Citrus Sponge Energy 328kcal/1381kJ; Protein 11.1g; Carbohydrate 53.7g, of which sugars 40.5g; Fat 8.8g, of which saturates 2.3g; Cholesterol 285mg; Calcium 66mg; Fibre 0.4g; Sodium 109mg.
Apple Cake Energy 653kcal/2751kJ; Protein 7.8g; Carbohydrate 105.4g, of which sugars 70.6g; Fat 25.3g, of which saturates 3.4g; Cholesterol 95mg; Calcium 215mg; Fibre 2.1g; Sodium 210mg.

Spicy Apple Cake

Hundreds of German cakes and desserts include the versatile apple. This moist and spicy *Apfelkuchen* can be found on the menu of Konditoreien, coffee and tea houses everywhere.

Serves 12

115g/4oz/1 cup plain (all-purpose) flour
115g/4oz/1 cup wholemeal (whole-wheat) flour
10ml/2 tsp baking powder
5ml/1 tsp cinnamon
2.5ml/½ tsp mixed (apple pie) spice
225g/8oz cooking apple, cored, peeled and chopped
75g/3oz/6 tbsp butter
175g/6oz/generous ¾ cup soft light brown sugar
finely grated rind of 1 small orange
2 eggs, beaten
30ml/2 tbsp milk
whipped cream dusted with cinnamon, to serve

For the topping

4 eating apples, cored and sliced
juice of ½ orange
10ml/2 tsp caster (superfine) sugar
45ml/3 tbsp apricot jam, warmed and sieved

1 Preheat the oven to 180°C/350°F/Gas 4. Grease and line a 23cm/9in round loose-bottomed cake tin. Sift the flours, baking powder and spices together in a bowl. Toss the chopped cooking apple in 30ml/2 tbsp of the flour mixture.

2 Cream the butter, brown sugar and orange rind together until light and fluffy. Gradually beat in the eggs, then fold in the flour mixture, the chopped apple and the milk. Spoon the mixture into the cake tin and level the surface.

3 For the topping, toss the apple slices in the orange juice and set them in overlapping circles on top of the cake mixture, pressing down lightly.

4 Sprinkle the caster sugar over the top of the cake and bake for 1–1¼ hours, or until risen and firm. Cover with foil if the apples brown too much.

5 Cool in the tin for 10 minutes, then remove to a wire rack. Glaze the apples with the jam. Cut the cake into wedges and serve with whipped cream, sprinkled with cinnamon.

Honey Cake

This cake is sweetened with honey and made with toasted hazelnuts and breadcrumbs instead of flour, which gives it a deliciously rich and moist texture. Bake in a brioche tin to give the cake an attractive shape.

Serves 12

15g/½oz/1 tbsp unsalted (sweet) butter, melted
115g/4oz/2 cups slightly dry fine white breadcrumbs
175g/6oz/¾ cup set honey, plus extra to serve
50g/2oz/¼ cup soft light brown sugar
4 eggs, separated
115g/4oz/1 cup hazelnuts, chopped and toasted, plus extra to decorate

1 Preheat the oven to 180°C/350°F/Gas 4. Brush a 1.75 litre/3 pint/7½ cup fluted brioche tin (pan) with the melted unsalted butter. Sprinkle the tin with about 15g/½oz/¼ cup of the fine white breadcrumbs.

2 Put the honey in a large heatproof bowl set over a pan of barely simmering water. When the honey melts a little, add the sugar and egg yolks. Whisk until light and frothy. Remove the bowl from the heat.

3 Mix the remaining breadcrumbs with the hazelnuts and fold into the egg yolk and honey mixture. Whisk the egg whites in a separate bowl until stiff, then gently fold in with the other ingredients, half at a time.

4 Spoon the mixture into the prepared tin. Bake in the preheated oven for about 40–45 minutes, until golden brown. Leave to cool in the tin for 5 minutes, then turn out on to a wire rack to cool. Sprinkle over the nuts and drizzle with extra honey to serve.

Cook's Tip
The cake will rise during cooking and then sink slightly as it cools – this is quite normal.

Apple Cake Energy 587kcal/2471kJ; Protein 5.5g; Carbohydrate 92g, of which sugars 69.7g; Fat 24.5g, of which saturates 10.6g; Cholesterol 40mg; Calcium 95mg; Fibre 2.5g; Sodium 129mg.
Honey Cake Energy 188kcal/791kJ; Protein 4.6g; Carbohydrate 23.5g, of which sugars 16.1g; Fat 9.1g, of which saturates 1.6g; Cholesterol 66mg; Calcium 39mg; Fibre 0.8g; Sodium 106mg.

Spiced Honey Cake

This classic honey cake is richly spiced, redolent of ginger, cinnamon and other sweet, aromatic scents.

Serves about 8

175g/6oz/1 ½ cups plain (all-purpose) flour
75g/3oz/⅓ cup caster (superfine) sugar
2.5ml/½ tsp ground ginger
2.5–5ml/½–1 tsp ground cinnamon
5ml/1 tsp mixed (apple pie) spice
5ml/1 tsp bicarbonate of soda (baking soda)
225g/8oz/1 cup clear honey
60ml/4 tbsp vegetable or olive oil
grated rind of 1 orange
2 eggs
75ml/5 tbsp orange juice
10ml/2 tsp chopped fresh root ginger, or to taste

1 Preheat the oven to 180°C/350°F/Gas 4. Line a rectangular baking tin (pan), measuring 25 × 20 × 5cm/10 × 8 × 2in, with baking parchment. In a large mixing bowl, mix together the flour, sugar, ginger, cinnamon, mixed spice and bicarbonate of soda until well combined.

2 Make a well in the centre of the flour mixture and pour in the clear honey, vegetable or olive oil, orange rind and eggs. Using a wooden spoon or electric whisk, beat until smooth, then add the orange juice. Stir in the chopped ginger.

3 Pour the cake mixture into the prepared tin, then bake for about 50 minutes, or until firm to the touch.

4 Leave the cake to cool in the tin, then turn out and wrap tightly in foil. Store at room temperature for 2–3 days before serving, to allow the flavours of the cake to mature.

Cook's Tip
This honey cake keeps very well. It can be made in two loaf tins (pans), so that one cake can be eaten, while the other can be wrapped in clear film (plastic wrap) and stored or frozen for a later date.

Old-fashioned Treacle Cake

The treacle gives this delicious cake a lovely rich colour and a deep flavour.

Makes a 20cm/8in cake

250g/9oz/2 cups self-raising (self-rising) flour
2.5ml/½ tsp mixed (apple pie) spice
75g/3oz/6 tbsp butter, cut into small cubes
35g/1oz/2 tbsp caster (superfine) sugar
150g/5oz/1 cup mixed dried fruit
1 egg
15ml/1 tbsp black treacle (molasses)
100ml/3½fl oz/scant ½ cup milk

1 Preheat the oven to 180°C/350°F/Gas 5. Butter a shallow 20–23cm/8–9in ovenproof flan dish or baking tin (pan).

2 Sift the flour and spice into a large mixing bowl. Add the butter and, with your fingertips, rub it into the flour until the mixture resembles fine crumbs. Alternatively, you could do this in a food processor. Stir in the sugar and mixed dried fruit.

3 Beat the egg and, with a small whisk or a fork, stir in the black treacle and then the milk. Stir the liquid into the flour to make a fairly stiff but moist consistency, adding a little extra milk, if necessary.

4 Transfer the cake mixture to the prepared dish or tin with a spoon and level out the surface. Bake the cake in the hot oven and cook for about 1 hour until it has risen, is firm to the touch and fully cooked through. To check if the cake is cooked, insert a small skewer into the centre of the cake – it should come out free of sticky mixture.

5 Leave the cooked treacle cake in the dish or tin to cool completely. Serve it, cut into wedges, straight from the dish.

Cook's Tip
Vary the fruit used in this cake, if you like. Try using chopped ready-to-eat dried apricots and stem ginger, or a packet of luxury dried fruit.

Spiced Honey Cake Energy 264kcal/1115kJ; Protein 3.8g; Carbohydrate 49.1g, of which sugars 32.4g; Fat 7.2g, of which saturates 1.1g; Cholesterol 48mg; Calcium 45mg; Fibre 0.7g; Sodium 23mg.
Treacle Cake Energy 2089kcal/8805kJ; Protein 37.4g; Carbohydrate 343g, of which sugars 152.4g; Fat 72.8g, of which saturates 42.2g; Cholesterol 356mg; Calcium 720mg; Fibre 11.1g; Sodium 676mg.

Moist Golden Ginger Cake

This is the ultimate ginger cake. Because it is made in the slow cooker the cake can be eaten straight away, but the flavour and texture improves if it is wrapped and kept for a day or two.

Serves 10

175g/6oz/generous 3/4 cup light muscovado (brown) sugar
115g/4oz/1/2 cup butter
150g/5oz/2/3 cup golden (light corn) syrup
25g/1oz malt extract
175g/6oz/1 1/2 cups self-raising (self-rising) flour
50g/2oz/1/2 cup plain (all-purpose) flour
10ml/2 tsp ground ginger
pinch of salt
1 egg, lightly beaten
120ml/4fl oz/1/2 cup milk, at room temperature
2.5ml/1/2 tsp bicarbonate of soda (baking soda)

1 Line the base of a deep 18cm/7in round fixed-base cake tin (pan) with baking parchment. Pour 5cm/2in of very hot water into the ceramic cooking pot. Switch to high.

2 Place the sugar, butter, golden syrup and malt extract in a heatproof bowl that will fit inside the slow cooker. Place in the pot and leave for 15 minutes, or until melted.

3 Remove the bowl from the pot and stir until smooth. Place an upturned saucer in the base of the ceramic cooking pot. Sift the flours, ginger and salt into a mixing bowl. Beat into the melted butter mixture until smooth. Mix in the egg.

4 Pour the milk in a jug (pitcher) and stir in the bicarbonate of soda. Pour the mixture into the ginger cake mixture and stir until combined. Pour the mixture into the cake tin, cover with foil and place in the cooking pot. Pour boiling water around the tin or dish to come just over halfway up the sides. Cover with the lid and cook for 5–6 hours, or until firm and a fine skewer inserted into the cake comes out clean.

5 Remove the cake from the slow cooker and place the tin on a wire cooling rack. Leave to cool for 15 minutes, then turn out and leave to cool completely, before serving in slices.

Whiskey Cake

This light, moist cake has the subtle flavours of lemon and cloves, making it seem especially tempting in winter.

Makes one 18cm/7in round cake

225g/8oz/1 1/3 cups sultanas (golden raisins)
grated rind of 1 lemon
150ml/1/4 pint/2/3 cup Irish whiskey
175g/6oz/3/4 cup butter, softened
175g/6oz/3/4 cup soft light brown sugar
175g/6oz/1 1/2 cups plain (all-purpose) flour
pinch of salt
1.5ml/1/4 tsp ground cloves
5ml/1 tsp baking powder
3 large (US extra large) eggs, separated

For the icing

juice of 1 lemon
225g/8oz/2 cups icing (confectioners') sugar
crystallized lemon slices, to decorate (optional)

1 Put the sultanas and grated lemon rind into a bowl with the whiskey, and leave overnight to soak.

2 Preheat the oven to 180°C/350°F/Gas 4 and grease and base line a loose-based 18cm/7in deep cake tin (pan). Cream the butter and sugar until light and fluffy. Sift the flour, salt, cloves and baking powder together into a bowl.

3 Beat the yolks into the butter and sugar one at a time, adding a little of the flour with each egg and beating well. Gradually blend in the sultana and whiskey mixture, alternating with the remaining flour. Do not overbeat at this stage.

4 Whisk the egg whites until stiff and fold them into the mixture with a metal spoon. Turn the mixture into the prepared tin and bake in the preheated oven for 1 1/2 hours, or until well risen and springy to the touch. Turn out and cool on a rack.

5 Meanwhile, make the icing. Mix the lemon juice with the icing sugar and enough warm water to make a pouring consistency. Lay a plate under the cake rack to catch the drips and pour the icing over the cake a spoonful at a time, letting it dribble down the sides. When the icing has set, it can be decorated with lemon slices, if you like.

Ginger Cake Energy 289kcal/1216kJ; Protein 3.4g; Carbohydrate 48g, of which sugars 31.1g; Fat 10.6g, of which saturates 6.4g; Cholesterol 48mg; Calcium 98mg; Fibre 0.7g; Sodium 211mg.
Whiskey Cake Energy 4691kcal/19,730kJ; Protein 48.1g; Carbohydrate 711.2g, of which sugars 577.8g; Fat 167g, of which saturates 97.1g; Cholesterol 1.06g; Calcium 735mg; Fibre 9.9g; Sodium 1.38g.

Boiled Fruit Cake

The texture of this cake is quite distinctive – moist and plump as a result of boiling the dried fruit with the butter, sugar and milk prior to baking. For special occasions replace some of the milk with sherry or brandy, and arrange cherries and nuts on the surface of the uncooked cake before putting it in the oven. It makes an ideal Christmas cake, too.

Makes a 20cm/8in cake
350g/12oz/2 cups mixed dried fruit
225g/8oz/1 cup butter
225g/8oz/1 cup soft dark brown sugar
400ml/14fl oz/1⅔ cup milk
450g/1lb/4 cups self-raising (self-rising) flour
5ml/1 tsp bicarbonate of soda (baking soda)
5ml/1 tsp mixed (apple pie) spice
2 eggs, beaten

1 Preheat the oven to 160°C/325°F/Gas 3. Lightly grease a 20cm/8in round cake tin (pan) and line it with a piece of baking parchment.

2 Put the mixed dried fruit in a large pan and add the butter and the brown sugar. Bring the mixture slowly to the boil, stirring occasionally.

3 When the butter has melted and the sugar has completely dissolved, bubble the mixture gently for about 2 minutes. Remove from the heat and cool slightly.

4 Sift the flour with the bicarbonate of soda and mixed spice into a bowl. Add this and the eggs to the fruit mixture and mix together well.

5 Pour the cake mixture into the prepared tin and smooth the surface. Bake for about 1½ hours or until firm to the touch and cooked through – a skewer inserted in the centre of the cake should come out free of sticky mixture.

6 Leave the cake in the tin to cool for about 20–30 minutes, then turn out and cool completely on a wire rack before cutting into wedges and serving.

Porter Cake

Porter was a key ingredient in many traditional Irish dishes, adding colour and richness. Stout is a good substitute in recipes like this one.

Makes one 20cm/8in round cake
225g/8oz/1 cup butter, at room temperature
225g/8oz/1 cup soft dark brown sugar
350g/12oz/3 cups plain (all-purpose) flour
pinch of salt
5ml/1 tsp baking powder
5ml/1 tsp mixed (apple pie) spice
3 eggs
450g/1lb/2⅓ cups mixed dried fruit
115g/4oz/½ cup glacé (candied) cherries
115g/4oz/⅔ cup mixed (candied) peel
50g/2oz/½ cup chopped almonds or walnuts
about 150ml/¼ pint/⅔ cup stout, such as Guinness

1 Preheat the oven to 160°C/325°F/Gas 3. Grease and base line a 20cm/8in round deep cake tin (pan). Cream the butter and sugar in a bowl, until light and fluffy. Sift the flour, salt, baking powder and spice into another bowl.

2 Add the eggs to the butter mixture, one at a time, adding a little of the flour mixture with each egg and beating well. Mix well and blend in any remaining flour. Add the fruit and nuts and enough stout to make quite a soft consistency. Mix well.

3 Turn the mixture into the tin and bake for 1 hour. Reduce the heat to 150°C/300°F/Gas 2 and cook for 1½–2 hours, or until the top is springy to the touch and a skewer pushed into the centre comes out clean. Cool the cake in the tin.

4 When cold, remove the lining paper, wrap in fresh baking parchment and store in an airtight container for at least a week before eating, to give the flavours time to develop.

Cook's Tip
Porter cake can be made by many methods, ranging from rubbed-in teabreads to the creaming method, as here.

Fruit Cake Energy 5150kcal/21689kJ; Protein 72.2g; Carbohydrate 796g, of which sugars 498.8g; Fat 209.1g, of which saturates 125.4g; Cholesterol 884mg; Calcium 2352mg; Fibre 20.1g; Sodium 3297mg.
Porter Cake Energy 6130kcal/25807kJ; Protein 80.2g; Carbohydrate 964.9g, of which sugars 696.9g; Fat 240.2g, of which saturates 125.7g; Cholesterol 1.16g; Calcium 1.42mg; Fibre 31g; Sodium 2.23g.

Caraway Seed Cake

This old-fashioned cake remains popular on farmhouse tea tables.

Makes 1 cake

225g/8oz/2 cups plain (all-purpose) flour
115g/4oz/½ cup butter, at room temperature
115g/4oz/generous ½ cup caster (superfine) sugar
2 large (US extra large) eggs
5ml/1 tsp baking powder
15ml/1 tbsp caraway seeds
30–45ml/2–3 tbsp milk, if necessary

1 Preheat the oven to 180°C/350°F/Gas 4. Butter and base line a 18cm/7in deep cake tin (pan) with lightly buttered baking parchment.

2 Sift the flour into a bowl. Cream the butter and sugar together in a separate bowl until fluffy, then add the eggs, a little at a time, with a spoonful of flour with each addition. Add the baking powder and most of the caraway seeds to the remaining flour, reserving a few seeds to sprinkle over the top of the cake.

3 Add the flour and caraway seeds mixture to the butter mixture, and blend in lightly but thoroughly; add a little milk to make a soft mixture if it seems too stiff.

4 Turn the mixture into the tin and sprinkle with the reserved caraway seeds. Put the cake in the preheated oven and bake for 15 minutes. Reduce the temperature to 160°C/325°F/Gas 3 and bake for a further 1 hour, or until the cake is well risen and golden brown.

5 Leave the cake to cool in the tin for about 10 minutes, then remove and finish cooling on a wire rack. When cold, remove the baking parchment and store in an airtight tin.

Cook's Tip
Aromatic caraway seeds come from a herb in the parsley family. They have a mild aniseed flavour and are often used in baking.

Poppy Seed Cake

This plain and simple cake is studded with tiny black poppy seeds that give it a nutty, distinctive taste that is utterly moreish. Serve with a cup of hot tea when you feel like a treat.

Serves about 8

130g/4½oz/generous 1 cup self-raising (self-rising) flour
5ml/1 tsp baking powder
2.5ml/½ tsp salt
2 eggs
225g/8oz/generous 1 cup caster (superfine) sugar
5–10ml/1–2 tsp vanilla extract
200g/7oz/scant 1½ cups poppy seeds, ground
15ml/1 tbsp grated lemon rind
120ml/4fl oz/½ cup milk
130g/4½oz/generous ½ cup unsalted (sweet) butter, melted and cooled
30ml/2 tbsp vegetable oil
icing (confectioners') sugar, sifted, for dusting

1 Preheat the oven to 180°C/350°F/Gas 4. Grease and base-line a 23cm/9in springform tin (pan). In a large mixing bowl, sift together the flour, baking powder and salt.

2 Using an electric whisk, beat together the eggs, sugar and vanilla extract for 4–5 minutes until pale and fluffy. Stir in the poppy seeds and the lemon rind.

3 Gently fold the sifted ingredients into the egg and poppy seed mixture, working in three batches and alternating with the milk. Gradually fold in the melted butter and vegetable oil until the mixture is well combined.

4 Pour the mixture into the prepared tin and bake for about 40 minutes, or until firm. Cool in the tin for 15 minutes, then invert the cake on to a wire rack to cool completely. Serve cold, dusted with icing sugar.

Variation
To make a poppy seed tart, pour the cake mixture into a par-cooked pastry crust, then bake for 30 minutes, or until the filling is firm and risen.

Caraway Energy 2252kcal/9448kJ; Protein 37.4g; Carbohydrate 295.7g, of which sugars 124.2g; Fat 110.8g, of which saturates 64.1g; Cholesterol 702mg; Calcium 465mg; Fibre 7g; Sodium 879mg.
Poppy Energy 485kcal/2023kJ; Protein 8.3g; Carbohydrate 42.7g, of which sugars 30.5g; Fat 32.4g, of which saturates 11.4g; Cholesterol 83mg; Calcium 267mg; Fibre 2.5g; Sodium 188mg.

Black Bread

This cake has a texture that is similar to pumpernickel and is slowly steamed rather than oven-baked. Empty fruit cans are perfect for producing bread in the traditional round shape.

Makes 2 loaves

50g/2oz/½ cup rye flour
40g/1½ oz/⅓ cup plain (all-purpose) flour
4ml/¾ tsp baking powder
2.5ml/½ tsp salt
1.5ml/¼ tsp cinnamon
1.5ml/¼ tsp nutmeg
50g/2oz/⅓ cup fine semolina
60ml/4 tbsp black treacle (molasses)
200ml/7fl oz/scant 1 cup cultured buttermilk
cherry jam, sour cream or crème fraîche and a sprinkling of ground allspice, to serve

1 Grease and line 2 × 400g/14oz fruit cans. Sift the flours, baking powder, salt and spices into a large mixing bowl. Stir in the semolina. Add the black treacle and buttermilk and mix until thoroughly combined.

2 Divide the mixture evenly between the two cans, then cover each with a double layer of greased pleated foil.

3 Place the cans on a trivet in a large pan and pour in enough hot water to come halfway up the sides of the cans. Cover the pan tightly and steam for 2 hours, checking the water level occasionally, and topping up if necessary.

4 Carefully remove the cans from the steamer. Turn the bread out on to a wire rack and cool completely. Wrap in foil and use within 1 week.

5 Serve the bread in slices, spread with cherry jam, topped with a spoonful of soured cream or crème fraîche and a sprinkling of allspice.

Cook's Tip

If you cannot get buttermilk, use ordinary milk instead, first soured with 5ml/1 tsp lemon juice.

Christmas Cake

Rich cakes need at least a month to mature, so Christmas cakes are best made by Hallowe'en. This cake may be finished in the traditional way with almond paste and white icing, or glazed with fruit and nuts.

Makes one 20cm/8in round or 18cm/7in square cake

225g/8oz/2 cups plain (all-purpose) flour
pinch of salt
7.5ml/1½ tsp mixed (apple pie) spice
900g/2lb/5 cups mixed dried fruit
50g/2oz/½ cup slivered almonds
115g/4oz/⅔ cup glacé (candied) cherries, halved
115g/4oz/⅔ cup chopped mixed (candied) peel
225g/8oz/1 cup butter, at room temperature
225g/8oz/1 cup soft dark brown sugar
15ml/1 tbsp black treacle (molasses)
finely grated rind of 1 orange
5ml/1 tsp vanilla extract
4 large (US extra large) eggs
150ml/¼ pint/⅔ cup Irish whiskey

1 Prepare a 20cm/8in round or an 18cm/7in square loose-based cake tin (pan) by lining it with three layers of greased baking parchment, extending 5cm/2in over the top of the tin. Attach a thick band of folded newspaper or brown paper around the outside of the tin, using string to secure it.

2 Sift the flour, salt and mixed spice in a large mixing bowl. Put the dried fruit in a separate large bowl with the almonds, cherries, mixed peel and 15ml/1 tbsp of flour taken from the measured amount.

3 In another bowl, cream the butter and sugar until light and fluffy, then add the treacle, orange rind and vanilla extract. Beat well. Add the eggs, one at a time, adding a little of the flour mixture with each egg and beating well after each addition. Fold in the fruit mixture and the remaining flour with 30ml/2 tbsp of the whiskey. Mix well.

4 Put the mixture into the prepared tin, smoothing down well with the back of a spoon and leaving a slight hollow in the centre. At this stage, the cake can now be left overnight or until it is convenient to start baking.

5 Preheat the oven to 160°C/325°F/Gas 3. Place the cake in the centre of the oven and bake for about 1½ hours, or until just beginning to brown. Reduce the heat to 150°C/300°F/Gas 2 and continue to bake for another 3 hours, or until cooked. Protect the top of the cake from over-browning by covering loosely with foil or brown paper.

6 When cooked, the top of the cake will feel springy to the touch and a skewer pushed into the centre will come out clean. Leave the cake to cool, then remove the papers and turn upside down.

7 Using a skewer, make small holes all over the base of the cake and pour in the remaining whiskey. Leave the cake to soak up the whiskey. When soaked, wrap the cake in a double layer of baking parchment, followed by a layer of foil. Store the cake in an airtight container in a cool place until about two weeks before Christmas, if you wish to add a topping.

Black Bread Energy 417kcal/1774kJ; Protein 12.3g; Carbohydrate 94g, of which sugars 25.1g; Fat 1.8g, of which saturates 0.3g; Cholesterol 4mg; Calcium 356mg; Fibre 4.7g; Sodium 103mg.
Christmas Cake Energy 9834kcal/41,553kJ; Protein 89.9g; Carbohydrate 1846.1g, of which sugars 1673.2g; Fat 247g, of which saturates 127.3g; Cholesterol 1.39g; Calcium 2.24g; Fibre 46g; Sodium 2.8g.

Barm Brack

The traditional yeasted Hallowe'en barm brack contains all kinds of symbolic tokens, of which the best known is a ring. Serve this version sliced and buttered while still warm.

Makes 2 loaves

450g/1lb/4 cups plain (all-purpose) flour
5ml/1 tsp mixed (apple pie) spice
2.5ml/½ tsp salt
2 sachets easy-blend (rapid-rise) dried yeast
75g/3oz/6 tbsp soft dark brown sugar
115g/4oz/½ cup butter, melted
300ml/½ pint/1¼ cups tepid milk
1 egg, lightly beaten
375g/13oz/generous 2 cups dried mixed fruit
25g/1oz/⅓ cup chopped mixed (candied) peel
15ml/1 tbsp caster (superfine) sugar

1 Butter two 450g/1lb loaf tins (pans). Mix the flour, spice, salt, yeast and sugar in a large bowl and make a well in the centre.

2 Mix the melted butter with the tepid milk and lightly beaten egg and add to the bowl. Add the mixed fruit and peel to the bowl and mix well.

3 Turn the mixture into the loaf tins. Leave in a warm place for about 30 minutes to rise. Meanwhile, preheat the oven to 200°C/400°F/Gas 6.

4 When the dough has doubled in size, bake in the hot oven for about 45 minutes, or until the loaves begin to shrink slightly from the sides of the tins; when turned out and rapped underneath they should sound hollow.

5 Make a glaze by mixing the caster sugar with 30ml/2 tbsp boiling water. Remove the loaves from the oven and brush over with the glaze.

6 Return the loaves to the oven for about 3 minutes, or until the tops have turned a rich shiny brown. Turn on to a wire rack to cool slightly for 5–10 minutes, before serving in warm slices with plenty of butter.

Bara Brith Teabread

The Welsh spiced loaf known as bara brith is similar to barm brack. Once the fruit has been plumped up by soaking it in tea, this version is easy to make with self-raising flour. Serve sliced, with a little butter, if you like.

Makes 1 large loaf

225g/8oz/1⅓ cups mixed dried fruit and chopped mixed (candied) peel
225ml/8fl oz/1 cup hot strong tea, strained
225g/8oz/2 cups self-raising (self-rising) flour
5ml/1 tsp mixed (apple pie) spice
25g/1oz/2 tbsp butter
100g/3¾oz/scant ½ cup soft light brown sugar
1 egg, lightly beaten

1 Put the fruit into a heatproof bowl and pour the hot tea over it. Cover and leave to stand at room temperature for several hours or overnight.

2 Preheat the oven to 180°C/350°F/Gas 4. Grease a 900g/2lb loaf tin (pan) and line it with baking parchment.

3 Sift the flour and the mixed spice into a large mixing bowl. Add the butter and, with your fingertips, rub it into the flour until the mixture starts to resemble fine breadcrumbs.

4 Stir in the brown sugar, then add the soaked fruit and its liquid along with the beaten egg. Stir well to make a mixture with a soft consistency.

5 Transfer the mixture to the prepared loaf tin and level the surface. Put into the hot oven and cook for about 1 hour or until a skewer inserted in the centre comes out clean. Turn out on a wire rack and leave to cool completely.

Cook's Tip
The flavour of the loaf can be varied subtly by using a variety of teas – try the distinctive perfume of Earl Grey.

Barm Brack Energy 2019kcal/8524kJ; Protein 34.9g; Carbohydrate 364.6g, of which sugars 193.2g; Fat 57g, of which saturates 32.8g; Cholesterol 246mg; Calcium 704mg; Fibre 11.7g; Sodium 590mg.
Bara Brith Energy 2024kcal/8588kJ; Protein 33.2g; Carbohydrate 432.7g, of which sugars 261.3g; Fat 29.9g, of which saturates 15g; Cholesterol 244mg; Calcium 565mg; Fibre 11.9g; Sodium 342mg.

Mango Chutney

No Indian meal would be complete without this classic chutney, which is ideal for making in the slow cooker. Its gloriously sweet, tangy flavour is the perfect complement to the warm taste of spices.

Makes 450g/1lb

3 firm mangoes
120ml/4fl oz/½ cup cider vinegar
200g/7oz/scant 1 cup light muscovado (brown) sugar
1 small red finger chilli or jalapeño chilli, split
2.5cm/1in piece fresh root ginger, peeled and finely chopped
1 garlic clove, finely chopped
5 cardamom pods, bruised
1 bay leaf
2.5ml/½ tsp salt

1 Peel the mangoes and cut out the stone (pit), then cut the flesh into small chunks or thin wedges.

2 Put the chopped mango in the ceramic cooking pot. Add the cider vinegar, stir briefly to combine, and cover the slow cooker with the lid. Switch to high and cook for about 2 hours, stirring the chutney halfway through the cooking time.

3 Stir the sugar, chilli, ginger, garlic, bruised cardamom pods, bay leaf and salt into the mango mixture, until the sugar has dissolved completely.

4 Cover and cook for 2 hours, then uncover and let the mixture cook for a further 1 hour, or until the chutney is reduced to a thick consistency and no excess liquid remains. Stir the chutney every 15 minutes during the last hour.

5 Remove and discard the bay leaf and the chilli. Spoon the chutney into hot sterilized jars and seal. Store for 1 week before eating and use within 1 year.

Cook's Tip
To make a more fiery chutney, seed and slice two green chillies and stir into the chutney mixture with the other spices.

Butternut, Apricot and Almond Chutney

Coriander seeds and ground turmeric add a deliciously spicy touch to this rich, slow-cooker chutney. It is ideal spooned on to little savoury canapés or with melting cubes of mozzarella cheese; it is also good in sandwiches, helping to spice up a variety of fillings.

Makes about 1.8kg/4lb

1 small butternut squash, weighing about 800g/1¾ lb
400g/14oz/2 cups golden sugar
300ml/½ pint/1¼ cups cider vinegar
2 onions, finely chopped
225g/8oz/1 cup ready-to-eat dried apricots, chopped
finely grated rind and juice of 1 orange
2.5ml/½ tsp turmeric
15ml/1 tbsp coriander seeds
15ml/1 tbsp salt
115g/4oz/1 cup flaked (sliced) almonds

1 Halve the butternut squash and scoop out the seeds. Peel off the skin, then cut the flesh into 1cm/½in cubes.

2 Put the sugar and vinegar in the ceramic cooking pot and switch to high. Heat for 30 minutes, then stir until the sugar has completely dissolved.

3 Add the butternut squash, onions, apricots, orange rind and juice, turmeric, coriander seeds and salt to the slow cooker and stir well.

4 Cover the cooker with the lid and cook for 5–6 hours, stirring occasionally. After about 5 hours the chutney should be a fairly thick consistency with relatively little liquid. If it is still quite runny at this stage, cook uncovered for the final hour. Stir in the flaked almonds.

5 Spoon the chutney into warmed sterilized jars, cover and seal. Store in a cool, dark place and allow to mature for at least 1 month before eating. It should be used within 2 years. Once opened, store jars of the chutney in the refrigerator and use within 2 months.

Mango Chutney Energy 1045kcal/4465kJ; Protein 4.1g; Carbohydrate 272.5g, of which sugars 271.1g; Fat 0.9g, of which saturates 0.5g; Cholesterol 0mg; Calcium 908mg; Fibre 11.7g; Sodium 1002mg.
Butternut Energy 2770kcal/11723kJ; Protein 41.7g; Carbohydrate 532.6g, of which sugars 524.1g; Fat 67.3g, of which saturates 5.9g; Cholesterol 0mg; Calcium 807mg; Fibre 31.6g; Sodium 5967mg.

Sweet and Hot Dried-fruit Chutney

This rich, thick and slightly sticky preserve of spiced dried fruit is simple to make in the slow cooker. It is a wonderful way to enliven cold roast turkey left over from your Christmas or Thanksgiving dinner.

Makes about 1.5kg/3lb 6oz

350g/12oz/1½ cups ready-to-eat dried apricots
225g/8oz/1½ cups dried dates, stoned (pitted)
225g/8oz/1⅓ cups dried figs
50g/2oz/⅓ cup glacé (candied) citrus peel
150g/5oz/1 cup raisins
50g/2oz/½ cup dried cranberries
75ml/2½fl oz/⅓ cup cranberry juice
300ml/½ pint/1¼ cups cider vinegar
225g/8oz/1 cup caster (superfine) sugar
finely grated rind of 1 lemon
5ml/1 tsp mixed (apple pie) spice
5ml/1 tsp ground coriander
5ml/1 tsp cayenne pepper
5ml/1 tsp salt

1 Chop the apricots, dates, figs and citrus peel, and put all the dried fruit in the ceramic cooking pot. Pour over the cranberry juice, stir, then cover the slow cooker and switch to low. Cook for 1 hour, or until the fruit has absorbed most of the juice.

2 Add the cider vinegar and sugar to the pot. Turn the slow cooker up to high and stir until the sugar has dissolved.

3 Re-cover and cook for 2 more hours, or until the fruit is very soft and the chutney fairly thick (it will thicken further as it cools). Stir in the lemon rind, mixed spice, coriander, cayenne pepper and salt. Cook, uncovered, for 30 minutes, until little excess liquid remains.

4 Spoon the chutney into warmed sterilized jars, cover and seal. Store in a cool, dark place. Open within 10 months and, once opened, store in the refrigerator and use within 2 months.

Variation
Pitted prunes can be substituted for the dates, and dried sour cherries for the dried cranberries.

Beetroot, Date and Orange Preserve

With its vibrant red colour and rich earthy flavour, this distinctive slow-cooker chutney is good with salads as well as cheeses, such as mature Cheddar, Stilton or Gorgonzola.

Makes about 1.4kg/3lb

300ml/½ pint/1¼ cups malt vinegar
200g/7oz/1 cup sugar
350g/12oz raw beetroot (beets)
350g/12oz eating apples
225g/8oz red onions, very finely chopped
1 garlic clove, crushed
finely grated rind of 2 oranges
5ml/1 tsp ground allspice
5ml/1 tsp salt
175g/6oz/1 cup chopped dried dates

1 Put the vinegar and sugar in the ceramic cooking pot. Cover the slow cooker and switch to high. Leave until steaming hot.

2 Meanwhile, scrub the beetroot, then cut into 1cm/½in pieces. Peel, quarter and core the apples and cut into a similar size.

3 Stir the vinegar mixture with a wooden spoon until the sugar has dissolved. Add the beetroot, apples, onions, garlic, orange rind, ground allspice and salt. Stir, then re-cover and cook for 4–5 hours, stirring occasionally, until very tender.

4 Stir in the dates and cook for a further hour until the mixture is really thick. Stir once or twice during this time to prevent the chutney from catching on the base of the ceramic cooking pot.

5 Spoon the chutney into warmed sterilized jars, cover and seal. Store in a cool, dark place and open within 5 months of making. Refrigerate after opening and use within 1 month.

Cook's Tip
For really speedy preparation and a deliciously fine-textured chutney, put the peeled beetroot through the coarse grating blade of a food processor. Alternatively, you can simply grate the beetroot by hand.

Sweet Chutney Energy 2873kcal/12248kJ; Protein 32g; Carbohydrate 714.3g, of which sugars 703.5g; Fat 6.8g, of which saturates 0.2g; Cholesterol 0mg; Calcium 1075mg; Fibre 52.1g; Sodium 2358mg.
Beetroot Preserve Energy 1632kcal/6949kJ; Protein 16.8g; Carbohydrate 413.7g, of which sugars 406g; Fat 1.5g, of which saturates 0.2g; Cholesterol 0mg; Calcium 278mg; Fibre 23.1g; Sodium 2241mg.

Apple and Sultana Chutney

Use wine or cider vinegar for this stovetop chutney to give it a subtle and mellow flavour. The chutney is perfect served with farmhouse cheeses and freshly made soda bread.

Makes about 900g/2lb

350g/12oz cooking apples
115g/4oz/⅔ cup sultanas (golden raisins)
50g/2oz onion
25g/1oz/¼ cup almonds, blanched
5ml/1 tsp white peppercorns
2.5ml/½ tsp coriander seeds
175g/6oz/scant 1 cup sugar
10ml/2 tsp salt
5ml/1 tsp ground ginger
450ml/¾ pint/scant 2 cups cider vinegar
1.5ml/¼ tsp cayenne pepper
red chillies (optional)

1 Peel, core and chop the apples. Chop the sultanas, onion and almonds. Tie the peppercorns and coriander seeds in muslin (cheesecloth), using a long piece of string, and then tie to the handle of a preserving pan or stainless steel pan.

2 Put the sugar, salt, ground ginger and vinegar into the pan, with the cayenne pepper to taste. Heat the mixture gently, stirring, until the sugar has completely dissolved.

3 Add the chopped fruit to the pan. Bring the mixture to the boil and then lower the heat. Simmer for about 1½–2 hours, or until most of the liquid has evaporated.

4 Spoon the chutney into warmed sterilized jars and place one whole fresh chilli in each jar, if using. Leave until cold, then cover and seal the jars and attach a label to each one. Store in a cool, dark place. The chutney is best left for a month to mature before use and will keep for at least 6 months, if correctly stored.

Variation
For a mild chutney, add only a little cayenne pepper. For a spicier one, increase the quantity to taste.

Christmas Mincemeat

In many mincemeat recipes, the raw ingredients are simply mixed together. Here, gentle simmering in the slow cooker develops and intensifies the flavours, so that the mincemeat can be used immediately without being left to mature. At the same time, heating it to simmering point helps prevent fermentation, and allows a longer shelf-life.

Makes about 1.75g/4lb

450g/1lb cooking apples
115g/4oz/¾ cup glacé (candied) citrus peel
115g/4oz/½ cup glacé (candied) cherries
115g/4oz/½ cup ready-to-eat dried apricots
115g/4oz/1 cup blanched almonds
150ml/¼ pint/⅔ cup brandy
225g/8oz/1 cup currants
225g/8oz/1⅓ cups sultanas (golden raisins)
450g/1lb/3¼ cups seedless raisins
225g/8oz/1 cup soft dark brown sugar
225g/8oz/1⅔ cups suet (US chilled, grated shortening) or vegetarian suet
10ml/2 tsp ground ginger
5ml/1 tsp ground allspice
5ml/1 tsp ground cinnamon
2.5ml/½ tsp grated nutmeg
grated rind and juice of 1 lemon
grated rind and juice of 1 orange

1 Peel, core and chop the apples, then roughly chop the citrus peel, glacé cherries, apricots and blanched almonds.

2 Reserve half the brandy and put the rest into the ceramic cooking pot with all the other ingredients. Stir until well mixed. Cover the ceramic cooking pot with the lid and switch the slow cooker to high. Cook for 1 hour.

3 Stir the mixture well, then re-cover the pot and reduce the temperature to low. Cook for a further 2 hours, stirring halfway through cooking to prevent the mixture from overheating and sticking to the sides of the pot.

4 Remove the lid and leave the mixture to cool completely, stirring occasionally. Stir the reserved brandy into the mincemeat and spoon the mixture into sterilized jars. Cover and store in a cool, dark place for up to 6 months. Once opened, store in the refrigerator and use within 2 weeks.

Apple Chutney Energy 1299kcal/5525kJ; Protein 10.9g; Carbohydrate 299.5g, of which sugars 297.7g; Fat 14.9g, of which saturates 1.1g; Cholesterol 0mg; Calcium 254mg; Fibre 10.4g; Sodium 3.97g.
Mincemeat Energy 7149kcal/30087kJ; Protein 55.6g; Carbohydrate 1114g, of which sugars 1088.3g; Fat 267.7g, of which saturates 106.3g; Cholesterol 0mg; Calcium 1228mg; Fibre 47.3g; Sodium 774mg.

Confit of Slow-cooked Onions

Onions are caramelized in the slow cooker in sweet-sour balsamic vinegar.

Serves 6

30ml/2 tbsp extra virgin olive oil
15g/½oz/1 tbsp butter
500g/1¼lb onions, thinly sliced
3–5 fresh thyme sprigs
1 bay leaf
30ml/2 tbsp light muscovado (brown) sugar, plus a little extra
30ml/2 tbsp balsamic vinegar, plus a little extra
120ml/4fl oz/½ cup red wine
50g/2oz/¼ cup ready-to-eat prunes, chopped
salt and ground black pepper

1 Put the oil and butter in the ceramic cooking pot and heat on high for 15 minutes. Add the onions and stir to coat. Cover the cooker, then place a folded dish towel on top. Cook the onions for 5 hours, stirring the mixture occasionally.

2 Season, then add the thyme, bay leaf, sugar, vinegar and wine. Stir until the sugar has dissolved, then stir in the prunes. Re-cover and cook for 1½–2 hours, until thickened. Adjust the seasoning, adding sugar and/or vinegar to taste. Store in the refrigerator.

Shallots in Balsamic Vinegar

These whole shallots, slowly simmered in balsamic vinegar and herbs, are a modern variation on pickled onions, but with a gentler, smoother flavour. Bay leaves and thyme are used here, but rosemary or oregano work just as well.

Serves 6

30ml/2 tbsp muscovado (molasses) sugar
several bay leaves and a few fresh thyme sprigs
300ml/½ pint/1¼ cups balsamic vinegar
500g/1¼lb shallots, peeled

1 Put the sugar, bay leaves, thyme and vinegar in a pan. Bring to the boil. Add the shallots, cover and simmer for 40 minutes.

2 Transfer the mixture to a sterilized jar, seal and label, then store in a cool, dark place. Alternatively, drain and transfer to a serving dish. Leave to cool, then chill until ready to serve.

Blushing Pears

As this slow-cooker pickle matures, the fruits absorb the colour of the vinegar, giving them a glorious pink hue. Their deliciously spicy, sweet-and-sour flavour is especially good with cold turkey at Christmas, or with game pie, well-flavoured cheese or paté.

Makes about 1.3kg/3lb

1 small lemon
450g/1lb/2¼ cups golden sugar
475ml/16fl oz/2 cups raspberry vinegar
7.5cm/3in cinnamon stick
6 whole cloves
6 allspice berries
150ml/¼ pint/⅔ cup water
900g/2lb firm pears

1 Using a sharp knife, thinly pare a few strips of rind from the lemon. Squeeze out the juice and add to the ceramic cooking pot with the strips of rind.

2 Add the sugar, raspberry vinegar, spices and water, and switch the slow cooker to high. Cover the cooker and leave to heat for about 30 minutes, then stir gently until the sugar has completely dissolved. Re-cover the cooker with the lid and heat for a further 30 minutes.

3 Meanwhile, prepare the pears. Peel and halve the pears, then scoop out the cores using a melon baller or small teaspoon. If the pears are particularly large, cut them into quarters rather than into halves.

4 Add the pears to the slow cooker, cover and cook for 1½–2 hours, turning them occasionally to coat them in the syrup. Check the pears frequently; they should be tender and translucent but still retain their shape.

5 Using a slotted spoon, remove the pears from the slow cooker and pack them into hot sterilized jars, adding the spices and strips of lemon rind.

6 Remove any scum from the surface of the syrup remaining in the ceramic cooking pot, then ladle it over the pears in the jars. Cover and seal. Store for a few days before eating, and use within 2 weeks.

Confit of Onions Energy 133kcal/556kJ; Protein 1.2g; Carbohydrate 16.5g, of which sugars 14.6g; Fat 5.9g, of which saturates 1.8g; Cholesterol 5mg; Calcium 26mg; Fibre 1.6g; Sodium 20mg.
Shallots in Balsamic Vinegar Energy 50kcal/209kJ; Protein 1g; Carbohydrate 11.8g, of which sugars 9.9g; Fat 0.2g, of which saturates 0g; Cholesterol 0mg; Calcium 24mg; Fibre 1.2g; Sodium 3mg.
Blushing Pears Energy 2133kcal/9086kJ; Protein 5g; Carbohydrate 560.3g, of which sugars 560.3g; Fat 0.9g, of which saturates 0g; Cholesterol 0mg; Calcium 230mg; Fibre 19.8g; Sodium 50mg.

Red Hot Relish

Make this tangy, stovetop relish during the summer months when tomatoes and peppers are plentiful. It enhances simple, plain dishes, such as a cheese or mushroom omelette.

Makes about 1.3kg/3lb

800g/1¾lb ripe tomatoes, skinned and quartered
450g/1lb red onions, chopped
3 red (bell) peppers, seeded and chopped
3 fresh red chillies, seeded and finely sliced
200g/7oz/1 cup sugar
200ml/7fl oz/scant 1 cup red wine vinegar
30ml/2 tbsp mustard seeds
10ml/2 tsp celery seeds
15ml/1 tbsp paprika
5ml/1 tsp salt

1 Put the chopped tomatoes, onions, peppers and chillies in a preserving pan, cover with a tight-fitting lid and simmer over very low heat for about 10 minutes, stirring once or twice, until the tomato juices start to run.

2 Add the sugar and vinegar to the tomato mixture and slowly bring to the boil, stirring occasionally until the sugar has dissolved completely. Add the mustard seeds, celery seeds, paprika and salt, and stir well to combine.

3 Increase the heat under the pan slightly and cook the relish, uncovered, for about 30 minutes, or until most of the liquid has evaporated and the mixture has a thick, but moist consistency. Stir frequently towards the end of the cooking time to prevent the mixture sticking to the pan.

4 Spoon the relish into warmed sterilized jars, cover and seal. Store the jars in a cool, dark place and leave to mature for at least 2 weeks before eating. Use the relish within 1 year of making.

Cook's Tip
Once opened, store jars of the relish in the refrigerator and consume within 2 months.

Carrot and Almond Relish

This Middle Eastern classic, usually made with long fine strands of carrot, is available from many supermarkets. This version, using coarsely grated carrots and gently simmered in the slow cooker, tastes much better.

Makes about 675g/1½lb

15ml/1 tbsp coriander seeds
500g/1¼lb carrots, grated
50g/2oz fresh root ginger, finely shredded
200g/7oz/1 cup caster (superfine) sugar
120ml/4fl oz/½ cup white wine vinegar
30ml/2 tbsp clear honey
7.5ml/1½ tsp salt
finely grated rind of 1 lemon
50g/2oz/½ cup flaked (sliced) almonds

1 Crush the coriander seeds using a mortar and pestle. Put them in the ceramic cooking pot with the carrots, ginger and sugar, and mix well.

2 Put the vinegar, honey and salt in a jug (pitcher), and stir until the salt has dissolved completely. Pour the mixture over the carrots. Mix well, cover and leave for 1 hour.

3 Switch the slow cooker to high and cook for about 2 hours, or until the carrots and ginger are almost tender, stirring only if the mixture looks dry around the edges.

4 Stir in the lemon rind and cook for a further 1 hour, until the mixture is thick. Stir once towards the end of the cooking time to prevent the mixture from sticking to the base of the ceramic cooking pot.

5 Put the almonds in a frying pan and toast over low heat until just beginning to colour. Gently stir into the relish, taking care not to break the almonds.

6 Spoon the relish into warmed sterilized jars, cover and seal. Store in a cool, dark place and leave to mature for 1 week. The relish will keep unopened for up to 1 year. However, once the jars have been opened, store them in the refrigerator and use within 2 weeks.

Red Hot Relish Energy 1270kcal/5392kJ; Protein 17.8g; Carbohydrate 306.2g, of which sugars 294.1g; Fat 5.6g, of which saturates 1.4g; Cholesterol 0mg; Calcium 320mg; Fibre 23.5g; Sodium 121mg.
Carrot Relish Energy 1407kcal/5947kJ; Protein 13.7g; Carbohydrate 289.6g, of which sugars 285.8g; Fat 29.4g, of which saturates 2.7g; Cholesterol 0mg; Calcium 268mg; Fibre 15.7g; Sodium 2898mg.

Papaya and Lemon Relish

This chunky relish is best made with a firm, unripe papaya. The long, gentle simmering in the slow cooker allows plenty of time for all the flavours to mellow. Serve the relish with roast meats, or with cheese and crackers.

Makes 450g/1lb
1 large unripe papaya
1 onion, very thinly sliced
175ml/6fl oz/generous 3/4 cup red wine vinegar
juice of 2 lemons
165g/5 1/2oz/3/4 cup golden caster (superfine) sugar
1 cinnamon stick
1 bay leaf
2.5ml/1/2 tsp hot paprika
2.5ml/1/2 tsp salt
150g/5oz/1 cup sultanas (golden raisins)

1 Peel the papaya and cut it in half lengthways. Remove the seeds and discard, then cut the flesh into small chunks of a roughly similar size.

2 Place the papaya chunks in the ceramic cooking pot, add the onion slices and stir in the red wine vinegar. Switch the slow cooker to the high setting, cover with the lid and cook for 2 hours.

3 Add the lemon juice, golden caster sugar, cinnamon stick, bay leaf, paprika, salt and sultanas to the ceramic cooking pot. Gently stir the mixture thoroughly until all of the sugar has completely dissolved.

4 Cook the chutney for a further 1 hour. Leave the cover of the slow cooker off to allow some of the liquid to evaporate and the mixture to reduce slightly. The relish should be fairly thick and syrupy.

5 Ladle the chutney into hot sterilized jars. Seal the jars and store the chutney for 1 week before using to allow it to mature a little and for the flavours to further develop. The chutney should be used within 1 year of making it. However, once a jar has been opened, the chutney should be stored in the refrigerator and consumed within 2 weeks.

Fresh Lemon Curd

This classic tangy, creamy curd is still one of the most popular of all the curds, and it is simple to make in the slow cooker. Delicious spread thickly over freshly baked bread or served with pancakes, it also makes a wonderfully rich, zesty sauce for fresh fruit tarts.

Makes about 450g/1lb
finely grated rind and juice of 3 lemons (preferably unwaxed or organic)
200g/7oz/1 cup caster (superfine) sugar
115g/4oz/1/2 cup unsalted (sweet) butter, diced
2 large (US extra large) eggs
2 large (US extra large) egg yolks

1 Pour about 5cm/2in very hot water into the ceramic cooking pot. Switch the cooker to high. Put the lemon rind and juice, sugar and butter in the largest heatproof bowl that will fit inside the slow cooker.

2 Put the bowl into the cooking pot, then pour near-boiling water around it to come just over halfway up the sides. Leave for 15 minutes, stirring occasionally, until the sugar has dissolved. Remove to cool for a few minutes. Turn the slow cooker to low.

3 Put the eggs and yolks in a bowl and beat together with a fork. Strain the eggs into the lemon mixture, and whisk well until combined. Cover the bowl with foil, then return it to the cooker.

4 Cook the lemon curd on low for 1–2 hours, stirring every 15 minutes, until thick enough to lightly coat the back of a wooden spoon.

5 Pour the curd into small warmed sterilized jars. Cover and seal. Store in a cool, dark place, ideally in the refrigerator, and use within 3 months. Once opened, store in the refrigerator.

Cook's Tip
To make sharp, tangy lime curd, replace the lemons with the grated zest and juice of 4 large ripe, juicy limes. Lime curd has a lovely pale greenish hue.

Papaya Relish Energy 1294kcal/5511kJ; Protein 8.4g; Carbohydrate 332.7g, of which sugars 332.7g; Fat 1.4g, of which saturates 0g; Cholesterol 0mg; Calcium 272mg; Fibre 16.1g; Sodium 1111mg.
Lemon Curd Energy 1968kcal/8224kJ; Protein 22.4g; Carbohydrate 215.3g, of which sugars 215.3g; Fat 118.9g, of which saturates 66.9g; Cholesterol 1102mg; Calcium 277mg; Fibre 0g; Sodium 895mg.

Fine Lime Shred Marmalade

There is something about lime marmalade that really captures the flavour and essence of the fruit. It is important to cut the slices very finely though, because lime skins tend to be tougher than those on any other citrus fruit and can result in a chewy marmalade if cut too thickly.

Makes about 2.25kg/5lb
12 limes
4 kaffir lime leaves
1.2 litres/2 pints/5 cups water
1.3kg/3lb/6½ cups sugar, warmed

1 Halve the limes lengthways, then slice thinly, reserving any pips (seeds). Tie the pips and lime leaves in a muslin (cheesecloth) bag and place the bag in a large pan with the sliced fruit.

2 Add the water to the pan and bring to the boil. Cover and simmer gently for 1½–2 hours, or until the rind is very soft. Remove the muslin bag, leave to cool, then squeeze it over the pan to release any juice and pectin.

3 Add the sugar to the pan, and stir over low heat until the sugar has dissolved. Bring to the boil, then boil rapidly for 15 minutes, stirring occasionally, until setting point is reached (105°C/220°F).

4 Remove the pan from the heat and skim off any scum. Leave to cool for 5 minutes, stir, then pour into warmed sterilized jars. Seal, then label when cold. Store in a cool, dark place.

Cook's Tips
• *To check for setting, spoon a little marmalade on to a chilled saucer and chill for 2 minutes. Push the surface with your finger; if wrinkles form, the marmalade is ready to bottle.*
• *Stirring marmalade after standing and before potting distributes the fruit rind evenly as the preserve begins to set.*

Whiskey Marmalade

Home-made marmalade is easy to make – it only needs slow simmering on the stove. It tastes delicious and flavouring it with whiskey makes it a special treat.

Makes 3.6–4.5kg/8–10lb
1.3kg/3lb Seville oranges
juice of 2 large lemons
2.75kg/6lb/13½ cups sugar, warmed
about 300ml/½ pint/1¼ cups Irish whiskey

1 Scrub the oranges, using a nylon brush, and pick off the disc at the stalk end. Cut in half and squeeze the juice, retaining the pips (seeds). Quarter the peel, cut away and reserve any thick white pith, and shred the peel – thickly or thinly depending on how you prefer the finished marmalade.

2 Cut up the reserved pith roughly and tie it up with the pips in a square of muslin (cheesecloth), using a long piece of string. Tie the bag loosely and hang it from the handle of the pan.

3 Add the cut peel, strained juices and 3.5 litres/6 pints/15 cups water to the pan. Bring to the boil and simmer for 1½–2 hours, or until the peel is very tender.

4 Lift up the bag of pith and pips and squeeze it out well over the pan to extract as much pectin as possible. Add the sugar to the pan and stir over low heat until it has completely dissolved.

5 Bring to the boil, and then boil hard for 15–20 minutes or until setting point is reached. To test, put a spoonful of marmalade on to a cold saucer. Allow to cool slightly, and then push the surface of the marmalade with your finger. Setting point has been reached if a skin has formed. If not, boil a little longer and keep testing until it sets.

6 Skim, if necessary, and leave to cool for 15 minutes, then stir to redistribute the peel. Divide the whiskey among eight to ten warmed, sterilized jars and swill it around. Pour in the marmalade.

7 Cover and seal the jars while the marmalade is still hot. Label when cold, and store in a cool, dark place until required. The marmalade will keep well for 6 months.

Lime Marmalade Energy 5250kcal/22386kJ; Protein 13.3g; Carbohydrate 1380.1g, of which sugars 1380.1g; Fat 2g, of which saturates 0.7g; Cholesterol 0mg; Calcium 1263mg; Fibre 0g; Sodium 112mg.
Whiskey Marmalade Energy 10,736kcal/45,734kJ; Protein 22.8g; Carbohydrate 2657.8g, of which sugars 2657.8g; Fat 1.3g, of which saturates 0g; Cholesterol 0mg; Calcium 1.74g; Fibre 15.6g; Sodium 187mg.

Rowan Jelly

This astringent jelly is made from the orange fruit of mountain ash trees, which flourish in areas where deer run wild. It is a traditional accompaniment to game, especially venison.

Makes about 2.25kg/5lb
1.3kg/3lb/12 cups rowan berries
450g/1lb crab apples, or windfall cooking apples
450g/1lb/2¼ cups sugar per 600ml/1 pint/2½ cups juice, warmed

1 Cut the rowan berries off their stalks, rinse them in a colander and put them into a preserving pan. Remove any damaged parts from the apples before weighing them, then cut them up roughly without peeling or coring. Add the apples to the pan with 1.2 litres/2 pints/5 cups water, which should cover the fruit.

2 Bring to the boil and simmer for about 45 minutes, until the fruit is soft, stirring occasionally and crushing the fruit with a wooden spoon to extract the pectin. Strain the fruit through a jelly bag or a fine sieve (strainer) into a bowl overnight.

3 Measure the juice and allow 450g/1lb/2¼ cups sugar per 600ml/1 pint/2½ cups juice. Return the juice to the rinsed out preserving pan and add the measured amount of sugar.

4 Stir over low heat until the sugar has dissolved, and then bring to the boil and boil hard for 10 minutes, until setting point is reached. To test, put a spoonful of jam on to a cold saucer. Allow to cool slightly, and then push the surface of the jam with your finger. Setting point has been reached if a skin has formed. If not, boil a little longer and keep testing until it sets.

5 Skim, if necessary, and pour into warmed, sterilized jars. Cover, seal and store in a cool, dark place until needed. The jelly will store well for 6 months.

Cook's Tip
For a less astringent jelly, an equal quantity of apples and berries may be used, such as 900g/2lb of each.

Barley Water

Like lemonade, barley water has long been enjoyed as a refreshing summer drink and, until a generation ago, it would always have been home-made. Barley water is usually served cold, but is also very good when served as a hot drink.

Makes about 10 glasses
50g/2oz/⅓ cup pearl barley
1 lemon
sugar, to taste
ice cubes and fresh mint sprigs, to serve

1 Wash the pearl barley, then put it into a large stainless steel pan and cover with cold water. Bring to the boil and simmer gently for about 2 minutes, then strain the liquid. Return the barley to the rinsed pan.

2 Wash the lemon and pare the rind from it with a vegetable peeler. Squeeze the juice and set aside.

3 Add the lemon rind and 600ml/1 pint/2½ cups cold water to the pan containing the barley. Bring to the boil over a medium heat, then simmer the mixture very gently for 1½–2 hours, stirring occasionally.

4 Strain the liquid into a jug (pitcher), add the lemon juice, and sweeten to taste with sugar. Mix until well combined. Leave to cool. Pour the liquid into a bottle and keep in the refrigerator to use as required.

5 To serve, dilute the barley water to taste with cold water, and add ice cubes or crushed ice and a sprig of fresh mint, if you like.

Variations
• *The barley water can also be used with milk, in which case omit the lemon juice as it would curdle the milk.*
• *Make up the barley water with hot water to be drunk as a cold remedy.*

Rowan Jelly Energy 2340kcal/9993kJ; Protein 15.8g; Carbohydrate 606.4g, of which sugars 606.4g; Fat 0.5g, of which saturates 0g; Cholesterol 0mg; Calcium 1.03g; Fibre 54g; Sodium 80mg.
Barley Water Energy 37.9kcal/161.6kJ; Protein 0.43g; Carbohydrate 9.44g, of which sugars 5.26g; Fat 0.08g, of which saturates 0g; Cholesterol 0mg; Calcium 3.8mg; Fibre 0g; Sodium 0.5mg.

Cranberry and Apple Punch

When you are throwing a party, it is good to have a non-alcoholic punch available. Here, the slow cooker extracts maximum flavour from fresh ginger and lime peel.

Serves 6

1 lime
5cm/2in piece fresh root ginger, peeled and thinly sliced
50g/2oz/¼ cup caster (superfine) sugar
200ml/7fl oz/scant 1 cup near-boiling water
475ml/16fl oz/2 cups cranberry juice
475ml/16fl oz/2 cups clear apple juice
ice and chilled sparkling mineral water or soda water, to serve (optional)

1 Pare the rind off the lime and place in the ceramic cooking pot with the ginger and sugar. Pour over the water and stir until the sugar dissolves.

2 Cover with the lid and heat on high or auto for 1 hour, then reduce the temperature to low or leave on auto and heat for a further 2 hours. Switch off the slow cooker and leave the syrup to cool completely.

3 When cold, strain the syrup through a fine sieve (strainer) into a large serving jug (pitcher) or punch bowl and discard the lime rind and ginger.

4 Squeeze the juice from the lime and strain through a sieve into the syrup. Stir in the cranberry and apple juices. Cover and chill in the refrigerator for at least 3 hours.

5 To serve, pour or ladle the punch over plenty of ice in tall glasses and add sparkling mineral water or soda water, if using.

Cook's Tip
You can now buy all kinds of different apple juices made from specific varieties of apple. They have distinctive flavours, and it is well worth searching them out.

Hot Spiced Wine

On a cold winter's evening, there is nothing more welcoming than a glass of warm spicy wine. The slow cooker is particularly useful when you are making the wine for guests: you can prepare the spiced wine up to four hours before your guests arrive, and the slow cooker will keep it at the ideal serving temperature until you are ready to serve.

Serves 8

50g/2oz/¼ cup soft light brown sugar
150ml/¼ pint/⅔ cup near-boiling water
2 small oranges, preferably unwaxed
6 whole cloves
1 stick cinnamon
½ whole nutmeg
1½ bottles red wine, such as Bordeaux
150ml/¼ pint/⅔ cup brandy

1 Put the sugar in the ceramic cooking pot and pour in the near-boiling water. Stir until the sugar has dissolved, then switch the slow cooker to high.

2 Rinse the oranges, then press the cloves into one and add it to the slow cooker with the cinnamon stick, nutmeg and red wine. Halve the remaining orange, then slice it and set aside until required.

3 Cover the slow cooker with the lid and cook on high or auto for 1 hour, then reduce to low or leave on auto and heat for 3 hours.

4 Stir the brandy into the spiced wine and add the reserved orange slices. Heat for a further 1 hour.

5 Remove the whole orange and the cinnamon stick from the cooking pot. The wine is now ready to serve and can be kept hot for up to 4 hours. Serve in heatproof glasses.

Cook's Tip
Use heatproof glasses with a handle, so that guests can hold the hot wine easily.

Cranberry and Apple Punch Energy 111kcal/475kJ; Protein 0.1g; Carbohydrate 27.9g, of which sugars 16.5g; Fat 0.1g, of which saturates 0g; Cholesterol 0mg; Calcium 8mg; Fibre 0g; Sodium 2mg.
Hot Spiced Wine Energy 162kcal/675kJ; Protein 0.2g; Carbohydrate 6.8g, of which sugars 6.8g; Fat 0g, of which saturates 0g; Cholesterol 0mg; Calcium 12mg; Fibre 0g; Sodium 10mg.

Spiced Coffee

This slow-cooker recipe combines the sweet-tart flavour of apples and spices to make a delicious, tangy coffee.

Serves 4

475ml/16fl oz/2 cups apple juice
30ml/2 tbsp soft brown sugar, to taste
2 oranges, thickly sliced
2 small cinnamon sticks
2 whole cloves
pinch of ground allspice
475ml/16fl oz/2 cups hot, freshly brewed strong black coffee
halved cinnamon sticks, to serve (optional)

1 Pour the apple juice into the ceramic cooking pot and switch the slow cooker on to high.

2 Add the brown sugar, orange slices, cinnamon sticks, whole cloves and allspice to the pot and stir. Cover the cooker with the lid and heat for about 20 minutes. Gently stir the mixture until the sugar has dissolved completely, then re-cover with the lid and heat for 1 hour.

3 When the juice is hot and infused with the spices, switch the slow cooker to the low setting to keep the juice warm for up to 2 hours.

4 Strain the juice into a bowl, discarding the orange slices and spices. Pour the hot coffee into the juice and stir. Quickly pour into warmed mugs or espresso-style cups, adding a halved cinnamon stick to each, if you like.

Cook's Tips

- *For a good flavour, use strong coffee – espresso or filter-/plunger-brewed at 75g/3 tbsp/scant ½ cup coffee per 1 litre/1¾ pints/4 cups water.*
- *To make an alcoholic version of this drink, replace a quarter of the apple juice with the French apple brandy, Calvados. Stir in the brandy after straining the spice-infused apple juice and removing the spices.*

Mexican Hot Chocolate

Blending or whisking the hot chocolate before serving gives it a wonderfully frothy texture. The slow cooker is particularly good for heating the milk in this recipe, because the gentle heating process allows the cinnamon and cloves to infuse and flavour the hot chocolate with their warm and spicy flavour.

Serves 4

1 litre/1¾ pints/4 cups milk
1 cinnamon stick
2 whole cloves
115g/4oz dark (bittersweet) chocolate, chopped into small pieces
2–3 drops of almond extract
whipped cream and unsweetened cocoa powder or grated chocolate, to serve (optional)

1 Pour the milk into the ceramic cooking pot. Add the cinnamon stick and cloves, cover with the lid and switch the slow cooker to high. Leave to heat the milk and infuse the spices for 1 hour, or until the milk is almost boiling.

2 Add the chocolate pieces and almond extract to the milk and stir until melted. Turn off the slow cooker.

3 Strain the mixture into a blender (it may be necessary to do this in a couple of batches) and whizz on high speed for about 30 seconds, until frothy. Alternatively, whisk the mixture in the ceramic cooking pot with a hand-held electric whisk or a manual wire whisk.

4 Pour or ladle the hot chocolate into warmed heatproof glasses. If you like, top each with a little whipped cream and a dusting of unsweetened cocoa powder or grated chocolate. Serve immediately.

Cook's Tip

Traditional Mexican hot chocolate is always warmly spiced. It is a popular breakfast drink, often served with delicious deep-fried churros, which are Mexican sugared doughnuts.

Spiced Coffee Energy 85kcal/363kJ; Protein 0.2g; Carbohydrate 22.2g, of which sugars 22.2g; Fat 0.1g, of which saturates 0g; Cholesterol 0mg; Calcium 11mg; Fibre 0g; Sodium 3mg.
Hot Chocolate Energy 262kcal/1102kJ; Protein 9.9g; Carbohydrate 30g, of which sugars 29.7g; Fat 12.3g, of which saturates 7.6g; Cholesterol 17mg; Calcium 309mg; Fibre 0.7g; Sodium 109mg.

Index